The
HIDDEN PLACES
of
IRELAND

Edited by
David Gerrard

Published by:
Travel Publishing Ltd
7a Apollo House, Calleva Park
Aldermaston, Berks, RG7 8TN

ISBN 1-902-00730-1

© Travel Publishing Ltd

First Published: 1995
Second Edition: 1997
Third Edition: 2000

Regional Titles in the Hidden Places Series:

Cambridgeshire & Lincolnshire	Channel Islands
Cheshire	Chilterns
Cornwall	Derbyshire
Devon	Dorset, Hants & Isle of Wight
Essex	Gloucestershire & Wiltshire
Heart of England	Hereford, Worcs & Shropshire
Highlands & Islands	Kent
Lake District & Cumbria	Lancashire
Norfolk	Northeast Yorkshire
Northumberland & Durham	North Wales
Nottinghamshire	Potteries
Somerset	South Wales
Suffolk	Surrey
Sussex	Thames Valley
Warwickshire & W Midlands	Yorkshire Dales

National Titles in the Hidden Places Series:

England	Ireland
Scotland	Wales

Printing by: Ashford Press, Gosport
Maps by: © MAPS IN MINUTES ™ (2000)
Line Drawings: Rodney Peace
Editor: David Gerrard
Cover Design: Lines & Words, Aldermaston

Cover Photographs: Giant's Causeway, Co. Antrim © Britain on View/Stockwave; Finny River & Maamturk Mountains, Co. Galway © Bord Fáilte - Irish Tourist Board; Dunguaire Castle, Kinvara, Co. Galway © Bord Fáilte - Irish Tourist Board.

Foreword

The Hidden Places series is a collection of easy to use travel guides taking you, in this instance, on a relaxed but informative tour of Ireland. Often called the "Emerald Isle", Ireland is indeed rich in greenery, but there is an abundance of every variety of landscape; rugged peaks and mountain ranges, scenic coasts and lush pasture. The country also offers the visitor plenty of fascinating historical sites, beautiful towns and villages and, above all, its people offer the most genuine of friendly welcomes.

The Hidden Places of Ireland explores this fascinating country in a relaxed narrative style. It guides the reader to some of the established visitor attractions and focuses on the more secluded and less well-known places of interest as well as venues for food, drink and accommodation, many of which are easy to miss unless you know exactly where you are going.

We include hotels, b&b's and other types of accommodation, restaurants, pubs and bars, historic houses, museums, gardens and many other attractions throughout Ireland, all of which are comprehensively indexed. Most places have an attractive line drawing and are cross-referenced to coloured maps found at the rear of the book. We do not award merit marks or rankings but concentrate on describing the more interesting, unusual or unique features of each place with the aim of making the reader's stay in the local area an enjoyable and stimulating experience. We would also like to direct you to the Calendar of Events - most of these take place annually - which can be found at the rear of the book

Whether you are visiting Ireland for business or pleasure or in fact are living in the country we do hope that you enjoy reading and using this book. We are always interested in what readers think of places covered (or not covered) in our guides so please do not hesitate to use the reader comment forms provided to give us your considered views. We also welcome any general comments which will help us improve the guides themselves. Finally if you are planning to visit any other corner of the British Isles we would like to refer you to the list of other *Hidden Places* titles to be found at the rear of the book.

Travel Publishing Ltd

Note: International Calling

All telephone numbers throughout the book are shown with local dialling codes. Please note that for Northern Ireland numbers callers outside the United Kingdom should first dial the country code of 00 44 followed by the number shown with the leading zero dropped. For numbers in the Republic of Ireland the country code is 00 353 and again the leading zero should be dropped prior to dialling the number shown.

Contents

1 Dublin City and County Dublin

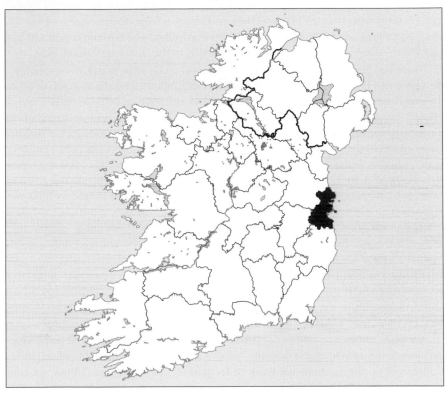

DUBLIN

The old ballad sings of *Dublin's Fair City*, the Irish poet Oliver St John Gogarty lauded it as *No Mean City*, while James Joyce - along with most of his contemporaries - always referred to *"dear, dirty Dublin"*. Anyone who spends any time in Dublin will almost certainly share Joyce's affection for the city, but it is "dirty" no longer. For one thing, the legendary Irish charm has beguiled the European Commission into lavishing more Euros per capita on the Republic than on any other of its member nations. The money hasn't always been wisely spent as some of the truly dreadful modern buildings spatchcocked into the elegant Georgian squares bear witness. But the new "Celtic Tiger" economy has brought a real buzz to the city and stemmed the flow of young emigrants to other countries that drained the country for so long. Today, more than half of Greater Dublin's population of around 3.7 million is under 25. The first record of this attractive and vibrant city appears on Ptolemy's famous map of AD140. It shows a settlement on the River Liffey which he named Eblana but which was known to its Celtic inhabitants as *Dubh Linn*, the "Dark Pool". The Vikings arrived in AD860, ejected the Celts and set up a trading post on the south bank of the Liffey. A century and a half of intermittent warfare followed until the Celts finally defeated the Vikings at the Battle of Clontarf in 1014. For another century and a half the Celts were left in peace. Then, in 1169, the Anglo-Normans arrived, the first chapter in a long and tragic saga of conflict between Ireland and England that would only end, (in the south, at least), with the establishment of the Irish Free State in 1922.

There was one short and glorious period however when hope of a peaceful resolution of Anglo-Irish hostilities seemed possible and even likely. During the last quarter of the 18th century, Ireland had its own parliament and although only Protestants could be elected, amongst their number were many liberal landowners who favoured Catholic emancipation. During this period, known as the "Anglo-Irish Ascendency", a building boom endowed the city with the dignified Georgian houses, squares and public buildings which still give Dublin such a distinctive architectural character. Then came the French Revolution and, in 1798, a countrywide rising by the United Irishmen. The rebellion failed but a panicky British government resumed direct control of Ireland in 1800, provoking yet another century of intermittent and violent resistance.

The ghosts of Henry II, the Earl of Essex, Cromwell, William of Orange and the Black & Tans still haunt Irish history but visitors to this friendly city will find only warmth, openness and a voracious appetite for "craic" - the delight in conversation and good fellowship. On Irish tongues, the English language sings and dances; a way with words also evidenced in the pantheon of Irish writers that ranges from Dean Swift, Sheridan and Oliver Goldsmith in the 18th century to Oscar Wilde, W.B. Yeats, James Joyce, George Bernard Shaw, Samuel Beckett and Seamus Heaney in more recent times.

We begin our exploration of the city at the O'Connell Bridge, a central point which provides a stirring view of the river and some of Dublin's most famous buildings. Facing College Green, the monumental **Bank of Ireland** was designed in 1729 but not completed until 1789. Regarded as one of the finest specimens of the 18th century neo-classical style, the grandiose building provided an imposing setting for the short-lived Irish Parliament that gathered here between 1783 and 1801. Two years later, the Bank of Ireland acquired the building for a colossal £40,000 and it's still in business here today. Guided tours, available during normal banking hours, lead visitors through the former House of Lords, where there's a magnificent coffered ceiling and a splendid Waterford chandelier dating from 1765, and to the old House of Commons which has two fine 18th century tapestries depicting two famous Protestant victories, the Battle of the Boyne and the Siege of Derry. Also on display is the Parliament's Golden Mace.

Across the busy main road from the Bank of Ireland is the entrance to **Trinity College** whose famous alumni have included Oliver Goldsmith and Edmund Burke, (both commemorated by statues), Dean Swift, J.M. Synge the playwright, Samuel Beckett and the author of *Dracula*, Bram Stoker. The college was founded in 1591 by Elizabeth I although the oldest surviving portion dates back to 1722. Trinity's design emulates the colleges of

Oxford and Cambridge, with buildings of cream-coloured stone set around cobbled quadrangles. There's a finely-proportioned Chapel and Examination Hall, (both 1787), and a Museum of 1857 whose walls contain some exuberant stone carvings by the famous O'Shea brothers. But the highlight here is the **Trinity College Library**, a gracious building completed in 1732. It contains well over half a million printed books, as well as more than 140 Irish manuscripts, some from the 6th century, Greek and Latin manuscripts, and Egyptian papyri. The Library's greatest treasure though is the priceless Book of Kells, a beautifully illuminated manuscript of the gospels created sometime in the 8th century. There are 680 pages in all, now bound in 4 separate volumes, and each day a page is turned to reveal yet more fantastic and intricate designs, so finely drawn that even when magnified they reveal no flaws. Of equal interest is the **Book of Durrow**, dating from between 650 and 680AD - the earliest surviving example of the great Irish illuminated manuscripts.

Also within the peaceful Trinity College campus are the redbrick **Rubrics**, the oldest part of the college dating from around 1700 and once occupied by Oliver Goldsmith as a student; the **Douglas Hyde Museum of Modern Art** which stages frequent exhibitions of major Irish artists; and the **Provosts' House**, a handsome mansion of 1760.

South of Trinity College, a stroll along pedestrianized **Grafton Street** takes you through the heart of the city's smart shopping area, well supplied with cafés, bars and restaurants, where the entertainment includes lively street theatre and buskers. At the southern end of the street is **St Stephen's Green**, laid out as a public park in 1890 by Sir Arthur Edward Guinness of the drinks dynasty. Tree-lined walks, shrubberies, colourful flowered gardens, an ornamental lake and lunchtime concerts during the summer make this a pleasant place to while away a quiet hour. In Georgian times, the houses surrounding the Green provided the smartest addresses in town. Sadly, most of these elegant buildings fell victim to ruthless "development" in the 1960s. (Nearby Ely Place and Harcourt Street were more fortunate and contain some of the best-preserved domestic Georgian architecture in Dublin).

Leading northwards from St Stephen's Green, Kildare Street contains the mightily impressive building frontage of **Leinster House**, built in 1745 as a town house for the Duke of Leinster. It is now home to not only the two houses of the Irish Parliament, the *Dáil Éireann*, but also the **National Library** and the **National Museum** (free), each with a huge rotunda over its entrance. The National Museum houses the treasures of ancient Ireland - beautifully crafted Celtic jewellery ranging from the 8th to the 1st centuries BC, along with spectacular medieval pieces such as the exquisite Tara Brooch, generally regarded as the finest piece of Irish metalwork to have survived. Incorporated in the National Museum is the **Natural History Museum** (free) which contains collections illustrating the wild life of Ireland, along with an extensive African and Asian exhibition. Children especially will be impressed by the two huge skeletons suspended from the ceiling of whales stranded on the Irish coast.

Backing on to Leinster House is the **National Gallery** (free) which boasts a collection of more than 2,500 works, representing every major European school of painting. Amongst them are works by Jack Yeats, (brother of the poet W.B.Yeats), Hogarth, Reynolds, Gainsborough and Turner, along with an extensive array of fine European painting from

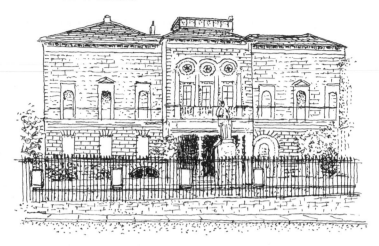

The National Gallery, Dublin

the Renaissance onwards. Highlights include a recently rediscovered Caravaggio, *The Taking of Christ* (1602), and Degas' *Ballet Girls*. A riveting collection of Irish portraits lines the grand staircase at the top of which is one of Countess Markiewicz, the fervent Nationalist who was incensed when she was pardoned for her rôle in the Easter Rising.

A few minutes walk from St Stephen's Green and located in the centre of Dublin's business district, **The Leeson Inn Downtown** offers a unique combination of stylish en suite accommodation in a prime location at an excellent price. A prominent Georgian building dating back to 1810, the Inn was thoroughly refurbished in 1998/99. All the rooms are attractively decorated and equipped with features such as satellite TV, direct dial telephone, hairdryer, iron and ironing board and even a computer modem point. Guests have the use of a spacious lounge and business services such as a fax, photo-

The Leeson Inn Downtown, 24 Lower Leeson Street, Dublin 2 Tel: 01 662 2002 Fax: 01 662 9963
e-mail: leesonin@iol.ie
website: http://www.iol.ie/leesoninn

copier and e-mail service are all available. The Leeson Inn's facilities will appeal to both business and tourist travellers and the genuinely friendly staff are committed to making your stay effortless and enjoyable. Within the immediate vicinity of the Inn you will find many of the city's leading attractions - St Stephen's Green, (one Dublin's most beautiful parks), the National Gallery and National Concert Hall, as well as a wide range of restaurants, bars and clubs.

On the south side of St Stephen's Green there is one outstanding Georgian survivor - **Newman House**. It is actually two houses, both built around 1738 and famous for their spectacular plaster decoration and magnificent 18ᵗʰ century interiors. The house is named after Cardinal Newman who in 1853 became first Rector of the newly-established Catholic University of Ireland which is still based here. The Jesuit priest and poet, Gerard Manley Hopkins, was Professor of Classics here from 1884 to 1889, and the room in which he lived has been restored in his honour. The University's most famous alumnus was James Joyce, a B.A. student here from 1899 to 1902; a classroom, decorated as it would have been in his time, survives and is included in the guided tour.

To sample contemporary Irish arts and culture, the place to make for is **Temple Bar**, just to the west of Trinity College. Clustered around Meeting House Square, a spectacular open air performance area, are the Gallery of Photography, the Irish Film Centre, the Temple Bar Music Centre, "Arthouse" - a multi-media centre for the arts, "The Ark" - a cultural centre for children and, every Saturday, The Book Market provides a gathering place for independent booksellers and readers of all tastes and genres. Temple Bar mounts a free programme of events throughout the day and into the evening and an additional attraction is the unique Food Market (Saturdays only) where small producers and growers offer a huge range of home produced goods - farmhouse cheeses, venison, smoked fish, organic vegetables, chocolate and fudge.

Across the road from Temple Bar is one of Dublin's most famous bridges, the pedestrian- only **Halfpenny Bridge**. Erected in 1821, it was one of the earliest cast iron structures

of its kind in Ireland. Until the early 1900s, a toll was charged to use - hence the name.

A few steps from Temple Bar, **Dublin's Viking Adventure** takes visitors on a fascinating journey back through time to the Viking town of "Dyflin", imaginatively and accurately recreated and brought to life. You can walk the narrow streets, chat to the "locals", observe

Halfpenny Bridge, Dublin

their daily work and experience the sounds and smells of the city. Within the complex, the Viking Museum features a collection of the artefacts discovered during the excavation of Viking Dublin, the most important collection outside Scandinavia.

Another short walk brings you to **Dublin Castle**, originally built for King John's visit here in 1207. Of that early fortress, only the massive stone Record Tower still stands, and the Great Courtyard is surrounded by an architectural medley that includes a graceful 18th century mansion, a rather fussy neo-gothic church of 1803, and an Inland Revenue office building as alluring as its function. But the superb State Apartments are well worth visiting. Built as residential quarters for the English Viceroy, they are now the venue for Ireland's Presidencies of the European Community, Presidential Inaugurations and other state functions.

Of Dublin's many churches, the grandest is **St Patrick's Cathedral** which stands on the site where, it is said, St Patrick baptised converts in a well beside the building. A church has stood here since 450AD but the present building dates from 1191 and was much restored in Victorian times. The national cathedral of the Church of Ireland, St Patrick's is the largest church in Ireland. Its interior is notable for some imposing tombs and memorials, the most striking of which is the flamboyant 17th century monument to the Boyle family, Earls of Cork. In the Choir are the Banners and the Stalls of the Knights of St Patrick (1783) and in the transepts hang the old Irish regimental banners.

St Patrick's contains several mementoes of Jonathan Swift, author of *Gulliver's Travels*, who was Dean of St Patrick's from 1713 to 1745. His pulpit, table and chair are here, and he himself is buried in the cathedral alongside his wife Stella. A plain black slab is engraved with the epitaph he wrote himself, but there's an even more telling inscription on a tablet at the east end of the church. In just two lines, William Taylour sums up the human condition: *As You are, so were Wee / And as Wee are, so shall You be.*

At the west end of the cathedral, the medieval door to the Chapter House has a roughly hewn hole in it which is believed to have given rise to the phrase "chancing your arm". In 1492, the Earl of Ormonde and his supporters were barricaded within the cathedral, resisting an attack by their enemies, the Earl of Kildare and his followers. Eventually, Kildare decided to make peace, hacked a hole through the door and put his arm through it, urging Ormonde to shake hands. Kildare's gamble paid off, Ormonde shook hands and peace was restored. Dublin's other Church of Ireland cathedral is **Christ Church**, some 30 years older than St Patrick's and with much more of its original fabric still intact. The crypt, dating from 1172, is unique in Ireland for its scale and size, being almost as large as the entire upper church. It contains some interesting relics, amongst them the punishment stocks from the old 'liberty' of Christ Church, and the 1689 candlesticks and tabernacle of James II.

Located beside Christ Church, **Dvblinia** tells the story of the development of Dublin from the arrival of Strongbow and his Anglo-Norman knights in the 12th century to the era of Henry VIII. Life-size reconstructions bring history to life, while medieval artefacts from the Wood Quay excavations are on display in the museum area. Visitors can take part in a Medieval Fayre and climb the 17th century St Michael's tower for a unique, panoramic view of the city. Just outside the main entrance to Christ Church, **Marsh's**

Library is the oldest public library in Ireland. Built in 1701 by Archbishop Narcissus Marsh, it contains some 25,000 volumes, most of them dating from the 16th to the 18th centuries, along with 250 volumes of manuscripts. The beautiful dark oak bookcases and the tiny reading cubicles are still here, so too are the 3 original wired 'cages' where readers consulting rare books used to be locked in.

To the west of Marsh's Library is one of Ireland's most popular visitor attractions, the **Guinness Hopstore** in St James' Gate. Arthur Guinness purchased a run-down old brewery nearby in 1759 and began brewing the famous black stout with its distinctive creamy head. The handsome 4-storey building houses the "World of Guinness Exhibition"; an Advertising Gallery displaying the inspired posters used over the years; an audio-visual show on the history of Guinness in Ireland; a model Cooperage and Transport Museum; and an Art Gallery devoted to the work of John Gilroy. There's also a coffee shop and a lively bar where you can sample what is probably the best pint of Guinness in the city.

Before crossing the Liffey to north Dublin, two more buildings on the southwest edge of the city are well worth a visit. The **Irish Museum of Modern Art** (free) is housed in a glorious classical building of 1680, formerly the Royal Hospital Kilmainham for wounded army pensioners. The Museum, opened in 1991, owns only a small number of paintings but puts on a regularly changing collection of works borrowed from other galleries.

From the Museum, a long tree-lined avenue leads to the forbidding bulk of **Kilmainham Gaol**, now the largest unoccupied gaol in Ireland and used as a location in the film *In the Name of the Father*. It was opened in 1796, just in time to receive the leaders of the rebellion of 1798. A roll-call of Irish nationalists - Robert Emmet, Charles Stewart Parnell, De Valera - followed them through its portals. The admission price to the gaol includes an audio-visual presentation, an exhibition and a guided tour which gives a realistic insight into 19th century notions of punishment and correction. Perhaps the most poignant moment of the tour is a visit to the chapel where, on 4 May 1916, Joseph Plunkett - one of the leaders of the 1916 Easter Rising - was married by candlelight to Grace Gifford. The ceremony concluded at 1.30am: at 3.30am Plunkett was executed by firing squad. He had spent a total of ten minutes alone with his wife.

NORTH OF THE LIFFEY

Extending northwards from the O'Connell Bridge is the widest city thoroughfare in Europe, **O'Connell Street**, a grand sight with its central strip dotted with statues. The most striking building is the **General Post Office** (GPO), opened in 1818 and almost a century later the scene of one of the most significant moments in the struggle for Irish independence. On Easter Monday 1916, a group of rebels led by Pádaig Pearse seized the building and proclaimed the Irish Republic from its steps. British troops surrounded the building and shelled it from a gunboat anchored in the Liffey, wrecking the building and much of O'Connell Street as well. The rebels held out for 5 days before being overwhelmed. Sixteen of the rebel leaders were summarily shot; 2000 others imprisoned. Inside the GPO, a superb sculpture by Oliver Sheppard of the mythical Celtic warrior Cúchullain honours the heroes of the Easter Rising.

The most recent sculpture to be erected in O'Connell Street was unveiled to celebrate Dublin's millennium in 1988. The **Anna Livia Fountain** shows a recumbent woman bathed by the waters of the fountain. It represents Joyce's character Anna Livia Plurabella, the personification of the River Liffey and of Dublin women, but is usually referred to irreverently as the "Floozie in the Jacuzzi".

The final statue at the northern end of O'Connell Street commemorates Charles Stewart Parnell (1846-1891), the Nationalist politician whose distinguished career ended with his involvement in a divorce case. The square behind his statue also bears his name and contains some of Dublin's earliest Georgian buildings. One of the most impressive is Charlemont House, built for the Earl of Charlemont in 1762 and now home to the **Hugh Lane Municipal Gallery of Modern Art**. The Gallery houses an extensive collection of 20th century Irish art as well as half the French Impressionist collection amassed by Sir Hugh Lane. Sir Hugh died when the *Lusitania* was torpedoed by a German submarine in 1915. In his will he bequeathed his collection to "the Irish nation", a bequest which caused problems when the Republic was established. The outcome was that half the paintings are now permanently held in Belfast. Since Sir Hugh's death, the most significant donation to the Gallery was the gift of the Francis Bacon Studio and his unfinished *Self-Portrait*. (Bacon was born in Dublin in 1906 and lived in Ireland until 1925).

Also in Parnell Square is the **Dublin Writers Museum** which celebrates Ireland's illustrious literary tradition. Housed in a magnificent 18th century mansion, the collection features the lives and works of the city's literary celebrities over the past 300 years. Swift and Sheridan, Shaw and Wilde, Yeats, Joyce and Beckett are among those presented through their books, letters, portraits and personal items. The museum holds exhibitions and readings and has a special room devoted to children's literature.

A short walk from Parnell Square, in North Great George's Street, a titan of Irish literature has his own personal museum - **The James Joyce Centre**. Located in a beautifully restored Georgian townhouse, the Centre is dedicated to promoting a great interest in the life and works of the author of *Ulysses*. The Centre provides audio-visual material relating to Dublin's most local and yet international writer, an excellent bookshop, lectures and walking tours through the heartland of Joyce's north inner city. There's also a coffee shop, the "Ulysses Experience" which contains a mural based on the people and events featured in Joyce's most famous novel.

Yet another Dublin literary shrine is the **Shaw Birthplace**, at 33 Synge Street on the southern edge of the city centre. It was here that George Bernard Shaw was born in 1856 and spent his early years. The interior of the neat little terrace house has been restored to its Victorian appearance and looks as if the family has just gone out for the afternoon. The displays provide a fascinating insight into domestic life in Victorian Dublin as well as celebrating the early years of one Dublin's Nobel prize winners for literature, a prize incidentally Shaw declined to accept.

Returning to the north bank of the River Liffey, a short walk eastwards from the O'Connell Bridge brings you to the famed **Abbey Theatre**, Ireland's national theatre. Founded in 1904 by W.B.Yeats, J.M.Synge and Lady Gregory, the Abbey has premiered the work of every leading Irish playwright, at times sparking off riots such as those that fol-

Custom House, Dublin

lowed the première of Sean O'Casey's *The Plough and the Stars*, a revisionist view of the heroes of the Easter Rising. A fire in 1951 destroyed the original theatre and the brutalist building that rose in its place now contains two theatres: the Abbey which is devoted to the Irish classics, and the smaller Peacock which specialises in experimental drama.

A little further east from the Abbey Theatre stands one of Dublin's finest heritage buildings, the **Custom House**, completed in 1791. Designed by the celebrated architect James Gandon (1743-1823), this noble building with its elegant portico and great dome stands on the quayside overlooking the River Liffey. During the War of Independence in 1921 the Custom House, as a symbol of English government, was set alight by Republicans and burned fiercely throughout five days and nights. It has twice been refurbished since then and once again houses government offices. The Visitor Centre has an exhibit recording the history of the Custom House, including the 1921 fire; displays on the many government characters who have worked in the building; and a Gandon museum detailing the great architect's life and work.

Another of Gandon's magnificent buildings also stands on the north bank of the Liffey, about half a mile west of O'Connell Bridge. **The Four Courts** were completed in 1786 as the seat of the High Court of Justice of Ireland and although they, like the Custom House, suffered massive damage during the 1921 civil war, they have been thoroughly restored. A graceful Corinthian portico supports a statue of Moses, and the figures of Justice and Mercy, while above the circular entrance hall rises a colossal pillared dome.

If you have a taste for the macabre, a visit to **St Michan's Church,** the oldest building in north Dublin, should prove very satisfying. An unusual combination of dry air, constant temperature, and methane gas from rotting vegetation beneath the 11th century crypt, has kept the bodies stored here in a state of mummification. The best preserved are on display, some of them more than three centuries old. The church also has an early 18th century organ which Handel played when he was in Dublin for the very first performance of *The Messiah* in 1742.

A mile or so to the west of the Four Courts is Dublin's playground, **Phoenix Park**, a huge lung covering 1,760 acres and with a circumference of 7 miles - about 5 times the size of London's Hyde Park. Originally priory lands, the area was seized in the 1640s and made into a royal deer park. A Viceroy's Lodge was built here which is now the *Aras an Uachtaráin*, the Irish President's official residence. Visible from most corners of the Park is the towering, 205 feet high **Wellington Monument**, erected in honour of the victor of Waterloo who was born in Dublin in 1769. The Iron Duke didn't seem particularly proud of his Irish origins. When someone remarked on Dublin being his birthplace, Wellington retorted, "Being born in a stable doesn't make one a horse".

Thirty acres of Phoenix Park are occupied by the landscaped grounds of **Dublin Zoo**, opened in 1830 and now home to some 700 animals and tropical birds from around the world. "Fringes of the Arctic" features polar bears, snowy owls and arctic foxes; "World of Cats" includes jaguars, lions and snow leopards; and an innovative "Meet the Keeper" programme allows visitors to learn about the many rare and endangered species which have found a sanctuary here. Other attractions include a train ride around the zoo, children's play areas, a pet care area, discovery centre, restaurants and gift shop.

One final "must see" attraction lies about a mile to the northeast of Phoenix Park. The **National Botanic Gardens** were founded by the Royal Dublin Society in 1795 and the 48 acre site contains some 20,000 species of plants and trees. There's an arboretum, rock garden and burren areas, extensive herbaceous borders, a student garden and an annual display of decorative plants, including a rare example of Victorian carpet bedding. Amongst the notable specimens thriving here are a fine, weeping Atlantic cedar, vener-

National Botanic Gardens, Dublin

able Chusan palms, and the "Last Rose of Summer" of the famous ballad. The botanical treasures are enhanced by a superb range of curvilinear glasshouses more than 400 feet in length, built and designed by the Dublin ironmaster Richard Turner between 1843 and 1869. Adjacent to the gardens is Prospect Cemetery, the final resting place of many famous Dubliners, including Michael Collins, Daniel O'Connell and Charles Stewart Parnell.

COUNTY DUBLIN

Though the county of Dublin only covers the city and a coastal strip to the northeast, it contains many places of interest, most notably Malahide Castle and Newbridge House. The best of the county is easily accessible thanks to DART - the Dublin Area Rapid Transit railway, which runs fast and frequent electric trains that run from Howth right around Dublin Bay to Bray just across the border in Co. Wicklow. The route offers some great views, especially between Dalkey and Killiney, so it's worth taking a trip even if you have your own transport. We begin by travelling northwards from the city centre.

MARINO   MAP 7 REF L10
3 miles N of Dublin city centre off the R105

Marino is an unassuming suburb but it does have one attraction well worth taking the trouble to find - the 18th century **Marino Casino**. It's not a gambling den but an extraordinary folly built for Lord Charlemont in the 1750s as a Neo-classical foil to his villa here. The villa has long since gone but the Casino with its massive columns and elaborate urns concealing chimney stacks was fully restored in 1984. Lord Charlemont's villa was designed to command a panoramic sea vista but a local painter named Ffolliot spitefully erected a row of town houses deliberately intended to block the view. To compound the insult, Ffolliot made the view of the backs of the houses in MarinoCrescent as unsightly as possible with ill-proportioned windows and ramshackle sheds.

SUTTON   MAP 7 REF M10
6 miles NE of Dublin on the R105

Located in the quiet residential area of Sutton, **Dun Aoibhinn** is a luxurious detached house where Mary McDonnell offers quality bed & breakfast accommodation. Mary is an assiduous host, determined to make your stay as relaxing and comfortable as possible. Her home stands on a large corner site in a peaceful quarter of this favoured and much sought-after Dublin suburb. The coast road runs close by, the DART train with its fast link to Dublin city centre is just a 5-minute walk away, as are some half a dozen bus routes. Dun Aoibhinn was purpose built as a guest house so it is well equipped with all up-to-date amenities. You'll find a spacious, well-furnished guest lounge instantly heated by a natural gas fire and complete with TV and video along with tea/coffee facilities available 24 hours a day. There are 3 guest bedrooms, all of them en suite, and all attractively furnished and decorated. Mary serves a copious breakfast offering a good choice of menu - more than enough to set you up for the day! Dun Aoibhinn is open all year except over

Dun Aoibhinn, 30 Sutton Park, Sutton, Dublin 13
Tel: 01 832 5456 Fax: 01 832 5213 e-mail: mary_mcdonnell@ireland.com

the Christmas period and provides a perfect base for exploring Ireland's capital city and the surrounding countryside.

HOWTH
9 miles NE of Dublin on the R105

MAP 7 REF M10

Howth (pronounced to rhyme with 'both') stands on a peninsula which forms the northern horn of the Dublin Bay crescent. Once the main port for the steam packets from Britain, today it is a popular seaside resort for Dubliners and a busy fishing centre. From Howth Head there are wonderful views across the bay to the Wicklow Mountains and even, on a clear day, to the mountains of Wales. From the harbour there are boat trips available, one of which will take you to **Ireland's Eye**, a small island bird sanctuary about a mile off shore which is a popular place for walkers and picnickers. On the west side of the town, **Howth Castle** is a long battlemented building dating from 1564. The castle itself isn't open to the public but you can wander through the extensive grounds (free) which provide a brilliant sight in early summer when the azaleas and rhododendrons are in flower. The grounds also contain the ruined square tower of Corr Castle and a huge dolmen made of ten enormous masses of quartzite, with a capstone said to weigh 70 tons. Known as **Aideen's Grave**, it is reputed to cover the grave of Aideen, wife of Oscar, who was slain near Tara at the end of the 3rd century. Also within the Howth Castle Demesne is the **National Transport Museum** which has specimens of just about every vehicle to have travelled an Irish road, from Victorian carriages to early trams and fire engines.

The renowned **King Sitric Fish Restaurant & Accommodation** stands in a magnificent position at the head of Howth's East Pier, overlooking Balscadden Bay. Established in 1971 by Aidan and Joan MacManus, the restaurant has earned an international reputa-

King Sitric Fish Restaurant & Accommodation, East Pier, Howth, Co. Dublin
Tel: 01 832 5235/832 6729 Fax: 01 839 2442 e-mail: info@kingsitric.ie

tion for superlative fresh seafood dishes and diners come from miles around to sample the outstanding fare on offer. Each day, Aidan selects the finest fish and seafood from the catches landed at nearby Howth harbour, one of the busiest fishing ports in Ireland. House specialities include fresh lobster and crab caught in Balscadden Bay and cooked to perfection, along with oysters and mussels from the West Coast. Other seasonal delights include black sole, John Dory, turbot, sea bass, squid and scallops. Diners have the choice of either à la carte or table d'hôte menus. Before your meal, enjoy a pre-dinner drink in the Wine Cellar while selecting a wine to complement your meal from the extensive Wine List which has earned the King Sitric the rating of "Outstanding Wine Cellar" in the *Good Food Guide 2000*. The restaurant is open for lunch and dinner, Monday to Saturday all year.

In 1999, Aidan and Joan extensively rebuilt their old Harbour Master's house, relocating the restaurant to the first floor, where diners can enjoy panoramic sea views, and adding 8 guest bedrooms of 4-star quality. All the bedrooms - each named after a Lighthouse!, have sea views and offer all modern amenities. Before sampling the excellent breakfast, you could take a gentle stroll along the Pier or a more energetic hike on the unspoilt Cliff Path and the trails of Howth Head. And if you plan some sightseeing in Dublin, the DART (Dublin Area Rapid Transit) train will get you there in just 25 minutes.

BALGRIFFIN
MAP 7 REF L10
5 miles NE of Dublin off the R107

To appreciate the elegance of Georgian Dublin at its best, book yourself into the **Belcamp-Hutchinson**, a noble 18th century mansion set in lovely, peaceful grounds. The house was built in 1786 and takes its name from the original owner, Francis Hely-Hutchinson,

3rd Earl of Donoughmore. Its generously proportioned rooms, high ceilings and ornate decoration all evoke a more gracious era. The present owner, Count Waldburg, took tremendous care during the house's recent refurbishment to ensure that the work was carried out with the greatest sensitivity, uniting the old elegance of the house with its modern amenities. He is now proud to offer guests the most up-to-date facilities in a setting unspoilt by the passage of time. After a carefree day golfing, attending the horse-racing, touring, shopping or walking the nearby long sandy beach of Portmarnock, the visitor may then return to Belcamp-Hutchinson, enjoy a

Belcamp-Hutchinson, Balgriffin, Dublin 17
Tel: 01 846 0843 Fax: 01 848 5703

leisurely meal in the old family dining room, take a stroll in the garden, or simply put their feet up with an after-dinner drink in the original family Drawing Room and savour the restful ambience. This outstanding guest house with its tranquil and extensive gardens sheltered behind high walls, is just a 20-minute drive from the centre of Dublin, 15 minutes from Dublin Airport, and only 5 minutes from one of Ireland's oldest and prettiest villages, Malahide. This beautiful village offers visitors golf, tennis, horse riding, sailing, a variety of upmarket restaurants, coffee houses, and pubs, as well as some very fine boutiques and shops.

Belcamp-Hutchinson offers its guests a truly memorable experience. Gracious surroundings; attentive, friendly and courteous service; fine cuisine; and, best of all, the irresistibly beguiling Irish gift for hospitality that transforms a stranger into a friend within minutes.

MALAHIDE   MAP 7 REF M10
9 miles NE of Dublin on the R126

With its fine sandy beaches, Malahide is another popular seaside resort for Dubliners, but its greatest glory is the splendid **Malahide Castle**, seat of the Talbot family from 1185AD until 1976. The oldest parts date back to the late 1100s but that simple fortification has been greatly extended over the years, with successive Talbots adding turrets, towers, Gothic windows and battlements to create a picture postcard medley of architectural styles. Many original 18th century furnishings are still in place together with an extensive collection of

Malahide Castle

Irish portrait paintings, most of them from the National Gallery. Also on display are the Boswell Papers, travel journals written by Dr Johnson's biographer. Boswell was related to the Talbots but these fascinating accounts of 18th century travel didn't come to light until a few years ago when they were discovered in a croquet box at the castle.

Malahide Castle's medieval Great Hall is particularly striking, the only one in Ireland to be preserved in its original form. It was in this room on the 1st July 1690 that fourteen members of the Talbot family sat down to breakfast. By nightfall they were all dead, killed in the Battle of the Boyne, William III's decisive victory over James II.

The castle is surrounded by beautiful gardens and parkland, and model railway buffs will be delighted to find within the castle grounds the **Fry Model Railway Museum**, a unique working collection of handmade models of Irish trains from the beginning of rail travel to modern times. The beautifully engineered models were created in the 1920s and 1930s by Cyril Fry, a railway engineer and draughtsman. The huge O-gauge layout includes immaculately crafted stations, bridges, trams, buses, barges and even the River Liffey. The museum also contains a book shop and model shop.

Any visit to this picturesque seaside village would be incomplete without calling in at **Duffy's** family pub on Main Street. Its impressive, multi-coloured frontage looks very inviting and the interior is even more so, with an exquisite blend of South American pine and oak used extensively throughout to great effect. In the conservatory area known as "The Marquee" another attractive feature is the full wall mural of the beach in Malahide

Duffy's, Main Street, Malahide, Co. Dublin
Tel: 01 845 0735

and Duffy's also boasts a Library Room - a rare phenomenon in Dublin pubs. Not so visible, but very welcome nevertheless, is the Clean Air system which has been installed. Duffy's is well known for its varied, and very reasonably priced, food. Lunches are served from 12.30 until 14.30 with a menu offering a wide range of snacks, sandwiches, main courses and desserts along with a good choice of non-alcoholic drinks. Duffy's lays on traditional Irish music on Mondays and Thursdays, and your host, Sean Farrell, is an expert at arranging any kind of special event or function. This popular tavern has a history that stretches back to the days when Malahide was a busy coal importing port. The boats had always to be unloaded on the tide, which meant the colliers worked irregular hours. It was thirsty work and particularly inconvenient in early morning when the local village pub was closed. Therefore, a special licensing dispensation was granted so that the workers could avail themselves of a drink. So it was not uncommon for "Parkinsons", as the pub was named then, to be busy and alive with sounds of laughter and merriment from early morning until late at night. Today, in the same tavern, that historic past is perpetuated in what is probably Dublin's most complete licensed premises, "Duffy's of Malahide".

DONABATE   Map 7 ref M9
12 miles N of Dublin on the N1

A good investment is to buy the joint ticket that gives you entry to both Malahide Castle and **Newbridge House**, just outside the trim little town of Donabate. Newbridge House is a delightful 18th century manor, set in 350 acres of parkland, which was built in 1737 for

Charles Cobbe, later Archbishop of Dublin. The house is reckoned by most experts to be one of the finest Georgian interiors in Ireland. Each room open to the public has its own style of antique and original furniture, and the period atmosphere is enhanced by a fully restored courtyard, surrounded by a dairy, estate worker's house, carpenter's shop and a blacksmith's forge, all displaying 19th century tools and implements The grounds also contain a 29-acre traditional farm, complete with farmyard animals. Collectors of curiosities will be pleased to find that the Cobbe family shared their interest. A charming small museum contains oddities from around the world, amongst them exotic weapons, an African chief's umbrella and the mummified ear of an Egyptian bull. And cinema buffs with a good memory may recognise Newbridge House as a major location for the 1965 film *The Spy Who Came in from the Cold*, starring Richard Burton and Claire Bloom.

SKERRIES
18 miles N of Dublin on the R127

MAP 7 REF M9

One of the largest resorts on the northeast coast, Skerries takes it name from the islands just offshore: in Gaelic, *skerries* means 'sea rocks'. There are boat trips to **St Patrick's Island**, where there's a ruined church in which a national synod was held in 1148, and to **Red Island** where some strange indentations in the rocks are said to be St Patrick's footprints.

When Skerries' local bank moved to new premises in 1983, Terry and Margaret McCoy bought the handsome old building and created **The Redbank**, a superb restaurant which has since won many awards and citations. The old bank vault was converted into a well-stocked wine cellar and the McCoys went on to forge a reputation as one of the best establishments of contemporary Irish cuisine. In 1997, they extended the Redbank's hospitality by opening the Redbank Guesthouse adjacent to the restaurant. These individually decorated en suite rooms offer a genuine welcome and a promise of comfort and relaxation in tranquil and pleasant surroundings. As the McCoys put it, "A perfect end to a perfect meal and without breaking the bank!"

A tremendous enthusiast, Terry is an avid supporter of local produce and suppliers and always keen to try out new ideas to make the most of them. Fresh seafood from Skerries harbour provides the backbone of his menus, but without limiting the vision - this is a man who

The Redbank, 7 Church Street, Skerries, Co. Dublin
Tel: 01 849 1005/849 0439
Fax: 01 849 1598
e-mail: redbank@eircom.ie

goes out at dawn to gather young nettles for soup! The luscious vegetables of this, the market gardening area of Ireland, feature extensively on his menus. Equally nurtured by this big-hearted chef are the local millers who supply him with stone ground floor for his delicious fresh brown bread and, of course, the farmhouse cheesemakers of Ireland who produce such mouth-watering cheeses.

The Redbank Guesthouse is an ideal base for forays to explore Dublin or for a round of golf at one of the 25 golf clubs within an hour's drive. If you would like to try your hand at sailing, Terry will be only too happy to arrange a course with the local sailing school. Tennis, cycling, bowls and horse riding can also be arranged and if you enjoy walking, the McCoys can provide their guests with detailed maps, whether it be for an energetic 6 mile walk through country lanes or a short stroll by the sea.

DUN LAOGHAIRE MAP 7 REF M10
4 miles SE of Dublin on the N31

"Dun Leary" for English tongues; "Dun Lay-ray" for the Irish, Dun Laoghaire still retains something of its character as a Victorian resort with brightly painted houses, broad promenades and tree-lined avenues. As well as being the major port of entry to the Republic, Dun Laoghaire is also Ireland's chief yachting centre with races held regularly during the summer months. For almost exactly one hundred years, it was known as Kingstown in commemoration of a visit by George IV in 1821. With the establishment of the Irish Free State the town reverted to its earlier name which refers to the 5th century High King of Tara, Laoghaire, who allowed St Patrick to begin his mission in Ireland.

The town's seafaring history is detailed in the **National Maritime Museum**, housed in the former Mariners' Church on Haigh Street. Amongst the prize exhibits are a French longboat, sent to aid the nationalist rebels but captured at Bantry Bay in 1796, and the massive old optic from the Baily Lighthouse on Howth Head.

About a mile south of Dun Laoghaire, at Sandycove, the **James Joyce Martello Tower** is an essential stop for anyone following the James Joyce trail. The tower features in the first chapter of *Ulysses* with "stately, plump Buck Mulligan" performing his morning ablutions on the open top of the tower. Mulligan is based on the Irish poet and wit, Oliver St John Gogarty, with whom Joyce spent a few days here in August 1904. His stay had been intended to be much longer but one night one of the other guests had a nightmare and fired several shots into the fireplace of the room where they were sleeping. Gogarty then shot at a row of saucepans above Joyce's head, shouting "Leave him to me!" Joyce departed early the next morning. The tower has a small museum set up by Joyce's publisher, Sylvia Beach, which contains memorabilia of the author, including a tie given by Joyce to Samuel Beckett. On the seaward side of the tower is the Forty Foot Pool where, in *Ulysses*, Mulligan has a morning dip in the nude. The pool was for many years a men-only swimming place where nudity was the rule. Today, women can also swim here but a curt sign advises "Togs required - By Order".

DALKEY

MAP 7 REF M10

5 miles SE of Dublin on the R119

Pronounced "Dawkey", this pleasant little seaside town was the birthplace of the Elizabethan composer, John Dowland, who is commemorated by a statue in the park. The town also provided the material for Flann O'Brien's satirical novel *The Dalkey Archive*. Another of Ireland's great writers, George Bernard Shaw, lived at Torca Cottage on Dalkey Hill between 1866 and 1874. From the harbour there are boat trips to **Dalkey Island**, a treeless, low-lying island crowned by another of the Martello Towers erected to defend the realm from attack during the Napoleonic wars. There's a bird sanctuary here and the fragmentary ruins of the early Irish St Begnet's Oratory.

Just south of Dalkey is Killiney *("kill-eye-nee")* where there's a public park atop **Killiney Hill** offering breathtaking views of Dublin Bay and the Wicklow Hills. You can also enjoy this stunning view by taking the DART train for the short trip from Dalkey to Bray, just over the county boundary in Co. Wicklow.

2 The East Midlands

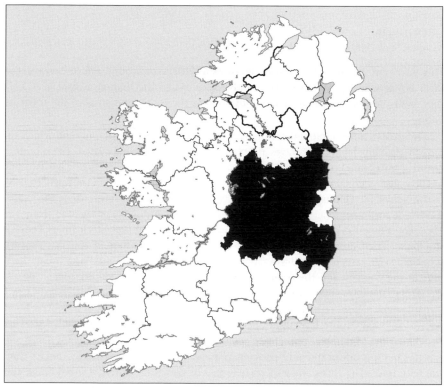

COUNTY LOUTH

The smallest of Ireland's 32 counties, Louth covers an area of only 317 square miles, most of it fertile, undulating country with a coastline of sandy beaches interspersed with rocky headlands. But the landscape changes in the north where the mountainous Cooley Peninsula looks across Carlingford Lough to the Mountains of Mourne. Part of the old province of Leinster, County Louth figures prominently in the epic stories of Ireland's misty past. The most famous of these tales tells of Queen Maeve of Connacht who started a war to win a bull she coveted. Maeve had the power to immobilise her enemies with a magical sickness - all save one, the warrior Cúchulainn who single-handedly defeated her troops.

Louth and the neighbouring county of Meath are both rich in prehistoric remains, and the ruins of the great religious foundations of Mellifont Abbey and Monasterboice testify to the religious preoccupations of medieval Leinster. There are only two towns of any size in County Louth, both with populations of around 28,000; the port and county town of Dundalk in the north, and Drogheda in the south which is where we begin our tour.

DROGHEDA   MAP 6 REF L8
35 miles N of Dublin on the N1

This busy port and industrial centre began as a settlement around a ford crossing the River Boyne where St Mary's Bridge stands today. When the Vikings arrived in 911AD they built the first *Droichead Atha*, "bridge across the ford", and so gave the town its name.

Drogheda's most dominant feature is **Millmount**, a huge earthen mound which reputedly contains prehistoric graves although it has never been excavated. The mount is crowned by a Martello Tower which was badly damaged during the 1922 Civil War but has been fully restored and now provides some grand panoramic views of the town. Housed in the nearby 18th century military barracks is the **Millmount Museum** where the exhibits include a wonderful period kitchen, complete with a hand-powered vacuum cleaner of 1860, and a Boyne coracle, the circular fishing boat in use from prehistoric times. Perhaps the most prized possessions though are the three large banners of the 18th century broguemakers', carpenters' and weavers' guilds. These are the only surviving Guilds' banners in the country and the beautifully woven drapes are wonderfully rich in detail. Drogheda's tradition of fine workmanship is maintained in the adjacent **Millmount Craft Centre** where the six resident craft workers offer a fascinating range of jewellery, hand painted silks, patchwork & appliqué, fashion knitwear, ceramics and decorative glass.

During the Middle Ages Drogheda city walls had no fewer than ten gates. Only one survives but it is one of the most perfectly preserved in the country. **St Lawrence's Gate** was built in the late 1200s and it's a miracle that its two drum towers, 4 storeys high and supporting a portcullis gate, somehow escaped Cromwell's savage assault on the town in 1649 when his troops massacred 2,000 of the garrison and citizens. Many sought refuge in **St Peter's Church** and were burnt to death when Cromwell's soldiers set the 13th century wooden structure on fire. The present church was erected in 1753, an elegant building with a fine porch and steeple designed by the eminent Irish architect Francis Johnston. The graveyard here contains the macabre Golding Cadaver tombstone slabs which depict the horrors of the Black Death and a gruesome, though finely sculpted, memorial of 1520 which dwells on the effects of bodily decomposition.

In Drogheda's main thoroughfare, West Street, there's another **St Peter's Church**. This imposing Roman Catholic place of worship was erected as a memorial to St Oliver Plunkett, Archbishop of Armagh, who was executed in London in 1681 for his alleged participation in the "Popish Plot" fabricated by Titus Oates. The archbishop's body was spirited away by his supporters and his head is now preserved at St Peter's in a special shrine which draws pilgrims from all over Ireland to venerate the relic. Oliver Plunkett was canonized in 1975, the first Irishman to be made a saint for more than 700 years.

About 6 miles west of Drogheda stand the ruins of **Mellifont Abbey**, established in 1142 as the first Cistercian monastery in Ireland. Construction of the Abbey took fifteen years and its consecration in 1157 was attended by a papal legate, the Irish primate, 17 bishops and the leading lords temporal of Ireland. For almost 400 years the Abbey was one of the most important religious foundations in the country, with 38 other monasteries under its jurisdiction. In 1539, Henry VIII closed them all. The glorious building with its huge pillars supporting a canopy of soaring arches was handed to Sir Edward Moore, ancestor of the Earls of Drogheda, who converted the church into a fortified mansion. His fortifications proved ineffectual against an onslaught by Cromwell's troops in 1649 and by the mid-1800s the shattered building was serving as a pigsty.

Few of the remains rise above shoulder height but a notable exception is the Lavabo, built around 1200. Originally octagonal, today only four walls remain standing. The monks would come to the Lavabo before meals to wash their hands in the jets that sprayed from a fountain in the centre. The only other substantial portions of the Abbey still in place are the two square towers of a former gatehouse.

Muiredach's Cross, Monasterboice

About 6 miles northwest of Drogheda, **Monasterboice** (*Mainistir Buite*, "Buite's Monastery") is notable for the remains of the monastic settlement founded by St Buite in the 5th century. This small, secluded site contains two of the most perfect 10th century high crosses in Ireland and one of the best surviving Round Towers. Muireadach's Cross stands 17 feet 8 inches high with every inch of its surface covered with exquisitely carved Biblical scenes and a depiction of the Last Judgement. Nearby, the West Cross is even taller, 21 feet 6 inches, and although more weathered is equally richly ornamented. Towering above the crosses is what must have been the tallest Round Tower in Ireland before it lost its conical cap. It still stands almost 110 feet high and is 51 feet across at its base.

ARDEE
MAP 6 REF L8
13 miles NW of Drogheda on the N2

This attractive little market town on the River Dee stands at a strategic crossroads and was often used as a mustering point by the English for their attacks on Ulster. This explains why the town has two castles: the 13th century Ardee Castle, whose square keep now houses a museum and gift shop, and Hatch's Castle in Market Street which dates from the same period. Ardee stood at the northern boundary of The Pale, the area controlled by the English since the days of Henry II. The territories "beyond the Pale" were regarded as outside the boundaries of a civilized society.

Conveniently located in the town's main street, the Bord Failte-approved **Setanta** is a fine old Georgian town house which has been sympathetically restored and converted into a unique family-run Bed & Breakfast establishment. The proprietors, Declan and Una Taaffe, will do all they can to ensure that your stay in this charming old house is a happy and memorable one. High-ceilinged rooms, original oak beams and wooden floors all add to the inviting atmosphere and blend happily with modern features such as the en suite

Setanta, 7 Castle Street, Ardee, Co. Louth
Tel: 041 685 3319 e-mail: setanta_ardee@ireland.com
website: www.dragnet-systems.ie/dira/setanta

bedrooms all of which have colour television. Breakfast is served in the large dining room overlooking Castle Street and the choice includes vegetarian options and a children's menu. Declan and Una named their house after the birth name of the famed Cúchulainn, champion of Ulster, who at Ardee gave battle to his foster brother, Ferdia, the champion of the South. After many days battle, Cúchulainn slew Ferdia and it was from the fallen hero that Ardee derived its name, *Atha Fhirdhia*.

Collectors of ecclesiastical curiosities should make the short journey from Ardee to the village of **Kildernock** and its **Jumping Church**. There are two theories as to why most of the end wall of the church here stands 3 feet away from the base on which it was built. The locals' logical explanation is that the wall moved of its own accord in order to exclude the grave of an excommunicated sinner. Meteorologists have come up with the fanciful idea that it was actually a ferocious storm in 1715 that shifted the stonework so neatly. The graveyard here is also interesting because of the plain, foot-high stone slabs which are some of the earliest tombstones to mark the previously unidentified graves of the poor.

SMARMORE   MAP 6 REF L8
2 miles S of Ardee off the N2

Archives show that **Smarmore Castle** has been inhabited continuously from 1320 when William Taaffe was recorded as having his seat here. The Keep of that castle still stands, its stone walls some 8 feet thick. The extensions on either side were added around 1720 and 1760 respectively. This striking building, brimming with archaeological and historic importance, has been recently refurbished and now combines the elegance and relaxed

Smarmore Castle, Ardee, Co. Louth Tel: 041 685 7167 Fax: 041 685 7650
e-mail: info@smarmorecastle.com website: www.smarmorecastle.com

atmosphere of a bygone age with the comfort and range of facilities of the most modern accommodation. The Castle's five bedrooms all represent a different perspective on the building's unique history. Each has a cosy sitting area and en suite bathroom. Opened in May 1999, the Castle also boasts a state-of-the-art Fitness and Leisure Club, the use of which is free to residents. In addition to a 22-metre heated swimming pool, the complex contains a toddler's pool, sauna, steam room and jacuzzi, as well as a fully equipped gym with a variety of modern cardiovascular and aerobic equipment.

Other major attractions at Smarmore Castle are the 40 acres of extensive grounds including woodland walks and the charming Courtyard Restaurant. Facilities for golf, walking, cycling, angling and equestrian pursuits are all available locally, and the Boyne Valley, the Hill of Tara, Mellifont Abbey and the Cooley Peninsula are just some of the historic and scenic attractions located nearby.

LOUTH   MAP 6 REF L7
6 miles N of Ardee on the R171

Why the county should have taken its name from this peaceful little village isn't clear, but it's worth stopping off just to visit **St Mochta's Church**. According to legend, the original church here was built during the course of a single night to provide shelter for its founder, St Mochta, who died in 534. The present remains date back to the 1100s and were part of a monastery dedicated to the saint. The high, vaulted roof, reached by way of a shoulder-scraping staircase, is surprisingly graceful for such an early date.

DUNDALK   MAP 6 REF L7
22 miles N of Drogheda on the N1

The county town of Louth, Dundalk is a busy manufacturing town, sitting at the head of Dundalk Bay. In Celtic times, as *Dún Dealga*, it was already a fortress (*dún*) guarding the pass through the mountains to the province of Ulster. Vikings, Anglo-Normans and the English followed each other in fighting tooth and nail to command this strategic site. Centuries of unremitting warfare have left few traces of the town's history before things finally settled down, more or less, in the 18th century. The 14th century tower of St Nicholas' Church and the belltower of a Franciscan friary of 1240 are the only significant witnesses to Dundalk's medieval past.

When more prosperous times at last provided Dundalk's Town Fathers with sufficient funds for erecting substantial civic buildings, but with no distinctive Irish tradition of public architecture to emulate, they genuflected to the past. **The Courthouse** for example, completed in 1818, is modelled on the Temple of Theseus in Athens. The Courthouse is a lovely, airy building whose classical poise and grace will be a little tarnished for modern-day English visitors by the uncompromising inscription beneath the statue of a Guardian Angel on the plaza outside. The sculpture is dedicated to "the martyrs in the cause of liberty who fought and died in the struggle against English Tyranny and foreign rule in Ireland".

Despite those understandable anti-English sentiments of the time, the architects of Dundalk's Roman Catholic **St Patrick's Cathedral** seem to have had no reservations about producing a virtual replica of the exterior of one of England's most distinctive ecclesiastical buildings, King's College Chapel, Cambridge, complete with needle spires, huge mullioned windows and crenellated walls. Financial constraints ruled out any attempt to replicate in St Patrick's interior the 15th century glories of its East Anglian model so the lively Gothic contours of the cathedral from outside are considerably more rewarding than the austere interior.

Two other locations are worth a visit. **Louth County Museum**, housed in an impressive 18th century distillery, uses some high tech displays and an audio-visual presentation to tell the story of local industries from coopering to cigarettes while the top two floors of the building host travelling art exhibitions. A rather unusual attraction, about a mile south of the town on the N1, is the **Carrolls Tobacco Factory**, a striking 1970 building designed by Scott Tallon Walker.

Dundalk makes a good base for exploring the **Cooley Peninsula**, a magically unspoilt area with enchanting views across Carlingford Lough to the Mountains of Mourne. The peninsula was the setting for one of Ireland's best-known myths, the Táin Bó Cúailnge, or the Cattle Raid of Cooley mentioned above. Although the story is set in the first century AD, the topographical descriptions in the epic tale are so precise that many of the places can still be recognised.

At the western end of the peninsula, near **Ravensdale**, stands the gigantic **Proleek Dolmen**, accessible via a footpath from the rear of the Ballymascanlon Hotel. The huge capstone that crowns it weighs an incredible 46 tons.

DROMAD
Map 6 ref L7
5 miles N of Dundalk on the N1

With its creeper-clad walls **Parkview House** makes an attractive picture, a view enhanced by a lovely garden and beautiful surroundings. In this attractive modern bungalow, David and Patrick Beagan offer top quality bed and breakfast accommodation in a friendly atmosphere. They have 6 guest bedrooms, 4 of them en suite and all attractively decorated and equipped with colour television. At breakfast time there's a choice of a full Irish or vegetarian meal along with a choice for children. Parkview is within easy walking distance of some good restaurants, bars and discos, there are facilities nearby for golf, fishing,

Parkview House, Dromad, Dundalk, Co. Louth
Tel: 042 938 0026

pony trekking and hill walking, and Parkview's convenient location makes it an ideal base for exploring this corner of the country.

CARLINGFORD   MAP 6 REF M7
14 miles NE of Dundalk on the R173

The main settlement on the Cooley Peninsula, Carlingford is an attractive seaside resort with some fine beaches and a distinctly medieval feeling in its narrow, terraced streets where at one time there were 32 castellated buildings. St Patrick is said to have made his first landfall in Ireland here, the Vikings arrived a few centuries later, but the oldest survival from the past is the impressive bulk of **King John's Castle** down by the water's edge. With walls rising some 70 feet, it is the largest Norman Castle in the country. It was built around 1210 and shortly after its completion King John stayed here, hence the name. Also worth seeking out in Carlingford are the well-preserved Taaffe's Castle and a fortified house called the Mint. Neither building is open to the public. Close to the Mint and forming an archway over the road, the Tholsel was originally a gate tower in the town walls and later served as Carlingford's gaol.

The hills behind Carlingford provide splendid walking country, with a particularly breathtaking view near the village of Omeath. Another striking feature is Windy Gap, a narrow ravine which, according to the Táin Bó Cúailnge, was carved through the hills by Fergus, Queen Maeve's chief warrior.

Whether you are looking for an active holiday, or just want to relax in idyllic surroundings, **Beaufort House** is ideal. This elegant guesthouse, smartly decorated in ochre and white, stands right on the shore of Carlingford Loch with breathtaking views across to the Mountains of Mourne. A premier establishment, Beaufort House offers the very highest standards of accommodation, achieving the AA's Premier Selected 5 Diamonds

Beaufort House, Ghan Road, Carlingford, Co. Louth
Tel: 042 937 3879 Fax: 042 937 3878

Award, and a cuisine prepared by the award-winning proprietor for the discerning guest. The company also operates two matching Elan 36 sailing cruisers, available either for charter, cruises, or for sail training activities. The Seaschool is an ISA recognised teaching establishment and runs courses from Competent Crew, to Yachtmaster offshore. Guests at Beaufort House also have a multitude of different walks to choose from and the wealth of bird life in the environs should satisfy the most demanding twitcher. If you are not feeling actively inclined, just settle down in the Chart Room where you can simply read the newspapers or write that postcard!

COUNTY MEATH

Until the mid-1500s, the "Royal County of Meath" - so called because it is home to Tara, seat of the High Kings of Ireland - was combined with Westmeath, making it Ireland's fifth largest, and most powerful, province. Even 5000 years ago this area was clearly an important population centre as the astonishing megalithic cemetery at Loughcrew bears witness. The valley of the River Boyne is also rich in prehistoric tombs with the county as a whole containing by far the richest bounty of such remains in Ireland.

Although the county does have a short coastline, barely 7 miles long, Meath is first and foremost an inland county of rolling green pastures divided into rich plantations and prosperous farmsteads. It was here that one of Ireland's most fateful battles took place, the Battle of the Boyne in 1690, and other memories of the past are vividly evoked by the splendid Norman castle at Trim, the high cross and round tower at Kells, and the holy Hill of Slane.

NAVAN
MAP 7 REF K9
25 miles NE of Dublin on the N3

Navan, the county town, stands at the meeting of the Boyne and Blackwater Rivers, a strategic location in times past. There is little in the town itself to detain the sightseer but about 1½ miles to the south, on the east bank of the River Boyne, are the impressive ruins of **Athlumney Castle**, a 15th century tower house with a Jacobean manor house added in the early 1600s. It was the home of Sir Lancelot Dowdall, a devout Catholic who after the defeat of James II at the Battle of the Boyne set fire to his home rather than have it fall into the hands of William's troops. It is said that he watched from the opposite bank of the river as the house blazed throughout the night and then set off for an exile from which he never returned.

Northeast of Navan, about 1½ miles along the Slane road, is **Donaghmore**, the site of an early Christian settlement of which only a well preserved 10th century Round Tower survives. Its only doorway is 12 feet from the ground, its keystone carved with a figure of the crucified Christ. About a mile further east are the remains of **Dunmoe Castle**, a 15th century building that was destroyed by fire in 1799. The ruins aren't particularly impressive but the glorious view along the River Boyne certainly is.

KELLS

MAP 7 REF K8

10 miles NW of Navan on the N3

This little town on the River Blackwater is best known for the celebrated Book of Kells, the illuminated manuscript produced by the scribes of Iona around 800AD and brought to Kells for safe keeping from Viking raids. No trace of Kells monastery, founded by St Columba in 550AD, has survived and the original Book is now on display in Trinity College, Dublin, but you can see a facsimile copy of it in the modern **St Columba's Church**. In the churchyard are two remarkable early Christian survivals. The **South High Cross** is the largest and probably the oldest of the five high crosses in the town, four of them here in the churchyard. The South High Cross is intricately carved with a wealth of detailed scenes from Biblical stories. The nearby **Round Tower** is one of the best preserved in the country, nearly 100 feet high and only lacking its original conical cap. The alignment of the five windows near the top is believed to have been intended to provide a clear view of the 5 roads entering the town. It's known that the tower was already standing in 1076: in that year Murchadh Mac Flainn, a claimant for the High Kingship, was murdered here.

Just outside the churchyard, **St Colmcille's House** is possibly even older than the Round Tower and miraculously well-preserved. Its walls are 4 feet thick and those at the sides continue upwards, inclining inwards, to meet in a ridge. Inside, it measures about 24 by 21 feet and its 38 feet height was originally divided into two floors. Modern day visitors enter by a ground floor doorway but the entrance used by the monks can still be seen in the west wall, some 8 feet from the ground.

A little over a mile out of Kells along the Oldcastle road, the R163, a short detour will bring you to the **Castlekeeran Crosses**, all that remains of the Díseart Chiaráin, or Hermitage of Ciaran. The four high crosses in this secluded spot are considerably older than those in Kells and their decoration is much simpler. One of them actually stands in the river. This unusual siting is explained by an old story that rather improbably claims that St Columba was caught red-handed by St Ciaran as he made off with the cross to his own monastery. In his shame he dropped the cross in the river and fled back to Kells.

The Castlekeeran site also has an early Christian grave slab and a fine example of an Ogham stone. Ogham was an early Irish script using just vertical and diagonal strokes in various combinations. It survived until well into the 19th century in some isolated peasant communities where it had the advantage of being completely impenetrable to outsiders.

CARLANSTOWN

MAP 6 REF K8

2 miles N of Kells on the N52

Less than 2 miles from historic Kells, **Teach Cuailgne** offers luxurious bed and breakfast accommodation in idyllic surroundings. Peggy O'Reilly and her family have lived here for some 30 years and their warm and friendly welcome makes Teach Cuailgne the kind of place visitors return to again and again. Peggy is a keen golfer and will be happy to arrange privilege prices for green fees at local clubs, or a day's fishing, shooting or horse riding, whatever your preference happens to be. Peggy is also an accomplished cook so it's a good idea to book the optional evening meal and to sample her home-baked bread, cakes, buns and home-made jams. Vegetarian options are available and there's also a

Teach Cuailgne, Carlanstown, Kells, Co. Meath
Tel/Fax: 046 46621

children's menu. The 4 guest bedrooms at Teach Cuailgne are all equipped with TV, hairdryer and orthopaedic beds, and have a private bathroom and toilet. Non-smoking rooms are also available. Children are welcome - a baby-sitting service can be arranged if required, and there are also facilities for pets. Open all year except over Christmas, Teach Cuailgne provides a perfect base for exploring this historic and beautiful corner of the country.

OLDCASTLE
MAP 4 REF J8

12 miles NW of Kells on the R154

This sleepy little town set on the broad plain between the Loughcrew and Cavan hills has some attractive Georgian buildings and was once the largest yarn market in Ireland. The main attraction lies about 3 miles to the southeast in the Loughcrew Hills, the highest of which is **Slieve na Caillighe** (900 feet), "the Mountain of the Sorceress". Scattered across the summits of the three main peaks is a remarkable group of 30 Neolithic chambered cairns. One of the major archaeological sites in the country, the area here was comprehensively studied by the archaeologist Martin Brennan in 1980. He produced a convincing theory that the cairns were aligned to receive the rising sun on significant days such as the spring and autumn equinoxes. Despite their importance, the cairns are little visited, partly no doubt because some fairly extensive walking is involved.

SLANE
MAP 7 REF L8

7 miles NE of Navan on the N2/N52

Standing at the central crossroads of this appealing village are four almost identical Georgian houses. According to tradition they were built by four spinster sisters with a view to keeping an eye on their siblings' behaviour. A different version claims that it was their brother who built the four houses because he was exasperated by their constant squabbling when they were together.

The village was laid out in the 18th century by Viscount Conyngham whose plans also included the fine Georgian mill of 1766 that still stands beside the River Boyne. Across the road from the mill is an imposing Gothic gateway, the entrance to the Conyngham family seat, **Slane Castle**. The castle is not normally open to the public but there are occasional rock concerts in the grounds - the Rolling Stones, Bob Dylan and Bruce Springsteen have all performed here. The present owner of the castle is Lord Henry Mountcharles, an entrepreneur with many interests in the rock music business. This presumably explains why there's a nightclub held in the castle basement every Saturday evening. If you drive to Slane from Dublin along the N2 you will find it is an unusually straight road. It was constructed, so it is said, to enable George IV to waste no time in travelling to Slane and the welcoming arms of his mistress, the Marchioness Conyngham.

To the northwest of the village rises the famed **Hill of Slane** (530 feet). It was here that St Patrick lit the first Paschal fire at Easter 433AD to proclaim the arrival of Christianity in Ireland. This was in direct defiance of Laoghaire, High King of Tara, who had decreed that the first fire should be lit on the Hill of Tara. Fortunately, Christian forbearance ensured that St Patrick was promptly forgiven. The hilltop views of the Boyne Valley are splendid, and even more impressive if you climb the 60 or so steps to the top of the Friary Church which was built in 1512 on the site of the church founded here by St Patrick.

After St Patrick, Slane's most famous son is the poet Francis Ledwidge who was born at Slane in 1887. His birthplace, a stone-built labourer's cottage about a mile to the east of the town, is now the **Francis Ledwidge Museum**. On a stone plaque outside the cottage are the lines he wrote for his friend, Thomas MacDonagh, also a poet, who was executed by the British for his involvement in the Easter Rising of 1916: *He shall not hear the bittern cry / In the wild sky, where he is lain / Nor voices of the sweeter birds / Above the wailing of the rain.* Although a nationalist himself, Ledwidge volunteered to fight on the British side in the First World War and died on the battlefield of Flanders on July 31, 1917.

To the east of Slane, within a great loop of the River Boyne is the area known as **Brú na Bóinne** which contains some of Ireland's most important neolithic remains. The most spectacular of them is **Newgrange**, a passage grave which predates Stonehenge by a thousand years. The man-made mound is about 300 feet across, rises to 30 feet at its highest point, and is retained by a wall of brilliant white quartzite stones. It's been estimated that some 20,000 tons of stone were dragged here from the Wicklow Mountains, south of Dublin, to build the mound. Access to Newgrange is through the Brú na Bóinne Visitor Centre and then by bus to the site. There are guided tours of the inner stone chamber with its intricately decorated stones and the tour concludes with a recreation of the climactic moment on the morning of the winter solstice, December 21st, when the interior is illuminated by the sun streaming through a narrow "roof-box". To witness the actual event within the tomb, you need to book years ahead and during the summer season you may also find yourself facing a long wait since the Office of Public Works limits the number of admissions to 600 each day. If you possibly can, visit out of season; if not, visit anyway.

Newgrange is the most astonishing of the 40-odd neolithic monuments in this area but **Knowth**, 2 miles to the northwest, where excavations are still under way, is likely to be acknowledged as the most complete of the **Brú na Bóinne** monuments. Twice the size of Newgrange and 500 years older, the site was occupied from around 3000BC until the 13th century AD. The tunnel to the central chamber is over a hundred feet in length and the chamber itself is richly decorated. The 250 or so decorated stones discovered here constitute around half of all the known Irish passage grave art. While excavations continue, only the exterior can be viewed but the Visitor Centre has some informative displays about Knowth and a third passage grave nearby, Dowth, as well as the other standing stones and cairns within the area.

DONORE Map 7 ref L8
3 miles SW of Drogheda off the N51 or the R152

This little town was chosen by James II as his base before the fateful Battle of the Boyne on July 1st 1690. Just north of here, his force of 25,000 Irish and French troops was routed by the 38,000 men of William III's army. James fled to permanent exile in France and William's domination of Ireland was assured. The battlefield itself is just off the N51, opposite the turn to Tullyallen. A panoramic plan at the site gives a clear picture of the events that day in which 500 of William's soldiers and 1500 of James' perished.

TARA Map 7 ref K9
8 miles S of Navan off the N3

One of the most venerated sites in Ireland, the **Hill of Tara** was the symbolic seat of the High Kings of Tara. Although little more than 300 feet high, the grassy, flat-topped hill enjoys extensive views over the plains of County Meath but, wisely, no attempt has been made to create a Tara Theme Park of wood-and-wattle reconstructions. The Visitor Centre

Hill of Tara

provides an informative audio-visual presentation that gives full weight to the romantic legend while making sense of the 4000-year-old earthworks which are the only ancient structures to be seen apart from the **Lia Fáil, the Stone of Destiny**, on which it is said the Kings of Tara were crowned.

The origins of the Kingdom of Tara are lost in the mists of time but it reached its peak of power in the 3rd century AD during the reign of the legendary Cormac Mac Art. The kingship was not a hereditary title but acquired through negotiation or battle. Medieval writers, especially the author of the 12th century *Book of Leinster*, created a whole mythology surrounding the High Kings, their great banquet hall on the summit of the hill and the five great roads of Ireland that converged on Tara. Only the roads can be authenticated but all the other details are ingrained in Irish folk lore and the stories invest this historic spot with a magic all its own.

The area that gave rise to the idea of a Banquet Hall consists of a long, sunken corridor about 750 feet long and 90 feet wide. Archaeologists believe that in Neolithic times this space was a theatre for priestly or royal processions.

In more recent times, the Hill of Tara was the setting for a mass meeting called by Daniel O'Connell in 1845 as part of his campaign against union with Britain. It was estimated that more than 1 million people gathered here - one in eight of Ireland's population at that time. A hundred years later the Hill saw a smaller scale invasion when a group known as the British Israelites began excavations in the belief that the Ark of the Covenant was buried here. Local people apparently encouraged them in their search by planting Roman coins where they would be easily found. That was all the British Israelites found however, and they soon returned to London.

From the Hill of Tara winding country lanes lead westward to **Bective Abbey**, a beautiful example of medieval Cistercian architecture in an idyllic riverside setting. Founded in 1146, the Abbey at one time owned one third of County Meath and its Abbot held the right to a seat in the British House of Lords, one of only fifteen such peerages granted to the whole of the Pale. The extensive ruins dating mostly from the 1400s provide a romantic picture and usually there is plenty of peaceful solitude in which to appreciate them.

TRIM
9 miles SW of Navan on the R154

MAP 7 REF K9

The best approach to this pleasant and historic town set beside the River Boyne is along the R154 from Dublin. This route opens up a striking view of the imposing ruins scattered throughout the town, the most impressive of them being **Trim Castle** which is the largest Anglo-Norman fortress in Ireland, dating back to 1190. The well-preserved ruins sprawl across 2 acres with an outer wall almost 500 yards long and an encircling moat which could be filled from the River Boyne. With its ten D-shaped turrets, sturdy gate towers, barbican and drawbridges, the castle is a noble sight and provided an atmospheric location for scenes in Mel Gibson's 1995 film *Braveheart*. The castle is also known as King John's Castle, after the English king who stayed at Trim for a few days in 1210. A later, more reluctant visitor, was Henry of Lancaster who was imprisoned here by Richard II but went on to depose Richard and ascend the throne himself as Henry IV.

The most prominent ruin in Trim is the **Yellow Steeple**, all that remains of the 13th century Abbey of St Mary's. It stands on a ridge opposite the castle overlooking the town, a gaunt stone skeleton 125 feet high which in the setting sun takes on the honey colour that gives the tower its name. In front of the Steeple is **Talbot's Castle**, a fortified manor house built in 1415 by the Lord Lieutenant of Ireland, Sir John Talbot. It later became a Latin school whose most famous pupil was Arthur Wellesley, 1st Duke of Wellington. He entered Parliament as MP for Trim and it was during his period as Prime Minister, 1828-30, that he reluctantly agreed to the Act of Catholic Emancipation. The Duke lived in Dublingate Street, and in nearby Emmet Street there's a statue commemorating his distinguished career.

Nearby stands another of Trim's copious ruins - the remains of the 13th century **Newtown Cathedral**. Destroyed by fire some 500 years ago, it is still worth exploring and trying out the eerie echo in the cloister. Out in the graveyard, look out for the famous **Tomb of the Jealous Man & Woman**. The Elizabethan stone effigies of Sir Lucas Dillon and his wife, Lady Jayne Bathe, are separated by a sword signifying, it is said, Sir Lucas' displeasure at the affair between his wife and brother. Incidentally, if you suffer from warts, soak them in the water trapped in the nooks and crannies of the tomb and they will disappear. The rusty pins lying on the tomb are thank-offerings from sufferers who have been cured.

Situated on an elevated site overlooking Trim Castle and the River Boyne, **Highfield House** is a beautiful period residence offering a relaxing and friendly place to stay within 2 minutes walking distance of Trim town centre. Just park in the private car park and stroll into town to visit the many quaint shops, pubs and restaurants. Highfield's owners, Geraldine and Eddie Duignan, look after their guests well and even provide a telescope on site so that visitors can make the most of the excellent views on offer. Inside, there are 7

Highfield House, Maudlins Road, Trim, Co. Meath
Tel: 046 36386 Fax: 046 38182

spacious en suite guest rooms, all with colour TV, direct dial telephone and tea/coffee-making facilities. Golfers will find 4 courses within a 10-mile radius; Moy Riding Centre is nearby and there's good fishing on the River Boyne. Also worth a visit is "The Power & the Glory", an audio-visual show which brings the world of medieval Trim to life.

Family owned and run since 1915, **Brogans Guesthouse and Bar** is famed for its hospitality and friendly atmosphere. The handsome building dates back to the mid-19th century and stands in the heart of this historic, medieval town. Gerry Merrick (née Brogan), with her husband Denys, is the 3rd generation of her family to own and run this out-standing hostelry; Ruth, their daughter, the 4th. The Merricks have moved with the times, adding some superb new accommodation in the former stables adjoining the main house

Brogans Guesthouse and Bar, High Street, Trim, Co. Meath
Tel: 046 31237 Fax: 046 37648 e-mail: brogangh@iol.ie

where there are now 8 superb, generously-sized guest bedrooms, all individually designed, furnished and decorated to an exceptional standard. The 4 bedrooms on the ground floor provide easy access for wheelchairs. Guests can enjoy the outdoor barbecue area on balmy summer evenings, and there's also the convenience of a private car park. The 6 bedrooms located in the main house have also been recently refurbished. All rooms have an en suite bathroom, direct dial telephone, colour TV, hairdryer and tea/coffee facilities. After a busy day of work, golf or sightseeing, where better to relax than in the warm atmosphere of Brogans Bar, located in the main house, where you can enjoy a pint of Guinness and listen to long stories and tall tales!

About 10 miles east of Trim, **Dunsany Castle** has been the home of the Plunkett family since the 16th century. The first castle here was built in the 1100s by Hugh de Lacy but the present building is one of the most thriving examples of an Irish castle you are likely to see. It is packed with fine furniture, some unusual Jacobite relics, and a notable art collection which contains a portrait of St Oliver Plunkett, hanged in London in 1682 on trumped-up charges that he was implicated in the "Popish Plot". (The Catholic Plunketts only survived all the vicissitudes of religious persecution because another branch of the family were Protestants and so able to protect their interests). The grounds at Dunsany Castle are also impressive but they, and the castle, are only open to the public during July and August, and then only from 9am until 1pm, Monday to Saturday, although these opening hours may change.

ASHBOURNE   MAP 7 REF L9
10 miles NW of Dublin off the N2

Only 20 minutes drive from Dublin, **Aisling House** offers a warm, friendly welcome in a homely atmosphere with the added bonus of excellent food and comfortable accommodation. Aisling is the luxurious home of Kathleen and Michael Davitt who provide their guests with all the traditional comforts of home in a peaceful, rural setting. Standing on

**Aisling House, Baltrasna, Ashbourne, Co. Meath
Tel: 835 0359/835 1135**

¾ of an acre of landscaped gardens, their modern house offers 10 bedrooms with private facilities, is fully centrally heated and parking is ample. There are fine views of the countryside from the bedrooms which are decorated and furnished to a very high standard. Aisling House is only 10 miles from Dublin city, about the same distance from Fairyhouse Race Course, just 7 miles from the famous Tattersalls horse sales, and the astonishing Stone Age site of Newgrange is only 15 miles away. Locally, there are golf courses, horse riding and clay pigeon shooting and royal Meath also has many historic associations.

BULLSTOWN   MAP 7 REF L9
12 miles NW of Dublin off the N2

Only 20 minutes from Dublin city and 15 minutes from Dublin airport, **Broadmeadow Country House and Equestrian Centre** stands in pleasant rural surroundings near the

Broadmeadow Country House & Equestrian Centre, Bullstown, nr Ashbourne, Co. Meath Tel: 01 835 2823 Fax: 01 835 2819 e-mail: broadmeadow@eircom.net website: www.equinenet.com/Broadmeadow

town of Ashbourne. This exceptional 4**** country house and equestrian centre is run by the Duff family who have been involved in all aspects of the horse industry for generations. The house has 8 luxurious en suite bedrooms, all tastefully decorated to meet the expectations of their guests, both business and pleasure. The house is surrounded by beautiful landscaped gardens and a tennis court - a wonderfully peaceful spot in which to unwind and relax.

Their equestrian centre offers superb facilities for customers: an indoor and outdoor arena, a number of natural cross-country jumps, a coffee shop, reception and toilet facilities. Broadmeadow has horses and ponies that cater for every standard of rider from beginners to the more advanced. The Duffs tailor make packages to suit both individuals and groups. They provide for the customer who wishes to compete, improve their equestrian knowledge or simply ride for pleasure. For the non-rider, golf, cycling and tours can also be arranged.

COUNTY WESTMEATH

Set in the heart of this placid county, the Hill of Uisneach was believed to mark the spot where the ancient provinces of Ireland converged, "the navel of Ireland". The hill is something of an exception in this land of woods, rivers and lakes, renowned for its first class angling. Four large lakes lie completely within the county boundaries, it shares beautiful Lough Sheelin in the north with County Cavan, and islet-dotted Lough Ree, over to the west, is noted for its scenic cruises.

The county town, Mullingar, is a busy agricultural centre surrounded by great huntin', shootin' and fishin' country and graced by a fine Palladian mansion, Belvedere House, notable for its gardens and a huge folly known as the Jealous Wall. The only other town of any size is Athlone, a bustling road, rail and waterway centre within easy reach of "Goldsmith Country", the area around Glassan ("The Village of the Roses") which has close associations with the 18ᵗʰ century author of *The Vicar of Wakefield*. And you will surely want to discover the Seven Wonders of Fore, hidden away in the Fore Valley, an area of outstanding natural beauty.

MULLINGAR
MAP 4 REF J9

54 miles W of Dublin on the N4

Standing on the River Brosna, halfway between Lough Ennell and Lough Owel, Mullingar is almost encircled by the Royal Canal. Standing at the centre of Ireland's cattle-rearing heartland, it's a lively place with some excellent pubs and grocery shops. The town's most striking building is the **Cathedral of Christ the King**, a neo-Classical building of white stone whose twin spires soar 140 feet into the sky and, whether intentionally or not, somewhat resemble devotional candles. Inside, there are two interesting mosaics by the Russian artist Boris Anrep, and an ecclesiastical museum which contains many penal wooden crosses and the vestments of St Oliver Plunkett.

Mullingar was formerly a garrison town and the history of those days is recorded in the **Military Museum** at the Columb Barracks. Housed in the old Guard Room, the museum has a display of arms, uniforms and flags from both World Wars, as well as exhibits devoted to the IRA, the War of Independence and the Civil War of the 1920s. Not particularly military but nevertheless fascinating are the long, canoe-like boats which have been found in the boggy floor of the nearby lakes. Originally thought to be Viking craft, they have now been dated as much earlier. Amongst the oddities in the museum is a Military Cycling Handbook which explores this arcane skill with a gravity worthy of the Monty Python team.

If that seems somewhat bizarre, you can learn all about a genuine local eccentric in the **Market House Museum** which is run by volunteers and what it lacks in priceless items it makes up for with enthusiasm. The eccentric was Adolphus Cooke who amongst other peculiar notions was convinced that one of the turkeys strutting about his yard was the reincarnation of his father. He also had the windows of his house made into the shape of spoon-backed chairs, the better to reflect the furniture within. Throughout his life, Adolphus was convinced that he would be reincarnated as a bee so he arranged to be buried in a tomb resembling a beehive. It stands in the graveyard of Cooksborough church, about 8 miles east of Mullingar.

If you are looking for quality bed and breakfast accommodation in Mullingar, look no further than **Turnpike Lodge**, about a mile from the town centre. The house takes its name from the old toll house that stood nearby on what was then an important toll road. The present house though is a spacious modern building in Tudor style, surrounded by a large garden. Turnpike Lodge is the home of Catherine and Tom Bennett who both possess a real knack for making their guests also feel at home. All of their 5 letting rooms are

**Turnpike Lodge, Dublin Road, Petitswood, Mullingar, Co. Westmeath
Tel: 044 44913**

en suite, non-smoking, exceptionally well furnished and decorated, and equipped with television. Downstairs, the residents' lounge overlooks the attractive garden and, on cooler evenings, is fragrant with the aroma of logs burning on the open fire.

Few equestrian centres, even in Ireland, enjoy such stately surroundings as **Ladestown House Riding Stables**. They are based in elegant 18th century stables and outbuildings, where you will also find top quality self-catering accommodation available. Ladestown Stables offers a superb selection of horses with a choice of mounts suitable for both beginners and skilled riders alike. Expert supervisors are always at hand to guide you through the surrounding countryside of lakes and gentle hills which provides a perfect terrain for exploring on horseback. The Ladestown Stables are owned and run by Brian and Tony

**Ladestown House Riding Stables, Mullingar, Co. Westmeath
Tel: 044 48218 Fax: 044 44253**

Peters, experienced equestrians who make every effort to ensure that you enjoy your riding here as much as they do. And as their children do. Brian's daughter, Philippa, for example, won the silver medal and team bronze medal for Ireland at the 1999 European Championships. Brian and Peter also provide the ideal arrangement for visitors looking for the combination of top-quality riding facilities and convenient self-catering accommodation. Part of the venerable old building has been ingeniously converted into 2 self-contained apartments, attractively furnished and decorated, with kitchens fully equipped with just about everything you could possibly need. Additional attractions at Ladestown House include the biggest maze in Ireland and a tropical orchid house whose historical importance there's no space to describe here. Book in at Ladestown and ask Brian or Peter!

About 3 miles south of Mullingar, on the shores of **Lough Ennell**, **Belvedere House & Gardens** is a popular destination for a summer afternoon's outing. This attractive Palladian house was built around 1740 for Robert Rochfort, later 1st Earl of Belvedere. Rochfort was a deeply unpleasant man by all accounts who kept his young wife a prisoner in a nearby house for 31 years after accusing her of adultery with his younger brother, Arthur. Arthur fled to England and didn't return to Ireland for 20 years when he was promptly sued by the Earl for adultery. Unable to pay the legal costs, Arthur spent the rest of his life in gaol. The Earl also quarrelled with another brother, George, who lived at Tudenham House just across from the Earl's home. To block out any view of Tudenham House, the Earl ordered the building of the **Jealous Wall**, an impressive Gothic folly said to be the largest man-made ruin in Ireland.

At the time of writing, the interior of Belvedere House is being renovated and is not open to the public. But visitors are welcome to wander through the gardens which are stocked with a wide variety of rare shrubs and trees, swim in the lake, follow the woodland walks or simply bring a picnic.

TYRRELLSPASS

MAP 4 REF J10

11 miles S of Mullingar on the N52/N6

This delightful Georgian village takes its name from Robert Tyrrell, a late-16th century hero who annihilated a large force of Elizabethan troops near here with the help of a small band of men. The winner of many Irish "Tidy Town" awards, the village is formally laid out around a semi-circular village green and amongst the buildings of note are an impressive tower house with a small museum and café, and **St Sinian's Church** which contains some elaborate tombs to the Belvedere family. One of them commemorates Jane, a countess "gifted with a masculine understanding".

Overlooking the village green, **The Village Hotel** was built as part of an elegant Georgian crescent by that very same Jane, Countess of Belvedere. The beer garden at the front of the hotel provides a perfect setting for watching the world go by in this outstandingly pretty village. The hotel's owner, Gerard Clery, has taken great pains to retain the gracious Georgian features of the building while providing all the amenities expected of a modern hotel - en suite guest bedrooms with TV and direct dial telephones for example. The hotel is beautifully and tastefully decorated throughout and nothing seems to be too

The Village Hotel, Tyrrellspass, Co. Westmeath
Tel: 044 23171 Fax: 044 23491

much trouble for the friendly and helpful staff. The restaurant has an excellent reputation for fine fare and an award winning Innkeeper's Buffet serving bar food all day. The restaurant also offers a superb selection of fine wines from around the world. The area's attractions include a championship golf course at Esker Hills; one of the world's oldest distilleries - Lockes; heavenly fishing at Lough Ennell, or you can enjoy a fantastic day out at Kilbeggan's famous racecourse.

KILBEGGAN   MAP 4 REF I10
14 miles SW of Mullingar on the N6

The main visitor attraction in this neat little town on the River Brosna is **Locke's Distillery**, believed to be the oldest pot still distillery in the world. Established in 1757, pot still Irish malt whiskey was produced here for almost 200 years. In recent years, the local community has been restoring the building and machinery so that the huge old water wheel is now turning again and visitors can follow the process from the grinding of the grain to the casking of the final product. There's a bar within the distillery, where you can sample "the water of life", and a restaurant where you can enjoy a meal in front of an open fire.

NORTH OF MULLINGAR

This is the most scenic part of the county, containing the loughs of Derravaragh, Lene and Sheelin, and the enchanting Fore Valley running close to the border with County

Meath. The area also boasts one of Ireland's largest and most romantic stately homes, Tullynally Castle, and the ancient ecclesiastical settlement of Fore Abbey. Visitors can also follow the Fore Trail which links the celebrated "Seven Wonders of Fore".

MULTYFARNHAM   MAP 4 REF J9
8 miles N of Mullingar off the N4

This winner of the "Tidy Towns" award stands on the River Gaine about half a mile from where it flows into Lough Derravaragh. The modern Franciscan **Friary** here stands on the site of one founded around 1260. It was suppressed by Henry VIII in 1540 but the monks maintained a presence here - "a nest of scorpions" as Elizabeth I described them - until they were scattered by Cromwell's troops in 1651. The old Friary was restored in 1973 and has some striking modern stained glass. The beautifully laid out grounds contain life-size stations of the cross, regarded as one of the finest outdoor shrines in Ireland.

Housed in an attractive stone building dating back some 200 years, **An Tintain** is both a fully licensed restaurant and a delightful guest house. Ian and Liz Milburn have owned this dual establishment since 1993 and during that time have earned an excellent reputation for both good food and comfortable accommodation. Their menu offers a

An Tintain, Multyfarnham, Co. Westmeath
Tel: 044 71411   Fax: 044 71434

mixture of European dishes as well as more traditional fare and vegetarian options. In the evening, meals can be enjoyed by the light of candles and the open log fire. An Tintain's 8 guest bedrooms are all en suite, tastefully decorated and furnished, and all equipped with television and direct dial telephone. If you are touring the lovely lake country of Westmeath, An Tintain provides an ideal base.

CASTLEPOLLARD
Map 4 ref J8
13 miles N of Mullingar on the R354

This neat little town was laid out in the late 17th/early 18th century by the Pollard family with attractive houses set around a large triangular green. Castlepollard is a popular base for anglers drawn here by the abundant roach, pike and trout in nearby Loughs Derravaragh and Lene, and for visitors to **Tullynally Castle**, hereditary home for ten generations of the Anglo-Irish Pakenham family, the Earls of Longford. One of the largest and stateliest homes in Ireland, the castle was built as a simple tower house in the late 1600s but was remodelled in the Gothic Revival style - bristling with battlements, towers and turrets, in the early 1800s. Guided tours of the house include the Great Hall whose superb acoustics make it an ideal venue for concerts and recitals; the Library started by the 1st Earl's wife in the 1760s and now containing more than 8000 volumes; and a vast Victorian kitchen.

The castle stands in 30 acres of romantic woodland and walled gardens laid out in the 18th and 19th centuries which contain many splendid trees, a grotto and two ornamental lakes. The grounds are open to visitors from May to September; the castle itself from mid June to mid August every afternoon and at other times by arrangement.

FORE
Map 4 ref J8
16 miles NE of Mullingar off the R195

The **Seven Wonders of Fore** are scattered across the Fore Valley but the local tourist board has produced a useful leaflet detailing the Fore Trail which links them and other places of interest in the valley. The traditional listing of the 7 wonders has "the anchorite in a stone" as number six. This refers to the **Anchorite's Cell**, a cubicle 8 feet by 12 feet in the

The Anchorite's Cell, Fore

tower of a tiny chapel on the hillside above Fore which was occupied by hermits right up until 1616. The last hermit was a man called Patrick Beglan who had vowed to stay in the cell until he died. Oddly, he broke his neck falling from the tower window. The chapel is kept locked but the key can be obtained from the appropriately named Seven Wonders pub nearby.

At the bottom of the hill is Wonder Number 2: "the monastery in the bog", the roofless remains of **St Fechin's Church**, named after St Fechin's Spring nearby from which bubbles up Wonder Number 5: "the water that will not boil". St Fechin founded his monastery here around 630AD but the present ruins date from the 11th to the 13th centuries. A notable feature of the church is the mighty lintel stone over its west doorway which is carved with a Greek cross within a circle. It weighs over two tons and could only have been put in place by means of a miracle, hence Wonder Number 7: "the stone raised by St Fechin's prayers". The remaining three Wonders are "the water that flows uphill", which refers to the river flowing out of Lough Lene where a trick of the light makes it seem as if the water is indeed running upwards; "the tree that will not burn", probably a petrified stump but now represented by a tourist board placement of a dead branch, and "the mill without a race", the only one of the Wonders that has not been satisfactorily explained. Other antiquities in and around Fore include the stone gateways that led into the medieval village, and no fewer than 18 crosses, some plain, others carved, of which the best preserved stands in the middle of the village.

The best starting point for an exploration of the enchanting Fore Valley and its Seven Wonders is Fore village; and the best base in Fore village is **Hounslow House**, a spacious 200-year-old farmhouse overlooking the valley and its historic Abbey. The house enjoys sweeping views and stands in extensive grounds in which there are swings for the children and a games room in the converted stables. Visitors are welcomed with tea on arrival

Hounslow House, Fore, Castlepollard, Co. Westmeath
Tel: 044 61144 Fax: 044 61847
e-mail: Eithne_Healy_Hounslow@MailAndNews.com

and your host, Eithne Healy, is happy to provide evening meals and packed lunches on request, and will cater for vegetarian tastes as well as offering a children's menu. And for the perfect place to relax, just settle down in the residents' lounge with its lovely views along the valley.

COLLINSTOWN
Map 4 ref J9

14 miles NE of Mullingar on the R395

Collinstown village, once known as the "Maypole", always presents a very pretty appearance, especially during the summer months, with flower filled gardens and a general air of neatness and order. The village stands close to the southern tip of Lough Lene, a European Blue Flag Lake and a popular venue for swimmers, anglers and scuba divers. The village also has its own pitch and putt course.

"When you arrive as visitors at **Cummerstown House** you leave as friends". Such is the attractive philosophy of Matt and Monica O'Donnell who have converted part of their sturdy farmhouse building (dating back to 1846) into a romantic 2-bedroom country cottage for self-catering visitors. The cottage provides the kind of setting that begs you

Cummerstown House, Collinstown, Co. Westmeath
Tel: 044 66316

not to leave: pine ceilings and floors, tasteful furnishings, and a kitchen fit for a gourmet cook. The farmhouse stands at the hub of a true working farm where younger children, particularly, will be entranced by the feel of farm life, surrounded by lots of animal friends: chickens, ducks, horses and even a donkey. All the family will find plentiful entertainment in the spacious games room which offers a choice of snooker, table tennis and a darts' board.

WEST OF MULLINGAR

About 10 miles southwest of Mullingar is **Uisneach Hill**, the "navel of Ireland", which in mythology was the seat of the High Kings before they moved to Tara. The only evidence for this are thick layers of ashes suggesting that it was the site for fire festivals such as the Beltane, held in the first days of May. *Bealtaine* incidentally is the Irish word for the month of May. An ancient boulder, the Catstone ("Stone of Divisions"), stands atop the hill and traditionally marks the geographical centre of the 4 ancient provinces of Ireland: Leinster, Munster, Connacht and Ulster. If you climb to the summit of the 250 feet hill there are views taking in 20 of the 32 counties that formed the 4 provinces.

ATHLONE   Map 4 ref H9
28 miles SW of Mullingar on the R390/N6

Straddling the River Shannon just before it flows into Lough Ree, Athlone has been an important strategic location since prehistoric times. Turlough O'Connor built a wattle bridge here and fortified the banks. Brian Boru, High King of Ireland, convened a great assembly at Athlone in 1001 and two centuries later the Anglo-Normans replaced an earlier castle with the sturdy fortress known as **King John's Castle** which was in use by the military right up until 1969. Although it has been strengthened and extended over the centuries, the castle still retains its classic, uncompromising Norman design. During its long history the castle has seen a great deal of action, most notably in 1690 when

Sheela-na-Gigs

supporters of James II withstood a week-long siege here, and again in 1691 when William III's artillery peppered the town and castle with some 12,000 cannonballs.

The circular keep of castle now houses an interesting museum of folk and local history where amongst other things you can learn the approved method of milking a cow, (begin by squirting a few drops on the grass for the fairies), and see the pairs of boots worn by ponies when rolling the lawn to avoid leaving any unsightly hoof prints. The collection also includes two fine examples of **Sheela-na-Gig sculptures**, (prehistoric fertility symbols), and a fascinating display devoted to John McCormack, the legendary tenor who was born at Athlone in 1884. The singer's own 78rpm gramophone is among the exhibits, along with a stack of his recordings - visitors can ask for their favourite to be played. A bust of McCormack, who was created a Papal Count in 1928 for his charity work, occupies a prominent position on the riverside promenade and a plaque marks his house in The Bawn, off Mardyke Street.

Outstanding cuisine served in unique surroundings is the appealing combination on offer at **Restaurant Le Chateau**, a temple of good eating which is housed in a former Presbyterian Church. The interior of this handsome waterside building has been transformed into a striking split-level restaurant designed like an old galleon, with raised floors upstairs to resemble the decks. At the back of the restaurant is an original Star of David stained glass window restored to its original splendour. Advantage was taken during the renovation of installing every

Restaurant Le Chateau, St Peter's Port, The Docks, Athlone, Co. Westmeath Tel: 0902 94517 Fax: 0902 73740 e-mail: lechateau@tinet.ie

modern convenience, from air conditioning to wheelchair access. Le Chateau's owners, Steven and Martin Linehan, are both qualified chefs with extensive careers ranging from Ashford Castle and the west of Ireland to as far-flung places as Hong Kong, America and Paris. They offer a fine choice of menus to suit everyone's taste, ranging from a 5-course dinner to an extensive à la carte. A very varied wine list is available, with vintages from 1968 to 1996, all at affordable prices. Understandably, this atmospheric restaurant has been showered with awards, many of them making special mention of the Candlelight Dinner Menu.

For clean, comfortable and well-appointed budget accommodation in the Athlone area, the place to seek out is **Lough Ree Lodge**, conveniently located on the Dublin Road.

Lough Ree Lodge, Dublin Road, Athlone, Co. Westmeath Tel: 0902 76738 Fax: 0902 76477

Owned and run by Gerry and Geraldine Barry, this smart, modern facility stands in its own grounds with large gardens and plenty of private parking spaces provided. There are 60 guest bedrooms, all en suite and equipped with TV, and of varying sizes. There's also a large common room where guests can enjoy a chat with other guests or simply sit and relax. A Continental breakfast is available and packed lunches are also available on request. The Lodge has a warm and friendly atmosphere and Gerry and Geraldine will be happy to share their local knowledge of where to go and what to do.

Especially popular with anglers, **Riverdale House** is a large, detached property, well located in a quiet residential area and yet close to Athlone town centre and within 200 yards of the River Shannon and the famous "Meadows Stretch". Riverdale enjoys an excellent reputation for ensuring clients receive well prepared food in comfortable and friendly surroundings, and good, up-to-date angling information. The house caters for a maximum of 18 guests, thus ensuring a high level of personal service and home-from-home

Riverdale House, Clonown Road, Athlone, Co. Westmeath
Tel: 0902 92480

comforts. All rooms have cable TV and constant hot water, and there's a large TV/video lounge to relax in after your day's sightseeing or fishing. Whether it is a family, or serious fishing holiday, Riverdale House will suit your requirements perfectly.

In a wonderfully peaceful and secluded spot just a couple of miles from Athlone, **Creaghduff Lodge** provides quality self-catering accommodation in a 300-year-old recently restored stone cottage. The Lodge is situated on an estate of natural woodland and has its own private harbour on Coosan Lough, renowned for excellent coarse fishing - specimen bream, tench, rudd and rudd/bream hybrids. Boats and engines are available for hire. There are 2 self-catering apartments within the Lodge, each with a fitted kitchen with electric cooker and fridge; dining/sitting area; and bedroom sleeping 4 with a bathroom en suite. Children are welcome and a baby-sitting service can be arranged if required.

Creaghduff Lodge, Creaghduff House, Athlone, Co. Westmeath
Tel: 0902 75891

The apartments are equipped with washing machine, colour television and free bed linen, and also provided is a bait and tackle room complete with fridge. Outside, there are large gardens and ample parking space. Facilities for a wide choice of activities are available locally, from nature walks and bird watching, to golf and horse-riding, with plenty of evening entertainment on tap in Athlone's pubs, hotels and night clubs.

BALLYKEERAN
3 miles NE of Athlone on the N55

MAP 4 REF H9

A popular choice for a day out in this area is to take a boat trip on Lough Ree which is actually an expansion of the River Shannon, about 15 miles long and varying from 1 mile to 6 miles across. Several of the islands on the lough have the remains of very early churches, one of them, **Inchclearaun**, boasting no few than six early Christian ruins. Your guide will regale you with stories of Queen Maeve, goddess of war and fertility, who it seems was very active around Lough Ree in mythological times. Also look out for the ruins of 13th century **Rindown Castle** which stands on a spit of land jutting out into the lake.

Lough Ree, with its legend-rich islands of Inchclearaun and Inchbofin, is a wonderfully scenic spot, and **Harbour House** is ideally situated to make the most of its many attractions. This luxuriously appointed modern bungalow enjoys an exceptionally peaceful location although barely a mile from the N55. Your host is Ann Meade who greets arriving guests with a friendly welcome and a refreshing cup of tea. Ann will do everything she can to make your stay as pleasant and relaxing as possible, arranging boat hire if you wish or providing a satisfying packed lunch. Breakfast is equally enjoyable with a good choice that includes a "Full Irish" and a vegetarian option. Ann doesn't provide

**Harbour House, Portaneena, Ballykeeran, Athlone, Co. Westmeath
Tel/Fax: 0902 85063 e-mail: ameade@indigo.ie**

evening meals but a short walk (150 yards) will bring you to local eating places and
Athlone town is just 3 miles away. All the comfortable guest rooms at Harbour House
have private facilities, colour television, hairdryer and tea/coffee-making facilities, and
non-smoking rooms are available if required.

CARTRONTROY
1 mile E of Athlone off the N6

MAP 4 REF H9

For those who agree that breakfast is the most important meal of the day, then there's
only one place to stay in the Athlone area. Situated in a quiet location just a mile or so
from Athlone town centre, **Shelmalier House** is the proud winner of the National Galtee
Breakfast Awards. Breakfast is indeed rather special here with home-baked bread accompanying the superbly cooked traditional Irish breakfast, supplemented by a fresh fruit
buffet and all the trimmings. There's a menu for children, another for vegetarians, and
you can extend your eating pleasure by booking a packed lunch. Shelmalier House is an

**Shelmalier House, Cartrontroy, Athlone, Co. Westmeath
Tel: 0902 72145 Fax: 0902 73190**

impressive modern building surrounded by large, attractive gardens, (complete with barbecue area), and its 7 guest bedrooms are exceptionally well furnished and decorated. All of them are en suite and equipped with TV, direct dial telephone, radio and tea/coffee-making facilities. Shelmalier House is the home of Jim and Nancy Denby who make every effort to ensure a comfortable and relaxing stay for their guests. Athlone's central position in the heart of Ireland makes this an ideal base for touring with excellent facilities for golf, fishing and family activities all within easy reach.

GLASSAN
4 miles NE of Athlone on the N55

Map 4 ref H9

> *Ill fares the land, to hastening ills a prey*
> *Where wealth accumulates and men decay.*

Those familiar lines from Oliver Goldsmith's poem *The Deserted Village* were written with Glassan in mind. The poet was lamenting the mid-18th century enclosures which were devastating rural life throughout Britain:

> *No busy steps the grassgrown foot-way tread*
> *For all the bloomy flush of life is fled.*

In his poem, Glassan appears as "sweet Auburn", the "village of the roses" and by a curious quirk of history it was a later enclosure of the neighbouring Waterstown estate which led to the building of this attractive estate village.

Built in the 1750s, **Grogan's** is a charming whitewashed building made colourful with window boxes and umbrellas shading the tables on the forecourt. Paddy, Moira and Miriam

Grogan's Pub, Glassan, Athlone, Co. Westmeath
Tel: 0902 85158 Fax: 0902 85685

Grogan are your hosts and they preside over a wonderfully atmospheric traditional Irish family inn which also incorporates an award-winning restaurant, Nannie Murph's Seafood and Steak Bar. Nannie Murph's menu offers a tantalising choice of appetising dishes: Sautéed Crab Toes with garlic on a bed of mixed salad leaves amongst the starters for example, a wide choice of main courses which includes Ostrich with a plum and Madeira sauce, fish, steaks, vegetarian dishes, and "Nannie's Favourites" - tried and tested treats such as a traditional Irish Stew "full of vegetables and spuds". If you plan to eat here at the weekend, you should certainly book ahead. The bar at Grogan's is also a very popular venue, especially midweek when there's live traditional Irish music to enjoy along with fine ales and good craic.

Just outside Glassan, in a rural location near the shores of Lough Ennell, **The Portlick Inn** provides all the delights of a traditional Irish inn with the added bonus of 2 comfortable self-catering apartments to let. Your host, Paddy Killmartin, and his "crew" offer a genuine Irish welcome, good bar food, and a superb atmosphere. The modern single-level building has some interesting decor - features such as oak beams, carved wooden fixtures,

**The Portlick Inn, Killenmore, Glassan, Co. Westmeath
Tel: 0902 85512**

and a half-size fishing rowboat sticking out of the wall! An additional attraction here is the live entertainment - anything from country to traditional Irish and folk. If you're staying, the self-catering apartments (which sleep 5 and 3 persons respectively) are both self-contained, with fully-equipped kitchen, TV, and with bed linen included in the rental. This is good fishing country and Paddy, or his bar manager, Rosie, will be more than happy to arrange boat hire, bait and tackle, and direct you to the best locations. Clay pigeon shooting can also be arranged and should you be planning a special event, there's a marquee area at The Portlick Inn with seating for up to 1,000 people!

Enjoying an idyllic location on the shore of Lough Ree, **St Mark's Accommodation** offers visitors to this lovely corner of the county a choice of either bed and breakfast or self-catering accommodation. Lough Ree is of course well-known as an anglers' Paradise and it's also popular with swimmers and sailing folk. If your particular preference is golf, then there's an 18-hole course just a few minutes drive away. St Marks itself provides residents with a tennis court and basketball pitch. Bed and breakfast guests stay in en

St Mark's Accommodation, Glassan, Athlone, Co. Westmeath
Tel/Fax: 0902 85125

suite bedrooms at the main house: self-catering visitors are accommodated in a quaint traditional cottage which has been sensitively modernised to provide all up-to-date amenities. Both properties command soothing, panoramic views across the lough. Bed and breakfast visitors are welcome all year round and have the additional options of staying on either a half or full board basis. Whichever option you choose, your hosts, Ann and Michael Hopkins will do all they can to ensure that your stay is as relaxed and comfortable as possible.

The local tourist authorities have been zealous in putting up brown and white signs directing visitors to any site connected with Oliver Goldsmith although it has to be said that some of them are less than rewarding. Of his childhood home, the parsonage at Lissoy, only the front and end walls still stand; nothing survives of the school he attended here. Forgney Church, where his father served as a curate, was rebuilt in 1830 but at Pallas, his supposed birthplace, the Oliver Goldsmith Society erected in 1974 a larger-than-life statue of the poet, incomprehensibly incarcerated behind bars in a curious kind of grotto.

COUNTY LONGFORD

A county of quiet farmlands and brown bogs, with only the occasional low hills, County Longford attracts relatively few tourists but plenty of anglers - there is prime fishing to be enjoy in its lakes and rivers. But for those who appreciate pastoral calm and a gentle pace of life the county will provide a refreshing change from the busier tourist counties. And it has its fair share of things to see and do. The prehistoric dolmen at Aughnacliffe and the Stone Circles near Granard are both fine specimens of these enigmatic monuments, while the Corlea Trackway at Kenagh is a unique timber "railway" dating from around 3000BC.

The county has several literary associations. Oliver Goldsmith (1730-74), whose play *She Stoops to Conquer* is still frequently revived, was born at Pallas; the novelist Maria Edgeworth (1767-1849) came from the family after whom the village of Edgesworthtown is named; and more recently, the poet and dramatist Patraic Colum (1881-1972) was born in Longford Town, which is where we begin our tour.

LONGFORD

MAP 4 REF I8

26 miles W of Mullingar on the N4

Set on a slope beside the River Camlin, Longford is dominated by its 19th century grey limestone **Cathedral of St Mel**. St Mel was bishop here around 480 and his crozier is one of the treasures in the ecclesiastical museum housed at the rear of the cathedral. Longford has not been lucky in preserving its past: the ancient fortress (*longphort* in Gaelic) of the O'Farrells and a Dominican priory of 1400 have both disappeared without trace, but some slight remains of a later castle erected by the 1st Earl of Longford in 1627 are incorporated in the old military barracks.

This quiet town really comes alive in July when the week-long **Longford Summer Festival** takes place, with the streets closed to traffic at 6pm and handed over to live pop and rock bands.

Although only a mile from the town centre, the house and gardens of **Viewmount House** provide a haven of intimate, restful tranquillity. Providing accommodation of the highest quality, Viewmount is a strikingly handsome Georgian house dating back to the 1750s. Originally owned by the Earl of Longford, Viewmount House was occupied by the landlord's agent. It was once a Church of Ireland school in the 1800s, and later a farm-

Viewmount House, Dublin Road, Longford, Co. Longford
Tel: 043 41919

house but has now been transformed into a real jewel with wood floors, an elegant staircase, open fires and a relaxing atmosphere. To start the day, you are guaranteed a quality breakfast from an extensive menu. The dining room boasts vaulted ceilings and is decorated to retain the charm of the period to which it belongs. The luxurious en suite bedrooms are individually styled, furnished with elegant period furniture, and each has its own particular view of the garden and surrounding countryside. A new restaurant is planned which will be beautifully set in the outstanding gardens.

The gardens are designed to allow you to meander and enjoy the extensive range of shrubs and herbaceous borders, ponds and places to sit and listen to bird song - far away from the noise of traffic. Local amenities include the Co. Longford 18-hole golf course whose fairways adjoin the property and there are also a number of other 18-hole golf courses within a half hour drive - most notably Glasson Golf and Country Club. Longford is ideally suited for fishing enthusiasts with Lough Gowna, Lough Ree and the River Shannon all nearby. While in Longford you could visit the villages of Ardagh and Newtowncashel, both of them winners of national and international Tidy Town Competitions. Also nearby are the 2000 year old Corlea Trackway near Keenagh, Carrigglas Manor, Strokestown House and Gardens, Tullynally Castle, and Ballinamuck which is famous for the battle of 1798. Lawn Tennis and bicycle hire are both available.

About 3 miles northeast of Longford, on the R194 road to Granard, **Carriglas Manor** is a striking Tudor-Gothic style mansion built in 1837 for Chief Justice Thomas Lefroy whose other claim to fame is that he enjoyed a brief romantic liaison with Jane Austen and may well have been the model for Darcy in *Pride and Prejudice*. The Lefroy family is still in residence and it will be one of them who shows you around the house with its elegant Waterford glass, Dutch furniture and family portraits. Visitors can wander around the attractive grounds and there's also a costume museum displaying a hoard of mid-18th century clothes which were discovered in old chests in the manor. The museum is handsomely housed in the former stable block, a striking Classical building designed by James Gandon who was also responsible for two of Dublin's finest buildings, the O'Connell Bridge and the Custom House.

ENNYBEGS   MAP 4 REF I8
5 miles NE of Longford off the R194

A couple of miles further along the road to Granard there's quite outstanding bed and breakfast or self-catering accommodation to be had at **Cumiskey's Farmhouse** which is in a class of its own. The Tudor-style farmhouse stands in extensive gardens surrounded by an old stone wall, its interior beautifully furnished and decorated with taste and flair. This lovely house has a huge residents' lounge from which a spiral staircase rises to the Library. The cosy bedrooms are as welcoming and comfortable as you would expect from an establishment which has an ITB 4 star rating and has won awards for its accommodation. The farmhouse is the home of Mrs Pat Cumiskey who greets her guests with a genuine Irish welcome and is known for her wonderful home cooking. As well as the full Irish breakfast included in the tariff, evening meals are also available.

Comiskey's Farm House, Ennybegs, Drumlish P.O., Co. Longford
Tel: 043 23320 Fax: 043 23516 e-mail: kc@iol.ie

Within the farmhouse grounds, a group of 4 stone cottages stands in a neat semi-circle. One is a Irish traditional cottage, the other 3 are purpose-built in traditional style for those visitors who prefer self-catering. Known affectionately as Red Door, Yellow Door and Green Door Cottages, one is thatched and all have stone fireplaces, oak or stone floors, a viewing balcony and gas central heating. All three cottages are wheelchair accessible. There's a fully equipped kitchen and laundry; a sitting room with raised ceiling, multi-channel TV and an open gas fire. All bed linen and towels are supplied and anglers are well-provided for with a Tackle Room and refrigerators, and bait is available. Another amenity, also within the grounds, is a Pitch and Putt course. The cottages are available to rent all year round; the farmhouse B & B from 1st March to 30th October. If you are looking for somewhere with real character to stay at in the Longford area, Comiskey's Farm House provides the answer.

EDGEWORTHSTOWN
8 miles E of Longford on the N4 and N55

MAP 4 REF I8

The Edgeworth family settled at this crossroads village (known then as Mostrim) in 1583 but it was in the 18th century that they first came to wider notice. Richard Lovell Edgeworth was an author and inventor who is credited with creating the formula for tarmac well before the name of his Scottish contemporary, Macadam, became irrevocably linked with the road-making material. Richard equipped his house with central heating and also devised a water pump that dispensed a coin to anyone who pumped up a certain quantity of water. Richard's brother was the Abbé Henry Essex Edgeworth, confessor to Louis XVI, whom he attended on the scaffold. The Abbé left an eye-witness account of the king's last moments before the guillotine fell and the confessor's robes were drenched in royal blood. Best known of all the Edgeworths, though, was Maria, one of Richard's 22 children. An early campaigner for women's education, Maria made her name at the age of 32 with the novel *Castle Rackrent*. It's an even-handed book, equally understanding of the Anglo-Irish gentry and the impoverished peasantry, and imbued with a truly Irish sense of fun. Sir Walter Scott was an admirer of Maria's work and presented her with an inlaid marble table which now stands in **St John's Church**. In the graveyard outside stands the Edgeworth family vault and, nearby, the grave of Oscar Wilde's sister, Isola, who died while on a visit to Edgeworthstown Rectory.

The Edgeworth family home, The Manor, where literary luminaries such as Scott and William Wordsworth were entertained, is now a nursing home run by the Sisters of Mercy and not open to the public. Another literary connection with Edgeworthstown has no visible memorial. The school on Pound Street where Oliver Goldsmith received his early education is currently just a derelict site. The school that replaced it, on the Athlone road, has now been converted into a Visitor Centre and community centre.

Located just outside the village, **Lackan Lodge** is a smart new bungalow farmhouse set in peaceful farm surroundings. Cattle, sheep and horses graze in the fields around the house. This tranquil spot is the family home of Charlie and June Murphy who offer a warm welcome to their bed and breakfast visitors. The house is wheelchair friendly with

Lackan Lodge, Edgeworthstown, Co. Longford
Tel/Fax: 043 71299

all 4 guest rooms, 2 of them en suite, on the ground floor. All rooms are equipped with television and tea and coffee making facilities and, like the rest of the house, are all non-smoking. There's a spacious dining room and a comfortable lounge with an open fire and, outside, a colourful garden and ample parking space. The Murphys are happy to provide evening meals if required and can direct you to the many attractions and amenities in the area. Edgeworthstown village is of course notable for its close associations with Oliver Goldsmith and the novelist, Maria Edgeworth. The Ardagh Heritage Village is just a couple of miles away and within a one hour drive you'll find the castles of Athlone and

Tullynally, Boyle Abbey and the remarkable monastic complex at Clonmacnoise, the Lifeforce Mill at Cavan and Strokestown House, Gardens and Famine Museum.

GRANARD MAP 4 REF I8

6 miles NE of Edgeworthstown on the N55

A popular angling and riding centre, Granard is a bustling market town with a fondness for festivals. The most celebrated is the **Granard Harp Festival**, held on the second weekend in August, which originated in 1781 and was revived in 1981. The festivities include parades, concerts, a harp workshop, competitions and ceilis. Then in late October comes the **Granard Pumpkin Festival** which features a wide range of activities from pumpkin baking and pumpkin carving to guess the weight competitions. If you are thinking of entering your own prize pumpkin bear in mind that recent winners have tilted the scales at around 180lbs. Each spring, the town also hosts an **Easter Eggstravaganza**. To quote from the publicity flyer: *"Eggsciting floats and, for the girls, eggciting blokes, and for the rest of you folks we have eggsciting yolks"*. Eggstraordinary. On a more conventional note, Granard also boasts the largest Norman motte and bailey in Ireland. Built in 1199 and rising some 540 feet above sea level, it is worth walking to the top where a statue of St Patrick gazes out a view that takes in nine counties, five lakes and a network of rivers. An even more venerable monument than this Norman earthwork is the Stone Circle about 3 miles outside the town. Also known as the **Druid Circle** and the only stone circle in the midlands, this prehistoric construction consists of 24 stones, 6 of them upright, 7 of them placed on their sides and the remainder having fallen.

A short distance from the Druid Circle and approached by a drive more than half a mile long, **Toberphelim House** is a splendid Georgian period farmhouse, the family home

Toberphelim House, Granard, Co. Longford
Tel/Fax: 043 86568 e-mail: tober@tinet.ie

of Dan and Mary Smyth. Here, visitors can enjoy a hideaway mini-break or overnight stay with all modern comforts in old world Georgian surroundings offering space and privacy. The house is situated in the centre of a 200 acre dry stock farm which is the Smyths' main enterprise. It consists of suckler cows, continental beef cattle and sheep, along with domestic animals. Visitors are welcome to walk the fields, view the lakes and hillsides and examine the flora and fauna. Rubber boots are a must if you wish to enjoy fully your visit to the farm! Toberphelim House has 3 bedrooms, two of them en suite with shower, each with a double and single bed, and a twin room with separate bathroom. There's a separate drawing room with television and a dining room with a large mahogany table. The Smyths family room is available for children and outside there's a children's playground. The cooking at Toberphelim House is wholesome traditional farmhouse fare, all home cooked, and dinner is also available if booked the previous day. The house has a wine licence and major credit cards are welcome. Advance booking is advisable and appreciated.

About 5 miles northwest of Granard, the **Aughnacliffe Dolmen** is a mightily impressive sight. Believed to be around 5000 years old, it consists of a huge block of stone about 12 feet long, 7 feet wide and 5 feet thick resting on two supports. The assumption is that these massive neolithic monuments were erected over the grave of a chieftain or other important person and that the stones were originally covered with earth.

ARDAGH
7 miles SE of Longford off the N4 or R393   MAP 4 REF 18

This pretty village, a National Tidy Towns winner, is surrounded by woods and believed to be the site of a church founded by St Patrick, although today the oldest surviving structure is the ruin of **St Mel's Cathedral**, dating back to around 900AD. The **Ardagh Heritage Centre**, housed in the former Victorian school, traces the story of this unspoilt village which has a number of pleasant but unremarkable 19th century buildings grouped around the village green.

ABBEYSHRULE
18 miles SE of Longford off the R393   MAP 4 REF 19

Just outside Abbeyshrule stand the mournful remains of a 12th century Cistercian abbey but the main reason for seeking out this small village near the border with Co. Westmeath is its lively pub. Famous for good food, drink and entertainment, the **Rustic Inn** stands on the village main street with the Royal Canal running past the garden at the back. The inn promises exclusive menus and exquisite cuisine, all served in its spacious restaurant which can seat up to 300 guests - ideal for weddings and other functions. The inn also serves tasty bar food and lunches. This area is, of course, prime fishing country and the owner of the Rustic Inn, Ted McGoey, has produced an informative leaflet giving details of the best locations in the many loughs and rivers all around. The local river, the Inny, for example, which runs through the village, "is a top class coarse fishery and..... provides in excess of 60kms of good bank pike fishing". From Ballymahon to Abbeyshrule, the Inny can be a productive wet and dry fly trout fishery and several angling competitions are fished each year on the river.

The Rustic Inn, Abbeyshrule, Co. Longford
Tel: 044 57424   Fax: 44 57742

Ted is also a keen flyer and actively involved in the Abbeyshrule Annual Fly-In and Airshow which is held in early August at the General Aviation Airfield just outside the village. The show attracts aircraft from abroad as well as a sizeable UK contingent and the programme includes a lively barbecue and Irish Night at the Rustic Inn. If you are planning to stay in the area, the inn has 4 guest rooms for bed and breakfast, all of them en suite, and there's also a delightful thatched cottage, "Mac's Cottage", which is available for those who prefer self-catering. Other amenities and attractions in the area include 3 championship golf courses within a 20-minute drive; the Hill of Uisneach, which is traditionally recognised as the centre of Ireland; and the historic town of Athlone.

BALLYMAHON
MAP 4 REF I9

14 miles S of Longford on the N55

One of the few places of any size in southern Co. Longford, Ballymahon (population 1,000) is mainly remarkable for its inordinately wide main street. The town stands on the River Inny, renowned for its fine trout, which is spanned here by a graceful 5-arched bridge. Ballymahon prides itself on being close to the heart of Goldsmith Country: his mother lived here as a young girl; the author was born at the village of Pallas, 3 miles to the east; and two years later the family moved to Lissoy, 5 miles to the southwest.

DERRYLOUGH
MAP 4 REF H9

5 miles W of Ballymahon on minor road off the R392

Hidden away in the southwest corner of the county, close to Lough Ree, **Derrylough Farmhouse** is a comfortable, secluded farmhouse offering good accommodation and fresh

Derrylough Farmhouse, Derrylough, Keenagh, Co. Longford
Tel: 043 22126   Fax: 043 22040

farm food. This is an ideal base if your passion is fishing. Lough Ree is the second largest lake on the Shannon, more than 21 miles long, and is particularly noted for its pike along the eastern shore. The countless bays of the lough have many bags of large bream taken each year, with roach and tench also widely available. Good fishing can be enjoyed from the shore in all locations and local information is available on the most productive locations. Game fishing is also a popular activity, with numerous locations where excellent catches can be taken.

The nearby village of Keenagh was an estate village but its big house has gone, demolished in 1962. The village offers sequestered walks alongside the Royal Canal; the ruins of Abbeyderg Augustinian Priory; a charming early-19th dovecote; and a clockhouse memorial tower erected in 1878 which still keeps perfect time. It is worked with its original weights and chains which demand manual winding each week. The mechanism was made by the same company that fitted out London's Big Ben. Just outside the village is the fascinating Corlea Interpretative Centre, a distinctive mustard-coloured building standing in splendid isolation surrounded by windswept bogland on all sides. At this spot, in 1985, a *togher*, an ancient trackway of oak planks, was discovered by men cutting turf. These ancient trackways date back to 3500 BC and were constructed to transport animals and personal belongings across marshy terrain. The one at Corlea is massive and sturdily built, having endured the pressure of wheeled vehicles over a long period.

NEWTOWNCASHEL   Map 4 ref H9
11 miles SW of Longford off the R392

Another of Co. Longford's "Tidy Towns", Newtowncashel has a small Cottage Museum,

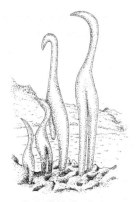

Bog Oak Sculptures

occupying a restored 19th century dwelling, furnished and equipped with typical utensils of the period. The village is perhaps better known for the famous **Bog Oak Sculptures** produced by the local artist, Michael Casey, from centuries-old oak retrieved from local bogs, allowed to dry out over several years, and then sculpted into intriguing shapes. Newtoncashel also hosts the **Larry Kelly Traditional Music Weekend** in early June. Established in 1991, the festival commemorates the legendary fiddle player Larry Kelly and his unique style of fiddle playing. The concerts, sessions and workshops attract traditional music lovers from all over Ireland.

LANESBORO
9 miles SW of Longford on the N63

Map 4 ref **H8**

Sitting at the northern tip of Lough Ree, Lanesboro is a noted centre for coarse fishing and for boat and barge trips around the lough or along the River Shannon. A rather unorthodox attraction, just outside the town, is the **power station** which offers guided tours. The station is fuelled by peat, a fossil fuel with which Ireland is still well-provided.

Standing only yards from the River Shannon and close to Lough Ree, it's easy to understand why **Moher Lodge** is so popular with anglers and, indeed, with anyone who appreciates peace and tranquillity in an unspoilt countryside. This modern 4-bedroomed bungalow is set within its own private grounds and fully furnished with every amenity you could possibly require, including a tackle shed and bait fridge. If you want to hire a boat to go out on the Lough, these are available in Lanesboro village. In addition to good

Moher Lodge, Knock, Lanesboro, Co. Longford
Tel: 043 21136 Fax: 043 21957

fishing, the lake is worth a trip to see the islands of Inchclearaun and Inchbofin. Both have remains of 6th century churches, 7 of them on Inchclearaun alone, and it was on Inchclearaun that the legendary Queen Maeve met her death. She was bathing in the lough when Furbaide, whose mother Maeve (or Medb) had murdered, let fly with a piece of cheese from his sling. It pierced her forehead and killed her. Another place of interest nearby is the Heritage Centre at Newtowncashel where a traditional Irish farmhouse has been restored. The living rooms have been furnished and decorated in the style of the early 1930s and there's a display of tools, implements, utensils and farm equipment from the turn of the last century.

CLONDRA
MAP 4 REF H8

5 miles W of Longford off the N5

At Clondra the Royal Canal meets with the River Shannon, a junction marked by an impressive harbour of cut stone. **The Richmond Inn** occupies a prime position in this pretty village, standing on the banks of the Royal Canal overlooking the harbour. Your hosts are Des and Frances McPartland who assure their patrons of a warm welcome and fine home cooking. The imposing 4-storey building provides everything you need for a holiday stay - clean, spacious accommodation in 7 guest bedrooms, all of them twin-bedded and en suite; a friendly and welcoming bar where there's live entertainment during the season; and an excellent restaurant. If you plan to go boating, the inn has life jackets and boats available; if you are fishing, Des and Frances "will do everything we can for you except catch the fish!" There's a drying room and bait store at the inn and within easy reach is the River Shannon and numerous small rivers and lakes. Des is more than willing

The Richmond Inn, Clondra, Co. Longford
Tel/Fax: 043 26126

to offer his advice as to where the latest "hot spots" are to be found and local catches include hybrids, perch, pike, bream, rudd, tench, and brown trout. As he points out, "The Royal Canal is so near to The Richmond Inn, your angling days can be extended into the evening, if you have the staying power". Fishing may be the most popular activity in this land of lakes and rivers, but there are plenty of other attractions and amenities to keep the visitor busy. Walking and cycling, indoor and outdoor swimming, 18-hole golf courses and Pitch & Putt, horse riding and greyhound racing, as well as a wealth of historic monuments and ancient sites, notably the Kenagh Interpretative Centre with its 2000 year old trackway and, in Roscommon town, the striking ruins of its venerable abbey and castle.

BALLINAMUCK

MAP 4 REF I8

11 miles N of Longford off the R198

This small town in the north of Co. Longford was the arena for the battle that ended the 1798 Rising against the English. The combined Irish and French armies were defeated by a much larger force commanded by Gen. Cornwallis. When the battle was over, 500 bodies lay scattered across the battlefield - most of them Irish rebels who had refused to surrender. Despite this drastic defeat, the north of the county remained a centre of resistance, so much so that in 1846 an imposing Royal Irish Constabulary barracks was erected in the village. This is now the **1798 Memorial Hall** which incorporates the Ballinamuck Visitor Centre. The exhibits recount the course of the fateful battle and deals with such exploits as the heroic stand of Gunner Magee and the atrocities of the "Walking Gallows".

COUNTY OFFALY

The topography of central Ireland is often described as "saucer-shape", and County Offaly represents the lower half of the saucer with the flood-plain of the River Shannon to the north and the heathery Slieve Bloom Mountains providing the rim in the southeast. Most of the county is level plain and bogland - indeed, some of the last remaining tracts of bogland can be visited at Clara and Mongans Bog. But there are also beauty spots such as Victoria Lock near Banagher which one writer compared, perhaps a little over-enthusiastically, with Jamaica. And this gentle, unassuming county is also home to one of Ireland's most important early Christian sites, Clonmacnois, and what most experts regard as the country's most perfect 18th century town, Birr, now designated as a Heritage Town. The Parsons family who created Georgian Birr and later became Earls of Rosse still live at Birr Castle where visitors can see the famous Rosse Telescope.

TULLAMORE

MAP 4 REF I10

60 miles W of Dublin on the N80

Offaly's county town, Tullamore owes its extraordinarily wide main street to an early aviation disaster. In 1785, a hot air balloon erupted in flames over the town and the resulting conflagration destroyed no fewer than one hundred houses. Thirteen years later the Grand Canal reached the town, providing the local brick manufacturers with economical transport for their product - and modern visitors with some pleasant towpath walks. You can also hire a narrowboat here and make your own way along the canal, passing through undulating pastureland and with a better-than-even chance of glimpsing a kingfisher or a lithe otter which can outpace your boat's regulation 4mph by a streamlined speed of 6mph.

The flavoursome whiskey liqueur Irish Mist was created at Tullamore and although the distillery itself has relocated to Clonmel you can sample this heady brew in the town's many lively pubs and bars.

To the southwest of Tullamore, **Charleville Forest Castle** is a flamboyant Georgian-Gothic mansion built in 1779 to the designs of Francis Johnston. Johnston was clearly a prime inspiration for the designers who created the sets for the Hammer House of Horror movies of the 1960s - dark recesses, gloomy archways, even a grotto in the grounds, all suggest a sinister medieval provenance but the overall effect is curiously light-hearted. The castle and grounds are open from 11am to 4pm from June to September; weekend afternoons during April and May; and at other times by appointment.

DURROW   Map 4 ref I10
2 miles N of Tullamore on the N52

A few miles north of Tullamore, just off the N52, is the site of **Durrow Abbey**, yet another of the monasteries founded by St Columba in the 6th century. The famous illuminated **Book of Durrow** was written here in the following century and is currently housed in Trinity College, Dublin. A medieval church now stands on the site of the Abbey but a 10th century high cross and some fine early tombstones can be seen in the disused cemetery. The church stands next to a grand Georgian mansion, (not open to the public), whose well-maintained grounds provide an elegant backdrop to the tumbledown graveyard.

DAINGEAN   Map 4 ref J10
9 miles E of Tullamore on the R402

Set beside the Grand Canal, this little town was once the seat of the chiefs of Offaly, the O'Conors and was also, briefly, the county town. In the 1500s it was renamed Philipstown in honour of Philip II of Spain, husband of Henry VIII's daughter "Bloody" Mary. The unhappy marriage only lasted four years (1554-58) but during that time Offaly became known as "King's County" and the title still lingers on.

Located in the very heart of Ireland, **Eskermóre House** is a lovely early-Georgian farmhouse set in the curve of a stream in wooded grounds surrounded by mature gardens. It was built originally for the Fossett family, wealthy landowners who expended much time and money on both the house and grounds. Approached by a tree-lined avenue, Eskermóre looks as if it has grown here rather than been built. Mellow, creeper-covered walls, neat lawns and well-tended gardens add to the sense of settled tranquillity. The house is the home of Ann Mooney and has been modernised in sympathy with its period, retaining original features and furnished with fine antiques. Bed and breakfast guests will find a welcoming family atmosphere, comfortable guest bedrooms, (3 of them, 2 en suite),

Eskermóre House, Daingean, Tullamore, Co. Offaly
Tel: 0506 53079 Mobile: 0868 249574

and wholesome home cooking at breakfast time. Ann, who has a well-deserved reputation as a fine cook, also offers 5-course evening meals if required. Ann is also happy to
arrange package holidays for activity breaks - golf, horse riding, hunting, fishing, for
which there are plenty of facilities close by. For a more relaxed break, there are walks
along the Grand Canal and scenic drives through the beautiful Slieve Bloom Mountains
in the immediate area. Or, if you prefer just to sit back and forget it all, Eskermóre House
guarantees plenty of peace and quiet.

BANAGHER
Map 4 ref H10

22 miles W of Tullamore on the R439/R356

This appealing little town is set beside the Shannon with its one long street descending
the hillside to the river and looking across to the Martello tower on the Galway bank.
With its handsome Georgian features, Banagher provides a good base for exploring both
the East Midlands and County Galway so some of the local shopkeepers are well-stocked
with wines, spices and exotic vegetables for Continental holidaymakers, while other stores
don't seem to have changed since the 1940s. Visitors can hire boats and canoes to explore
the Shannon, and there's even a vintage barge offering luxury cruises along the river.

An early vacationer at Banagher was Charlotte Brontë who spent her honeymoon
here in 1854. (Sadly, she died the next year in pregnancy). Another literary resident was
Anthony Trollope who worked here as a GPO surveyor in the 1840s and wrote his first
novel *The Macdermots of Ballycloran* while staying at Banagher.

About 2 miles outside Banagher, **Lime Kiln Cottages** combine the promise of a wholly
enjoyable self-catering holiday with excellent value for money. These lavishly refurbished
old farm houses have been fully modernised and immaculately furnished to provide maximum comfort while retaining their nostalgic, pastoral charm. The ground floor bedrooms
sleep 5 plus a cot and have been designed to be wheelchair and disabled friendly. Children are welcome and a baby's high chair and cot are provided, along with free bed linen
and heating. There's colour TV in the attractively furnished lounge/dining area and the

**Lime Kiln Cottages, Corgrave South, Lusmagh, Banagher, Co. Offaly
Tel: 0509 51224 e-mail: joanlarkin@tinet.ie**

kitchen is comprehensively equipped with extras such as microwave, washing machine and dryer. The peaceful garden is supplied with outside furniture and includes a barbecue area along with secure private parking. Joan and Tom Larkin are warm and attentive hosts who offer a wealth of local knowledge to help visitors to make the most of their stay.

There is much to see and do in the area. Banagher, perched on the banks of the River Shannon, has an excellent marina where boats can be hired for an exhilarating day out. The town is peppered with lively pubs featuring traditional music, glorious Guinness and great craic! Further afield, the Slieve Bloom Mountains, historic sites such as Cloghan Castle and Clonmacnoise, and a full range of sporting activities provide plenty to keep the holiday maker busy.

A few minutes drive from Lime Kiln Cottages will bring you to **Clonagh Castle**, the oldest inhabited castle in Ireland. There was a monastery here in the 7th century but the present massive tower house dates from Norman times. It has a magnificent medieval dining room and the castle is furnished with a fascinating collection of antiques, along with weapons and armour going back to Cromwell's time.

SHANNONBRIDGE
Map 4 ref H10
8 miles N of Banagher on the R357/R444

At Shannonbridge a fine, but narrow, 16-arched bridge crosses the River Suck just before it meets the Shannon, and a grey Napoleonic fort guards this strategic junction where 3 counties meet - Offaly, Roscommon and Galway. The town's main visitor attraction is the "Bog Railway", more properly known as the **Clonmacnoise and West Offaly Railway**. This narrow-gauge railway offers a 5 mile circular tour around the Blackwater Bog and is preceded by a 35-minute video explaining the complex flora and fauna of the area. The railway is operated by the National Peat Board which uses peat from the bog to fuel the massive power station that dominates the landscape. According to the Board, "A few hundred years from now the bog will be an integrated tapestry of fields, woodlands and wetlands" - a prospect which has exasperated conservation bodies trying to save Ireland's fast diminishing areas of natural bogland.

CLONMACNOISE

MAP 4 REF H10

12 miles N of Banagher on the R444

One of the largest and most impressive monastic sites in Ireland, **Clonmacnoise** stands in emerald green fields beside the River Shannon. In 548 AD, St Ciaran founded a monastery here, which was to become the most important religious establishment of its kind in the country, famed as a centre of art and learning throughout Europe. Several of its early treasures have been removed for safe keeping to Dublin, amongst them the superb gold and silver Crozier of Clonmacnoise, and the *Book of the Dun Cow*, one of the earliest and most famous manuscripts in the Irish language.

The extensive site, bounded by an encircling stone wall, contains an astonishingly rich variety of ecclesiastical monuments - the ruins of a 14th century Cathedral, two lofty Round Towers, the finest collection of High Crosses in Ireland, nine churches and numerous carved gravestones. To protect them from the weather, three of the High Crosses, including the magnificent 12 feet high Great Cross, are now housed in the Visitor Centre which also has displays illustrating the history of the site and a video presentation of the life of St Ciaran whose fame still draws pilgrims here for his festival on 12 September.

Clonmacnoise occupied an isolated position, protected on two sides by the river and on the other sides by a boggy plain, passable only by a single *esker*, or raised ridge. Even so, it suffered a series of attacks by Irish, Viking and English raiders, all hoping to plunder not just the riches of the monastery but also the treasures of the Royal City of the High Kings of Connacht who had made Clonmacnoise their capital. The last of them, Rory O'Conor, was buried here in 1198.

After surviving so many depredations, the 1000-year-old history of Clonmacnoise was abruptly ended in 1552 when English troops from the garrison at Athlone looted the monastery and left the buildings beyond repair. So much remains, though, that there is a constant stream of tourists visiting the site and for many Irish people Clonmacnoise is perhaps the most evocative of all Ireland's holy places.

BIRR

MAP 4 REF H11

22 miles SW of Tullamore on the N52/N62

Standing at the junction of the Rivers Camcor and Little Brosna, Birr is one of Ireland's finest Georgian towns, beautifully laid out with wide streets and elegant squares and with many dignified houses. The people of Birr have the Parsons family, later the Earls of Rosse, to thank for their handsome town. The lands here were granted to Sir Laurence Parsons in 1620 and became known as Parsonstown. But it was a descendant of his, another Sir Laurence, who began a thoroughgoing "improvement" of the town in the 1740s. **Emmet Square** is the oldest part, completed in 1747 and dominated by the lofty Cumberland Pillar which originally was crowned by a statue of the Duke of Cumberland, the "Butcher of Culloden". Dooly's Hotel, also 1747, is here too, a fine old coaching inn that was accidentally set on fire one night in 1809 by revellers from the Galway Hunt. Since that day, the Hunt has been known as the Galway Blazers.

West of Emmet Square is **John's Mall**, distinguished by some fine Georgian houses with elegant fanlights above the doors. The noble classical building here, with its pillared and porticoed entrance, is John's Hall which now houses the town's Tourist Information Centre where you can pick up a leaflet describing a pleasant 50-minute Town Trail which takes in all the major sights.

One of the finest Georgian streets is the majestically tree-lined Oxmantown Mall which leads to the main gates of Birr Castle. Overlooking the Mall is the **Stables Restaurant and Townhouse**, a handsome late-Georgian building with a striking fanlight window over the front door. The restaurant began as the brainchild of Dan and Rita Boyd in 1977. They converted the stables and coach house of the building to create a restaurant which at that time had seating for just 16 guests. The original stone walls and beamed ceilings, the glow of flickering candles against the honey-coloured walls, the crisp white linen and the lantern-lit courtyard provide an ambience of comfort and old world charm. Famed for its reputation as one of the leading restaurants in the midlands, The Stables is now owned and managed by Donal and Caroline Boyd. The restaurant is fully licensed and open every Tuesday to Sunday, serving lunch from 12.30pm to 2.30pm (even on Christmas Day); snacks from 12.30pm to 5.30pm; and dinner from 6.30 to 10pm. Traditional Sun-

The Stables Restaurant and Townhouse, Oxmantown Mall, Birr, Co. Offaly
Tel: 0509 20263 Fax: 0509 21677

day lunches are served from 12.30pm to 3pm. Large parties, functions, weddings and meetings are also catered for with menus provided to suit any occasion and any price.

Over the years, The Stables has grown and developed and is now incorporated into the main house. Here you can enjoy a coffee or a drink before and after your meal in the sumptuous Georgian style lounge with its open fire and comfortable armchairs. Accommodation at The Townhouse is an exquisite retreat offering luxurious old world bedrooms combined with modern comforts. All bedrooms are en suite and are overlooking Oxmantown Mall or the courtyard. It is ideally located for golfing, horse riding, hunting, fishing, hill walking, sight-seeing or just for relaxation.

Birr Castle, hereditary home of the Earls of Rosse, is not normally open to the public but visitors are welcome to stroll through the castle's 100 acres of pleasure grounds laid out by the 2nd Earl in the 1830s and 1840s. The gardens contain many rare specimen trees and shrubs, and also boast the tallest box hedges in the world, about 33 feet high. There are delightful walks around the huge ornamental lake and alongside the rivers created specially to enhance the landscape. Apart from the imposing Gothic exterior of the castle itself, the most fascinating structure here is the famous **Rosse Telescope** constructed by the 3rd Earl in 1845. With its 72-inch diameter reflector, it was for 75 years the largest telescope in the world. The 4th Earl used it to make the first accurate measurement

Birr Castle

of the temperature of the moon and to catalogue the spiral nebulae. Also within the castle grounds is the Historic Centre, housed in the former stable block and celebrating the scientific achievements of other members of the Rosse family, amongst them the Lunar Heat Machine invented by the 4th Earl whose younger brother, incidentally, invented the steam turbine.

About 2 miles south of Birr, **Minnocks Farmhouse** is a spacious, comfortable farmhouse set in mature gardens on a working dairy farm. Your hosts, Noel and Veronica Minnock, welcome you to their farm to experience the peaceful atmosphere which is enhanced by a fine reputation for hospitality and excellent cuisine. Guests are made to feel relaxed and comfortable and a warm welcome is assured. Over the years, the Minnocks

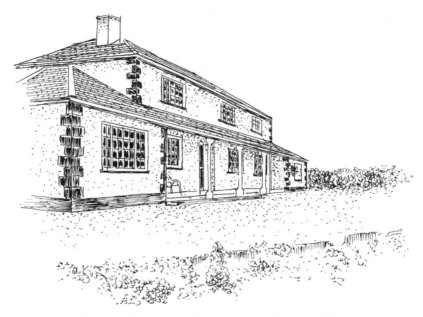

Minnocks Farmhouse, Roscrea Road, Birr, Co. Offaly
Tel: 0509 20591 Fax: 0509 21684 e-mail: c.village@oceanfree.net

have enjoyed the company of visitors of numerous nationalities, many of whom return again and again. All 6 guest bedrooms are en suite and equipped with colour TV, direct dial telephone and hair dryer. A full Irish breakfast is included in the tariff and evening meals are available on request. Minnocks is handily located for a whole range of activities and places of interest. There are 4 golf courses within easy reach, horse riding and indoor swimming at Birr, and angling at numerous locations. A list of the many attractions in the area begins with the famous heritage town of Birr nearby with its historic buildings, lovely riverside walk and Birr Castle Demesne, the world-renowned garden park and arboretum. Children will be delighted with the Lusmagh Pet Farm, the Ashbrook Open Farm and the West Offaly Railway which offers a 5-mile circular tour on a narrow gauge track around the Blackwater Bog. The important monastic centre of Clonmacnoise is also within easy reach and an excellent way to enjoy the heartland of Ireland is to follow the Slieve Bloom Way, a scenic 31-mile drive that runs through wooded hills and desolate moorland, and along the bed of a pre-Ice Age river valley. En route, you could stop off at Cadamstown and join the brave locals bathing in the chilly waterfall there!

KINNITTY
MAP 4 REF I11
8 miles E of Birr on the R440/R421

Set at the foot of the Slieve Bloom Mountains, Kinnitty is a picturesque village and here you'll find **Ardmore House**, an impressive stone house built in the 1840s and set in a beautiful 2-acre garden. The house was originally built for the Bernard family of Kinnitty Castle and is now the home of Christina Byrne. With its turf fire, brass beds, good home

Ardmore House, The Walk, Kinnitty, Co. Offaly
Tel: 0509 37009 e-mail: chrisbyrne@eircom.net

cooking (which includes home made bread, scones and jam), and friendly, relaxed atmosphere, this old Victorian town house is a place one wants to linger in. Ardmore has 4 non-smoking guest bedrooms, 2 of them en suite.

Opposite the house stands the extraordinary Kinnitty Pyramid, an exact replica of one of the pyramids in Egypt. Built by Richard W. Bernard, its construction took four years until its completion in 1830. It stands in the graveyard behind the Church of Ireland and serves as a tomb for four members of the Bernard family. The High Cross which stands in the grounds of Kinnitty Castle came from a nearby monastery founded by St Kinian Cam nearby in the 6th century.

Behind Kinnitty rise the foothills of the **Slieve Bloom Mountains** which offer a wealth of tranquil havens and places of interest for the nature enthusiast, a walker's paradise. You can follow the **Slieve Bloom Way** or many mapped walks such as the Circuit of Knocknaman, (Christina can provide you with a map). Guided walks are also a regular activity during the summer months and a walking festival is held annually in May. Other places within easy reach of Kinnitty are Lough Boora Parklands, a creative combination of cutaway bogs, wetlands and lakes, and the Heritage Towns of Roscrea and Birr. For anyone with a love of Irish music, the traditional music sessions held every Friday night in Kinnitty Castle are not to be missed. If you are feeling active, facilities for most country pursuits are to be found in the neighbourhood: three 18-hole golf courses at Birr and Tullamore; fishing at Banagher and an equestrian centre at Kinnitty.

COUNTY LAOIS

As County Offaly was known as King's County, so Laois (pronounced *leash*) was Queen's County, named after Mary I who "planted" the county with her Catholic supporters in the late 1550s. A new town, Maryborough, was established, now better known as Portlaoise, the county town. Those early settlers were mainly smallholders so Co. Laois has none of the great estates like those handed out by Cromwell and Charles II in the southwest counties some 90 years later. But the colonists built some attractive towns and villages, as well as some notable mansions such as those at Abbeyleix and Emo.

Geographically, Laois has two distinct landscapes: the Slieve Bloom Mountains running along its northwestern border with Co. Offaly, and the green plains that cover the rest of the county. An old traveller's tag proclaims that the Laois landscape is, like the local accent, flat and boring: a more sympathetic visitor will appreciate the quiet byways and the gentle, unhurried rhythms of everyday life.

PORTLAOISE   Map 4 ref J11
52 miles SW of Dublin off the N7

When Portlaoise was established in 1556 as Maryborough the town was heavily fortified as part of a plan to subdue the local chiefs but these fortifications were comprehensively destroyed by Cromwell's troops and only the outer wall of a tower survives. Depressingly, the most substantial building in Portlaoise today is its top-security gaol which stands in the same street as the county mental hospital. Inevitably, a local wit renamed the street "Nuts'n'Bolts Road". A more cheerful aspect of the town is its abundance of lively pubs - 22 of them at the time of writing.

About 4 miles to the east of Portlaoise, the **Rock of Dunamase** rises from the plain, a geographical feature so distinctive that it even appears on Ptolemy's 1st century map as "Dunum". Successive generations of warrior-kings made good use of the Rock's strategic position which enjoys uninterrupted views of the low-lying country all around. The Rock's lumpy contours are dotted with the weathered ruins of early fortifications, culminating in the remains of the hilltop 12th century castle erected by Dermot MacMurrough, King of Leinster. In 1650 it suffered the same fate as so many of Ireland's medieval fortresses - cannonballed into uselessness by Cromwell's artillery.

A mile or so to the east of the Rock of Dunamase, steam buffs will find the **Stradbally Hall Railway** which operates during the summer season. A 19th century steam locomotive, formerly used at the Guinness brewery in Dublin, chuffs along the narrow gauge track and a steam engine rally is held here on the first weekend in August. Also in the village is a **Traction Engine Museum** which also houses a fine collection of vintage cars.

MOUNTMELLICK   Map 4 ref J11
6 miles N of Portlaoise on the N80

Set within a bend of the River Owenass, Mountmellick was founded in the 17th century by Quakers and flourished as a centre for cotton, linen and woollen manufacturing. One of the town's products, "Mountmellick work", became extremely popular in the 1700s.

Currently, local people are trying to revive the production of this elegant white-on-white embroidery, decorated with flowers and plants. To the west of Mountmellick rise the Slieve Bloom Mountains "as sweet and delightful as their name" declared one writer. "At any season of the year they fill the eye with beauty and the lungs with their fragrant delicious air". The 31-mile- long **Slieve Bloom Way** provides a circular walk around the mountains. The most outstanding views are to be found at the Glendine Gap and the Ridge of Capard.

PORTARLINGTON
12 miles NE of Portlaoise on the R4/R420

MAP 4 REF J11

Handsome Georgian houses with gardens stretching down to the river and a "French" church where many of the tombstones are engraved with names such as Champ and Le Blanc bear witness to Portarlington's Huguenot forebears. They arrived here in the late 1600s and their industrious way of life brought prosperity to this little town. There's an unusual reminder of the town's Huguenot past in the **French Week** held here in July - complete with a snail-eating competition. The **People's Museum** in the Catholic Club has some interesting relics of the Huguenot era and also offers an overview of the town's history stretching back to 4000-year-old axe heads found nearby.

Arlington Tower Hotel is an impressive building which dates back to 1725 when it began as a Huguenot School known as St Germain. Over the years, the hotel has been modernised and refurbished to the very high standard appreciated by guests today. An especially attractive feature of the hotel is its garden which extends parallel to the func-

Arlington Tower Hotel, Portarlington, Co. Laois
Tel: 0502 23225 Fax: 0502 23901 e-mail: arlington.tower@oceanfree.net

tion room. Very well foliaged trees and shrubs, a garden fountain, seats, tables and umbrellas, provide the ultimate in privacy. The hotel restaurant boasts a warm and cosy atmosphere, and offers both à la carte and table d'hôte menus with the emphasis on freshly prepared local produce, complemented by excellent service. Superb lunches and high teas are also served in the comfortable surroundings of the Lounge, where music is provided each weekend in an atmosphere that is both entertaining and relaxing. Arlington Tower has 12 guest bedrooms, all en suite, tastefully decorated, and equipped with direct dial telephone, multi-channel TV and tea/coffee-making facilities. And if you are planning a special event, the hotel's Function Room with its own bar provides the perfect atmosphere. The hotel's exciting night club is also open every weekend.

EMO   MAP 4 REF J11
8 miles NE of Portlaoise on the R419

This attractive village in the north of the county is dominated by the works of James Gandon (1743-1823), the English-born architect who spent most of his professional life in Ireland. He is probably best known for the dignified Custom House in Dublin, often described as "one of the noblest buildings in Europe". Gandon was also involved in the design of Dublin's Four Courts, the Carlisle (O'Connell) Bridge, and the Bank of Ireland. A lucrative commission from the 1st Earl of Portarlington enticed Gandon from the capital city to this rural corner of County Laois. The Earl desired a stately residence here: Gandon obliged with **Emo Court**, a massively imposing building crowned by a great dome. During the summer season, visitors on guided tours can admire its interior, lavishly appointed with costly Siena marble. All year round, you are free to wander through the extensive landscaped grounds. In addition to Emo Court, Lord Portarlington's commission to James Gandon also specified the building of a church at nearby Coolbanagher and an inn to service the stage coaches bringing guests to his noble home. Gandon delivered, both on time and in budget. Few inns anywhere can claim such a distinguished architect as the one that bears his name.

The Gandon Inn has another claim to fame as Ireland's oldest family pub, owned and run by the Treacy family for many generations. The present manager is Tom Treacy and he and his friendly staff are always on hand to ensure that your stay here is a memorable one. Arriving guests step into a reception area which reflects the "Gandon era" with its highly stained woodwork and display cases, and the period theme continues throughout the premises. The bar has a series of intimate nooks and crannies, ideal for both small and large parties. Vintage memorabilia, wooden floors, and stained and leaded glass all help to create a warm, informal atmosphere.

The quality ethos of the restaurant is reflected in the excellent cuisine - from the highest *repas* to your candlelit gourmet meal. The Inn has 10 luxury en suite bedrooms and an elegant Bridal Suite, all with direct dial telephone, TV and tea/coffee making facilities. The Bridal Suite combines contemporary elegance in a period setting, complete with 4-poster bed and en suite facilities which include a Steam Room and a Jacuzzi. The Inn's Function Room is a popular venue for weddings, special occasions, private parties, dinner

The Gandon Inn, Emo, Portlaoise, Co. Laois
Tel: 0502 26622 Fax: 0502 46781

dances etc., and all events are expertly catered for with a choice of tailor-made venue available. With its beautiful Conservatory, overlooking a panoramic landscaped garden, the Function Room is ideal for photographs.

ABBEYLEIX   MAP 4 REF I12
10 miles S of Portlaoise on the N8

The village of Abbeyleix grew up around the Cistercian monastery founded here in 1183. The Abbey has long since disappeared but very much in evidence is the "improving" work carried out by Abbeyleix's 18th century landlord, Viscount de Vesci. He decided to relocate his uncomfortably close tenants and labourers to a new, elegantly laid-out village set alongside the main coach road, a mile or so away. so that their humble though well-constructed dwellings no longer marred the view from his own mansion.

It was the 3rd Viscount de Vesci who, in 1840, built what is now the **Hibernian Hotel** as a dowry for his wife. This imposing building now incorporates two other houses of the same period and provides spacious, comfortable and attractive accommodation. The Hibernian's owner, Frank Harding, has been in the hospitality business for more than 45 years so he knows how to look after his visitors well. The hotel has an excellent bar and a superb restaurant. Take your pick from either the bar snacks, served all day, or the appetising à la carte meals served in the restaurant every evening. Sunday lunch at the Hibernian is always something special, and always great value for money. The 10 guest rooms here are all en suite and attractively furnished and decorated.

Although no traces remain of Abbeyleix's original Cistercian monastery, the Abbeyleix Heritage House has garnered abundant materials to present a series of rich displays exploring local and county history. One of them tells the story of the de Vesci family whose handsome mansion designed by James Wyatt, Abbeyleix House, adds a distinctive note to the village but sadly is closed to the public although its gardens are occasionally open on

**Hibernian Hotel, Pembroke Terrace, Abbeyleix, Co. Laois
Tel: 0502 31252 Fax: 0502 31888**

summer weekends. Other exhibits include the re-created interior of the Abbeyleix Carpet Factory which made the carpeting for the *Titanic,* and the lovingly restored Sexton House in which visitors can travel back in time to the 1800s and a world of open fires, decorated dressers and brass beds.

BORRIS-IN-OSSERY
Map 4 ref I11

16 miles SW of Portlaoise on the N7

Close to the southern tip of the Slieve Bloom Mountains, **Ballaghmore House** is a striking modern building set in extensive gardens which contain some impressive ornamental features. This outstanding guest house is located at the heart of a 75-acre working farm where horses are also bred. At the time of writing, Ballaghmore's owner, Carole England, is designing a Bogland Walk through the farm - a feature which should be in place by the time you read this. Another of Carole's projects, currently under way, is the creation of a private coarse fishing lake about half a mile from the house.

Ballaghmore House itself is an imaginatively designed building with distinctive features such as the large entrance hall with its sweeping staircase making a deep impression on visitors. The 6 guest bedrooms, all of them en suite, are attractively decorated and furnished, and supremely comfortable. Breakfast at Ballaghmore House is also definitely something special, with as much as possible of the fare on offer deriving from the farm's own produce.

Carole is a member of the Laois Tourist Development Council, so she is eminently qualified to guide you to the most interesting of the many attractions in this historic area. They range in time from the 292 prehistoric standing stones at Timoney to the Workhouse Museum at Donaghmore; and in variety of activities from golf, pitch & putt, and canoeing, to fishing, horse riding and craft making. As for ancient castles: 15th century

Ballaghmore House, Ballaghmore, Borris-in-Ossery, Co. Laois
Tel: 0505 25166

Ballaghmore Castle is just up the road; 13th century Roscrea Castle only a little further away and, a few miles to the northwest, what was reputedly the most haunted castle in Ireland. Leap Castle is a ruin now, but until it was ravaged by fire in 1922 visitors such as W.B.Yeats and Oliver St John Gogarty all testified to the presence within its rooms of a revoltingly smelly spectre.

COUNTY KILDARE

County Kildare is traversed by several of the arterial roads leading away from Dublin and these convey visitors along without taking them near the best that Kildare has to offer. One of the best ways to discover the county is by following the Grand Canal either by hiring a cruiser or just walking along the towpath. The landscape is relatively flat, offering panoramic views of rolling farmland and the stone walls surrounding the old estates.

The Irish love of horses is legendary and Kildare is famous for its racecourses at Punchestown, Naas and, most famous of all, The Curragh at Kildare Town where the Irish National Stud is also located. Amongst the county's most notable buildings are the magnificent Classical pile of Castletown House at Celbridge and Kilkea Castle at Castledermot, a largely 19th century restoration but none the less impressive for it.

NAAS   MAP 7 REF K10
20 miles SW of Dublin off the N7

Barely 20 miles from the centre of Dublin, the county town of Naas (pronounced *Nace*) is fast becoming a commuter suburb of the capital. Although it was once one of the seats of the Kings of Leinster, all that remains of that regal past is a large *motte*, or man-made hill, in the centre of the town. The principal attraction for visitors is nearby **Punchestown Racecourse** whose main meeting of the year is the 3-day steeplechasing festival in late

April. Motor-racing enthusiasts will find racing events most weekends at the **Mondello Park** circuit where, for a fairly substantial fee, they can experience the thrill of driving a single-seater racing car around the track.

PROSPEROUS   Map 7 ref K10
6 miles NW of Naas on the R403

Prosperous is a well-known centre for coarse angling but the derivation of its optimistic name is a mystery. An interesting place to stay here is **Hillview House** where guests can not only enjoy excellent country house accommodation but also undertake one of any number of local leisure pursuits and holistic therapies. If golf is your sport, Hillview is within easy reach of K-Club (the Ryder Cup venue for 2005), Knockanally, Curragh,

Hillview Guest House, Prosperous, Naas, Co. Kildare
Tel: 045 868252 Fax: 045 892305 e-mail: hillview@eircom.net

CityWest, Luttrelstown Castle, and Kilkea Castle. If your interest is racing and equestrian pursuits, a short drive will take you to Curragh, Naas, Punchestown, Goffs and Kill International Equestrian Centre. Guests at Hillview are very well looked after. The bedrooms are all en suite and equipped with multi-channel TV, direct dial telephone, hairdryer and tea/coffee making facilities. There are restful guest lounges, peaceful gardens, and the wholesome food on offer is complemented by an extensive wine list.

At Hillview, holistic courses are run for groups of 6-8 people, covering a wide range of subjects including Feng Shui in your Home, Reiki Attunements, and the Power of Crystals. Guests are welcome to book a Reiki, Crystal or Spiritual Healing treatment.

STRAFFAN   Map 7 ref K10
6 miles NE of Naas off the R403

Occupying a former Victorian church which has been transplanted here stone by stone from Dublin, the **Straffan Steam Museum** contains some surprisingly smooth-running steam engines, a display of miniature models of steam engines and exhibits detailing the impact of the Iron Horse on Ireland's history. At the nearby **Straffan Butterfly Farm** huge colourful butterflies flitter around freely while various creepy-crawlies, reptiles and tarantulas are considerately displayed behind glass.

CELBRIDGE   MAP 7 REF L10
12 miles NE of Naas on the R403

The little village of Celbridge on the River Liffey boasts two major visitor attractions. **Castletown House** is Ireland's largest and finest Palladian country house, built around 1722 for the Speaker of the Irish House of Commons, William Conolly. Conolly began life as the son of a publican in Donegal and made his fortune trading in forfeited estates following the Battle of the Boyne. The house was conceived on a massive scale. Conolly engaged the "best architect in Europe", the Italian Alessandro Galilei, to design the palatial mansion and while the exterior is restrained and formal with its regular rows of pedimented windows, the interior is much more flamboyant. The person mainly responsible for the striking decoration was Conolly's daughter-in-law, Lady Louisa Lennox, (one of the wayward Lennox sisters featured in the 1999 TV series *The Aristocrats*). It was she who commissioned the Lanfranchini brothers to produce the great hall's dazzling plasterwork; created the charming Print Room; and ordered the incongruous Murano glass chandeliers for the delightful Long Gallery, decorated in the Pompeiian style. After extensive restoration and refurbishment in 1998/9 , the house is once again home to a fine collection of 18th century Irish furniture and painting.

The grounds of Castletown House are equally satisfying, the extensive views enhanced by the follies erected by Conolly's widow. One has been described as "140 feet of what appears to be a monument to chimney-sweeping" while another, an Obelisk, enraged Lady Conolly's sister because of its cost - "Three or four hundred pounds at least". Yet another, the "Wonderful Barn", is a curious conical structure 5 storeys high which Lady Conolly nonchalantly erected on somebody else's property. Like so many follies of the time, they were erected to provide relief work in time of famine or unemployment.

Celbridge Abbey Grounds, situated on the River Liffey and its Millrace, are being developed by the St John of God Order as a historical, cultural and environmental amenity for the public. The magnificent grounds were planted by Vanessa Homrigh for her friend and admirer Jonathan Swift who was a frequent visitor. "Vanessa's Bower" is a delightful, secluded spot with a view of the weir where they spent many hours together. The nearby Rockbridge is believed to be the oldest remaining stone bridge over the Liffey. Celbridge Abbey, built in 1697 for Vanessa's father, Bartholomew Van Homrigh, Lord Mayor of Dublin, is a private residence and not open to the public but its handsome crenellated exterior provides an attractive focus to the grounds. A popular venue for family outings, the Abbey Grounds contain a well-stocked Garden Centre, a model railway reproducing a typical Irish railway in the 1950s, a children's playground, picnic areas, a restaurant, and there are also themed walks and an ecology trail.

KILCOCK
14 miles N of Naas on the R407

MAP 7 REF K10

Way back in 1830 the Ordnance Survey described what is now **Larchill Arcadian Garden** as "The most fashionable garden in all of Ireland". It's also one of the most fascinating, a rediscovered rococo fantasy in an Irish pastoral setting. The 63 acres of landscaped gardens enjoy breathtaking views of the Dublin mountains and contain Europe's only remaining *ferme ornée* - an "embellished farm". A circular walk links 10 Gothic and castellated follies, amongst them a romantic island fortress and temple on an 8-acre lake, an exquisite shell-lined tower in a formal walled garden, and the notorious "Fox's Earth" - a refuge prepared for the 18th century Mr Watson's re-incarnation as a fox. The gardens are also home to a large collection of rare breeds of cattle, ponies and 4-horned sheep, and there's also a pets' corner for children and a pleasant tea room.

RATHMORE
5 miles E of Naas on minor road between the N7 and N81 and north of Blessington

MAP 7 REF L10

About halfway between Dublin and Kildare, and set in peaceful countryside, **Springfield** is a delightful farmhouse offering warm and welcoming bed and breakfast accommodation. The family home of Margaret and Willy Gillespie, Springfield has 3 comfortable guest bedrooms, a residents' TV Lounge, and a charming garden where visitors can on warm evenings settle down, relax and unwind. Margaret serves a hearty breakfast, with

Springfield, Rathmore, Naas, Co. Kildare
Tel: 045 862116

options for vegetarians and children, and will also be happy to provide you with a packed lunch. Springfield is an ideal base for touring, with Dublin, Glendalough, the National Stud and Russborough House all within easy reach. Local amenities include golf, pitch & putt, horse riding, fishing and horse racing at Punchestown, the Curragh and Naas.

BALLYMORE EUSTACE   MAP 7 REF K11
7 miles S of Naas on the R411

Just outside this tranquil village beside the River Liffey, the majestic **Ardenode Hotel** stands proudly on 6 acres of beautifully landscaped gardens. This outstanding country house hotel is owned and managed by Tom and Jean Browne, warm and welcoming hosts whose top priority is the comfort and enjoyment of their guests. Quality cuisine is also of major importance. The Garden Restaurant is renowned for its superb menus ranging from traditional Irish dishes to locally caught game and served in a spectacular ambience cre-

The Ardenode Hotel, Ballymore Eustace, Co. Kildare
Tel: 045 864198 Fax: 045 864139 e-mail: ardenode@iol.ie

ated by the floodlit garden. The accommodation at Ardenode meets the same exacting standards, offering 16 luxury bedrooms, all of them en suite and equipped with satellite TV and tea/coffee-making facilities. Guests also have the use of an elegant drawing room and the friendly Garden Lounge bar. The Ardenode's lovely setting makes it a perfect location for weddings, no matter what time of year. The immaculately maintained land-scaped gardens are resplendent throughout each season and provide a wonderfully photogenic backdrop for photographs. Business guests are also well provided for at The Ardenode which can cater for any number of delegates up to a maximum of 300 people, with the added bonus of special secretarial services.

KILDARE

Map 7 ref K11

12 miles SW of Naas on the N7

Kildare owes its foundation to Ireland's most revered female saint, Brigid, who came here sometime in the 6th century and spread her handkerchief on the ground. The area it covered was granted to her in perpetuity by the local king and here she built a convent. **St Brigid's Cathedral** stands beside the market square but little of its 13th century fabric remains. It was pillaged and burnt many times and between 1641 and 1875 lay in ruins. The present building is notable for some fine monuments and a 3-light stained glass window depicting Ireland's greatest saints - Brigid, Patrick and Columba. Nearby stands a 10th century Round Tower which is open to visitors during the summer months; from its summit there are grand views of the rolling horse country all around.

Kildare's most famous hostelry is undoubtedly **Silken Thomas** with its 3 lively bars, restaurant and large Function Room. The main lounge bar, which serves excellent bar food, is attractively styled with oak beams and wooden alcoves, while the Sports Bar (also known as the Squires Gannon Bar) is crammed with sporting memorabilia. Lil Flanagan's

Silken Thomas, The Square, Kildare, Co. Kildare
Tel: 045 522232/521264 Fax: 045 520471

bar is a separate building, a delightful thatched cottage-style building where you step back in time to a world of wooden floors, brick walls, oak beams and open fire. Traditional Irish music adds to the marvellous atmosphere and visitors are welcome to join in if they wish. The restaurant at Silken Thomas offers exceptional cuisine at remarkable value-for-money prices, offering a menu that includes steaks, seafood and poultry dishes as well as vegetarian options and a children's menu. Specialities of the house include a wonderful Supreme of Chicken Lord Edward - breast of chicken, stuffed with fresh salmon, dill and cream, poached and served with Champagne Sauce. Not to be missed!

Incidentally, the inn takes its unusual name from a member of the Fitzgerald family, Lords of Kildare, who was dubbed Silken Thomas because of the richness of his clothes and the silken banners carried by his standard bearers. In 1536, duped into believing that his father had been executed in the Tower of London, he led an uprising against Henry VIII. The rebellion was ruthlessly suppressed and Silken Thomas was beheaded at Tyburn.

With its brightly painted shop-fronts, busy pubs and, of course, well-patronised betting shops, Kildare is a lively place but its three major visitor attractions are located just outside the town. **The Irish National Stud** was the brainchild of a Scotsman, Col. William Hall-Walker, who in 1900 decided to breed thoroughbred horses at Tully Farm. The Colonel was convinced that the moon and stars dictated the destiny of all living creatures so he insisted on skylights being incorporated into the roofs of the stables. His theories seem to have been vindicated since one of his horses was the Derby winner, Minoru. In 1915 the Colonel presented the estate and horses to the Crown and it was handed over to the Irish state in 1943. Visitors can tour the trim buildings, watch the horses being exercised and groomed, or just roaming free in the paddocks. Also within the grounds are the Irish National Stud Museum where, amongst many other exhibits devoted to horses and racing, stands the skeleton of the legendary steeplechaser, Arkle.

Next door to the Stud and in complete contrast are the **Japanese Gardens**. These were also the inspiration of Col. Hill-Walker who commissioned the Japanese landscape gardener Tassa Eida and his son Minoru to create what are now acclaimed as the finest Japanese Gardens in Europe. They symbolise the journey of a soul from Oblivion to Eternity, the 20 different stages including a Marriage Bridge, a Hill of Ambition and a Tunnel of Ignorance.

Just south of the town is the **Curragh Racecourse**, the centre of the Irish racing world and host to all the classic Irish races. The racecourse is surrounded by some 6000 acres of grassland where in the early morning you can see strings of magnificent thoroughbred racehorses exercising.

RATHANGAN   MAP 7 REF J10
6 miles NW of Kildare on the R401

For centuries, peat has been a vital part of rural life in Ireland. A cheap and efficient fuel in bad times and good, the peat fire provided a focal point in the hearths of cottages and farmhouses. At **Peatland World**, in the heart of the **Bog of Allen**, visitors can discover some more versatile aspects of this ancient fuel which in recent years has been used in cosmetics, clothing, insulation, and even postcards. The past is represented by prehistoric artefacts preserved in bogland, a reconstruction of a typical Irish cottage kitchen from the early 1900s with a turf fire and traditional hearth, and examples of turf-cutting implements and equipment.

LACKAGH   MAP 7 REF J11
2 miles W of Kildare off the N7

For quality farmhouse accommodation in tranquil surroundings, the place to seek out is **Castleview Farm**, tucked away in the countryside but only a couple of miles from Kildare

Castleview Farm, Lackagh, Kildare, Co. Kildare
Tel/Fax: 045 521816

town, and with the airport and ferries only an hour's drive away. This spick and span modern bungalow is the home of Liz Fitzpatrick who delights her guests with some superb home cooking. Vegetarians and children are catered for and Liz will also provide a packed lunch on request. Castleview has 4 guest bedrooms, all en suite, a residents' TV Lounge and lovely, beautifully maintained gardens. The house is conveniently located close to the area's major attractions, Curragh Race Course, the National Stud and Japanese Gardens, and Kildare town, with its historic St Brigid's Cathedral and Round Tower, are all just a few minutes drive away.

ATHY   MAP 7 REF J11
14 miles S of Kildare on the N78 and R415

Located on the border with County Laois, near the point where the Grand Canal meets the River Barrow, Athy is the largest town in County Kildare. Overlooking the bridge over the River Barrow is **White's Castle**, built in the 16th century by the Earl of Kildare to protect this strategic crossing. There are some fine Georgian houses, an elegant market square, and a curious, pentagon-shaped modern church built of massed concrete about whose architectural merits opinions vary from dubious approval to outright hostility.

Just minutes from Athy, **Tonlegee House** is set in 4½ acres of its own private grounds. A beautifully proportioned Georgian house, owned by Marjorie and Mark Molloy, this family-run hotel and restaurant offers relaxed and friendly hospitality. The restaurant enjoys an international reputation for the excellence of its cuisine and is featured in many good food guides, including Egon Ronay and Bridgeston Good Food. With seating for only 40 covers, the restaurant is intimate and cosy with service that is courteous and attentive without being fussy. Mark is the chef and uses herbs and vegetables grown in Tonlegee's garden, and locally caught fish as well as other fresh produce. The residents' lounge, with bar, is the ideal place to unwind after a day out sightseeing, and all the 9 en

Tonlegee House & Restaurant, Athy, Co. Kildare Tel/Fax: 0507 31473
website: http://homepage@eircom.net/-tonlegee

suite bedrooms provide the perfect atmosphere for a comfortable night's rest. Beautifully
furnished and decorated throughout, in a style in keeping with the age of the building,
Tonlegee House is a lovely country house, full of character and charm. It is also ideally
situated for touring the Wicklow Mountains, and there are many activities available close
by, including four 18-hole golf courses and five race courses.

Few bed & breakfast establishments can have been showered with as many awards as
Ballindrum Farm, located about 4 miles northeast of Athy. It received a Family Farm of
the Year Award in both 1997 and 1999, boasts a National Award of Excellence, and is also

Ballindrum Farm, Athy, Co. Kildare
Tel/Fax: 0507 26294 e-mail: ballindrumfarm@eircom.net

a National Agri-Tourism Award winner. The farmhouse is a striking modern building set in the tranquil 200 acres of a working dairy and tillage farm. It's the home of Vincent and Mary Gorman, friendly hosts who greet arriving guests with a warm welcome and homemade scones and jams along with a cup of tea or coffee. Indeed, complimentary tea, coffee and drinking chocolate are always available throughout your stay. Ballindrum Farm has five bright and spacious guest rooms, four of them en suite, one with its own private bathroom. Each room enjoys a view of undulating countryside, preserved hedgerows and mature deciduous trees. Guests also have the use of a comfortable television lounge and, if they are feeling active, can play table tennis in the elegant conservatory.

CASTLEDERMOT
9 miles SE of Athy on the R408/N9

MAP 7 REF K12

This little town in the southeast corner of the country is notable for its rich cluster of ecclesiastical remains. The group includes the substantial ruins of a 13th century **Franciscan friary**, two finely carved 10th century High Crosses and a truncated Round Tower. Castledermot was once a place of some importance - a walled town in which Hugh de Lacy built an Anglo-Norman fortress. The castle was sacked by Cromwell's troops in 1649 and only one of the town gates still stands, but Castledermot seems at peace with its much quieter modern rôle.

"Dine in Style, Sleep in Comfort" is the motto adopted by Marion Greene for **Kilkea Lodge Farm**, the superb Georgian house that her husband Godfrey's forebears have lived in since 1740. Set in 260 acres of prime tillage and parklands, the Lodge possesses an

Kilkea Lodge Farm, Castledermot, Co. Kildare
Tel/Fax: 0503 45112

abundance of character and charm, and is ideal for guests who want to get away from it all. If you are an animal lover, you will feel very much at home here. Marion runs an equestrian livery and training yard specialising in Dressage Courses for event riders. Kilkea is also a most congenial venue for sightseers or race-goers who wish to entertain their friends in a house party atmosphere, sampling excellent food and imaginative cooking. Facilities for tennis, golf and fishing are all available in the locality, with Kilkea Castle Hotel leisure centre and golf club right next door. During the year, Kilkea Lodge hosts occasional musical workshops, painting courses and health breaks, and Marion can also arrange visits to local private gardens of interest.

COUNTY WICKLOW

Dubbed the "Garden of Ireland", Wicklow offers visitors a rich mix of attractions. Family holiday-makers flock to the golden sandy beaches at Arklow and Bray; inland, the rolling Wicklow Mountains with their deep heather-clad glens, cascading waterfalls and serene lakes contain some of the finest scenery in Ireland. Glendalough, in the Wicklow Mountains National Park, is one the most important of all early Christian sites in the country, its origins dating back to the 6th century and its later monastic remains amongst the most extensive and impressive to have survived.

The county also boasts some magnificent houses and gardens, most notably the glorious Palladian mansion of Russborough House near Arklow, which also boasts a superb art collection, and the world-famous gardens at Powerscourt, laid out in the mid-1800s to a classical pattern. Despite the county's proximity to Dublin, it is surprisingly underpopulated and unspoilt - characteristics which have made it a popular location with film and television directors. The county has had starring (if silent) rôles in films such as *Excalibur* and *Braveheart,* and in the hugely successful TV series, *Ballykissangel.*

In this tour of the county we begin by following the coast southwards from Bray before turning inland to explore the Wicklow Mountains National Park.

BRAY   Map 7 ref M11
12 miles SE of Dublin off the M11

Bray developed as a genteel Victorian resort when the railway arrived here in the 1850s and it remains a popular weekend destination for Dubliners so, in addition to its safe, mile-long beach of sand and shingle, the town is well-supplied with all the usual amusements. James Joyce lived at Bray from 1889 to 1891, his residence duly noted in the **Bray Heritage Centre** which also has a good collection of photographs, maps and artefacts illustrating the town's history, and a folklore room.

Other attractions include the **National Aquarium**, home to a wonderful variety of native and tropical fish and, just outside the town, **Killruddery House & Garden**. The Brabazon family have lived at Killruddery since 1618 and the 17th century garden here is one of the oldest in Ireland still surviving with its original layout. The house itself contains some interesting features - carvings by Grinling Gibbons, Chippendale furniture and a water-powered clock. Just south of the town, **Bray Head** (791 feet) provides an exhilarating coastal walk, overlooked by a huge cross erected to commemorate the Holy Year of 1950.

Sea Breeze House is well-named since it stands on the sea front at Bray and commands some splendid views along the coast. Thomas and Mary O'Hara's attractive Victorian terraced house, with its bright colour-washed frontage, offers comfortable and relaxing bed and breakfast accommodation in a warm, family atmosphere. Guests have the use of a TV lounge but there are also TVs in the 4 spacious guest bedrooms, (3 family, 1 twin), all of which are en suite and most of which share those superb views. There's also a separate

Sea Breeze House, 1 Marine Terrace, Bray, Co. Wicklow
Tel/Fax: 028 68337

bathroom. To the rear of the house, there's a large garden, complete with barbecue area for warm summer evenings. The O'Hara's provide a generous spread at breakfast time with vegetarian and children's options available. Bray town centre is just a few minutes away and a short drive will take you into the scenic splendours of the Wicklow Mountains.

ENNISKERRY
Map 7 ref L11
3 miles W of Bray on the R117

The picture-postcard village of Enniskerry, with its splendid backdrop of the Great Sugar Loaf Mountain, was built to serve the 14,000 acre estate of **Powerscourt House** nearby. But an impressive drive, more than half a mile long, only leads to the shell of what was once a magnificent Palladian mansion, designed in 1740 by the German architect Richard Castel. The parlous state of the house seems particularly unfair since it was destroyed by a fire in 1974 just before it was due to be re-opened after a major restoration programme. But Powerscourt remains one of Wicklow's major visitor attractions because of the glorious gardens where spouting fountains and winged horses, mosaic terraces created with pebbles from Bray beach, tranquil lakes and superb specimen trees create an Arcadian landscape of utter serenity. Apart from a fragrant Japanese garden added in Edwardian times, the gardens were originally laid out in the mid-1700s and redesigned a hundred years later by Daniel Robertson, an eccentric character who suffered grievously from gout. He directed operations while being trundled around the grounds in a wheelbarrow, swigging the while from a large bottle of sherry. When the sherry was exhausted, so was Daniel and he retired for the rest of the day. Also within the estate grounds but approached by a different entrance, is the **Powerscourt Waterfall** which plunges some 400 feet over a jagged rock face. There are some pleasant riverside walks in the valley below, a popular venue for picnics with tables provided and kiosk refreshments available.

ASHFORD
MAP 7 REF M11
4 miles NW of Wicklow on the N11

This pretty little village on the River Vartry is close to two celebrated beauty spots. To the northwest, **Devil's Glen** is a deep ravine where there are some breathtaking walks high above the rushing river which at one point falls almost 100 feet into the "Devil's Punchbowl". Closer to the village, **Mount Usher Gardens** have grown from a mere potato field in 1860 to one of Ireland's finest informal gardens today. Four generations of the Walpole family have tended the trees, shrubs and flowers, many of them rare species, introduced from all around the world and planted in harmony with the natural woodland. The 20-acre gardens are laid out along the banks of the River Vartry with its weirs and waterfalls. Attractive suspension bridges provide vantage points from which to enjoy some spectacular and romantic views. At the courtyard entrance, there are several craft and clothing shops, and a pleasant tea room overlooking the river and gardens.

Owned and managed by the Caprani family for more than 20 years, **The Chester Beatty Inn** offers 12 superbly appointed bedrooms to complement its already renowned award winning Restaurant, (Winner of the Tourist Menu of the Year Award in 1996). Enjoy the convivial and authentic Irish atmosphere of the Lounge and Traditional Irish Bar - both with open log fires. All the bedrooms have been tastefully furnished and finished to a 5-star standard. Facilities include direct dial telephone, TV, tea/coffee-making facilities, trouser press, hair dryer and spacious Italian marble en suite bathrooms. The Traditional Irish Bar is open daily from 12 noon; there are Carvery Lunches daily from 12.30pm to 2.30pm and the Restaurant is open for Sunday lunches. Evening meals are served in the Traditional Irish Bar and the Restaurant is open for evening meals from 6pm with menus and wine lists to tempt the most discerning of palates.

If snooker is your preferred game, you will be delighted to know that the Inn has no fewer than 4 championship tables. At weekends, Clouseau's Night-club is the place to be seen, offering a variety of music to make the night enjoyable for everyone, relayed on one of the most up to date sound systems in Europe.

Chester Beatty Inn, Ashford, Co. Wicklow
Tel: 0404 40206 Fax: 0404 49003

The Capranis have produced a helpful 4-page list of the many attractions within easy reach of the Inn. They range from Avoca village, which was the setting for the famous TV series *Ballykissangel,* to the 6th century monastic settlement of Glendalough. Within a 3-minute walk of the inn, Mount Usher Gardens are regarded as the most exotic in Ireland and within the grounds you can also browse around the Brian Keogh Pottery studio. A little further afield are the glorious sandy beaches of Brittas Bay and the multiple attractions of Dublin are only 28 miles distant.

WICKLOW TOWN

Map 7 ref M11

30 miles SE of Dublin off the N11

The Danes named it *Wyking alo*, "Viking meadow" and it became one of their most important settlements. Today, Wicklow's county town is a pleasantly sleepy place overlooking a crescent-shaped shingle bay with a ruined Norman castle at its eastern end. Contrasting with the town's brightly-painted houses, the grey stone walls of the former **Wicklow Gaol** (1702) now house a museum dedicated to the 1798 Rebellion with some poignant exhibits detailing the wholesale transportation of rebels and criminals and also the tribulations of the years of the Great Famine. A good antidote to this rather sobering display is a walk around **Wicklow Head** which provides some exhilarating views along the coast and across to the strange profiles of Great and Little Sugarloaf Mountains. On the headland is **Wicklow Lighthouse**, or lighthouses rather, since there are actually 3 separate towers.

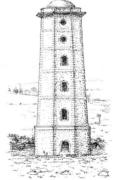

Wicklow Lighthouse

Back in the town, **MacReamoinn Town House,** with its primrose-coloured walls and trimly-maintained gardens, makes a pretty picture indeed. MacReamoinn is the Gaelic version of the family name of Peter and Una Redmond whose home this is. They moved here in 1996, carried out a comprehensive refurbishment, and now provide a warm welcome for bed & breakfast guests. They have 4 letting rooms, all attractively furnished and all en suite, (3 with showers, 1 with bath). Adjoining the house, there's a charming patio,

MacReamoinn Town House, Summerhill, Wicklow Town, Co. Wicklow
Tel: 0404 61113

colourful with flower boxes and plants, where guests can sit out and enjoy fairweather days. The tariff includes a hearty Irish breakfast. MacReamoinn Town House is non-smoking, has its own private parking and is open all year round. Located on the edge of the town, it's well-placed for touring this attractive part of the country with scenic treasures such as the Vale of Avoca just a few miles away.

Located just 1 mile outside Wicklow, **Lissadell House** is a handsome part Georgian-style house set in spacious and beautifully-maintained gardens. There are delightful views of the Wicklow hills and countryside and the surrounding area with its combination of mountains, forests and coast, is one of the most scenic regions of Ireland. Lissadell House is the home of Patricia Klaue who has been welcoming bed and breakfast guests for some 14 years, many of them returning again and again. There are 4 guest bedrooms, 2 of them en suite, and all attractively furnished and decorated. A full Irish breakfast is included in the tariff and Patricia will also provide an evening meal if required. Facilities for golf, fishing and horse-riding are all nearby, the celebrated Mount Usher Gardens are just a few

Lissadell House, Ashtown Lane, off Marlton Road, Wicklow, Co. Wicklow
Tel: 0404 67458 e-mail: lissadellhse@eircom.ie

miles away, and the scenic Vale of Avoca lies a little further to the south. And if you enjoy live Irish music, there are some lively pubs in Wicklow Town where you will be well entertained.

Set in peaceful countryside overlooking Blainroe Bay, the **Blainroe Hotel** offers excellent food and accommodation in luxurious surroundings. The hotel has recently been totally refurbished, adding a new reception area and bar while retaining traditional features such as the open log fire and baby grand piano. The 13 spacious en suite bedrooms are all beautifully decorated, comfortably furnished and well equipped. Good food is a major priority at the Blainroe. At breakfast time there's a choice of a full Irish or a Healthy Options meal to set you up for the day. Dinner is always rather special, too, with a full à la carte menu proffered along with special menus for vegetarians and children. The ac-

Blainroe Hotel, Coast Road, Wicklow, Co. Wicklow
Tel: 0404 67500 Fax: 0404 69737 e-mail: blainroehotel@oceanfree.net

complished chefs are always happy to cater for any particular requirements their guests may have. The service in the splendid Atrium Restaurant, and indeed, throughout the whole hotel deserves special commendation. The Blainroe is owned and personally run by David Ellis and his courteous and efficient staff are always ready to assist in any way they can, and will willingly help you plan your stay and advise on your itinerary. The hotel itself has a fully equipped gym, swimming pool, sauna and jacuzzi, and a short drive will bring you to facilities for golf, fishing, horse riding or hill walks through the enchanting Wicklow Mountains.

KILBRIDE
5 miles SW of Wicklow on minor road off the N11

MAP 7 REF M12

South of Wicklow Town stretches the 3-mile-long expanse of white sandy beach at Brittas Bay, with Mizen Head, which features so often in fishing forecasts, at its southern tip. A mile or so inland a warm Irish welcome awaits visitors to **Gormanstown Manor Farm Guest House**, a charming family-run country guest house. Set in spectacular and wonderful surroundings, Gormanstown Manor Farm exudes a peaceful, stress-free atmosphere - guests are free to enjoy the large, landscaped gardens, wander along the nature walks on the farm or take advantage of the golf driving range on the farm. (There are also 20 golf courses within easy reach!). The Manor is a new, large and comfortable house, built to the highest standards. Its bright, spacious, en suite bedrooms have direct dial telephones and televisions; there's a residents' lounge and sitting room with TV and open log fires as well as central heating throughout. Your hosts, Martin and Margaret Murphy will welcome you after a day of fresh air and country pursuits with the best of good, traditional home cooking, fresh Irish food and superb personal services. The farm is situated off the Dublin to Rosslare road, the N11, at the Lil, Doyle's and Beehive pubs just outside Wicklow.

Gormanstown Manor Farm Guest House, Gormanstown, Kilbride,
Co. Wicklow Tel: 0404 69432 Fax: 0404 61832
e-mail: gormanstownmanor@tinet.ie

The guest house is ideally located for touring this beautiful county, dubbed the Garden of Ireland, with its breathtaking scenery of picturesque mountains, valleys, rivers, lakes and woodlands. Enjoy the golden beaches of Brittas Bay or take advantage of the facilities for sailing, fishing, cycling, horse riding, polo, golf, tennis, mountain climbing and much more. The Manor is also close to the famous Mount Usher Gardens, Powerscourt Gardens and Waterfall, Russborough House, (home of the Beit family and a world-famous art collection), and the scenic delights of the Vale of Avoca and Glendalough.

ARKLOW   Map 7 ref L12
14 miles S of Wicklow on the N11

Set around the estuary of the River Avoca, Arklow claims to be one of the ports identified on Ptolemy's famous 2nd century map of Britannia. It was certainly an important port in medieval times and there's still a thriving shipbuilding industry here. Sir Francis Chichester's celebrated transatlantic yacht *Gypsy Moth IV* was built here at John Tyrell's yard, although the boat itself is now moored at Greenwich in London. The town's **Maritime Museum** houses a wonderfully motley collection of items with a seafaring connection - a whale's tooth and eardrum and a model ship made with more than 10,000 matchsticks amongst them. Arklow's own white sand beach has the docks on one side and a gravel extraction plant on the other but about 5 miles south of the town, **Clogga Beach** is quiet and sheltered.

THE CROGHAN VALLEY

The extreme southern tip of Co. Wicklow is a peaceful area of leafy glens, mountain streams and gentle rivers. In ancient times gold was mined from Croghan Mountain (2000ft) and when a sizeable nugget was found there in 1796 a "Gold Rush" ensued during which 2000oz were discovered within a few months.

SHILLELAGH   Map 7 ref K12
24 miles SW of Wicklow on the R749/R725

This pleasant village lies in a wooded valley almost surrounded by hills. The surrounding area was once completely covered by the extensive **Shillelagh Wood**, famous for its oak trees. The oak roofing of St Patrick's Cathedral in Dublin came from Shillelagh oaks.

Shillelagh is "old Coollattin Country, a corner of County Wicklow, known the world over as The Garden County of Ireland". Here, **The Avalon** offers good food and drink with People Who Care. It has 10 guest bedrooms, full bar restaurant and dance licence, and has been home to the Pratt family for over 30 years. The Avalon dates back to when it was known as The Railway Hotel. Shillelagh (population 300) is largely a 17th century estate village with attractive granite stone houses and walls. The Courthouse has a weathervane in the form of a fox on top of its clock tower, matching the cock on the top of the church spire. The village is steeped in history as the whole area was once owned by Lord Wentworth Fitzwilliam, an Englishman who used Coollattin House, one mile away,

The Avalon, Shillelagh, Co. Wicklow
Tel: 055 29149/29127

as his hunting lodge, and hundreds of acres of oak woodland for his hunting or fishing. Today, it's owned by Coollattin Golf Club and the park is now an 18-hole course. Only 18 miles from the sea, Shillelagh and district remains unspoiled,

THE VALE OF AVOCA AND AVONDALE

The late 18th century Romantic poets adored this corner of County Wicklow. Wordsworth toured these enchanting valleys in the 1790s and was captivated. The Irish poet, Thomas Moore, spent many hours in contemplation on a hill overlooking the Meeting of the Waters (where the River Avonbeg flows into the Avoca) and wrote some of his best-known lines:

> *There is not in this wide world a valley so sweet*
> *As that vale in whose bosom the bright waters meet;*
> *Oh! The last rays of feeling and life must depart*
> *Ere the bloom of that valley shall fade from my heart.*

The valleys are particularly glorious in late spring when the wild cherry trees are in blossom but they are delightful throughout the year which means that the main road is nearly always busy. Fortunately, you only have to walk a short distance from the road to find peaceful Arcadian vistas opening up in every direction.

AVOCA   MAP 7 REF L12
12 miles SW of Wicklow on the R752/R754

This charming little hamlet of trim white houses set beside the river is the home of **Avoca Handweavers** whose appealing range of woollens and knitwear provide popular and practical souvenirs of a visit to their workshops here, housed in a group of whitewashed buildings which also contain the oldest surviving handweaving mill in Ireland, dating from 1723. The Wynne sisters who established the business more than 40 years ago, proudly claim to be the inventors of the car rug. There are daily demonstrations of handweaving and the little complex also has a shop and tea room.

This village is also the setting for the BBC TV series *Ballykissangel*. This Irish comedy/ drama, frequently referred to as BallyK or Ballykea, is filmed in Avoca. The beautiful scenery is matched by wonderful characterization and well crafted writing.

Nestling in the picturesque setting of the Vale of Avoca, **Cherrybrook Country Home** enjoys a quiet scenic location less than 4 miles from the N11. A real Irish welcome awaits bed and breakfast visitors to this handsome modern house set in landscaped gardens complete with picnic and barbecue areas. Cherrybrook is the home of Mrs Bernie Ivers who will be only too glad to make your holiday in this beautiful corner of Ireland a happy and enjoyable experience. Guests can stay on either a B & B or half board basis but you

Cherrybrook Country Home, Avoca, Co. Wicklow
Tel/Fax: 0402 35179

really shouldn't miss sampling Bernie's excellent home cooked food, all prepared from fresh local produce and including vegetarian options. Packed lunches are also available. Cherrybrook has an elegant residents' lounge with soothing countryside views, and all 4 guest bedrooms are en suite, attractively furnished and decorated, and non-smoking. Each is equipped with colour TV, hair dryer and tea/coffee maker. Children are welcome, with a cot and baby-sitting service available if required. Devotees of the TV series *Ballykissangel* will be delighted to know that "Fitzgerald's Pub" is just a few minutes walk away!

MEETING OF THE WATERS
11 miles SW of Wicklow on the R752

MAP 7 REF L12

Overlooking the Meeting of the Waters, where the Avonmore and the Avonbeg merge, you will find **The Meetings** which is owned and run by Peter and Marion Moore. This

The Meetings, Vale of Avoca, Co. Wicklow
Tel: 0402 35226 Fax: 0402 35558

small complex offers the traveller almost everything he could need in just one stop: add to this the beautiful views and scenery and you have the perfect place to sit and rest awhile. The Restaurant and Grill Room serves a wide variety of dishes, from bar food to à la carte, with a full grill menu also available. The bar food is served throughout the day, with dinner and grill menu served from 6pm until 10pm. The Craft Shop sells a wide selection of traditional Irish souvenirs and crafts such as wools, mohair, tweeds, china and glass, and also has a Bureau de Change attached to it so that changing money should never be a problem. Both the Restaurant and Craft Shop overlook the Meeting of the Waters which was made so famous by the great poet Thomas Moore in 1807. Outside, you will find a large beer garden with umbrellas to shade you on those balmy afternoons, an inviting spot to sit and enjoy a bar snack accompanied perhaps by a glass of wine.

LARAGH   MAP 7 REF L11
9 miles W of Wicklow on the R755

From Rathdrum, the R752 winds through the Avonbeg Valley, also known as the Vale of Clara, to the pleasant village of Laragh, set around a major crossroads and close to one of Ireland's most important spiritual sites, **Glendalough**. Some time in the late 6th century St Kevin, a scion of the royal house of Leinster, came to this secluded valley and for many years he lived here as a hermit, sometimes sleeping in the hollow of a tree. Gradually, his sanctity and wisdom attracted many disciples and by the time of his death, at a great age in 618, Glendalough was known across Europe as a centre of learning. St Kevin's foundation continued to flourish, despite being sacked twice by Vikings and once again by the English. Each time, the monks patiently restored the buildings until they were finally ousted by Henry VIII.

The oldest surviving building is the **Church of the Rock** which stands on the site of St Kevin's original oratory and has to be reached by boat. The building is about 24ft by 14ft on the inside and entered by way of a doorway made of large granite blocks. To the east of the church, in the cliffside about 30ft above the lake, is **St Kevin's Bed** - a tiny hole in the rock which was reputedly used by the saint for meditation and prayer. An ancient legend says that he also used it as a refuge from the unwelcome attentions of a young maiden. When she eventually found his hiding place, St Kevin responded by pushing her into the lake. The extensive Glendalough site contains a wealth of other ancient buildings - a Cathedral built in two phases in the 10th and 12th centuries, a well-preserved Round Tower with a doorway 10 feet above the ground, and numerous crosses, of which the most impressive is the 8th century St Kevin's Cross. An excellent introduction to all these ecclesiastical treasures is provided at the Visitor Centre where your admission charge includes entrance to an informative exhibition and video show as well as the option of a guided tour if you wish.

Adjoining the Glendalough site is the **Wicklow Mountains National Park Visitor Centre**. The Centre has exhibitions, free lectures during the summer, education courses, and provides comprehensive information about the 49,420 acres of the Park which covers most of upland Wicklow.

Located in the heart of the Wicklow National Park and with the River Avonmore flowing softly past, **Tudor Lodge** offers quality bed and breakfast accommodation in wonderfully peaceful surroundings. The Lodge is a modern Tudor-style house which was custom built for guests with very spacious and comfortable bedrooms enjoying en suite facilities. Your hosts, Des and Liz, serve a generous breakfast, with vegetarian and children's options available. The Lodge stands in attractive gardens with a large patio, barbecue area and lovely riverside views. Des and Liz can make arrangements locally for walking tours and nature trails with experienced guides, horse riding and much more. The monastic city of St Kevin is less than a mile away, as is the Wicklow Way, and the spectacular

Tudor Lodge, Laragh, Glendalough, Co. Wicklow
Tel/Fax: 0404 45554

Wicklow Mountains are all around. Dublin City is about 1 hour, Dun Laoghaire is 40 minutes and Rosslare is only 1½ hours away.

About a mile to the east of Glendalough, there's outstanding food and accommodation at **Laragh Lodge**, a charming 16th century stone house with latticed windows and a creeper trying to smother the porch. Inside, stone floors, beamed ceiling and beechwood furniture all add to the appeal. The owner/managers, John Grehan and Tracey O'Neill, have had catering experience all around the world and their menu offers an excellent choice of dishes with an international flavour. The Lodge also has 6 guest rooms, all of

Laragh Lodge, Laragh, Co. Wicklow
Tel: 0404 45302 Fax: 0404 45235 e-mail: laralodge@tinet-ie.

them en suite and all with enchanting views of mountains or countryside. Outside, there's an inviting patio, beautiful landscaped gardens, and ample parking. The area around Laragh is famed for its striking scenery, with the Valley of the Two Lakes running northwestwards to Wicklow Gap where there's a spectacular viewpoint. This is grand walking country, but visitors with different interests will also find facilities for trout fishing and horse riding.

Surrounded by lovely countryside and set in 7 acres of garden and pastureland, **Glendale** enjoys an outstandingly peaceful location. The house overlooks some outstanding views and the garden runs down to the tranquil Avonmore river. Christy and Valerie Merrigan built their attractive single-storey home a few years ago and they now offer a warm Irish welcome to bed and breakfast guests. They have 4 letting rooms, 3 of them with showers, 1 with shower and bath, and all non-smoking. The dining room has tea and coffee-making facilities and there's also a TV lounge for guests. Glendale has ample parking space and, if you are planning a day out in the countryside, packed lunches can be provided. If you prefer a self-catering holiday, by the time you read this Christy and

Glendale, Laragh East, Glendalough, Co. Wicklow
Tel: 0404 45410 e-mail: merrigan@tinet.ie

Valerie should have available 5 cottages, each of them with accommodation for up to 6 people. These will be rented on a weekly basis and available all year round. Children are welcome for both bed & breakfast and self-catering accommodation.

ROUNDWOOD
12 miles NE of Wicklow on the R755

MAP 7 REF L11

Set on the banks of the River Vartry, close to the point where it enters the Vartry Reservoir, this attractive village is a popular angling and horse-riding centre. The village is also well-known to lovers of good food who make their way to **The Roundwood Inn**, a former coaching inn on the Wexford to Dublin route. Parts of the attractive black and white building date back to 1623. The inn is a member of the "Taste of Wicklow Good Food Circle", a group of hostelries ranging from homely converted stables to elegant Georgian mansions but all owner run and all dedicated to providing their guests with the very best in comfort and cuisine. The Roundwood has been owned and run by Jurgen and Aine Schwalm since 1966 and they are now assisted by son-in-law Michael and nephew John. Credit for the superlative food goes to Paul, the excellent chef who has been in charge of the Roundwood's kitchen since 1981. His appealing menus offer the best of Irish and European cuisine with specialities such as Roast Wicklow Lamb and prime fish dishes vying with game and poultry for your attention. More difficult choices when you come to study the wine list which contains more than 100 bins. Reservations are essential for lunch or dinner in the restaurant, (closed Monday, Tuesday and Sunday evening), but you can enjoy tasty bar food every day, including such dishes as Irish Stew, Seafood Platter, Lobster Salad and Oysters. Roundwood itself enjoys the distinction of being the highest village in Ireland, 780 feet above sea level, and was also the home of the great Irish writer James Joyce as a boy. The village lies on the edge of the Wicklow Mountains National Park

The Roundwood Inn, Roundwood, Bray, Co. Wicklow
Tel: 01 281 8107/281 8125

where red deer and grouse may still be seen and there are opportunities for wonderful nature walks. Wicklow County is also famous as "The Garden of Ireland" with celebrated public gardens at Powerscourt and Mount Usher.

BLESSINGTON

Map 7 ref L11

20 miles W of Bray on the N81

Tucked away in the northwestern corner of the county, Blessington enjoys a dreamy location alongside the gleaming waters of a lake and with the Wicklow Mountains as a dramatic backdrop. Once a staging post on the coach route from Dublin to Carlow, this attractive village has a wide main street lined by trees and handsome Georgian buildings.

But there's an even more impressive sight nearby, the stately pile of **Russborough House**, a grand Palladian mansion built in the 1740s for Joseph Leeson, 1st Earl of Milltown, a prosperous Dublin brewer. Leeson spared no expense. The house was designed by Ireland's leading architect of the day, Richard Castel; the swirling plasterwork was created by the Francini brothers, and one of the most fashionable painters in Europe at the time, Claude Vernet, was specially commissioned to provide four of the sea-scapes for which he was celebrated.

The palatial building with its two pillared and curving wings looks across to a placid lake, a commonplace of 18th century landscaping, but this lake is actually a thoroughly modern 20th century reservoir formed by damming the River Liffey and providing Dublin with some 20 million gallons of water a day.

The interior of Russborough House is furnished with a dazzling collection of antiques, tapestries and exquisite porcelain, but the greatest glory of the house is its sumptuous array of paintings - works by Goya, Velazquez, Gainsborough, Rubens and Frans Hals are just some of the masterpieces on display. The paintings come from the collection of Alfred Beit, co-founder with Cecil Rhodes of the De Beer Diamond Company, and they arrived at this obscure corner of County Wicklow when Beit's nephew, Sir Alfred Beit, bought Russborough Hall in 1952. Such a treasury of art attracted some unwelcome attention. In 1974, Bridget Rose Dugdale stole 16 of the paintings, worth £18 million, to raise funds for the IRA. These were all recovered within a week. There was a second burglary in 1986 and although some of those stolen paintings were retrieved, security at the Hall is now understandably tight.

DUNLAVIN
MAP 7 REF K11

26 miles SW of Bray on the R756/412

Close to the border with Co. Kildare, **Tynte House** is a lovely 19th century farmhouse nestling in the peaceful village of Dunlavin. At this splendid guest house, owned and personally run by Caroline and John Lawler, you can expect a warm and friendly welcome to this charming house. Tynte House has 7 spacious en suite bedrooms where you can be sure of a comfortable, relaxing sleep. Breakfast is a traditional home-cooked meal, and dinner in the evening is available by arrangement.

In the courtyard of this charming Georgian house is a beautifully renovated stable block which now contains 4 luxury self-contained mews holiday homes. As with the

Tynte House, Dunlavin, Co. Wicklow
Tel: 045 401561 Fax: 045 401586 e-mail: jclawler@iol.ie

house, the apartments are tastefully decorated with antique furnishings and, varying in size with accommodation for between six and eight people, they all have fully equipped kitchens. With a children's play area and an all-weather tennis court in the grounds, there is something here for all the family. Tynte House has been showered with awards and recommendations, amongst them a 1998 Agri-Tourism Award and the AA's Top 20 Land-lady (UK & Ireland) Award for 1998.

3 Southeast Ireland

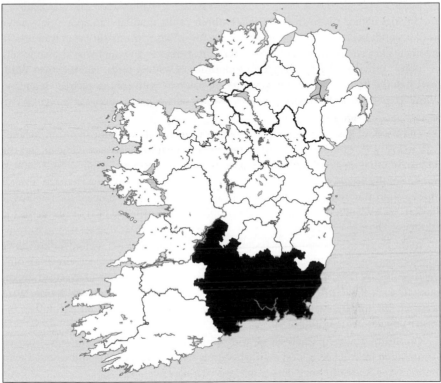

COUNTY WEXFORD

The southeast corner of Ireland is the sunniest and driest part of the country and County Wexford is conveniently provided with some excellent beaches lining almost the whole of its east coast. The strands at Curracloe and Rosslare are particularly extensive and even in July and August never overcrowded. Curracloe has an additional interest for film buffs since it was the location for the 'Normandy' beach landings in Stephen Spielberg's film *Saving Private Ryan*. Inland, the gentle countryside of low hills, lush valleys and trim farms is shaped by three great rivers, the Nore, the Barrow and the Slaney. To the northwest, the Blackstairs Mountains form a natural boundary with County Carlow.

Although County Wexford has many prehistoric and medieval monuments, they tend to be on a modest scale with the many 14th century tower houses, for example, merging into the later farmhouses which have grown up around them. The county boasts some

outstanding gardens, notably at Johnstown Castle near Wexford Town and the JFK Arboretum at New Ross which was established as a memorial to President Kennedy whose
forebears lived at nearby Dunganstown.

WEXFORD   MAP 7 REF L14
89 miles S of Dublin on the N11

The Vikings named the town *Waesfjord* - harbour of the mudflats, an appropriate name
since it stands beside the muddy estuary of the River Slaney whose silt-laden waters have
gradually clogged the once busy deep-water port. However, the mudflats, known locally
as "slobs", provide a perfect habitat for thousands of wading birds. The **Wexford Wildfowl Reserve** (free) is famous for its wintering wildfowl with species such as Greenland
White-fronted Geese, Brent Geese, Bewick's Swans and Wigeon amongst the regular visitors.

Old Wexford has been described as "one of the most atmospheric towns in Ireland"
with many of its winding streets so narrow you could shake hands across them. But the
only substantial medieval building to have survived is **Westgate.** Built around 1300, it
was one of the 5 gates of the walled city. Now designated the West Gate Heritage Tower it
offers a short film retracing the history of the town. Also interesting are the remains of
Selskar Abbey where Henry II spent the whole 40 days of Lent, 1171, atoning for the
murder of Thomas à Becket.

In the centre of Wexford, a small square called the Bull Ring is a reminder of the once
popular sport of bull-baiting. The square is now dominated by a statue commemorating
the rebellion of 1798 when armed only with pikes the townspeople of Wexford fought
valiantly against overwhelming odds. A century and a half earlier, Cromwell's troops had
occupied the town, destroyed many of its churches and massacred all but 400 of the
town's population of around 2000.

On nearby Crescent Quay stands the statue of a vigorously striding naval officer,
Commodore John Barry, a local man who emigrated to Philadelphia and credited with
founding the American Navy during the War of Independence.

Internationally, the town is probably best known for its annual **Wexford Festival
Opera**, "Europe's most enjoyable Festival" according to *Reader's Digest.* Held in October,
the festival offers the opportunity of seeing lesser-known works by major composers in a
wonderfully unstuffy, festive atmosphere. Performances take place in the tiny Theatre
Royal, so tickets are hard to come by, but the Festival also offers recitals, concerts, lectures
and a lively fringe programme. Wexford's cultural life isn't just confined to the Festival.
Throughout the rest of the year the Theatre Royal puts on drama performances and the
Wexford Arts Centre, housed in an 18th century market house in Cornmarket, has an
ever-changing programme of exhibitions, dance and music performances.

Situated overlooking the fabulous Slaney Estuary, **Ferrycarrig Hotel** offers a unique
mix of stunning scenery, superb leisure facilities, excellent food and luxurious accommodation. Its ambience conjures up an Ireland of peaceful, unhurried days, with the cries of
gulls wheeling out to sea, friendly faces, good food and fine music. You'd like a room with
a view? At the Ferrycarrig Hotel, that's no problem - every bedroom enjoys a breathtaking

Ferrycarrig Hotel, Ferrycarrig Bridge, Wexford, Co. Wexford
Tel: 053 20999 Fax: 053 20982 e-mail: ferrycarrig@griffingroup.ie

view over the River Slaney, along with colour television, tea and coffee making facilities, and direct dial telephones. And whether your taste is for traditional Irish or modern French cuisine, the hotel's two superb, award-winning restaurants make every meal an occasion to remember. The Tides Restaurant, (2 Rosettes from the AA for 4 years running), has a striking interior, unrivalled cuisine, an enviable cellar and, of course, that marvellous view. The Boathouse Bistro vibrates with a lively, contemporary atmosphere that accords well with the exciting local and international dishes on offer. There's also the Dry Dock Bar where you can enjoy your drink or bar meal either inside, or on the beautiful riverside deck.

The Ferrycarrig's outstanding Health and Fitness Club boasts a fully equipped fitness suite, a 20 metre swimming pool, sauna, steam room, jacuzzi and beauty treatment rooms. Golfers will find that a 15 minute drive brings them to the hotel's associated golf course, the 18-hole Championship golf course at St Helen's Bay, situated on a beautiful cliff-top position overlooking the historic Tuskar Rock lighthouse.

The hotel makes a perfect base for exploring the lush, green countryside around Wexford with its picturesque villages, tranquil seaside towns, and miles and miles of unspoilt beaches. Saunter around the historic towns of Wexford or Kilkenny, discover attractions like the nearby Irish National Heritage Park, or simply take an evening stroll along the river to Wexford's historic castle.

A short distance from the Ferrycarrig Hotel is one of Wexford's must-see attractions, the **Irish National Heritage Park**. The 35-acre site depicts man's settlements in Ireland from 7000BC until the arrival of the Normans in the 12th century. Visitors can wander through carefully reconstructed full scale models of ancient homesteads and places of ritual. Burial modes are explained and the county's abundance of archaeological remains interpreted. Guided tours are available and the site includes a nature reserve, a restaurant and a crafts and book shop. The Park is open daily from early April until the end of October.

Johnstown Castle Gardens, Wexford

A couple of miles south of the Park is another major visitor attraction. **Johnstown Castle Gardens** surround Johnstown Castle, a splendid Gothic Revival castellated mansion which is now an Agricultural College, and contain a wealth of colourful shrubs and flowers, ornamental lakes, shady woodland and beautifully maintained walled gardens. The grounds are open daily all year round and during the winter months entrance is free. Also within the grounds of Johnstown Castle is the **Irish Agricultural Museum** which has extensive displays on all aspects of rural life - farming machinery, domestic objects, carts and carriages, country furniture and reconstructed workshops, and an exhibit on the Great Famine.

TAGOAT   MAP 7 REF L14
9 miles SE of Wexford on the N25

To the southeast of Wexford, the popular resort of Rosslare offers safe bathing on a 6-mile long beach that curves around the bay. A mile or so further south is the village of Tagoat, well worth seeking out if you appreciate top class accommodation. A sense of tranquillity descends on you from the moment you step inside the beautifully appointed **Churchtown House**. Winner of the AA award for Guest Accommodation of the Year, Ireland, 1998, this charming period house dating back to 1703 is set in eight and a half acres of mature trees and shrubbery. Churchtown House is the home of Patricia and Austin Cody, two of the greatest hosts you could ever wish to meet. Their guests return again and again to enjoy the superb hospitality at this elegant country guest house. Arriving visitors receive a warm welcome from the Codys and probably from their two friendly golden retrievers, Alex(andra) and Cleo(patra) as well. With its prime location and pastoral setting, the

Churchtown House, Rosslare, Co. Wexford
Tel/Fax: 053 32555

house is perfect for an overnight stay or a longer break to enjoy golf at one of the 3 local courses, fishing, swimming, walking, horse riding and many other activities. There's an excellent choice of local restaurants and evening entertainment, or you could choose to stay in and sample Churchtown House's own fine cooking, based on fresh produce, organically produced wherever possible. Your hosts offer each guest a glass or two of sherry before the meal and if you enjoy wine with your meal, the house also has a wine licence. The 14 spacious bedrooms, all with bath/shower, are individually decorated and comfortably furnished with a mixture of antique and traditional pieces. One of them has been adapted to be wheelchair friendly. This corner of Co. Wexford is particularly rich in visitor attractions. In Tagoat village itself is the **Yola Farmstead Folk Park**, an 18th century themed village, while Johnstown Castle with its wonderful gardens and Agricultural Museum is just a few miles away, as is Old Wexford Town, an historic medieval walled town with narrow streets running down to the Quay.

ROSSLARE HARBOUR   MAP 7 REF L14
9 miles SE of Wexford on the R740

Although well-known to ferry passengers arriving from Wales or France, Rosslare Harbour itself has little to detain visitors - except for golfers who will find an excellent links course here. A short drive inland though will bring you to the village of Kilrane and a great place to stay.

KILRANE   MAP 7 REF L14
10 miles SE of Wexford on the N25

No-one is quite sure when the house at **O'Leary's Farm** was built - all the local records were destroyed by fire in 1840. The house is certainly older than that and has been in the same family for 5 generations. The present "matriarch" of the O'Leary family is Kathleen,

O'Leary's Farm, Killilane, Kilrane, Rosslare Harbour, Co. Wexford
Tel: 053 33134

a charming lady who began offering bed and breakfast accommodation back in 1956, so she must be doing something right since visitors return time and again. Kathleen is assisted now by her daughter Philomena in running this charming old house with its attractive features such as vintage oil lamps, antique furniture and an open fire. If you're lucky, Philomena's daughter Nora may give an impromptu recital on her cello. Nora has been chosen as one of the Top 40 Young Musicians in Ireland and has played at the National Concert Hall. Philomena believes that the encouragement Nora received from visitors has contributed to her daughter's success.

The farmhouse has 10 attractively furnished and decorated guest bedrooms, 7 of them en suite. At breakfast time you'll find a good spread of cheeses, fruits and cereals, along with a full traditional Irish breakfast complemented by fresh home-baked bread. If you prefer a self-catering arrangement, there's also a cottage in the grounds which sleeps 4 people.

Despite its lovely rural setting, O'Leary's Farm is just a 10-minute drive from Rosslare Harbour and the regular ferries to Wales and France, and only 25 minutes from the county town of Wexford. In the neighbourhood of the farm there are some delightful walks to unspoilt beaches with some grand sea views along the way. This stretch of the coast is also a favourite with bird watchers - the Wexford Slobs, Lady's Island Lake and Tacumshin Lake are all internationally significant for their waterbirds, and the Saltee Islands renowned for their seabird colonies.

A couple of miles south of Kilrane, **Lady's Island** as well as being a great location for bird-watching is also a place of pilgrimage. Each year, between August 15th and September 8th, pilgrims make their way across the causeway that links the island to the mainland in order to pay their devotions at the shrine of Our Lady. The most fervent worshippers crawl around the perimeter of the island on their knees; others progress around the shoreline with one foot in the water. Also on the island are the ruins of a 13th century Augustinian priory, a Norman castle and a Round Tower which leans even more alarmingly than the one at Pisa.

KILMORE QUAY

MAP 7 REF K15

14 miles SW of Wexford on the R739

This charming fishing village is set around a busy little harbour with whitewashed thatched cottages running alongside the narrow main street. The cottages have walls two to three feet thick, made of clay, straw and stones, and roof frames often made from the strong timbers of ships wrecked by southwesterly storms. Kilmore's modern marina has 55 fully serviced berths and there are regular trips from the quayside during the season to the nearby Saltee Islands, two large granite outcrops which support eleven different species of breeding seabirds in summer. Boats are also available for fishing trips or cruises along the coast and an event unique to Kilmore is the annual **Blessing of the Boats**, a service held each year at the end of the summer season.

Kilmore Quay has had its own lifeboat since 1847 and since that date its crew members have saved 111 lives. The history of the lifeboat and the town is recorded in the **Guillemot Maritime Museum**, housed in an old lightship alongside the marina.

If you enjoy seafood, the time to visit Kilmore is in mid-July when the village hosts the 10-day **Kilmore Quay Annual Seafood Festival** which features events such as a seafood barbecue, a talent competition, outdoor games and activities on the pier, live entertainment and, of course, an abundance of seafood caught by the local fleet and available at prices to suit every budget.

Just a short walk from the beach, **Groveside** is the farmhouse for a 120-acre tillage farm owned and run by Sean and Mary Cousins. They also rent an additional 400 acres where the barley waving in the fields is destined eventually for the mash-vats at the Guinness brewery. Groveside itself is a spacious modern house, built in 1984 and opened for bed and breakfast guests in 1992. It stands in extensive and secluded gardens which

Groveside, Bally Harty, Kilmore, Co. Wexford
Tel/Fax: 053 35305 e-mail: groveside@infowing.ie

are ideal for children and equipped with a play area specially for them. The grounds also include a fish pond, sitting areas, a barbecue which guests are welcome to use, and a private car park. The house has 3 guest bedrooms, all en suite, and all individually furnished and decorated. Because the emphasis at Groveside is on peace and relaxation, the bedrooms are not provided with TVs but a set can be provided on request or you can watch in the comfortable guest lounge with its attractive traditional furniture and antiques. Breakfast at Groveside is a satisfying experience with a handsome spread of cheeses, fruit, yoghurts, cereals, and a good choice of egg dishes. An additional attraction is the selection of home baked bread and cakes which are always available throughout the day - just help yourself whenever you feel a little peckish. Kilmore Quay is of course famous for its fishing and there's a good choice of facilities for sea angling. The neighbourhood also offers plenty of other things to see and do. The Cousins will be happy to arrange horse riding for you; boat trips to the Saltee Islands, Ireland's largest bird sanctuary, are a popular excursion; the renowned gardens at Johnstown Castle are just a short drive away, and in the evenings you'll find plenty of good Irish music in the local pubs.

Occupying a lovely position overlooking the sea and the Saltee Islands, **Mill Road Farm Cottages** offer 4-star self-catering accommodation in a tastefully converted 19th century barn. The cottages have been furnished and decorated to a very high standard and are well equipped with just about every mod. con. you can think of. There are 6 of them in all, 3 with two bedrooms, 3 with one bedroom. All of them have central heating, colour TV, fully fitted kitchen and ample private parking. All bed linen and towels are supplied, a cot and high chair is available if required, and the cottages have their own

Mill Road Farm Cottages, Kilmore Quay, Co. Wexford
Tel/Fax: 053 29633 e-mail: millfarm@iol.ie

natural water system. The cottages stand within the grounds of a working dairy farm just outside Kilmore Quay and if you prefer bed and breakfast accommodation, that is available in the main farmhouse. This is the home of Greg and Philomena Stafford and has 5 guest bedrooms, all of them en suite and fully equipped with such features as TV and hairdryer. If you are travelling on one of the morning ferries from Rosslare, the Staffords will happily provide you with an early morning breakfast. Before you leave, though, there is much to see and do in the area. A trip to the Saltee Islands and the bird sanctuary there is a popular excursion, while on the mainland there are beautiful unspoilt beaches, facilities for horse riding, angling, boat hire and golf, with 3 championship golf courses within a 20-minute drive. Scuba diving and off-shore fishing are other options availiable. A particularly good time to visit Kilmore Quay is in July when the Seafood Festival takes place, offering nightly entertainment and delicious seafood barbecues. The village is also a popular choice for accommodation in October when the Wexford Opera Festival is in full swing.

DUNCORMICK   MAP 7 REF K14
15 miles SW of Wexford on the R736

Walkers along the Slí Charman, Wexford's Coastal Pathway, will be familiar with the little village of Duncormick, set back from Ballyteige Bay and with splendid beaches within easy reach. Conveniently, Duncormick also has an excellent place to stay. In Gaelic, **Áras-Muillin** means "Mill House " and there is indeed an old mill next door to this attractive modern guest house about a mile outside the village. Áras-Muillin is set in a lovely garden

Áras-Muillin, Ambrosetown, Duncormick, Co. Wexford
Tel: 051 563145 Fax: 051 563245

sheltered by a cypress hedge which creates a warm micro-climate where palm trees find it easy to flourish. Here, and in a separate garden beside the mill, are ideal places to relax with just the sound of birds to disturb the peace. Áras-Muillin is the home of Mary Parle and her family who have been welcoming bed and breakfast guests here since 1995. Residents have the use of a comfortable lounge and also of a delightful Sun Room in the conservatory overlooking the garden. In this family-run guest house the mood is easy and the service is the best. Breakfast is served in the dining room off the Sun Lounge when there's a good spread that includes fruit, yoghurt and juices, as well as a full Irish breakfast. The 3 guest bedrooms have all been recently refurbished with 2 of them en suite and all of them smartly furnished and decorated. Children are welcome, with a cot available if required, and pets too can be accommodated. Locally, there are facilities for a wide range of activities. Golf, fishing and horse-riding are all available with a 3-mile radius, and there are many beautiful walks and some excellent beaches all within easy reach. The National Heritage Park, the JFK Botanical Gardens, Johnstown Castle with its superb gardens, are all just a short drive away, or you could visit Wexford, a small, lively town where the hospitality is truly Irish!

CULLENSTOWN STRAND
18 miles SW of Wexford off the R733

MAP 7 REF K15

A few miles further to the west, Cullenstown is a peaceful little seaside village with an excellent sandy beach. **Ocean View** is situated on the Bannow Drive Route at Cullenstown beach and occupies a prime position looking out over the Celtic Sea to the bird watchers' paradise of the Saltee Islands. There's a golden beach nearby, and since the sea here is warmed by the Gulf Stream, it's a pleasure even on a winter's day to stroll along the sands. It is rare indeed for this corner of the county to ever experience a frost. Ocean View enjoys a peaceful location in a quiet cul-de-sac and its owners, Eleanor and John Browne, offer visitors a choice of either bed and breakfast or self-catering accommodation. B&B guests stay in the spacious main house with its large, glassed-in terrace overlooking the sea. There are 3 double bedrooms, all en suite and all well-appointed. The 3 self-catering apart-

Ocean View, Cullenstown Strand, Duncormick, Co. Wexford
Tel: 051 561270

ments have 1 double bedroom and 2 twin rooms each and all are fully equipped with just about every mod.con. you can think of. With its safe beaches, (14 of them within a 30-minute drive), and thriving fishing industry, the area is well-provided with facilities for a wide range of seaside activities. But you'll also find tennis, a par 3 golf course, pitch and putt, and surf fishing for bass all within easy reach. And if you feel like a pint or two in the evening, a 1-minute walk from Ocean View will bring you to the local pub where you can be assured of passing a pleasant evening.

FOULKSMILL
MAP 7 REF K14
4 miles N of Wellington Bridge off the R736

On the outskirts of this delightful small village, **Mill House** offers a choice of self-catering accommodation in a peaceful, rural setting. There are 3 properties to choose from, all of them standing within Aidan and Mary Theresa Redmond's family farm and all within a few minutes walk of the village with its two lively pubs. One of them has 4 bedrooms, (2 doubles, 2 twins), lounge, dining room, kitchen, an upstairs bathroom and an additional powder room on the ground floor. The second cottage sleeps 5 people in 3 bedrooms, (1 double, 1 twin, 1 single). There's a lounge/dining area, a well-equipped kitchen and a

Mill House, Foulksmill, Co. Wexford
Tel: 051 565683/565695

bathroom. The third property is a bungalow with 4 double bedrooms, lounge, dining room, kitchen and bathroom. All three houses have central heating as well as open fires for which adequate fuel is supplied and each represents excellent value for money. Mill House itself takes its name from the splendid old corn mill in the village which was in operation until a few years ago when the miller, who was in his 80s, passed away. Foulksmill village is a pleasant place to while away the time but if you are feeling active, there are facilities for golf, pony riding, and fishing (both fresh and saltwater), within easy reach along with some fine beaches and excellent little restaurants.

BALLYCULLANE   Map 7 ref K14
17 miles W of Wexford off the R733 or R374

A few miles west of Wellington Bridge, the village of Ballycullane also has a station on the railway linking the two county towns of Wexford and Waterford. But it remains a quiet, peaceful place, set amidst a pastoral landscape, and ideal as a holiday base. A good place to stay is **Ballytarsna House** where visitors arriving at for a self-catering holiday will find that their host, Ann Walsh, has also been doing some catering. They will be welcomed by a smiling face and a supply of freshly home baked scones, cakes and fresh cream flan along with tea or coffee. The accommodation is just as inviting - two spacious old farmhouses, both with a 4**** rating from the Irish Tourist Board. Each of the houses has 4 bedrooms capable of sleeping up to 8 people and each house is fully equipped with just

Ballytarsna House, Ballycullane, New Ross, Co. Wexford
Tel: 051 562397 Fax: 066 9792116

about everything you could possibly need. One is semi-detached with the owner living next door. It is set on a working farm where visitors are welcome to help out with milking or collecting the chicken eggs if they wish. A leisurely 10-minute stroll will bring you to the village and pub; J.F.Kennedy Park is about 5 miles away, and there's a lovely beach about 7½ miles distant. In fact, there are no fewer than 14 beaches all within a 15-minute drive. The other property is a refurbished farmhouse standing in its own grounds in a quiet, rural location. It has a ground floor en suite bedroom. Both houses are open all year, children are welcome and a cot is available if required. Ballycullane provides an ideal touring base for the southeast, east and Dublin with plenty of facilities in the area for golf, horse riding and walking. If you fish, the local trout fishing is excellent and so is sea fishing for bass. Waterford and its famous crystal factory is less than a 30-minute drive away, as is the county town of Wexford and the busy harbour of Rosslare with its ferries to England and France. Even closer are the ruins of Tintern Abbey, only 3 miles or so from Ballycullane.

Wexford's **Tintern Abbey** should not be confused with the glorious ruins near Chepstow in South Wales immortalised by Wordsworth in a famous elegiac poem. Wexford's Tintern was in fact named after the Welsh abbey by its founder, William Marshall, Earl of Pembroke. While sailing from Wales to southern Ireland, William's ship was caught in a violent storm. Falling to his knees on the wind-tossed deck, William vowed that he would build an abbey wherever his ship came safely to land. He was true to his word and building began in 1200. The riverside setting is picturesque and the substantial remains, which include the nave, chancel, tower, chapel and cloister of the original building, are imposing and dignified. The Abbey was partly converted into a private residence in 1541 and further adapted over the centuries by the Colclough family who lived here for more than 400 years, right up until the 1960s.

SALTMILLS   MAP 7 REF K14
18 miles SW of Wexford off the R733 or R734

Just a 10 minute walk from Tintern Abbey and close to the beaches of Bannow Bay, **The Grove Farmhouse** offers comfortable bed and breakfast accommodation in a delightful old farmhouse which dates back some 200 years. The house has been in Rita and Michael Powers' family for 4 generations and has that indefinable charm of a much-loved family home. There are 4 spacious guest rooms, all en suite and well equipped, and all enjoying restful views across the Bay. A highlight of a stay at The Grove is Rita's delicious home baking so it's a good idea to take advantage of the optional High Tea or evening meal.

The Grove Farmhouse, St Kearns, Saltmills, Fethard-on-Sea, Co. Wexford
Tel: 051 562304

Packed lunches are also available on request. The Grove is handily located for exploring the Hook Head Peninsula which offers a wide variety of things to see and do. There are castles at Fethard and Ballyhack, abbeys at Tintern and Dunbrody, and an Elizabethan fort at Duncannon. Within easy reach of The Grove you'll find safe beaches, and facilities for sea angling and pony trekking, and the area is also popular with bird watchers especially when the Brent Geese and Baltic Sea Wigeon pay their annual visit. American visitors will be interested in paying a visit to the cottage in Dunganstown where President J. F. Kennedy's great-grandfather was born and to the nearby J.F. Kennedy Arboretum & Forest Park.

FETHARD-ON-SEA
21 miles SW of Wexford on the R734

Map 7 ref K15

A quiet little resort nowadays, Fethard was once a place of some consequence - important enough for James II to grant it the status of a borough. Little more than a hundred years later though, Fethard's population was so diminished it was stripped of its parliamentary seat. In compensation, the village landlord was granted the then-colossal sum of £15,000. On the edge of the village are the remains of **Fethard Castle**, an L-shaped fortified hall house built in the 1400s and incorporating the gate tower of an even older castle.

Located in the heart of this picturesque village, the **Hotel Naomh Seosamh** is one of the focal points of the Hook Head Peninsula because of its close proximity to all amenities and its access to scenic tours. The hotel's owners, Nicholas and Maureen Tweedy, assure their guests of a warm, friendly welcome to their comfortable, cheery hostelry. Good food is a priority at the Naomh Seosamh, whether it's a tasty snack or meal from the bar food menu, or a full feast chosen from the extensive menu on offer in the Helen Blake

Hotel Naomh Seosamh, Fethard-on-Sea, Co. Wexford
Tel: 051 397129 Fax: 051 397560 e-mail: seosamh@indigo.ie

Room. Amongst the fish dishes, look out for the Symphony of Locally Caught Fish, and do save yourself for one of the fresh home made desserts, in particular the House Special Pavlova. Complement your meal with a selection from a wine list which offers a choice of both European and New World wines. Nightly entertainment is provided during the high season in the pleasant and comfortable Lounge Bar, and at weekends in the off season. For the more active, and the young at heart, the hotel boasts "Saints" Niteclub every Saturday night throughout the year, and the best of live bands and entertainment during the holiday periods. As for daytime activities, the hotel can arrange boat fishing at reasonable rates and also offers group packages for golfers with green fees included at one of the several 18-hole courses nearby. The clear waters off the Hook, where visibility can be as much as 35 feet, are ideal for snorkeling and scuba diving, and Fethard also has facilities for canoeing and sailing. Beach lovers are well-provided for, with a different beach to visit each day for a fortnight, some of them within easy walking distance of the hotel. The area's attractions also include the Hook Lighthouse, the oldest in Europe and 4th oldest in the world, Tintern Abbey, Dunbrody Abbey, the John F. Kennedy Memorial Park, and Johnstown Castle with its famous gardens.

DUNCANNON
Map 7 ref J14
25 miles SW of Wexford on the R733

A pleasant holiday resort boasting a sandy Blue Flag beach, Duncannon stands on a rocky promontory jutting out into Waterford Harbour. It was here that Conan is reputed to have built his *dun*, (hill fort), from which the town takes its name. The Normans also built a castle here but the site is now occupied by **Duncannon Fort**, a star-shaped citadel built in 1588 in expectation of an attack by the Spanish Armada. Visitors can examine the gruesome dungeon in which the "Croppy Boy" of the well-known rebel song was held. Guided tours are available daily during the season, (June to September).

ARTHURSTOWN
Map 7 ref J14
25 miles SW of Wexford on the R733

This small fishing village on the western coast of the Hook Peninsula is a pleasant place to visit and also boasts an outstanding restaurant as well as first-class B&B or self-catering accommodation.

Occupying a beautiful position overlooking the King's Bay, the **Waterfront Restaurant** offers the traveller a wide variety of culinary delights in a relaxed and friendly atmosphere. The building was originally the Dispensary for the Chichester Estate and dates back to the mid-1800s. Slate floors, a timber dado and rustic furniture make this a charming place to dine. It was converted to a restaurant in 1996 by Colleen Murphy and her husband and now enjoys an excellent reputation for the quality of the cuisine on offer. Colleen deliberately keeps the menu short so that each dish can be carefully prepared, with the emphasis on fresh local produce cooked to perfection. Daily specials are based on the seafood catch of the day and there's always at least one vegetarian option. To round off your meal, there's a choice of home made desserts or a selection of Irish cheeses

Waterfront Restaurant, Arthurstown, Co. Wexford
Tel: 051 389534

and crackers. Children have their own menu or can choose a half portion from the main menu. The wine list at the Waterfront is also quite short but offers good value for money and wines chosen to complement the food. The Murphys spent some 12 years working in the restaurant trade in New York and have imported the high standards of American service exemplified by friendly, courteous and efficient waiters and waitresses. The Waterfront Restaurant is open from 18.00 each day during the period from Easter to the end of September with Sunday lunch served from 12.30. Its reputation is such that it is definitely advisable to book ahead. The restaurant is only 5 minutes from the Waterford car ferry.

Arthur's Rest : what an appropriate name for a comfortable and welcoming B&B and self-catering accommodation. Arthur's Rest is an impressive building which was erected in the mid-1800s as a barracks for the Royal Irish Constabulary. It has however been thoroughly modernised and refurbished to a very high standard by its owners, Peggy and Kevin Murphy, and now offers real home from home comforts for guests. Arthur's Rest is a place where you can really spread yourself and relax. In addition to the residents' lounge and dining room with a separate sitting area, there is also a conservatory and courtyard garden. The house has 5 guest bedrooms, all with en suite facilities, with one of them incorporating a single bedroom - ideal for a group of three. Peggy's breakfasts are something to relish, offering an extensive choice which includes, of course, the famous Full Irish Breakfast. She bakes her own bread and scones each day, and should you feel a little peckish during the day, these are always available. Peggy works closely with other tourism

Arthur's Rest, Arthurstown, Co. Wexford
Tel: 051 389192 Fax: 051 389362 e-mail: arthursrest@hotmail.com

providers in the area such as the renowned Neptune Restaurant & Cookery Centre in the nearby fishing village of Ballyhack. The Murphys have also restored a lovely old 3-storey stone corn loft beside Arthur's Rest which offers self-catering for up to 7 people and has stunning views of the River Barrow from the top floor. They also have a lovely restored Fisherman's Cottage on Strand Road, Arthurstown, which offers comfortable self-catering for up to 6 people. Arthurstown itself is ideally situated for exploring this historic corner of the Sunny Southeast, with the local car ferry at Ballyhack providing a short and easy crossing to Waterford City, home of the world famous Waterford Crystal. There are also excellent golfing and horse riding facilities within a few minutes' drive of Arthur's Rest.

BALLYHACK
MAP 7 REF J14
25 miles SW of Wexford off the R733

Ballyhack is best known locally for its year round vehicle ferry across the harbour to Passage East in County Waterford. But the village is also worth visiting to see **Ballyhack Castle**, a sturdy tower house occupying a steep slope and a commanding position overlooking Waterford estuary. The castle is thought to have been built around 1450 by the Knights Hospitallers of St John, one of the two great military orders founded in the 12th century at the time of the Crusades.

CAMPILE
MAP 7 REF J14
10 miles SE of New Ross on minor road off the R733

On the outskirts of Campile stand the extensive remains of **Dunbrody Abbey**, one of the finest ecclesiastical ruins in Ireland. The Abbey was founded in 1210 and because it held the right of sanctuary became known as the Monastery of St Mary of Refuge. The site also contains the ruins of Dunbrody Castle which now houses a craft shop selling quality hand-made local crafts. There's a tea room containing a small museum mostly concerned with family genealogies, a large doll's house in the form of a scale replica of the castle, a small pitch and putt course and a full size yew tree hedge maze - one of only two in Ireland. The Abbey site is open from April to September.

For anyone who appreciates gardens, the only place to stay in Co. Wexford is **Kilmokea Country Manor & Gardens**, an alluring location which offers a unique combination of country house accommodation and the additional attraction of superlative gardens. The gardens at Kilmokea cover some 7 acres and fall into two distinct parts. Around the house are formal walled gardens where one design feature leads to another. The Italian loggia and pool with its fine stone pillars is the perfect resting area from which to view the quarter garden brimming with Iris and Roses and on to the "old English" style herbaceous

Kilmokea Country Manor & Gardens, Great Island, Campile, Co. Wexford
Tel: 051 388109 Fax: 051 388776 e-mail: kilmokea@indigo.ie
website: www.kilmokea.com

border. Set into the stone wall, a heavy wooden door leads you into the magical world of the woodland garden where the acid soil provides a perfect environment for Rhododendrons, tender Camellias, Eucryphias and Magnolias, not to mention Echiums - the giant borage closely associated with Kilmokea. With over 130 different species, the garden is a delight to both the keen amateur and the more serious horticulturalist.

Accommodation at Kilmokea is provided in the handsome Georgian manor house, built in 1794. Here, Emma Hewlett and her husband offer the very best of Irish country accommodation with 4 elegant and spacious guest bedrooms available, one of them boasting a sumptuous 4-poster bed. Breakfast is excellent, with a choice of freshly baked breads, fruit and yoghurt, as well as a full Irish breakfast. Light lunches and Garden Teas are served in the Georgian Conservatory in the walled garden, and dinner is served at 8pm.

As far as possible, the dishes are based on home grown organic produce and fish. If you prefer self-catering, the Hewletts also have 2 apartments to let, both of them with 2 bedrooms. Emma is a qualified aromatherapist and this sybaritic treatment is available by arrangement. Emma is also a keen member of the Wexford Festival Singers and rides with the local Hunt. So, if you want to know anything about the area, just ask Emma!

DUNGANSTOWN   MAP 7 REF J14
4 miles S of New Ross on the R733

This unremarkable little village close to the River Barrow is well-established on the tourist route because of **The Kennedy Homestead**, the birthplace of Patrick Kennedy, great-grandfather of President J.F. Kennedy. Patrick Kennedy left the homestead in 1848 and set sail from New Ross on a wet October day. Now a Cultural Museum and Visitor Centre, the homestead celebrates a family history like no other, one that moves from the steerage quarters on an immigrant vessel to the slums of Boston; from the Court of St James to the White House. The Kennedy family still own and run the farm here and JFK himself visited the house in June 1963. The Homestead is open daily from May to September and at other times by appointment.

A couple of miles to the east, on the slopes of Slieve Coillte, the **John F. Kennedy Arboretum** covers an expanse of some 620 acres and boasts a plant collection of international standing with some 4500 types of trees and shrubs from all the temperate regions of the world. Designated a National Park, the site includes a lake, a visitor centre with an audio-visual show and is open daily all year round from 10am.

NEW ROSS   MAP 7 REF J14
23 miles NW of Wexford on the N25

Set on a steep hill overlooking the River Barrow, New Ross is one of the oldest towns in County Wexford. It still has a medieval feel to it with narrow winding streets which in some places are stepped and so only open to pedestrians. At the time of writing the town is still waiting for its major tourist attraction to be put in place - a full scale reconstruction of the original **SS Dunbrody**, a splendid 176ft long 3-master which conveyed thousands of emigrants across the Atlantic. Plans for the ship include an interactive visitor centre and a comprehensive data base of all Irish immigration into the US from 1820 to 1920. The JFK Trust which has financed the building of the boat is now hoping that the Dunbrody will be open to visitors from Easter 2000. Meanwhile, visitors can take advantage of the river cruises which depart from the bridge at New Ross during the summer season. Meals are included in the tariff and the boat is fully licensed.

About 4 miles north of New Ross, the **Berkeley Costume and Toy Museum** displays a wonderful private collection of 18th and 19th century toys, dolls and costumes dating back to the 1720s. Rare dolls, toy carriages and embroidered textiles such as wedding dresses from 3 generations of one family are amongst the exhibits, a small, pretty garden is included in the visit and on certain occasions Victorian goat-carriage rides are available for children.

BALLINABOOLA   Map 7 ref K14
20 miles W of Wexford on the N25/R736

This small crossroads village on the N25 is well known to local gardeners since the **Fuschia Nursery** is the only specialist fuschia grower in Ireland. Plants are propagated from a private collection of more than 1000 varieties, a collection which is constantly updated with imports from around the world. Small cuttings right up to tall fuschia standards are usually available, along with various other tender perennials, garden plants and shrubs.

The village also boasts an excellent hostelry. For some 30 years the **Horse and Hounds Inn** has been owned and run by the Murphy family. When the Murphys acquired the Horse and Hounds it was just a small country pub but as its reputation for good food, good company and welcoming atmosphere became established the building has been greatly extended. The lively public bar is known as the Fox Hunters Bar in tribute to the

Horse and Hounds Inn, Ballinaboola, New Ross, Co. Wexford
Tel: 051 428323/428482 Fax: 051 428471

local hunt which meets outside during the hunting season to partake of a warming Stirrup Cup. There's also a spacious and comfortable Lounge Bar, an ideal place to relax with a bar meal and a drink. Food is taken very seriously at the Horse and Hounds. The restaurant here has, for more than 25 years, prospered under the "watchful eye" of Christy Murphy whose à la carte menu offers an extensive choice of expertly prepared and attractively presented dishes. Vegetarian options are available and there's also a special section for children. The wine list is also rather special, presenting a wide range of European and New World wines at affordable prices. A welcome feature of the list is its small selection of wines by the quarter bottle for those who prefer just a glass or so. Ballinaboola makes a convenient base for touring southeast Ireland so if you are thinking of staying in the area, the Horse and Hounds Inn is an excellent place to put up. The inn has 12 rooms, all comfortable and well-appointed, with some rooms adapted for wheelchair access. Located roughly half-way between Wexford and Waterford, the inn is close to an 18-hole golf course, the J.F. Kennedy Park is just 4 miles away, while a little further afield is Enniscorthy Castle and the Blackstairs Mountains.

ENNISCORTHY   MAP 7 REF K13
14 miles NW of Wexford on the N11/N30

Generally regarded as County Wexford's most pleasing town, Enniscorthy was founded
way back in 510AD by St Senan. A thriving market town, Enniscorthy's most ancient
surviving building is the imposing **Enniscorthy Castle** erected in the early 1200s and
restored around 1586. The Elizabethan Poet Laureate, Edmund Spenser, owned it for a
while shortly after its restoration. The castle now houses the **Wexford County Museum**
which has an extensive collection illustrating the storied past of the county in all its
varied aspects. The displays include such objects as an ogham stone and a sedan chair,
and there are particularly good exhibits commemorating the risings of 1798 and 1916.

The 1798 rebellion is explored in even greater detail at the **National 1798 Centre**
which boasts what is possibly the best interactive centre in Ireland. The Centre traces the
progress of the rebellion, together with events as they happened in Europe, the United
States and Australia. The highlight of the show is a dramatic audio visual display, using a
curved screen, to simulate the battle of Vinegar Hill which took place just outside the
town. A bronze statue in Market Square also recalls the 1798 Rebellion with a fine sculpture of one of its leaders, Father Murphy, and a soldier armed only with a pike.

The town's most impressive church is **St Aidan's Cathedral**, a grand Gothic Revival
building of the 1840s designed by Pugin at the time he was also working on London's
Houses of Parliament. The Cathedral stands on a commanding site overlooking the River
Slaney and provides some grand views along the valley.

COUNTY CARLOW

Shaped like an inverted triangle, County Carlow is the second smallest county in Ireland
with an area of just 346 sq. miles and a population of less than 50,000. Most of the county
is devoted to agriculture, especially the cultivation of sugar beet which is processed at a
huge factory in Carlow Town.The most attractive areas are the Blackstairs Mountains in
the south, and along the valley of the River Barrow which, for most of its length, forms
the border with County Kilkenny. The river has long been of immense importance to
Carlow as a means of communication and though no longer a commercial waterway is
still busy in season with pleasure craft, river cruisers and anglers.

The county has few grand houses or churches although it does boast the largest dolmen
in Ireland at Browne's Hill near Carlow Town and a ruined Norman castle in the town
itself. Generally however this is not a county for sightseeing but for enjoying the gentle
landscape where traditional farming methods have preserved an unspoilt countryside
with hedges and trees in abundance.

CARLOW   MAP 7 REF K12
50 miles SW of Dublin on the N9

Carlow was for centuries an Anglo-Norman stronghold at the edge of a fiercely Gaelic
county. Little remains to indicate its former status apart from the remains of **Carlow**

Castle, a 13th century rectangular keep of which a wall and two flanking towers still stand near the bridge over the River Barrow. Its ruined state is only partly the result of the many battles that took place at this strategically sited town. Further damage was caused in 1841 by a certain Dr Philip Middleton. Attempting to reduce the thickness of the walls in readiness for converting the castle into a mental hospital, the good doctor rather overestimated the amount of explosives required!

Perhaps the most impressive building in Carlow is the fine classical-style polygonal **Courthouse**, built in 1830 and with a Doric portico modelled on the Parthenon at Athens. It stands on a high plinth beneath which is a basement maze of cells and dungeons. This noble building was apparently intended for Cork but the plans were mixed up and it was erected in this small country town instead. Another striking architectural feature of the town is the 151ft high lantern tower on the **Cathedral of the Assumption**, one of the first Roman Catholic churches to be built after the Emancipation Act of 1829. The driving force behind the building of the cathedral was James Doyle, Bishop of Kildare,

Carlow Courthouse

who is commemorated inside the church by an acclaimed statue, the work of the celebrated sculptor James Hogan. Apparently Hogan forgot to include the bishop's ring and was so distressed by this professional lapse he committed suicide.

On the western bank of the River Barrow is a more sombre memorial which marks the **Croppies Grave**. This handsome monument rises above the site of an old sand pit where following the failed Rebellion of 1798 the bodies of 640 slaughtered Carlow insurgents were thrown and covered with quick lime. The Croppies were so named because they cropped their hair to demonstrate their allegiance to the cause of Irish independence.

Back in the town centre, look out for the **Cigar Divan** in Dublin Street. There is another Cigar Divan in Mallow, Co. Cork, but this is the older of the two. The name dates from the time when Turkish cigarettes were highly fashionable and the Victorian shop front has elaborate iron panels beneath the windows and several engraved glass advertisements.

Just 4 minutes walk from the town centre, **Barrowville Town House** enjoys a lovely location in its own grounds on the south side of Carlow town on the exclusive Kilkenny Road (N9). This Regency house (which enjoys listed status) has lots of antiques and was

Barrowville Town House, Kilkenny Road, Carlow Town, Co. Carlow
Tel: 0503 43324 Fax: 0503 41953

comprehensively renovated in the late 1980s. Owned and professionally managed by Randal and Marie Dempsey, Barrowville is a registered 3-star guesthouse and recommended by this and many other good guide books. The 7 guest bedrooms are all en suite, (most with bath and shower), and equipped with colour television, radio, direct dial phone, and hairdryer. The bedrooms are all non-smoking, however there is a sitting room overlooking the garden where you may smoke and where you'll find tea, coffee, TV and about 150 books. Breakfast at Barrowville is definitely something to look forward to. There's a choice of a traditional or buffet breakfast, with an extensive menu which includes smoked salmon, cheese board, lamb's liver or kidney, (and do try their scrambled eggs). The buffet is laid out in the elegant conservatory, with a grapevine, overlooking a beautifully maintained semi-formal garden which is available to guests. Barrowville Town House is an ideal centre for touring the southeast, the midlands, with Kilkenny and the scenic attractions of the Wicklow Mountains just a short drive away.

About 2 miles to the east of Carlow Town stands the **Browns Hill Dolmen**, arguably the most impressive sight in the county. A field monument of huge proportions, it has a tilted capstone which weighs 100 tonnes and is believed to be the largest in Europe. The location, setting and purpose of this Megalithic structure have been the subject of conjecture for centuries. The most likely explanation is that it marks the burial place of some prehistoric local king but the extraordinary monument has been invested with a rich overlay of myth and legend.

LEIGHLINBRIDGE
8 miles S of Carlow on the N9/R705

Map 7 ref J12

Overlooking the River Barrow, the **Black Castle** (1547) stands on the site of an earlier fortress built in 1181, one of the first Norman strongholds to be erected in Ireland. There are even more venerable remains in Old Leighlin, a couple of miles to the west. Here, the

7th century **Cross of St Lazerain** and his holy well are still venerated and attract many votive offerings. St Lazerain founded a monastery here which at one time accommodated some 1500 monks and was the location for an important church synod in 630 which was summoned to devise a formula for determining the date of Easter each year. The 13th century **Cathedral of St Lazerain** stands on the site of the monastery and has some interesting architectural features. Guided tours are available on request.

Located in the heart of picturesque Leighlinbridge, **The Lord Bagenal Inn** has developed a reputation for fine food, and excellent value for money. The Inn enjoys a lovely position beside the River Barrow and at the time of writing a Marina complex is under construction. This outstanding facility should be up and running by the time you read this. The Inn itself is a charmingly rambling structure with lots of individual gathering spots as well as a very spacious lounge, a restaurant, bars and function rooms. The Lord

The Lord Bagenal Inn, Leighlinbridge, Co. Carlow
Tel: 0503 21668 Fax: 0503 22629 e-mail: info@lordbagenal.com
website: http://www.lordbagenal.com

Bagenal's à la carte restaurant has won many national and international awards with a wide selection of fresh seafood in season its speciality. There's also an appetising Carvery served every day. The Inn has 12 guest bedrooms, all of them en suite, comfortably furnished and attractively decorated. Every effort is made to ensure that your stay is as relaxed as possible and the beautifully maintained gardens provide a peaceful place to spend a quiet hour.

BAGENALSTOWN (MUINE BHEAG) Map 7 ref J12
13 miles S of Carlow on the R705/R724

When Walter Bagenal began building the town that bears his name, his plans were enormously ambitious - nothing less than a mirror image of Versailles with fine street scapes and classical buildings. He made an impressive start with an imposing **Courthouse** which, like the one in Carlow Town, is modelled on the Parthenon at Athens. Then his grandiose scheme faltered. He failed to get the stage coach re-routed through his new town and serious financial problems finally put paid to his plans. All that remains are the Court-house and his own home, **Dunleckney Manor**, just outside the town. This impressive Georgian house is open for guided tours on weekdays during March, May and August.

Situated in the Barrow Valley, beneath Mount Leinster and the Blackstairs Mountains, **Lorum Old Rectory** is a warm and welcoming family home. It was built by the Church of Ireland for the Rev. William Smyth-King in 1864 and is now home to Bobbie Smith, Don (her New Zealand-born husband), and their three daughters. The house is a wonderful example of a mid-Victorian cut stone granite Rectory, providing spacious and comfort-

Lorum Old Rectory, Kilgreaney, Bagenalstown, Co. Carlow
Tel: 0503 75282 Fax: 0503 75455 e-mail: bobbie@lorum.com
website: http://www.lorum.com

able accommodation in its 5 en suite guest bedrooms. Food is definitely something spe-cial at the Old Rectory. Dinner is served in the red dining room at the long mahogany dining table and Bobbie, who is a member of Euro-Toques, (the European community of cooks), enjoys a fine reputation for country-style cooking using organic and home-grown ingredients whenever possible. And since the Old Rectory is licensed for wine, you can enjoy a glass or two with your meal. Breakfast, too, is a meal to be savoured. Guests can relax in the informal drawing room or the Library, and will find plenty to keep them busy during the day. Lorum is the base for Celtic Cycling, and there are facilities for golf, horse riding and fishing all within easy reach.

BORRIS

Map 7 ref J13

16 miles S of Carlow on the R702

Set in a fertile valley of the River Barrow beneath the gentle curve of the Blackstairs Mountains, Borris is a handsome estate town created by the McMurrough Kavanaghs, lineal descendants of the Kings of Leinster. The family still live in the town at **Borris House**, a stately Tudor-style house which is open to group tours by arrangement. In the mid-1800s it was the home of Arthur McMurrough Kavanagh who amongst many other achievements was responsible for building the spectacular 16-arch railway viaduct at the lower end of the town. Arthur was born without arms or legs but nevertheless learned to ride, shoot and fish, and was an inveterate traveller. As a prominent landlord, he threw himself into improving the life of his tenants, largely rebuilding the villages of Borris and Ballyragget, establishing a sawmill and initiating a local lace industry. In 1866 he entered politics and was elected as Conservative Member of Parliament, first for County Wexford and later for County Carlow.

Just across the road from Borris House, **The Step House** is a stately Georgian building offering superb food and superior accommodation in elegant and gracious surroundings. The house was built in the 1820s as a dower house for the Borris House demesne and constructed on a grand scale with spacious rooms and lofty windows. The owners, Cait and James Coady, have furnished the house with classic Irish and French furniture and kept such features as the welcoming open fires. The guest bedrooms are also appropriately furnished, (with a 4-poster bed if you wish), along with fresh flowers and up-to-date

The Step House, Main Street, Borris, Co. Carlow
Tel: 0503 73209 Fax: 0503 73395

amenities such as colour television. The restaurant here enjoys an excellent reputation and since The Step House is fully licensed the beverage of your choice will almost certainly be available. And in the evening, you can step next door to the Step House Bar which is run by James - a friendly place where you can be sure the craic is good!

Inside **The Green Drake Inn** on Main Street there's a fascinating old menu on display which offers a dish of Porridge for 2d (0.6p), a pot of tea for 2½d (1p) and, if you really wanted to splurge out, a chunky round of back bacon cost all of 3d (1.2p). Prices have escalated a little since those halcyon days but The Green Drake Inn still provides very satisfying value for money. Built in the 1890s, the long, 2-storeyed building has an ingeniously designed frontage with a front door apparently extending its arms in welcome.

The Green Drake Inn, Main Street, Borris, Co. Carlow
Tel: 0503 73116/73746

Inside, there's a cosy front bar, a spacious lounge and an even larger function room which is a popular venue for all kinds of events throughout the year, including traditional Irish funeral parties. The Green Drake is also well known for its excellent traditional music which is provided Wednesday and Sunday evenings all year round. The food is good too, with snacks and lunches available until 6pm and larger meals until 9.30pm. Outside, the huge rear garden is secure and ideal for children.

From Borris the circular **Mount Leinster Drive** strikes northeastwards through the Blackstairs Mountains, skirting the foot of Mount Leinster which at 795ft is the highest peak in the range. It's possible to drive right up to the summit where the Nine Stones viewing point provides superb views over Carlow, Wexford, Kilkeeny and Wicklow, and, on a fine day, across the Irish Sea to the Welsh coast. The Drive continues through the picturesque village of Bunclody in County Wexford and on to Clonegal in the Derry Valley, sometimes referred to as the "Switzerland of Ireland". The Drive then strikes westwards to Bagenalstown and back to Borris.

BALLON
10 miles SE of Carlow on the N80

Map 7 ref K12

The charming village of Ballon lies just a few miles from the famous **Altamont Gardens**. These delightful formal and informal gardens lie in the grounds of Altamont House and are regarded by many as the "jewel in Ireland's gardening crown". Tended lawns sweep down to the large man-made lake whose perimeter walk provides a succession of ever-changing vistas of rare trees and shrubs. Within the grounds there's also a well-stocked garden centre and a large wild garden, stocked with many rare shrubs, which leads to a dramatic Ice Age glen overlooking the River Slaney.

Nearby, nestling amid rolling parklands and tranquil countryside, **Sherwood Park House** provides timeless elegance and a warm family welcome. Built in the early 1700s by Arthur Bailie, this beautiful Georgian residence is set on a working estate of some 120 acres and is the family home of Maureen and Patrick Owens. Guest accommodation con-

Sherwood Park House, Kilbride, Ballon, Co. Carlow
Tel: 0503 59117 Fax: 0503 59355 e-mail: infor@sherwoodparkhouse.ie
website: www.sherwoodparkhouse.ie

sists of 4 delightful bedrooms with brass and canopy beds, all en suite and with tea/coffee making facilities provided. Enjoy the experience of dining out while staying in and indulge yourself in the delights of Irish country house cooking based on fresh, local produce and served by the light of candles. Diners are welcome to bring their own wine. As guests, you are free to wander about the farm and the quiet country roads, overshadowed by the splendour of Mount Leinster. Salmon and trout fishing on the River Slaney can be arranged, as can rough shooting, golf, and horse riding, while horticultural classes are available locally on a daily basis. Situated just off the main N80, midway between Dublin and Rosslare, Sherwood Park House is an ideal touring base for the southeast, with attractions such as the renowned Altamont Gardens within easy reach.

TULLOW
MAP 7 REF K12
9 miles SE of Carlow on the R725/N81

The largest town in County Carlow, Tullow is a popular centre for anglers fishing the River Slaney for salmon and trout. There's a fine statue in the market square of Father John Murphy, the insurgent leader who was captured near Tullow and executed here on July 2nd, 1798. Otherwise, there is little to detain the visitor although you might care to travel a little further north to the delightful village of **Rathvilly** which has the distinction of having won the All Ireland Tidy Town competition three times over.

COUNTY KILKENNY

With Ireland's medieval capital at its heart, County Kilkenny is rich in heritage and its lush, well-cultivated landscapes offer some of the most appealing scenery in the south-

Caravan Touring, Co Kilkenny

east. The county's importance in medieval times is reflected in the string of dramatic castles set along the river valleys of the Nore and the Barrow; the splendid ruins of Kells Priory and Jerpoint Abbey; and most notably in Kilkenny Town itself with its magnificent castle and the largest concentration of medieval churches in the country. Outstanding natural features include the extraordinary underground chambers of Dunmore Cave and, as the self-styled "Creative Heart of Ireland" and home to the Irish National Design Centre, the county prides itself on having fostered the survival of traditional skills, producing an impressive range of original works and giftware in glass, clay, precious metals, leather and textiles.

KILKENNY   Map 7 ref J13
73 miles SW of Dublin on the N10

Despite having a population of less than 9000, Kilkenny insists on being called a city, and with some justification. Before the Normans arrived, it was the capital of the Kingdom of Ossary, and the Confederate Parliament sat here between 1642 to 1648. Kilkenny suffered grievously from the vandalism of Cromwell and his troops when they were quartered here in 1650, but the city retains an astonishing wealth of medieval buildings.

Kilkenny has been described as a mini-Edinburgh because, like the Scottish capital, it has a main thoroughfare lined with fascinating buildings and bracketed at one end by a cathedral, at the other by a castle. **Kilkenny Castle** stands on high ground overlooking the river and dates back to the late 1100s when it was erected by Theobald Fitzwalter, Chief Butler of Ireland. His family took the name Butler and, as Earls, Marquesses and Dukes of Ormonde, lived in the castle until 1935. Extensive additions took place in the 18th and 19th centuries but the castle's medieval origins are plain to see in the grand scale of the rooms, the deeply recessed windows and mighty fireplaces. The Butler family's long tenure of the castle is reflected in the serried lines of family portraits dating back to the 13th century which are displayed in the spectacular Long Gallery. The castle is set in extensive grounds which also contain the Butler Gallery, dedicated to exhibitions of modern art, and the Irish National Design Centre, housed in the 18th century stables, which offers a wide range of high quality Irish products.

From the castle, The Parade runs parallel to the River Nore and just off to the right, in Rose Inn Street, is the **Shee Alms House**, a lovely 16th century building which is one of the very rare Tudor almshouses to be found in Ireland. It now houses the tourist information office which has a video presentation of Kilkenny's history and also runs regular walking tours around the city, an excellent way of discovering its many treasures.

A little further north along The Parade is the arcaded **Tholsel**, built in 1761 of black Kilkenny marble as a toll-house or exchange, and now serving as the Town Hall. Beyond The Tholsel the road becomes Parliament Street, running through the heart of medieval Kilkenny with its narrow "slips", or alleys, darting off in all directions. **Rothe House** is a striking Tudor building of 1594, the only surviving example in Ireland of a wealthy merchant's town dwelling. It has three distinct houses, connected by courtyards, spacious lodgings necessary to house John Rothe's family of 12 children . The house is now home to Kilkenny's Archaeological Society Museum and a Costume Museum with a fine collection of waistcoats, bonnets and gowns from the 18th century onwards. Just across the road from Rothe House rises the stately **Court House** built in 1794 and, a little further north, **St Francis's Brewery** which occupies part of the site of a 13th century Franciscan friary whose remnants stand nearby. The Brewery is open to visitors during July and August, offering a video of the production process and a tasting in the cellar bar. Tickets are free and can be obtained at the Tourist Information Centre.

At the northern end of the main street, **St Canice's Cathedral** is a magnificent 13th century building which boasts the second longest nave in Ireland after St Patrick's Cathedral in Dublin. It has an important Library with more than 3000 early and rare volumes, a wealth of carvings and a remarkable collection of tombs and monuments. The oldest one is dated 1285 and many of them commemorate members of the Butler family of Kilkenny Castle. In the Cathedral precinct, a Round Tower is all that remains of the monastic settlement founded here in the 6th century by St Canice. It's possible to climb the tower and there are some superb views from the top. Scattered across the city are many other medieval remains. The most notable are the **Black Abbey**, founded in 1225 and carefully restored, which has some fine stained glass and some interesting carvings and sepulchral slabs, and **St John's Priory** with a roofless chancel and an impressive seven-light window dating from 1250. A secular building of interest is **Kyteler's Inn**, the oldest dwelling in Kilkenny. It has changed little since 1324 when it was owned by Dame Alice Kyteler. Alice outlived four wealthy husbands but her good fortune wavered when she was charged with witchcraft by the local bishop. She made a speedy departure for France and it was her maidservant Petronella who was burned at the stake in her place.

Another grand old building is **Butler House**, a superior hotel located in a secluded and quiet spot in the heart of medieval Kilkenny. Established in 1770 by Walter Butler, the 16th Earl of Ormond, Butler House was an integral part of the Kilkenny Castle estate

Butler House, 16 Patrick Street, Kilkenny, Co. Kilkenny
Tel: 056 65707/22828 Fax: 056 65626 e-mail: res@butler.ie website: www.butler.ie

and many of the superb Georgian features remain, amongst them sweeping staircases, magnificent plastered ceilings, marble fireplaces, and a lovely walled garden. Now an elegant and distinctive hotel, Butler House was refurbished in a contemporary and unique manner by Kilkenny Design in the early 1970s. Along with its important collection of Irish art, the house was acquired by the Kilkenny Civic Trust in 1989. Comfortable and tranquil, the hotel has 13 beautiful bedrooms and suites, each with its own individual character, and all with en suite bathrooms. All rooms are equipped with television and telephone, and some rooms and suites have large bay windows overlooking the secluded gardens and the Castle beyond. The Basement restaurant at Butler House is an intimate and stylish venue for dining. Award-winning chefs emphasise presentation and fresh ingredients in the historic cellar of the house. Part of the history of Kilkenny, Butler House is also renowned for its splendid reception rooms which provide an ideal venue for executive conferences, training and business events, weddings and receptions. The largest of the 3 splendid reception rooms accommodates up to 120 persons and meals and refreshments of the highest standard are provided. Secretarial services and audio-visual equipment are also available. With its enviable architectural heritage, comprehensive amenities and quiet, city centre location, Butler House makes the perfect base for exploring both the city and the county. An important centre for crafts, Kilkenny also has a superb championship golf course at Mount Juliet, and within easy reach there are ample facilities for fishing and equestrian activities.

Situated in the very centre of the city, **Troysgate House** combines three enterprises in one convenient location. Firstly, there's the welcoming guest house which occupies a building originally built as the city jail. Don't be put off! The property has been comprehensively refurbished and now provides comfortable accommodation with all 20 rooms fully en suite, and all of them pleasantly decorated and furnished. Also incorporated into

Troysgate House, Kilkenny, Co. Kilkenny
Tel: 056 61100 Fax: 056 51200

the building is Bambrick's renowned Old World Pub which has been an ale house since 1843 and still retains its nostalgic charm. A great place for a friendly pint and good craic. The third element in the Troysgate House complex is being completed at the time of writing but a smart new restaurant offering top quality cuisine should be in full operation by the time you read this. The owner of Troysgate House, Michael Bambrick, is confident that his new restaurant will be a significant and welcome addition to Kilkenny's top eating places.

Indian restaurants are still something of a novelty across most of Ireland so Kilkenny is lucky to have one of the best. **Shimla**, located in the heart of the city, is owned and run

by Lilu Miah whose family has an extensive chain of restaurants in Britain but have only recently made Kilkenny their first enterprise in Ireland. The air conditioned restaurant is opulently decorated and provides an appropriately sumptuous setting for the excellent cuisine on offer. The restaurant is small and intimate but with the individual tables well spaced apart. Shimla specialises in Tandoori and curry dishes and has already attracted a loyal clientele. The restaurant is open every day for lunch from noon until 14.30. In the evenings, it is open from 17.00 to 23.30 (Sunday to Thursday), and 17.00 to midnight on Fri-

Shimla, 6 Dean Street, Kilkenny, Co. Kilkenny
Tel: 056 23788

days and Saturdays. On Sundays, Shimla also serves a tasty buffet offering a wide selection of Indian specialities.

Just two minutes from the city centre, **Sundown** provides comfortable bed and breakfast accommodation in a location which is also convenient for buses and the railway station. Your hosts are Nora O'Connor and her daughter Helen, both of whom are very bubbly and outgoing and dedicated to making sure that your stay will be as pleasant and relaxing as possible. There are 4 guest bedrooms in this striking-looking building, all of them en suite and all equipped with radio and hairdryer. Non-smoking rooms are available. Sundown also has a large family room and, outside, a delightful garden in which to relax with a good book, and ample off-street private parking. At breakfast time, the

Sundown, 8 Greenfields, Freshford Road, Kilkenny, Co. Kilkenny
Tel: 056 21816

O'Connors serve a good spread, with all the trimmings and a choice of menu. I.T.B. Approved, Sundown is open all year except over the Christmas period. Kilkenny's historic buildings are all within easy walking distance of the house and a short drive will bring you to the lovely scenery of the south Kilkenny countryside.

Only five minutes walk from the centre of medieval Kilkenny, **Hotel Kilkenny** stands in the rural tranquillity of parkland and beautifully landscaped gardens. The core of the

Hotel Kilkenny, Rosehill House, College Road, Kilkenny, Co. Kilkenny
Tel: 056 62000 Fax: 056 65984 e-mail: kilkenny@griffingroup.ie

hotel is the restored 19th century home of the noted architect, Sir William Robertson, who in 1825 undertook the elaborate alterations to Kilkenny Castle at the request of the Marquess of Ormond. In an early instance of creative recycling, Sir William made use of some of the Castle fabric in building his own residence. Since then, the building has been greatly extended and the Hotel Kilkenny has recently completed a major development which has seen the addition of a fabulous new Active Health and Fitness Centre with a 20 metre swimming pool, 24 new de luxe rooms, the comprehensive refurbishment of all the existing rooms, and the addition of an elegant conservatory to the front of the original house.

It would be easy to spend an enjoyable holiday here without ever leaving the hotel grounds. You wake up in one of the elegant bedrooms, all equipped with direct dial telephone, multi-channel television, trouser press and hairdryer. After a leisurely breakfast, you could enjoy some time in the Fitness Centre or just stroll around the lovely grounds. Take a light lunch, perhaps, in the conservatory's Rosehill Bar where music and song is provided each weekend in an atmosphere that is both entertaining and relaxing. In the evening, you could dine in the sophisticated ambience of Brooms Bistro where the menu offers a choice selection of international cuisine, before retiring to your sumptuous bedroom. At some point, though, you really should drag yourself away to explore the historic city and the lovely scenery of the surrounding countryside.

In a quiet location off the N76 and directly opposite the entrance to the Hotel Kilkenny, **The Laurels** is a luxurious, warm family home where Brian and Betty McHenry provide comfortable and relaxing bed and breakfast accommodation. The Laurels is a

The Laurels, College Road, Kilkenny, Co. Kilkenny
Tel: 056 61501 Fax: 056 71334 e-mail: laurels@eircom.net

striking modern building with a high-pitched roof standing in an attractive garden and just a 5 minute walk from the city centre. The interior has been recently refurbished to hotel standard and has good access for disabled guests with a helper. The house is non-smoking and the 8 guest bedrooms are all en suite and equipped with television, ortho-paedic beds, hairdryers and tea/coffee making facilities. A bedroom with a jacuzzi bathroom is also available on request. At breakfast time there's a choice of menu and although evening meals are not available there's a wide choice of pubs and restaurants within easy walking distance. This top of the range establishment is open all year except over the Christmas period and provides quality food and accommodation at value for money prices.

For good quality bed and breakfast accommodation in a convenient location just half a mile from the city centre, **Majella** is hard to beat. This modern detached bungalow, set well back from the main Kilkenny to Waterford road, is the home of Rita Byrne who offers

Majella, Waterford Road, Kilkenny, Co. Kilkenny
Tel/Fax: 056 21129

a warm welcome, comfortable lodging and a tasty breakfast with plenty of choice. Majella has a charming garden and plenty of off-road car parking. There are 4 guest bedrooms, all of them en suite and, since one of Rita's enthusiasms is for interior design and decorating, each has a character of its own, very stylish and tasteful. Non-smoking rooms are avail-able and credit cards are accepted. Within a 3 mile radius of the house, you'll find facilities for fishing, golf and horse riding, and Kilkenny itself has much for the visitor to see and do. Please note that Majella is open from April 1st to October 31st.

Situated on the Dublin to Carlow road, (the N10), **Dunromin** guest house is very easy to find. It's a handsome looking building, its whitewashed walls colourful with creepers and its front garden bounded by a low, railinged wall. Built in the 19th century, this spa-cious house is the home of Tom and Val Rothwell who warmly welcome you to their family home and assure you of a pleasant and enjoyable stay. At Dunromin, they say, "the kettle is always boiling!". There are 3 guest bedrooms, all of them individually decorated, non-smoking, and provided with en suite facilities and TV. A hearty, full Irish or a conti-

Dunromin, Dublin Road, Kilkenny, Co. Kilkenny
Tel: 056 61387 Fax: 056 70736 e-mail: valtom@oceanfree.net

nental breakfast is included in the tariff. It's just a 10-minute walk from Dunromin to Kilkenny town centre and the Rothwells can give you advice on the town's many attractions, including places to eat, drink and listen to traditional music. They can also guide you to the sporting facilities available locally such as swimming, angling, golf and horse riding.

One of the most popular of the town's bed and breakfast establishments is **Shillogher House**, located about half a mile from the town centre and set in two acres of scenic gardens. Professionally managed by the proprietors, Bill and Margaret Morgan, Shillogher House sets new standards of excellence, providing hotel standards at a bed and breakfast price. To enhance the excellent service, Margaret has successfully completed a Tourism Practitioners' course. This modern, purpose built house offers all the usual facilities plus some extra touches such as electric blankets, hairdryer and iron in all of the spacious

Shillogher House, Callan Road, Kilkenny, Co. Kilkenny
Tel: 056 63249/64865 Fax: 056 64865 e-mail: shillogher@tinet.ie
website: http://www.travel-ireland.com/irl/shiloger.htm

guest bedrooms, each of which is en suite and equipped with colour TV and tea/coffee making facilities. There's a tranquil and beautiful conservatory room overlooking the extensive back garden where you'll always find complimentary tea and coffee, cookies and lollies. As part of their service, the Morgans will also ferry you from the train or bus station, and in every respect will do their best to make your stay a memorable one. This outstanding establishment is just a pleasant 10-minute walk from the centre of Kilkenny where any visit would be incomplete without seeing Kilkenny Castle,- the jewel in the city's crown!

One of the special attractions of staying at **The Gables** for a self-catering holiday is the sight of deer roaming freely around the estate on which it stands. They are bred here on this 200-acre working farm, and so too are horses. (If you are interested in horse riding,

The Gables, Archersgrove, Bennettsbridge Road, Kilkenny, Co. Kilkenny
Tel: 056 61869 Fax: 056 51788 Mobile: 086 8286863

there's an equestrian centre at the adjoining farm). The Gables will also appeal to fly fishermen since the River Nore actually flows through the farm. The house itself was originally a coach house, a handsome stone building dating from the 1700s and standing close to the main house. It has been imaginatively modernised, attractively furnished and decorated, and provides creature comforts such as electric central heating along with just about every possible mod. con. you could possibly require for a self-catering holiday. The comfortable main living room features a striking black marble fireplace, constructed from marble quarried on this very farm. Visitors will find a good supply of free firewood for the open fire it surrounds. The Gables, which enjoys a 3*** ITB rating, sleeps 5 guests and is conveniently located about a mile from the city centre to which it is linked by a pleasant walkway. Historic Kilkenny City has a wealth of visitor attractions and should you exhaust those, a short drive will take you out into some of the most scenic countryside in Ireland.

Hillgrove is less than half a century old but with its creeper-clad walls and white-columned porch it has the presence and style of a much older building. Your host at Hillgrove, Margaret Drennan, used to work with the Irish Tourist Board so she has a very good understanding of her visitors needs and interests, and can also provide you with sound information about the area's manifold attractions. This charming house is beauti-

Hillgrove, Warrington, Bennettsbridge Road, Kilkenny, Co. Kilkenny
Tel: 056 51453/22890 Fax: 056 51453 e-mail: hillgrove@esat.ie

fully decorated and attractively furnished with antiques and the 5 en suite guest bedrooms are well-equipped with additional features such as orthopaedic beds and electric blankets as well as tea and coffee-making facilities. Breakfast is definitely something to look forward to at Hillgrove since Margaret is a National Breakfast Award winner and offers a fine spread with a choice of hot dishes and all the trimmings! This outstanding guest house, recommended by major travel guides, provides a very convenient base for exploring historic Kilkenny City and the scenic countryside of Co. Kilkenny.

The Visitors Book at **Newlands Country House** says it all: *"Brilliant weekend, totally relaxing, pampered. Hospitality first class, and as for the chef!!!"* Another visitor was the famous American author and journalist Sandra Lambert who wrote the following in an American publication "Seamus and Aileen [Kennedy, the owners] do all the cooking, creating seven course gourmet feasts for dinner and enormous breakfasts offering an incredible variety of dishes". (Breakfast is served until noon, incidentally, giving you the chance of that precious lie in, or why not really indulge yourself and have breakfast in bed). Sandra Lambert also wrote about all the small farm animals in the 3 acres of grounds,

Newlands Country House, Sevenhouses, Kilkenny, Co. Kilkenny
Tel: 056 29111 Fax: 056 29171 Mobile: 086 8510358
e-mail: newlands@indigo.ie

including hens, ducks and lambs. She then finished the article by saying how much she enjoyed her stay in "the plush, yet unspoiled ambience of Newlands Country House".

The dining room is a bright sunny conservatory. The best of ingredients are gathered from the lush farmlands and clear rivers of Kilkenny, then lovingly prepared to produce hearty breakfasts and memorable dinners which include succulent steaks, lamb, farm chickens and wonderful salmon, complemented by only the freshest herbs and vegetables. Coeliacs are especially catered for. The attractive residents' lounge at Newlands is decorated in navy and dusky pinks, with deep pile carpet and soft, comfortable couches. On chilly evenings it's an ideal place to relax in front of the open fire. The bedrooms are beautifully appointed with peace and quiet assured. All cosy and warm, they each boast canopies over the beds, clock radios, TVs, electric blankets, tea/coffee making facilities, direct dial phones and fridges. Each bedroom has either shower or bath, while the suites have a full bathroom, with the luxury of your own whirlpool bath and large, comfortable beds. Staying at Newlands Country House is an experience you won't forget - sheer luxury, superb food, peace and quiet, and that little bit of extra "Tender Loving Care"!

A good indication of the quality of the hospitality on offer at **Launard House** is the fact that it holds a Customer Care and Service Award for Kilkenny. This luxurious house overlooking the Ring Road and backed by woodland, was built in 1993 with the express purpose of accommodating bed and breakfast guests. Your hosts, John and Sandra Cahill, have spared no effort to make sure that your stay is as relaxed and comfortable as possible. The house is non-smoking and the 5 attractive guest bedrooms are all en suite and all equipped with orthopaedic beds, TV, hairdryers and tea & coffee making facilities. At

Launard House, Maiden Hill, Kells Road, Kilkenny, Co. Kilkenny
Tel: 056 51889 Fax: 056 71017 e-mail: launardhouse@email.com

breakfast time, there's an inviting spread and a choice of either a full Irish or a continental breakfast. Launard House, which is open all year round except over Christmas, stands just 200 yards from the Hotel Kilkenny & Springhill Court Hotel, and about half a mile from the city centre with its magnificent Castle and Cathedral.

One of County Kilkenny's major visitor attractions is **Dunmore Cave**, about 7 miles northeast of Kilkenny Town off the N78. The series of chambers here were formed over millions of years and contain some of the finest formations of stalactites and stalagmites to be seen in Ireland. You may well share the response of one visitor who described Dunmore Cave as having "a dreadful romantic appearance, as if one stood in the mouth of a huge wild beast". The cave is first mentioned in the 9th century Irish Triads and the Annals tell of a Viking massacre here in 928AD. In 1967, the skeletons of 46 women and children were found in the cave along with coins dating from between 897 to 926. The well-presented caverns are open daily during the season; at weekends and Bank Holidays only in the winter. Access is by guided tour only.

KELLS
7 miles S of Kilkenny on the R697   Map 7 ref J13

Not to be confused with Kells, Co. Meath, the origin of the famous *Book of Kells*, this Kells is a delightful riverside village with a huge bridge and an ancient stone water mill standing beside the river. Nearby, set within emerald green fields, are the ruins of **Kells Priory**, a walled monastery with the appearance of a medieval town. The remains of the 12th century foundation are immensely impressive, with a complete curtain wall fortified with square towers and a sturdy gatehouse. Extending over 5 acres, Kells is one of the largest and most satisfying ecclesiastical sites in Ireland - definitely not to be missed.

About two miles south of this beguiling little village are the **Kilkree Round Tower**, one of many such structures in this area, and a High Cross with some badly-weathered biblical carvings.

THOMASTOWN   MAP 7 REF J13
11 miles SE of Kilkenny on the R700/N9

South of Kilkenny Town, the valley of the River Nore is renowned for its beauty. The river flows through fertile pastures, past peaceful villages and ancient ruins. The most striking of the ruins are the substantial remains of **Jerpoint Abbey**, near Thomastown. This outstanding Cistercian abbey, founded in the late-1100s and built in oat-coloured stone, is noted for the unique carvings of medieval lords and ladies in the cloister, some fine tombs and the serene peacefulness of its setting. The small Visitor Centre houses an informative exhibition and there's good access for visitors with disabilities.

Looking out over the River Nore and towards Jerpoint Abbey, **Belmore Country Home** occupies a superb, elevated position with grand views that include the site of the old medieval town of Newtown Jerpoint. Belmore, and its attached, very fine stable yard was built around 1800 for the then Lord Belmore. After many years in the Hunt family, many of whom are buried in the churchyard on the land, the house came into the possession of the Teesdale family in 1953. Rita and Joe Teesdale are both working farmers and dispense traditional Irish farmhouse hospitality to all their guests. When this gracious old house

Belmore Country Home, Belmore, Jerpoint Church, Thomastown, Co. Kilkenny
Tel: 056 24228

was built, Lord Belmore spared no expense and many of the attractive original features are still in place, complemented by antique furniture and artefacts all around the house. The 3 guest bedrooms, all en suite, are also furnished and decorated in appropriate style. Americans, Japanese, French and English visitors have all found their way to this outstanding guest house with its lovely garden and amenity area, which includes a croquet pitch and covers around 3 acres.

The farm, devoted to sheep and barley production, extends to 120 acres, including woodland. Visitors are welcome to enjoy these facilities and explore the grounds. There's free fishing on the farm's own 1-mile stretch of the River Nore, and there are extensive local club waters available at very reasonable rates. (A licence is required for fishing salmon). Golfers will find 4 courses within easy reach, including the Championship course at Mount Juliet; there are several horse riding establishments locally, and clay pigeon shooting is also available in the neighbourhood. A variety of good restaurants are established in the area, and there are craft, historical and garden tours available as well as walking tours. Belmore is an ideal base for touring the southeast since, in addition to Jerpoint Abbey, there are many other places of interest within easy reach - Kilfane Gardens, Woodstock Gardens, Duiske Abbey and the charming towns of Inistioge, Thomastown and Graignamanagh.

Two miles north of Thomastown, **Kilfane Glen and Waterfall** is one of County Kilkenny's prime beauty spots. Its Romantic-era garden, laid out in 1790, was only rediscovered a few years ago and has been beautifully restored. This magical garden, complete with waterfall, hermit's grotto and a cottage orné, is reached by winding paths which open up some lovely views.

GRAIGNAMANAGH
22 miles SE of Kilkenny on the R703/R705

MAP 7 REF J13

Picturesquely sited on a mountain ravine, Graignamanagh is a prosperous market town popular with anglers who come to fish for salmon and trout in the River Barrow. Graignamanagh was once an important ecclesiastical centre, based on **Duiske Abbey** which dominates the town. Founded in 1204, the Abbey was the largest Cistercian abbey in Ireland, its precincts including much of the area of the present town. The Abbey's interior has been lovingly restored and amongst many interesting features are a superb effigy of a knight in chain and a richly decorated, marvellously preserved Romanesque processional door. Outside in the churchyard are two 9th century stone crosses and a 6th century font.

For a fishing, shooting or walking holiday, **Brandon View House**, a couple of scenic miles from Graignamanagh, is absolutely ideal. Set in its own grounds in the lovely Barrow Valley, the McCabe family's splendid 18th century house gazes upwards to Brandon Hill smothered in multi-coloured gorse. Fishing has always been a way of life in these majestic valleys. Large stocks of salmon and trout are available on the River Barrow close by and the river boasts large stocks of bream, rudd, perch, dace and roach. In 1993, Michael McCabe built his own 2.5 acre fishing lake, just 50 yards from the house. This purpose built lake with its natural spring feeder holds some excellent stocks of tench and bream

Brandon View House, Graignamanagh, Co. Kilkenny
Tel: 0503 24191 Fax: 0503 24451

and is fishable all year round. Michael is also one of the largest stockists of fishing bait in the southeast of Ireland, with purpose built cold rooms to keep your bait fresh at all times. The area around Brandon View is also ideal for the walking enthusiast and for those who enjoy game shooting, the McCabes have extensive shooting rights on the slopes of Brandon Hill.

Accommodation at Brandon View House consists of 4 guest bedrooms, comfortably furnished, all with hot and cold water, and a tastefully appointed reception area. The house features a restful old world sitting room where, should the mood take you, you are invited to participate in an informal piano session. If not, simply relax in peace by a crackling log fire. The dining room at Brandon View is renowned for its good food, based on fresh, home-grown fruit and vegetables. For those who prefer self-catering, the McCabes can also offer accommodation in a newly restored and completely refurbished stone built farmhouse, adjoining the main dwelling, which has 3 bedrooms, 2 with hot and cold water, a combined dining room and kitchenette, toilet and shower. Visitors' year round comfort is assured by central heating throughout.

CLIFDEN   Map 7 ref J13
6 miles NE of Kilkenny off the N10

Hidden away in the north-eastern corner of the county and located about 2 miles off the main Kilkenny to Carlow road, **Glenview** offers first class self-catering accommodation in a peaceful, rural setting. The house was originally built in the 1840s with unbelievably thick walls to ensure warmth and comfort. Over the years, Glenview has been continually upgraded and improved to provide all modern comforts in a traditional Irish home, including full central heating. There's a huge lounge with a large open log-burning fire and the 3 double bedrooms all have a genuinely Irish atmosphere. The house can sleep 6 people and is comprehensively equipped with just about everything you could possibly need for a relaxed and comfortable holiday. Glenview overlooks the picturesque ruins of a 16th century church and is ideally located as a convenient base for exploring the many

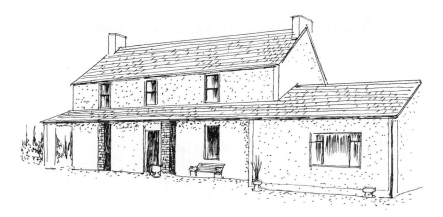

Glenview, Freneystown, Clifden, Co. Kilkenny
Tel: 056 59755

attractions of the area, along with the East and South East of Ireland. Historic Kilkenny town with its famous castle and cathedral is just a few minutes drive away, while Dunmore Cave and Kells Priory are both within easy reach.

COUNTY WATERFORD

More than any other of the southeast counties, Waterford offers a wide variety of landscapes. To the west, unspoiled uplands provide some splendid mountain scenery; in the heart of the county, wooded river valleys wind through fertile farmlands; while the fretted coastline opens up panoramic views of broad bays lined with low cliffs and sandy beaches. Strung along the coast are a handful of fishing villages and holiday resorts of which Tramore is the best known. It is around Tramore that the earliest known inhabitants of the county left their impressive monuments and human remains dating back to 9000BC. At Ardmore, near the County Cork border, St Declan disembarked in the early 400s, the first Christian missionary to land in Ireland, preceding St Patrick's arrival by several years. Ardmore's splendid 13th century Cathedral, standing on the site of St Declan's monastery, maintains the continuity of Christianity in this area, widely known as Old Parish because it was the first to be established in the country.

Norman survivals in the county include the sturdy Reginald's Tower in Waterford Town while amongst later buildings of note is Curraghmore House at Portlaw, a magnificent Georgian mansion, home of the Marquesses of Waterford for many generations.

WATERFORD   MAP 7 REF J14
95 miles SW of Dublin on the N9

Centuries ago Waterford was described in the *Lebor Gabala*, or Book of Invasions, as standing at a "sweet confluence of waters, a trinity of rivers", the three rivers being the Suir, the

Nore and the Barrow. This favoured position fostered Waterford's development as the major commercial centre of the southeast and it is still a busy working port.

It was the Vikings who established the first major settlement here in 853AD. They ruled the local Celtic tribe, the Désaí, with an iron rod, forcing them to pay a tribute known as *Airgead Sróine,* or Nose Money. Anyone who defaulted on the payment had his nose chopped off. One of the later Viking leaders, Ranguald, built a tower to guard the harbour. It was re-built after the Norman invasion of 1170 and, now known as **Reginald's Tower**, is the oldest surviving building in the town, indeed the oldest civic building in Ireland. The massive circular tower has been used as a mint, a prison and military store but now houses the city's museum. Nearby, the **Waterford Heritage Museum** is well worth a visit. The museum houses two interesting collections. The ground floor displays fascinating artefacts from Viking and medieval times which were recovered during recent excavations in the city centre. The mezzanine floor contains one of Ireland's greatest collections of civic regalia and decorated char-

Reginald's Tower, Waterford

ters, including one from Richard II dating back to 1399. King Richard is also linked to the city's other major medieval survival, the Franciscan **French Church**, founded in 1240. It was here that Richard received the submission of the Irish Chiefs in 1395, consolidating Anglo-Norman power in the city for generations. After the suppression of the monasteries, the church served as an almshouse but reverted to being a place of worship when French Huguenot refugees arrived at Waterford in the late 1600s. The church's tower and fine east window are still complete but the building is now roofless.

Two other churches stand close by. The Church of Ireland's **Christ Church Cathedral** is a noble edifice of the 1770s, its handsome Georgian appearance somewhat undermined by one of the tombs preserved from a much older church on the site. The monument to James Rice, Lord Mayor of Waterford, who died in 1482, displays the effigy of a corpse in an advanced state of decomposition. Few details of corporeal decay are omitted, with various creepy crawlies faithfully included in the design. More palatable is the cathedral's 45-minute audio presentation, *Let the Pillars Speak,* which relates Waterford's stirring story from the Norman invasion to the present time.

Christ Church was designed by John Roberts who, unusually, was also the architect for the Catholic **Holy Trinity Cathedral** just a few hundred yards away. The Cathedral was built in 1793 but considerably altered in late-Victorian times which accounts for its ornate, very un-Georgian appearance.

Another of Roberts' buildings has fortunately been left untouched. **City Hall** in the Mall was built in 1788 and now houses **Waterford Municipal Art Collection** which includes important works by Jack Yeats, Louis le Brocquy, Paul Henry, Lamb and Keating. On request, visitors can also view the dazzling Waterford crystal chandeliers in the council chamber. City Hall is also the venue for The Waterford Show, an evening entertainment of Irish music, story, song and dance presented by performers in Georgian costume. Tickets can be obtained at the Tourist Office on The Quay.

The **Chamber of Commerce** (1785) in George Street was yet another of John Roberts' buildings and contains what is generally regarded as his *pièce de résistance*, a magnificent cantilevered oval staircase adorned with brilliantly decorative stucco work. Visitors can view the staircase during normal office hours.

Wherever you go in Waterford, you'll find the famed Waterford Crystal on display. If you want to see how this exquisite translucent glass is made, there are regular tours of the **Waterford Crystal Glass Factory**, about a mile from the city centre. The theatre at the visitor centre shows a 17-minute audio-visual presentation which traces the ancient craft of glassmaking to the present day.

For those who know Waterford well, **McCluskeys Bistro** is the favoured venue for tasty, appetising food served in pleasant surroundings by friendly staff. The menu changes every week but always offers an interesting choice of dishes, all imaginatively prepared and attractively presented. The lunchtime menu thoughtfully includes a number of asterisked dishes for those in a hurry - pan fried fillets of Dunmore plaice, for example, with a lemon, chilli, mint and olive oil dressing; or linguine with Knockalara cheese, tomatoes, herbs and olive

McCluskeys Bistro, 18 High Street, Waterford, Co. Waterford Tel: 051 857766

oil. The dinner menu is served from 6pm until 10pm, Tuesday to Saturday, and it's defi-nitely a good idea to make a booking. Again, the menu changes weekly but you may well find Bannow Bay mussels with tomato, chillies and coriander amongst the starters, and Cashel blue potato cakes with flageolet beans, cider and rosemary, and side salad, listed in the main courses. Home made breads and freshly made desserts all contribute to a memo-rable eating experience.

Occupying a prime position on The Quay, the **Granville Hotel** is one of the oldest hotels in the country and also one of the most historical with many famous people enjoy-ing its hospitality over the years. It was originally the home of Thomas Meagher, Mayor of Waterford in the early 1800s, and Daniel O'Connell, "The Liberator" and famous ora-tor was a constant visitor to the house. Meagher's son, Thomas Francis Meagher, was to achieve fame as the Brigadier General of the "Fighting 69th" in the US Civil War, and later

Granville Hotel, The Quay, Waterford, Co. Waterford
Tel: 051 855111 Fax: 051 870307

Secretary of State and Governor of Montana. Charles Stewart Parnell, "The Uncrowned King of Ireland", also stayed here and one of his last speeches was made from a first floor window of what is now the Parnell Room. By the 1970s, though, this splendid old house was deteriorating rapidly but was rescued in 1980 by "locals" Liam and Ann Cusack who graciously restored it to its former grandeur, combining modern comforts with "olde worlde" charm and elegance. The hotel's many amenities include two restaurants - the well established and renowned Bianconi's which seats 90 people and serves national and international cuisine daily in a relaxed atmosphere, and the newer Bells, seating 36 and offering delicious gourmet food served in elegant yet friendly surroundings. Bar food is also served daily in the Thomas Francis Meagher Bar with its homely fires, library and conservatory areas. The Granville's 80 guest bedrooms are all en suite with direct dial telephone, 12-channel TV, radio, electric clothes presser and hair dryer, and there are suites available proffering that extra touch of luxury. The hotel also boasts one of the most gracious conference/function rooms in Ireland, the Tapestry Room, where tapestries line the walls and create a very special ambience.

If you are looking for luxury self catering accommodation in Waterford, **Crystal Apartments** have the very thing. Opened in January 1997 and with a Bord Fáilte 3*** rating, Crystal Apartments is centrally located just opposite the Bridge Hotel. The apartments are

beautifully furnished to a high standard and comprise 2 bedrooms, shower room, an open plan living/dining area and a fully equipped kitchen. Each apartment contains all mod. cons., including direct dial telephone, microwave cooker, bed linen, and multi-channel/ Cablevision colour TV with teletext. There are also a washing machine, dryer and ironing facilities available and daily room service if required. The building is monitored by security cameras throughout and business facilities such as a fax machine are also available. The apart-

Crystal Apartments, 3 Bridge Street, Waterford,
Co. Waterford Tel: 051 843533 (day); 051 879500 (night)
Fax: 051 879501

ments are just 100 yards from the bus and train stations and less than 15 minutes from top beaches, tennis and squash courts, an equestrian centre, the racecourse at Tramore and no fewer than 4 championship golf courses. A few more minutes will take you to Mount Juliet, regarded as one of the best-maintained estates in Ireland.

Popular with visitors from the USA, **Brookdale House** offers comfortable bed and breakfast accommodation in a quiet location just 400 metres off the Waterford to Cork road, the N25. This modern bungalow stands in landscaped surroundings not far from the Crystal Glass factory and almost next door to a well-equipped swimming and leisure complex. Visitors receive a warm welcome from Mrs Phil Harrington, whose home this is, and will soon feel completely at ease in the relaxed, home from home atmosphere. Open from May 1st to October 31st, Brookdale House has 4 guest bedrooms, all of them attractively decorated, en suite and equipped with TV and tea/coffee-making facilities. One of the winners of the CIE "Best Home Stay in Ireland, 1999" awards, Brookdale House offers

Brookdale House, Carrigrue, Ballinaneeshagh, Waterford, Co. Waterford
Tel: 051 375618

a discount of 25% for children. At breakfast time you'll find a good choice and a hearty spread to set you up for a day of exploring the city or the lovely surrounding countryside and coastline.

Just half a mile from the city centre, **St. Alban's** is a spacious, detached villa with a huge rear garden and plenty of parking space. The house is about the same distance from Waterford's famous Crystal Glass Factory, a must-see attraction for anyone visiting the southeast. St. Alban's is the home of Helen Mullally who in the short time she has been

St. Alban's, Cork Road, Waterford, Co. Waterford
Tel/Fax: 051 358171

welcoming bed and breakfast visitors, (she only moved here in the summer of 1999), has already gained an appreciative clientele. The house has 8 guest bedrooms, all of them en suite, appealingly furnished and decorated, and fully equipped. Helen serves a generous breakfast with a choice of either "The Full Irish" or continental. The house has a warm and welcoming atmosphere and is handily placed for exploring the City of Waterford itself and its many historic buildings, or the Waterford coast with its picturesque fishing villages such as Dunmore East.

Situated overlooking Bellake, which is famous for its coarse fishing, **Lakefield House** is adjacent to some of the most scenic countryside in the southeast. This spacious modern house, set in extensive gardens, is the home of Cally Carney who has spent many years in hotel management and is also a committee member of the Waterford Tourist Board so she knows all about looking after her guests well. Cally is also a gifted cook so it's definitely a good idea to sample her gourmet evening meals. The 6 guest bedrooms at Lakefield House

**Lakefield House, Dunmore East Road, Waterford, Co. Waterford
Tel: 051 382582**

are all en suite and, like the rest of the house, beautifully furnished and decorated, and equipped with all creature comforts. The picturesque fishing village of Dunmore East is just a few minutes drive away and offers excellent beach facilities as well as being a major angling centre and pleasure boating base. Woodstown beach and Tramore, one of Ireland's premier seaside resorts, are also within easy driving distance. The historic City of Waterford with its famous Viking fortification, Reginald's Tower, is just 5 miles away, and tours of the world renowned Waterford Crystal factory can easily be arranged.

SLIEVERUE
Map 7 ref J14
2 miles NE of Waterford off the N25

About half a mile off the N25 Waterford to New Ross road, **Suncrest** is a handsome modern building where you'll find top quality bed and breakfast on offer. Suncrest's owner, Maureen Wall, has been in the hospitality business for some 30 years and still loves wel-

Suncrest, Slieverue, Waterford, Co. Waterford
Tel: 051 832732 Fax: 051 851861

coming guests to her spacious house. It was built in 1965 by members of her family, a family which has a long tradition of producing skilled carpenters. The interior of Suncrest displays some excellent examples of their work, all adding to the charm of this inviting house. There are 5 guest bedrooms, all of them en suite, and equipped with TV and tea/coffee-making facilities, and non-smoking rooms are available if you wish. Children are welcome, with a cot and baby-sitting service available if required. Breakfast at Suncrest is something to look forward to: fill in the order form the previous night, indicate the time you would like to eat, and Maureen will see to the rest! Suncrest stands in an extensive and beautifully maintained garden and in a quiet and peaceful area. It's conveniently located close to the golf course and the Waterford Crystal factory, with facilities for horse riding also within easy reach. Suncrest is open from March 1st too November 30th and provides the perfect base for exploring Co. Waterford.

PORTLAW
10 miles NW of Waterford off the R680

Map 7 ref I14

A popular excursion from Waterford is to the village of Portlaw, founded as a model village by a Quaker family, the Malcolmsons, who also established a cotton industry which became noted for its durable tweeds. Adjoining the village is the stately home of the Marquesses of Waterford since 1170, **Curraghmore**. The present building is a grand Georgian mansion set in parkland with gently sloping hills rising behind. The grounds of Curraghmore are considered one of the most beautiful demesnes in the country. They contain an outstanding Arboretum, a bridge built in 1205 for King John to cross the River Clodagh, and a fascinating Shell House, designed and decorated by Catherine, Countess of Tyrone, in 1754. Opening hours of the house and grounds are limited, (details on 051 387102), but group tours are welcome all year round on weekdays by prior appointment.

COMERAGH MOUNTAINS
10 miles S of Carrick-on-Suir on the R676

Map 2 REF I14

Just off the N25 Waterford to Dungarvan road, **Kilmacthomas** is built on steep slopes either side of the Mahon River. To the west rise the Comeragh Mountains, a fine range with many peaks above 2000ft. The highest point, Fascoum (2597ft) towers above Lough Coumshingaun. The lough gives its name to an outstanding guest house, **Coumshingaun Lodge**, where a warm welcome, good food and great scenery await visitors. This comfortable, tastefully furnished house of character nestles in unspoilt countryside at the foot of the Comeragh Mountains. The Lodge requires care to find but lies to the east of the R676

Coumshingaun Lodge, Kilclooney, Kilmacthomas, Co. Waterford
Tel/Fax: 051 646238 e-mail: coumshingaun@eircom.net
website: http://homepage.eircom.net/~coumshingaunlodge

exactly 10 miles south of the bridge at Carrick-on-Suir. Coumshingaun Lodge is the home of Pauline and Ken Humphreys, both of whom are keen musicians: Ken plays the fiddle, tin whistle and melodeon, Pauline is a pianist and also sings. With any luck, you will be entertained to an evening session of traditional Irish music. Pauline is also a professional cook so it's a good idea to order the optional evening meal at which you can also take advantage of the Lodge's wine licence. Breakfast is special, too - a hearty repast which includes freshly squeezed orange juice, fruit compotes, cereal or porridge and a choice of cooked breakfasts served with freshly made soda bread. The Lodge has 5 guest rooms, all en suite and with tea/coffee-making facilities; a lounge with an open fire, dining room and drying room. The dining room and lounge are non-smoking areas, as are 3 of the bedrooms. The ground floor and 2 of the bedrooms are suitable for wheelchair users.

The Comeragh Mountains are great walking country and you can start walks from the front door of the Lodge. You can also drive round the Comeraghs on the Comeragh Drive, or visit the majestic Mahon Falls only 6 miles away. There are 19 lakes in the area, including the fabulous Lough Coumshingaun, (pronounced *com-shin-awn*). Surrounded on three sides by 1000 feet cliffs, it is the finest example of a corrie lake in Europe. The area is very popular with rock-climbers. Other scenic drives include the Waterford coastal drive and the Knockmealdown Drive. Local facilities include pony trekking and horse riding; cycle hire; angling in river, lake or sea; safe, clean beaches; musical pubs and many fine golf courses. Maps and guidebooks are available during your stay at Coumshingaun Lodge and you are also welcome to borrow from the Humphreys' extensive collection of books.

WOODSTOWN   MAP 7 REF J15
6 miles SE of Waterford on minor road off the R684

Well-known for its beautiful sandy beach backed by woodland, Woodstown is an ideal place for a gentle stroll or a quiet swim. Nearby are two excellent places to stay. **Woodstown House Country Estate** nestles in 35 acres of wooded parkland just a few minutes from Woodstown Beach and offers unique self-catering accommodation in idyllic, peaceful and quiet surroundings. At the heart of the estate stands Woodstown House, an elegant Regency house which was built around 1823 by Lord Carew as a gift for his wife. As a young girl, Lady Carew is said to have danced with the Duke of Wellington at the famous Ball in Brussels given by the Duchess of Richmond on the eve of the Battle of Waterloo. She lived to the great age of 103, dying at Woodstown House in 1901. The house was

Woodstown House Country Estate, Woodstown, Co. Waterford
Tel: 051 382611 Fax: 051 382644 e-mail: stay@granville-hotel.ie

bought in 1945 by Major C.D. Cholmeley-Harrison who let it during the summer of 1967 to Mrs Jacqueline Kennedy, widow of the American President.

Then, in 1991, Liam and Ann Cusack purchased the house and restored it to its former grandeur, tastefully transforming the Dower House, Stables and Carriage Houses into the luxurious Woodstown House Country Estate. The spacious mews-style houses are beautifully furnished and consist of an hallway, living room, kitchen/dining room, 2/3 bedrooms, and bathroom. All have an open fireplace, central heating and direct dial telephone. The houses are totally self-contained, equipped with all modern conveniences, and there's an attractive walled garden with play areas and two hard tennis courts. Most houses have a private patio and all are set in beautifully landscaped gardens with tree-lined avenues leading to Woodstown Beach which is ideal for swimming, windsurfing, walking, fishing or just relaxing. On the estate itself, in addition to the two tennis courts, there's a croquet lawn, putting green, boulles pitch, barbecue area and a network of paths for jogging. There's also a Par 3 golf course just 5 minutes away and no fewer than 10 golf courses within a 10-40 minute drive.

Surrounded by densely packed woodland, **Ardilaun** is very much a Hidden Place but well worth seeking out. It is located close to Woodstown, with its beautiful sandy beach, and the picture-postcard resort of Dunmore East. This well-designed, detached house was built in 1970 and is set in beautifully maintained gardens - a wonderfully peaceful retreat and an ideal base for exploring the scenic delights of this southeast corner of Ireland. Ardilaun is the home of Anne-Marie Newport who possesses the inestimable knack of making her guests feel instantly at home. The house has 3 guest bedrooms, all furnished and decorated with great style, and the huge lounge with its stone divider provides a relaxing and comfortable place to settle down with a good book. Breakfast at Ardilaun is equally satisfying - a hearty spread with a good selection of dishes to choose from. It will set you up well for a day of touring the Waterford countryside, taking advantage of the many facilities for active pursuits, such as golf or

Ardilaun, Woodstown, Co. Waterford
Tel: 051 382231

horse riding available locally, or simply enjoying the peace and tranquillity of this rural retreat.

DUNMORE EAST
11 miles SE of Waterford on the R684

MAP 7 REF J15

Standing at the mouth of Waterford Harbour, Dunmore East is a picturesque seaside resort with a delightful main street that follows a twisting course from the east cove down to the busy little quay with its crooked harbour wall. The village is framed by red sandstone cliffs overlaid with emerald green turf dotted with golden gorse. Safe bathing beaches boasting the Blue Flag accolade lie at the foot of the cliffs and there are copious facilities for every kind of water sport. Dunmore is a very active fishing port, busy with brightly coloured fishing vessels, and also home to the long-established **Waterford Harbour Sailing Club**. The town takes its name from the *dun*, or hill fort, of which a few traces remain on nearby Brownstown Head.

Offering luxury accommodation in a peaceful village setting, **Springfield** is a striking modern bungalow set in beautiful surroundings beside a wooded hill. Despite its tranquil location, the house is only 200 yards from the beach and within walking distance of the Golf Club, tennis courts, restaurants and bars. The house has been well designed, with large comfortable rooms, and non-smoking throughout. Guests have the use of a residents' lounge and a light and airy conservatory, overlooking the garden, where tea and coffee are always available. Springfield is the home of Tony and Winnie Brooke, welcoming hosts who will do all they can to make your stay as comfortable and relaxed as possible.

Springfield, Dunmore East, Co. Waterford
Tel: 051 383448 e-mail: springfieldbb@esatclear.ie

They have 6 guest bedrooms in the main house, all of them en suite and with TV. The Brookes serve a generous breakfast with a good choice of menu and for those who prefer self-catering, there's a 4-bedroomed detached bungalow within the grounds which can sleep up to 8 people and is comprehensively equipped with everything you could possibly need. Springfield is open from March 1st until November 30th and it provides a perfect base for touring and exploring this scenic corner of the country.

Located in the centre of this picturesque fishing village, **Church Villa** is an impressive Victorian town house dating back to 1856. Originally built as a constabulary house within a complex constructed by Lord Waterford, Church Villa is now the home of Phyllis and Ed Lannon who welcome bed and breakfast guests to their delightful house. The grand

Church Villa, Dunmore East, Co. Waterford
Tel: 051 383390 Fax: 051 383023 e-mail: churchvilla@eircom.net

Victorian rooms at Church Villa have an appealing olde worlde charm. There are 6 guest bedrooms, all of them en suite with TV and tea/coffee-making facilities, and with a choice of either family, double, twin or single. Children over 4 are welcome and a cot is available if required. Open all year, except over the Christmas period, Church Villa is ideally situated just yards from the Blue Flag beach, close to restaurants, shops and pubs, and with no fewer than 5 golf courses within a 20-minute drive.

TRAMORE
MAP 7 REF J15
6 miles S of Waterford on the R675

A delightful town where the houses rise one street above another climbing up the hill-side, Tramore is the major seaside resort in the southeast and offers a huge range of holiday amusements in its extensive fun park. **Splashworld** is an all-water experience featuring a bubble pool, river ride, wave machine and water slides, all in chlorine-free, hygienic waters. Outdoors, there's a sandy bathing beach 3 miles long, a fine promenade, good facilities for boating and angling, and the Tramore races are a popular event in the Irish racing calendar, especially the traditional festival meeting in August.

Its walls almost smothered in ivy, **Belair** is a lovely old Georgian house built on a high point of Tramore Town and commanding a beautiful view of Tramore bay and beach. Its extensive grounds contain many beautiful plants, such as Californian poppies, and many centuries-old trees. There's also a gazebo and tables with sun shades where you can enjoy

Belair, Old Waterford Road, Tramore, Co. Waterford
Tel: 051 381605/386800 Fax: 051 386688

your afternoon tea. Children are well catered for in the spacious grounds and there is ample car parking for all residents. Belair is an exceptional guest house, a home from home in friendliness. All rooms are equipped with tea-making facilities, TV and internal telephone system. The resident's lounge with its beautiful Kilkenny marble fireplace also has colour TV and video. Although you will be living in the middle of Tramore Town, Belair is peaceful and private within its walled-in grounds. The house is a 10-minute walk from the beach, and is very close to the race course, golf course, pitch & putt, tennis, sea fishing, surfing, horse riding, amusements and the many other amenities that Tramore offers.

Occupying a superb position on the sea front, **Killerig House** is a lovely 200 year old Georgian town house overlooking Tramore Bay. The fine sandy beach is just a few yards away and if the weather is poor you can still enjoy water sports in Splashworld, just across the road. Killerig House is the home of Maria Byrne who welcomes bed and breakfast guests to her spacious and comfortable house. There are 4 guest bedrooms, all of them en suite and fully equipped with television and tea/coffee-making facilities. Maria serves a hearty breakfast with plenty of choice and although she doesn't provide an evening meal

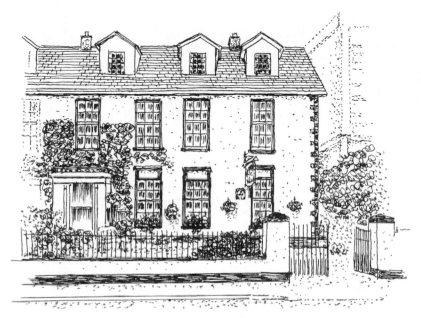

Killerig House, Lower Branch Road, Tramore, Co. Waterford
Tel: 051 381075

there are plenty of pubs and restaurants within easy walking distance. Golf, fishing and horse riding are all available locally and this popular holiday resort is particularly good for children. They will love the 50-acre amusement park which has a miniature railway, paddle steamer, boating lake, adventure island, marina and much more.

BUTLERSTOWN   Map 7 ref J14
3 miles W of Waterford off the N25

Just 3 miles from Waterford, **The Coach House** at Butlerstown Castle provides the oppor-tunity for relaxation in elegant yet affordable accommodation in a small country house steeped in history. It's situated on an elevated site in the grounds of Butlerstown Castle which dates back to 1248 and is now in ruins. The same fate nearly happened to the Coach House. It was built in 1874 by the Northern Nationalist, Samuel Ferguson, and occupied until the late 1960s when it was abandoned for 30 years during which time it

The Coach House, Butlerstown Castle, Butlerstown, Co. Waterford
Tel: 051 384656 Fax: 051 384751 e-mail: coachhse@iol.ie

became derelict. Then in 1991, the shell was bought by Des O'Keeffe who began a total restoration. The Coach House is now an appealing building of stone and warm brick facings, providing en suite accommodation in 7 bedrooms, all with direct dial telephone, colour TV and tea/coffee-making facilities. Many of the bedrooms enjoy commanding views of the surrounding countryside, Castle and mountains. The interior furnishings of The Coach House are most impressive, with real leather chairs and sofas, and deep pile carpets. Crackling open fires add to the charm and you can settle down comfortably here with a glass of wine if you wish, since the Coach House has the added advantage of holding a wine licence. And after a hard day's touring and exploring, why not relax in the private sauna and ease those aches away.

Although a mere half mile from the main Waterford to Cork road, (watch for the sign for Butlerstown Church on the N25), tranquillity is guaranteed here. There are delightful country walks, with the megalithic Knockeen and Gaulstown Dolmens a short distance away, and the banks of the River Suir just 2 miles to the northeast. Golfers will find 5 of the country's top golf courses within a 20-minute drive, and from the grounds of the Coach House the Comeragh Mountains beckon, gentle, alluring and scenic. You can be on the scenic Comeragh Drive or the Nire Valley route within half an hour.

CLONEA

MAP 2 REF I15

4 miles E of Dungarvan on the R675

The beautiful strand at Clonea is one of only 3 Blue Flag beaches along the Waterford coast, an excellent location for a family holiday or a quiet stopover. Handily located less

Butler's Cottage, Ballin Road, Clonea, Co. Waterford
Tel: 058 41188

than a couple of miles from Dungarvan town centre and only 200 yards from Dungarvan Golf Club, **Butler's Cottage** offers quality self-catering accommodation in a modern detached bungalow with spacious gardens at the front and rear. The house is centrally heated and equipped with all the modern conveniences visitors could possibly need for a relaxed and comfortable stay. Butler's Cottage has 3 large bedrooms which sleep up to 6 people and its location is ideal in an area where there's a shortage of self-catering properties. The superb beach at Clonea is close by, the 72 par Championship Golf Course even closer and picturesquely set with the Comeragh Mountains as a backdrop. If you want to see the mountains at closer quarters, there are facilities at Cappoquin for pony trekking with guides available for both novice and proficient riders, and there are also guided or self-guiding coastal, hill and inland walks.

DUNGARVAN

MAP 2 REF I15

29 miles SW of Waterford on the N25

A busy fishing port and the administrative centre for the county apart from Waterford Town, Dungarvan enjoys a picturesque setting, surrounded by low cliffs and gentle hills smothered in pine trees. A pretty arched bridge spans the River Colligan and on the edge of the town are the remains of a castle built by King John in the early 1200s. A maze of narrow alleyways winding between warehouses leads down to the bustling harbour where the attractive old inns naturally specialise in sea food. Collectors of curiosities should make the short trip to the junction of the R672 and N72, northwest of the town. Here stands the **Master McGrath Memorial**, a plain stone monument with an elegant spire erected in 1873. It commemorates not some local worthy but a legendary greyhound which won the Water Cup for coursing 3 times during the 19th century. The hound is also remembered in popular ballads and in the name of a superior brand of dog food.

Dungarvan is a convenient place to stay and whether your preference is for bed and breakfast or self-catering accommodation, **The Old Rectory** can oblige with either. Bed and breakfast guests stay in The Old Rectory itself, a spacious building set in 2½ acres of

The Old Rectory, Abbeyside, Dungarvan, Co. Waterford
Tel/Fax: 058 41394 e-mail: tournore@tinet.ie
website: http://homepage.tinet.ie/~1108

its own grounds on the outskirts of Dungarvan and adjacent to the Championship Golf
Course. Attractive gardens with an ornamental pool and tranquil surroundings make this
former Minister's house a very pleasant and relaxing place to stay. Your hosts are Rosaleen
and Jim Prendergast from whom a warm *"céad mile fáilte"* ("a hundred thousand welcomes") is assured. The house has five inviting guest rooms, all of them en suite and
equipped with TV and tea/coffee-making facilities. There's a large residents lounge and a
dining room where you'll find a generous choice of menu available at breakfast time.
Both Rosaleen and Jim are keen golfers, officials of the Dungarvan Golf Club, and thus in
a good position to furnish you with all the information and assistance you might need.
The Old Rectory is open from February 1st to December 20th and provides an excellent
base for touring the area. Should you opt for self-catering, accommodation is available in
a smart modern apartment block on the Quay, just yards from the town centre.

PULA   MAP 2 REF I15
4 miles S of Dungarvan on minor road off the N25

Located about 4 miles south of Dungarvan, **Seanachie** is an absolute gem of a traditional
Irish pub. It lies within the area known as An Rinn, or Ring, an enclave where Gaelic is
still the first language for the population of around 1500 and Irish traditions still thrive.
Seanachie looks a picture with its neat thatched roof and when you step inside it's like
stepping back into the 1930s. The furniture and decoration, and lots of interesting bric-à-
brac around the rooms, all accord with that period and the owner of Seanachie, Seamus

Seanachie, Pula, Dungarvan, Co. Waterford
Tel: 058 46285

McGrath, has lovingly preserved the old-world atmosphere. As you might expect, there's a wonderful ambience, with a large open fire adding to the attraction, and the regulars ensuring that there's plenty of good craic. There's also plenty of good food, with fish a speciality, and the separate dining room offers a relaxed and sociable setting in which to enjoy the superb fare. Yet another attraction at Seanachie is the excellent live entertainment which is provided every evening from Thursday to Sunday inclusive. For summer days, there's a pleasant Beer Garden and the location enjoys splendid views over Dungarvan Bay. If you want to experience a traditional Irish pub at its best, Seanachie is not to be missed.

ARDMORE   MAP 2 REF H15
14 miles SW of Dungarvan on the R673

This attractive seaside village boasts a splendid Blue Flag beach, exhilarating views across a wide bay, and the distinction of being one of the earliest Christian settlements in Northern Europe. St Declan brought Christianity to the region as early as 416AD, almost 30 years before St Patrick's mission began. The area around Ardmore is still known as Old Parish, reflecting its status as the first parish to be established in Ireland. Declan's remains are supposedly buried in St Declan's Oratory and St Declan's Well, to the east of the village, still bubbles up beneath three simple stone crosses. Pilgrims traditionally wash in the cool, fresh water and devotees are especially numerous on the Saint's Day, July 24th.

Ardmore Cathedral, which is mostly 12th century, stands on the site of the monastery founded by Declan. The cathedral's exterior is decorated with some remarkably vigorous, if rather weathered, carvings of Biblical scenes such as the Judgement of Solomon, and inside there are several ogham stones which pre-date St Declan. Nearby rises an imposing **Round Tower**, reputedly built by the saint in the course of a single night. The graceful tower, 97ft high, is remarkably well-preserved but cannot be the one so miraculously erected by Declan since it dates from the 11th century.

As its name suggests, the **Round Tower Hotel** stands close to the famous monument. The hotel building was originally a convent but is now a friendly and lively hostelry offering comfortable accommodation and wholesome food at very competitive prices. Locals meet for a pint and a snack in the Victorian-style bar (which can be busy when holidaymakers swell the crowds during the summer), and more formal fare is served by friendly staff in the hotel dining room. The simple food has a home made character - easily explained by the fact that the cooking is done by three capable home cooks from

Round Tower Hotel, Ardmore, Co. Waterford
Tel: 024 94494/94382 Fax: 024 94254 e-mail: rth@tinet.ie

the locality. There's always a vegetarian option alongside the local seafood from Ardmore harbour, poultry, traditional red meats and respectfully prepared vegetables. The homely, freshly-prepared desserts will often include old-fashioned favourites such as Bakewell Tart or Apple Crumble, as well as ice creams and fresh fruit in season. Daytime food, including Afternoon Tea, is served in the bar or the pleasant conservatory area that links the original building with a recently completed extension. The hotel has 10 simple bedrooms, all of them en suite with shower.

Located in the heart of this delightful village, **Whitehorses Restaurant** has established a fine reputation for its seafood specialities with regular customers coming from as far afield as Cork. This outstanding eating place is owned and run by two sisters, Geraldine Flavin and Christine Power, and Christine's husband, Joe. Their menus change regularly but are always based on prime quality seafood, locally caught, lovingly prepared and attractively presented. A speciality of the house is lobster, prepared in various ways but consistently delicious. Whitehorses has a wine licence so you can complement the excellent food with a glass or two of wine if you wish. Service is friendly and courteous, and the prices represent extremely good value for money. Whitehorses seats about 50 diners and the popularity of the restaurant is such that it is definitely a good idea to book in advance.

Whitehorse's Restaurant, Main Street, Ardmore, Co. Waterford
Tel: 024 94040

The restaurant is open daily from May 1st to September 30th, and on Friday, Saturday and Sunday evenings throughout the rest of the year, offering at all times a memorable eating experience.

KINSALEBEG
13 miles SW of Dungarvan on the N25

MAP 2 REF H15

Just a couple of miles from the historic and picturesque village of Ardmore, **Summerhill Farmhouse** is located on a 90-acre working dairy farm and enjoys breathtaking views

Summerhill Farmhouse, Kinsalebeg, Ardmore, Co. Waterford
Tel: 024 92682 Fax: 024 92682

across green rolling countryside to the Atlantic Ocean. The stylish modern building is spacious and light, with an attractive conservatory which overlooks the garden and where visitors can help themselves to tea and coffee. Summerhill is the home of the Budds family who are perfect hosts, warm, friendly and very relaxed. The house has 6 letting rooms, all en suite and appealingly furnished and decorated, and at breakfast time guests will find a hearty farmhouse spread. Visitors are welcome to watch the cows being milked and a central roadway through the farm enables you to absorb the scenic view and also to meet some friendly animals, and observe the wildlife and abundant flora. There are three sandy beaches within a 5-minutes drive and Summerhill is also a convenient base for visiting a whole host of attractions: the Rock of Cashel, Lismore Castle, Fota Wildlife Park, the Waterford Crystal factory, the scenic Vee Drive and much, much more.

CAPPOQUIN
10 miles NW of Dungarvan on the N72

MAP 2 REF H15

From Ardmore the long-distance footpath, St Declan's Way, links the historic village to the Rock of Cashel in Co. Tipperary. En route, the path passes through Cappoquin at the head of the tidal estuary of the River Blackwater, noted for its excellent coarse fishing. This quiet market town is surrounded by attractive wooded hills and the river valley to the west, skirting the **Knockmealdown Mountains**, is particularly lovely. If you take the **Glenshelane River Walk** it will bring you, after about 3 miles, to Mount Melleray Abbey, a functioning Cistercian foundation where visitors who wish to take time for quiet contemplation are welcome.

On the outskirts of Cappoquin and originally built in 1704 by the Earl of Cork and Burlington, **Richmond House** is a stately building which has been lovingly renovated

Richmond House, Cappoquin, Co. Waterford
Tel: 058 54278 Fax: 058 54988 website: www.amireland.com/richmond

and refurbished to the highest standards. Today, Richmond House provides luxurious accommodation and superb restaurant cuisine in one of the finest country house hotels in the country. Bill and Jean's son, Paul, has taken over as chef after wide-ranging experience in other Irish and Swiss hotels. Strongly influenced by the classical French cuisine he learned in Switzerland, and then by the honesty and appreciation of Irish foods which is taught at Darina Allen's famed Certificate Course at Ballymaloe, Paul gradually replaced Jean's traditional cooking with what he describes as "Modern Irish Cuisine". He cooks a set dinner every day, comprising 5 starters, a soup and sorbet, 6 main dishes and a selection of desserts. The ingredients all come from specially selected local producers. Paul and his wife, Claire, who is also well-experienced in the hospitality business, have settled happily into the pastoral surroundings of Richmond House which features in the *Bridgestone Guide to 100 Best Places to Stay* and *The Best Restaurants in Ireland*.

The accommodation at Richmond House is as splendid as the cuisine, with each of the 10 en suite bedrooms displaying a blend of Georgian elegance and modern comfort. All bedrooms feature period furniture, central heating, direct dial television, trouser press and tea-making facilities, with rooms enjoying lovely views of the surrounding countryside. Richmond House is a place where you will want to linger, but when you are ready for extramural activities, there are plentiful facilities for golf, angling, pony trekking, swimming and walking all within easy reach.

LISMORE
16 miles W of Dungarvan on the N72

MAP 2 REF H15

A designated Heritage Town, Lismore lies in the broad plain of the Blackwater Valley and has the distinct feel of a 19th century estate town. The estate in this instance was the property of **Lismore Castle**, the Irish home of successive Dukes of Devonshire since 1753. Earlier owners of the castle included Sir Walter Raleigh who sold it to Richard Boyle, later 1st Earl of Cork, whose 14th child, Robert, the celebrated chemist and formulator of Boyle's Law was actually born in the castle. Parts of the grey stone, castellated building overhanging the river date back to the days of King John but it was extensively remodelled by the 6th Duke of Devonshire in the mid-1800s. The noble old castle is not open to the public but visitors are welcome to explore the attractive gardens, in the afternoons only, from May to September.

Lismore's origins go back to 636AD when St Carthage founded a monastic complex for both monks and nuns, a foundation which became an important centre of learning despite repeated attacks by Vikings and Normans. The most disastrous visitation however was by the troops of Elizabeth I who almost totally destroyed the medieval cathedral. Its site is now occupied by the Church of Ireland's **St Carthage's Cathedral**, consecrated in 1633 and given a neo-Gothic facelift in the 1820s. The cathedral enjoys a beautiful setting, surrounded by ancient yews and pollarded limes, while the interior contains some interesting tombs and some dazzling stained glass by the English Pre-Raphaelite Burne-Jones.

If you are in search of quality bed and breakfast accommodation in this historic little town, look no further than **Pine Tree House**, an exceptionally spacious modern house

Pine Tree House, Ballyanchor, Lismore, Co. Waterford
Tel: 058 53282 e-mail: pinetreehouse@oceanfree.net

standing in an extensive garden amidst peaceful surroundings. The house has 3 large guest rooms, all of them en suite and well appointed, and at breakfast time you'll find a very good spread with plenty of choice. Pine Tree House is the home of Daphne and Shaun Power, a young couple with a keen interest in golf. They can provide you with all the information you need about golfing opportunities in the area, as well as the many other activities and visitor attractions to be enjoyed in and around Lismore. Fishing, pony trekking and scenic walks, naturally, and Lismore Castle of course is a "must-see" attraction for anyone visiting the town. Also well worth visiting is the Lismore Heritage Centre, housed in the former Courthouse. At this award-winning multi-media presentation, "Brother Declan" takes you on an enthralling journey through time, beginning with the arrival of St Carthage in 636 AD and bringing viewers right up to the present.

COUNTY TIPPERARY

Tipperary is the largest of Ireland's inland counties and also the richest. The county's wealth come from the undramatic central Golden Vale, a limestone plain that is prime beef and dairy cattle territory, 'planted' with Cromwell's soldiers after his conquest of the country. The Golden Vale is bounded by mountain ranges, the finest of which are the Comeragh and Galtee mountains, and the Glen of Aherlow, but perhaps the most striking landscape feature is the dramatic Rock of Cashel which rises abruptly from the central plain. Its summit is crowned by a wonderful succession of medieval towers, turrets and spires, and the Rock's historic associations with St Patrick and King Brian Boru have made Cashel the most visited site not just in Tipperary but in the whole of Ireland.

The county can also boast some enchanting towns, Clonmel and Birr for example; one of the country's largest and best preserved castles at Cahir; and a uniquely beautiful Tudor mansion, Ormond Castle, at Carrick-on-Suir. We begin our tour of the county where most visitors tend to begin: in the southeast.

CARRICK-ON-SUIR
Map 7 ref I14
15 miles NW of Waterford on the N24

A thriving market town today, Carrick was founded in 1640 by the Duke of Ormonde whose family, the Butlers, had for generations made this area their stronghold. It was an earlier Duke, "Black Tom" Ormonde, who in the 1560s built the superb Elizabethan fortified mansion known as **Ormonde Castle.** "Black Tom" reputedly built the house in expectation of a visit from Elizabeth I, a visit which never came about. The first completely unfortified great house in Ireland, Ormonde Castle is regarded as the finest example of a Tudor manor house in the country, its State Rooms elegantly embellished with decorative plasterwork, including plasterwork portraits. The Long Gallery has a magnificent carved fireplace which adorned Kilkenny Castle for many years before being returned to Ormonde when the house was restored in the 1990s. An old tradition claims that Ann Boleyn was born at the castle but this has never been authenticated. Ormonde Castle is open daily from mid-June to September and the optional guided tours are strongly recommended.

Carrick town itself, although a pleasant enough place, has little else to encourage the visitor to stay although devotees of local history might like to spend an hour or so in the Heritage Centre which occupies the former Protestant church. The Centre's prize exhibit is the 17th century church silver presented to the parish by the current Duke of Ormonde. Cycling enthusiasts will be pleased to note that Carrick's minuscule main square has been renamed after the champion cyclist Sean Kelly who was born in the town.

Just outside Carrick however, at Ballynoran, is one of the county's major visitor attractions, **Tipperary Crystal Craft.** Housed in two thatched cottages, the display area and factory lie close to the banks of the Suir River, opposite an ancient tower house. Visitors can watch glass being created by the age-old hand craft method - a skilful use of mouth, hand and timber moulds. In addition to a show room and retail shop where you can view and buy the beautiful crystal items, there are also restaurant facilities and a bureau de change. The site is open daily all year, (no demonstrations on weekdays), and admission is free. Five miles north of Carrick, the little village of Ahenny is worth a short detour to see the two beautiful high crosses in the churchyard. Dating back to the 8th century they are unusual examples of the transitional style between the austere simplicity of the early Christian shaft crosses and the much more elaborately carved crosses seen at Monasterboice and Kells.

MULLINAHONE
Map 2 ref I13
15 miles NE of Clonmel on the R690

North of Carrick the N76 crosses a range of hills, of which Slievenamon (719ft) is the loftiest, then drops into the valley of the River Anner. Mullinahone sits beside the river, a small village best known for its associations with the writer and patriot Charles Joseph Kickham (1828-1882) whose best novel, *Knocknagow*, is based on rural life in this corner of Co. Tipperary. A plaque marks the house in Fethard Street where he lived and a Celtic cross stands over his grave beside the Catholic church.

Just 300 yards outside the village, **Killaghy Castle** is a unique place to stay for bed & breakfast. The first castle on this site, a motte and bailey construction of 1206, can still be seen to the left of the present building. St Aulyus lived here for eight years and then

Killaghy Castle, Mullinahone, Co. Tipperary
Tel: 052 53112

erected a stone castle, four storeys high and with a stone spiral stairway. During Tudor times, a long house was added at the rear and between that time and 1800 two further buildings were added, making Killaghy what it is today. Set in 300 acres of working farmland, the Castle is now the home of Maria and Pat Collins who have a Bord Fáilte Approved Farm Guesthouse rating. There are 5 guest bedrooms, 3 of them en suite and two with private bathrooms. The tariff includes a full farmhouse breakfast and evening meals are available on request, when guests can take advantage of the Castle's wine licence. The Castle also has a games room and outside there's a lovely walled garden and two tennis courts. Definitely a place not to be missed!

CLONMEL
Map 2 ref H14
24 miles SE of Tipperary on the N24

The county town of Tipperary and its largest settlement with a population of around 13,000, Clonmel enjoys a lovely riverside setting looking across to the Comeragh Mountains of Co. Waterford. The town is a great centre for the greyhound world and the elegant animals can often be seen as they are exercised along the roads, much as racehorses are in Kildare.

A goodly portion of Clonmel's medieval town walls still survive around **St Mary's Church**, a Protestant church with a striking octagonal tower. Although it looks medieval, the West Gate which arches across Main Street was actually rebuilt in 1831 on the site of the earlier gate. The most imposing building in Clonmel is the **Main Guard** in O'Connell Street, said to have been built to a design of Christopher Wren for the main guard of the garrison. The façade bears two panels dated 1675 showing the coats of arms of the town and of the Palatinate of Ormonde, an administrative district which was dissolved in 1715.

Clonmel's **Town Hall** has a display of civic regalia which includes the mayor's gold chain to which each incumbent adds a new link. A former mayor of Clonmel, an Italian named Charles Bianconi, established Ireland's first public transport system when he began running his "Bianconi Cars" (stage coaches) between Clonmel and Cahir in 1815. They departed from Hearns Hotel where the original clock which timed the system can still be seen. At one period Bianconi was running up to 100 of his cars at any one time and his achievement is still celebrated with costumed festivities on his birthday, July 6th.

Clonmel boasts an interesting clutch of literary associations. Laurence Sterne, author of the inimitable *Tristram Shandy*, was born here in 1715; Anthony Trollope worked for a while in the local post office; and George Borrow (1803-81) went to school here.

An unusual, if not unique, attraction at Clonmel is the weekend evening entertainment **Celebrated Tipperary Trials**. This is staged in the former Courthouse where the trials originally took place and each performance depicts a different trial, based on dialogue from the official court transcripts and newspaper reports of the time. The show also includes a presentation of the history of Tipperary in song, dance and story. Tickets are available from the Clonmel tourist office and the admission price includes pre-performance refreshments as well as a sample of the famous local cider.

KNOCKLOFTY   Map 2 ref H14
4 miles W of Clonmel on the R665

Only a few minutes drive from Clonmel, **Knocklofty House Hotel** is a magnificent mansion superbly set in 105 acres of sweeping parkland, Formerly the country residence of the Earls of Donoughmore, the house dates from the 17th century with subsequent 18th and 19th century additions. Internally, the house embodies the best of Irish Georgian decorative architecture and, externally, commands glorious views of the surrounding countryside. Guests can relax in the spacious comfort of the Library, a beautiful sunny two-storey room with, along three walls, an upper gallery with wrought iron balustrade and ornamented bookcases containing a wealth of books. A finely decorated Georgian ceiling and marble inlaid fireplace add to the elegance of this handsome room.

The hotel's Egon Ronay recommended Restaurant is situated in the West Wing and has superb oak-panelled walls and fireplace. The room is south facing and enjoys extensive views over the River Suir, which runs through the demesne, the Comeragh and Knockmealdown mountains, and the rolling Tipperary parklands.

In keeping with the rest of the hotel, the guest bedrooms are spacious and distinctive in design, with every effort taken to retain the elegance of a bygone age. All bedrooms

Knocklofty House Hotel, Knocklofty, Clonmel, Co. Tipperary
Tel: 052 38222 Fax: 052 38300 e-mail: knocklofty@tinet.ie
website: http://www.tipp.ie/knocklof.htm

have en suite facilities, colour television and hospitality tray. Guests at Knocklofty House also have the use of the hotel's large swimming pool.

With its extensive amenities and picturesque grounds, Knocklofty House is a popular venue for wedding parties. The hotel has two elegant suites available: the Palatine Suite, which seats approximately 60, and the Donoughmore Suite which can accommodate up to 70 people. The suites are also suitable for larger parties of up to 130 people since the Palatine Suite adjoins the Donoughmore Suite through a wide pillared entrance.

American visitors in particular will be interested in the history of the Hutchinson family, later Earls of Donoughmore. In 1633, the Hutchinsons emigrated to New England and one of them, William, married Ann Marbury who owned Rhode Island. Later, they were ejected from the island by the Puritans; Ann and her children were killed by Indians in 1643. Another Hutchinson, Thomas, became the first Governor of Massachusetts Bay. In 1648, Richard P. Hutchinson returned to England where his support for Cromwell's Irish campaign earned him the reward of extensive lands in Tipperary and Waterford and the house at Knocklofty. The family continued to live here right up until 1983.

NEWCASTLE
10 miles SW of Clonmel on minor road off the R665 or R671

Map 2 ref H14

Newcastle village lies beneath the intriguingly named Knockmealdown Mountains on a bend of the River Suir. For a taste of the real Ireland, you can't do better than stay here at one of Helen and Liam McGrath's two self-catering properties, **Tailor's Cottage** and **Mulhough Cottage**. Helen teaches Gaelic to schoolchildren and is also a registered Local Tour Guide. If you join one of her walks through the Knockmealdown mountains you will hear traditional Irish music on the mountain, played by Helen on the accordion and tin whistle.

Both of the McGrath's two cottages are 3-star Board Fáilte approved and well-equipped with amenities such as washing machine and dryer. They both enjoy grand views of the

Tailor's Cottage, Newcastle Village, Clonmel, Co. Tipperary
Tel: 052 36359 Fax: 052 36612 website: http://www.tipp.ie/nscater.htm

Galtee, Commeragh and Knockmealdown mountains. Tailor's Cottage, which sleeps 5, is a beautifully restored 2-storey cottage, built around 1890, with an old fashioned open fire in the sitting room (fuel is provided). Molough Cottage sits on one acre of grounds overlooking the River Suir just one kilometre away. The area is ideal for touring and fishing, and the coast is just 30 minutes away. As Helen would say, "Céad Míle Fáilte!"

CAHIR
MAP 2 REF H14

14 miles SE of Tipperary on the N24

Beautifully set on the River Suir, this appealing little town is dominated by the magnificent 15th century **Cahir Castle**, one of those which Cromwell's troops "knocked about a bit" but which has recently been superbly restored. The castle stands on a rocky islet in the Suir, its great outer walls enclosing three separate 'wards', the inner one protected by a sturdy gate and portcullis. The Irish chieftain Conor O'Brien, was the first to build a fortress here but the present building Cahir Castle was built as a stronghold of the Butler family, Dukes of Ormonde. The massive structure survived largely unscathed from both the assault of the Earl of Essex in 1599 and of Cromwell in 1647. The castle's attractions include an excellent audio-visual show, "Partly Hidden and Partly Revealed", which introduces visitors to all the major sights of south Tipperary.

The town itself has considerable charm, with colourfully painted houses, a broad main square and many traditional shops looking as if they have not changed for decades. Another attractive feature of the town is that Cahir has always been noted for its lack of religious bigotry - at one time Protestants and Catholics used to worship simultaneously in the now-ruined church with only a curtain wall between them. The famous Regency architect, John Nash, has two strong connections with the town. St Paul's Church was built around 1820 to one of his designs and a very different kind of structure, also designed by him, stands just outside the town on the Clonmel road. The **Swiss Cottage** is an interesting oddity, a delightful thatched "cottage orné" built in the early 1800s for Richard Butler, 1st Earl of Glengall. Recently restored, the interior of this rustic summerhouse contains a graceful spiral staircase and some elegantly decorated rooms. The original hand-painted wallpaper in the Salon, manufactured by the Dufour factory, is one of the first commercially produced Parisian wallpapers. The Cottage is open from March to November and access is by guided tour only.

Another attraction within easy reach of Cahir is **Mitchelstown Cave**, just off the N8 road to Mitchelstown. Visitors are guided through almost half a mile of incredible dripstone formations - stalagmites, stalactites, huge calcite columns and one of Europe's finest columns, the inspiring Tower of Babel which stands some 30ft high. There are three massive caverns - one of them measuring 200x160 feet. The cave is open daily throughout the year.

POULNAMUCKY Map 2 ref H13
6 miles NW of Clonmel on the R687

Conveniently located in the triangle formed by Clonmel, Cashel and Cahir, **Farrenwick Country House** offers luxury accommodation in a spacious modern house. All the rooms are en suite with TV, telephone and tea/coffee making facilities. Children are welcome, with a family room available. Farrenwick, which is a non-smoking house, is the home of Denis and Kay Fahey who provide a genuinely warm welcome to all their guests. Denis is a regular tour guide and is happy to take you around the area or direct you to the many places of interest within easy reach. One of the nearest is Cahir Castle, just 6 miles away, this was one of the most important castles in Ireland. It is picturesquely set on a rocky island in the River Suir and is well worth a visit. Historic Cashel with its famous Rock should also not be missed. Other attractions just a short drive away include the Fethard

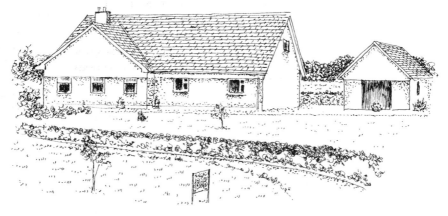

Farrenwick Country House, Poulnamucky, Curranstown, Clonmel, South Tipperary Tel: 052 35130 Fax: 052 35377 e-mail: kayden@clubi.ie website: www.theaa.co.uk/regionlb/81934.html

Farm Museum, St Patrick's Well, Mitchelstown Caves, the Nire Valley, Lismore Castle, Mount Mellary Abbey and, at Carrick-on-Suir, the splendid Ormonde Castle, one of the finest examples of an Irish manor house. It was built by "Black Tom", the 10th Duke of Ormonde, in preparation for a visit by his cousin, Elizabeth I. Sadly, she never arrived.

TIPPERARY
Map 2 REF G13
24 miles NW of Clonmel on the N24

An important dairy-farming centre, Tipperary is very much a traditional Irish town, its amenities geared up for local people rather than tourists. This honest-to-goodness approach is refreshing, providing as it does an authentic feel of the real Ireland. Despite its agricultural preoccupations, Tipperary suffered badly during the Anglo-Irish and Civil War strife. Various granite statues around the town commemorate heroes of those conflicts and the town's small museum displays some poignant memorabilia of the time. There are letters written from prison by Seán Tracey, a violin belonging to Joseph Mary Plunkett, (a poet executed in the 1916 rising), and some moving photographs of the young, fresh-faced officers of the old IRA who were involved in the uprising.

Tipperary is surrounded by wonderfully scenic countryside, with the Glen of Aherlow and the grand Galtee Mountains lying just a few miles to the south. There is some splendid ridge-walking in the mountains, especially around Lyracappul, but before leaving the town you should try out one of the town's atmospheric hostelries. Highly recommended is **Donovan's Pub** in O'Brien Street, one of only 3 pubs in the town which have passed down through three generations of the same family. The present landlord is John Dono-

Donovan's, O'Brien Street, Tipperary Town, Co. Tipperary
Tel: 062 51384 e-mail: padroigoc@tinet.ie
website: http://www.tipp.ie/donovans-pub.htm

van who presides over this bright and spacious hostelry with its lovely welcoming atmosphere. A feature to look out for in the pub is John's fine collection of sporting memorabilia. Donovan's hosts Irish music nights every night of the week except for Tuesday and Thursday - a splendid opportunity for visitors to enjoy a relaxing traditional Irish night out. Food is taken very seriously at Donovan's with all the dishes prepared from top quality fresh ingredients and attractively presented. The dinner menu might include a starter of finest oak-cured Irish salmon served with home made wholemeal brown bread; a main course of prime Sirloin Steak accompanied by a whiskey and mushroom sauce, with the meal rounded off by a delicious dessert. Meals can be enjoyed either in the attractive restaurant area or, in good weather, in Donovan's extensive Beer Garden. Lunch is served daily from 12.30pm to 2.30pm; evening meals from 5.30pm to 9pm every day. The pub is happy to cater for family functions and celebrations, and bus tours are also welcome.

MONARD   Map 2 ref G13
3 miles NW of Tipperary on the N24

The village of Monard lies right on the county boundary, just a few steps away from Co. Limerick. Tipperary Racecourse is little more than a mile away and the village boasts its very own 18-hole golf course. Located right next to the Golf and Country Club, **Ballykisteen Lodge** offers high quality bed and breakfast accommodation in a wonderfully peaceful setting. Your welcoming hosts are Angela and Douglas Edinborough who make every effort to ensure that guests in their spacious home enjoy their visit to the full. The Lodge is open all year round and all the comfortable rooms are en suite, with colour television, tea/ coffee-making facilities, and central heating, and there's also a residents'

Ballykisteen Lodge, Ballykisteen, Monard, Co. Tipperary
Tel: 062 33403

TV lounge. Breakfast comes with a choice of menus. The Lodge stands in beautiful gardens and it's just a short drive to the Heritage Town of Tipperary. The historic town of Cashel with its famous Rock and Cathedral is only a few miles further.

DUNDRUM
8 miles NE of Tipperary on the R661/R505

MAP 2 REF H13

Gardeners will want to pay a visit to the **Celtic Plantarum Dundrum** on the edge of the village. The 8-acre site offers a dazzling display of some 60,000 plants of more than 2000 varieties, specialising in native Irish plants. Features within the Plantarum have a Celtic theme - a crannóg, dolmen, fairy fort, and so on, and the site includes lakes, a waterfall and water display, and an extensive garden centre.

Dundrum is an attractive village, sitting at the edge of the Galtee Mountains surrounded by wooded hills and farmland. A couple of hundred years ago, 29,000 acres of this land formed the estate of Lord Maude whose agent, or factor, occupied the charming house which now provides the nucleus of **Rectory House Hotel**. (The house became a Church of Ireland rectory in Victorian times, finally being converted to a hotel in 1980).

Rectory House Hotel, Dundrum, Co. Tipperary
Tel: 062 71266 Fax: 062 71115

It's an appealing building, an appeal enhanced by the 10 acres of beautiful grounds in which it stands. A tree planted to commemorate Queen Victoria's visit to Ireland stands proudly on the front lawn and a path leads from the hotel gardens to the Plantarum mentioned above. Inside the house there are many interesting features such as the wooden beam which slides out of the wall to barricade the front door. Elegant rooms with high ceilings, period furniture and mirrors, all contribute to the gracious atmosphere and there's also that warm, indefinable quality you only seem to find in family-run hotels. In this case the family is Jimmy Sheils and Tina Doyle, ably abetted by their daughter Jennifer. Jimmy and Tina settled here a few years ago after many years in the hospitality business and their experience ensures that guests are very well looked after indeed.

A member of the Best Western family of hotels, Rectory House takes its cuisine very seriously, offering an excellent à la carte menu with choices ranging from Traditional Irish Stew to Picatta Fillet of Pork Italienne, along with seasonal game and fish dishes and vegetarian options. The accommodation at Rectory House is equally satisfying. Of the 10 guest bedrooms, 2 are so large they could be described as "semi-suites", while downstairs there are 4 purpose-built bedrooms all with easy wheelchair access. An exceptional hotel in every way.

CASHEL   Map 2 ref H13
11 miles E of Tipperary on the N74/N8

Cashel is one of Ireland's most historical sites with a magical cluster of medieval buildings crowning the great limestone outcrop, the **Rock of Cashel**, that rises spectacularly from the surrounding plain. Legend has it that the Rock was created by the Devil who in one of his understandable rages had bitten a huge chunk of rock from the Slieve Bloom Mountains. He was flying across the plain with the massive rock in his mouth when he caught sight of St Patrick standing ready to found a new church on the site. Startled, he dropped

Rock of Cashel

the rock which fell to earth thus creating this striking feature. It was at Cashel also that St Patrick plucked a shamrock and used it to explain the doctrine of the Trinity - God the Father, God the Son and God the Holy Ghost. Since that time the shamrock has become Ireland's unofficial emblem.

A good way to get your bearings in this memorable town is to take the tram tour which departs from the Heritage Centre at the Town Hall. The highlight of the tour is of course the buildings on the Rock itself. The oldest structure here is the lofty **Round Tower**, constructed during the 1100s and with an entrance some twelve feet above the ground. **Cormac's Chapel**, built between 1127 and 1134, is the oldest and most beautiful of Ireland's surviving Romanesque churches, its walls ornately carved with beasts and human figures. The chapel takes its name from Cormac, King-Bishop of Munster, who is believed to be buried here in an exquisitely decorated sarcophagus. The largest structure in this rich complex is the roofless 12th century **Cathedral** which despite its ruined state is still remarkably graceful. In 1647 the cathedral witnessed one of the worst atrocities of Cromwell's war. As his troops, under the command of Lord Iniquin, approached the town, the citizens of Cashel fled to the sanctuary of the cathedral. Iniquin, ordered his soldiers to pile turf around the walls and set it alight. Hundreds were roasted to death.

The nearby **Hall of the Vicars** was built in the 1400s as a grace and favour residence for senior members of the cathedral choir; it now contains a museum displaying St Patrick's Cross, a unique kind of high cross which stands on a broad plinth believed to be the coronation stone of the High Kings of Munster.

In the town itself, the **GPA Bolton Library** houses an impressive collection of almost 12,000 antiquarian books and rare manuscripts, the oldest of which date back to the 12th century. The Library also has a fine collection of church silver and a display of the altarware used in the original cathedral on the Rock. (The GPA in the Library's name refers to Guinness Peat Aviation which provided the major funding for a complete renovation of the 160 year old dwelling in which the Library is housed).

In Dominic Street, the **Cashel Folk Village** has a fascinating range of reconstructions of traditional thatched village shops, a forge and other businesses. (Vegetarians would be well-advised to decline a visit to the butcher's shop). There's also a penal Chapel and an extensive display of signs and other commercial memorabilia.

During the summer season, devotees of Irish traditional music can indulge their interest at the **Brú Ború** which presents a colourful performance of Irish music, song and dance every evening from Tuesday to Saturday inclusive. The complex includes a restaurant and a centre for the study and celebration of native Irish traditions.

Located right in the heart of Cashel, **Ashmore House** is a classical Georgian town house, built in 1740 with spacious rooms 12 feet high. Ornate plasterwork, beautiful fireplaces and mirrors, and elegant furniture all contribute to the olde-worlde charm. The sitting room is also in the Georgian style with a large open fireplace, a relaxing setting in which to sit and make your plans for the next day's exploration of Cashel and the Tipperary countryside. Ashmore House is the home of Brendan and Laura Ryan who have been welcoming guests for bed and breakfast accommodation for more than a decade. They

Ashmore House, John Street, Cashel, Co. Tipperary
Tel: 062 61286 Fax: 062 62789 e-mail: ashmorehouse@yahoo.iol

have five tastefully decorated letting rooms, 3 of which are en suite. They include double, twin and family rooms, each offering both old-world and modern comforts. In the morning, guests will find an extensive breakfast menu with everything freshly cooked to order and served in the spacious dining room. Ashmore House also boasts its own walled garden, a lovely and peaceful sanctuary, as well as private off-street parking. The house's central location means that all the town's attractions are just a short walk away. The world-famous Rock of Cashel, crowned by historic buildings, is a must-visit site and also not to be missed is the famous Bolton Library, right next door to Ashmore House, which contains the smallest book in the world. During the summer months, nearby Brú Ború offers an authentic celebration of traditional Irish culture in music, song and dance.

Carmel is a delightful place to use as a base for exploring County Tipperary and **Ardmayle House** offers visitors a choice of either bed and breakfast or self-catering accommodation. Ardmayle is the family home of Annette Vere Hunt, located on a 300 acre working farm. It's a handsome Georgian house with creeper covered walls outside and a warm welcome inside. Annette and her family have a great love of horses so there are usually some of their equine friends in the spacious stables. Ardmayle has a relaxing, away from it all atmosphere and it's here that bed and breakfast guests stay. Breakfast is included in the tariff and evening meals are available by arrangement. Annette also has 2 inviting old cottages for those who prefer self-catering. These attractive properties have

Ardmayle House, Cashel, Co. Tipperary Tel: 0504 42399 Fax: 0504 42420
e-mail: ardmayle@iol.ie   website: http://www.iol.ie/tipp/ardmaylh.htm

been sensitively modernised to combine up-to-date amenities with old-world charm. Ardmayle is just a few minutes drive from the historic Rock of Cashel, the 12th century Cormac's Chapel, and the famous Bolton Abbey whose collection of 12,000 volumes includes the "Smallest Book in the World".

BALLYNURE   Map 2 ref H13
4 miles NE of Cashel on the R691

This peaceful village in the Slieveardagh Hills is best known locally for the quality farmhouse cheeses made here and for an outstanding guest house. As it happens, both attractions are at the same address. Set in a panoramic scenic location on a 120-acre working farm, **Derrynaflan** is a handsome 18th century farmhouse which stands on the site of a 15th century castle. Generations of the O'Sullivan family have lived here for more than 200 years, with Sheila and Ned O'Sullivan the present incumbents. The farm is well-known for its award-winning cheeses, one of which has won the top Irish prize for semi-soft farmhouse cheese. Derrynaflan stands in attractive gardens with pleasant views across the Tipperary landscape. The house is furnished with elegant antique furniture throughout and has 5 guest bedrooms, 4 of which are en suite and 2 are large family rooms. In addition to breakfast, light meals and evening meals are also available. The choice includes dishes prepared with beef from the farm, local salmon, lamb and fresh vegetables - and of course some of that prize-winning cheese. Packed lunches can be provided on request. Children are welcome at Derrynaflan and the O'Sullivans also organise walking holidays. Other activities available in the neighbourhood include pony trekking, golfing, and fishing, and in the evening you'll find good country pub entertain-

Derrynaflan, Ballynure, Cashel, South Tipperary
Tel: 052 56406 e-mail: dnaflan@iol.ie website: http://www.tipp.ie/derrynaf.htm

ment nearby. Not to be missed is a visit to Cashel, just 4 miles away, with its famous Rock, cathedral and medieval chapel.

HORSE AND JOCKEY   MAP 2 REF H13
6 miles N of Cashel on the N8

Where else in the world, one wonders, would you find a village that has taken its name from an inn? The **Horse and Jockey Inn** was already well-established here in the mid-1700s, sitting at an important crossroad in the heart of County Tipperary. The village

Horse and Jockey Inn, Horse and Jockey, Thurles, Co. Tipperary
Tel: 0504 44192

grew up around the inn and eventually assumed its name. And the name is significant since several of Ireland's leading racecourses and training stables are only a few miles from the inn. It's not unusual for guests to find themselves rubbing shoulders with key players in this cherished sport - and often in a celebratory atmosphere! The inn's legendary reputation for hospitality continues to attract luminaries from not just the sporting world, but also from the political, commercial and cultural communities. Even while playing host to such local, national and international dignitaries, a homely and friendly Tipperary atmosphere prevails throughout. The Horse and Jockey has recently completed an extensive renovation programme and now offers its customers a spacious lounge and bar, a high quality restaurant and a modern conference centre. The 33 bedrooms and suites are all equipped with state-of-the-art facilities and include specialised accommodation for asthma sufferers and disabled persons. Happily, the thorough face-lift hasn't changed the heart of the inn. The words of an old poet who sang the praises of the Horse and Jockey Inn many years ago still ring true:

> *It is there you will find it,*
>
> *More friendship than is in all Ireland's grounds.*
>
> *God bless you my Inn, Horse and Jockey.*
>
> *O where can your likes be found.*

HOLY CROSS
4 miles SW of Thurles on the R660/R661

MAP 2 REF H13

The story of **Holy Cross Abbey** is an uplifting saga that spans more than eight centuries and, unusually for Irish medieval churches, has a happy ending. The tale begins in 1168 when Donal O'Brien, King of Munster, founded the Abbey as a worthy shrine for a particle of the True Cross which had been presented to his father by Pope Paschal II. Pilgrims flocked in their thousands to the Abbey to venerate the holy relic. Their donations enabled the Cistercian monks to employ the most accomplished craftsmen to embellish the Abbey with superb features such as the traceried windows and the stone *sedilia*, (seats reserved for the clergy), so delicately sculpted in limestone they resemble the work of a master woodcarver. When Henry VIII officially suppressed the monastery in 1536, the protection of the local magnates, the Earls of Ormonde, allowed the monks at Holy Cross to stay in residence for another century. But Cromwell's ruthless repression of Catholicism finally closed the Abbey. Over the years the fabric deteriorated, the roof collapsed and for 200 years Holy Cross Abbey stood forlornly as one of the *"bare, ruined choirs"* that Shakespeare alluded to. Then, in 1975, funds made available as part of the European Architectural Heritage Year made possible a complete restoration of the Abbey. It is now once again in full use as the parish church for the village.

If you are touring this northern corner of the county, an excellent place to stay is **Boherna Lodge**. Enjoying lovely views of the Tipperary countryside, Boherna Lodge offers first class bed and breakfast accommodation in this historic village. Decked in summer with hanging baskets of flowers, the Lodge is the home of Anna and Robert Stakelum and their two daughters Laura and Sinèad. Anna has been in the hospitality business for some 25 years, spending sixteen of those managing a 4-star hotel so she certainly knows how to

Boherna Lodge, Tipperary Road, Holy Cross, Thurles, Co. Tipperary
Tel: 0504 43121

pamper her guests, welcoming them on arrival with complimentary tea or coffee and scones. The Lodge is a spacious modern bungalow, purpose-built as a guest house with 4 letting rooms - 2 doubles and 1 twin en suite, 1 twin with its own bathroom just across the corridor. Each bedroom is bright and airy and individually decorated with quality modern furnishings. The house has a separate dining room for guests overlooking the rear garden which visitors are welcome to use. A full Irish breakfast is served and special dietary needs can be catered for, and Anna is also happy to provide evening meals and packed lunches on request. Boherna Lodge provides an ideal base for the Rock of Cashel and Kilkenny, with golf, fishing and forest walks all available nearby.

THURLES   MAP 2 REF H12
20 miles NE of Tipperary on the R661

Thurles is a busy, workaday market town and also the cathedral town of the archdiocese of Cashel and Emly. The late-Victorian cathedral of 1875, with its lofty 125ft-high campanile, is a landmark for many miles around but until 1998 Thurles featured on very few visitor itineraries. Then in July of that year the south of Ireland was presented with its first Microbrewery, Pub and Restaurant. Housed in a striking mid-Victorian building, **Dwan** is the brainchild of Bill Dwan whose family has a long and proud tradition of producing quality Irish minerals and importing fine wines and spirits from around the world. Bill has united these traditions to create a delicious and authentic range of beers brewed in his very own craft brewery.

Dwan beers are made from the best of Irish ingredients - Irish water, Irish malted barley and wheat, and their own unique yeast,- combined with the finest hops from the United States, the United Kingdom and Germany. In Bill's opinion, small is beautiful. His hops are flown in from their country of origin in small amounts to maintain their flavour and aroma. The beers are brewed in small batches so they do not need to be pasteurised. This means that every beer is at its peak in terms of freshness when you drink it, with no additives or preservatives.

The brewery produces about 6,000 litres of beer a week. The range of 5 beers includes a traditional Irish extra stout named An Dubháin, (The Dark One); Rich Ruby, a fruity and aromatic ale which won a gold medal at the Stockholm Beer Festival only 3 months after it was first produced; a European pilsener style beer, Cool Amber; Black Pearl; and Silver Frost, an American style lager.

The old granary provides a dramatic setting for the restaurant, its ceiling rising the full 3-storey height of the building. There's also a spacious pub area with high tables and stools. During the day, the restaurant offers a good selection of well-presented starters, snacks and main meals supplemented by

Dwan Brew Pub and Restaurant, The Mall, Thurles, Co. Tipperary Tel: 0504 26007 Fax: 0504 26060 e-mail: dwan@eircom.net website: http://www.tipp.ie/dwan.htm

Specials of the Day. In the evening, the Dwan's chef excels himself by providing a menu of delicious choices which always include vegetarian options. If you appreciate superb food and prime beers served in an unusual setting, Dwan is definitely the place to seek out.

NENAGH
23 miles NW of Thurles on the R498/N7

Map 2 ref G12

The administrative centre of north Tipperary, Nenagh was once an important Anglo-Norman settlement and then a major Franciscan centre until Cromwell's troops destroyed their Friary. Nowadays there's little to detain visitors here apart from the remains of **Nenagh Castle**, built in 1217, whose massive circular Keep with walls 20ft thick still dominates the town. The rest of the castle succumbed partly to the ravages of time, partly to the badly-placed explosives of a farmer trying to rid the castle of its infestation of sparrows' nests.

ARDCRONEY
5 miles N of Nenagh on the N52

Map 2 ref G11

From the moment guests arrive at **Ashley Park House** they realise that this is no ordinary bed & breakfast accommodation. The long driveway to the house offers some superb views of Lough Ourna, framed by the ring forts on the shore and the Slieve Bloom Mountains beyond. Set in 76 acres of beech woodland and formal gardens, the house is an 18th

Ashley Park House, Ardcroney, Nenagh, Co. Tipperary
Tel: 067 38223 Fax: 067 38013 website: http://www.ashleypark.com/

century mansion which has been faithfully restored to its original splendour, complete with fine period furniture. Visitors enter through the octagonal hallway and are guided to their rooms past the grandfather clock on the hallway and upstairs past the stained glass windows. True to the period, the bedrooms have a generous aspect and retain the original decorative features. Most rooms have views of the lake and all are en suite.

After freshening up, visitors are served afternoon tea in the drawing room, after which they might like to take a walk around the gardens or maybe row around the lake, visiting the ruins of the fort on the island.

Dinner can be booked in advance and taken in the large dining room, looking out across the lake. All tastes are catered for, including vegetarians. After dinner, coffee is served in the Chinese Reading Room or on the terrace. If it's too cold outside, visitors can settle down in front of a roaring fire before retiring to the large comfortable beds with crisp white cotton sheets.

After breakfast, (either full Irish or Continental with fresh fruit), the area offers a wide range of indoor and outdoor activities including fishing, golf, sailing, horse riding and hiking. In the evening, for those seeking a little entertainment, traditional Irish music can be heard in many of the local pubs.

Ashley Park House has a long history. Back in 1786 the *Post-Chaise Companion* noted that it was *"pleasantly situated, near a fine lough"*. More than 200 years later, Ashley Park still provides an 18th century escape from the hustle of a 20th century lifestyle.

TERRYGLASS   MAP 2 REF G11
12 miles N of Nenagh on the R493

"Relax in rural bliss!" is the message from Lucy and Tom Sanders whose family home, **Riverrun**, is situated in the heart of Terryglass, one of Ireland's prettiest villages, (a winner of Ireland's Tidiest Towns competition). It is indeed a great place to relax and wind down, whether sunning yourself in the secluded south-facing garden or strolling down to the village pub for a pint and a meal. A five minute walk will bring you to the harbour on Lough Derg, the largest lake on the Shannon, and if you enjoy fishing, the Sanders have

Riverrun House, Terryglass, Nenagh, North Tipperary
Tel: 067 22125 Fax: 067 22187 e-mail: riverrun@iol.ie

two boats available for hire. Riverrun has its own hard tennis court and there are four 18-hole golf courses within half an hour's drive. One of them is just 5 miles away at Portumna where it's also worth visiting the ruined Priory, the early 17th century Portumna Castle, and the Portumna Forest Park. Riverrun itself is a charming, pink-washed house which was built in 1992 but since it was designed in traditional style looks as if it has been standing here for ever. There are 5 guest bedrooms, all en suite and provided with telephone and tea/coffee making facilities. A baby sitting service is available if required and the house has secure private parking. It's no surprise to find that Riverrun has been widely recommended in many guide books to Ireland.

4 The Southwest

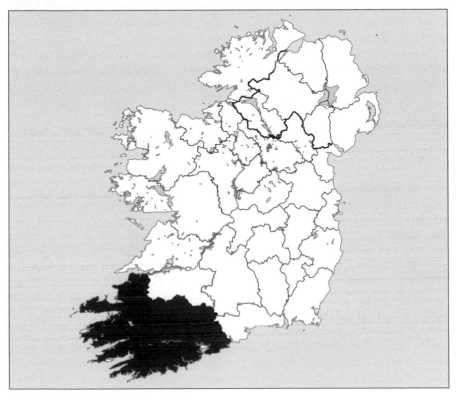

© MAPS IN MINUTES ™ (1998)

COUNTY CORK

The tourist board slogan "Ireland in Miniature" is actually a faithful description of this appealing county. In the north, the beautiful Blackwater Valley is framed by high mountains, while in the east a gentler landscape extends to the coast with its historic ports of Youghal and Cobh. To the west, a series of rocky peninsulas grope out into the Atlantic and scattered islands create some magical seascapes.

The southwest corner is where the Gulf Stream first hits land. Its moderating warmth creates a wonderfully mild climate that varies very little over the year. Wonderful subtropical gardens like the one on Garinish Island flourish in these benign conditions and the accompanying rainfall has helped make Cork an important dairy county.

The county is also home to one of Ireland's premier attractions, the Blarney Stone at Blarney Castle where hundreds of visitors each day kiss the stone in the hope of acquiring the gift of eloquence. The Castle itself is an outstandingly well-preserved 15th century building but the county has comparatively few grand buildings that pre-date the 19th century cathedral building boom which saw the construction of ornate Gothic structures such as St Finbarr's in Cork and St Colman's at Cobh. A notable exception is Bantry House, in the west, a gracious Georgian mansion packed full of fine furniture and works of art.

What it lacks in ancient buildings, Cork County makes up for with a wide range of holiday activities, most notably angling. If your interest is fine cuisine, the historic port of Kinsale is considered the gourmet capital of Ireland, and wherever you go in the county you'll never be far from a traditional pub resounding to the plangent strains of Irish music.

CORK

Ireland's second largest city and capital of the Republic's largest county, Cork is a captivating place with a character all of its own. It stands on an island in the River Lee so creating a compact city centre and a pleasing townscape of elegant bridges and old stone quaysides, all bathed in the soft reflected light of the water. This is a city to savour on foot - strolling the quaysides, browsing for bargains in Coal Quay Market (not too proud to describe itself as a "flea-market"), or wandering along French Church Street with its modish restaurants and pavement cafés.

The city's name comes from the Gaelic *Corcaigh*, meaning a marshy place, which is exactly what it was when St Finbarr established an Abbey and school here in the 7th century. The imposing triple-spired **St Finbarr's Cathedral**, an exuberant 19th century Gothic building designed by William Burges, stands on the site of the long-vanished Abbey. Most of Cork's major buildings date from the same era as the Cathedral, with some outstanding works by Pugin and Pain: together they give the city a satisfying architectural unity.

The city's lack of older buildings is the consequence of its unfortunate knack for invariably supporting the losing side in any conflict that might be under way - and getting ransacked as a result. The people of Cork rallied to Perkin Warbeck in his rebellion against Henry VII, they fought for Charles I against Cromwell, and threw in their lot with the hapless James II in 1690. It was this last misguided enterprise that led to the demolition of the city's medieval fortifications along with its Tudor and Stuart period houses.

Fortunately, some later buildings have survived, most notably the fine Georgian **Church of St Anne's**, Sandon (1750). It's easy to find - just scan the skyline for a tower topped by a huge weathervane in the form of an 11-feet long salmon. A climb to the top of the tower is rewarded by some grand views and the chance to ring out a tune on its famous bells. (Sheet music provided).

Close by is the **Cork Butter Exchange**, a complex of sturdy 19th century buildings in the Classical style which now house an interesting colony of up-market craft shops. Also

19th century is the castle-like **Cork City Gaol** where an imaginative taped tour will guide you through the routine horrors of life in a Victorian penitentiary. The impact is heightened by amazingly lifelike figures and evocative sound effects. A separate exhibition within the gaol precincts is called the **Radio Museum Experience**. Back in 1927, the Governor's House was chosen as the unlikely base for radio station 6CK and this recently opened exhibition is housed in the original studio. It incorporates the Radio Telefis Éireann Museum Collection along with displays illuminating with the early days of Irish and international radio broadcasting.

Cork is the undisputed cultural capital of southern Ireland, hosting a major Film Festival in early October, a popular International Jazz Festival later that month, an International Choral Festival in early May, and a lively Folk Festival in September. Throughout the year, the Triskel Arts Centre, the Cork Opera House, the Kino art house cinema, and the Firkin Crane dance centre between them offer a huge variety of concerts, plays and ballets sufficient to sate the appetite of the most voracious culture vulture.

EAST OF CORK

FOTA ISLAND   MAP 2 REF G16
6 miles E of Cork on the R624

A popular excursion from Cork is to **Fota Wildlife Park** on Fota Island, one of several islands lying within Cork Harbour. Fota teems with wildlife - birds thronging the mudflats; apes, cheetahs, red pandas and giraffes roaming the landscaped acres of the Fota House estate. The house itself, a striking early 19th century mansion designed by Richard Morrison, is currently not open to the public but its elegant proportions can be admired from the park. Visitors are welcome at the estate's Arboretum which is stocked with many species rarely seen elsewhere in Ireland.

COBH   MAP 2 REF G16
12 miles E of Cork on the R624

Cobh (pronounced Cove) is a complete delight and should on no account be missed. Its huge neo-Gothic **cathedral**, designed by Pugin and built of blue-grey Dalkey granite, dominates the picturesque little town and its bustling harbour. Despite having one of the finest natural harbours in the world, this small fishing village was virtually unknown up to the early 1800s, (although Sir Francis Drake did take refuge here when his ships were outnumbered by those of the Spanish Armada). With the advent of the French Revolutionary and Napoleonic wars, between 1792 and 1815, the harbour became an important refuelling point for naval and commercial ships. Tall ships called to transport convicts to Australia and to carry Irish emigrants to North America. Later, the early transatlantic steamers and finally the great ocean liners continued the task of carrying the Irish to new lives in new lands. From 1848-1950 over 6 million adults and children emigrated from Ireland - about 2.5 million embarked at Cobh making it the single most important port of emigration.

Today, Cobh's unique origins, its history and the legacy are dramatically recalled at **The Queenstown Story** - a multi-media exhibition housed in Cobh's Victorian railway station. (Cobh was renamed Queenstown following a visit by Queen Victoria in 1849, a name it retained until the establishment of the Irish Republic in 1922). The exhibition also recalls two great ships associated with the town. The *Lusitania* was sunk by a German submarine off the coast here in 1915 and several hundred of the 1198 passengers who perished are buried in Cobh's old graveyard. Three years earlier, Cobh had been the last port of call for the ill-fated *Titanic*.

A more cheerful claim to fame is the town's historic **Yacht Club**, founded in 1720 and the oldest yacht club in the world. The Club hosts an annual Regatta in mid-August and in early September the town is the home port for the International Sea Angling Festival.

If you plan to stay in Cobh, the ideal place for an intimate weekend or a relaxing family break is the **Bella Vista House Hotel**.. This beautiful Victorian villa occupies a perfect location above the picturesque town and enjoys tremendous views of Cork harbour and St Colman's Cathedral. Bella Vista has an interesting history. James Verling, the doctor who attended Napoleon on St Helena, lived in the manor house and died there in 1858, a connection which is marked by the naming of the Napoleon and Josephine suite, and also of the Napoleon restaurant. The guest reading lounge is another room steeped in history. It was here that Fr. Browne, the now famous photographer, gave his magic lantern show of photographs of the *Titanic* on her maiden voyage from Southampton to Cobh. This is a charming room with beautiful oil paintings lining the walls and views through the many windows of real life landscapes that would challenge any artist's brush. The views from Napoleon's Restaurant are equally breathtaking. This conservatory dining room is becoming increasingly famous for the quality of the food, with chef Michael Hourigan offering a superb menu along with additional specials such as Baked Duo Breast

Bella Vista House Hotel, Bishop's Road, Cobh, Co. Cork
Tel: 021 812450 Fax: 021 812215
e-mail: bellavis@indigo.ie website: http://indigo.ie/~bellavis

of Guinea Fowl with an onion compote Madeira jus or, as "Catch of the Day", Poached fillet of Brill stuffed with shrimp and crabmeat on a dill & pernod flavoured sauce. The accommodation at Bella Vista is just as splendid. The house has been completely renovated to provide the ideal combination of modern comfort and traditional style and hospitality. The hotel now offers 16 spacious, individually decorated guest rooms, all with private bath, satellite TV and direct dial telephones. Ten of the rooms command magnificent views of the harbour and cathedral. Other attractions at Bella Vista include a welcoming bar, wheelchair friendly rooms and courteous, friendly service.

Heather Bird paid her first visit to Cobh in 1966, fell in love with the area, and some 12 years ago acquired **The Lodge**, just 5 minutes drive from the town centre. Heather had the old house substantially modernised while still keeping much of its original character and it is now available for self-catering visitors. Situated in the countryside, with views of

The Lodge, Bookings through Mrs Heather Bird, Ballydulea, Cobh, Co. Cork
Tel: 021 811260

sea and farmland, The Lodge is attractively furnished and equipped with every conceivable mod. con. including electric cooker, fridge, washing machine, drier, microwave, colour TV/video, and pay phone. Bed linen and towels are also provided, as well as electric blankets in all beds. As an extra welcoming touch, you will find a pack of fresh Irish produce waiting for you on arrival.

The accommodation downstairs consists of a small kitchen/dining room with an open fire, a large sunny conservatory (ideal for dining), two bedrooms (1 twin, 1 single), and shower/w.c. An unusual feature of the house is the small stairway which leads from the kitchen, upstairs to a third bedroom, twin-bedded with en suite shower/w.c. Although The Lodge is semi-detached, it is completely separated from the small apartment next door and is very quiet and private with its own entrance and parking. There's a grassed area in front and a gravelled courtyard at the rear, surrounded by old style farm buildings.

This is a place where you can relax and read some of the many books in the house, but Heather has also prepared "Take 5", a long list of all the things you can do within a 5 minute drive from The Lodge. You can take a boat trip around the harbour, visit a bird sanctuary, sample smoked salmon fresh from the smoke-house, hear a recital on a 49-bell carillon, browse around quality gift shops, visit the magnificent St Colman's Cathedral, and much, much more. If you want to drive for 10 minutes, then you can visit Fota Wildlife Park, take a stroll around the world-famous arboretum, or play golf on an 18-hole course.

CARRIGTOHILL   Map 2 ref G15
9 miles E of Cork on the N25

Back on the mainland, near the village of Carrigtohill, stands **Barryscourt Castle** (Dúchas), the seat of the Barry family from the 12th to the 17th centuries. The present castle is a fine example of a 15th century tower house with 16th century additions and alterations. The original bawn (enclosure) wall with three corner towers is largely intact. Stage 1 of an ambitious restoration programme has been completed and successive areas of the castle will be opened to the public as the work proceeds. The ground floor houses an exhibition on the history of the Barrys and Barryscourt Castle and there's also a restaurant, tea shop and crafts shop.

MIDLETON   Map 2 ref G15
12 miles E of Cork on the N25

A bustling market town, Midleton was founded in the late 1600s by the Brodrick family, later Earls of Midleton. The Brodricks also established Midleton College as a free grammar school and later benefactors provided the town an elegant 18th century Market House in the main street. But the town is perhaps best known as the home of **Jameson's Distillery** where visitors can join a guided tour, test their expertise at tasting, and marvel at the colossal copper pot still, the largest in the world, with a capacity of 32,000 gallons. The tour also takes in the old water wheel, which is still in operation, before concluding with a complimentary glass of *uisce beatha* - the "water of life".

Popular though it is with visitors, the East Cork region has suffered from a shortage of quality, affordable accommodation. **Lynwen Lodge Guesthouse**, recently refurbished and upgraded, is helping to change all that. Located a mile to the west of Midleton, the Lodge is surrounded by 12 acres of lovingly tended gardens and orchards, a tranquil haven just a sparrow's hop from the N25. Thomas and Carol Scoutts-Gould arrived here in 1998 and their improvements have ushered in a new era for the Lodge which had already been a popular guest house for more than a quarter of a century. All the spruced-up en suite bedrooms are stylishly decorated: two of them on the ground floor have been made easily accessible for disabled people. The Lodge boasts an elegant dining room in which you can savour your full Irish breakfast and also, if you wish, linger later in the day over a table d'hôte 5-course sumptuous dinner or choose from the à la carte menu. You might then want to settle down in the Lodge's appealing sitting-room, decorated and furnished in a relaxing, modern style. Another attractive feature of Lynwen Lodge is the impressive

Lynwen Lodge, Midleton, Co. Cork
Tel/Fax: 021 631934

staircase which rises to the first floor where a rich red carpet leads you, royalty style, to whichever of the 8 en suite rooms is booked in your name. Children and groups are especially welcome at the Lodge, with special reductions available for groups. Tom and Carol can also offer conference facilities for small private or business parties and the Lodge's rural surroundings, despite being so close to Cork, make it an ideal venue where business and pleasure can be happily combined. A private car park with space for 40 cars may not be the most alluring of the Lodge's attractions, but it's certainly a useful one.

CLOYNE
MAP 2 REF G16

5 miles S of Midleton on the R629

About 5 miles south of Midleton, the somnolent village of Cloyne was an important religious centre for a thousand years and more. St Colman founded a monastery here in the 6th century on a site now occupied by the **Cathedral** bearing his name. This building dates back to 1250 but suffered badly at the hands of Victorian restorers. Nevertheless, it contains some striking monuments, amongst them the splendid alabaster tomb of the philosopher George Berkeley who was Bishop here from 1734 to 1753. Within the cathedral precincts stands the **Round Tower**, one of only two of these distinctive structures to be found in County Cork. Built in the 11th century, the Tower lost its conical roof in 1754 when it was struck by lightning. The 90 feet climb to the top of the Tower opens up some spectacular views.

CASTLEMARTYR
MAP 2 REF G16

5 miles E of Midleton on the N25

Standing on lands once owned by Sir Walter Raleigh, **The Demesne** is a striking 18th century farmhouse, one wing of which is available as a beautiful self-catering apartment. The estate was granted to Sir Walter by Elizabeth I but when he fell from grace and was imprisoned in the Tower of London he sold the lands to Richard Boyle, later Lord Shannon. The estate remained in his family for more than 300 years and The Demesne was built as a home for the Estate Steward. The Demesne is surrounded by 250 acres of mixed

The Demesne, Castlemartyr, Co. Cork
Tel: 021 667210

farming and set in peaceful wooded countryside. It is now the home of Bill and Barbara Bateman, having been in Bill's family since 1931. The self-catering wing has a large, comfortable sitting room with colour TV and an open fire for which the logs and lighting are provided free. The kitchen is well-equipped with electric cooker, fridge/freezer, toaster and microwave, and the electricity is paid for by meter. There are two bedrooms, one with a double bed, the other with two singles. Linen and electric blankets are supplied and a cot is available if required. The bathroom has a bath, shower and toilet, and the apartment also includes a Utility Room-cum-Playroom equipped with an automatic washing machine and tumble drier, snooker table, ring board and other games. (Please note that the whole of the apartment is *definitely* non-smoking). Outside, there's a beautiful garden which has been a labour of love for Barbara over some 20 years and is a delightful place to settle down with a good book. Garden furniture is provided. There are sandy beaches about 5 miles away, and facilities for lake or sea fishing available in the neighbourhood. Secluded though it is, The Demesne is easy to find. Turn off the N25 about a mile west of Castlemartyr, signposted to Cloyne, and you'll see the entrance straight ahead at Gate Lodge. Then just follow the signs.

GARRYVOE
MAP 2 REF G16

10 miles SE of Midleton on the R632 off the N25 Cork/Rosslare road at Castlemartyr

Just a few minutes from the 4-mile stretch of fine sandy beaches at Ballycotton Bay, **Moloney's Farmhouse** commands some panoramic scenery and offers a choice of either bed and breakfast or self-catering accommodation. B&B guests stay at Pat and Marion Maloney's smart modern bungalow where they are greeted with a warm welcome and, quite possibly, with the inviting aroma of bread and scones being baked. They make a

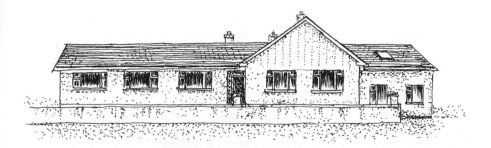

Moloney's Farmhouse, Garryvoe, Ladysbridge, Co. Cork
Tel: 021 66 7421 (end of 2000 changes to 021 466 7421)

delicious addition to the generous Irish breakfast provided by the Maloneys. The house
has 4 guest bedrooms, 3 of them en suite and 1 with a private bathroom, and all furnished
in an attractive traditional style. Pat and Marion moved here a few years ago from their
original family home nearby. This is where self-catering guests will find accommodation
comprising 3 bedrooms, a large well-equipped kitchen, dining and sitting rooms, and a
bathroom. The local attractions include Ballymaloe House & Cookery School, Trabolgan
Holiday Village, Fota Wildlife Park,Cobh Heritage, the Jameson Whisky Heritage Centre
and the Stephen Pearce Pottery.

YOUGHAL   MAP 2 REF H15
30 miles E of Cork on the N25

Unlike Cork, Youghal (pronounced Yawl) managed to be on the winning side during the
various conflicts that troubled the land. Consequently its town walls, originally built on
the orders of Edward I in 1275, are the best preserved in Ireland. The town is picturesquely
set at the mouth of the River Blackwater and for many centuries was a thriving port. The
prosperity of those days is reflected in some striking buildings: **Tynte's Castle** in Main
Street is a fine 16th century tower house; the **Red House** of 1710 is an attractive building
in the then-popular Dutch style; and there are some lovely old almshouses founded by
Richard Boyle, Earl of Cork, in the early 1600s.

Of special historical interest is **Myrtle Grove**, an Elizabethan gabled house which was
for a while the residence of Sir Walter Raleigh. Amongst the guests he entertained here
was his fellow-colonist, the poet Edmund Spenser. Three other buildings in the town are
also worth a look. There's a handsome **Clock Tower** built in 1777 to replace one of the
medieval town gates; a 19th century **Lighthouse** which stands on the site of St Anne's
Tower, a 12th century lighthouse which was manned by nuns until the mid-1500s; and in
William Street, the **Collegiate Church of St Mary's**. This is the largest medieval parish
church in Ireland and also one of the oldest still in use. It dates back to the early 1200s
and although much restored contains some outstanding medieval tombs and monuments.

About 3 miles outside Youghal, **Carn na Radharc** is a delightful modern bungalow
whose Gaelic name means "Hill of the View" and it does indeed enjoy magnificent views
of the wooded valley of the River Blackwater and the surrounding mountains. These

Carn na Radharc, Ardsallagh, Youghal, Co. Cork
Tel: 024 92703

superb vistas change not only with the seasons but even by the hour as the light alters. Located in a quiet cul-de-sac, Carn na Radharc provides a wonderfully peaceful spot where guests can relax in a spacious, landscaped garden with its pond and small waterfall. Your hosts, Maura and Pat Coughlan, will greet you with a warm welcome and tea or coffee along with home baked scones and cakes. If you arrive late from the ferry, a light meal of bread & cheese and cooked meats is available if you wish. Maura and Pat have 3 guest bedrooms, all of them en suite and non-smoking. There are 2 family rooms, one with 2 double beds, the other with 1 double bed and a single, while the third room is really a suite, with plenty of space to spread yourself. Children are welcome of course, with a cot available if required. The Coghlans serve a substantial breakfast, complete with an "Irish Fry" and although they do not provide evening meals, there are good pubs and restaurants within easy reach. Carn na Radhac is open from April 1st until October 31st and is an ideal base for exploring the counties of Cork and Waterford. A short walk from the house leads to the River Blackwater, there are some fine beaches locally, as well as facilities for golf, fishing and pony trekking. Only a little further afield are the heritage towns of Lismore, Cobh and, of course, Cork with its many historic and contemporary attractions.

NORTH AND WEST OF CORK

BLARNEY
5 miles NW of Cork on the R617

Map 2 ref F15

The **Blarney Stone** is sometimes referred to as Ireland's equivalent of the Crown Jewels and the queue waiting to perform the ritual of Kissing the Blarney certainly equals that at the Tower of London. The stone itself is an unremarkable limestone slab, 4 feet by 1 foot, but it is embedded in the outer wall of Blarney Castle, 83 feet above the ground. Those in

Blarney Castle

search of the gift of eloquence must lie on their back hanging over the parapet, legs held by two trusted friends, and then reach up to kiss the stone. If you have no head for heights, (or two reliable friends), resign yourself to a life of being tongue-tied and inarticulate.

The custom of kissing the Blarney Stone became popular with tourists in late-Victorian times but the legend originates in a story from the reign of Elizabeth I. The Lord of Blarney at that time was a silver-tongued Irishman, Dermot MacCarthy, who "could talk himself out of a noose". While apparently enthusiastically co-operating with the Queen's colonising ambitions, he managed to do absolutely nothing to put them into effect. Receiving yet another of MacCarthy's procrastinating letters, Elizabeth fumed "This is Blarney, all Blarney".

Blarney Castle itself is one of Ireland's oldest and most historic castles. It was built in 1446, with walls 18 feet thick in places, by another Dermot MacCarthy, King of South Munster, and was one of the strongest fortresses in Munster. The castle is open daily all year except over Christmas. Before the Blarney Stone put the village on the tourist map, the main local industry was producing woollen goods, an industry which has been revived at the **Blarney Woollen Mills** whose factory shop offers some outstanding bargains along with a large selection of crystal, china and gifts.

If you are planning to stay in the Blarney area and appreciate accommodation with a difference, **Maranatha Country House** is in a class of its own. Built in 1887, this impressive mansion is set on a hill and surrounded by 27 acres of beautiful private woodlands and meadows, well-tended gardens and lawns. A leisurely walk through the grounds runs past wonderful monkey puzzle trees and banks of mature rhododendrons.

The interior of Maranatha is even more striking. Olwen Venn, whose family has owned the property since 1945, is an accomplished interior decorator and every room in the house is an eye-opener. Swagged curtains and soft draperies create a romantic atmosphere in the high-ceilinged rooms which still retain the original plasterwork. Olwen's designs are daringly imaginative and exuberant - in one room, for example, the draperies contain

Maranatha Country House, Tower, Blarney, Co. Cork
Tel: 021 385102 Fax: 021 382978 e-mail: maranatha@cork-guide.ie
website: http://www.cork-guide.ie/blarney/maranatha/welcome.html

more than 400 yards of material. Each of the 6 bedrooms is individually designed but the decor in each is equally sumptuous. One of them has a flower garden theme, in another is an opulent 4-poster bed topped by a crown, its draperies of deep burgundy and pinkish reds refreshed by real lilacs. The lavish decor may recall a more gracious age but the en suite rooms also provide all modern amenities such as hairdryers, and there's even a jacuzzi in one of the rooms. Another useful feature is a baby sitting service to ensure a relaxed evening if you are on holiday here with a youngster.

The very special "Maranatha Experience" continues at breakfast time when your meal is served in the lovely flower-filled conservatory. Also remarkable is the very reasonable tariff for staying at this exceptional establishment, (currently around IR£25.00 per person, with a discount for Senior Citizens). Maranatha is open from March to October, has ample parking facilities and is a non-smoking house.

Just outside Blarney, **Pine Forest House** is the family home of Janet Murphy-Hallissey who has been welcoming bed and breakfast guests here for more than 20 years. This

Pine Forest House, Elmcourt, Blarney, Co. Cork
Tel: 021 385979 e-mail: pineforest@cork-guide.ie

attractive and spacious bungalow, set in lovely landscaped gardens, is beautifully situated in a quiet, scenic area on the main Blarney to Killarney road, the R617. Bed and breakfast guests are accommodated in 5 comfortable guest bedrooms (which are non-smoking) and there's a TV lounge for the use of residents where smoking is permitted. A breakfast menu is available with an excellent choice of dishes to set you up for the day. Pine Forest has good access for the disabled and ample private parking. Children are welcome and there's a baby sitting service available if required. The house is open all year round, except over the Christmas period, and is handily located for exploring Co. Cork's many and varied attractions, starting of course with Blarney Castle which is within easy walking distance.

KILLARD
Map 2 ref F15
4 miles NW of Cork off the N20

Less than a mile from Blarney, in the hamlet of Killard, **Hillview House** is a family-run B & B offering quality accommodation in delightful rural surroundings. Hillview is the home of Fran and Tony Cronin who bought the house in 1997 and have thoroughly renovated the whole building, creating 4 comfortable, tastefully decorated guest bedrooms, all of them en suite and with full central heating. All rooms are equipped with television, hairdryer and tea/coffee-making facilities and all of them are on the ground floor. A cot is available if required. There's a relaxing sun lounge where visitors can settle down with a good book and, on fairweather days, the spacious garden is a wonderfully peaceful spot. There's also a large car park, well back from the road. Fran serves a splendid breakfast with an extensive menu to choose from and is happy to help you work out the day's itinerary. Hillview is within walking distance of historic Blarney village with its impressive Castle and of course the famous Blarney Stone, while County Cork's many visitor attractions are just a short drive away, amongst them the Jameson Irish Whisky

Hillview House, Killard, Blarney, Co. Cork
Tel: 021 385161 e-mail: hillview_blarney@yahoo.co.uk
website: http://www.geocities.com/TheTropics/Coast/1491/index.html

Heritage Centre at Midleton, the Royal Gunpowder Mills at Ballincollig, and Cork City's wealth of interesting buildings and shops. The gourmet town of Kinsale and Cobh, the heritage centre, are also within a half-hour drive.

CLOGHROE   MAP 2 REF F15
6 miles NW of Cork on the R579

About 3 miles west of Blarney the village of Cloghroe tends to be overshadowed by its more famous neighbour. There's a very good reason for visiting however. With its white-washed walls and abundance of hanging flower baskets and window-boxes, **Blairs Inn** looks as pretty as a picture. Occupying a secluded, riverside setting in the heart of the country, this inviting hostelry is an outstanding example of an authentic traditional, family run pub. John and Anne Blair are your hosts, a warm and friendly couple who extend a sincere welcome to regulars and newcomers alike. Anyone visiting for the first time will soon understand why Blairs Inn has been showered with awards and rave reviews. In 1998, the Blairs were given the *Licensing World Pub Lunch Award* accompanied by a citation praising the "welcoming atmosphere, with open fires and friendly management prepared to cosset their customers". The Inn has also received the accolade of *Irish Pub of Distinction*, one of only 175 establishments in the whole of Ireland to be so honoured.

Also much praised is the cuisine on offer here, with the emphasis on international dishes imbued with a nostalgic Irish flavour. Extensive day and evening menus feature varied dishes which include a large selection of seafood prepared from freshly-caught fish delivered daily from Kenmare and Dingle; poultry such as French-reared Poussin (baby

Blairs Inn, Cloghroe, Blarney, Co. Cork
Tel: 021 381470

chicken) and Irish-reared Duckling; lamb and steaks from prime Munster herds; and seasonal game that ranges from pheasant and partridge to quail and venison. Imaginative starters and delicious desserts round off the menus which are changed daily. Meals can be enjoyed in the Bar Lounge, Snug and Pantry or, if the weather is fine, in the peaceful garden bounded by the Owennageara, the Sheep River where, in summer, trout can be seen to "rise".

Much sought out by visitors to the area, Blairs Inn is also a popular "local", a lively Irish pub where traditional music is featured each Monday evening during the season, and there are fireside guitar sessions on Sunday evenings throughout the year. Definitely an inn for all seasons.

MALLOW
MAP 2 REF F14
21 miles N of Cork on the N20

From Cork City the N20 strikes northwards through the rolling wooded foothills of the **Boggerach** and **Nagles mountains** to Mallow. Surrounded by good farming country, Mallow is a prosperous town which still bears signs of its fashionable past as a spa town with a Spa Well still in existence and a quaint half-timbered Clock House adding a distinctive touch to the main street. Nowadays the town is best known for its excellent angling and for its racecourse.

CROOKSTOWN   MAP 2 REF E16
15 miles W of Cork on the N22

Travelling west from Cork, the inland route follows the Lee Valley to Crookstown, a small town standing at the head of the lovely Bride Valley. As many thousands of visitors have discovered, to stay at **Bridelands Country House** just outside the town is to enjoy a memorable experience, something very special indeed. This historic country house, dating back to 1840, is set in 8 acres of the Lee Valley in an idyllic location overlooking the River Bride. Arriving guests are presented with an Irish coffee, courtesy of the management, and will also find a complimentary decanter of port in their bedroom. Such hospitality is typical of this gracious hotel which is owned and run by Siun and Peter

Bridelands Country House, Crookstown, nr Macroom, Co. Cork
Tel: 021 7336566 Fax: 021 7336604

Tiernan. Siun is also Bridelands' gifted chef, offering an outstanding cuisine based on freshly caught fish and other local produce such as beef and lamb. These tasty dishes are accompanied by organic vegetables and home-baked bread. Participating in a candlelit dinner here, beneath high ceilings and chandeliers of Waterford crystal, is a memory to be cherished. Diners, incidentally, are invited to bring along their own wine. After dinner, return to your room, sample the port perhaps, and snuggle down in the antique 4-poster bed. Next morning, breakfast is also rather special with some difficult choices to make: smoked salmon or kippers; a traditional Irish breakfast or a selection of cold meats.

Bridelands is especially popular with anglers. There's good sport to be had in the River Bride, and the hotel provides a drying room for clothing and fridges for bait. Students of Irish history will know, or be interested to learn, that it was while he was on his way to

Bridelands that Michael Collins, commander of the Irish Free State Army during the Civil War, was ambushed and killed. That violent episode, almost 80 years ago, seems very remote now from this most tranquil and engaging of Irish country house hotels.

MACROOM   MAP 2 REF E15
22 miles W of Cork on the N22

Macroom enjoys a beautiful setting beside the Sullane River, backed by the Boggerach Mountains. The town is dominated by its massive square **castle** which dates back to the 1400s. Cromwell granted the castle to Admiral Sir William Penn whose son later gave his name to the state of Pennsylvania. The younger Penn was a tireless missionary for Quakerism, but when his colonists demanded a more representative form of government he returned to England, harassed by financial problems and suffering from apoplexy.

About 10 miles southwest of Macroom the Pass of Keimaneigh leads to the **Gougane Barra Lake**, a broodingly romantic stretch of water which provides the source of the River Lee. In the centre of the lake rises a tiny half-acre island, reached by a causeway. This was once St Finbarr's hermitage, founded in the 7th century. A diminutive chapel and the remains of an 18th century building emphasise the loneliness of this secluded spot.

THE CORK COUNTY COAST

KINSALE   MAP 2 REF F16
18 miles from Cork on the R600

Set around a broad sheltered harbour, Kinsale has witnessed two of the most critical events in Irish history. The Battle of Kinsale in 1601 sounded the death knell of the old Irish aristocracy. The rebellious Earls were supported in their defiance of Queen Elizabeth's troops by a sizeable Spanish fleet anchored in the harbour but bungled communications prevented them taking part in the battle. Six years later came the "Flight of the Earls" when they fled en masse to the Continent and abandoned their hereditary lands.

By that time, **James Fort** had been built on the spit of land that curls around the harbour mouth. The fort is in ruins now, covered with creeper, but the location is a pleasant place to wander around. A much more impressive building is **Charles Fort** (Dúchas) on the other side of the harbour. Built in 1677, it's a classic example of a star-shaped fort and one of the largest military citadels in Ireland. Charles Fort played its part in the other great event in Kinsale's history - the arrival of the deposed James II in 1690. His troops were billeted here before marching north to their decisive defeat at the Battle of the Boyne. James returned to Kinsale and set sail for France and an inglorious exile.

There are more military echoes at **Desmond Castle** (Dúchas), a striking 16th century tower house in Cork Street which is also known as the "French Prison". At the height of the Napoleonic Wars, as many as 600 French prisoners were incarcerated here. Earlier, in 1754, a dreadful fire swept through the gaol and 54 prisoners, mostly French seamen, perished. Today, Desmond Castle houses the **International Museum of Wine** which docu-

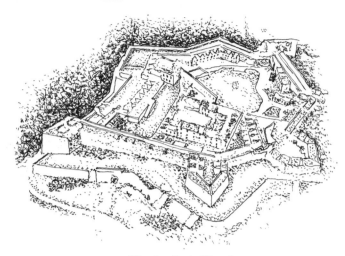

Charles Fort, Kinsale

ments the intriguing story of Ireland's wine links with Europe and the wider world from the early modern period to the present day.

Kinsale's own history is entertainingly brought to life in the **Kinsale Museum**, located above the old market with its Dutch-style façade. Within the same building is the former Courtroom, its 18th century interior left just as it was in 1915 when the inquest into the sinking of the *Lusitania* was held here. That appalling incident took place just off Kinsale Head with the Germans later maintaining that the ship was carrying munitions, a claim that the Americans hotly denied. Whatever the truth, the 128 American deaths among the 1198 victims swayed public opinion in the US in favour of entering World War I.

Over recent years Kinsale has acquired a formidable reputation as the gourmet centre of southern Ireland with many excellent, (if sometimes expensive), restaurants and a Gourmet Festival which begins on the first Thursday in October. If you plan to attend the Festival, make sure you get your accommodation arranged well ahead and, if you possibly can, book into **The Lighthouse**, arguably Kinsale's most famous Tudor-style bed and breakfast. "The Lighthouse is not just a place to sleep, it really is an experience" wrote one visitor. This outstanding establishment is run by the colourful Carmel Kelly-O'Gorman who will whisk you into her domain with breathless enthusiasm. She's a great talker and laugher, indulging in typical "Irish arabesque conversation!" Every room at The Lighthouse is appointed with antiques, and one private suite has its own sitting room. The 4-poster and canopy beds in the Georgian and Empire suites are beautiful. The Victorian dining room is in Regency style with prints of London that provide a perfect match for the period decor. The rooms are small and feminine with a lot of pinks, lace bedhead drapes, chocolates placed on the bed, and with some quite rare items of Irish lace flattened beneath glass-topped bedside tables. Lace is a particular interest of Carmel's who embroiders her own sheets. The quilts are all hand-made too, hand-me-downs from her family. Each room has a theme which has been lightly adhered to. The "Out of Africa"

The Lighthouse, The Rock, Kinsale, Co. Cork
Tel: 021 772734   e-mail: lighthouse@cork-guide.ie

room, for example, has a lace mosquito net and two small David Shepherd paintings on the wall. Carmel is an enthusiastic traveller so you'll find all kinds of souvenirs she has collected from her trips in Asia and America. As you might expect, breakfast at The Lighthouse is also memorable. One of Carmel's specialities is smoked salmon with scrambled egg which, according to another visitor, "beats most five star hotels out of sight".

Set in three acres of woodland on a scenic walking trail but less than a mile from Kinsale town centre, **Rocklands House** occupies a superb position on Compass Hill, overlooking much of Kinsale's maritime environment with beautiful views to all points of the

Rocklands House, Compass Hill, Kinsale, Co. Cork
Tel/Fax: 021 772609 e-mail: rocklandshouse@tinet.ie

compass. John and Eleanor Bateman bought this outstanding property in the early 1990s with the intention of extending it and creating a superior guest house offering both bed and breakfast and self-catering accommodation. They added a second floor, and rooms with balconies commanding magnificent views of the Bandon River. All six guest bedrooms (4 doubles, 1 twin and 1 triple) are en suite, equipped with TV, tea/coffee-making facilities and, like the rest of the house, are non-smoking. There's a residents' lounge, about the size of a small hotel, comfortably appointed with antique and traditional furniture. John and Eleanor are thoughtful and helpful hosts who, along with their 4 golden retrievers, provide a warm welcome for their guests. The B&B tariff includes a hearty Irish breakfast but if you prefer self-catering, John and Eleanor also have a cottage available to let. Rocklands House is open all year, except over the Christmas period, and provides a perfect base for both exploring Kinsale and Co. Cork, or for taking advantage of the huge range of activities available in the area.

DUNDERROW

Map 2 ref F16

3 miles NW of Kinsale on the R605

Beautifully situated on the banks of the Brandon River, **Leighmoneymore Farmhouse** is a lovely period house built in 1912 and surrounded by a 60-acre beef farm which has been in the O'Sullivan family for decades. The house stands in a delightful garden with broad lawns and mature trees, a perfect place to relax with a good book. Michael and Dominique O'Sullivan-Vervaet are your hosts, a charming couple who have made this grand old house a very special place to visit. High ceilings, wooden floors and antique furniture add to the appeal. There are 5 guest bedrooms, all of them en suite with bath & shower, and they are all non-smoking - as is the rest of the house. The rooms are spacious enough for even claustrophobics to feel at ease, and are equipped with traditional brass beds, telephone and hair dryer. In one of the bathrooms there's a magnificent claw foot bath evoking the style of yesteryear. Guests have the use of the light and airy conservatory where they can enjoy afternoon tea or coffee, and also take their breakfast there if they

Leighmoneymore Farmhouse, Leighmoneymore, Dunderrow, Kinsale, Co. Cork
Tel: 021 775312 Fax: 021 775692 e-mail: leighmoneymore@tinet.ie

wish. Children are welcome at Leighmoneymore and there's even a playroom just for them. It would be easy to enjoy a satisfyng holiday without ever leaving the grounds of Leighmoneymore, but if you are feeling active there's a huge range of activities and attractions within easy reach. Sea angling, horse riding, golf, shooting, tennis, swimming and sailing are all available locally, historic Kinsale is just a few minutes drive away, and all around lies the scenic countryside of south County Cork with its fretted coastline dotted with picturesque villages and offering wonderful vistas at every turn of the road.

BANDON
19 miles SW of Cork on the N71

MAP 2 REF F16

The thriving town of Bandon stands at a major crossroads with good access to all areas of the county. So it's an appropriate location for the **Irish International Morris Minor Festival** in late July when devotees of these durable old cars gather in the town.

TIMOLEAGUE
14 miles SW of Kinsale on the R600

MAP 2 REF E16

This trim little village on the estuary of the Ardigeen river is dominated by the sprawling ruins of **Timoleague Abbey**, destroyed in 1649 but still very impressive. Much less so are the minimal remains of Timoleague Castle but the big attraction here is the **Castle Garden** with its fragrant walled garden a palette of dazzling colours during the season. Westwards from Timoleague stretches the **Seven Heads Peninsula**, its fretted coastline dotted with small fishing villages and providing good walking as well as excellent bird watching.

BUTLERSTOWN
15 miles SW of Cork on minor road off the R601

MAP 2 REF E17

A network of winding country lanes leads southwards from Timoleague. Tucked away in the countryside near Dunworley Bay, the **Dunworley Cottage Restaurant** is very much a Hidden Place, but decidedly well worth seeking out as anyone who has sampled the outstanding fare on offer here will confirm. The owner, Katherine Norén, hails from Sweden though she has lived in Ireland for some ten years, most of that time at Butlerstown. Katherine says her aim in life is to give enjoyment to others through her food - her customers' appreciation is her pleasure. And the food is wonderful. As Katherine points out, "nothing has travelled far to reach your plate". Potatoes and vegetables are home-grown, eggs come from Katherine's free-range hens, pork from her black saddlebacks, fish from nearby Courtmacsherry, beef from around the corner, fruit from local orchards, while the bread and ice-creams are all made on the premises. Only the whiskey, from Jameson, and the wines come from rather further afield. A typical menu might include a tasty nettle soup, pie filled with home-grown artichokes, organic salads, seasonal seafood, and an appetising lamb or veal dish served with a delicious home-made sauce.

"Make a day of your visit" Katherine urges. Park your car at the restaurant and enjoy a pleasant coastal walk on Seven Heads or take a swim in Dunworley Bay, famous for its

Dunworley Cottage Restaurant, Butlerstown, Clonakilty, Co. Cork
Tel: 023 40314

red cliffs. Then stroll back to the restaurant for a peaceful drink and a pleasant meal. You can book in advance and special diets can be catered for. Katherine can't promise you good weather, but she can certainly guarantee a memorable meal!

CLONAKILTY
14 miles SW of Bandon on the N71

MAP 2 REF E16

Clonakilty stands at the head of one of the countless inlets along this stretch of coastline. A bustling little town, Clonakilty boasts one of southwest Ireland's best beaches on Inchadony Island, an "island" which is now permanently linked to the mainland by a causeway.

The Republican leader, Michael Collins, was born at Clonakilty in 1890 but the town's main claim to fame nowadays is its status as a major centre for traditional Irish music. There are plenty of lively pubs and the music-making comes to a climax during the **Clonakilty Festival** in late June/early July.

Especially popular with children, the **West Cork Model Railway Village** depicts, in a miniature scale of 1:24, life and industry in West Cork as they were 50 years ago. The theme is enhanced by the miniature working railway which re-creates the long-closed West Cork Railway. The already extensive layout will become even larger as other West Cork towns are added to the display. The most recent visitor attraction to open at Clonakilty is the **Lisnagun Christian Ring Fort** where children particularly will be fascinated by the inventive reconstruction, on the original site, of a 10th century village. The exhibit includes a thatched central house and replica weapons, clothes and tools of the period. The complex also contains a small wildlife park, home to a variety of animals ranging from rabbits to reindeer.

About a mile north of the town, the **Templebryan Stone Circle** has lost five of its original nine stones but not the mystical atmosphere that seems inseparable from these prehistoric monuments with which southwest Ireland is so liberally sprinkled.

From Clonakilty the N71 runs mostly inland, just touching the coast at the small resorts of **Rosscarbery** and **Glandore**. About halfway between these two towns, a short detour will take you to the mightily impressive **Drombeg Stone Circle**, splendidly sited in a field overlooking the sea. Dating from around 1500 BC, the 17 stones encircle a recumbent stone which is aligned to the position of the sun at the midwinter solstice. A little to the west of the stones stands a group of hut circles and troughs which would have been used for cooking, the water heated by hot stones tossed into them from a fire. This fascinating settlement has been dated to roughly AD 200. When the circle was excavated a cremated body was discovered in the centre of the ring.

The nearby village of **Leap** is renowned for Connolly's Bar, generally acknowledged to be the best live music venue in West Cork. From Leap, another detour along country lanes will bring you to the coastal village of **Castletownshend**, perched on a steep hill that dives down to a minuscule quay. A flourishing tree stands defiantly in the centre of the village's main road, an unexpected hazard which acts as an effective traffic calming feature. Castletownshend is something of a shrine for devotees of *The Irish RM* series of stories which recount the risible experiences of an English Resident Magistrate who is perpetually outwitted by the wily locals. The stories were written jointly by Edith Somerville and her cousin, Violet Ross, who assumed the nom-de-plume of Martin Ross. Edith spent her childhood at Skibbereen before settling down in Castletownshend where both she and her cousin are buried in the village graveyard.

ROSSCARBERY

MAP 2 REF E17

9 miles SW of Clonakilty on the N71

Set around a broad bay, Rosscarbery is a pleasantly old-fashioned little town standing on an elevated position above the shore. The sea here offers good bathing and fishing, and for those in search of history, the **Drombeg Stone Circle** (see above) can be found a mile or so outside the town, commanding lovely views across pastures and cornfields to the sea.

Drombeg Stone Circle, Co. Cork

Located on the outskirts of this picturesque little town, **Rosalithir** is an attractive building with steep gables, colour washed walls and arched windows and doorways. The house, which is the home of Catherine O'Sullivan and her family, has 4 comfortable

Rosalithir, Frehanes, Rosscarbery, Co. Cork
Tel/Fax: 023 48136

rooms - 3 of them en-suite. It is furnished and maintained to a high standard with impressive decor and plenty of off-road parking. Breakfast at Rosalithir is definitely rather special, with free-range eggs and other produce from the farm featuring on the menu. Guests are made to feel very welcome here with tea or coffee offered on arrival.

Located nearby is the original farmhouse, which now offers excellent self-catering accommodation. It enjoys a peaceful, rural position with its own garden, on a working dairy farm, only 3 minutes drive from a lovely sandy beach. Facilities include central heating, dishwasher, microwave, tumble dryer, fridge/freezer, colour TV, video/radio/CD player, barbecue, bed linen, cot and a high chair with a welcome pack awaiting them.

Incidentally, Rosalithir - meaning "place of pilgrims", was the original name of Rosscarbery during the 6th century when St. Fachtna founded a monastery. The monastery became famous for its school and after the saints' death, it attracted pilgrims from all over the country. Nothing remains now of the monastery, but Rosalithir house makes a visit to this historic town worthwhile in itself.

SKIBBEREEN
20 miles SE of Bantry on the N71

Map 1 ref D17

A lively market town, with a cattle market on Wednesdays and a country market on Fridays, Skibbereen stands at the gateway to the most southerly of the Cork and Kerry peninsulas. The town is home to the **West Cork Arts Centre** which puts on monthly exhibitions and occasional music and dance events.

For anyone with even a passing interest in gardens there are two of them close to the town which should not be missed. **The Liss Ard Experience** is a New Age garden where the emphasis is on conservation and natural growth - the landscaped garden here has been left unchanged since 1924. An extraordinary feature which is still in the process of being created is the Sky Garden, the work of an American artist, James Turell. The project when completed will include a pyramid, a crater, a mound, a sky walk and a grotto. At the time of writing, only the crater is finished, a vast grassy saucer with a single flat stone slab at its centre, an altar on which visitors lie down to view and to contemplate.

Creagh Gardens are somewhat more conventional, with woodland walks, grassy slopes leading down to the Illen estuary, and an early-19th century walled garden. But its late owner modelled this superb garden on the jungle paintings of Henri Rousseau - filling it with lush vegetation and sub-tropical plants. All that's missing is the occasional lion or tiger which Rousseau used to include in his tableaux.

BALTIMORE
60 miles SW of Cork on the R595

MAP 1 REF D17

Standing near the tip of the Skibbereen peninsula, Baltimore is the last mainland settlement on this, the most southerly part of Ireland. It's a charming fishing village clustering around its busy harbour and overlooked by a 16th century castle. Back in the 1920s, Baltimore achieved a certain fame since it was here that the *Saoirse*, "Freedom", was built - the first Irish ship to sail round the world. Almost 300 years earlier, in 1631, the town suffered a much more inglorious episode when a shipload of Algerians sailed in, massacred many of the inhabitants and carried off others to a fate worse than death as white slaves.

Baltimore's harbour always provides a colourful and active scene with regular ferries during the season sailing to the nearby islands of **Sherkin** and **Clear**, and across the aptly-named Roaringwater Bay to Schull on the Mizen Head Peninsula. The harbour becomes especially busy during the last two weeks of July and the first weekend in August when the annual Regatta takes place.

Baltimore is a delightful place to linger in and there's an equally delightful hotel to stay at. Your hosts at **Caseys of Baltimore**, Ann and Michael Casey, have a very attractive philosophy. "We take immense pleasure in seeing people enjoy themselves and indeed welcoming them back again and again". Once you've stayed at this outstanding hotel it's easy to understand why one visit is not enough. The hotel occupies a stunning, serene location overlooking the natural harbour and commands grand views of the wild, rugged scenery which typifies this region. The building was completely renovated in 1997 and its 14 en suite bedrooms have all the comforts one associates with quality accommodation - satellite TV, radio and video channel, direct dial telephone, tea/coffee-making facilities, a hairdryer and trouser press have all been provided for the convenience and comfort of guests. The rooms have been decorated to the highest standard, the bright, cheerful decor complementing the crisp white linen and pine furniture.

The hotel's light and airy restaurant with its breathtaking views of the sea has a well-deserved reputation for superb food, especially seafood from Baltimore's fleet and farm-fresh produce from the locality. Diners can also enjoy succulent steaks and a variety of vegetarian options. The restaurant's origins go back to the days when Michael was himself a

Caseys of Baltimore, Baltimore, West Cork
Tel: 028 20197 Fax: 028 20509 e-mail: caseys@tinet.ie
website: http://www.sleeping.giant.ie/baltimore/caseys/welcome.html

fisherman and brought some of his own catch to be served in the bar and at tables on the pavement outside the original inn. From such modest beginnings the restaurant has evolved to become one of West Cork's best eating places.

Adjacent to the restaurant, Casey's cosy traditional pub with its open fires and traditional music at weekends is a world apart. The convivial atmosphere created by the staff will have you relaxed and feeling "abroad" within minutes! And for fair-weather days, there's an attractive beer garden overlooking the bay. The tranquillity surrounding Caseys of Baltimore makes it an ideal setting for weddings, anniversaries and other special events, as well as for business meetings, with restaurant accommodation for up to 80 guests. As the Caseys say, "Get away from it all - Baltimore is wonderful!"

SHERKIN & CLEAR ISLANDS   MAP 1 REF D17
3 miles S of Baltimore off the coast

Not to be missed if you are staying in Baltimore is a trip on the ferry to the islands of Sherkin and Clear. **Sherkin Island** is the nearer of the two and it's extremely picturesque. The ruins of a 15th century Franciscan friary stand beside the harbour and fine sandy beaches stretch along the island's western coast. In June each year Sherkin Island, along with Baltimore and Clear Island, hosts the O'Driscoll clan gathering whose members vastly outnumber Sherkin's resident population of fewer than a hundred. Festivities centre on the lively Jolly Roger pub which is also very active throughout the rest of the year. Its traditional music evenings attract many aficionados from the mainland and if a band has been booked you'll usually find that a late night boat has been laid on to carry you and other revellers back to the mainland.

A little further south, **Clear Island** is the most southerly point in all Ireland. On your way there you may well see basking sharks, seals, and even occasional dolphins frolicking alongside the boat. About 3 miles long and barely a mile wide, Clear Island is a birdwatcher's dream come true, one of the most rewarding locations in Ireland for viewing seabirds. A bird observatory was established here in 1959: it welcomes visitors and has hostel-style accommodation available for the really dedicated twitcher. On Clear Island, Irish is still a living language and there are regular summer schools for those wishing to master Gaelic's arcane vocabulary and beguiling rhythms. The island also hosts the County Cork Story-telling Festival in early September and a music and arts festival in late October. The island's **Heritage Centre** is tiny but nevertheless succeeds in presenting a vivid record of local history, including the story of St Kieran who was born here in the mid-6th century. A holy well attributed to the saint stands close by the north harbour. The most impressive building on the island is **Dún an Óir**, "Fort of Gold", an O'Driscoll fortress impaled on a great slab of vertical rock which becomes an island at high tide. It can be admired at a distance but, sadly, is not open to the public.

Across the water from the islands and sweeping out into the Atlantic, the **Mizen Head Peninsula** has a spectacular coastline of sea-beaten cliffs which are particularly dramatic along the northern shore. There are some fine sandy beaches, especially at **Barley Cove** on the western tip, a location which is also popular with surfers riding the great Atlantic rollers. At the neck of the peninsula, the colourful little town of **Ballydehob** was once known as the hippy capital of the West because of the large numbers of disillusioned young Europeans who came here in the '60s to "drop out". Most have returned to the rat race, leave behind a legacy of health food and craft shops to supplement the town's extraordinarily generous complement of pubs.

SCHULL
MAP 1 REF C17
16 miles SW of Bantry on the R592

One of the most appealing little towns on the Mizen Head Peninsula, Schull is a popular seaside resort and yachting centre. It enjoys a splendid setting around its large sheltered harbour, looking out to **Carbery's Hundred Islands** and with the great bulk of Mt Gabriel (1339 feet) rising to the east. During the season, there are regular ferries to Clear Island with its famous ornithology centre and to Sherkin Island. Should you happen to fancy some shark fishing, just call in at the Black Sheep Inn where they'll arrange everything you need!

This attractive yachting centre is at its busiest during sailing events such as the **international sailing festival for children** in July, and the **Calves Week regatta** in early August. At these times it is wise to book well ahead. For excellent bed and breakfast accommodation and a truly memorable eating experience, **Adèle's** in Main Street is the place to stay. Adèle Connor has been in the business for more than 15 years and the reputation of her pastry-shop and restaurant is second to none. Overnight visitors wake to the delicious smell of baking, - wonderful pies, pastries and breads and even pasta are all made on the premises. The daytime restaurant menu ranges from light snacks to full meals, available in a variety of food styles. There's also a takeaway menu and the staff will happily make up a picnic lunch for you. In the evening, Simm Connor takes over as chef, offering a different table d'hôte menu each evening. The emphasis is always on seasonal and local produce, including freshly caught fish and organic vegetables. The menu always includes a vegetarian option. Adèle's wine list is also outstanding. It specialises in wines from small vineyards which are mostly organic or semi-organic. Like the food, these are offered at very reasonable prices - unless you

Adèle's, Main Street, Schull, Co. Cork
Tel: 028 28459

want to really indulge yourself with a glass of one of the very special vintage dessert wines!

CROOKHAVEN
28 miles SW of Bantry on the R591

Map 1 ref C17

About 12 miles from Schull, this remote village near the western tip of the peninsula has a sheltered anchorage which makes it a popular meeting place for yachtsmen. It also boasts the most southerly Bord Failte Quality Approved guest house in the whole of Ireland - **Galleycove House**, located just 6 miles from Mizen Head. The house occupies a

Galleycove House, Crookhaven, West Cork, Co. Cork
Tel/Fax: 028 35137

splendid position overlooking the Atlantic Ocean and the Fastnet Rock lighthouse, the last landfall between here and America, and just 5 minutes walk from Crookhaven village with its pubs, restaurants and sandy beaches. Maureen and Jimmy Newman have been welcoming bed and breakfast guests to their friendly and comfortable house for some 20 years. Arriving visitors are greeted with genuine warmth and the offer of tea, coffee, scones or cakes. They are then shown to one of the guest bedrooms, all individually decorated and furnished, and enjoying wonderful sea views. (Some guests have told Maureen that they noticed lightning out at sea during the night but heard no thunder. It was, of course, the lighthouse beam they had seen). Two downstairs bedrooms have patio doors opening on to a terrace with seating and tables, overlooking the nearby islands, the Atlantic Ocean and countryside. At breakfast time you'll find an excellent spread in the conservatory-type dining room with its high wooden ceiling and breathtaking views of passing ships, fishing boats and well-tended gardens. The meal, which is complemented by home made bread, will certainly set you up for the day. Do note that Galleycove House is non-smoking throughout and closed during January and February. One place particularly well worth visiting in the neighbourhood is the "Mizen Vision", set on dramatic cliffs at the most southwesternly point of Ireland. Maureen was one of the founder members of the group which in 1993 opened this former Mizen Head Fog Signal Station as a Visitor Centre with a variety of fascinating displays dedicated to the area's maritime history. The centre stands on Cloghane Island, linked to the mainland by a narrow suspension bridge 150 feet above sea level, crossing which is an experience in itself!

Just beyond the village, the peninsula divides into three: **Brow Head**, **Mizen Head** and **Three Castle Head**. The most dramatic scenery is at Mizen Head - sheer cliffs with an offshore lighthouse. Standing on this exhilarating spot, it takes little imagination to see why such a great number of ships have foundered in Dunlough Bay to the north. A walk around the bay, (taking care as the ragged cliffs have a notorious habit of ending abruptly), brings you to Three Castle Head where a curtain wall and two turrets of an O'Mahoney stronghold still stand. They were once part of the chain of 12 castles built along the peninsula in the 15th century. From this point, the peninsula turns sharply east along a north coast that is all empty wild cliffs with breathtaking views.

BANTRY   MAP 1 REF D16
57 miles SW of Cork on the N71

"Were such a bay lying upon English shore, it would be the world's wonder". That was the opinion of William Makepeace Thackeray when he visited Bantry Bay in the mid-1800s. Its northern shore dramatically framed by the Caha Mountains, the bay stretches for some 30 miles before it loses itself in the Atlantic Ocean. This appealing town has a refreshing sense of space - "It breathes" said one writer. At its heart is a large square which is the setting for a traditional country market every first Friday of the month.

The waters of Bantry Bay have twice been violated by major French invasions. In 1689, French ships sailed up the Bay in a doomed attempt to restore James II to the British throne. Just over a century later, in the winter of 1796, a formidable French Armada of 40 ships carrying 15,000 soldiers arrived with the intention of putting an end to British rule and establishing an independent Irish Republic. As with the Spanish Armada in Eliza-bethan times, it was the weather that confounded the enterprise. For 6 days the French battled against storms but at times were "close enough to toss a biscuit on shore". Finally, with 10 of their ships lying at the bottom of Bantry Bay, the fleet turned for home.

The invasion had been urged on the French by the Irish nationalist, Wolfe Tone, who sailed with the fleet. His rôle in the luckless adventure is detailed at the **1796 Bantry French Armada Exhibition** which contains a life-size model of the famous Irish patriot. Another model, a giant 1-to-6 scale replica of a frigate vividly illustrates life in the French Navy some 200 years ago. The Exhibition is housed in one of the courtyards of **Bantry House**, a gracious Georgian house occupying a superb position overlooking the bay. Built in 1765 by Richard White, 1st Earl of Bantry, the house and its contents provide a reveal-ing insight into the lifestyle of the Anglo-Irish aristocracy during the Protestant Ascendancy. Gobelin tapestries, Aubusson carpets and fine furniture, Russian icons and mosaics from Pompeii, and a host of art treasures testify to a privileged way of life.

There's more history on display at the **Bantry Museum** but here it's mostly of a do-mestic nature. The museum is run by Bantry's Local History Society and contains an eclectic collection of vintage household paraphernalia, old newspapers and other ephem-era. The oldest artefact to be found in Bantry, however, stands in a field just south of the town. The **Kilnaruane Pillar** is a striking early-Christian carved stone depicting a cross, an apostle and four figures in a rowing boat.

Set on the outskirts of the town and enjoying a panoramic view of Bantry Bay, the **Atlantic Shore** is a spacious purpose-built bungalow offering quality bed and breakfast accommodation. Maggie and Tim Doyle have been welcoming visitors here since 1994 and their 6 guest bedrooms (5 of which are en suite) includes one specially designed to provide good disabled access and also has a shower for the disabled. All the rooms are equipped with television and tea/coffee-making facilities and all of them are non-smok-ing. Open all year round, the Atlantic Shore is close to amenities such as golf, angling and horse-riding, and if one of your interests is scuba diving, just have a word with Tim: he

Atlantic Shore, Newtown, Bantry, Co. Cork
Tel: 027 51310 Fax: 027 52175 e-mail: divebantry@aol.com

runs the local scuba diving centre. If you've come to enjoy the famed scenery of West Cork, then you will be spoilt for choice. In whichever direction you strike out from Bantry, superb vistas unfold - whether it's the rugged heights of the Caha Mountains, the miles of fretted coastline, or the wooded inland hills.

GLENGARRIFF
10 miles NW of Bantry on the N71

MAP 1 REF C16

The huge mass of rock which gave the secluded deep Glengarriff valley and harbour their name is now covered by verdant growths of holly, arbutus, fuchsia, yew, pines and oaks. The natural shelter afforded by the surrounding mountains has endowed the valley and village with one of Ireland's most pleasant micro-climates and this is a lovely spot for boating, fishing and swimming. During your visit you will almost certainly be accosted by a boatman offering a trip to **Garinish Island** and this is an offer you should not refuse. Some 80 years ago, this 37-acre island was just barren rock. Then its owner, Annan Bryce, had tons of soil shipped over from the mainland and in collaboration with the architect and garden designer Harold Peto created a miniature botanical paradise. Garinish is known to horticulturists and lovers of trees and shrubs all around the world as an island garden of rare beauty. Garinish's sheltered position allows fragile species from every continent to flourish here and provides a dazzling contrast to the bare mountains of the Beara Peninsula.

From Glengarriff, the R572 follows the northern shore of Bantry Bay with the **Caha Mountains** rising majestically to the right. This scenic route along the **Beara Peninsula** leads to Castletownbere which, confusingly, is also known as Castletown Bearhaven.

CASTLETOWNBERE
22 miles SW of Glengarriff on the R572

MAP 1 REF C16

Castletownbere boasts the second largest natural harbour in Ireland and is still an active international fishing port where you are as likely to hear Spanish and Portuguese being spoken in the bars, mingling with the soft Irish brogue of the locals.

A mile or so outside the town there's an impressive stone circle and to the southwest stand the ruins of **Dunboy Castle**. Dunboy has been a mere shell ever since the day in 1602 when an English force of 4000 men surrounded the fortress, battered their way through its walls and killed the castle's defenders. Close by is **Puxley's Castle**, another shell. This Victorian Gothic mansion was once the home of the Puxley family who made their fortunes from copper mining. Their story provided the inspiration for Daphne du Maurier's novel *Hungry Hill*. The house fell victim, not to the English, but to the IRA who set fire to it during the civil War of the 1920s. The story is depressing but the setting of Puxley's Castle is idyllic, a picturesque scene encompassing an inlet of Bantry Bay, leafy woodland and wild mountains.

West of Castletownbere, only a few small settlements have taken root and if you want to feel really remote, pay a visit to **Dursey Island**, a last fragment of Ireland flanked by 3 huge sea pillars named **The Bull, The Cow** and **The Calf**. There's no pub or shop and reaching the island involves a hair-rising trip in a Heath Robinson-designed cable car across the narrow and treacherous sound. The reward is breathtaking views and the satisfying sense of having sought out one of the most isolated outposts of County Cork.

About 2½ miles from Castletownbere, in a lovely countryside setting, **Teer-na-Hillan** offers two charming traditional cottages for self-catering holiday-makers. Nestling at the foot of a hill and overlooking the bay, both cottages are attractively furnished and decorated with pine floors in the lounge and bedrooms carpeted. There are fully equipped

Teer-na-Hillan, Castletownbere, Co. Cork
Tel: 027 70108 e-mail: ostnah@indigo.ie

kitchens, a dining area and an open-plan lounge with an open peat fire. Both cottages also have well-kept gardens and the owners, Seán and Ruth O'Sullivan, will be happy to provide you with a barbecue for those (hopefully) warm summer evenings. The O'Sullivans, who are organic farmers, also have 3 ponies which are available for trekking through the scenic countryside that lies all around. They can arrange sea fishing and boat hire, too, and there's good rock fishing virtually on the doorstep. And if you are wondering where the peat for that open fire comes from, Seán will give you a demonstration, at a peat bog near the ringfort, of the time-honoured skill of peat-cutting!

COUNTY KERRY

The most-visited county in Ireland, Kerry offers some of the most beautiful scenery in the country, and some of the friendliest people. Ireland's most impressive mountain range, **Macgillycuddy's Reeks**, are crowned by Ireland's tallest peak, **Carrauntoohil** (3411 feet), and rise majestically above the lakes surrounding Killarney, the county's largest town. Killarney is a good starting point for the Ring of Kerry, the famous scenic drive around the Iveragh peninsula. Perhaps the most enchanting corner of this captivating county is the

Dingle Peninsula, running westwards from Tralee. Irish is still a living language here and the wealth of prehistoric and early Christian remains all contribute to the indefinable, mystical quality of the area. Within the county boundaries lie the now-uninhabited Blasket Islands, and the Skellig Islands where St Patrick exterminated the last of Ireland's venomous snakes.

KILLARNEY MAP 1 REF D15
54 miles NW of Cork on the N22

Killarney's tourism history goes back to the 1750s when the local landowner, Lord Kenmare, capitalised on the newly-discovered appreciation of "Romantic" scenery by creating a purpose-built resort around the village of Cill Áirne (Church of the Sloes) for the well-heeled travellers of the time. Killarney's surroundings are indeed glorious - magnificent vistas of loughs and mountains open up in every direction, with much of this superb scenery lying within the boundaries of the **Killarney National Park**. A popular excursion from the town is a day trip through the park in a "jarvey" or "jaunting car" (pony-trap) driven by a silver-tongued guide who will regale you with some highly inventive history along with fanciful tales of leprechauns and legends. Their charges can also be somewhat fantastic so do negotiate a price before you set off.

Another satisfying excursion is a boat trip around the 3 lakes, Lough Leane, Muckross Lake and the Upper Lake - all of them framed by the highest mountains in Ireland, **Macgillycuddy's Reeks** which rise to 3410 feet. Killarney is also a natural starting-point for the **Ring of Kerry**, a 112-mile circular drive around the Iveragh Peninsula which takes in some of the finest scenery in Ireland. **The Kerry Way** is the walker's alternative - a 38-mile hiking trail across the neck of the peninsula which takes in some especially dramatic scenery around Torc Mountain and Windy Gap.

Killarney itself, despite its long history as a tourist resort, is surprisingly lacking in architectural interest. Its one building of any consequence is the Catholic **Cathedral of St Mary**, a flamboyant exercise in neo-Gothic style designed by Augustus Pugin and consecrated in 1855. Its construction was halted by the Great Famine of 1845-51. During those years, the completed part was used as a hospital for the victims of starvation and disease.

Just across the road from the Cathedral is the entrance to the Knockreer Estate where the main path leads to the impressive ruins of 15th century **Ross Castle**, the last fortress in southwest Ireland to succumb to Cromwell's forces in 1652. (The interior of the castle is not open to the public). The Knockreer Estate extends to the banks of Lough Leane where there are grand views of Macgillycuddy's Reeks and Innisfallen Island, the largest of the 30-odd islands scattered across the lough. It's well worth hiring a boat for the short trip to the island to see the picturesque ruins of **Innisfallen Abbey**, an important ecclesiastical centre for more than a thousand years. The 11th century High King, Brian Boru, is believed to have been educated here and it was monks at the Abbey who compiled the Annals of Innisfallen, a fascinating chronicle of world and Irish history recording events between 950 and 1350.

Situated just outside Killarney in the heart of the Kingdom of Kerry, **Darby O'Gills Country House Hotel** is an ideal spot to stop and enjoy the atmosphere of an Irish country house. It takes its name from the lovable hero of the Walt Disney film, *Darby O'Gill and the Little People*. Made in 1959 with a star-studded cast that included Sean Connery, the movie depicts Ireland in its best light - a heady brew of beguiling and enchanting stories, ancient legends, beautiful traditional music, and an excellent insight into the Ireland of yesteryear. It's only a rumour, but it is said that the owner of Darby O'Gills, Pat Gill, is a distant relation of "Darby" himself! Pat and his wife Gill have a long experience in the catering industry and have transformed the small country pub they

**Darby O'Gills Country House Hotel, Lissivigeen, Mallow Road, Killarney, Co. Kerry
Tel: 064 34168 Fax: 064 36794 e-mail: darbyogill@eircom.ie**

bought in the mid-1990s into an inviting country house hotel. The guest bedrooms here are some of the most charming in the Kingdom - all en suite and finished to a very high standard. All are furnished in country pine to give a very homely atmosphere. There's a spacious Lounge Bar where daily plate lunches are served and entertainment is hosted nightly during the summer, and also a cosy Bar which is just as an Irish pub should be - the art of conversation still lives, and darts, rings, and cards are actively played. Darby's Restaurant is an ideal setting for dinner each evening when only the best of Irish cuisine is served: Poached Darne of Killarney Lake Salmon, perhaps, served with a white wine and mushroom sauce. À la carte and table d'hôte menus are on offer, there are half portions for children, and a wine list is also available. For special events, meetings or parties, the newly refurbished Lissivigeen Room provides a perfect venue. It has its own entrance, toilets and bar, and there's ample parking.

MUCKROSS
3 miles S of Killarney off the N71

Map 1 ref D15

Located about 3 miles south of Killarney, the 11,000 acre **Muckross Estate** was a gift to the nation by an American, Bowers Bourne, and his son-in-law Senator Arthur Vincent. Now part of a 25,000 acre National Park (where cars are banned), the estate covers most of the lake district and contains the beautifully situated ruins of **Muckross Abbey**, founded in 1448 and the best preserved abbeys in the country despite being despoiled by Cromwell's troops in 1652. The Abbey's lovely setting is enhanced by superb gardens, dominated by a gigantic yew tree. Also within the Park is **Muckross House**, a magnificent early-Victorian mansion built in the Tudor style. The main rooms are furnished in opulent fashion and the rest of the house has been transformed into a museum of Kerry folk life where blacksmiths, weavers and potters demonstrate their time-honoured skills. Within the extensive grounds there's a traditional working farm, an excellent tea room and superb gardens noted for their dazzling rhododendrons and azaleas during early summer. A short walk brings you to two of Killarney's most famous beauty spots, the lovely Meeting of the Waters and the spectacular Torc Waterfall which tumbles 60 feet down the flank of Torc Mountain.

About 2 miles further south, the park's boundary is formed by the shore of the **Upper Lake**. The lakeside road leads to Ladies' View which provides a stunning view of the Gap of Dunloe and the remote and cheerless Black Valley beyond the lake.

GAP OF DUNLOE   MAP 1 REF C15
7 miles SW of Killarney on minor road off the N72

Running south from Beaufort, the **Gap of Dunloe** is one of Kerry's premier attractions so this beautiful glacial valley, 4 miles long, that lies between Macgillycuddy's Reeks and the Purple Mountains can become congested with cars and jarveys during the season. But a tour of County Kerry would be seriously incomplete if you missed out on its magnificent views of mountains, loughs and tarns. Kate Kearney was a well-known beauty in Ireland during the years before the Great Famine of 1845-49 and her legend has captured the imagination of people from far and wide over the years. At her cottage Kate distilled her famous poitín, "Kate Kearney's Mountain Dew", which was described as "very fierce and wild, requiring not less than seven times its own quantity to tame and subdue it". It was, of course, illicit. However, Kate flouted the law and invited the weary traveller to partake of her fiery brew.

Today, Mary Coffey, whose family has run **Kate Kearney's Cottage** for more than 150 years, continues the tradition of hospitality made famous by the legendary Kate herself.

Kate Kearney's Cottage, Gap of Dunloe, Killarney, Co. Kerry
Tel: 064 44146 Fax: 064 44641

The restaurant and coffee bar have established a fine reputation, with good food served all day at reasonable prices. Groups and small functions are welcome. In the evening there is a choice of full à la carte and dinner menus, served between 18.00 and 21.00, and followed perhaps by the speciality of the house, Irish Coffee. The Cottage's comfortable lounge bar with its open fire is full of atmosphere and attracts locals and visitors alike. Every Wednesday, Friday and Sunday during the season Kate's hosts an "Irish Night" which features traditionally costumed Irish dancers, and guests are invited to take part in old time and Irish set dancing. And on Saturday evening, there's traditional music played by local musicians. An additional attraction at Kate's is its 2 craft shops which feature many Irish crafts and souvenirs.

Kate's is also the ideal starting point for a scenic pony trek through the mountains, or to embark on the Gap of Dunloe boat trip, one of the most spectacular in the world. Walkers can join the Kerry Way, perhaps the most famous walk in Ireland, and hike or ramble past enchanting lakes and rugged mountain terrain. And golfing enthusiasts can indulge their passion at the nearby courses of Dunloe and Churchtown.

KENMARE
20 miles SW of Killarney on the N71

Map 1 ref C15

If you travel the scenic Ring of Kerry route in a clockwise direction from Killarney, (both directions are equally satisfying, incidentally), the first town of any size you come to is Kenmare. Picturesquely set on the estuary of the River Kenmare, this prosperous little town is well supplied with craft and speciality shops, bars, restaurants and cafés, and its position at the meeting point of both the Iveragh and Beara peninsulas makes Kenmare a popular base for tourists.

There's evidence of early occupation of this pleasant site in the **Druid's Circle**, standing just outside the town on the banks of the River Kinnihy. The 15 small stones form a circle about 50 feet across around a dolmen supporting a large capstone. Another relic from the past is **St Finan's Holy Well**, southeast of the town, whose waters are credited with healing powers and which still attracts many pilgrims seeking a cure. Nearby are the ruins of a church traditionally associated with the saint.

But modern Kenmare's history really began in the mid-1600s, thanks to Sir William Petty, Cromwell's Surveyor-General. Sir William amassed a colossal fortune wheeling and dealing in Irish real estate following the Civil War. The cash-strapped Commonwealth government had rewarded its supporters with confiscated lands in Ireland but many of these beneficiaries baulked at the idea of actually removing themselves to what was seen as virtual exile. Sir William came to the rescue, providing ready cash in return for the freeholds. His acquisitions provided the basis for the vast Lansdowne estate that once surrounded Kenmare where he established mines and ironworks and helped develop a fishing industry. In addition to being a canny businessman, Sir William was gifted in other ways - he became a professor of music at Oxford at the age of 27, was a founder member of the Royal Society in London, and so politically adroit that when Charles II was restored to the throne Sir William managed to acquire yet more land - and a knighthood. It was his descendant, the 1st Marquess of Lansdowne, who in 1775 laid out the town on a pleasing X-plan. The story of the town's development is recounted in the **Heritage Centre** in the main square, where you'll also find the **Kenmare Lace & Design Centre**.

Kenmare is still noted for its lace-making, (point lace and other varieties), and **Willow Lodge** has an interesting connection with this historic industry. When Poor Clare's Convent was established here in 1861, the nuns created work for local people by training them in lace-making. Willow Lodge stands in the grounds of the Convent's garden - a wonderfully quiet and peaceful place although only a few minutes walk from the centre of the town. Willow Lodge is the home of Gretta Gleeson O'Byrne who welcomes her guests with a ready smile, a pot of tea and a selection of her delicious home baking. Gretta's cooking skills are equally evident at breakfast time when you'll find an extensive menu to choose from; you'll need to stay several days if you want to work your through

Willow Lodge, Convent Garden, Kenmare, Co. Kerry
Tel: 064 42301

all the choices! The 8 guest bedrooms at Willow Lodge, each one bearing the name of a tree, are spacious and attractively furnished and decorated. They are all en suite and equipped with TV, hairdryer and tea/coffee-making facilities, and three of them have the added luxury of a jacuzzi in the bathroom. Guests have the use of a large lounge with an inviting open fireplace. Willow Lodge's location makes it an excellent starting point for touring both the Ring of Kerry and the Ring of Beara - scenic drives through some of the most enchanting scenery in Ireland. Facilities for a huge range of activities are all within easy reach of Willow Lodge, from gourmet restaurants to golf, sailing and water-skiing, from hill-walking to deep-sea fishing. And if you would like to know more about lace-making in Kenmare, do pay a visit to the Heritage Museum where you can watch artisans at work and perhaps purchase one or two pieces as a souvenir. Admission to the Museum is free.

Occupying a prime position on Main Street, **d'Arcy's** restaurant and guest house has a long and varied history. The building is first recorded in 1832 when it was leased to Samuel Kingston Maybury at a rent of 2s6d (12½p) a year. A few years later it had become a boarding house run by a Ms. L. Murphy. She was to shock her friends by marrying one of her lodgers and later, on her deathbed, shocked her husband by making a will which excluded him from any inheritance. After a period when it was used as a girls' secondary school, the building served as Kenmare's first bank. When the bank moved elsewhere, the premises housed various kinds of restaurant until 1992 when Aileen and Matthew d'Arcy purchased the business and opened as The Old Bank House. After a year or so, realising

d'Arcy's, Main Street, Kenmare, Co. Kerry Tel/Fax: 064 41589
e-mail: patgath@iol.ie website: www.kerry-insight.com/darcy/

that there other "Bank Houses", they changed the name to d'Arcy's. The restaurant flourished but following Matthew's untimely death in 1998, Aileen leased it to Pat Gath who, together with his brilliant chef, James Mulchrone, has maintained d'Arcy's excellent reputation. The ambience of the restaurant is relaxed, with candles, oil lamps and an open fire, and a gentle musical background of jazz and blues. Non-smokers get to dine in what was the manager's office and in the old vault; smokers are accommodated in the customer area. The à la carte menu is based on prime quality local produce such as Kerry lamb and beef and seafood from Kenmare Bay as well as local free range ducks, all organically fed. The vegetables too are organically grown. D'Arcy's is open all year except from mid-January to mid-February and reservations are essential. And if you are planning to stay in this popular little town, Pat Gath also has 5 guest rooms, (3 doubles and 2 family), all en suite and attractively furnished.

Definitely worth a visit, **The Square Pint and Café Indigo** Restaurant, Grill and Late Night Bar are located in the heart of this beautiful heritage town. The Square Pint Bar is recognised as one of Ireland's leading live music venues. Since opening in 1996 it has already played host to many of the country's leading musicians, including The Fureys, Sharon Shannon, Stockton's Wing and Honor Heffernan, as well as many acclaimed international acts. Buzzing with people of all ages and from all walks of life - by day and night - there is also an exceptional bar menu servedfrom 12.30pm to 5.00pm daily.

Situated directly above the Square Pint, the award-winning restaurant Café Indigo is, quite simply, so blue it sings! Acclaimed as one of Ireland's most stylish eateries, Café

Indigo's talented young head chef, Vanessa Falvey, has created an internationally inspired menu that sparkles with originality and utilises only the highest quality, seasonally available ingredients. Diners can choose from an extensive à la carte or grill bar menu. There is an exceptional, reasonably priced wine list and a full late night bar serving a wide selection of beers, cocktails and spirits. At the weekends, there is also

The Square Pint & Café Indigo, The Square, Kenmare, Co. Kerry Tel: 064 42356/42357

entertainment and a late night disco until 1.00am. Café Indigo is the perfect venue for an enjoyable night out - with friends old and new - in a contemporary and welcoming environment.

Both establishments are owned and managed by Christopher MacDermott who, with his professional team of friendly staff, look forward to welcoming you.

If you are looking for first-rate bed and breakfast accommodation within walking distance of Kenmare town centre, the place to make for is **Tara Farm**. Occupying an outstanding position overlooking Kenmare Bay and the Caha mountains, this substantial modern farmhouse offers exceptionally spacious, warm and comfortable accommodation with all 6 bedrooms having full en suite facilities and fine views of sea and mountains to be enjoyed from their balconies, patios or mini-conservatories. The well-stocked garden with its flourishing palms has an almost Mediterranean flavour. Proprietor Anne Maybury greets her guests with the warmest of welcomes - and also serves a superb Irish breakfast with an extensive menu. You would be well-advised to take up the option of having either High Tea or an evening meal at Tara Farm where the speciality of the house is delicious seafood dishes. There are 6 guest bedrooms here, (2 twin/double, 3 triple, 1

Tara Farm, Tubrid, Kenmare, Co. Kerry
Tel: 064 41272 Fax: 064 41377

family): all of them are en suite and some with TV. Children are welcome at Tara Farm and pets can also be accommodated. An especially attractive feature of Tara Farm is the river that runs through its grounds. This is a great place to relax, but if you are feeling active there are facilities for golf, fishing, boating, horse riding and walking all within easy reach.

Not many guest houses have a prehistoric stone circle, standing stones, and the romantic ruins of a 12th century castle within their grounds but **Dunkerron**, on the outskirts of Kenmare, has, and much more besides. The old castle was once the stronghold of a warlike local chieftain, O'Sullivan Mor. Nowadays, kestrels nest in its picturesque remains.

Dunkerron, Sneem Road, Kenmare, Co. Kerry
Tel: 064 41102

These noble birds are not the only wildlife attraction to be seen here. Rise early in the morning, quietly follow the woodland paths to the sea and you may well see otters frolicking in the little inlet that forms parts of the grounds. There are many other beautiful walks on the 70-acre estate where at any moment you may come across wild deer and other game. And if you enjoy golf, there's a pitch and putt course within the grounds or a 5-minute drive will bring you to two first-class golf courses.

Dunkerron house itself is a handsome 200 year old building, but it was in a sorry state when Moya Gubbins bought it in the 1980s. Painstaking work over the years has restored the house to its former state of grace and Dunkerron now offers a choice of bed & breakfast or self-catering accommodation in idyllic surroundings. Bed & breakfast guests stay in the main house which has 10 very large double rooms, all en suite and comprehensively equipped. They also have the choice of several elegant rooms in which to relax, all of them hung with choice works by contemporary Irish artists. The Green Room is especially cool and tranquil while the spacious conservatory is a green and pleasant place to laze away a summer afternoon. Another striking feature of the house is the vestibule with its large, sweeping staircase and chandelier of Waterford crystal.

As well as a hearty breakfast, evening meals, complemented by an extensive wine list, are also available at Dunkerron, and for those who prefer self-catering, there are attractive, well-equipped cottages set within the tranquil grounds.

From Kenmare, the R571 crosses the River Ken to the Beara Peninsula which County Kerry shares with County Cork. The peninsula here is a rocky, wild and barren place but the R571 clings to the shoreline, opening up marvellous views of mountains, loughs and the estuary of the River Ken.

KILGARVAN   MAP 1 REF D15
7 miles E of Kenmare on the R569

Another short diversion from the Ring of Kerry brings you to this busy little town set beside the River Kenmare and backed by the foothills of the Derrynasaggart Mountains. Anyone with an interest in motoring history will want to pay a visit to the **Kilgarvan Motor Museum** which displays a large collection of vintage and classic cars and is open all year.

Just outside the town and set in 1½ acres of gardens, **Birchwood** is a spacious, modern house offering excellent bed and breakfast accommodation in beautiful surroundings. It stands on a hillside overlooking a lovely river valley, a view that can be savoured from the comfort of the large sun room that runs the length of the house. Tom and Mary MacDonnell have been welcoming guests for B&B at Birchwood since the late 1980s. It's well worth taking up the option of having an evening meal here since you'll be treated to a tasty repast prepared from best quality local produce. Should you happen to arrive late in the evening, Tom and Mary will still make sure you don't go to bed hungry. Breakfast at Birchwood is also something to look forward to, with a hearty spread of cereals, fruit, yoghurts and juices along with a full Irish Fry. And if you feel a little peckish during the day, home-cooked scones and breads are always available, along with tea and coffee. The house is attractively decorated with lots of timber and tiled floors, and the 5 guest bed-

Birchwood, Kilgarvan, Co. Kerry
Tel: 064 85473 Fax: 064 85570

rooms, all of them with private bathrooms, are so spacious they could almost be called suites. Guests also have the use of a large and comfortable residents' lounge. Children are welcome, with a cot and baby-sitting service available if required. Golfers and anglers will feel particularly at home at Birchwood since Tom is a keen golfer and fisherman and will be happy to arrange either for you. In fact, you only have to cross the road to find good trout and salmon fishing. Horse riding, boat trips, cycling, hill walks and lively traditional pubs are all within easy reach and Birchwood is also an ideal base for touring the Ring of Kerry and the Beara Peninsula.

SNEEM   MAP 1 REF C15
12 miles W of Kenmare on the N70

Westwards from Kenmare, the **Ring of Kerry** skirts the Kenmare Estuary, passing some wonderful river and mountain scenery, leading to the well known beauty spot of **Parknasilla** where palms and tender shrubs thrive in the mild Gulf Stream climate. At Parknasilla, the road turns inland for a mile or so and brings you to the picture-postcard village of Sneem, its colour-washed cottages set beside the River Ardsheelaun. Locals will assure you that the different hues have a very practical purpose - the varying colours make it easier to distinguish your own residence after a long evening of merry-making! There's good fishing hereabouts, a fact celebrated by the salmon-shaped weathercock that crowns the tower of the Protestant church which dates back to Elizabethan times. The village's Catholic church was built much later, in 1865, and contains the grave of Father Michael Walsh, Sneem's parish priest in the mid-1800s and immortalized in the popular song, *Father O'Flynn*. An even more famous figure is commemorated by a monument on the village green to Gen. de Gaulle who once spent two weeks here: local people refer to it affectionately as "Da Gallstone". They also have their own term, "The Pyramids", for the **Sneem Sculpture Park** where the exhibits are inspired by the beehive huts of prehistoric Staigue Fort, (see below).

About 3 miles from Sneem, **Brookvilla** offers a perfect arrangement for golfers and for anyone who would like to learn the game. While staying at Brookvilla, you can enjoy quality bed and breakfast and also improve your golfing skills with some tuition from Charlie McCarthy, one of Ireland's most experienced teaching PGA golf professionals. Charlie and his wife Geraldine offer special packages that include golf lessons and B&B in their spacious newly-built house which enjoys wonderful light and lovely views. Charlie

Brookvilla, Tahilla, Sneem, Co. Kerry
Tel: 064 45172

has created a golf tuition area in the spacious grounds of Brookvilla where absolute beginners can learn the elements of the game before venturing on to the local golf course under Charlie's watchful eye. No need to bring clubs - you can rent clubs, golf balls and caddy cart for around £10 a day, and you can also buy clubs, golf bags, waterproof clothing and other golfing accessories.

Even for non-golfers, Brookvilla is a great place to stay. Arriving guests are greeted with a warm welcome and offered tea or coffee, biscuits and scones. In fact, tea and coffee are available at any time of day. The food at Brookvilla is excellent and guests would be well-advised to book the optional evening meal. If you fancy eating out, though, there are good restaurants in both Sneem and Kenmare. Guests at Brookvilla have the use of a spacious residents' lounge and all 4 guest bedrooms are en suite and enjoy some breathtaking views. If you prefer self-catering, Charlie and Geraldine can offer you a well-equipped 3-bedroom house, sleeping up to 7 people, which can also be rented as part of a golf & accommodation package. Whichever option you choose, you'll find Brookvilla an ideal base for exploring the Ring of Kerry and the Beara peninsula.

Continuing clockwise around the Ring of Kerry, the road passes through an area rich in ancient forts and standing stones, one of the best of which is **Staigue Stone Fort**, signposted off the main road between Nedanone and Caherdaniel. This extremely well preserved ring fort, some 3000 years old, is believed to have been a fortress of the Kings of Munster. The walls, 13 feet wide at the base and around 18 feet high, enclose a space of about 90 feet across. The only entrance is through a small doorway with sloping sides. From the bank on which the fort stands there are superb panoramic views. (Don't forget to respond to the notice on the honesty box which requests a small sum to compensate the farmer for "trespass").

DERRYNANE
MAP 1 REF B16
28 miles W of Kenmare on the N70

This pleasant little village with its expanses of sandy beaches and dunes, was the home of one of Ireland's most significant and attractive statesmen, Daniel O'Connell (1775-1847), the nationalist leader and social reformer. A powerful orator and skilled organizer, O'Connell's election as MP to the Westminster Parliament in 1829 forced the British government to repeal legislation which banned Roman Catholics from sitting in the House of Commons. **Derrynane House**, remodelled by "the Great Liberator" himself, is a rather austere building but it enjoys a lovely setting overlooking the sea and is surrounded by a 300-acre park. The house contains a wealth of family memorabilia and it's well worth watching the video which commemorates the life and times of a man who ringingly declared that "no political change whatsoever is worth the shedding of a single drop of human blood".

WATERVILLE
MAP 1 REF B15
35 miles W of Kenmare on the N70

From Derrynane, the Ring of Kerry twists its way through the spectacular Coomakista Pass to the resort town of Waterville with its sandy beach, thriving palm trees and wild Atlantic views. According to legend, Waterville was founded by Noah's grand-daughter, Cessair. Having filled his Ark with animals, the patriarch discovered he had no room left for Cessair so she set sail with a retinue of 49 women and 3 men for an island which, she was assured, was "free of monsters, reptiles and sin, and would therefore escape the flood". Two of the men died after arriving at Waterville; the sole surviving male flinched from facing his awesome responsibilities and ran away. These stirring events took place, apparently, in the year 2958 BC.

Waterville stands on a narrow neck of land that separates Ballinskelligs Bay and **Lough Currane**, one of the most beautiful lakes in Ireland and noted for its salmon fishing. The town developed in Victorian and Edwardian times and still retains a rather dignified air despite the advent of some more recent and less appealing tourist "amenities".

VALENTIA
MAP 1 REF B15
45 miles SW of Kenmare on the R565

Linked to the mainland by a bridge at **Portmagee**, **Valentia** is an intensively cultivated island, 7 miles long and 2 miles broad, which boasts the most westerly harbour in Europe, Knightstown. It was from here that the first transatlantic cable was laid in 1857, and for decades Valentia enjoyed far superior communications with New York than with Dublin. If you were to travel due west from Valentia, the first landfall would be Newfoundland,

Puffin Island

1900 miles distant, but a much shorter boat trip, about 9 miles to the southwest, will bring you to the fascinating **Skellig Islands** which rise abruptly and forbiddingly from the sea. Little Skellig is a sanctuary for some 40,000 gannets and landing is not permitted but, if you are able and willing to negotiate a ladder set into its harbour wall, you *can* visit Great Skellig, or Skellig Michael as it's also known. Another steep climb, on steps carved out of the solid rock, leads to a remarkable cluster of ecclesiastical ruins - the arched stone remains of St Fionan's Abbey (560 AD), a somewhat larger church dating back to the 10th century, several burial enclosures, some rough-hewn crosses and two wells. The most evocative remains, though, are the six distinctive beehive cells in which monks of the Dark Ages passed an appropriately murky existence. It's difficult to credit that these neat and intricate drystone constructions have survived almost a millennium and a half of onslaughts from Atlantic gales. The cliffs of Great Skellig rise

Beehive Huts, Great Skellig

some 700 feet and it was from their awful summit that St Patrick drove the last venomous snakes of Ireland into the sea. Several local companies offer boat trips to the Skelligs but if you book with **The Skellig Experience**, at Portmagee on the mainland, the package includes entry to the visitor centre which provides informative audio-visual displays on all aspects of the island's history.

Returning to the mainland and the Ring of Kerry, the road now runs northwards to the resort town of **Cahersiveen**, birthplace of Daniel O'Connell, and about 10 miles further on, joins the southern coastline of Dingle Bay. From this point, there are grand views across the bay almost all the way to Killorglin. A worthwhile stop en route is at **Glenbeigh** where the **Kerry Bog Village Museum** is a unique development which includes theme cottages, an old forge equipped with all its utensils, a stone hen house, vegetable garden and a bog. The dwellings are exact replicas of those built in Ireland in the early 1800s.

KILLORGLIN
MAP 1 REF C14
12 miles NW of Killarney on the N72

This pleasant little town stands on a hill above the River Laune with Macgillycuddy's Reeks dominating the landscape to the south. The ruins of 13th century Conway Castle are a rather minor attraction and the town is best known for its **Puck Fair**, held in August every year. Originating in pagan times, the fair is believed to have been a celebration of the approach of harvest time. Another tradition claims that it commemorates an occasion when the stampeding of goats (pucks) alerted the townspeople to the approach of English forces. The festivities begin when a wild goat is captured in the mountains, brought to Killorglin and, its horns beribboned, is enthroned in a cage in the centre of the town. The "coronation" signals the beginning of 3 days of cattle and horse sales, and "unrestricted merry-making".

CASTLEMAINE
MAP 1 REF C14
14 miles NW of Killarney on the N70/R761

Castlemaine stands on the River Maine whose sprawling estuary separates the Iveragh and Dingle peninsulas. Although there is little of interest in the village itself, the surrounding countryside is some of the most enchanting in all Ireland.

Just outside the town, **Murphy's Farmhouse**, dating back to around 1800, is a handsome Georgian building with attractively colour-washed walls partly hidden beneath luxuriant creeper. The house has been extended and renovated over the years and since 1964 has been run as a guest house by Mary Murphy, the 6th generation of her family to live here. The fact that guests return year after year testifies to the quality of the hospitality on offer. Mary is assisted by her daughters, Mary and Eileen, and all three ladies make sure that their visitors quickly feel at home. Open all year round, Murphy's Farmhouse provides its residents with an excellent breakfast and the home-cooked 3-course evening meal is prepared from only the very best of local produce and served in the rustic-style dining room with its two areas separated by a feature brick fireplace. Indeed, Murphy's Farmhouse seems to have all the amenities of a country house hotel, except for a drinks

Murphy's Farmhouse, Boolteens, Castlemaine, Co. Kerry
Tel: 066 9767337   Fax: 066 9767839

licence. No problem. Just 300 yards away is Murphy's Pub which, as you may have guessed, is run by Mary's son so you can be sure of a great welcome there.

The farmhouse itself is comfortably furnished in traditional style, with elegant open fireplaces and walls adorned with old family portraits and photographs. The 14 guest bedrooms are all en suite and visitors have the use of an inviting residents' lounge complete with TV. The appealing little village of Boolteens is a 5-minute walk away and there are facilities locally for golf, fishing, walking and hill climbing. A short drive will bring you to the great expanse of Inch Beach, which featured prominently in the classic film *Ryan's Daughter*, and Murphy's Farmhouse also provides an ideal base for exploring the Dingle Peninsula and the scenic Ring of Kerry.

THE DINGLE PENINSULA

The most northerly of County Kerry's promontories, the Dingle Peninsula stretches westwards for 30 miles with the Blasket Islands scattered off its southwestern tip. The dramatic scenery of its mountain backbone, a spectacular coastal road, a wealth of ancient remains and traditional customs, crafts and lore have made the peninsula one of the most popular tourist destinations in the west. There's a lively music scene in this Irish-speaking enclave and a visit is made even more enjoyable by the excellent seafood available, especially in and around the delightful fishing port of Dingle. We begin this survey in the southeastern corner, at Inch, and travel clockwise around the peninsula to Tralee, the capital town of County Kerry.

DINGLE (*AN DAINGEAN*)   MAP 1 REF B14
40 miles NW of Killarney on the N86

Dingle bills itself as "the westernmost town in Europe", a busy fishing port with brightly-coloured houses clustered around the huge natural harbour. Fishing is still carried on in the traditional way with small boats and low-tech methods, but the catches are still copious and excellent fresh seafood features on most menus in the town's many restaurants and cafés. The town also boasts a first-class bookshop/café, An Cafe Liteartha, several good craft shops, an internet café, The Dingle Web, and plenty of good old-fashioned pubs where you'll find music most evenings. In medieval times Dingle was a major port, trading mostly with Spain. When that commerce petered out, the town took advantage of its remote position to become an active centre for smuggling. Now its prime industry is tourism, with visitors drawn here by the town's scenic location, surrounded on three sides by hills, its good angling and attractions such as **Oceanworld** which reveals the fascinating species that inhabit the nearby waters and offers a journey through the Peninsula's ancient sea culture from pre-Christian times to the present. Interactive screens allow visitors to follow in the footsteps of St Brendan the Navigator and to examine some artefacts salvaged from wrecked ships of the Spanish Armada. The highlight of a visit is an underwater walk through the Tunnel Tank with long-snouted sharks gliding eerily above you.

To enjoy Dingle's famed seafood at its best, look no further than the **Beginish Restaurant** in Green Street. This outstanding eating place takes its name from one of the Blasket Islands, Beginish, - from the Gaelic *beag inis* meaning "small island". The name is appropriate since the now uninhabited island has been owned by John Moore's family for generations. John and his wife, Pat, opened the restaurant a few years ago and Pat's training in cookery on the Continent quickly ensured its success. Pat's appetising menu is prepared from prime quality fresh fish with daily specials based on the day's catch landed at Dingle Harbour. Begin with steamed mussels, perhaps, served with lemon grass, coriander and wine; follow it with a main course of Lobster Beginish (lobster in a brandy, cream and herb sauce) or Medallions of Monkfish with herb crust and provençale sauce. (Incidentally, the herbs used come from Pat's own herb garden). Although fish dishes predominate, the menu also offers meat dishes and a vegetarian dish of the day. The delicious desserts at Beginish include such

Beginish Restaurant, Green Street, Dingle, Co. Kerry Tel: 066 91 51588

treats as Rhubarb Soufflé Tart with crème anglaise, and assorted home made ice creams in tuille. Complement your meal with a choice from the excellent wine list which is especially strong on French wines and even includes some premier cru vintages.

The restaurant is part of the Moores' family home and has three distinct areas. The largest has a fully licensed bar and a tank for fresh lobster; the second is a small and intimate dining "nook", and the third is a Conservatory with a delightful view of a terraced garden which is illuminated at night. Beginish is open from mid-March to mid-November and should on no account be missed.

Situated in Dingle town centre, **The Captain's House** has a long tradition of hospitality going back to 1886 when Captain Tom Williams, after meritorious service in the Royal Navy and Irish Lights, started taking lodgers. His guest house, served by its kitchen garden, earned a reputation for homeliness, comfort and good food which has lived on through various owners.

In the late 1980s, the seafaring connection was renewed when the property was bought by Jim and Mary Milhench - Jim, a retired Sea Captain; Mary, a local girl brought up in the guest house tradition. Approached by a footbridge over the Mall river and passing through award-winning gardens, the three-star Guesthouse has been renovated and furnished with antiques and items collected on the Captain's voyages, creating a soothing atmosphere of peace and tranquillity. Fine furniture and paintings, turf fires and fresh flowers generate a warm, friendly and relaxing atmosphere which is also evident in the bedrooms. With orthopaedic beds, direct dial telephones, satellite TV, hospitality trays and other home comforts, they are invitingly warm and cosy. En suite bathrooms with loads of hot water

The Captain's House, The Mall, Dingle, Co. Kerry
Tel: 066 9151531   Fax: 066 9151079   e-mail: captigh@tinet.ie

complete the pleasure. Breakfast at The Captain's House is a memorable experience. It's served in the Conservatory overlooking the garden and the menu offers some difficult choices: traditional Irish fry, free-range egg creations, smoked fish, home-baked hams and local farmhouse cheeses. The buffet of home-made muesli, cereals, fruit and yoghurts provides a welcome change, and home-baked brown bread and scones add to the gastronomic pleasure.

The Kitchen Garden of Captain William's day has been extended along the banks of the Mall river and now boasts a thriving Garden Shop where guests can browse and search for that distinctive, different souvenir. If you are planning a longer stay on the Dingle Peninsula, Jim and Mary can also offer you beautiful self-catering accommodation, a seaside bungalow named *Bun An Tsrutháin* just a few miles outside Dingle Town.

Only a 5 minute walk from the centre of Dingle, **Ard na Greine House** enjoys soothing country views over a gentle hillside. Ard na Greine was purpose-built as a guest house in 1975 and has recently been refurbished by its owners, the Houlihan family. Each of the 4 rooms is en suite with full bathrooms and very well-equipped, complete with a fridge,

Ard na Greine House, Spa Road, Dingle, Co. Kerry
Tel: 066 91 51113 Fax: 066 91 51898

direct dial phone, television, hair-dryer, as well as ironing and tea/coffee making facilities. Ard na Greine would be worth visiting for the breakfast alone. The extensive choice includes such treats as scrambled eggs with locally-smoked wild salmon, fresh fruit and freshly squeezed juices, kippers, various omelettes, along with a traditional Irish breakfast, all served with home made bread. Just the thing to set you up for a day spent exploring the marvellous scenery of the Dingle Peninsula.

ANASCAUL
9 miles E of Dingle on the N86

MAP 1 REF B14

In this tiny village, a mile or so inland, you can get a drink at the South Pole, or more precisely, at the South Pole Inn, so named because it was once owned by Thomas Crean, a member of Scott's expedition to the Antarctic. Another pub in the village, run by the magician Dan Foley, is much photographed because of its shocking-pink frontage. A more conventional attraction is **Minard Castle**, about 3 miles outside the village. The largest fortress on the peninsula, it was a stronghold of the Knights of Kerry but was virtually destroyed by Cromwell's troops in 1650.

INCH (*INSE*)   MAP 1 REF C14
14 miles E of Dingle on the R561

At Inch a long narrow sandbar stretches across the mouth of Castlemaine Harbour providing shelter for the bird sanctuary on its eastern side. In the 18th century Kerry wreckers had the brilliant wheeze of tying a lantern to a horse's head and leaving it to graze on the dunes on stormy nights. Sailors would mistake the moving light for another boat, steer towards it and find themselves aground on the strand.

Three miles long and with a backdrop of the **Slieve Mish** mountains, the beach at Inch is probably the finest in Ireland. It featured in the film *Ryan's Daughter* and you could easily imagine Robert Mitchum striding across the sands towards you. This lovely setting is where you will find **Sammy's Store & Café** which offers a wide range of snacks, home made pies, pastries and cakes, along with substantial meals such as steaks or fresh seafood

Sammy's Store & Café, Inch Beach, Inch, Co. Kerry
Tel: 06691 58118

when available. Sammy's is owned and run by Mahmoud and Iris Hussain, assisted by their sons Mark & George, daughter Zarah, and mother Kitty. If you're planning to stay in this beautiful spot, the family have 9 self-catering houses overlooking the beach, each fully equipped with all mod. cons., and they can also offer 3 bed & breakfast rooms.

KNOCKAVROGEEN   MAP 1 REF B14
3 miles NW of Dingle on minor road off the R559

Staying for bed and breakfast at **Bróigín** really does feel like a home from home since you have free run of this attractive modern bungalow set on a dairy farm of some 47 acres in

Bróigín, Knockavrogeen East, Dingle, Co. Kerry
Tel: 066 91 51292

the secluded little village of Knockavrogeen. Make yourself a snack in the kitchen if you wish, have a game of tennis on the adjacent tarmac court, or hire a bicycle from Bróigín's owners, Anne and John Joe Curran, and explore the lovely countryside all around. Anne and J.J. are always happy to give advice on local walks, drives around the Dingle Peninsula, and the area's many other attractions - places to visit and things to do. There are facilities for golf, pony trekking and hill walking all within easy reach. The Currans serve a breakfast designed to satisfy the heartiest appetite and will also provide an evening meal on request. Bróigín has en suite rooms available, there's a TV lounge and the attractively decorated house is full of traditional furniture and ornaments. There is always someone on call - day and night! Set in a beautiful and peaceful location, Bróigín provides an ideal base for exploring the scenic delights of the Dingle Peninsula.

VENTRY   Map 1 ref B14
4 miles W of Dingle on the R559

Like Dingle, Ventry boasts a fine natural harbour but the wide curve of sandy beach, dotted with a sprinkling of houses, shops and a pub, gives little indication that this was once the main port on the peninsula. Westwards from Ventry the road is carved into the precipitous flank of Mount Eagle (1696 feet) and passes through an area renowned for its abundant archaeological remains. Perhaps the most dramatic site is **Dún Beag**, an Iron Age cliff-top fort about 4 miles west of Ventry. A great wall, 22 feet thick, is girdled by four rings of earthworks, beehive huts stand nearby, and an elaborately constructed souterrain, or underground escape passage, testifies to the engineering sophistication of the prehistoric occupants of this lonely outpost. Dún Beag is part of the astonishing **Fahan Group** which includes no fewer than 414 clochans, (unmortared beehive huts), 19 souterrains, 18 standing, inscribed stones, 7 earthen ring forts and 2 sculptured crosses. Not to be missed.

Continue westwards along the R559 to **Slea Head** where there's a magnificent panoramic view of the **Blasket Islands**, a group of 7 islands and many rocks. These bare, inhospitable islands, uninhabited since 1953 except for summer stayovers, nevertheless proved to be a fertile source of memorable literature. Books such as Maurice O'Sullivan's

Twenty Years A-Growing and Thomas O'Crohan's *The Islander* give a vivid impression of life on these sequestered isles where few could read or write but all contributed to a rich tradition of oral folk lore and legend. During the summer, there are boat trips to Great Blasket island where you can land and wander the many paths or find a secluded beach. Boats leave from **Dunquin**, a small village on the mainland where you'll also find the **Blasket Island Centre**, *Ionad am Bhlascaoíd Mhoír*, which provides an introduction to the islands and houses a comprehensive archive of books, tapes, films and photographs relating to the Blaskets.

From Dunquin, the R559 continues around the western tip of the peninsula to **Ballyferriter** and the broad inlet of **Smerwick Harbour**, overlooked by **Dún an Óir**, "the Golden Fort". In September 1580 the beach here, wonderfully peaceful now, became an abattoir. Spanish, Italian, English and Irish supporters of the Catholic rebellion against Protestant England were defeated at Smerwick by English forces led by Lord Grey. Despite having surrendered, some 600 men, women and children were slaughtered on the sands. A monument erected in 1980 records this dismal event.

A mile or so inland from Smerwick Harbour stands one of the best preserved early Christian church buildings in Ireland. **Gallarus Oratory** dates from somewhere between 800 and 1200 AD and at that time its design, (shaped rather like an inverted boat), was a major architectural advance on the earlier beehive constructions. A doorway that narrows towards the top leads into a space just 15 feet by 10 feet, with just a single loophole window at the eastern end providing a "dim, religious light". Despite the fact that the Oratory was built so many centuries ago, with unmortared stone, it remains completely watertight. Only a slight sagging in its roofline admits to the weight of years.

BALLYDAVID
MAP 1 REF B14
7 miles NW of Dingle on minor road off the R559

Sometime in the 5th century AD, St Brendan set sail from Ballydavid Head in search of the "Islands of Paradise" which had been revealed to him in a vision. His course lay due west, giving rise to the enduring legend that he was the first European to discover the Americas. He would have set off in a currach, a boat whose construction is peculiar to the west of Ireland. The currach's wooden framework is covered by a tarred canvas and its high prow is well-designed to slice through oncoming waves. Ballydavid is one of the very few places in Ireland where these sturdy craft are still built. It's not known whether St Brendan's currach did indeed convey him to America some 900 years before Columbus arrived there, but whether he did or not, Brendan has been adopted as the patron saint of County Kerry and the mighty hill that rises to the east of Ballydavid has been named Mount Brandon in his honour. A gruelling pathway up the mountainside leads to a shrine at the summit, marking the place where the saint received his vision of the "Islands of Paradise".

Nestled at the foot of the mountain is **Coill an Róis**, ("Forest of the Roses"), an enchanting new bed and breakfast establishment. Surrounded by natural wild scenery, it is only 7 miles from bustling Dingle Town, yet seems light years away. Named for an ancient stone fort nearby that is covered in wild roses during the summer, this lovely B&B starts the "rose" theme by being painted in two shades of rose. Stained glass roses on the front

Coill an Róis, Ballyganeen, Ballydavid, Dingle, Co. Kerry
Tel/Fax: 066 91 55475 (Off season: 066 91 55198)

door add to the whimsy. Guests are welcomed warmly by Jimmy Bruic with the offer of tea or coffee which is served in a comfortable sitting room whose floral carpeting continues the rose motif. Your engaging host enjoys chatting with guests about the area, and the sightseeing and dining options.   The bedrooms at Coill an Róis are tastefully furnished with pine beds, wardrobes and a vanity desk area with a mirror and chair. Pine woodwork and door accentuate the well-kept rooms. Comfortable beds are made up with plump, flowered comforters that co-ordinate with the black-out drapes covering large picture windows overlooking the quiet countryside. Reading lamps are located on bedside chests and plenty of electric outlets are provided for the convenience of guests. Some of the rooms are provided with TV. Spotless bathrooms contain either a steam shower, or body shower with multiple spray heads. Shampoo, liquid soap and plenty of fluffy towels and washcloths add to the comforts. A separate jacuzzi room is also available for those who enjoy a soak while contemplating the mountain vista.

Breakfast at Coill an Róis is an experience to remember. Jimmy, who was a pastry chef at Manhattan's famous Harbor Lights Restaurant and London's Corning and Barrow Wine Company, prepares a wonderful breakfast to satisfy all tastes and includes many home made and home grown delights.

CLOGHANE   MAP 1 REF B14
7 miles NE of Dingle on minor road off the N86

As the crow flies, Cloghane is less than 8 miles from Ballydavid but with the bulk of Mount Brandon intervening it's necessary to return to Dingle and then take the dramatically scenic route northwards through the Conor Pass. Cloghane boasts some lovely beaches and, nearby, one of the best bed and breakfast establishments in the peninsula, Loch an Dúin. A real Irish welcome awaits guests arriving at **Loch an Dúin**, the home of Veronica and Michael Maunsell who have a real knack for making visitors feel immediately at

Loch an Dúin, Ballyhoneen, Conor Pass Road, Cloghane, Co. Kerry
Tel: 066 713 8163   e-mail: lochandúin@eircom.net

home. Their house is set on a 60-acre sheep farm at the foot of the Conor Pass where you'll find some of the most spectacular views in this county of breathtaking vistas. A word of advice: do take advantage of the optional evening meal on offer at Loch an Dúin. Veronica was chosen as National Winner in the Canderel Cookery Competition for a 3-course dinner and has won many other awards for her cooking which are displayed throughout the house. Her culinary expertise is also evident in the extensive breakfast menu. A smart, modern bungalow, Loch an Dúin combines all the up-to-date amenities along with traditional features such as an open turf fire in the TV room. En suite bedrooms are available and families are very welcome - a baby-sitting service can be arranged if required. Loch an Dúin serves as an excellent base from which to explore the Dingle Peninsula and Killarney, and if you are an active sort of holiday-maker there is plenty to keep you occupied within easy reach of the house. Fermoyle and Cappagh Strands, two of Kerry's most beautiful beaches are just a 5-minute drive away and are ideal for wind-surfing. There's good fishing nearby at Lough Adoon, (Loch an Dúin), deep sea fishing from the harbours at Brandon and Maharees, and off shore at Fermoyle beach. If golf is your passion, there are excellent courses at Castlegregory and Ceann Sibéal, and the whole area is ideal for hill walking and exploring. All around are links with an eventful past: beehive huts, Bronze Age field systems, ring forts, cross slabs, and those enigmatic designs picked out on boulders and megaliths which are often referred to as rock art.

FAHAMORE
15 miles W of Tralee on minor road off the R560

Map 1 ref B13

Hidden away on the northern tip of the Dingle Peninsula, the seaside village of Fahamore is well worth seeking out for its sandy beaches and for **Spillane's Bar** which has been in the Spillane family since 1875. The present incumbents are Michael and Marilyn Spillane and in the 25 years they've been running the bar have maintained a reputation for excellent food. Everything is locally produced with the menu giving pride of place to fresh fish

Spillane's Bar, Fahamore, Maharees, Castlegregory, Dingle Peninsula, Co. Kerry Tel: 066 71 39125

- wild salmon or crab claws, for example. But you'll also find prime Kerry beef and all dishes are served with local fresh vegetables. (Kerry carrots are known throughout Ireland for their superb taste). An interesting feature in the bar is the curragh suspended from the ceiling. These small canvas-covered rowing boats are made locally and nowadays are used for racing. This friendly bar and restaurant is open from 13.00 until late during the high season, and from 18.00 during the shoulder seasons. Closed November to mid-March.

From Fahamore boats are available for a visit to the **Maharees Islands**, the "Seven Hogs", a mile or so offshore. The most interesting of the islands is **Illauntannig** where there are the remains of an early Christian monastery attributed to St Seanach. A protective wall encloses the ruins of two oratories, three beehive cells and a small cross.

TRALEE   Map 1 ref C14
15 miles NW of Killarney on the N22

If you are female and can claim some Irish ancestry, you too could be the "Rose of Tralee". As part of the Kerry Festival, held in the last week of August, any lady of Irish descent can compete in an old fashioned beauty contest to win the title of "Rose Queen". The sentimental Victorian song, *The Rose of Tralee*, was written by a local man, William Mulchinock, who lived near the town at Cloghers House, Ballymullen.

Tralee enjoys festivals. There's another one that takes place over the Easter weekend, the **International Pan Celtic Festival**, founded in 1970. The festival is designed to strengthen the bonds of friendship between the 6 Celtic nations - Ireland, Scotland, Wales, Brittany, Cornwall and the Isle of Man, and to promote their traditional music, song and dance. The week-long festivities culminate on the Sunday with an inter-denominational Mass which features musical contributions from all 6 nations. The town calls itself "the Happy Holiday Centre" and there is plenty here to keep visitors entertained - historic buildings, spacious parks, quality food and shopping, a bowling centre, horse and greyhound racing, golf, arts and crafts, a vibrant night life and a range of all-weather visitor attractions unmatched anywhere else in Ireland. One of the most popular is the **Aqua**

Dome, Ireland's largest waterworld, where visitors can battle raging rapids, splash out in the wave pool or plummet down the water flume. Children have their own pool and slides, while adults can relax in the extensive Sauna Dome. Other amenities include a restaurant and ice cream parlour, and a shop selling a variety of water-related items such as buoyancy aids and water toys.

On a more cultural level, the outstanding **Kerry the Kingdom** contains 3 separate attractions. "Kerry in Colour" provides a panoramic, multi-image audio-visual tour of County Kerry celebrating its scenery, historic sites, people and traditions. In the "Geraldine Tralee" exhibit, visitors are seated in time cars and transported 600 years back in history to the reconstructed streets, houses, Abbey and Castle of medieval Tralee, complete with sounds and smells. The Museum itself uses interactive media and life-size models, along with priceless treasures dating from the Stone and Bronze Age, to recount the story of Kerry and Ireland over 8000 years. Just along the road from Kerry the Kingdom, the **Siamsa Tíre Theatre** is the home of the acclaimed National Folk Theatre of Ireland whose aim is to present on stage a dance/theatre entertainment based on the wealth of Irish music, folklore and dance. The performances do not use dialogue and so are immediately accessible to visitors from every land.

A disastrous fire in 1580 consumed Tralee's ancient buildings and the heart of the town is mostly Victorian with a sprinkling of Georgian houses. Two churches are well worth visiting - the neo-Gothic Dominican **Church of the Holy Cross**, designed by Pugin with some fine stained glass by Michael Healy, and the prominent landmark of **St John's Church**, a masterpiece of the Gothic Revival style in Ireland which also has some dazzling Victorian stained glass and a sculpture of St Brendan by Gabrielle Hayes.

Amongst its many other attractions, Tralee offers some lively pubs. One of the most inviting is **Betty's** pub in Strand Street which takes its name from Betty Sugrue, the legendary character who presided over this welcoming traditional inn for some 40 years. Long though her tenure was, it comprised only a modest part of the hostelry's long history which stretches back to the mid-1800s. Betty's was bought in 1980 by Marie O'Sullivan and Pat Franklin who have faithfully preserved its traditional atmosphere. Pat is a Kerry man, born and bred; Marie's par-

Betty's, 99-101 Strand Street, Tralee, Co. Kerry
Tel: 066 71 21405

ents were also Kerry people, although she herself was born and brought up in Yorkshire. Both of them have inherited the Irish gift for making a complete stranger a welcome friend within a matter of a few minutes. At Betty's you may well find your quiet evening pint at the bar enlivened by an impromptu musical session provided by players and singers who just happen to have dropped in. On Friday and Sunday evenings there are scheduled performances of traditional music; on Saturday evenings, ballads and folk music predominate. Betty's is such a popular venue that Marie and Pat are, at the time of writing, enlarging the premises. By the time you read this, the next door property to Betty's should be offering an extension to the original inn where you'll find the same hospitable atmosphere, an appetising menu offering the best of fresh local produce and, of course, the inimitable allure of a heartfelt, Irish welcome.

Devotees of steam railways will be delighted with the **Tralee & Dingle Steam Railway** whose station is located on the southern outskirts of the town, close to the River Lee. This is Europe's most westerly line and was part of the famous Tralee & Dingle Light Railway which functioned from 1891 to 1953. During the season, steam trains depart on the hour, every hour, from 11am to 5pm, for the 2-mile jaunt to **Blennerville**.

Blennerville was the main port of emigration from County Kerry during the Great Famine and that story is told in an exhibition and audio-visual presentation at the **Blennerville Windmill Visitor & Craft Centre**. The windmill itself is the largest working mill in the British Isles and is beautifully set beside the bridge with the Slieve Mish Mountains as a backdrop. A miller is always on hand to explain the flour making process and the complex also includes craft workshops, gift shop and restaurant.

Tralee & Dingle Steam Railway

Ten miles east of Tralee, **Crag Cave** is a remarkable cave system stretching for some 2 miles underground. Grotesquely shaped stalagmites and stalactites a million years old line the caves which were only discovered in 1983. Guided tours are available and there's also a restaurant and craft shop.

NORTH KERRY

North of Tralee, the Stacks Mountains stride eastwards into County Limerick while the rest of this area is undulating farmland bounded by the Atlantic to the west and the River Shannon to the north. There are fine beaches at Banna and Ballyheige, and Ballybunnion, near the mouth of the Shannon, is a delightful resort, famous for its seaweed baths. There are few ancient buildings although Ardfert boasts a fine Norman cathedral and Carrigafoyle Castle occupies a striking location overlooking the Shannon. Listowel is well known for its annual Writers' Week while at Tarbert the Bridewell Jail is worth a visit. From Tarbert you can also take a ferry across the Shannon to County Clare.

ARDFERT   MAP 1 REF C13
5 miles NW of Tralee on the R551

The town's principal attraction is **Ardfert Cathedral**, a noble Norman building dating back to the 13th century. It stands on the site of a monastery founded by St Brendan in the 7th century and in medieval times the cathedral was County Kerry's ecclesiastical centre. An effigy of a bishop of those days was discovered here in 1830 and now stands in a niche in the building. Just down the road and also worth visiting is a rather austere 15th century Franciscan friary and church.

About a mile west of Ardfert, **Banna Strand** commands splendid views over Tralee Bay. In April 1916, on the eve of the Easter Rising, the Irish patriot Sir Roger Casement who had been trying to get Germany to commit troops to an invasion of Ireland was brought here by a German submarine. Casement was promptly arrested, tried and executed as a traitor. His plea to be buried in Ireland was rejected at the time but his body was finally returned to his homeland in 1965 and buried at Glasnevin Cemetery in Dublin.

LISTOWEL   MAP 1 REF D13
17 miles NE of Tralee on the N69

This quiet little town bursts into life in the third week of September when the annual **Listowel races** attract farming people, their harvests gathered in, from all over Ireland. A more sedate event takes place in June when the town hosts a week-long festival of writers' workshops and meetings. Several notable writers live and work in Listowel although the town's most famous author is probably John B. Keane whose *Man of the Triple Name* is a lively account of matchmaking shenanigans in North Kerry in the 1930s and 1940s.

Set beside the River Feale, Listowel has a ruined 15th century castle in the town square which belonged to the Lords of Kerry and was the last to resist the Elizabethan forces during the Desmond revolt. When the castle finally fell to English troops in 1600 the whole garrison was put to the sword.

BALLYBUNION   MAP 1 REF D13
20 miles N of Tralee on the R553

This decorous resort at the mouth of the Shannon has some good sandy beaches, and with its caves, coves and rugged cliffs is popular with families. The town boasts a magnificent clifftop 18-hole golf course, boats are available for angling or pleasure trips, and during the season there's a variety of stage performances and dances. Ballybunion's most unusual attraction however is its **Seaweed Baths** which occupy two 1920s bathing houses on the North Beach. Bathers settle down in their own private bathroom, supplied with an inexhaustible stream of hot sea water and a generous quantity of seaweed gathered earlier in the day from the Black Rocks. A good soak relieves any aches and pains you may have and afterwards you can take a tray of tea and apple tart onto the beach.

TARBERT   MAP 1 REF D12
11 miles NE of Listowel on the N69

The small village of Tarbert stands on a steep slope overlooking one of the most attractive stretches of the River Shannon. A year-round vehicle ferry operates from here making the short crossing to County Clare in a matter of minutes. While waiting for the ferry, you might care to spend a while in the **Bridewell Courthouse & Jail** (1831) which has been restored with tableaux and exhibits to show how the judicial system worked in those days. Open from April to October, the Bridewell also serves an excellent afternoon tea!

About 4 miles west of Tarbert, stand the marvellously photogenic ruins of 15th century **Carrigafoyle Castle.** A stronghold of the O'Connors, the castle suffered frequent attacks and has been in ruins since its partial destruction by the Cromwellians in 1649. If you climb the winding stone staircase to the battlements, there are stunning views across river and countryside.

5 Shannonside

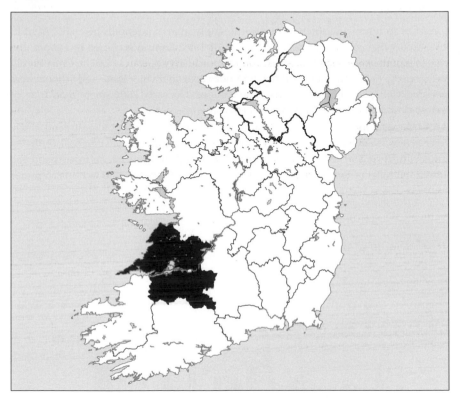

COUNTY CLARE

The landscape of County Clare is defined by water and you are never far from it - nearly three-quarters of the county boundary is formed by either the Atlantic, the mighty River Shannon or the great expanse of Lough Derg. There is some outstanding coastal scenery in the southeast, around Loop Head, while further north the dramatic Cliffs of Moher tower almost 700ft above the Atlantic. Inland, Clare displays stark differences between the productive gentle pastures and fertile land by the Shannon and the lunar rockscape of the Burren, a wild wasteland irresistibly attractive to botanists, geologists and archaeologists exploring its many prehistoric sites.

Clare is known as both the "banner county" and the "singing county". The former epithet was earned by the fighting prowess of Clare's soldiers at the Battle of Ramillies, and later because of the courageous struggle of its people for Catholic emancipation. The "singing county" is self-explanatory - wherever you go you can be almost certain of finding a pub offering regular or impromptu sessions of traditional music.

ENNIS
MAP 2 REF E11

20 miles S of Galway on the N18

Ennis has an unusual distinction - proportionately more households here are linked to the Internet than anywhere else in the world. In 1997, Ennis was chosen by Eircom, the Irish telecommunications company, for an extraordinary social experiment. Every family was offered a new computer, with free Internet access and voice mail, and schools were provided with a computer for every nine students. By early 2000, more than 82% of households had computers and were linked to the Internet.

A busy and attractive town, the county capital grew up around a great bend of the River Fergus. Narrow, winding streets thread their way through the compact centre of Ennis with its quaint shops and shopfronts. Right in the heart of the town stand the substantial ruins of **Ennis Friary**. Founded around 1240, the friary is rich in sculptures

Ennis Friary

and decorated tombs, most notably the 15th century MacMahon tomb with its striking alabaster carvings of the Passion.

Dominating the main street is a much-maligned statue of **Daniel O'Connell**, the great 19th century nationalist leader who was elected MP for Clare in 1828. As a Catholic he was legally barred from membership of the House of Commons but the Government, fearing violent civil unrest, was forced to pass the Catholic Emancipation Act the following year. Another statue, opposite the neo-Classical Courthouse of 1852, commemorates Eamon de Valera who represented the county in the Dáil from 1917 until he was elected President in 1959.

The town's small **museum** specialises in items associated with famous Clare people. Fans of Percy French, the Victorian painter and entertainer, for example, can see the old steam engine he immortalised in his song about the West Clare Railway (1887-1961), *"Are you right there, Michael, are you right?"* French's satirical song made fun of the WCR's propensity for its engines to stop anywhere other than stations and it led to him being sued for libel by the railway directors.

If you would like to know more about Irish traditional music and dance, there are evening sessions every Wednesday during the season where you can learn some Irish dancing steps. Tea and brown bread is included in the small admission charge. And every Saturday night from May to October there are Oiche Céilí evenings featuring traditional Irish music where again guests are invited to participate.

COROFIN   MAP 2 REF E11
8 miles N of Ennis on the R476

Set in pretty countryside near the shore of Lough Inchiquin, Corofin is worth seeking out in order to visit the **Clare Heritage Centre**, housed in the former St Catherine's Church which was built in 1718 by a cousin of Queen Anne. The centre has a museum which opens a fascinating window on the story of 19th century Ireland and, the first of its kind in the country, a Genealogical Centre which brings together the most comprehensive research material to help anyone with Clare roots to trace their ancestry - parish and civil records, census returns, tombstone inscriptions and information from many other sources provide details of more half a million people. The Centre is open weekdays all year round and also at weekends during the summer.

A couple of miles south of Corofin, **Dysert O'Dea Castle** is an uncompromising rectangle with blank walls pierced by a few narrow slits. This 15th century tower house is now home to the Clare Archaeology Centre whose extensive museum displays hundred of artefacts from the Stone Age to the War of Independence. A 20-minute audio-visual presentation introduces visitors to the 25 historic monuments to be found in the surrounding fields. The most notable are two Celtic forts, a ruined Round Tower, two Romanesque churches, a 12th century High Cross and a Holy Well.

LISSYCASEY   MAP 2 REF E12
10 miles SW of Ennis on the N68

If you were allowed to visit only one village pub in the Republic, the village would have to be Lissycasey and the pub **Fanny O'Dea's** - Ireland's oldest family-run pub. With its long, low thatched roof and orange-washed walls Fanny O'Dea's is a wonderfully picturesque building and the interior is equally inviting. There's a clock which featured in the pub scene in the film *Ryan's Daughter*, and an open fire which has been burning continu-

Fanny O'Dea's, Lissycasey, Co. Clare
Tel: 065 34143

ously for 200 years. The pub's history goes back to 1695 when Denis O'Dea settled in Lissycasey and set up a small inn which doubled as a Shibìn (unlicensed alehouse). When he retired, the inn was bought by his niece Fanny who immediately displayed a remarkable flair for innkeeping - a great housekeeper and a charming host.

A particular attraction for her customers was the invigorating hot egg flip she had created to her own recipe, a recipe which contained a liberal lacing of Jameson whiskey. One winter night in 1790, a High Court judge was caught in a blizzard and sought refuge at the inn. As he dried himself out by the fire, Fanny served him the speciality of the house, her famous egg flip. The judge sipped the concoction appreciatively and then remarked that he tasted spirits in the drink. Did she have a licence to sell spirits, he enquired. Fanny replied that she could not afford to pay for a licence and that she gave this drink to friends only. On hearing this, the judge opened a travel case and, taking out a form, filled it in, signed it Robert Vere O'Brien and handed it to Fanny, saying "There is your licence, now you may sell intoxicating drink".

The present owners are direct descendants of Denis and Fanny O'Dea - the eighth generation of the family to have owned and run this delightful pub. They continue to serve the potent egg flip which provided the unlikely means by which Fanny's hostelry acquired its first licence. Today, Fanny O'Dea's is the perfect place to stop for a drink, sample some of the wholesome bar food, enjoy the craic, and listen to impromptu sessions of traditional Irish music. Definitely not to be missed!

QUIN   Map 2 ref F12
7 miles SE of Ennis on the R469

Just southeast of Ennis, **Quin Abbey** is a well-preserved 15th century Franciscan friary set in beautiful surroundings. The Macnamaras who founded the Abbey cannibalised much of the fabric of Ennis's Anglo-Norman castle to build it. Although roofless, the church is remarkably complete, with a high altar, cloisters and a graceful tower from the top of which there are excellent views.

Close by is **Craggaunowen Castle**, a fortified tower house built in 1550 and restored in 1975. Inside there's an impressive collection of 16th century European wood carvings but even more interesting are the reconstructions of ancient Irish homes and farmsteads in the surrounding grounds. The exhibits include a reconstructed *crannog*, (a Bronze Age lake dwelling), a ring fort and a *souterrain*, or underground chamber. These are all replicas but the *Brendan* is the real thing - the leather boat in which the journalist and adventurer Tim Severin sailed from Ireland to Newfoundland in 1976 to prove that St Brendan the Navigator could have made the journey in the 6th century as old chronicles relate. Another genuine artefact is an actual Iron Age road, excavated from Corlea Bog in Co. Longford, and moved to this site. It's made of large oak planks placed over birch and alder branches, an ingenious solution to the problem of crossing spongy bogland.

A couple of miles further south, **Knappogue Castle** is a massively impressive fortress also built by the Macnamara family (in 1467) and held by them until 1815 with the exception of a brief period when they lost it to Cromwell. He used it as his headquarters, thereby saving it from the major damage he inflicted elsewhere. Fully restored, the castle has become a major tourist attraction and hosts medieval-style banquets.

SHANNON Map 2 ref F12
12 miles SE of Ennis on the N19

Shannon is effectively a dormitory town for the nearby international airport, the single most important employer in Co. Clare. The airport boasts several firsts. In 1947 it introduced duty free shopping for international travellers; it was the first to provide pre-flight US immigration clearance facilities; and it also claims to have invented Irish coffee to placate stranded transatlantic passengers in the days when smog-bound Heathrow was often closed and many planes were forced to land here. Shannon is also one of very few airports in the world to have an 18-hole golf course right next to it.

BUNRATTY Map 2 ref F12
16 miles SE of Ennis on the N18

Bunratty village overlooks Ireland's greatest river, the Shannon, which at 240 miles is also the longest in the British Isles. A broad, slow-moving river, the Shannon drains almost one fifth of the area of the country and drops a mere 400ft in the course of the journey from its source in the hills of Co. Cavan. As the river approaches the estuary its waters are harnessed to provide a major source of hydroelectricity.

About 2 miles to the east of Shannon, **Bunratty Castle** stands on what was once an island. The Vikings were the first to fortify the site and the moat they constructed is still in place. The present impressive building, set beside a small stone bridge over the River Ratty, was erected by the Macnamaras around 1460 and fully restored 400 years later. The massive rectangular Keep houses an outstanding collection of furniture, tapestries, and paintings from the 14th to the 17th centuries. The imaginative restoration of the castle has created an authentic 15th century atmosphere, best experienced during one of the medieval-style banquets held here twice nightly at which guests are served and serenaded by winsome colleens in medieval costume.

In the grounds of the castle the **Bunratty Folk Park** contains a fascinating series of replicas of rural and urban Irish houses as they would have looked in the late 1800s. There's a grey limestone cottage from north Clare, a whitewashed mountain farmhouse from west Limerick, a smallholder's comfortable home from Tipperary's Golden Vale and nearby the kind of basic hovel his hired hands would have lived in. Additional attractions include a complete village street with shops and a pub, gift and tea rooms, and the well known tourist pub, Durty Nelly's.

A striking modern building with colour-washed walls and arched windows, **Bunratty Villa** evokes a Mediterranean setting, an impression heightened by the thriving palm trees in the immaculate gardens. This attractive building was purpose built in 1988 as a guest house with 6 letting rooms, all of them en suite, stylishly furnished and decorated, and equipped with all modern amenities including Sky TV, clock radio, hairdryer and

Bunratty Villa, Low Road, Bunratty, Co. Clare
Tel: 061 369241 Fax: 061 369947 e-mail: bunrattyvilla@eircom.net

tea/coffee making facilities. Bunratty Villa is the home of Jackie and Jack Burns, along with Jackie's parents, Kevin and Phyl O'Callaghan, and they are all adept at making their visitors feel welcome. There's always a pot of fresh coffee brewing in the comfortable guest lounge, along with a choice of herbal teas. At breakfast time, Jackie provides a good spread, ranging from fruit, cereals and yoghurt to salmon and scrambled eggs or a full Irish breakfast. Outside, the lovely spacious gardens are quiet and peaceful, and there is ample parking space. With Shannon Airport just a 15-minute drive away, Bunratty Villa is an ideal stopping place either on arrival or departure. (Please note that Bunratty Villa is closed through December and January). This area of East Clare provides a plentiful choice of things to see and do. The 15th century Bunratty Castle and Folk Park is just a 5 minute walk away, as is the popular Durty Nelly's bar, and Bunratty village with its pubs and restaurants only a little further. Fishing, angling and horse riding are all available within a 3-mile radius and if you are of an historical turn of mind, there's a wealth of ancient churches, (such as St Flannan's Cathedral and Oratory at Killaloe), and hundreds of archaeological sites scattered around the countryside.

Surrounded by lovely landscaped gardens and backed by woodland, **Park House** is a purpose-built luxurious bed and breakfast establishment where you will find a warm

Park House, Low Road, Bunratty, Co. Clare
Tel: 061 369902 Fax: 061 369903 e-mail: parkhouse@eircom.net
website: http:///homepage.eircom.net/~parkhouse

welcome from your hostess, Mairead Bateman, and a relaxing atmosphere. Built in 1997, this spacious house is elegantly furnished with attractive features such as maple wood floors and pine furniture helping to create a stylish ambience. The 8 guest bedrooms are all en suite and equipped with television, clock radio, hairdryer and tea/coffee-making facilities. Like the rest of the house, the bedrooms are all non-smoking. Children are welcome at Park House, with a cot and baby-sitting service available if required. Breakfast, served in the sunny dining-room, offers a wide choice that includes yoghurts, fresh fruit and pancakes. Open from mid-February to mid-December, Park House enjoys a peaceful setting with Bunratty Castle just a couple of minutes away; Shannon Airport a mere 10 minutes drive.

KILLALOE   MAP 2 REF G12
13 miles NE of Limerick on the R494

Killaloe lies at the southern end of Lough Derg, where the Shannon narrows and passes beneath a lovely 13-arched stone bridge. Picturesquely set beside the lough, Killaloe is an excellent base for lough cruises or boat rentals and you can also hire wind-surfers, canoes, wet-suits and dinghies from the University of Limerick Activity Centre a couple of miles outside the town.

The centre of Killaloe is a network of narrow lanes running up the hillside and leading to **St Flannan's Cathedral**, an austere 13th century building with a squat tower and sturdy buttresses. Just inside the cathedral is a strikingly decorated Romanesque doorway from an even older church and next to it the massive Thorgrim Stone (c.1000AD) inscribed with unique ogham and runic inscriptions and believed to be the memorial to a

Viking convert. In the churchyard stands St Flannan's Oratory, built in the 1100s and with its barrel-vaulted roof still intact.

On the east bank of the Shannon is Killaloe's twin town, Ballina, and about a mile south of Ballina is **Rathmore House,** an impressive modern house set in superb gardens close to the River Shannon and surrounded by farmland. Rathmore has the spaciousness and comfort of a large hotel combined with the charm of a family home. It is in fact the home of Patricia and Christopher Byrnes and visitors very quickly find themselves regarding the house as a home from home. Rathmore House has 6 guest rooms, 4 of them en suite, a comfortable private guest lounge with an open fire and an extensive selection

Rathmore House, Ballina, Killaloe, Co. Clare
Tel: 061 379296 e-mail: rathmorebb@oceanfree.net

of books to browse through, and a breakfast room where guests will find home made bread and scones included in the comprehensive breakfast spread. Rathmore is an ideal venue for touring the counties of Clare, Limerick and Tipperary and this scenic area also offers a host of activities: fishing, boating, sailing, water sports and hill walking, with golf available at the nearby Boydke, Nenagh and Limerick clubs. An attraction not to be missed if you appreciate fine crystal is the Tipperary Crystal Design Centre, just a couple of miles from Rathmore House. The Centre boasts a magnificent display of Tipperary Crystal and its gift department offers a mix of Irish-made products, amongst them Eden Pottery, Newbridge Cutlery and Jewellery, Linen, Rynhart Bronze, Louise Kennedy Clothing, scarves, soaps and candles.

From Killaloe a scenic road (the R463) runs northwards alongside Lough Derg, passing en route the great earth fort of Beal Boru from which King Brian Boru took his title, then through the fishing centre of Scarriff and the pretty lakeside village of Mountshannon before entering Co. Galway near Lough Alewnaghta.

SOUTHWEST CLARE

KILKEE
MAP 1 REF D12

30 miles SW of Ennis on the N67

This popular seaside resort, sheltered from the Atlantic by the reef-like Duggerna Rocks, is well-provided with all the essentials for a family holiday - amusements, cafés and restaurants, and a major all-weather attraction, **Kilkee Waterworld**. Opened in 1998, Waterworld offers a Crystal Tower Flume ride more than 60yds long, a Lazy River ride with some unexpected geysers and gushers, a Bubble Pool, children's pool, and other fun features to keep all the family amused. For fairweather days there's a safe sandy beach with a Blue Flag rating which slopes very gently into the bay and some marvellous clifftop walks stretching for miles in both directions. The town is a favourite with scuba divers and snorkellers, sea angling is easily arranged and inland the rivers Creegh and Cooraclore offer some excellent trout and salmon fishing.

"The fashionable bathing place" of Kilkee is mentioned in writings of the 18th century as a place to visit and immerse oneself in the healing waters of the Atlantic. So the **Kilkee Thalassotherapy Centre** is continuing a tradition in Co. Clare. Thalassotherapy, from the Greek *thalassa*, the sea, and *therapia,* to heal, is based on the healing virtues of the sea, originally developed in France to treat illnesses ranging from respiratory problems to heart conditions. Today it is recommended therapy for men and women suffering from skin disorders, muscular and circulatory problems, backache and stress. Modern thalassotherapy philosophy combines the traditional healing power of water, in the form of seaweed baths, with beauty treatments using products derived from the sea. On an-

Kilkee Thalassotherapy Centre, Gratton Street, Kilkee, Co. Clare
Tel: 06590 56742 Fax: 06590 56762

other level, thalassotherapy can be a treat, and provides a time out for self-indulgence and relaxation.

The Kilkee Centre offers treatments as varied as Natural Seaweed baths, balneotherapy, algeotherapy/seaweed body wraps, cryotherapy and massage. Confused? Don't be, since resident therapists Grainne Cashman and Tara Deasy provide a free initial consultation and assessment as to how thalassotherapy can benefit you. Beauty salon treatments are also available, including waxing, facials and manicures. The sauna, steamroom and sunbed complete the Centre's unique range of facilities. This outstanding amenity was established by Eileen and Padraig Mulcahy in 1999 and proved an instant success. Eileen organises the day-to-day running of the Centre while Padraig is busy harvesting tonnes of seaweed and collecting, so far, more than 24,000 gallons of seawater for use in the baths! The Centre is also a Bord Failte 3*** approved guesthouse with en suite accommodation ideal for those wishing to enjoy individual treatments, or day/weekend tailor-made packages. Open all year round, except for Christmas and the month of February, the Kilkee Thalassotherapy Centre has made the town a "fashionable bathing place" once again.

Occupying a prime position in this popular resort town, the **Stella Maris Hotel** is a small family run establishment owned and run by Ann and Martin Haugh assisted by friendly, welcoming staff. The Stella Maris was built more than 100 years ago as a hotel

Stella Maris Hotel, Kilkee, Co. Clare
Tel: 065 905 6455 Fax: 065 906 0006

with spacious rooms, open peat fires and a breakfast veranda which overlooks the beautiful expanse of the horse-shoe bay. Food is taken seriously at the Stella Maris. Martin is also the local butcher so only the freshest and best cuts reach the hotel kitchen for dishes such as Rack of Lamb or Chargrilled Steak. The menu will also appeal to lovers of seafood, offering a selection of dishes prepared from fresh, locally caught fish. Add starters such as the Chef's own Seafood Chowder and tempting desserts like the Fresh Fruit Crumble, complement your meal with a choice from the extensive wine list, and you have an infallible recipe for a memorable meal.

In the evening the hotel bar is a lively place, with traditional music creating an authentic Irish atmosphere and the bar meals menu also offers a tempting choice of tasty, well-prepared meals. And at bedtime, the hotel's 10 comfortable en suite bedrooms promise a relaxed and refreshing good night's sleep.

Kilkee itself is a bustling place during the season when its resident population of 2,000 increases to some 20,000. In addition to the superb sandy beach with its countless rock pools to explore, there's plenty to keep the visitor busy: - deep sea diving, an 18-hole Championship Golf Course, dolphin-watching trips from the picturesque fishing village of Carrigaholt nearby, spectacular beach and cliff walks, or you can follow the breathtaking Loop Drive around the peninsula which takes in some of the highest cliffs in Ireland.

KILRUSH   Map 1 ref D12
22 miles SW of Ennis on the N68

A lively maritime and market town overlooking the Shannon estuary, Kilrush has a Blue Flag beach, an adventure centre offering a wide range of activities for all ages from archery to windsurfing, a golf club which claims to be the friendliest in Ireland, and a 420-acre woodland park with a restored Victorian walled garden.

The pubs in Kilrush live up to Clare's reputation as the "Singing County" but for a real feast of traditional music the time to visit is mid-August when the 4-day **Éigse Mrs Crotty** takes place. Elizabeth Crotty was a famed concertina player in the early part of the 20th century and a pioneer of the movement to preserve Irish traditional music. The festival includes céilís, concerts, lectures, classes, traditional sessions in pubs throughout the town and a memorial mass. Other events in Kilrush include the Kilrush Maritime Festival in the second week of July and a traditional horse fair and market in March, June, October and November.

The town once boasted a muddy tidal harbour but now has an excellent modern marina. From the marina there are daily cruises setting off in search of Ireland's only known resident population of bottlenose dolphins. More than 100 individual dolphins have been identified in the Shannon estuary and the cruise boat's hydrophone allows you to hear them communicating with each other. Another popular excursion is to **Scattery Island**, about 2 miles out in the estuary. The site of a 6th century monastery founded by St Senan, the island has the ruins of five medieval churches, a well-preserved Round Tower 120ft high and around one thousand years old, and a gun battery from the time of the Napoleonic wars. The battery stands high on the southern tip of the island and offers a good chance of seeing dolphins at play.

A mere 5 minute walk from Kilrush and its bustling harbour, **Hillcrest** is an attractive, spacious bungalow, the home of Ethna and Austin Hynes who have been offering quality bed and breakfast accommodation here for some 11 years. Visitors are greeted on arrival with a welcoming cup of tea or coffee and soon discover that they have found a home from home. Wooden floors and a delightful conservatory overlooking the garden add to the charm. Guests can stay on either a B & B or half-board basis but it would be a shame to miss Ethna's superb cooking which can accommodate all tastes and diets. Hillcrest has

Hillcrest, Doonbeg Road, Kilrush, Co. Clare
Tel: 065 905 1986 Fax: 065 905 1986 e-mail: ethnahynes@hotmail.com

6 very spacious guest rooms, all en suite, non-smoking, and enjoying soothing views across this quiet and peaceful spot. Children are welcome, with a cot and baby-sitting service available if required. There are also facilities for pets.

Hillcrest provides an excellent base from which to sample the diverse attractions of the area. From Kilrush harbour during the season, there are regular boat trips to the Shannon Estuary to see the dolphins - pods of up to 100 bottle nose dolphins have made the estuary their home. Or you could take the ferry to Scattery Island which is named after a mythical monster which once prowled the island. The island contains the remains of a 6th century monastic settlement founded by St Senan, the ruins of five churches, and a unique 10th century Round Tower with an entrance at ground floor level, unlike most of these historic buildings which have the doorway several feet above the ground as a protection against attackers. Finally, if you are a deep sea angler, there are skippers who will take you out for bottom angling or even in search of sharks.

About 5 miles to the southeast of Kilrush is **Killimer Agricultural Zoo**, offering a close view of llamas, wallabies, pot-bellied pigs and many other farmed animals, and a little further east you can catch the regular vehicle ferry for the 20-minute trip across the Shannon to Tarbert in Co. Kerry.

COORACLARE
7 miles NE of Kilrush on the R483

Map 1 ref D12

Set beside the River Doonbeg, Cooralclare is a typical West Clare village, peaceful and quiet but offering an abundance of outdoor activities all within easy reach. The village also boasts the excellent **Tubridy's Bar & Guest House** which stands on the main street and is easily recognised by its distinctive ochre coloured frontage. More than a century

Tubridy's Bar & Guest House, Cooraclare Village, Co. Clare
Tel: 065 9059033 Fax: 065 9059388

old, the bar has been owned and run by 4 generations of the Tubridy family. Anne and Martin Tubridy are the present incumbents and they extend a warm welcome to all their guests. Visitors will find the very best of Irish home cooking on offer, along with lively entertainment in the bar and comfortable en suite accommodation. The bar menu includes home made soups, assorted sandwiches, an all day breakfast, and wholesome main dishes such as smoked salmon salad. The dinner choices are equally appetising, ranging from a starter of melon and kiwi in a vinaigrette dressing to a hearty steak. The dining room is a recent addition and is an inviting sight with its separate booths and tables laid with gingham cloths. After your meal, step into the bar where there's live entertainment at weekends and on other days during the summer season.

With the sea nearby, lakes and rivers all around, the area guarantees anglers the best of shore and game angling. Tubridy's provides a tackle shed, cool room and wash room, and boats can be hired from Kilrush and Quilty piers, both just a few miles away. Most lakes and rivers are accessible thanks to the help of local anglers and the hospitality of the farming community.   Facilities for golfing, sailing and horse riding are all available locally and other attractions in the vicinity include fine beaches at Kilkee and Miltown Malbay, boat trips on the River Shannon, and a wealth of historic remains: ruined Abbeys, Round Towers, ring forts and dolmens.

NORTHWEST CLARE

LAHINCH   MAP 1 REF E11
20 miles NW of Ennis on the N67

Overlooking the broad sandy beach of Liscannor Bay, Lahinch has a permanent population of little over 500 but in summer that number is multiplied several times since this is
one of Co. Clare's most popular resorts. It boasts two 18-hole golf courses - one of them
a championship course known as the "St Andrews of Ireland". There's also an entertainment centre with a theatre, cinema, seawater swimming pool, aquarium, children's pool
and play area, and Lahinch is a favourite destination for surfers enjoying the rolling
Atlantic breakers.

If you appreciate prime fresh sea food, beautifully prepared and presented, the place
to make for is **Mr Eamon's Restaurant**. It's not hard to find - a distinctive colour-washed
building located in the heart of Lahinch. Mr Eamon's is the oldest established fine dining
restaurant in the area and it enjoys a reputation for consistently serving delicious, top-
quality food. Culinary fashions may come and go but Eamon and Rita Vaughan have
remained faithful to what they know best, a policy which is obviously popular with their
appreciative customers. Eamon is the chef and the daily hand-written menu lists a wide
choice of appetising dishes. Local fish and shellfish have pride of place, with hot buttered
lobster one of the house specialities along with fresh crab, monkfish and turbot dishes,
and treats such as poached
Aran Scallops in a ver-
mouth sauce. Vegetarians
will find options like grilled
St Tola goat's cheese with
tapenade, or courgettes
stuffed with stir-fry vegetables. Meat eaters are also
well catered for with steak
and poultry choices as well
as local delicacies such as
calf's tongue. Home baked
breads add to the eating
pleasure. Desserts include
home made ice cream in a
ginger snap basket served
with butterscotch sauce, a
chocolate roulade filled
with Bailey's Cream, and a
traditional bread and butter
pudding which comes ac-
companied by cinnamon
ice cream.

**Mr Eamon's Restaurant, Kettle Street, Lahinch,
Co. Clare Tel: 065 7081050 Fax: 065 7081810**

Rita presides over the smooth running of the dining room, aided by a courteous and efficient team who together help to create a warm and relaxed atmosphere. This outstanding restaurant is open from 19.00 until 21.30 every evening but is closed throughout the month of February. Well-behaved children are welcome at Mr Eamon's, (a high chair is available if required), and the restaurant has full access for wheelchair users.

A mere 100 metres from Lahinch's beautiful beach and the famous golf links, the **Sancta Maria Hotel** is owned and run by the McInerney family who have welcomed holiday-makers here since 1956. Comfortable and with a relaxing ambience the hotel has 30 bedrooms, each with private bathroom, direct dial telephone, TV and hair-dryer. Many

Sancta Maria Hotel, Lahinch, Co. Clare
Tel: 65 708 1041 Fax: 65 708 1529

of the attractive bedrooms overlook the famous Lahinch Championship Golf Links while the quiet elegance of the spacious lounge provides the perfect atmosphere for relaxing conversation, or just day-dreaming!

The Sancta Maria offers extensive dining facilities with only the finest quality foods being prepared and presented to guests. The restaurant specialises in fresh produce, with special emphasis on local sea foods and home baking. For example, the evening menu offers fresh Liscannor Bay plaice, or wild Atlantic salmon, while amongst the breakfast choices is fresh Liscannor Bay mackerel. There is a good selection of wines to enhance the freshly prepared traditional dishes. Outside, the hotel's own private car park ensures that guests are not inconvenienced during the holiday period.

Lahinch is at the heart of some of Ireland's most spectacular scenery with many top attractions within easy reach. The dramatic Cliffs of Moher, just 7 miles from the hotel, are one of Ireland's most scenic spots, defiantly standing as giant natural ramparts against the might of the Atlantic. A little further north is the Burren National Park whose geology, flora, fauna, caves, archaeology, legends and history make it unique in Europe. Hundreds of stone forts and tombs remain as reminders of our ancient past. And just 5 miles off the coast are the Aran Islands, one of the last outposts of Gaelic civilizations where Irish is still the spoken word. In addition, Lahinch offers superb golf, (there are 2 excellent 18-hole courses), watersports, fishing, surfing and canoeing, with varied entertainment available in the evenings. There's also an exciting Aquarium and Leisure Centre amongst the abundance of attractions and activities makes Lahinch a very special holiday location indeed.

Set just outside the village, on the coast road to Miltown Malbay, **Le Bord de Mer** occupies a superb site on rising ground overlooking the sea. From the stylish dining room with its tiled floor and elegant furniture there are breathtaking views to be enjoyed through the panoramic windows. This outstanding bed and breakfast establishment is the home of Annie and Desmond O'Brien and if you're wondering why the name is French, the answer is that Annie *is* French and a teacher of French Art. Annie's Gallic origins are

Le Bord de Mer, Miltown Malbay Road, Lahinch, Co. Clare
Tel/Fax: 065 708 1454 e-mail: annieobrien@boinet.ie

evident in her welcoming charm and in the quality of the cooking. They probably also explain why fragrant brewed coffee is always available - Annie declares that she cannot stand the instant variety. Le Bord de Mer has a wonderfully relaxed atmosphere, (perhaps "laissez-faire" is the right term to describe it), and Annie recalls having guests who began a conversation over the breakfast table and were still there in the early afternoon. The glowing comments in the Visitors' Book record her guests' appreciation of the atmosphere and amenities on offer at Le Bord de Mer. The house has 5 guest rooms, all en suite and all attractively and stylishly furnished and decorated. Lahinch's many attractions and amenities are close by, with the Cliffs of Moher, the Burren and the Aran Islands all within easy reach.

LISCANNOR
14 miles NW of Ennis on the R478

MAP 1 REF D11

This small fishing village was the birthplace of John P. Holland (1841-1914) who invented the submarine but it is better known locally because of the **Holy Well of St Brigid** to the

Cliffs of Moher

northwest of the village. A major place of pilgrimage, the well is approached by a narrow stone passage whose entrance is guarded by a remarkably lifelike full size plaster model of the saint. About 3 miles beyond the village are the famous **Cliffs of Moher**, defiantly standing as giant natural ramparts against the might of the Atlantic. The cliffs stretch along the coast for some 5 miles and rise in places to 700ft. On the highest cliff stands **O'Brien's Tower**, built in the early 19th century as a viewing point for Victorian tourists. From its exceptional vantage position you can view the Clare coastline, the Aran Islands and mountains as far distant as Kerry and Connemara. There's a visitor centre here with a tourist information centre, crafts souvenir shop and tea room.

DOOLIN   MAP 1 REF D11
30 miles NW of Ennis on the R478

Famous for the quality of its traditional music, this small village set around a sandy cove is also the embarkation point for ferries to the **Aran Islands** of Inisheer, Inishmaan and Inishmore which are actually part of County Galway. Life on these windswept islands provided the raw material for J.M. Synge's early play *Riders to the Sea* (1904) and little has changed since those days. The rugged beauty, the sweeping views and the astonishing wealth of prehistoric and early monastic ruins make a visit to the islands a memorable, even mystical, experience.

Back on the mainland, just outside Doolin, **Ballyvara House** stands in splendid isolation, surrounded by 20 acres of its own grounds and open countryside. The owner of this wonderfully peaceful and secluded property is John Flanagan, the youngest of a family of six, who was left Ballyvara House when his parents died. A carpenter and builder by trade, John dismantled the original 19th century cottage and then used the stone and timber to

Ballyvara House, Ballyvara, Doolin, Co. Clare
Tel: 065 7074467 Fax: 065 7074868 e-mail: bvara@iol.ie

build this spacious house. The result is really something special, retaining the atmosphere of the old cottage with an imaginative use of the original fabric. At the same time, the right of way across a field where John recalls his parents driving a donkey and cart is now a proper road. This labour of love was completed in 1996 so the house is equipped with all up-to-date amenities - the 7 guest bedrooms all en suite and provided with facilities such as multi-channel television. Breakfast comes with home baked bread and a choice of either a full Irish or continental breakfast. Children are welcome at Ballyvara House, and there's a cot and baby-sitting service available if required.

Ballyvara's location is very handy for exploring the attractions of Clare and Galway, with the Cliffs of Moher, the Burren and the Aran Islands all easy to reach. There are regular ferries from Doolin to the Arans which are well worth visiting for their many pre-Christian and early Christian remains, and for the starkly beautiful scenery. Doolin itself is regarded as the "capital of the singing county", the village's three pubs vying with each other every night during the summer to provide the best of live traditional music.

CRAGGY ISLAND
28 miles NW of Ennis on the R477

MAP 1 REF E11

Craggy Island is so named for two reasons. Firstly, because this welcoming bed and breakfast establishment is situated between the two townlands of "Island" and "Craggycorradon"; secondly, because Craggy Island is the name of the mythical island of the *Father Ted* television programme which was filmed in this area and on the island of Innisheer. Craggy Island looks out across the Atlantic with the Cliffs of Moher to the left and the Aran Isles to the right. The house itself is traditional in style, with stone-flagged and pine floors downstairs. The dining room/lounge is spacious and comfortable, with a wooden floor and ceiling and an open turf fire. All bedrooms are en suite with shower,

Craggy Island, Ardeamush, Doolin, Co. Clare
Tel: 065 7074595 e-mail: cragisle@gofree.indigo.ie

w.c. and washbasin and the house is fully centrally heated, making it very comfortable even on the chilliest of summer evenings. When it comes to food, your hosts, Adrian and Bev O'Connor, do their best to cater for all tastes. There is always a choice between the traditional Irish, vegetarian or continental breakfast, all served with home made bread. Dinner is available on request, except during the summer months when there is a good selection of local restaurants to choose from. Please note that the O'Connors request that guests do not smoke in the house.

Adrian is a musician, singer and guitar player and if the weather is poor in the evening often entertains Craggy Island's guests with ballads and traditional music as they settle with a drink beside the open fire. In summer, Adrian often invites them to join him in a visit to the local pubs when he and his band are playing. Nearby Doolin is, or course, known as the traditional music capital of Ireland, its three pubs renowned for good music, good food and good craic!

LISDOONVARNA MAP 1 REF E11
24 miles NW of Ennis on the N67

Ireland's premier Spa town, Lisdoonvarna is also famous for hosting Europe's largest matchmaking festival. Its origins go back to the days when, having gathered their harvest in, local farmers came to the town in search of a wife. Today, the festival attracts visitors from all over the country for the month-long jamboree of singing, dancing and drinking.

The matchmaking festival takes place in September but throughout the year the Victorian **Spa Complex & Health Centre** offers restorative baths, saunas, showers and massages using the spring waters which contain elements of magnesia, iodine and iron and are believed to cure a wide variety of ills. A very different process is on view at **The Burren Smokehouse** huge slabs of salmon are deftly filleted and then smoked over an aromatic smouldering fire of wood chippings. A free video explains the procedure and the final product can be bought here or sampled in the next door tavern.

Situated just two minutes walk from the centre of Lisdoonvarna, the **Carrigann Hotel** is a small, quiet and friendly 3*** hotel standing in its own landscaped grounds. The hotel is owned and managed by Gerard and Mary Howard who during the past 10 years

Carrigann Hotel, Lisdoonvarna, Co. Clare
Tel: 065 707 4036 Fax: 065 707 4567 e-mail: carrigannhotel@eircom.net

have built up an excellent reputation for the quality of the welcome, service and food. This is evident in the large number of repeat visitors to the Carrigann. Mary, a qualified hotel manager, is the chef and along with her team produces and presents cuisine of the highest quality using fresh local produce. Gerard, as well as contributing to the management of the hotel, runs his own butcher shop in the village, from where he supplies the hotel with top quality meat products.

There is a relaxed and friendly atmosphere at the Carrigann at all times, where guests are made to feel "at home" and where even the bar is for their own private use. A sitting room with an open peat fire and an extensive library add to the relaxed ambience. Outside, the grounds around the hotel have been expertly landscaped and include rose beds, rockeries, shrubberies, ornamental trees and lawns, and the hotel also boasts its own extensive herb garden. Mary is a keen walker and for the past ten years the Carrigann has operated walking and environmental type holidays for both small groups and individuals. The unique limestone terrain of the Burren region provides superb walks to suit everyone from the complete beginner to the experienced hill walker. Mary has mapped and noted numerous walks in the area and is always available to give her advice and suggestions. Many other activities are also available within easy reach of the Carrigann - golf, pitch & putt, fishing, cycling, pony trekking and water sports. There are good beaches just a few miles away and a popular excursion is the daily boat trip from Doolin to the Aran Islands.

Just a 5-minute walk from the town centre, **Sunville** is an attractive old house, dating back some 200 years. It can also lay claim to being the first guest house in Lisdoonvarna. Known then as The White House, it opened more than 25 years ago and has been run by the Petty family throughout that time. Sunville has a great feeling of spaciousness with its high ceilings, large rooms and wide windows, and the Pettys' genuinely warm welcome

Sunville, off Doolin Coast Road, Lisdoonvarna, Co. Clare
Tel/Fax: 065 7074065 e-mail: thepettyfamily@indigo.ie

adds to the relaxing atmosphere. The house has 6 guest bedrooms, all of them en suite with bath and shower, and all are equipped with TV, hair dryers, electric blankets and tea/coffee making facilities. Therese Petty lays on a splendid spread at breakfast time - fruits, yoghurts, fresh cheeses, as well as a full Irish breakfast. The repast is accompanied by home baked breads and breakfast rolls. An evening meal is also available if required, or you could sample one of the excellent restaurants in the town. Sunville is open all year and guests can stay on either a B&B or partial board basis. Children are welcome - there's a cot and baby-sitting service available if required. The house is also suitable for a disabled person with a helper.

The area around Lisdoonvarna provides plenty to see and do. There are facilities available locally for golf, sea and lake fishing, pony trekking and cycling, along with beaches at Lahinch and Fanore. The Cliffs of Moher are just a short drive away and even closer is the ferry from Doolin to the famed Aran Islands. Sunville is also the "Gateway to the Burren", the strange lunar-like landscape covering some 100 square miles to the north and northwest of Lisdoonvarna.

To the east of Lisdoonvarna stretches the unique landscape of the **Burren**, an eerie moonscape of bare domed hills and limestone pavements called *clints*, perforated with vertical fissures called *grikes*. Water filters through these grikes into a vast underworld of caves, the most spectacular of which is Aillwee Cave near Ballyvaughan (*see below*). Although the treeless plateau of the Burren looks harsh and uninviting it is actually amazingly rich in plant life, with 1100 of Ireland's 1400 species to be found here. And bleak though it is, the area was widely settled by Stone Age people who left around 120 massive dolmens and wedge tombs. The most photographed of these is the **Poulnabrone Dolmen** about 4 miles south of Ballyvaughan off the R480. Dramatically sited on a limestone pavement, the dolmen with its massive capstone was built more than 6000 years ago, probably as a ceremonial cemetery for tribal leaders.

A popular way to explore the 100 square miles of the Burren is by way of the circular drive from Lisdoonvarna along the coast to Black Head and Ballyvaughan, returning along the Corkscrew road to Lisdoonvarna. And for an informative introduction to the area and its history, a visit to the **Burren Centre** at Kilfenora is strongly recommended. An additional attraction at Kilfenora is the array of medieval high crosses of which the most striking is the beautifully decorated 12th century **Doorty Cross** depicting Christ's entry into Jerusalem.

BALLYVAUGHAN

MAP 3 REF E10

24 miles NW of Ennis on the N67/R480

In striking contrast to the bare, treeless wastes of the Burren, Ballyvaughan is an attractive little port set in a green, wooded valley and looking across the bay to the Galway hills. The village has several interesting craft shops and Newtown Castle nearby is unusual in being a circular fortified tower standing on a square base. Ballyvaughan is an ideal base for exploring the Burren and has a good choice of quality places to stay.

With its colourful garden and walls half-smothered in creeper and hanging baskets, **Rusheen Lodge** looks absolutely charming. The interior is equally inviting with its elegant decoration and furnishings. So it's no surprise to discover that the Lodge is the

Rusheen Lodge, Ballyvaughan, Co. Clare
Tel: 065 7077092   Fax: 065 7077152   e-mail: rusheenl@iol.ie
website: http://members.xoom.com/Ballyvaughan/page8.html

proud recipient of the RAC's "Small Hotel and Guest House of the Year for Ireland" Award. The owners, John and Rita McGann were particularly pleased to be the first ever Irish Guest House to achieve the necessary standard to merit the award. The Lodge is also one of the few guest houses to achieve a 4**** rating from the Irish Tourist Board.

John and Rita are renowned for their friendly, warm welcome and personal service. Together with their family and staff they do everything possible to ensure that your stay is one to remember. The Lodge has 6 individually designed bedrooms and 2 suites, all generously apportioned, en suite and offering all modern comforts such as complimentary tea/coffee-making facilities, fitted hair dryers, and direct dial telephones. Fax and photocopying facilities are also available.

Breakfast is a very important part of the Rusheen Lodge experience, with an extensive choice that includes both the traditional Irish and continental variety. In the evening, visitors can dine at one of the enticing restaurants to be found in Ballyvaughan and neighbouring villages, and enjoy the friendly atmosphere of the many local pubs which are noted for their traditional music, dancing and sing-songs.

Rusheen Lodge is the ideal base from which to explore the varied attractions of counties Clare and Galway: the world-famous Burren with its extraordinary rock formations, the spectacular coastline, and the magical Aran Islands. Another attraction which has a particular interest for the McGanns is the famous Aillwee Cave. This natural geological wonder, incorporating a waterfall and 1000 metres of passages, was discovered in 1941 by Jacko McGann, John's father.

Located just outside Ballyvaughan and overlooking Galway Bay, the **Whitethorn Restaurant and Craft Shop** makes an ideal stopping place for visitors to North Clare. Originally the site housed the Coast Guard station and although the station no longer exists, the original boat house and slipway still do, right beside the restaurant with the boathouse now used by the Ballyvaughan rowing club. Between the mid-60s and mid-70s, a fish factory was built and operated here for the breeding and processing of fish and

Whitethorn Restaurant & Craft Shop, Ballyvaughan, Co. Clare
Tel: 65 77044 Fax: 65 77155 e-mail: whitethorne@tinet.ie

shellfish. Then in the late '80s the factory was converted to its present use as a craft shop and restaurant by a local couple and is now run by their daughter and her husband, Sarah and John McDonnell. The restaurant has a huge picture window providing spectacular views over Galway Bay to the Connemara Mountains and is the perfect place for anything from a simple home made snack to a wedding banquet. The wine list is particularly notable and has won the Georgina Campbell Wine List of the Year 2000 Award. As the *Irish Times* put it, "The list is not extensive. Neither is it expensive. What marks it out as special is that it presents an intriguing selection of wines, hand-picked with conviction and described with humour".

The Craft Shop carries a wide range of work from Irish craftspeople, so whether it's glass, pottery, woodwork, knitwear, presents or just a browse you want, this is an excellent place to step in for a wander. Another attraction at the Whitethorn is the Burren Exposure, housed in a striking building of natural stone and glass. The exhibition gives a fascinating overview of the Burren area, with the help of aerial photographs and a 35-minute audio-visual display. It may well make you want to stay longer in this special place: if so, there are 6 self-catering apartments available. Standing on the shores of Galway Bay, each is totally self-contained and suitable for 2 people.

Standing at the northern tip of the Burren, Ballyvaughan is an appealing little port looking out over the bay to the Galway coast. It provides an excellent base for exploring this unique region and **Burren Wee Cottages** offer top quality self-catering accommodation. These two semi-detached cottages were originally built in 1860 by a family who had emigrated to America, prospered and then returned home. The cottages have been thoroughly modernised and equipped with comforts such as full central heating - along with open fires. Attractively furnished and decorated, these spick and span cottages are owned by Teresa and Mort O'Loughlin who also returned here after living abroad for many years,

Burren Wee Cottages, Glenfort, Ballyvaughan, Co. Clare
Tel: 065 7077031/7077297 Fax: 065 7077031 e-mail: mortol@iol.ie

in their case in London. They consider the Burren the most beautiful place on earth and want others to enjoy its very special atmosphere. They will be happy to direct you to the most interesting places in the area. One of the nearest is Aillwee Cave with its astonishing chambers of stalactites and stalagmites. Nearby, Newtown Castle is an interesting 16th century fortified tower house and the Newtown Castle Trail, lasting about 1½ hours, incorporates history, folklore and botany into the 1-mile walk. A little further afield, there are regular ferries from Doolin to the Aran Islands and the Galway coast.

Located just a couple of miles south of Ballyvaughan, **Aillwee Cave** is Ireland's premier show cave. There's a whole labyrinth of caves, pot-holes, underground lakes and streams beneath the surface of the Burren, but Aillwee is the only one that can be explored without the aid of special equipment. Discovered by a local herdsman in 1941, the cave has more than 3500 feet of passages. Visitors are guided through beautiful caverns, over bridged chasms, beneath weird rock formations, and alongside the thunderous waterfall which can sometimes gently spray the unsuspecting visitor. At one point, there's a column from floor to ceiling formed by a stalactite and a stalagmite meeting. Unique to these islands are the Bear Pits - hollows scraped out by the brown bear, one of the cave's original inhabitants.

Aillwee Cave, Ballyvaughan, Co. Clare
Tel: 065 7077036 Fax: 065 7077107
e-mail: aillwee@eircom.net

The visitor centre at Aillwee houses a distinctly different craft shop, with fossils, crystals, mineral specimens and clothing, along with personalised souvenirs of an unusual style. On the top terrace of this award-winning building there's a Potato Bar where large, floury potatoes are served, bursting with flavour and filled with blue cheese or smoked salmon & avocado. Tastiest of all perhaps are the potatoes filled with the Burren Gold cheese which is made daily at the nearby farm shop. Here, the smell of wood smoke lingers in the air, drifting from the smoker where this delicious cheese is smoked. Burren Gold is on sale in the shop, along with other local cheeses and a huge range of other produce, most of it sourced locally in Ireland: Clare jams, Burren Wild Flower Honey, Crossogue and Ownabwee Preserves, Celtic chocolates, and much, much more. Finally, if you are feeling energetic, you could tackle the steep climb up the mountain behind the cave and reward yourself with an incomparable view over the sweep of Galway Bay.

COUNTY LIMERICK

Bordered by the popular tourist counties of Cork, Kerry and Clare, Co. Limerick tends to get overlooked by visitors in search of better known attractions. But this mainly agricultural county has a quiet charm of its own and also some sights as rewarding as anywhere in the country. King John's Castle in Limerick City is one of the best examples of fortified Norman architecture in Ireland, Castle Matrix is a beautifully restored 15th century tower house, and there's an impressive collection of prehistoric monuments in the area around beautiful Lough Gur. The ruins of many Norman castles and monasteries are dotted around the county's green pastures, noted for their lushness - the best dairy cattle come from Limerick and the county is also famous for its horse-breeding. And Adare is certainly a strong contender for the title of "Ireland's Prettiest Village".

Limerick City has been a centre of trade for well over a millennium and although it was once described as having "the grave, grey look of Commerce", in recent years it has revitalised itself, especially around the City Hall area, its Art School has produced some talented clothes designers, and for a city of its size it has a surprisingly vibrant nightlife.

LIMERICK

MAP 2 REF F12

65 miles N of Cork on the N20

The lowest fording point on the Shannon, Limerick was settled by Vikings around 922. They were ousted by the Irish under Brian Boru in 1014 who in turn were conquered by the Anglo-Normans. King John came here in 1210 and built one of the finest castles in his realm. **King John's Castle** rises impressively from the waterside, its sturdy round tower

King John's Castle, Limerick

guarding the fording place across the river. Badly damaged by Cromwell's troops, the castle was fully restored in 1990 and now houses an interesting re-creation of what life was like for the medieval garrison.

Nearby **Castle Lane** celebrates a more recent period - the 18th and 19th centuries, in a streetscape comprising buildings from Limerick's urban architectural heritage. It includes a traditional tavern; an "Officer's Club" which hosts a dinner/theatre entertainment that features a cast of young entertainers displaying the artistry and originality of modern Irish music and dance; and the Limerick Civic Museum. The Civic Museum documents the city's prosperity in Georgian times when it was famous for its production of silverware and lace.

There are even more extensive collections at the **Hunt Museum** in the University campus area. Donated by the art historian and antiquarian John Hunt, the collection includes some fine paintings by Renoir, Picasso and Yeats; a superb display of Celtic and medieval art; and an eclectic range of objects from all periods of the past. Amongst the many important items are the personal seal of Charles I, the Mary Queen of Scots Cross, a coin revered since the Middle Ages as being one of Judas' 30 pieces of silver, and a magnificent bronze horse by Leonardo da Vinci.

About halfway between the Hunt Museum and King John's Castle, **St Mary's Cathedral** dates back to the late 1100s with major additions and rebuilding in the 15th century. The cathedral's greatest treasures are its misericords, beautifully carved choir seats of black oak depicting a whole menagerie of real and imaginary animals - boars and griffins, sphinxes and cockatrice.

The Irish Chamber Orchestra re-located to Limerick in 1995 and music festivals and performances in the city are now so numerous it's difficult to keep track of them all. In addition to the Summerfest of classical music, the city also hosts the International Marching Band Competition and the "most user-friendly" festival, the Paddy Music Expo, which takes place over the May Bank Holiday and features a full programme of jazz, blues, folk and rock performances as well as talent competitions.

A more recently established celebration is the **Limerick Good Food Festival** in mid-August when international chefs from 3 continents compete for the Grand Prix Mondial, an open-air barbecue is held in the gardens of City Hall and the city's restaurants vie with each other to produce the most tempting food possible.

Activity of a different kind is reflected in Limerick's claim to be the "Sports Capital of Ireland" - Limerick-born athletes have won no fewer than 6 Olympic gold medals. Rugby, hurling and soccer are undoubtedly the most popular sports but the city also has a modern golf course, a National Hunt horse racing track and greyhound racing every Monday, Thursday and Saturday evening all year round.

In addition to its world-class athletes, Limerick boasts several other famous sons. Amongst them are the TV personality Terry Wogan, the actor Richard Harris, and Frank McCourt, author of the Pulitzer Prize-winning book *Angela's Ashes*, the film of which was shot in and around the city.

KILCORNAN
11 miles W of Limerick on the N69

MAP 2 REF F12

This small village boasts two major tourist attractions and an outstanding place to stay. Guests arriving at **Killeen House** will find a warm welcome from their hosts, Marie and Vincent Keran, whose hospitality even extends to giving you a lift to the local pub if you wish. (The publican will organise the return trip). Killeen House is an attractive modern

Killeen House, Cowpark, Kilcornan, Paliskenry, Co. Limerick
Tel: 061 393023

building set in spacious gardens at the edge of the Currahchase Forest Park. The interior is furnished in traditional style and although the house is fully centrally heated, there's an open fire to give that extra welcoming touch. The house has 8 guest bedrooms, all of them en suite, comfortable and well equipped. Breakfast is included in the tariff and an evening meal is available on request: - a tasty repast based on good old-fashioned home cooking and prepared from the freshest of local produce. Nearby **Currahchase Forest Park** is one of the finest landscaped grounds in Ireland. For some 300 years the estate was the home of the de Vere family whose most notable scion was the poet and author, Aubrey de Vere (1814-1902). The family's magnificent mansion, Currahchase House was destroyed by fire in 1941 and only the outer shell remains, but the grounds are superb. The 600 acre plantation is maintained by the Irish Forest and Wildlife Service which has provided detailed nature trails, forest walks, picnic areas and an arboretum. Also close to Killeen House is the **Celtic Park and Gardens**, located on an original Celtic settlement. The Park interprets Ireland's past with exhibits that include a stone circle, a dolmen, a lake dwelling, a stone church and holy well, and a fine example of an early surviving Ringfort. These two attractions are virtually on the doorstep of Killeen House and you don't have to travel much further to find facilities for lake trout fishing, golf and horse riding, while at Kilcornan itself you can enjoy Karting on Co. Limerick's only outdoor track.

FOYNES
MAP 2 REF E12
18 miles W of Limerick

Between 1939 and 1945, the port of Foynes was an important staging post for air traffic between the United States and Europe. The famous flying boats landed in the bay here, carrying a diverse range of people from celebrities, high-ranking British and American military officers, to refugees. The **Foynes Boat Museum**, housed in the terminal of the original Shannon Airport, recalls this era with a comprehensive range of exhibits, vintage film, graphic illustrations and an audio-visual show.

ADARE
MAP 2 REF F13
9 miles SW of Limerick on the N21

With its brightly coloured thatched cottages, romantic medieval ruins, ancient stone-work and trim gardens, Adare makes every effort to maintain its reputation as "Ireland's Prettiest Village". This model estate village snuggles in a wooded setting beside a graceful old bridge over the River Maigue, at its heart a beautifully preserved 14th century Augus-tinian Priory, part of which is still in use as the Church of Ireland parish church. The story book appearance of the village owes its special qualities to the 2nd Earl of Dunraven who

Adare Village

in the 1830s when landlords in general were replacing thatch with slate, went against the trend and rebuilt Adare with larger thatched houses. Before the Earl's improvements, Adare was notorious for its scruffy, run-down character; today its quaint old cottages are interspersed with upmarket restaurants, crafts and antiques shops.

The Earl also built a grand mansion for himself and his family. Noble Adare Manor is now the **Adare Manor Hotel** and a delight in every sense. Ranked among Ireland's finest baronial residences when it was completed in 1862, the dream home of the 2nd Earl of Dunraven is a showpiece of Irish architecture, a breathtakingly monumental building which imaginatively combines delicate local craftsmanship with the finest design influences from abroad. Set beside the gently flowing River Maigue, the Manor remained the home of the Earls of Dunraven until the 1980s. Then, in 1987, Thomas and Judy Kane from New Jersey, bought the Manor and carried out a faithful restoration that lovingly transformed the grand old house into Ireland's premier luxury resort. Arriving visitors step through an imposing portal to a cathedral-style high-arched Lobby, warmed by glowing open firelight, and a genuinely inviting welcome. Pause to admire the Minstrel's Gallery,

Adare Manor Hotel, Adare, Co. Limerick
Tel: 061 396566 Fax: 396124 e-mail: Reservations@adaremanor.com
website: http://www.adaremanor.ie

more than 40 yards long and almost 10 metres high, which was inspired by the Hall of Mirrors at Versailles, with 17th century Flemish choir stalls on both sides. Enjoy the peace of the superb Library or settle down to afternoon tea in the old world charm of the Drawing Room. The guest rooms are equally impressive. One of them, Room 203, the apartment of the former Lady of the Manor, is a wonderful example of painstaking craftsmanship and can probably be called the most beautiful bedroom in Ireland.

Within the Manor Estate's 840 acres of rolling countryside is the superb 7138 yard championship Golf Course designed by Robert Trent Jones Sr., regarded as amongst the finest created by this world renowned golf architect.

Adare Manor provides the visitor with every service and amenity needed to ensure that their stay is truly memorable. In addition to golf, there are facilities for horse riding, fishing, clay pigeon shooting, an indoor swimming pool, sauna and fitness centre, as well as comprehensive conference facilities.

One of the most highly recommended places for bed and breakfast in this enchanting village is **Beech Mount**, a peaceful family home in a quiet cul-de-sac opposite the Golf Club. Visitors are welcomed by Mary Hogan with a cup of tea, or coffee, and biscuits, a foretaste of the warm hospitality that has made Beech Mount so popular. Built in 1974, this spacious house stands within an extensive garden and enjoys some magnificent views. The residents' TV Lounge has a traditional open fire and the 3 en suite guest bedrooms are equipped with orthopaedic beds, hairdryers and tea/coffee making facilities. Non-smoking rooms are available. Children are welcome at Beech Mount, (with a 25% discount); the house has its own ample parking, and credit cards are accepted. Open from March 1st

Beech Mount, Ardshanballa, Adare, Co. Limerick
Tel/Fax: 061 396285

until October 31st, Beech Mount is close to facilities for fishing, golf and horse riding, and the village itself has a wealth of historic buildings to explore, most notably the ruins of the 15th century Franciscan friary which provides an unusual feature on the nearby golf course.

RATHKEALE
MAP 2 REF E13
16 miles SW of Limerick on the N21

The second largest town in Co. Limerick, Rathkeale has a long main street with a fine early-19th century Courthouse and, just outside the town, one of the most striking medieval tower houses in the country, **Castle Matrix**. Built around 1410 for the 7th Earl of Desmond, the castle follows the usual plan for these mini-fortresses - four or five storeys high with the upper floors used as living quarters, the windowless ground floor for storage. The young Walter Raleigh stayed here in 1580 and years later, following his return from his colonising voyage to Virginia, presented his host with some potatoes. The Desmonds claimed that they were the first to grow potatoes in Ireland, a claim hotly contested by Youghal in Co. Cork.

In the 1980s the castle was bought by Seán O'Driscoll, an Irish-American military expert who used his knowledge of medieval fortifications to restore the building as near as possible to its original state. A tiny chapel was re-created on the top floor and a medieval bedroom on another. The house is furnished with some wonderful Irish pieces, most notably an exquisite 19th century jewel encrusted harp. The house is now the headquarters of the Irish Heraldry Society but can be visited by arrangement. (Tel: 069 64284).

Rathkeale developed alongside the River Deel and just along from the Deel Bridge is **An Seabhac Wine Bar & Coffee Shop**, a fascinating place which contains the essence of traditional Ireland in 4 small rooms. The building dates back some 300 years, with stone floors, timber beams and ceilings, and open fires creating a wonderful olde-worlde atmosphere. Low doorways, where it's wise to "Duck or Grouse", add to the charm. The rooms are furnished with vintage tables and chairs, and lighting by candles provides an additional romantic touch. Local crafts are displayed around the rooms and in one corner there's a pile of old books which look as if they've been there a lifetime.

An Seabhac was a pub until the 1950s, when it became a private residence, but in 1997 Ann and Gerald Fennell opened the premises as a uniquely inviting wine bar and coffee shop. Also unique are the catering arrangements. An Seabhac doesn't have a menu. If you plan to dine here, phone Ann the day before and tell her what you would like to eat, and at what hour. Your meal will be prepared from the freshest ingredients and ready for you at the appointed time. If you're not dining, An Seabhac offers a large selection of carefully chosen wines which are served with complimentary snacks.

An Seabhac, Church Street, Rathkeale, Co. Limerick
Tel: 069 64888

Another major attraction here is the music. Gerald is an accomplished musician himself and is often joined in impromptu sessions by musicians from all over the world who drop in and avail themselves of the selection of instruments stored in the Music Room. These impromptu entertainments can happen any time but there are also scheduled traditional music sessions on most weekends. Definitely not to be missed. Combine your visit to An Seabhac with a browse around the nearby Craft Shop which concentrates on the work of local craftsmen and also stocks some interesting bric-à-brac as well as gifts for all occasions.

CROOM   MAP 2 REF F13
11 miles S of Limerick on the N20

This pleasant little town in the heart of the county has two literary credits to its name. In the 18th century it was the meeting place for the Maigue poets, an early movement dedicated to revitalising Gaelic poetry, and a century or so later the comic verse form, the limerick, was first popularised here.

ROCKHILL   MAP 2 REF F13
19 miles S of Limerick on the N20

Country House accommodation in a house once lived in by the novelist Dorothea Connyers, in a landscape captured by the painter Lionel Edwards, is an experience to be savoured. **Ballyteigue House** is the home of Dick and Margaret Johnson who are enjoying having guests sharing their lovely home. Every window reveals a picture: - the Ballyhoura Mountains and the Miauge Valley in the distance; the shrubbery and garden to the west. The rooms at Ballyteigue House are spacious and furnished with antiques; the

Ballyteigue House, Rockhill, Bruree, Co. Limerick Tel/Fax: 063 90575
e-mail: ballyteigue@tinct.ie   website: http://homepage.tinet.ie/~ballyteigue

bedrooms are large and en suite with modern comforts. There are 4 double or twin rooms, and 1 single. The house may be taken privately on a weekly basis for one to a maximum of 9 people on a B&B arrangement with full use of dining room and drawing room at the same price. Dinner is available on request.

Hunting can be arranged with local packs, and there are golf courses in abundance, with championship courses such as Ballybunnion, Lahinch and Killarney one and half hours away. The house is an ideal base for touring well known spots like Blarney, Adare, Cashel and, locally, Bruree on the Maigue river with its museum where the historic figure Eamonn de Valera is well documented. Ancient Kilmallock and archaeological Lough Gur with its stone circle is not far away. All in all a magical place - and only one mile off the N20.

LOUGH GUR   MAP 2 REF F13
16 miles S of Limerick off the R512

The only lake of any size in Co. Limerick, **Lough Gur** is surrounded by one of Ireland's most important archaeological sites although the most important artefacts discovered here have been distributed to museums around the world. In the mid-1900s the lake was partly drained, lowering its level by around 9 feet and uncovering such quantities of prehistoric items that whole cart-loads were carried away. The most dazzling discovery was an almost perfectly preserved bronze shield dating from 700BC, the only blemish to its design of concentric bosses being two nicks caused by the sickle of the reed cutter who unearthed it. At the interpretive centre near the lough there are facsimiles of weapons, tools and pottery found in the area, models of stone circles and burial chambers, and an audio-visual presentation recording the story of man's 5000-year-long presence at Lough Gur. During the season the centre runs regular walking tours around the most interesting archaeological features of this historic site.

6 The West of Ireland

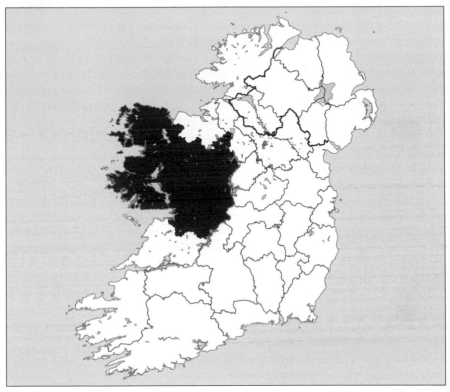

COUNTY GALWAY

The second-largest county in Ireland, Galway has an unusual shape - split into two distinct parts with the great expanse of Lough Corrib almost separating them completely. Only a narrow strip of land around Galway City links the Connemara area in the west to the more extensive inland districts. For many, Connemara is archetypical Ireland, a region of magnificent scenic grandeur typified by the rocky mountain range known as the Twelve Bens. Most of the inhabitants are Irish speakers and the ancient Gaelic culture is enthusiastically preserved. To the east stretch fertile fields corralled by dry stone walls, meandering rivers and streams and the houses and castles of a bygone age.

The unofficial "capital of west Ireland", Galway City has a population of around 60,000 - almost one third of the county's inhabitants but despite its enormous growth over the last 20 years it has retained its intimate and friendly atmosphere. Dating back to medieval times, this fishing port, and thriving commercial and cultural centre is a vibrant, cosmopolitan place where there always seems to be an event of some kind in progress.

GALWAY CITY
43 miles NE of Ennis on the N6

MAP 3 REF E10

Despite being the third largest city in Ireland, Galway has a village-like atmosphere, a place where everyone seems to known everyone else. It is not over-endowed in the way of top-flight historical sites or conventional visitor attractions but the city makes up for it by its vivacity and sense of fun. There are lively pubs, frequent concerts featuring top-calibre Irish folk groups and a succession of popular festivals and events. The most popular of these are the 6-day Race Week at the end of July, the **Galway International Oyster Festival** in late September, and the **Galway Arts Festival** in mid-July, a two-week-long celebration of the performing and visual arts which is widely regarded as Ireland's most popular arts extravaganza.

A good way to explore the city is to start by parking your car at the Eyre Square Centre, a modern shopping centre with more than 200 different shops which, amazingly, manages to blend up-to-date shopping facilities with a respect for the past. Incorporated within the Centre is a large section of the medieval town wall, built by the Anglo-Normans who settled here on the banks of the River Corrib in the 13th century. A short walk from the Centre brings you to the **John F. Kennedy Memorial Park** where the American President addressed the people of Galway when he received the freedom of the city in 1963. Also within the park are some strong iron cannons which were used in the Crimean War of 1853-6; a statue of Pádraic O'Conaire (1882-1928) who was a pioneer of the Irish Literary Revival; and, a real oddity, the freestanding Browne Doorway. This 2-storey portal was removed here in the 1920s from an old town house and bears the arms of the Browne and Lynch families, dated 1627.

The Lynch, or Lynche, family was one of the "14 Tribes of Galway" - leading Anglo-Norman families who dominated the county in the Middle Ages and whose surnames still take up many pages of the telephone directory. The Lynch family is also recalled by **Lynch's Castle** in the city centre, an imposing building with an elaborately decorated frontage which dates back to 1320 and is regarded as one of the finest medieval town houses in Ireland. It is now a branch of the Allied Irish Bank but in 1493 it was the home of James Lynch Fitzstephen, Mayor of Galway. In that year the Mayor's son, Walter, was found guilty in that year of murdering a Spanish visitor who had "made eyes" at Walter's girl friend, Agnes. As Chief Magistrate, James was forced to condemn Walter to death and when no-one could be found to carry out the sentence, the Mayor hanged his own son himself. A broken man, he retired into seclusion and died soon afterwards. Historians dispute that this tragic event ever took place but the story is now firmly entrenched in Galway's folk lore.

Mayor Lynch's tomb can be seen in **St Nicholas' Church**, a couple of hundred yards from Lynch's Castle. It's the largest medieval parish church in Ireland and an enduring tradition asserts that Christopher Columbus prayed here before crossing the Atlantic - St

Nicholas of Myra, better known now as Santa Claus, but in those days much more important as the patron saint of sailors. Whether Columbus prayed here or not, it is a fact that a Galway man named Rice de Culvy did accompany the great explorer on his pioneering voyage.

Just around the corner from St Nicholas' Church, number 8, Bowling Green Lane was the home of Nora Barnacle, the fiery-tempered, auburn haired woman who married the novelist James Joyce in 1931. Joyce regularly visited the tiny house where she grew up and the small museum here contains, amongst other Joycean memorabilia, copies of the letters they wrote to each other.

A short walk from Nora Barnacle's house leads to the riverside and one of the city's most historic landmarks, the **Spanish Arch**. This rather plain but functional building dates back to the 1500s when it was used to store barrels of wine and rum being offloaded from Spanish galleons. The Arch leads to the famous Long Walk where in times past Galway gentryfolk strolled along the river bank.

Right next to the Spanish Arch and situated in the heart of Galway's Latin Quarter, the **Hotel Spanish Arch** is every bit as exotic as it sounds. This unique building is the creation of Easter McDonagh who in the mid-1990s transformed a dilapidated site into one of the finest hotels in the country, a truly cosmopolitan place. The sumptuous interior design is also Easter's work, as intriguing in its way as her unusual Christian name - the consequence, incidentally, of being born on a Good Friday and christened on Easter Day. In the Victorian bar, for example, there are beautifully carved wooden panels which were salvaged from the home of the English actress Lillie Langtry, "Jersey Lily", confidante to King Edward VII. Engraved with the entwined initials "L" and "E" they impart a regal and intimate touch to this incomparable hotel. In this fine bar, the ancient timbered floors are resonant of a bygone age, adds a further touch of sophistication. During the development of the hotel, the wall of a 16th century Carmelite convent was uncovered. This wall has been tastefully integrated into the bar and restaurant

Hotel Spanish Arch, Quay Street, Galway
Tel: 091 569600 Fax: 091 569191
E-mail: emcdgall@iol.ie
website: http//www.beourguest.ie/
listcountydetails.cfm?id+117

areas, creating a dramatic and historic atmosphere. Here, locals and visitors can relax and savour the very best in beers, wines, coffees, tea, fine food and tasty snacks.

Easter's flair for interior decoration is most inventively demonstrated in the 20 en suite guest bedrooms, each one individually designed with a different colour scheme. Lavish soft furnishings evoke an air of unashamed opulence, romantic and relaxing, but complemented by modern amenities such as TVs and direct dial telephones.

Hotel Spanish Arch enjoys a prime position in this attractive city, with medieval Galway right outside its doors. Cosmopolitan cafés and restaurants, traditional Irish pubs, and the Druid and Taibhdhearc theatres nestle in nearby historic lanes.

To the east of the Hotel Spanish Arch is the harbour where you can catch one of the regular ferries to the famous **Aran Islands**, about 30 miles out in Galway Bay. The three islands, Inishmore, Inishmaan and Inisheer, are unique in their archaeology, in their Celtic and early Christian heritage and in their landscape which is akin to the stark limestone moonscapes of the Burren in County Clare. The other-worldly nature of the islands is enhanced by the fact that most of the 1500 islanders speak Gaelic as their native tongue. They still use the traditional canvas-covered boats, *curraghs*, for fishing and for access to the smaller islands where the ferry cannot dock.

The island's prehistoric sites are too numerous to detail here but one that should not be missed is **Dún Aengus** on Inishmore, a spectacular ring fort covering about 11 acres and perched on the edge of cliffs that plummet 300ft into the sea. The fort's three concentric ramparts are 18ft high and 13ft deep; their precise age and purpose still a mystery.

In addition to the Galway ferry, the islands can be reached by ferries from Doolin in County Clare and by air from the airstrip near Inveran on the Galway coast. All forms of transport are dependent on the west coast's unpredictable weather.

SALTHILL   Map 3 ref E10
1 mile S of Galway City on the R338

Salthill is Galway City's seaside suburb, one of Ireland's leading resorts offering a promenade 2½ miles long, good bathing, sailing, band concerts, amusements and an entertainment complex, Leisureland, providing a wide range of all-weather activities. The spacious sandy beaches are rarely crowded and they enjoy splendid views across the sparkling bay to the Burren hills of county Clare. Perhaps the most appealing of the beaches are Silver Strand to the west, and Ballyloughrun to the east.

Customer service in the United States is arguably the best in the world, something that Peter and Aideen Byrne came to appreciate during the years they lived there. Returning to Ireland in 1997, they purchased **Ocean Wave** and introduced the same ethos of friendly, prompt and courteous service. Arriving guests, for example, are unburdened of their luggage, (no tip expected, incidentally), and offered a refreshing cup of tea or coffee and fresh scones. This luxury 8-bedroomed property stands on the main junction of the Salthill to Barra road - the "Gateway to Connemara", a convenient location which provides easy access to both the city and the countryside. The property has been immaculately maintained, with wooden floors and staircases giving extra character to the modern, strik-

Ocean Wave, Knocknacarra Cross, Salthill, Galway City, Co. Galway
Tel: 091 520620

ingly designed building. The guest bedrooms are all en suite and equipped with TV, telephone, hairdryers, tea/coffee-making facilities and a safe for valuables. Bed & breakfast guests at Ocean Wave have the additional bonus of enjoying uninterrupted views of Galway Bay and the Burren. Visitors have the use of a spacious sitting room whose bay window looks out across Galway Bay, and the attractive garden with its fountain also enjoys this superb view. The food at Ocean Wave is also of a high standard and, if you are staying on a half-board basis, your evening meal will be based on the best of fresh, local produce and home cooked to perfection. If your passion is golf, you will feel very much at home at Ocean Wave since the local golf course is close by. Peter and Aideen are golf addicts themselves and offer golf package holidays with a choice of courses to play on. Another feature of the outstanding service they provide is that your golf clubs will be cleaned for you and stored in a secure area.

"At **Marian Lodge** you are not a tourist - you belong!" So declares Celine Molloy, the owner of this inviting family-run guesthouse which stands in lovely gardens close to the promenade, beach and Leisureland in Upper Salthill. The Salthill golf course and driving range is just around the corner and there are facilities for tennis, fishing, horse-riding, windsurfing and fishing all within easy reach. A 2-minute walk will take you to a quiet pub, a little further to Salthill's wide range of restaurants, pubs and shops. Celine hails originally from Co. Donegal but fell in love with the Galway area and now provides a warm welcome and a home-from-home atmosphere in her spacious modern house. An excellent cook, Celine bakes her own bread, which provides a tasty addition to the extensive choice at breakfast time. The meal is served from 8.10 until 9.30 in the dining-room with its elegant Waterford glass chandelier and splendid views overlooking Galway Bay. Another interesting feature of the house is a collection of vintage pots and pans displayed around a rustic fireplace.

Marian Lodge has 6 guest bedrooms, all en suite and non-smoking, and all comprehensively equipped with cable television, orthopaedic beds, direct dial telephone, hairdryer,

Marian Lodge Guest House, Knocknacarra Road, Salthill, Co. Galway
Tel: 091 521678   Fax: 091 528103   E-mail: celine@iol.ie
website: www.marian-lodge.com

clock radio and tea/coffee-making facilities. Open all year, except over the Christmas period, Marian Lodge offers top-quality accommodation and exceptional value for money.

Overlooking Galway Bay and with Leisureland and beaches close by, **The Connaught** is a spacious modern house which was purpose-built in 1984 as a guest house. Outside, huge tubs of flowers provide a colourful foil to the house with its pink-washed walls and white-railinged balcony. The Connaught is the home of Tom and Colette Keaveney and one very good reason for staying here is that Tom is a professional chef with many years experience in the hotel industry. A Lecturer in food production at the Galway and Mayo

The Connaught, Barna Road, Salthill, Co. Galway
Tel/Fax: 091 525865   e-mail: tcconnaught@eircom.net

Institute of Technology, Tom is responsible for the superb breakfasts served at The Connaught. The spread includes fresh croissants, bread, muffins, pancakes, waffles, French crêpes and French toast; a full Irish breakfast with egg dishes of every kind; or anything you particularly favour if ordered the previous day. Evening meals are not provided at The Connaught but the house is only a few minutes from the town centre where there's an abundance of restaurants and pubs. The house has 6 non-smoking guest bedrooms, all en suite, and fully equipped with television, electric blankets and hairdryers. Peaceful and relaxing, this outstanding guest house provides an excellent base for touring the area with Connemara and the Aran Islands within easy reach, and facilities for golf, fishing, horse-riding and wind-surfing all virtually on the doorstep.

BARNA VILLAGE   MAP 3 REF E10
5 miles W of Galway on the R336

An excellent way of exploring Connemara is to follow the **Great Figure Eight Tour**, a 150 mile drive that describes a figure of eight through one of the most beautiful regions of Ireland and also one of the most barren. Much of it lies in the Gaeltacht area where Irish is still spoken so be prepared for road and town signs in Gaelic and for the fact that the spelling of Gaelic words is highly variable. Beginning the tour at Salthill and travelling westward, the first place of note is the picturesque little fishing village and resort of Barna - or *Bearna*. If you plan to stay in this charming location, two places are highly recommended.

With its neatly thatched roof and colour washed walls, **The Twelve Pins Hotel** makes a very inviting picture and your hosts, Pat and Geraldine Lohan and their three daughters, offer a warm welcome second to none. The hotel and its restaurant are renowned for their olde tyme decor and ambience, and the famous restaurant excels in quality food, specialising in freshly caught seafood, steak and succulent duck. You can

The Twelve Pins Hotel, Barna Village, Galway, Co. Galway
Tel: 091 592368 Fax: 091 592485

select your own lobster from the tank or, if your preference is for vegetarian dishes, you'll find a choice of tasty, wholesome options. The restaurant is open seven days a week and is a perfect venue for small parties. The Twelve Pins also offers an excellent bar menu which is available throughout the day. There's a wonderful atmosphere in the bar, especially so at weekends when live music attracts both locals and visitors alike. In summer, the beer garden makes a pleasant setting for an outdoor pint.

This picturesque village is a great place to stay and the hotel has 18 luxurious bedrooms, all en suite with television and direct dial telephones. Two of the rooms are purpose built and wheelchair friendly. At breakfast time, the choice at The Twelve Pins includes a full Irish breakfast which is served right up until noon.

Barna village is just 10 minutes from Galway City, and just 20 minutes from the ferries to the famous Aran Islands. Superb golf courses, swimming, country walks, horse riding, beautiful beaches and fishing are all available in the immediate area. The Twelve Pins Hotel is also the perfect base for touring Connemara, Galway, Salthill, North Clare and the Cliffs of Moher.

Situated just 50 metres from the shoreline of Galway Bay, **An Faoilean** (The Seagull) offers outstanding bed and breakfast accommodation in this quaint little fishing village. The home of Geraldine and Enda Folan, An Faoilean is a beautifully laid-out house with plenty of character. The views from the house of Galway Bay and the Clare Hills are absolutely breathtaking and within a short distance of this fine guest house visitors will

An Faoilean, Freeport, Bearna, Co. Galway
Tel/Fax: 091 592498   e-mail: efolan@iol.ie
website: http://www.wombat.ie/pages/faoilean

find a wealth of holiday amenities - a Blue Flag Silver Strand beach, Riding Stables and Pony Trekking, the new Bearna Golf Club (1km); a Tennis Club and Galway Golf Club (2km); Salthill Promenade and beach, swimming pool and watersports (3km); and Galway City with its multifarious attractions is just 7km away. Visitors to An Faoilean will find comfortable, well-equipped bedrooms, a relaxing sitting room with panoramic countryside views and multi-channel TV and stereo system. The food here is superb, a fact testified by the many complimentary entries in the visitors' book. At breakfast time there's a choice of a traditional Irish breakfast or a self-service buffet offering a selection of fresh fruit, cereals, yoghurts, cheese board and home-baked breads. Delicious packed lunches are also available.

SPIDDAL (AN SPIDÉAL)
MAP 3 REF E10
10 miles W of Galway on the R336

The small coastal town of Spiddal is a charming little holiday resort with a fine sandy beach. It lies in the heart of the Gaeltacht (Gaelic-speaking area) and has some lively pubs and a Craft Centre where a collection of workshops produces some top quality sculpture, ceramics, weaving and jewellery. But the village is perhaps best known for its outstanding seafood restaurant, **Bolvisce.** Owned and run by Stewart and Barbara Brooke, Bolvisce has been in Barbara's family since 1993 and over the years has established a well-deserved

Bolvisce, Spiddal, Co. Galway
Tel: 091 553286

reputation for its quality food. The appetising menu offers wonderful dishes of locally caught fish - sole, salmon, monkfish; lobster and oysters in season. Especially popular is Bolvisce's famous offering of oysters and Guinness served with home-made bread. The menu also includes locally produced lamb, beef and duck along with vegetarian choices. The restaurant is fully licensed and boasts an impressively long (and reasonably priced) wine list. Bolvisce's informal and friendly atmosphere, soft lighting and open fireplace create just the right ambience for a relaxed and enjoyable meal. It is open all year round, between 12.30pm and 10pm every day.

From Spiddal the Figure Eight Tour continues along the coast as far as the little airport at Inveran (which has regular flights to the Aran Islands) and then turns inland to the village of Casla (*Costello* in Gaelic), home to the Gaelic radio station *Raidió na Gaeltachta* and the recently opened Tropical Butterfly Centre. North of Casla the route passes through wild and scenic countryside to Maam Cross, the crossover point of the figure-of-eight, which has been dubbed the "Piccadilly of Connemara". The drive continues northwards through the beautiful Maam Valley to the area known as Joyce Country - nothing to do with the great novelist but named after the Joyce family who settled here in the 13th century and whose name is still common in the district.

The attractive village of **Leenane** is an angling resort, a centre for climbers tackling the nearby Maamturk Mountains, and perhaps best known as the major location for the 1990 film *The Field*, starring Richard Harris and John Hurt. West of Leenane the route passes **Kylemore Abbey**, a 19th century mock-Tudor extravaganza of towers and turrets erected by an English shipping magnate and enjoying a spectacular lakeside location. Now a boarding school run by Benedictine nuns, the Abbey welcomes visitors to its craft shops and tea rooms.

About 4 miles further west at the quiet village of **Letterfrack** is the entrance to the **Connemara National Park**, a wild expanse of bog, heath and granite mountains which includes part of the famous Twelve Bens range. The Park's Visitor Centre has copious information about the fauna, flora and geology of the area, and the helpful staff can guide you to safe hiking trails in this potentially dangerous terrain.

CLIFDEN
37 miles NW of Galway on the N59

MAP 3 REF C9

The main town of Connemara, (although with a population of little more than 1000), Clifden is beautifully set on the edge of the Atlantic with the elegant spires of its two churches rising against a magnificent backdrop of mountains. The town is the centre of Connemara pony breeding and its annual **Connemara Pony Show** on the third Thursday of August is the main event in the Clifden calendar.

About 3 miles east of Clifden at Lettershea, **Dan O'Hara's Homestead** is the restored cottage of Dan O'Hara, a man made famous in song and story. A tenant farmer, he was evicted from his home in the 1830s and forced to emigrate. During the voyage to America he lost his wife and three of his children and arriving penniless in New York was reduced to selling matches on the street. His 8-acre holding is farmed as it would have been in pre-famine times. An old style pony and trap takes visitors on a guided tour and in addition to Dan's humble cottage the site includes a visitor centre with an audio-visual presentation; reconstructions of a *crannóg*, (a prehistoric lake dwelling), a ring fort and a *clachaun* (an early Christian oratory); a large craft shop and a tea room.

From Lettershea, the Figure Eight Drive returns eastwards, passing the much photographed Derryclare Lough, and on through the crossover point at Maam to the little town of Oughterard.

OUGHTERARD MAP 3 REF E9
14 miles NW of Galway on the N59

Although it lies a mile or so inland from **Lough Carrib**, is a major centre for anglers with plenty of boats available to rent either for fishing or to visit the uninhabited islet of Inchagoill in the centre of the lough. It has two ruined churches - St Patrick's, believed to date back to the 5th century, and the 12th century *Teampall na Naomh* (Church of the Saints) which has an impressive Romanesque doorway and some interesting carvings. The atmosphere on the island is quite magical.

The **Corrib House Hotel** in Oughterard promises "Character at the Gateway to Connemara" and it certainly delivers on its promise. Built in 1886, one of the hotel's early clients was the Russian revolutionary, Leon Trotsky, but the Corrib House's customers today are a more amiable mix of locals and visitors drawn by the lure of lovely Connemara. The interior of the hotel is an appealing blend of old time features such as wood

**Corrib House Hotel, Bridge Street, Oughterard, Connemara, Co. Galway
Tel: 091 552329**

panelling, high ceilings and traditional and antique furniture. The cosy bar is stocked with everything that the most fastidious could require, from vintage port to a humble pint. There's always good craic here and also regular sessions of traditional Irish music.

The Owenriff Restaurant at the Corrib House offers fine dining with the added advantage of an abundance of seafood and game in season, coupled with an excellent wine list. The hotel has 27 guest rooms, all en suite and provided with direct dial telephone and multi-channel TV. Some rooms are in the original building, the remainder in the annex surrounded by beautiful landscaped gardens and with ample, secure parking. Whatever your interests, you'll almost certainly find them catered for locally. Lough Corrib, 68½ square miles of water dotted with beautiful wooded islands has probably the finest brown trout fishing in Ireland; the local Oughterard Golf Club spent £2 million in 1999 to bring their course into contention as one of the finest golf clubs in the country. Hill and mountain walking, and racing at Ballinrobe and Galway, are just some of the many other activities and pastimes available.

PORTACARRON   Map 3 ref E9
15 miles NW of Galway off the N59

Occupying a superb lakeside setting, **Corrib Wave Guesthouse** commands magnificent views (from all bedrooms, lounges and dining-room) of Lough Corrib, the Twelve Bens, Maamturk and the Cloosh Mountains. The most up-to-date guesthouse in Connemara, Corrib Wave is built on its own lakeside farm where visitors can walk, mix with animals and wildlife, or take a boat and tour Lough Corrib. The guesthouse is the home of Michael

Corrib Wave Guesthouse, Portacarron, Oughterard, Connemara, Co. Galway
Tel: 091 552147 Fax: 091 552736

and Maria Healy and their family who assure visitors of a warm welcome and every comfort - Irish hospitality, superb home cooking (fresh meat, fish and vegetables), excellent wines, relaxation by an open turf fire, and beautiful bedrooms all of which are en suite with television, hairdryer and other amenities. If you are looking for peace and tranquillity, you will certainly find them at Corrib Wave, but there's also a wide range of activities available if you are feeling more energetic. Lough Corrib is known world-wide for its great free fishing and the Healeys can arrange anything from a rowing boat to a fishing rod for your angling. And nearby Oughterard has its own famous 18-hole golf course and a Horse Riding Centre.

AUGHNANURE

MAP 3 REF E9

15 miles NW of Galway off the N59

A couple of miles east of Oughterard, **Aughnanure Castle** is a 6-storey tower house occupying a daunting position on a rocky island surrounded by a fast flowing stream. In the 1500s it was the main stronghold of the O'Flahertys and said to be one of the strongest fortresses at the time Cromwell was blockading Galway. Visitors to the castle will hear of an interesting device constructed by the O'Flahertys to deal with unwelcome visitors. In the main hall, one of the flagstones was hinged downward so that the offending character could be tipped into the stream below. The hall has followed the same route, collapsing over the years into the rushing water, but the rest of the castle has been restored and is open daily throughout the season. At other times, the key can be collected from the caretaker.

This corner of Connemara is a delightful place to stay and walkers, anglers, pony trekkers and golfers especially will all find an excellent base at the **Mountain View Guesthouse**. It's just a five minute walk to Oughterard's famous golf club which has an 18-hole championship course for the avid player, and pitch and putt for the beginner. Walkers and pony trekkers will find many scenic trails through the breathtaking beauty of the Connemara countryside, while anglers are pampered by the abundant stocks of salmon

**Mountain View Guest House, Aughnanure, Oughterard, Connemara, Co. Galway
Tel: 091 550306 Fax: 091 550133**

and trout in nearby Lough Corrib. The owners of Mountain View, Richard and Patricia O'Connor, will happily help visitors make arrangements for any of these activities. They can also direct you to the many sites of cultural and historic significance in the area: the castles of Ross and Aughnanure, Kylemore Abbey, Pease Cottage and Joyce Country, for example. After a day in the fresh air, guests can relax in the lounge with its open peat fire and sample some of the excellent cuisine, all based on fresh local produce and complemented, if you wish, by a choice of wines. Retire later to a comfortable en suite bedroom, fully equipped with television, direct dial phone, tea/coffee-making facilities and hairdryers.

MOYCULLEN   MAP 3 REF E9
8 miles NW of Galway on the N59

Nestling in the heart of Moycullen village, **White Gables Restaurant** enjoys an outstanding reputation for the quality of its cuisine - in particular the excellent fresh seafood
dishes. Fresh lobster from the restaurant's own sea-water tank, mussels steamed in white
wine, pan-fried John Dory, Monkfish Thermidor, and daily specials fresh off the boat are
just some of the delicacies offered by chef Kevin Dunne. After training on the continent,

White Gables Restaurant, Moycullen, Co. Galway
Tel: 091 555744 Fax: 091 556004

Kevin and his wife Ann acquired White Gables in 1991. An attractive white-washed
building which dates back to the 1820s, it served for a time as the village police station.
Now fully renovated, the restaurant has a wonderfully relaxed and informal style while
maintaining the very highest professional standards. In addition to his appetising fish
dishes, Kevin also offers a good choice of meat and poultry dishes - and some heavenly
desserts. Affable informality and the trusted familiarity of the cooking is the White Gables
recipe for mopping up various consumer awards, and for ensuring that it continues to be
one of the most popular and highly regarded restaurants in Galway. During the season,
White Gables is open 7 days a week from 7pm until 10pm and also at Sunday lunchtime
from 12.30pm until 3pm. During the off season, the restaurant is closed on Mondays;
and from December 23rd until February 14th.

EAST OF GALWAY CITY

ORANMORE   MAP 3 REF F10
5 miles E of Galway on the N6

The picturesque village of Oranmore lies on the shore of Galway Bay to the south of the
city in the area known as "Oyster Country", the focus of the celebrated **Galway Interna-**

tional **Oyster Festival** in late September. This popular event attracts visitors from all over the world to sample the succulent delicacy, usually washed down with a pint of rich, creamy Guinness, and to enjoy the street theatre, free concerts and parades that take place in Galway City.

Another attraction at Oranmore is **Rinville Park**, an attractive amenity created around an ancient castle, a stately home, and a fine estate demesne which dates from the 16th century. Open all year round, the park has an extensive network of walks through woodlands, open farm land and by the sea. There are some fine views of Galway Bay, Galway City and the Burren of Co. Clare and ravens, grey herons and otters are among the fascinating fauna to be seen here. The park has picnic areas, a children's playground, a coffee shop (summer season only) and - an additional attraction, admission is free.

Located in the heart of Oranmore village and just a 10 minute drive from Galway City, **Keanes Pub** is an ideal place to break your journey and unwind for a while in a comfortable and relaxing atmosphere. Walls of exposed stone and the unusual feature of tree trunks supporting the main roof beam all help to give this inviting hostelry a character all its own. Food and drink at this "Irish Pub of Distinction 1999" is of the highest standard with an extensive menu available, including a special selection of meals for children. The main menu ranges from 8oz steaks, through seafood dishes such as char-

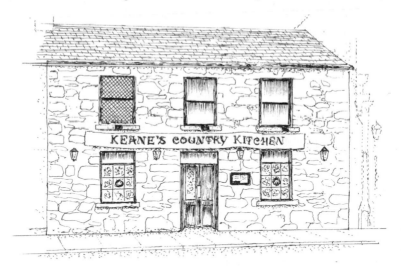

Keanes Pub, Oranmore, Co. Galway
Tel: 091 794075

grilled Salmon Supreme, to soups and sandwiches. Adding to the choice, there are vegetarian options and daily specials served from 12.30pm until 2.45pm. Irish traditional music is another attraction at this welcoming pub which also has a large function room (with dance floor), a popular venue for special events of every kind. Coach tours are welcome and Keanes Pub is ideally located just off the Galway road to Dublin and Limerick - a great place to stop!

CLARINBRIDGE
10 miles SE of Galway City on the N18

MAP 3 REF F10

At Clarinbridge you can ignore the old rule about only eating oysters if there's an 'r' in the month. The ones raised in the calm tidal waters around the village are farmed ones from Portuguese stock and it's perfectly safe to eat them at any time of the year. Under the banner "The World is your Oyster....Clarinbridge is its home", the village hosts its very own Oyster Festival a couple of weeks before Galway City's more extensive celebrations.

Less than a mile outside Clarinbridge, **Rock Lodge** is the home of Mrs Bernie Diskin who has been welcoming bed and breakfast guests here since the early 1980s. This attractive modern bungalow is located in a quiet cul-de-sac close to the sea with its own private

Rock Lodge, Stradbally North, Clarinbridge, Co. Galway
Tel: 091 796071

walkway to the shore. Recommended by the *Guide du Routard*, Rock Lodge provides its guests with comfortable accommodation in its 3 non-smoking guest rooms, 2 of which are en suite and all of them equipped with television and tea/coffee-making facilities. At breakfast time there's a choice of a full Irish Fry or, for lighter appetites, a selection of cereals, fruit, cheeses and yoghurts. Rock Lodge doesn't cater for evening meals but there's a good choice of restaurants and pubs within easy reach. If you have a taste for oysters, then Clarinbridge is the place to be during the second weekend in September when the Oyster Festival celebrates these slurpy bivalve molluscs.

KINVARA
18 miles S of Galway on the N18

MAP 3 REF F10

Set on an inlet of Galway Bay, Kinvara is a delightful quayside village and a popular destination for day visitors from Galway City. **Dunguaire Castle**, an outstanding example of an early-16th century tower house, overlooks the village with its thatched inn and harbourside cafés.

About 2 miles east of Kinvara, in a peaceful rural setting, **Clareview House** is a spacious farmhouse dating back to 1890. It's the home of Brenda and Micheal McTigue who have been welcoming guests here since 1993. Their non-smoking house has 5 guest

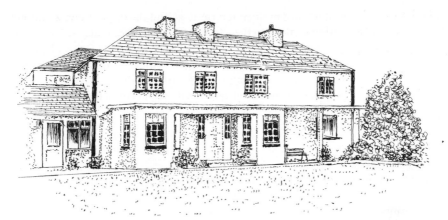

Clareview House, Kinvara, Co. Galway
Tel: 091 637170

bedrooms, all en suite, and all pleasantly furnished and well-equipped. Pets are welcome. If booked in advance, Brenda is always happy to provide an evening meal - wholesome fare based on locally-caught fish and locally-produced meat. The house stands in 120 acres of beef and dairy farmland and one of Clareview's special attractions is the pony which is available for guest use. The house provides an ideal base for touring the Burren, the Cliffs of Moher, Ailwee Caves, Coole Park and the W.B.Yeats tower, while the charming little port of Kinvara is just a couple of miles away. Well worth visiting in Kinvara is **Dunguaire Castle**, a fine example of a 16th century tower house which stands proudly on the site of the 7th century stronghold of the Kings of Connaught. In the 1920s, it was the retreat of Oliver St John Gogarty, contemporary and friend of W.B. Yeats and Lady

Dunguaire Castle

Gregory. Now it has been restored by Shannon Heritage and the displays give an insight into the lifestyle of the people who lived there from 1520 to modern times. Reflecting the great entertainments that took place here during the Middle Ages, the Castle plays host during the season to twice-nightly Medieval Banquets "with food to please the palate and entertainment to lift the soul". A harpist plays softly as you enjoy your meal and Dunguaire's artists present humorous and inspirational excerpts from the work of Synge, Shaw and O'Casey. All in all, a memorable evening.

GORT   MAP 3 REF F11
22 miles S of Galway on the N18

Just north of this small town is **Coole Park**, the former demesne of the house of Lady Gregory, much visited by W.B. Yeats and the subject of some of his most famous work. Little remains of the house but the grounds and lake are now a particularly beautiful forest park. The 'autograph tree' which bears the graffiti of George Bernard Shaw, Sean O'Casey and Augustus John amongst others now stands behind railings to deter anyone else with a literary bent adding their thoughts. In late September the park is the setting for a 3-day annual **Autumn Gathering** which features a programme of plays, lectures and visits to places in the locality associated with Yeats and Lady Gregory.

One such place is **Thoor Ballylee** nearby. Yeats bought this ancient Norman tower and the adjoining cottages in 1916. It was to became his inspiration and his retreat. His collection of poems, *The Tower*, contains several pieces written at or about Thoor Ballylee. The ivy-clad tower has been lovingly restored and now looks much as it did in the 1920s when Yeats and his family lived here. An audio-visual presentation evokes Yeats' life and times, there's a bookshop specialising in Anglo-Irish literature, an excellent tearoom, picnic area and a beautiful riverside walk leading to an ancient mill.

PORTUMNA   MAP 4 REF G11
38 miles SE of Galway on the N65

The traditional market town of Portumna stands on the northern shore of Lough Derg, well known as a fishing centre and now with a busy marina serving the lough and the Shannon. On the south side of the town are the easily accessible ruins of a **Dominican Priory**, built in 1426, and **Portumna Castle**, a 17th century mansion currently undergoing restoration but open to the public. The castle's estate is a wildlife sanctuary with a resident herd of fallow deer. Nearby, the 1000-acre **Portumna Forest Park**, bordering **Lough Derg**, is also a wildlife sanctuary with a well laid out nature trail and many pleasant woodland walks.

Located a couple miles northwest of Portumna, **Green Acres Cottage** offers visitors luxurious self-catering accommodation, peaceful free golfing and the unique experience of exploring the area by horse drawn caravan. Guests have free use of the 9-hole Green Acres Course and there's also an 18-hole pitch and putt. The course has its own welcoming club house with a coffee shop overlooking the green. Clubs, golfballs and trolleys are all available for hire. Anglers are also well-catered for at Green Acres. There's a tackle shed

Green Acres Cottage, Oldthort, Portumna, Co. Galway
Tel: 0509 41123 Fax: 0509 41174

and bait fridge on site, and boat hire can be arranged through the owners, Agnes and Michael Walsh. The Walshs can also arrange hire of a horse drawn caravan, a marvellous way to explore the quiet lanes of unspoilt rural Ireland. You will be given instruction and practice in leading and driving the horse and caravan before leaving on your tour. The instructor will travel with you for some distance to teach you the correct method of controlling the horse on the road. Then you are on your own to enjoy this most satisfying way of exploring the Irish countryside.

The beautifully appointed cottage at Green Acres overlooks the golf course green and can sleep 7-9 people. If necessary, it can be divided into two modern apartments. One has two double rooms, en suite, and can sleep 4-5. The other has one double and twin room and is capable of accommodating 3-4 people. Both kitchens are fully equipped with all

Clonfert Cathedral

modern conveniences and there are facilities for washing, drying and ironing. Electricity, central heating, bed linen and towels are all included in the tariff. The cottage is safe for children and a reliable baby sitting service is available if required. And for those balmy summer evenings, the attractive garden has its own private barbecue. Once experienced, Green Acres is a place you will want to return to again and again.

About 4 miles north of Portumna, tiny **Clonfert Cathedral** stands on the site of a Benedictine monastery founded around 560 by St Brendan. The present cathedral was built in the late 1100s and has an outstanding Romanesque doorway made up of six perfect semi-circular arches radiating outwards from the portal, each decorated with carvings of heads, plants and animal figures. There are more bizarre animal heads adorning the tops of the pillars and the chancel arch is decorated with angels, rosettes and a mermaid admiring herself in a mirror. The Bishop's Palace in the cathedral precincts was the home of the English fascist leader, Sir Oswald Mosley, following his release from prison but the building was later badly damaged by fire and is now derelict.

LOUGHREA   MAP 3 REF G10
20 miles SE of Galway on the N6

This little market town sits on the north bank of the lough from which it takes its name and at its centre survive the well-preserved remains of a **Carmelite priory** built by the de Burgh family in the 1300s. Little remains of the medieval town walls apart from the southeastern gate tower which is now a museum with some interesting exhibits - notably some exquisite 16th century gold and silver chalices. Alongside the tower stands the cathedral, completed in 1903, which features some stained glass created by the modern Dublin School of Stained Glass.

Just a short walk from the town centre, **Fairhill House** is a spacious modern house surrounded by beautifully laid out gardens. It's the home of Ann and Noel Donnellan who after some 20 years experience in the hospitality business opened their attractive house to bed and breakfast guests in 1996. Fairhill House is set well back from the road

Fairhill House, Athenry Road, Loughrea, Co. Galway
Tel: 091 841218

and enjoys enchanting views across the lough. A vista to savour. Guests have the use of a large and comfortable residents' lounge and the 4 guest bedrooms here are all en suite and comprehensively equipped. At breakfast time, you'll find a more than generous spread to set you up for whatever activities you've planned for the day. A few minutes drive will bring you to the scenic Slieve Aughty Mountains where there are some delightful walks, facilities for golf, fishing and pony trekking are all available in the neighbourhood, and the lively city of Galway is just a 20-minute drive away.

Few guest houses anywhere can have enjoyed such a long and interesting history as the **Old Mill Weir** on Bride Street. Part of the house was originally the old East Gate to the walled medieval town and was built around 1200. Later it became a Mill, its water-wheel driven by the river that runs past, and partially under, the building. A bakehouse was conveniently adjacent to the house, making good use of the Mill's products. The Mill continued operating until approximately 1910. The great-grandfather of the present owner used to trap silver eels

Old Mill Weir, Bride Street, Lochrea, Co. Galway
Tel: 091 841737

under the water wheel of the Mill. The season for silver eels only ran between September and November, during which time the catch was despatched to Billingsgate Market. The delicacy became renowned as the original Loughrea Silver Eel. The Mill building was later converted into a restaurant and a glass floor panel was installed through which diners could watch the water flowing past. Since 1993, however, Joseph and Philomena Fahey have run the Old Mill Weir as an excellent guest house, full of character and charm. There are exposed beams in the dining room where amongst the family portraits is one of Joseph's uncles who is a remarkable look-alike for Prince Charles. This is a delightful and unique place to stay, don't miss it!

More than 200 years have passed since what is now **O'Dea's Hotel** was built; more than a century has elapsed since the O'Dea family first opened this impressive 4-storey building as "The Railway Hotel". Today, Mary O'Neill (née O'Dea) continues the family tradition of offering first class accommodation and catering in an atmosphere which is both warm and relaxed. The dining room, with its welcoming open fires and elegant furnishings, serves a comprehensive à la carte menu each evening from 18.30. Carvery

lunches and succulent steaks garnered from locally raised cattle are
the chef's speciality, but there's also a
good choice of vegetarian dishes, all
of them complemented by a fine list
of wines at affordable, realistic prices.
O'Dea's is a place where you can not
only eat well, but also lodge well. The
hotel is very proud of its quiet and
comfortable, luxurious en suite bedrooms. Each of the 24 bedrooms at
O'Dea's has its own en suite bathroom, direct dial telephone, hair
dryer, and tea and coffee making facilities.

The hotel sits at the centre of a
web of manifold attractions, located
halfway between the important and
historic religious centre of
Clonmacnoise and the scenic attractions of the Cliffs of Moher. The
medieval walled town of Athenry is
just 12 miles away as is Thoor Ballylee,
the home of W.B.Yeats. A 15-mile
drive will bring you to the Burren and
its stark, lunar landscapes; travel 15
miles in the opposite direction and
you can visit Portumna Castle, one
of the very few Jacobean mansions

O'Dea's Hotel, Loughrea, Co. Galway
Tel: 091 841611 Fax: 091 842635

in Ireland to have survived both conflict and neglect. You don't have to travel even that
far to witness one of Loughrea's most colourful events. Once a month during the hunting
season, the famous Galway Blazers Hunt musters at O'Dea's Hotel.

About 4 miles north of Loughrea, signposted from the hamlet of Bullaun, stands the
Turoe Stone, the finest stone of its kind in Ireland. It's a rounded pillar, just over 3ft high,
richly decorated with an eddying mass of spirals, a form of decoration known as the
Celtic La Tene style and much more commonly found in Brittany. Dating from the 1st
century AD at the latest, the stone is believed to be a fertility symbol used in pagan rituals.

CRAUGHWELL
Map 3 ref F10
14 miles E of Galway on the N6

This pleasant little village set beside the River Raford was for some years the home of the
celebrated film director John Huston who lived at the house named St Clerans. A gregari-

ous man, he made the most of the village's 3 pubs which are famed for their music and dance sessions. Less well-known outside Galway, the poet Ó'Reachtaire is buried in the churchyard here.

A striking sight in the village is the porticoed entrance porch and curious "toothed" roof-ridge of **Acara Lodge Guesthouse**. Built in the late 1800s, the spacious house has been the residence of the Jennings family for more than a century and is now the home of Cyril and Mary Jennings. It was Cyril's grandmother who began a small drapery business here. The enterprise prospered and moved to larger premises. The rambling old house is

Acara Lodge Guest House, Craughwell Village, Co. Galway
Tel: 091 846755

full of character, replete with attractive features such as period fireplaces, high ceilings and antique furniture, but is also right up to date in providing all modern conveniences - en suite bedrooms, Cable TV and direct dial telephones for example. (Hair dryer and trouser press are also available on request). Guests have the use of a peaceful Reading Room and breakfast is served in a spacious dining room. Best of all is the excellent Restaurant where a top-ranked chef creates appetising dishes based on prime local produce and varying according to the season.

Craughwell village itself is steeped in history, not least as being the home of the Galway Blazers Hunt. A day's hunting with the Hunt is something no keen rider should miss and it can be arranged at short notice. Pony trekking and cross country eventing also take place locally. Craughwell is ideally suited for the keen golfer. Choose one of the many 18-hole golf courses in the area: - Loughrea, Athenry, Gort, Portumna or Galway Bay Golf & Country Club where you can watch the sun go down on Galway Bay. Shooting, fishing and cycle hire are all available locally, and because of Craughwell's rural setting there are many secluded walks to be enjoyed. The village has 3 pubs which are renowned for their lively music and dance sessions and, if you really want to pass on Acara Lodge's own fine restaurant, there is a large selection of top class eating places in the area.

ATHENRY   MAP 3 REF F10
14 miles E of Galway on the R348/R347

In a way, the people of Athenry should be grateful to Red Hugh O'Donnell who in 1597 attacked the town with such savagery that it didn't recover for centuries. The town became fossilised with the result that Athenry today is the classic Irish medieval town with an unmatched wealth of re-mains from the Middle Ages.

Visitors to **Athenry Her-itage Centre** will find a focal point for the many medieval monuments to be found in the town, including Athenry Cas-tle (1235), the Dominican Priory (1241), Market Cross, North Gate, and the longest medieval walls in Ireland. They will also find receptionists dressed in luxurious medieval garb whilst a variety of leather goods and handmade dolls are among the local crafts on of-fer in the Centre's shop.

At the time of writing, the walled garden located to the rear of the Centre is being de-veloped as an area of recreational activity. This par-ticular feature will enhance visitors' appreciation of the town's medieval experience. Allied to this is the inclusion of a fully supervised archery shoot

Athenry Heritage Centre, St Mary's, The Square, Athenry, Co. Galway Tel: 091 844661

where so-called "have-a-go" sessions will be held in a self-contained area. The area will also feature interactive art workshops and a miniaturized version of the town incorporat-ing replica walls, towers and gates. Also included in this phase is the construction of a pathway linking the rear of the Heritage Centre to the nearby entrance of Athenry Castle. By the time you read this, much of this new development may already be in place, but in any case the Centre is well worth visiting for the insights it provides into Athenry's medieval past. The Centre is open daily from Easter to September.

The area also boasts several tourist amenities, including three 18-hole golf courses, a pitch and putt course, as well as the annual **Medieval Festival** (held in mid-August) which celebrates the town's historic past in an explosion of vibrant colour and lavish spectacle.

Located at the heart of this historic little town, **Dobbyn & Coffeys** is a landmark for hospitality, good food and entertainment. An interesting feature of this fully air-conditioned building is the ancient stone wall which provides an intimate character to the restaurant and is a link with the town's long and varied history. The restaurant, "The Jostlestones", can seat 80 people and provides excellent cuisine complemented by fine

Dobbyn & Coffeys, Northgate Street, Athenry, Co. Galway
Tel: 091 845111   Fax: 091 845154

wines and discreet, friendly service. The owners, Olive and Paddy Coffey, promise "fantastic value, quality and choice of menu" and they certainly deliver on their promise. The Jostlestones is an ideal venue for Sunday lunches, evening dinners and intimate meals.

Dobbyn & Coffeys boasts no fewer than 3 different bars, each uniquely designed to meet a variety of tastes. Each bar has a contrasting character and guests will find a perfect setting in which to relax, soak up the friendly atmosphere and enjoy a great night out. Excellent bar food is available all day.

For party functions, there's the De Bermingham Function Room, named after the founder of Athenry Castle, Meyler de Bermingham. This spacious room provides an ideal setting for weddings and other special events. The Coffeys can offer expert advice on menus and wines, and their attention to detail will ensure that your special day will be one to remember. Private meeting rooms and conference facilities are also available.

The fun at Dobbyn & Coffeys continues late into the night at DC's Nightclub which provides a mixture of the latest sounds along with genuine classics. No expense was spared to install the very best in sound and lighting equipment. And after your night out, you can retire to one the 12 guest bedrooms here, all of them en suite and one of them adapted for disabled use.

For a wholesome snack, light meal or just a cup of tea or coffee, the recommended place to go in Athenry is **The Baron's Den** in Northgate Street. With its distinctive red and black frontage, the Den is easy to find. It was opened a few years ago by Anne and Bob Zonenblick, both caterers by profession, and their son Robert. Anne taught catering at Westminster College in London but returned to Ireland in the 1970s and, together with her husband, established a very successful outside catering business. They felt that there was a need in Athenry for a specialist coffee shop where locals and visitors alike could enjoy tasty food in attractive surroundings. And so the Baron's Den was born. This is not the place to find hamburger and chips - the food is light, fresh and predominantly organic. The menu offers an extensive range of options, indeed, Anne refers to it as "The

The Baron's Den, Northgate Street, Athenry, Co. Galway
Tel: 091 845301

Library" since the choice is so wide. Everything is prepared on the premises from the best of fresh, organic produce: even the salad dressings, vinegars and chutneys are all made by Anne and her staff, along with Irish soda bread freshly baked each day. An exception to the organic style is the traditional Irish Fry breakfast which is available all day. An interesting feature of The Baron's Den is a display in honour of the poet Padraic Fallon who includes several references to Athenry, the town of his birth, in his poem *The Fields of Athenry*. Set to music, it is now heard around the world and has been adopted by thousands of Glasgow Celtic supporters as their theme song. Fallon's son, Connor, is an accomplished sculptor and an example of his work, created in honour of his father, holds pride of place in the town.

For bed and breakfast accommodation in Athenry, the place to seek out is definitely **Tower View** on the Dublin Road. Antoinette Judge is a welcoming host with an ever ready smile and a determination to make sure you make the most of your stay. Some distinguished visitors have stayed at Tower View, amongst them Ireland's most famous contemporary poet, Seamus Heaney. Antoinette proudly displays a photograph of the Noble Laureate and herself together. Tower View itself is an attractive modern house with 3 spacious and comfortable guest rooms, all of them en suite and well-equipped. There's an inviting residents' lounge where "guests meet as strangers and part as friends". If you

Tower View, Dublin Road, Athenry, Co. Galway
Tel: 091 844147 e-mail: towerview@come.to
website: www.come.to/towerview

get immersed in the craic, don't worry about the time - Antoinette and her family will just take themselves off to bed and leave you to it. Breakfast arrangements are equally easy-going. Sleep in if you feel like it and when you are ready for breakfast, that's when it will be cooked. Naturally, there's a traditional full Irish breakfast on offer, along with a wide choice of egg dishes, fruit, cereals, juices, and bread & cheese. Athenry town has plenty to interest the visitor and it is also an ideal place for the visitor to use as a hub while explor- ing East Galway, the Burren in Co. Clare, Galway City and Connemara.

If you prefer self-catering, then **Raheen House** offers an excellent range of choices. The house itself was bought in the 1980s by Kathleen and Tom Coffey as a family home. Kathleen is a local doctor, Tom a Civil Engineer, and together they spent much love, time and effort restoring the 200-year-old house to its former state of grace. The self-catering units at Raheen House have been created by converting some of the attractive old out-buildings or, in one case, building a bungalow on the site of the former Gate Lodge. The Old Coach House, built in a lovely mellow pink stone, stands in an enclosed yard behind the main house and has been converted into 2 double-storey semi-detached cottages. In another enclosed courtyard behind the old coach house are a number of single storey

Raheen House, Athenry, Co. Galway
Tel: 091 844372/567673 Accommodation Fax: 091 844519

apartments ingeniously created from the former stables. All the units have been furnished and decorated to the highest standards, and are equipped with all modern conveniences such as dishwasher, washer-dryer, microwave and refrigerator. All the apartments are centrally heated, the 3 bedrooms have a solid fuel stove, complete with stacks of peat, firelighters and even matches! The property also has its own tennis court and there's a delightful walled garden where you can savour the peace and quiet. When you arrive at Raheen House, you will find milk, Irish cheese and butter in the fridge, along with tea, coffee and freshly baked Irish brown bread. The hospitality doesn't end there. Kathleen and Tom are immensely proud of their town and the area in general and are the kind of hosts who are prepared to invite you down to the local for a drink - an invitation you should definitely rush to accept!

COUNTY MAYO

The County Mayo coastline from Killary Harbour to Killala provides a marvellous sequence of vistas - rugged headlands, rough-moulded cliffs, sandy beaches and **Achill**, the largest island off the Irish coast (although it is now linked by road to the mainland). Inland, the landscape is also wonderfully varied with ranges of mountains rising from limestone plains and moorlands studded with countless lakes. It was on one of those mountains, Croagh Patrick, that St Patrick fasted for 40 days and pilgrims on their way to climb the mountain would break their journey at Ballintubber Abbey where Mass has been celebrated daily since its foundation in 1216.

Although Co. Mayo is roughly the same size as Co. Cork, its total population (110,000) is considerably less than that of Cork City alone. Surprisingly, Mayo has never been high on visitor itineraries although that has changed a little since the opening of Knock International Airport, constructed in 1986 to serve the million and a half pilgrims each year who visit the Basilica at Knock where the Virgin Mary appeared in a vision in 1879. But apart from Knock and a few other places such as the delightful Georgian town of Westport, Co. Mayo remains "undiscovered country".

CASTLEBAR
56 miles N of Galway on the N5

MAP 3 REF E7

Located in heart of Mayo's lake country, the county town of Castlebar was founded in the early 1600s by John Bingham, ancestor of the Earls of Lucan. The infamous fugitive Lord Lucan was actually born here. More creditable sons of Castlebar include the inventor of the monorail and the torpedo, Louis Brennan; the former Taoiseach Charles Haughey; and the world-famous soprano Margaret Burke Sheridan.

The town centre has an attractive tree-lined green and Mall which was once the cricket pitch of the Lucan family. An especially appealing feature of Castlebar is its **Sculpture Trail**, a series of sculptures in various materials - glass, stone, steel, bog pine, scattered around the town.

Originally a market town, Castlebar has kept this tradition and is one of the major shopping centres in the west of Ireland, offering a wide range of interesting shopping areas. The town gets even busier during the annual **International Blues Festival**, held over the Whitsun Bank Holiday weekend. A more unusual event is the annual **Celebration of the Senses Festival** in October with inventive performances and displays exploring the five senses of sight, sound, touch, taste and smell. And in early July the **Castlebar International Walking Festival** is a non-competitive event designed to encourage people to rediscover the bogs, rivers, mountains and unspoilt beauty of the area.

If you are planning to stay in Castlebar, the **Traveller's Friend Hotel & Theatre** on Old Westport Road provides an unusual combination of first class entertainment and accommodation. The theatre regularly presents the cream of national and international

**Traveller's Friend Hotel & Theatre, Old Westport Road, Castlebar, Co. Mayo
Tel/Fax: 094 23111   e-mail: tfhotel@anu.ie**

artists, has hosted many major drama groups, musicals, ballets and concerts as well as the Castlebar Blues International festival and the Castlebar International Song Contest. Christy Moore, Johnny Cash and Kris Kristofferson are just some of the international stars to have performed in this 1000-seat theatre. The Traveller's Friend Hotel itself offers exclusive, value for money packages combining travel arrangements, show tickets and top quality accommodation in its newly refurbished bedrooms, all of which are comprehensively equipped with bath/shower, television/text, radio, VCR, trouser press and hair dryer. The hotel's Tamarind Seed restaurant, with its appealing 1920s ambience, offers a varied choice of traditional and international cuisine. Luncheon is served daily, bar food is also available and the popular John Moore Carvery restaurant is also open every day. A recent addition to the hotel's many amenities is a dedicated business centre which provides seminar suites and conference rooms catering for anything from 4 to 1000 persons.

"You can do it all.....or sit back and do nothing at all!" is the motto adopted by **Lough Lannagh Village**, a superb holiday complex situated on the outskirts of Castlebar. Set within a mature landscape with a lakeside view of Croagh Patrick mountain, the village combines the peaceful tranquillity of an Irish lakeside village with traditional Mayo style houses and a Lodge House. A variety of accommodation is provided here to

Lough Lannagh Village, Castlebar, Co. Mayo
Tel: 094 27111   Fax: 094 27295   e-mail: llv@eircom.net
website: http://www.loughlannagh.ie

suit all tastes. Macalla Lodge is an elegant guest house built in traditional style and offering modern comforts which include en suite bedrooms, a breakfast café, residents' lounge and visitor information centre. The Lodge takes its name from the Echo Stream, (*macalla* is the Irish word for echo), which runs alongside the village entrance.

Self-catering visitors stay in one of the attractive cottages spaced around the village. These, too, are all built in traditional style, and equipped with all the conveniences of a home away from home. Also available is a site for touring caravans, discreetly tucked away in the landscaped grounds. At the Fitness Centre (which contains a shop with every day essentials), you can work out in the gym, relax in the steam room, or avail yourself of aromatherapy and reflexology, or hire a bicycle. Another feature of Lough Lannagh Village is Macalla Hall Rural Conference Venue which provides a refreshing and popular venue for meeting, exhibitions, presentations and private dining.

Within the village there is plenty to keep you occupied and a short walk will bring you to the hustle and bustle of the busy market town of Castlebar. A little further afield are the visitor attractions of Ballintubber Abbey, Croagh Patrick mountain, the Shrine at Knock, the moonscape country of the Burren and the Stone Age monuments at Céide Fields.

THE BARONY OF MURRISK

Southwest of Castlebar, the fist-shaped tract of rugged mountains and sparsely-populated plains is known as the Barony of Murrisk from the little town of that name near Westport. The scenery is as splendid as you'll find anywhere in the west of Ireland with two ranges of hills, the Mweelrea Mountains and the Sheefry Hills, providing terrain for serious walkers, and the holy mountain of **Croagh Patrick**, Mayo's most famous landmark, attracting pilgrims to the summit where in 441 St Patrick fasted for 40 days and nights. In return for this protracted abstinence the saint received a promise from God that the Irish would never lose their Christian faith. At the top of the 2510ft mountain there is a small modern chapel built with 716 bags of cement carried up the hillside by devout barefoot pilgrims. Nearby stands a statue of St Patrick commanding astounding views extending from the Galway mountains in the south to Achill Island to the north.

WESTPORT   Map 3 ref D7
11 miles SW of Castlebar on the N5/N59

Set around Clew Bay, Westport is unique among Irish towns in that it was designed to the plan of the well-known Georgian architect James Wyatt. The central Mall with its trees lining both sides of the Carrowbeg River is one of the most gracious thoroughfares in the country; Bridge Street's cheerful shop and pub fronts is a pleasant place for a stroll, and **The Octagon**, the town's central square, is the venue for a regular weekly market. The town is noted as a sea fishing centre and holds an annual **Sea Angling Festival** in late June, followed by the **Westport Arts Festival** in October.

The town's grandest building and Co. Mayo's only stately home open to the public is **Westport House**, standing in fine parkland near Westport Quay. Designed in the 1730s by Richard Castle with later additions by James Wyatt, the mansion is the seat of the Marquesses of Sligo who have successively lived on this spot for more than 400 years. The house is beautifully furnished inside with Irish Georgian and Victorian antiques, Waterford Crystal, Chinese wallpapers and an outstanding collection of paintings, including a *Holy Family* by Rubens. Some of the doors are made of Jamaican mahogany imported from West India by the 1st Marquess who was governor there. (For his time, the Marquess was a comparatively liberal man who freed many of his slaves). The dungeons beneath Westport House are a survival from an earlier building. Children of course love them and they are also well-provided for in the grounds by a rather incongruously inelegant collection of attractions and side-shows, and there's also a children's zoo, flume ride, model railway, boating lake with pedalos, horse-drawn caravan rides and gift shops.

Adjacent to the harbour and Westport House, **Ard Caoin** offers warm and friendly Irish hospitality in comfortable surroundings. This inviting guest house is set in peaceful surroundings just 5 minutes drive from the centre of Westport and within walking distance of some superb restaurants and bars. Ard Caoin has 4 spacious and superbly appointed bedrooms, all of them en suite, and outside there's a pleasant secluded garden

Ard Caoin, The Quay, Westport, Co. Mayo
Tel: 098 25492

where guests are welcome to settle down and relax. The owners of Ard Caoin, Mary and Sean O'Malley, do everything they can to make their visitors feel at home and if your interest is fishing Sean will be happy to arrange day sea fishing trips and supply the rods, bait and boats.

Located within easy walking distance of the town centre, **St Anthony's** is an attractive town house dating back to 1820. It occupies a lovely position beside the river, set in an acre of its own grounds and with a secure car park. Robert and Sheila Kilkelly have

St Anthony's, Distillery Road, Westport, Co. Mayo
Tel: 098 28887 Fax: 098 25172 e-mail: sk@achh.iol.ie

been in the B & B business for some 30 years and they certainly know how to make their guests feel relaxed and at home. The 6 spacious guest rooms at St Anthony's are all en suite, non-smoking, and equipped with colour TV and tea/coffee making facilities. Two of the upper bedrooms still retain the original oak beams of 1820. The Kilkellys offer both a vegetarian and children's menu and are happy to provide packed lunches on request.

With its smart white-washed walls set off by colourful window boxes of flowers, **Drummin House** has a very inviting appearance. It stands on Tubberhill overlooking the town and although the house looks quite small from the outside, the century-old build-

Drummin House, Tubberhill, Westport, Co. Mayo
Tel: 098 27427

ing has 5 spacious guest rooms and a large garden to the rear. This appealing bed and breakfast establishment is owned and run by Jackie and Ann Burns who possess a real flair for making their visitors feel instantly at home. The old oak floors and attractive furnishings help create a warm and cosy atmosphere and your hosts do everything they can to make your stay as relaxing and comfortable as possible. A hearty traditional Irish breakfast is included in the tariff and there are also vegetarian alternatives and a children's menu. Packed lunches are available on request. Drummin House is within easy reach of the town's renowned pubs and restaurant and the many local amenities include golf, sea & freshwater fishing, horse riding, hill walking, Blue Flag beaches and much more.

KNOCKRANNY

MAP 3 REF D7

2 miles E of Westport off the N5

Situated on the outskirts of Westport, one of Ireland's loveliest towns, **Knockranny Lodge** is a purpose-built guest house equipped with every feature the discerning guest might desire. Built to Bord Fáilte 4**** standard, the quality accommodation is ideal for both business and personal requirements. In the elegant, wooden-floored guest lounge

Knockranny Lodge Guesthouse, Knockranny, Westport, Co. Mayo
Tel: 098 28595 Fax: 098 28805 e-mail: knockranny@anu.ie
website: www.anu.ie/knockrannylodge

antique feature pieces catch the eye immediately. Stylish, comfortable seating invites you to relax and help yourself to a cup of tea or coffee, available 24 hours. Knockranny Lodge has 12 individually designed double and family rooms, all with en suite bathrooms, pressure jet showers, direct dial telephone and satellite TV. Breakfast at Knockranny Lodge is also something special, a tasty meal using the freshest of local ingredients and served in the sunny dining room.

LOUISBURGH

MAP 3 REF D7

14 miles W of Westport on the R335

In 1758 a nephew of the 1st Marquess of Sligo took part in the capture of Louisburgh, Nova Scotia from the French. In his honour, the proud uncle re-named this little coastal village after the great victory and replaced its rather shabby buildings with some handsome Georgian houses. The village is still little more than a crossroads but a pleasant base from which to explore the sandy beaches stretching eastwards from the promontory known as **Old Head**.

This corner of County Mayo has strong associations with a remarkable woman, Grace O'Malley or Gráinne Ni Mháille, whose exploits are still vividly remembered even though she died in the same year as Elizabeth 1 -1603. Grace's ancestors had been Lords of the Isles for 200 years and Grace fought hard to maintain her regal position against the encroachments of the English. A forceful woman, she unilaterally divorced her second husband by slamming the castle door in his face and then stealing all his other castles. A typical story relates that at the age of 45 Grace was on a sea voyage when she gave birth to her first son, Toby. An hour later, her ship was boarded by Turkish pirates. The battle on the deck was almost lost when Grace appeared wrapped in a blanket and shot the enemy captain with a blunderbuss. Her men rallied, captured the Turkish ship and hanged the crew. Grace O'Malley's colourful life is documented at the **Granuaile Centre** in Louisburgh, open from June to mid-September, which also has a harrowing display on the horrors of the Great Famine.

Reached by passenger ferry from Roonagh Quay, a few miles west of Louisburgh, **Clare Island** was part of Grace O'Malley's domain. The island is dominated by the sheer-sided mass of **Knockmore Mountain** which rises to more than 1500ft and although the island is quite small, only 15 miles square and with a population of around 150, there's good walking here, some little-used sandy beaches, and facilities for pony trekking, water-skiing, sailboarding and fishing. The ruins of Grace's massive castle stand above the tiny harbour and the redoubtable lady herself is reputedly buried in a tomb near the ruined 13th century Cistercian Abbey on the south coast which also has some striking medieval wall paintings.

CARROWKENNEDY

MAP 3 REF D8

10 miles S of Westport on the N59

Right in the heart of the Barony of Murrisk, the village of Carrowkennedy lies in the plain between the Sheefry Hills and Partry Mountains, an out of the way place but well worth seeking out for a rather special traditional hostelry.

On the outside wall of **Darby's** pub there's a vintage "Guinness for Strength" advertising placard, an encouraging indication that this appealing old inn with its colour-washed walls maintains the great traditions of the authentic Irish pub. Inside, wooden floors and seating, and open log fires create exactly the right atmosphere and your hosts, Mike and Susan Flynn, are always ready with a warm and friendly welcome. As you'd expect, the Guinness is superb and it goes down well with the selection of pub grub on offer which

Darby's, Clifden Road, Carrowkennedy, Westport, Co. Mayo
Tel: 098 21244

includes a children's menu and vegetarian options. Sunday nights at Darby's are especially enjoyable since these are Irish folk music nights with live music and, if the mood takes you, a bit of a jig also.

AROUND CASTLEBAR

KNOCK

MAP 3 REF F8

18 miles SE of Castlebar on the N17/R323

More than one and half million pilgrims each year make their way to **Our Lady's Shrine** in the basilica at Knock, the "Lourdes of Ireland". It was here, one rainy evening in 1879, that the Virgin Mary appeared on the gable of the parish church with St Joseph on her right and St John the Evangelist on her left. Angels hovered above the Apparition and the scene was enveloped in a bright light which was seen several miles away. No fewer than 15 people of varying ages witnessed the manifestation. Located in the heart of one of the most desolate and depopulated areas of Ireland, Knock immediately became an important centre of pilgrimage and although no major miracles have been claimed, a huge basilica seating 15,000 was completed in 1976. Architecturally uncompromising, the huge church nevertheless contains some interesting examples of modern art and architecture, and the 32 pillars each contain stone from a different Irish county. Three years after the basilica was consecrated, Pope John Paul II visited the shrine to mark the centenary of the original vision. The opening of **Knock International Airport** in 1986 brought visitors from all around the world to within a 10-minute drive of the village.

As with most centres of pilgrimage, the village is abundantly provided with shops selling a huge range of religious souvenirs but the **Museum of Folk Life** provides a straightforward account of the visitation and displays artefacts related to it and details of those miracles associated with it.

Just 2 minutes walk from the famous Basilica, **Providence Villa Guest Home** is a striking building with elegant windows, two storeys high, flanking the front door, and walls made interesting with a pattern of differently coloured bricks. It was designed and built by Desmond and Ann O'Neill who own and run this peaceful and relaxing guest

Providence Villa Guest Home, Drum, Knock, Co. Mayo
Tel: 094 88875

house and possess the knack of making all their guests feel immediately welcome. Providence Villa stands in large gardens which include a barbecue area and there's ample private parking. At breakfast time, the O'Neills serve a hearty full Irish breakfast and evening meals are also available on request, as are packed lunches. There are special dishes for vegetarians and children, with home baked bread adding a special extra tastiness. The TV lounge has an inviting open log fire and the 6 individually decorated guest bedrooms are all en suite, very comfortable and very well-equipped with useful extras such as toiletries in generous supply.

MAYO ABBEY

MAP 3 REF E8

12 miles SE of Castlebar on minor road off the N60

This tiny village, hidden away in the countryside south of Castlebar, was once the administrative centre of the Diocese of Mayo from which the county takes its name. **Mayo Abbey** was the seat of the bishop but little remains of the once splendid Abbey founded in the 7th century by St Colman. The abbey later became the centre of a famous university where, according to legend, Alfred the Great came to study. One of his sons is reputedly buried here.

Standing at the heart of this historic little village, **Malachy Byrne's Traditional Irish Pub** has everything one expects from an authentic Irish hostelry. Malachy and Margaret Byrne are the second generation of the Byrne family to own and run the inn

Malachy Byrne's Traditional Irish Pub, Mayo Abbey, Claremorris, Co. Mayo
Tel: 094 65005

which also incorporates the village shop where you'll find everything from animal feeds to footwear, fuel to funeral furnishings. The Byrnes are a friendly, welcoming couple who have earned a good reputation for their tasty bar food, delicious afternoon teas and the lively barbecues that take place in the secluded courtyard at the rear of the inn. Any time is a good time to visit Malachy Byrne's but it's especially true at weekends when traditional Irish music is played in time-honoured style.

BALLINTUBBER   MAP 3 REF E8
7 miles S of Castlebar on the N84

Ballintubber Abbey has been called "The Abbey that Refused to Die". Founded in 1216 by Cathal, King of Connaught, near the site of a church built by St Patrick in 441, the abbey was suppressed by Henry VIII along with all the other monastic establishments in Britain and Ireland. After the destruction by Cromwell in 1653, the abbey was left roofless but for 250 years the people of Ballintubber continued to attend Mass in wind, rain and snow. The abbey now has the unique status of being the only one in Ireland where Mass has been celebrated every day for more than 780 years. Almost completely restored now, the abbey stands in attractive grounds which are landscaped to portray spiritual themes and the interpretive centre has an informative video which includes scenes of local people performing the annual passion play. Leading westwards from Ballintubber Abbey, the **Tóchar Phádraig** is the ancient pilgrim path that winds for some 22 miles through the Mayo countryside to the holy hill of Croagh Patrick.

BALLINROBE   MAP 3 REF E8
18 miles S of Castlebar on the N84

Located on the Robe River near the eastern shore of Lough Mask, Ballinrobe is a noted angling centre for this lough and the neighbouring lakes of Carra, Conn, Corrib and Cullin. A 4-day wet fly-fishing competition is held here each year, usually in August, but the little town is at its busiest during the race meetings in July which completely fulfil one's expectations of Irish racing - a picturesque course, fine horses and a great atmosphere. Collectors of curiosities will be interested in the huge, stone-stepped pyramid just outside the town. Partly-effaced Roman numerals date it some time in the 1700s. It bears the name of George Browne, a member of the family who owned the magnificent Westport House at Westport but the reason why this strange folly was erected has been lost in the passage of time. About 2 miles southwest of the town is the great stone fort of **Cahernagollum** and further on stands the **Killower cairn**, a 22ft high pillar of stones which probably covers a Stone Age passage grave.

Back in Ballinrobe and tucked away in a peaceful pedestrian precinct, **Flannery's Bar & Restaurant** is a dazzling sight with its colour-washed walls and profusion of hanging baskets. Flannery's is the epitome of a traditional Irish pub where visitors soon find

**Flannery's Bar & Restaurant, Cornmarket, Ballinrobe, Co. Mayo
Tel: 092 41055/41724**

themselves sharing in a friendly chat and a pint with the locals. Michael Flannery is the third generation of his family to own and run the bar which is renowned for its wholesome food served daily from 12.30pm until 10pm, either in the cosy bar or in the à la carte

George Moore Room restaurant. Regular music sessions add to the character of this welcoming hostelry and in the likely event that you want to linger a while longer in this quaint little town, Flannery's has two 2-bedroom self-catering apartments just across from the pub.

CONG
Map 3 ref E9

24 miles S of Castlebar on the R346/345

In Gaelic *"cong"* means isthmus, in this case the 3-mile wide nexus of land that separates Lough Corrib from Lough Mask. In fact, the two lakes are linked by a river which flows underground for part of its course. Along the way it has formed great caves in the limestone, the most accessible of which is Pigeon Hole.

One of Cong's claims to fame is that the village was the shooting location for much of *The Quiet Man*, the immensely popular 1956 film starring John Wayne and Maureen O'Hara. At some point, the stars would no doubt have dropped in at **Lydon's Lodge**, Carmel and Frank Lydon's friendly hostelry in the heart of the village. Wooden floors, and wooden seating in alcove form, along with an open log fire mark this out as an

Lydon's Lodge, Cong, Co. Mayo
Tel: 092 46053/46715   e-mail: lydonslodge@tinet.ie

authentic traditional Irish pub. For the total "Irish Experience", try to arrive when the live folk and country music performers are in full swing. The Lodge serves good food, either in the bar or in the intimate dining area. If you are planning to stay in the area, look no further: Lydon's Lodge has 11 comfortable guest bedrooms, 10 of which are en suite. This is a delightful place, well worth seeking out.

Cong is a notably picturesque little town which was once a significant religious centre. One of its most impressive sites is the substantial ruin of **Cong Abbey**, founded in 1128 by Turlough O'Connor, King of Ireland. In its heyday the abbey was home to more than 3000 and its prosperous status is reflected by the exquisite Cross of Cong, a 12ᵗʰ century richly ornamented Celtic cross which is now on display at the National Museum in Dublin. But there is still much to admire here - fine stone carvings and atmospheric cloisters which give little sign of their partial rebuilding in 1860. The last high king of Ireland, Rory O'Connor, spent the last 15 years of his life at Cong in peaceful meditation following his defeat by the Anglo-Normans. An extraordinary medieval survival here is the monks' fishhouse, a tiny stone building on a platform overhanging the river where they would catch salmon for the refectory table.

PONTOON
9 miles NE of Castlebar on the R310

MAP 3 REF E7

Pontoon, standing on the neck of land that separates Lough Cullen from Lough Conn, is regarded as one of the most important freshwater angling centres in Ireland, the nearby lakes offering some of the best brown trout and salmon fishing in western Europe. The village is also popular with bird-watchers since the lakes attract a remarkable variety and number of wildfowl.

Nestled in woodland and overlooking Lough Cullen, **Healys Hotel** looks irresistibly inviting with its creeper-covered walls, masses of flowers and tables shaded by colourful parasols. Healys has mastered the art of relaxation - just 15 minutes from the conveniences of both Castlebar and Ballina, the hotel is far from all their hassles! This traditional old world 14-bedroomed hotel has recently been refurbished. All bedrooms are en suite with state of the art direct dial telephone, tea and coffee making facilities and colour television as standard. Amenities include the relaxing Bianconi Room lounge, a traditional public bar, and the elegant and intimate Lough Cullen Room restaurant serving

Healys Hotel, Pontoon, Foxford, Co. Mayo
Tel: 094 56443   Fax: 094 56572   e-mail: healyspontoon@tinet.ie

sumptuous cuisine and excellent wines. With sweeping landscaped grounds and the lakeview patio, what more could you ask for on a beautiful West of Ireland day! Fishermen will be in their element here. The hotel is only 15 minutes from the River Moy, probably the best salmon fishing river in Europe. Healys is also central to Mayo's best golfing locations: 15 minutes from Ballina and Castlebar, 30 minutes from the fabulous Enniscrone Golf Links and Westport Golf Course, and one hour from the magical Carne Golf Links in Belmullet.

BALLINA   Map 3 ref E6
23 miles NE of Castlebar on the N26

Ballina has a population of around 7000 which makes it the largest town in Co. Mayo. It stands beside the River Moy, one of Mayo's richest salmon and trout rivers. The original settlement here was at Ardnaree on the east side of the river, a site marked by the ruins of an Augustinian friary dating from 1427 and now dwarfed by the Victorian cathedral of St Muredach which boasts some particularly beautiful stained glass.

Enjoying an elevated view of the famous River Moy and Belleek Woods, **"Brigown"** is a delightful place to stay for bed and breakfast. It's the home of Marjorie Nolan who is well known in Ireland as the author of cookery books such as *Favourite Recipes from Marjorie's Kitchen* and for her weekly spot on local radio. Marjorie has also appeared on BBC1's *Ready, Steady, Cook* so, as you might expect, breakfast at "Brigown" is something rather special. The extensive menu boasts 18 main course breakfasts ranging from home made pancakes to scrambled egg with smoked salmon, complemented by delicious home made

Brigown, Quay Road, Coast Road, Ballina, Co. Mayo
Tel: 096 22609   Mobile: 087 2304986   e-mail: marjorie@mayo-ireland.ie
website: http://www.mayo-ireland.ie/brigown.htm

bread, buns and cakes. Vegetarians, children and those on gluten free diets are all catered for and packed lunches are also available if required. "Brigown" has 4 attractive guest rooms, 3 of them en suite, and all equipped with colour TV, hair dryer and tea/coffee-making facilities. Outside, there's a charming garden and patio, and "Brigown"'s convenient location, only a mile or so from the famous Ridge Pool, makes it an ideal base for exploring Co. Mayo and Co. Sligo. "Brigown" is Bord Failte approved and recommended by several guides including *Le Guide du Routard*.

During the 18th century Ballina, (pronounced *bally-nah*, incidentally), developed on the west side of the river and is today a thriving industrial, commercial and tourist centre. One of the most remarkable sights in Ballina is the **Dolmen of the Four Maols**, three large rocks capped by a massive boulder dating back to the Bronze Age. A much later legend asserts that the dolmen marks the graves of a quartet of 6th century foster brothers who killed their eminent tutor, Ceallach, Bishop of Kilmoremoy. They were hanged together by Ceallach's brother across the river at Ardnaree and then buried here.

Standing on the outskirts of Ballina, **Belvedere House** is a large Georgian-style modern house set in extensive well-maintained gardens. It's the home of Mary Reilly who welcomes bed and breakfast guests to her charmingly furnished and decorated house.

Belvedere House, Foxford Road, Ballina, Co. Mayo
Tel: 096 22004

There are 4 attractive bedrooms, all en suite and equipped with TV and tea or coffee making facilities. Children are welcome, with a cot available if required. A full Irish breakfast is included in the tariff and Mary is happy to provide packed lunches if required. Belvedere House is about a 10-minute walk from the town centre and within a 3-mile radius there are facilities for fishing, golf and horse riding as well as many delightful walks.

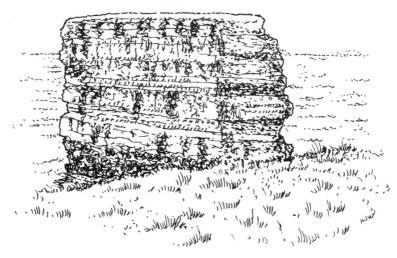

Downpatrick Head, Co. Mayo

To the north and west stretches the unspoilt north coast of Co. Mayo, wonderfully wild and remote. Not to be missed here is the spectacular view from **Downpatrick Head** where the Atlantic has gouged a huge bay from the mighty cliffs, their summits scoured of all vegetation except grass by the ceaseless ocean winds.

FOXFORD
Map 3 ref F7

13 miles NE of Castlebar on the N58

Situated on the banks of the River Moy and nestling between the Ox and Nephin Mountains, Foxford's main visitor attraction is the **Foxford Woollen Mills and Visitor Centre**. Visitors can watch rugs, blankets and tweeds being made, purchase the end products in the Mill Shop and browse around the craft workshops offering original paintings, wood crafts and jewellery.

CALLOW
Map 3 ref F7

15 miles NE of Castlebar on the N26

Winners of a National Tourism Award for "excellence in standards of self-catering accommodation", **Culduff Cottages** are perfect examples of sympathetic and imaginative restoration. The Old Granary, which was built before 1800 and used as a depot for grain distribution during the Great Famine, has attractive features such as an open fireplace and pine furniture. The 2 bedrooms can accommodate 4 adults but the cottage is not suitable for children. The second property, the 17th century Old House, is fronted by a large lawn and has been the traditional farmhouse to many generations of the Keane family. It has a unique blend of homeliness, space and comfort which is complemented by the modern facilities and rural surroundings. The house can sleep 8 people in 4 bedrooms, (2 en suite), and is usually enjoyed by fishermen, large parties or two families

Culduff Cottages, Culduff, Callow, Foxford, Co. Mayo
Tel/Fax: 094 51183

sharing. Children are welcome. The third property, The Stables, is a 19th century stone building, full of character and restored to the highest standards. It enjoys panoramic views over farmland, bog land, lake and mountain. The Stables has 4 en suite bedrooms, capable of accommodating 7 guests. The owners of Culduff Cottages, Tom and Mary Keane, are happy to arrange angling advice, permits and ghillies; estuary and sea fishing outings; landscape painting lessons; golf outings, and indeed will try to meet any reasonable request!

SWINFORD

MAP 3 REF F7

16 miles NE of Castlebar on the N26

"Enjoy the Wild, Warm and Wonderful West from the comfort of **Cashel Schoolhouse**" says Imelda O'Hara who offers this Bord Failte 4-star Approved self-catering property to let in this scenic corner of Co. Mayo. Built around 1900 and at a very interesting time in Irish history, Cashel Schoolhouse has been converted to meet the standards of today's discerning tourist while retaining attractive features, lovingly restored. This unique building has a large lounge with open stone fireplace, wooden floor and gallery area; a kitchen/dining room which is very spacious and well equipped with all modern conveniences; 4 bedrooms, sleeping 7, and a separate bathroom with shower. Bed linen and towels are supplied, and for anglers there's a useful tackle shed. Mrs O'Hara also has another property to let - The Cottage at Ardhoon Meelick which is a typical Irish cottage with a wonderful atmosphere and sleeps 5 people. It has a Bord Failte 3-star Approved rating. Both properties are close to some excellent fishing; golfers will find three

**Bookings through Mrs I. O'Hara, Carrick, Callow, Foxford, Co. Mayo
Tel: 094 51656/56732 Fax: 094 51025**

18-hole championship courses within easy reach as well as a 9-hole course in Swinford itself; trekking is available from the local riding school; there are beautiful safe beaches within easy driving distance and many good walks for which maps are available.

CHARLESTOWN   MAP 3 REF F7
18 miles NE of Castlebar on the N5/N17

Only 5 minutes from Knock Airport and 20 minutes from Knock Shrine, **Ashfort** is a spacious Tudor-style house, surrounded by large gardens, where you'll find excellent bed and breakfast accommodation. It's the home of Philip and Carol O'Gorman who have

**Ashfort Country House, Galway Knock Road, Charlestown, Co. Mayo
Tel: 094 54706**

been welcoming guests here since 1988, many of whom return again and again. They have 4 guest bedrooms, (2 double, 1 family, 1 twin), all of them en suite and with non-smoking rooms available if required. The hearty breakfast includes a choice for vegetarians and children, and packed lunches are available on request. A true home from home, Ashfort is open from March 16th until October 30th. This is a peaceful place to stay and an ideal base for touring the west of Ireland.

NEWPORT   MAP 3 REF D7
12 miles W of Castlebar on the R311

This orderly little 18th century town overlooks **Clew Bay** with its frantically serrated coastline of many-fingered headlands and splattered blobs of islands. Newport is primarily geared to the service of the angling fraternity and rather sadly takes pride in the fact that one of Grace Kelly's ancestors lived for a while at nearby Drimurla. The town is dominated by a huge arched bridge that once carried the railway linking Westport to Achill Island. The railway was built following a public outcry in the 1850s when a boat crowded with migrant workers sailing from Achill to Westport foundered in Clew Bay and everyone on board perished.

The **Westport to Achill** railway was a delightfully scenic but hopelessly uneconomic venture and in 1936 the company directors had no option but to close it down. Created in response to a terrible tragedy, the railway expired in the wake of another. A few days before its official closure a party of children from Achill who had been harvesting potatoes in Scotland died in a fire at the farmhouse where they were staying. The very last train from Westport to Achill carried the small coffins containing their remains.

About ten miles west of Newport, **Achill Island** is the largest island in the Republic and, since it is now linked to the mainland by a road bridge, one of the easiest to reach. The island offers a wonderful amalgam of dramatic mountains and cliffs, sparsely-patronised beaches and, inland, a rich scattering of prehistoric standing stones, stone circles and

Launching a currach at Keem Bay

dolmens. A generous influx of government subventions has transformed this once bitterly poverty-stricken area into what is now a comparatively prosperous region. The downside is the large number of characterless modern buildings that have been plonked down seemingly at random and appear totally out of context in such enchanting scenery. Fortunately, their impact on this grand landscape is, so far, still quite negligible. Ignore them and just stand above **Keem Bay** to watch the local fishermen launch into the waves a *currach*, the canvas-covered boat that has served them so well for centuries. You don't need to take a photograph: the image will stay in your mind for years.

COUNTY ROSCOMMON

An inland county, Roscommon nevertheless has an abundance of water. The River Shannon and Lough Ree form its eastern boundary and Loughs Key, Gara and Arrow encircle the county to the north. Smaller bodies of water are scattered across the fertile central plain and the River Suck, beloved of coarse fishermen, forms the boundary with Co. Mayo in the west. The only high ground to be found is on the Sligo and Leitrim border where the Curlew Mountains rise high and wild.

The county boasts some fine buildings, most notably the fine Palladian mansion, Strokestown Park, and the magnificent King House in Boyle. But the pre-eminent attractions of this peaceful county are its uncrowded towns and villages, and its people who seem still to have the time and warmth to make visitors feel truly welcome.

ROSCOMMON
MAP 4 REF H8
50 miles NE of Galway on the N63

The county town is an appealing little place with attractively restored Georgian and Victorian shops lining the main street, a stately Georgian courthouse, (now a bank), and a grim castellated Old Gaol which in the 18th century had the dubious distinction of providing regular employment for Ireland's only hangwoman. "Lady Betty" had been condemned to death herself for the unwitting murder of her own son but when the regular hangman fell ill she volunteered to carry out his duties on condition that her own life be spared. Her position was later made official and she was provided with a salary and accommodation in the gaol. She lived there for some 30 years, dispatching condemned felons from a hinged board fixed outside her third floor window. The Old Gaol now houses a collection of shops.

The town also boasts two striking medieval ruins. Standing in fields on the edge of the town are the ruins of the colossal **Roscommon Castle**, a 13th century structure which survived centuries of local feuding before succumbing to Cromwell's troops. The impressive remains include the rounded bastions at the corners and a double-towered entrance gate. In the town itself, **Roscommon Abbey** contains the tomb of its 13th century founder, Félim O'Conor, king of Connaught. The tomb is carved with the figures of eight *galloglasses*, the soldiers forming the retinue of an Irish chief. The Abbey stands on the site of a much earlier monastery founded by St Coman from whom the town and county take their names.

Located on the outskirts of the town, **Westway House** provides the kind of bed and breakfast accommodation one always hopes to find - warm, inviting and friendly. Your host is Catherine Campbell who for some 20-odd years now has been welcoming visitors here, many of whom return again and again. It's easy to understand why. Comfortable,

**Westway House, Galway Road, Roscommon, Co. Roscommon
Tel: 0903 26927**

en suite rooms all furnished and decorated to a high standard and equipped with both double and single beds, TV and tea/coffee-making facilities, are just part of the appeal. Breakfast at Westway House is another: an inviting repast that includes a choice of fruits, cereals, yoghurts, juices, egg dishes and, of course, a traditional full Irish breakfast. Evening meals are not provided at Westway House but a gentle, 10-minute walk into the town will provide you with a wide choice of restaurants, pubs and hotels. Quiet and peaceful, Westway House provides a perfect base for exploring the manifold attractions of the area.

RAHARA
MAP 4 REF H9

5 miles SW of Roscommon off the R362

Hidden away in the rural peace of "the undiscovered Ireland", **Lacken House** is a unique cut stone manor dating back to the 1820s which now offers guests a choice of bed and breakfast or self-catering accommodation. This lovely property was for generations the home of the McDonnell dynasty but when the last scion of the family died in 1972, the house was closed and allowed to fall into decay. Fortunately, in 1996 the estate was bought by Jan and Gertina Cammeraat who undertook an extensive programme of restoration and refurbishment, as well as adding 4 comfortable self-catering chalet-style lodges in the grounds of the ancient orchard of Lacken House. At the time of writing, they are also completing the conversion of the old stables which will provide a recreation room, (with table tennis and other games), a place to sit and enjoy the peaceful silence and maybe read a book, a coffee corner where you can buy a cup of coffee or tea, and a laundry room with washing machine as well as extra showers. Bed and breakfast guests stay in the main house where there are 6 individually designed and decorated rooms, one

Lacken House, Rahara, Athleague, Co. Roscommon
Tel/Fax: 0903 23449   e-mail: info@lackenhouse.findhere.com
website: www.lackenhouse.findhere.com   or www.lackenhouse.web.com

of which is a Bridal Suite. All the rooms are spacious, non-smoking and en suite with shower and toilet, and there are ground floor bedrooms available. Children are welcome, with a cot and high chair available if required. The Cammeraats have bicycles for hire, there's a golf course nearby and good fishing too, as well as some delightful walks. They also offer a full organised day trip, with driver, with the price depending on the itinerary, and if you are flying to Ireland they can arrange to pick you up at the airport.

CASTLEREA
17 miles NW of Roscommon on the N60

Map 4 ref G8

The third largest town in the county, Castlerea has little to detain the visitor in the town itself, (although it was the birthplace of Sir Walter Wilde, father of the celebrated Oscar), but on the outskirts stands **Clonalis House**, the ancestral home of the O'Conor clan which claims to be the oldest family in Europe. Hereditary kings of Connaught, the O'Conors' genealogical tree has been traced back to a certain Feredach the Just in 75AD although an optimistic chart preserved in the house extends the lineage back to the 15th century BC.

By comparison, **Clonalis House** (which is still lived in by the O'Conor family) is a relative newcomer - an appealing Victorian mansion in the Italianate style completed in 1878. It contains an interesting miscellany of priceless early-Irish archives, sumptuous antiques, family portraits documenting the O'Conors' colourful exploits at home and abroad, and a fascinating collection of mementoes. The chapel has a chalice which un-screws into three parts, a useful feature in the days when Catholic worship was proscribed, but perhaps the greatest treasure is the harp once owned by the celebrated blind harpist Turlough O'Carolan (1670-1738), "last of the Irish bards".

Cloonakerney House, just over 2 miles to the east of Castlerea, is an attractive modern country house with large gardens and a patio standing in unspoilt farmland. It's the home of Maura Donnellan who offers self-catering accommodation for visitors staying in this friendly part of the county. The apartment is beautifully decorated and comfortably furnished, comprehensively equipped with all modern amenities. Maura will go out of her way to make sure you enjoy your holiday and she can guide you to all

Cloonakerney House, Castlerea, Co. Roscommon
Tel: 0907 21001

the manifold attractions and activities in the area. Maura will even arrange transport via a minibus to local inns and restaurants. Golf and good walking are available locally and one attraction which shouldn't be missed is Clonalis House, home of the O'Conor family, formerly Kings of Connacht. In Castlerea High Street the Hell's Kitchen pub attracts many visitors to marvel at its astounding collection of antiques, "the only national museum with a liquor licence" as the owner describes it! And over to the west, it's a short drive to the lakes where you'll find many scenic routes along quiet roads.

STROKESTOWN   MAP 4 REF H8
12 miles NE of Roscommon on the R368/N5

The busiest visitor attraction in Co. Roscommon is undoubtedly **Strokestown Park House** and the associated **Irish Famine Museum** which is housed in the stableyards of the fine Georgian house. Strokestown Park was the seat of the Pakenham Mahon family from the 1660s until 1979 when it was sold to the local garage owner with all its contents intact - everything from antique furniture and furnishings to family archives and toys, even school exercise books from the 1930s. The old schoolroom is still here, with its blackboard, desks and school books, and the main living room, dining room, nursery and library all reflect the family's comfortable rather than ostentatious lifestyle. A unique feature of the house is the gallery in the kitchen from which the lady of the house could keep on an eye on the staff. This lofty distance was maintained even with the weekly list of menus which would be dropped over the railing each Monday morning.

An additional attraction at Strokestown Park is its lovely 4-acre **Walled Garden**, laid out in the 18th century and now fully restored. The pièce de resistance here is the herbaceous border which has been confirmed by the *Guinness Book of Records* as the longest herbaceous border anywhere in the British Isles. A stark contrast to the peaceful garden is the harrowing story recounted in the Irish Famine Museum which uses a combination of original documents and images in an attempt to explain the circumstances and consequences of the calamitous potato blight of 1845-51 that destroyed the staple, almost the only, food of rural Ireland. Within a matter of days an apparently healthy field of potatoes would be reduced, in the words of one eye-witness, to *"one wide waste of putrefying vegetation"*.

Individuals and charitable organisations in England attempted to relieve the appalling distress but the Whig government of the time refused to commit the really substantial funds necessary - with incredible callousness it decided that this was a problem for private enterprise to resolve. The result was that more than a million Irish died of starvation, another million and a half emigrated to an uncertain future in the United States or Canada. The effects of the famine were aggravated by an epidemic of typhus that caused a further 300,000 deaths: within the space of five years, it's been estimated, Ireland's population of 4 million had declined to a little over 2 million.

ELPHIN
12 miles N of Roscommon on the R368

MAP 4 REF H8

Oliver Goldsmith went to school here; the village has been the seat of a bishopric since the days of St Patrick; but the main visitor attraction nowadays is **Elphin Windmill**, the only working mill in the west of Ireland. It was built in the early 1700s to grind oats and wheat into meal. The mill worked for around a hundred years and was then abandoned. In 1992, the derelict tower was acquired by Elphin Area Community Enterprise Ltd and fully restored. Guided tours are given daily throughout the year and if you arrive on a day when there's a stiff breeze blowing you can see the mill in operation.

Elphin Windmill

BOYLE   MAP 4 REF G7
26 miles N of Roscommon on the N61

Generally regarded as the most appealing town in Co. Roscommon, Boyle stands beside
the river of the same name with the Curlew Hills rising to the northwest. The most venerable building here is **Boyle Abbey** which despite its town centre location enjoys a
tranquil setting beside a rushing stream. The abbey was founded by the Cistercian order in
1161 and even though it suffered the usual succession of attacks by warring Irish tribes,
a surprising amount of the fabric is still intact although for almost 200 years following the
suppression of the monasteries the building housed a military garrison. The 12th century
church has some striking Gothic and Romanesque arches and some interesting carvings.

The town also boasts some fine Georgian houses, most notably **Frybrook House**
which has some exquisite 18th century plasterwork and the nearby **King House** built by
Sir Henry King around 1730. Half a century later his descendants decided to remove
themselves to Rockingham House just outside the town and this stately building became
the home of the Connaught Regiment from 1788 and later the Irish Army. In the 1990s,
King House was comprehensively restored and re-opened as an intrepretive centre with
inventive high-tech special effects and life size models taking visitors through the history
of the house and of the people who lived in this corner of north Roscommon.

Located in the grounds of King House, the **Una Bhán Tourism Co-operative Society** is an innovative enterprise which was a well-deserved winner of the National Rural
Tourism Award for 1998. The Co-operative is a group of families who have joined

**Una Bhán Tourism Co-operative Society, Main Street, Boyle, Co. Roscommon
Tel: 079 63033   Fax: 079 63077   e-mail: infor@unabhan.com**

together to provide prospective and actual visitors to the area with all-in holiday arrangements, covering accommodation and activities connected with life on the land and local heritage. Call in, phone, fax or e-mail Una Bhán with your specific requirements and they will respond with comprehensive information. Whether you are looking for bed and breakfast or self-catering accommodation, want details about facilities for fishing, golfing, equestrian or water sports, craft trails, or places to see and visit, Una Bhán has copious, up-to-date information on its files and the helpful staff are all local people who know the area inside out. Another good reason for visiting Una Bhán is to sample the fare on offer in its cottage-style Restaurant and Coffee Shop. Snacks and full meals are available in friendly, comfortable surroundings, along with freshly baked scones and croissants, home made soup, an all day breakfast, and a great selection of ice creams and desserts. The Una Bhán complex also includes a Craft Shop stocked with a wide range of hand made traditional crafts, pottery, jewellery, stationery, cards, leather goods, wood creations and much more. Una Bhán incidentally is pronounced Oona Wawn and refers to the legend of a beautiful daughter of a local Celtic chieftain. Forbidden by her father to marry the man she loved, Una died of a broken heart and was buried on Trinity Island in nearby Lough Key. Her lover used to swim to the island every night to keep vigil at her grave. He was eventually buried beside her and tradition says that two trees grew up over their graves, entwining together to form a Lover's Knot.

A modern house on the outskirts of Boyle, **Avonlea** offers comfortable bed and breakfast accommodation in a warm and welcoming environment. Carmel and Martin Dolan are your hosts, a friendly couple who will do everything they can to ensure that your stay is as relaxed and comfortable as possible. Their attractive, non-smoking, home is furnished and decorated to a high standard, with lots of traditional and antique

Avonlea, Carrick Road, Boyle, Co. Roscommon
Tel: 079 62538

furniture, and the additional inviting feature of a blazing open fire. Avonlea has 5 guest bedrooms, 2 of them en suite and all equipped with television. Children and family groups are welcome, with a baby-sitting service available if required. Breakfast at Avonlea comes with an extensive menu and although the Dolans do not cater for an evening meal, there's a good choice of hotels, restaurants and pubs within easy reach. Avonlea enjoys a convenient location: just a 5-minute walk from the town centre; just a 5-minute drive from Lough Key Forest Park. Locally, there are facilities for fishing, golf, shooting, horse riding and forest walks; for a scenic drive just point your car in any direction, or if you just want to relax and wind down, settle into a comfortable armchair in Avonlea's residents' lounge.

To the east of the town stretches the **Lough Key Forest Park**, formerly part of the vast Rockingham estate. Rockingham House itself was burnt to a shell in 1957 but the grounds have been planted with conifers and the attractions on offer include forest walks, boating, fishing and cruising, a bog garden and picnic sites, and a caravan park and camping area.

In the opposite direction, about 3 miles along the R294, stands the Drumanone Dolmen, one of the largest in Ireland with an immense capstone 12 feet long and 9 feet wide. There are more prehistoric remains on nearby Lough Gara where no fewer than 300 *crannógs* have been found. These man-made islands were used by Iron Age farmers as refuges for themselves and their cattle. Astonishingly, some of them remained in use until the early 1600s. The excavations which uncovered these artificial islands also retrieved 31 dug-out wooden boats from the bottom of the lake.

7 Northwest Ireland

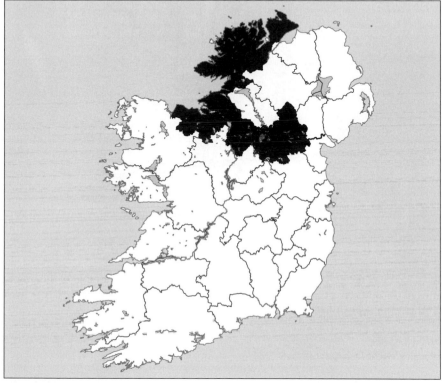

© MAPS IN MINUTES ™ (1998)

COUNTY DONEGAL

Attached to the rest of the Republic by a mere sliver of land near Ballyshannon, County Donegal is geologically a continuation of the Scottish Highlands and boasts the highest cliffs in Europe at Slieve League. Few would disagree that the county also has the most spectacular scenery in Ireland - sweeping ranges of mountains, deep glens and shimmering lakes, and a frayed coastline that extends for more than 650 miles. The third largest county after Cork and Galway, Donegal has the largest Gaeltacht (Irish speaking community) in Ireland, partly because the English never troubled to colonise this remote corner of the country with its rich scenery and impoverished soil.

Another result of the absence of the English is the lack of any stately homes in the county but in compensation there's a rich variety of prehistoric and medieval remains,

Transasrossan Bay, Co. Donegal

and a wealth of delightfully unspoilt villages and towns. We begin our tour of the county at its most southerly point, Bundoran, and travel northwards to Malin Head, the most northerly point in all Ireland.

BUNDORAN
MAP 5 REF H5
19 miles SW of Donegal on the N15

One of Ireland's older seaside resorts, Bundoran is set on the south shore of Donegal Bay looking across to the Donegal hills. The town offers all the usual variety of seaside amusements as well as a golf course which is one of the best known in the country.

A mere 500 yards from the centre of Bundoran, close to the lovely Blue Flag beach of golden sands and with all the local amenities nearby, **Macduff & Annehan Cottages** provide excellent self-catering accommodation in this popular seaside resort. Both cottages are bungalows, built in 1988 and fully equipped with up to date facilities. Bed linen, towels and just about everything you're likely to need are all included in the rental. Bundoran itself is known world-wide for possessing one of the most adrenaline-pumping surfing beaches and the mighty Atlantic Sea creates another major visitor attraction, the Puffing Hole, where the incoming tide produces spectacular spumes of water. Rather more sedate watersports are available at Waterworld, located on the seafront. Here you will find a choice of heated pools, along with a wave machine, water slides and seaweed baths. If you prefer outdoor activities, the town also has a riding school from which you

Macduff & Annehan Cottages. Book through Anne McCauley, Rose Cottage, Lisahully, Ballyshannon, Co. Donegal Tel: 072 52205

can go pony trekking along the coastal sand hills, and also a cycle rental shop if you want to explore the country lanes round about.

BALLYSHANNON
14 miles S of Donegal on the N15

MAP 5 REF H5

The people of Ballyshannon seem to like nothing better than a festival. They kick off in March, around St Patrick's Day, with an **Amateur Drama Festival**; on the first weekend of August the town is crowded for the **Music Festival** which has attracted performers such as Donegal's own Altan; in September the long-established **Harvest Fair** celebrations take place; and towards the end of November, there's the **Allingham Arts Festival for Writers**. This festival is named after the poet William Allingham (1824-89) who was born at Ballyshannon and became a member of an artistic circle that included Tennyson and the Pre-Raphaelites. He is buried in Ballyshannon churchyard beneath a stone slab inscribed with the word "Poet".

Ballyshannon is also noted for a variety of china known as Parian ware, (because it resembles the clear white Greek marble quarried on the island of Paros). It is produced at the **Donegal Parian China Factory** on the Sligo road where visitors can join a free guided tour, browse in the Exhibition Room, purchase one of the delicate, hand-crafted products, or settle down for a cup of tea in the refreshment room.

This attractive small town, set on the steep banks of the River Erne, is home to what is believed to be Ireland's oldest custom built hotel. A stately Georgian building with smart, ochre-washed walls, **Dorrian's Imperial Hotel** dates back to 1781. For the last 60 years or so, the hotel has been owned and run by the Dorrian family. The present incumbents, Ben and Mary Dorrian, recently undertook a major programme of improvement, extension and refurbishment. All of the 49 en suite rooms have been handsomely furnished and redecorated, and the hotel now boasts a fitness suite and modern gym facility. And by the time you read this, the new basement bar should be up and running. Excellent cuisine is also a priority with the Dorrians. The stylish restaurant offers an à la carte menu featuring dishes prepared with tasty fresh produce such as locally caught salmon. And to complement your meal, there's an extensive and well-chosen wine list. Do find time to wander up the street to Dorrian's Wine & Spirit Store, a charming thatched pub where

Dorrian's Imperial Hotel, Main Street, Ballyshannon, Co. Donegal
Tel: 072 51147   Fax: 072 51001

you are assured of a warm Irish welcome and plenty of good "craic"! Dorrian's also provides an ideal base for touring, golf and fishing. Ballyshannon is always a lively place but never more so than in the first week of August when its Music Festival is in full swing. This is one of the most popular celebrations of traditional Irish music: if you plan to attend, book well ahead.

Set on the hillside, **Mullac na Sí** takes its name from the old Irish words meaning "Mound of the Fairies". According to legend, the hill was the burial place of the early King, Aodh-Ruadh, and the fairies act as guardian spirits. Mullac na Sí is the home of

Mullac na Sí, Bishop Street, Ballyshannon, Co. Donegal
Tel/Fax: 072 52702

Bridget Nolan-Coyle and her husband who provide a warm Irish welcome for their bed and breakfast guests. Bridget is from Ballyshannon originally but spent 30 years in the United States before returning from Philadelphia with her husband to run this guest house. There are 3 en suite letting rooms, all of them huge and all with an additional sofa bed. One of the rooms, the honeymoon suite, has a king-sized bed 7 feet by 7 feet. Outside, in the beautifully maintained gardens, there's also a trim modern chalet to let. This spacious home is situated on 3 acres of land within the town's boundary. Mullac na Sí has private parking and is close to all the local amenities - lake, river and sea fishing, pony trekking, golfing, swimming and more.

Located on the east side of Ballyshannon, just a short walk from the town centre, **Carrickboy House** assures visitors of a warm welcome. This typical post-Victorian town house is the home of Doreen and John A. McGee who are members of the Town and Country Homes Association and have a Bord Failte Quality Approved rating for their bed and breakfast accommodation. The house has recently been completely refurbished and re-painted, with all new carpets and curtains fitted. Open all year round, Carrickboy has 4 guest bed-rooms, all of them en suite and well-appointed. A full breakfast is included in the tariff and the McGees will also provide an evening meal if required. There is also private car parking available for guests.

**Carrickboy House, East Port, Ballyshannon, Co. Donegal
Tel: 072 51744**

On the outskirts of Ballyshannon are the minimal re-mains of Abbey Assaroe, founded by Cistercian monks in the late 12th century. In 1989, the Abbey Mill Restoration Trust acquired the der-elict mills, restoring the mill buildings and water wheels for use an auditorium and coffee shop. It's a peaceful and picturesque spot and visitors to the interpretive cen-tre, **The Water Wheels**, can view a video film on the heritage of the monastery and mill.

Just a mile to the west of Ballyshannon stands **Portnason House**, a lovely old Georgian house of great character dating back to around 1750. It is approached by way

Portnason House, Ballyshannon, Co. Donegal
Tel/Fax: 072 52016

of an avenue lined with mature sycamore trees which gradually reveals the handsome building which was originally built to house British Army officers when Ballyshannon was the garrison town for south Donegal. The quality of the workmanship and materials is reflected in the fact that the house is still in excellent condition after almost 250 years. Madge and Barry Sharkey are the owners of this lovely house which they completely restored and redecorated in 1995 to a very high standard, at the same time providing the 10 spacious and airy guest rooms, some of them boasting antique fireplaces, and all of them with full en suite facilities. The three large reception rooms also have antique marble fireplaces. The property includes some 54 acres of good quality limestone land enclosed by drystone walls, its northern boundary formed by more than 1000 yards of foreshore which is ideal for horse-riding. It's possible to travel from Ballyshannon to Bundoran (about 4 miles distant) along the seashore which is mostly firm sandy beach. Guests are welcome to bring their own horses, with stabling, a large paddock and grazing all available. Madge and Barry breed Connemara ponies and other outdoor features include a spring-fed freshwater boating pond, two original stone piers and a 2.5 acre walled garden and orchard. From the courtyard of Portnason House there is direct access to the Erne Estuary with its magnificent sand dunes, ideal for horse-riding, beach-walking, salmon and sea-trout fishing and birdwatching - in fact, the Erne Estuary is a designated area for the preservation of birdlife. Other facilities nearby include two championship 18-hole golf courses, two pitch and putt courses, a driving range, year-round surfing, water skiing and board sailing, and an abundance of locations for fresh water fishing. Sea angling is also available with boats for hire in several locations nearby.

About 3 miles north of Ballyshannon, on the N15, look out for the entrance to **Cavangarden House**. Turn off here and follow the half a mile of driveway which leads to a stately Georgian residence set in 380 acres of working farmland. Built in 1750,

Cavangarden House, Donegal Road, Ballyshannon, Co. Donegal
Tel: 072 51365   e-mail: cghouse@iol.ie

Cavangarden House is a fine example of that golden age of Irish architecture with well-proportioned rooms, high ceilings and lofty windows. Elegant furnishings and decor reflect the character of that bygone age, as do the lush green lawns surrounding the house. This appealing old house is the family home of Agnes McCaffrey who offers her guests a warm and friendly welcome along with good food and peaceful, relaxing surroundings. Cavangarden's 6 guest rooms are all en suite, attractively decorated and furnished, and equipped with television. Laundry service is available on request. Evening meals at Cavangarden are something to savour, with a menu offering a home cooking at its best for which only the very finest of fresh Irish produce is admitted to the kitchen. After your meal, settle down in the tranquil surroundings of the residents' lounge. If you enjoy active pursuits you will find a good choice within easy reach: golf, fishing, pony trekking, nature walks and miles of sandy beaches.

LISAHULLY   MAP 5 REF H5
2 miles SE of Ballyshannon on minor road off the N3

Located close to the County Fermanagh border and just 2 miles from Ballyshannon, **Green Acres** offers comfortable self-catering accommodation in a peaceful, rural setting. This attractive modern bungalow was purpose-built in 1977 with self-catering guests in mind so it is exceptionally well-designed and equipped with all up-to-date conveniences. Attractively decorated as a typical family home, Green Acres has 3 bedrooms and can sleep up to 6 people. There are spacious lawns both back and front, just right for lounging in the sun or for an alfresco picnic.

Nearby Ballyshannon is one of the oldest towns in Ireland - legend has it that the first people to reach Ireland settled on Inish Saimer, an island in the Erne Estuary, just off the

Green Acres, Lisahully, nr Ballyshannon, Co. Donegal
Tel/Fax: 072 51642

Mall Quay in the town. A popular excursion from Lisahully is to Lower Lough Erne, just a few miles distant. This scenic area is where the region's earliest inhabitants settled. Many of the small islands that dot the lake are actually *crannógs*, or artificial islands created by Celtic settlers in prehistoric times. During the summer season, there are regular cruises around Lough Erne, or you can hire a boat and explore it for yourself.

CREEVY
3 miles NW of Ballyshannon off the R231

MAP 5 REF H5

This tiny seaside hamlet is the base for **Creevy Co-op Ltd**. which offers visitors in search of quality   self-catering accommodation a choice of three attractive stone-built cottages in their own individual locations. These are faithful modern reconstructions of tradi-tional Donegal cottages with features such as flagstone floors, open fireplaces, half-doors and sash windows. This old world charm has been carefully married to all the modern

Creevy Co-op Ltd., Creevy, Ballyshannon, Co. Donegal
Tel: 072 52896 Fax: 072 52896 e-mail: creevy@iol.ie

conveniences which include en suite bedrooms, fully fitted kitchens and oil-fired central heating. Outside, there are paved patios and substantial walled gardens. Guests can choose between cottages nestled by the shore or languishing deep in quiet countryside, each with spectacular views of mountain and sea. All of the cottages have been designed to be wheelchair-friendly, with shower and kitchen facilities adapted to suit the disabled. And since the Donegal coast is a fisherman's dream, the cottages also have bait and tackle rooms as well as freezing and drying facilities. Shore angling is enjoyed along the stretch of coastline at Creevy while beach casting is popular at nearby Rossnowlagh Strand. In 1997, 21 species of marine fish, ranging from mackerel to tope, were landed at Creevy. Deep sea trips on a 33ft, fully equipped boat can be booked through the Co-op office whose staff will also be happy to prepare breakfast or evening meals if you get tired of self-catering.

The Donegal coast also provides some of the best conditions in Ireland for surfing and other water sports. Golf and pony trekking facilities are within easy reach, there's a 3 mile stretch of golden strand at **Rossnowlagh** and some enchanting walks in the area. The Co-op has constructed a 6 mile cliff walk which opens up some breathtaking views. The route passes over moor and farmland and is equipped with fence stiles and direction markers. This walk is most suited for the physically fit. For those who wish to stroll at a sedate pace, the countryside around Creevy is laced with meandering country roads.

ROSSNOWLAGH
MAP 5 REF H5

5 miles NW of Ballyshannon off the R321

Best known for its magnificent beach Rossnowlagh is also home to the modern **Franciscan Friary Centre of Peace and Reconciliation** where visitors are welcome to share in the peace of its lovely seaside setting. The centre is open daily from 10am until 9pm but if you wish to stay longer, the Friary has overnight accommodation available in rooms with splendid sea views.

A much more rigorous regime is in effect at **Station Island** in Lough Derg, about 15 miles inland. According to legend St Patrick spent 40 days and nights fasting in a cave on the island. The cave has been a place of pilgrimage for centuries, even during the years that Catholic observances were prohibited. During the period of the St Patrick's Purgatory Pilgrimage between June 1st and August 15th only genuine pilgrims are allowed on the island. During the 3-day penitential exercise they must go barefoot whilst making the Stations of the Cross and only one meal each day of dry bread and black tea is permitted. The first night is spent in a vigil in the basilica; on the two successive nights, pilgrims stay either in the modern hospices or in the "Penitential Beds" - remains of the stone cells of the early Christian monks.

LAGHY
MAP 5 REF H4

3 miles S of Donegal on the N15

The small village of Laghy just south of Donegal Town makes a very convenient base for exploring the Donegal coastline and the gentle hill country inland dotted with small lakes. An excellent place to stay for bed and breakfast is **Hillcrest**, the home of Sheila

**Hillcrest, Ballyshannon Road, Laghy, Donegal, Co. Donegal
Tel: 073 21837 Fax: 073 21674 e-mail: gatins@eircom.net**

Gatins who offers her guests a warm welcome. As the name implies, Hillcrest sits high on the hillside enjoying superb views over the Donegal countryside and is situated in the village within walking distance of pubs, restaurant and supermarket. It's a large modern house and has been beautifully furnished and decorated by Sheila who clearly has a real flair for interior design. There are 4 guest bedrooms, 2 of them en suite, all provided with TV and tea/coffee-making facilities - and they all share those lovely views. Guests also have the use of the attractive residents' lounge. Parking space is ample. Sheila serves a hearty breakfast which will certainly set you up for the day. If you enjoy fishing, don't forget to bring your tackle with you as there is good sport in the nearby lakes; Donegal Golf Course and a lovely sandy beach are both just 3 miles away.

DONEGAL   Map 5 ref H4
45 miles SW of Londonderry on the N15

Despite its name, Donegal is not the county town - that honour is held by Letterkenny in the north near the Ulster border. But Donegal has the atmosphere of a county capital, always busy with visitors especially around the central Diamond, or market square. A 25ft high obelisk here commemorates the compilers of the **Annals of the Four Masters**, the encyclopaedic work which aimed to incorporate every known fact (and myth) about Ireland from 2958BC (when Noah's granddaughter visited Ireland) up to the year of completing the book, 1616AD.

Just off the Diamond, in Tyrconaill Street, is the well-restored **O'Donnell's Castle** which is actually a combination of a Norman-style tower house built in 1474, with a square tower and turrets added by the O'Donnells in 1505, and a Jacobean house built by Sir Basil Brooke, the English military commander of Donegal, in 1610. It's an attractive building both from the outside, with its mullioned windows, arches and gables, and inside where there are no fewer than 14 fireplaces, the most imposing of which bears the carved escutcheons of the Brooke family.

Also on Tirconaill Street is the **Donegal Railway Heritage Centre** where there's a model of the old County Donegal Railway which ran from Ballyshannon to Londonderry until its closure in 1959. The centre has some lovingly restored railcars, carriages and other steam age memorabilia.

Irish pubs are famous world-wide for their genuinely welcoming atmosphere, good craic and good music. At **McGroarty's Bar** in the centre of Donegal Town you can also add good food to the list. Located within this lively inn, the fare on offer at Stella's Salad Bar has attracted unstinting praise from a host of food writers. "Clever, concerned and mightily regenerative" enthused the *Irish Food Guide*; "great soups, good salads, lovely stir-fry filled pitta bread" was *The Times'* commendation, and the *Vegetarian Guide to Ireland* declared that "This is one of few pubs which makes a conscious effort to cook something original and creative for vegetarians".

As well as vegetarian dishes, Stella McGroarty, who compiled the appealing menu, also offers a wide choice of other dishes. They range from freshly cut sandwiches to hearty

**McGroarty's Bar, The Diamond, Donegal Town,
Co. Donegal   Tel: 073 21049**

hot dishes of the day, available either as a regular portion or large for those with a more robust appetite. Somewhere in between are the McGroarty Doorsteps - 3 slices of bread, lightly toasted with the filling of your choice on the lower level; lettuce, tomato and coleslaw up top. Home-made soups, salads and melts extend the choice even further. Although the choice is so wide, should you have any particular requirement it doesn't satisfy, a note on the menu invites you to feel free to ask "as our aim is to please". (Do note that food is not available after 6pm).

Stella's Salad Bar is one very good reason for a visit to McGroarty's Bar; another is the bar itself, hosted by Stella's husband, Jack. It's the epitome of a traditional Irish bar and renowned for the quality of its music. Thursday is the night for traditional music and other music is played at weekends.

The striking, ochre-washed **Abbey Hotel** stands at the heart of the town, facing the triangular market square called The Diamond. The Abbey embodies all the charm and character associated with Donegal, and provides a perfect example of Irish hospitality at its most friendly and courteous. For decades, the management's attention to detail and the staff's pride in accommodating every personal taste and request have made the Abbey the only place to stay for anyone who has once sampled the atmosphere.

The Abbey Restaurant offers an extensive menu which includes both local flavours and many international dishes in a relaxed and inviting atmosphere. As with other hotel services, the Chef will be delighted to cater for your individual tastes. The Eas Dun Bar is, in itself, a good enough reason for staying at the Abbey. Ornately designed in a unique two tier fashion, the bar provides the ideal setting for a pre-dinner drink or informal chat. Also well worth a visit is the Corabber Lounge with its commanding views of the River Eske and tranquil Donegal Bay. As you might expect, the 80 bedrooms are equipped to the highest specification to help make your stay a memorable experience. Teletext TV, video and satellite system, direct dial telephone, radio, hairdryer and trouser press are just some of the facilities provided as standard. Most rooms enjoy panoramic views of the river and bay, and also offer full access to wheelchair users and the less able bodied.

The Abbey is also an ideal venue for conferences and functions of all kinds with attentive, efficient staff and comprehensive facilities ensuring a successful event. And when you do finally leave the hotel, there's a whole gamut of activities to enjoy, from

Abbey Hotel, The Diamond, Donegal Town, Co. Donegal
Tel: 073 21014   Fax: 073 23660

shopping for Donegal's famous hand-woven tweeds to angling in the bounteous trout and salmon waters of the rivers Eske and Eany.

Less than a mile outside Donegal Town on the Ballyshannon road, the **Forbairt Craft Village** has a number of craft workshops, attractively grouped around a central courtyard, where traditional crafts are expertly finished by skilled craftspeople. A good place to pick up a souvenir, be it hand made pottery, batik, an uilleann pipe or some handwoven Donegal tweed for which the town is famous. The complex includes a coffee shop and picnic area.

Lough Eske, a couple of miles north of Donegal, is well known as one of the most scenic places in the county and Gráinne McGettigan's welcoming B & B, **Rhu-Gorse**, makes the most of its splendid position high above the lake. All the bedrooms enjoy extensive views across Lough Eske. The name means "Lake of the Fish" and the main catch here is char, a small and tasty member of the salmon family. Also needing explanation for non-gaelic speakers, Rhu-Gorse is the name of a champion bloodline dog of the Red Setter breed. Gráinne has adopted him as the logo on her stationery. Animals are important to Gráinne who also breeds the horses which can be seen grazing in the fields

Rhu Gorse, Lough Eske, Donegal Town, Co. Donegal
Tel/Fax: 073 21685

around the house. The house itself is a spacious building in the Swiss style with attractive interior features such as wooden stairways and huge rooms. Breakfast comes with a choice of menu, after which you might care to explore the Lough Eske Drive, a scenic route which circles the whole of the lake. A curiosity to look out for on the way is the colossal Famine Pot, almost 6 feet high and 6 feet round. During the potato famine, cauldrons like this were filled with maize provided by English landlords whose tenants would then fill their own household pots from it.

NORTH & WEST OF DONEGAL TOWN

MOUNTCHARLES
Map 5 ref H4

3 miles W of Donegal on the N56

The birthplace of the celebrated Irish writer, Seamus McManus, the little town of Mountcharles clings to a steeply rising hill with splendid views over Donegal Bay. At the summit of the hill is a bright green pump commemorating McManus, *"poet and seanachie"* (storyteller), who is buried in the churchyard at nearby Frosses village. Mountcharles and the neighbouring villages were once famous for hand embroidery work and it's still possible to find some embroidered linen on sale.

Just a mile outside Mountcharles, **Shore Cottage** offers outstanding self-catering accommodation. As the name suggest, the property is situated on the shore, just 20 feet from the water's edge. There are sublime views, both outside and from inside, over Donegal Bay to the hills of southern Donegal. The cottage was built in the early 1800s for the gamekeeper on the Marquess of Conningham's estate. The estate was originally the seat of the Mountcharles family from whom the nearby village takes its name.

The interior of Shore Cottage has been refurbished to the standard of a 4-star hotel, with a decor of the very highest quality. The beautifully furnished sitting room is huge,

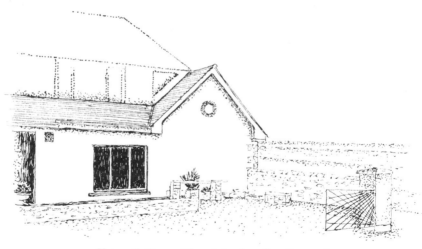

Shore Cottage, Mountcharles, Co. Donegal
Tel: 73 35044 Fax: 73 35437 website: www.shorecottage.com

has an open fire and large windows overlooking the sea and garden. In the spacious kitchen cum dining area, the old Stanley solid fuel cooker has been retained but an up-to-date microwave and dishwasher have also been installed. On the same level, there are 2 bedrooms, (1 double, 1 twin), and a bathroom with bath, shower and bidet. The cottage also has a utility room complete with washing machine and drying facilities.

Safe bathing is virtually on the doorstep and there are some lovely seashore walks, with shellfish picking nearby. Quiet though the area is, there's plenty to do. Boat trips and bicycles for hire are available either at Mountcharles or in Donegal; you can join mountain walks organised by a local walking club and there are also historical walks. There are scenic drives in abundance and inviting traditional pubs offering musical entertainment. As the owner of Shore Cottage, Evanna Schorderet, says: "If it's ambling and scrambling through the beautiful countryside, or drinking in Atlantic breezes, Shore Cottage is the place to be!"

KILLYBEGS
15 miles W of Donegal on the R263

MAP 5 REF G4

The busiest fishing port in Ireland, Killybegs hosts a huge **International Sea Angling Festival** in mid-July each year but throughout the year boats are available to hire for sea angling expeditions. If you have neither the time nor inclination to catch the fish yourself, you can always wander down to the quay in the early evening when the fishing fleet arrives, accompanied by flocks of raucous seagulls, and choose from that day's newly-arrived catch.

Killybegs is a picturesque place with sparkling whitewashed houses lining the narrow streets running up the sloping hillside from the harbour. But there's little in the way of other visitor attractions to detain you once you've sampled the fish and northwards from the town beckon the scenic splendours of west Donegal. Or you can strike due west along the coast road that tumbles and rolls over the cliff tops to Kilcar and Carrick. A mile or so south of Carrick the mighty cliffs of **Slieve League** rise almost 2000ft from the shore, the loftiest sea cliffs in Europe. The view of the cliffs from the tiny village of Teelin is awe-inspiring.

GLENCOLUMBKILLE
30 miles NW of Donegal on the R263

MAP 5 REF G4

Reached by a spectacularly scenic road from Killybegs, this peaceful and picturesque little resort takes its name from St Colmcille (c.521-97) who had a retreat house here. At midnight on the saint's day, June 9th, pilgrims begin a barefoot procession around the area, stopping to pray at the 15 Turas associated with St Colmcille, amongst them his chapel, holy well and the stone slab that served as his bed. The procession concludes at 3am with Mass in the village church.

The area surrounding Glencolumbkille is dotted with more than forty prehistoric monuments - portal dolmens, souterrains and cairns from the Bronze Age, some of them erected more than 5000 years ago. This remote corner of Co. Donegal has always suffered from chronic poverty and unemployment. In 1951 a newly appointed parish priest, the energetic Father James MacDyer, began several initiatives to provide employment for local people and stem the constant drain of emigration. The most visible of Father Macdyer's projects is the **Folk Village and Museum** which features three reconstructed dwellings, replicas of those typical in the area during the 1720s, 1820s and 1920s. Each cottage is appropriately furnished with furniture, artefacts and utensils, and there's also a replica of a National School which has a display of interesting vintage photographs. There's a Shebeen where you can have a free taster of unfamiliar beverages such as fuchsia, honey or seaweed wine, and the site also includes a tearoom serving more traditional fare - home made scones and soup. You're unlikely, however, to want to sample the unappealing brew of maize porridge that is prepared daily for the "famine pot" standing in the yard outside.

ARDARA
23 miles NW of Donegal on the N56

Map 5 ref H4

From Glencolumbkille a staggeringly beautiful route passes through the spectacular Glengesh Pass to the sizeable town of Ardara, attractively located at the head of a deep sea-lough. A centre for weaving, knitwear and homespun tweed for generations, Ardara is definitely the place to purchase your souvenir Aran sweater, either in the high street shops or in the half dozen factory shops where you can watch the manufacturing process in operation. The town's major product is celebrated in the town's **Heritage Centre** and also by the annual **Weavers' Fair** in midsummer, a popular local event when Ardara's many pubs are alive with traditional music and good craic.

Ardara's buildings are quietly pleasing rather than outstanding in any way but it's worth stepping inside the **Church of the Holy Family** to look at the striking stained glass window created by Evie Hone, one of the most important Irish artists of the 20th century.

Brook Cottage, a couple of miles outside Ardara, is the genuine article, a traditional Irish cottage more than 200 years old. The thatched and whitewashed, single-storeyed dwelling has been in Margot McGill's family for more than a century. All modern amenities have been introduced without marring the old world charm and the cottage is now available for self-catering holidays. The property sleeps up to 5 people and stands in

Brook Cottage, Cashel, Ardara, Co. Donegal
Tel: 075 41552

peaceful countryside, an ideal base for exploring this scenic corner of Donegal with its fretted coastline and the dramatic Blue Stack Mountains which provide a challenge even for experienced walkers and climbers. A short drive southwards will bring you to the busy fishing port of Killybegs where keen fishermen will find a good choice of boats offering sea angling trips.

Beagh Cottage and **Oitir Cottage**, situated approximately 3 miles from the Heritage Town of Ardara, occupy a tranquil setting surrounded by scenic countryside, ideal for a peaceful and relaxing self-catering holiday. The cottages are both close to a European Blue Flag beach, a 900-acre Nature Reserve and Narin Portnoo 18-hole links golf course. Beagh Cottage is a charming thatched and whitewashed traditional Irish cottage which

Beagh Cottage & Oitir Cottage, Sandfield, Ardara, Co. Donegal
Tel: 075 41444

has been sensitively restored and equipped with all modern conveniences. Oitir Cottage is a neat purpose-built bungalow which stands only yards from the nature reserve. Both cottages sleep up to 5 people. Each has its own entrance and private garden, and both dwellings have electric central heating. The properties are available all year round and the owner, Bernadette Shovlin, offers special rates for off season bookings. No traveller in this part of Donegal should leave without paying a visit to one of the wool mills in Ardara. The town has been a centre for weaving and knitwear for generations and its most famous product, Aran Sweaters, can be purchased here at spectacularly low prices. At Ardara's Heritage Centre there's a fascinating exhibition on the history of hand-weaving and a real-life weaver works away at his hand loom while regaling the audience with lively tales about the industry.

GLENTIES
18 miles NW of Donegal on the N56

MAP 5 REF H4

The outstanding scenery around Glenties provides a popular location for film and TV producers. *The Hanging Game* was filmed here and most recently *Dancing Lunacy* in which Meryl Streep plays the leading rôle. She also attended the première of the film in Glenties.

So it's perhaps not surprising to discover that the town has won the "Ireland's Tidiest Town" award five times, and the "Tidiest Small Town" title a further five times. Picturesquely situated where two glens converge, Glenties' wooded surroundings display a marked contrast with the ruggedness of much of the surrounding country.

This part of Donegal has always been noted for its strong tradition of Irish music and Glenties has a flourishing traditional music school which is constantly turning out a new generation of musicians. To experience this tradition at its best, visit the town on the first weekend of October when the **"Fiddlers Weekend"** attracts fiddlers from many parts of Ireland and around the world.

The most striking building in the town is the Roman Catholic **St Connell's Church**, a lovely modern church designed by the Derry architect Liam McCormack and consecrated in 1974. Imitating the nearby mountains, the church has a long sloping roof which sweeps down to within 6 feet of the ground. When it's raining, the water drips off the tiled roof and forms gleaming ornamental pools.

Glenties' most famous son is Patrick MacGill (1890-1963) whose life got off to a poor start when his parents sold him at a hiring fair for servants. He escaped to Scotland where he worked as a farm labourer and navvy before his writing skills earned him a position with the *Daily Express*. His best-known book is *Children of the Dead End*, a semi-autobiographical account of the lives of itinerant navvies. In early August each year the town hosts the **McGill Summer School** in honour of his work, a very Irish event celebrating his work with literary debates, lectures, workshops and exhibitions.

An excellent base for touring this corner of County Donegal is the **Avalon Guest House**, a smart, modern bungalow where Mary Ita and Hugh Boyle welcome guests for either bed and breakfast or half board accommodation. Avalon has 4 comfortable guest

Avalon Guest House, Glen Road, Glenties, Co. Donegal
Tel/Fax: 075 51292 e-mail: miboyle@eircom.net

rooms, (3 doubles and 1 twin), three of which are en suite. The food served here is really rather special, always home made and with extra treats such as home-baked bread, buns and cakes. There are menus for coeliacs, gluten free diets and children, and packed lunches are also available on request. The Glenties area has plenty to keep visitors occupied. Golf, fishing, and horse riding are all within easy reach and a 10-minute drive will bring you to a lovely golden sandy beach.

DUNGLOE
50 miles NW of Donegal on the N56

Map 5 ref H3

Dungloe lies in the heart of the Rosses, one of Ireland's *gaeltacht* (Irish-speaking) areas so the name you will see on signs for the town is *An Clochán Liath*, referring to the stepping stones which were once the only way to cross the river. This lively and thriving little town with a population of fewer than a thousand is well known throughout Donegal for its **"Mary from Dungloe Festival"** which takes place over the August Bank Holiday each year. A relaxed local version of the Miss World beauty contests, it provides a grand excuse for general celebration and extended licensing hours.

On Dungloe's main street stands the headquarters of the **Templecrone Co-operative Agricultural Society**, known locally as the "Cope". The Society was founded in 1906 by a local farmer, Paddy Gallagher, who took note of the fact that the price of manure was considerably less when purchased in quantity by societies. He extended this principle to buying more generally marketable commodities with the broad aim of helping local people shake off their dependence on the dreaded gombeen men, (moneylenders). By the time of his death in 1966 the "Cope" was a flourishing business with branches throughout the Rosses.

Just 500 yards from the town centre, **Lake View House** occupies a prime position overlooking Lake Dungloe. Bed and breakfast visitors staying here will receive a very warm welcome from Roisin Bonner. Her spacious modern bungalow, which was designed and built by the Bonner family, has 4 guest bedrooms, 3 of them en suite, and all of them

Lake View House, Carnmore Road, Dungloe, Co. Donegal
Tel: 075 21897

large, bright and attractively furnished. Pets are welcome and so too are smokers. Lake View House has an inviting home-from-home atmosphere and an additional attraction for visitors is free use of the Bonners' boat for trips around the lake. Angling can also be arranged. At breakfast time there's a choice of Irish or continental breakfast and Roisin is also happy to provide packed lunches. Golf, horse-riding and the beach at Lake Maghery are all within a few miles of the house and Dungloe is a good starting point for some splendidly scenic walks and drives through The Rosses.

The name given to the area around Dungloe, "The Rosses", means "place of many lakes", some 130 in all. The majority of them lie within 5 miles of the **Ostan na Rosann** hotel near Dungloe, making it an excellent centre for anglers who are provided with a surfeit of choices. The hotel is also a convenient base for visiting the many safe, unspoiled beaches dotted along the 200-mile coastline with its stunning cliffs, bays and inlets. Walkers, too, will enjoy the peacefulness of this secluded region, and for those who prefer to explore the Rosses on four wheels the quiet roads wind through picturesque scenery.

Ostan na Rosann is a stylish modern hotel standing on a hill overlooking Dungloe. It's owned and run by the McBride family whose enthusiastic commitment to the comfort and happiness of their guests has made the hotel so popular. The whole building is wheelchair-friendly, the 48 attractive bedrooms are all en suite, and there's a relaxing

Ostan na Rosann, Mill Road, Dungloe, Co. Donegal
Tel: 075 22444   Fax: 075 22400

residents' lounge. Ostan na Rosann is also a good place to eat, offering a range of menus which cater for all tastes and are based on fresh local produce. Bar meals are served in the informal atmosphere of an Irish pub, or you can choose from an à la carte menu where you'll find a wide selection of contemporary dishes amongst which, of course, locally caught salmon and trout take the place of honour. Children have their own special menu. Staying at Ostan na Rosann also means that you have direct access to one of the area's most modern leisure centres. The complex includes a heated swimming pool, a sauna, steam room, jacuzzi, solarium, and of course a gymnasium. As the McBrides point out, "It will keep you and the children occupied for hours on the odd day when it rains in Donegal!"

FALCARRAGH
24 miles NW of Letterkenny on the N56

MAP 5 REF H2

If you are planning to stay in this spectacular area, the village of Falcarragh provides a good base, well-supplied with pubs, shops and excellent bed and breakfast accommodation at the **Ferndale Guest House**, a smart modern bungalow set in a charming garden. Open from April to September, Ferndale is the home of Margaret Murphy who offers a warm Irish welcome to all her visitors. The house has 6 guest bedrooms, 2 of them en suite,

Ferndale Guest House, Ballina, Falcarragh, Co. Donegal
Tel: 074 65506

and all pleasantly decorated and furnished. Anglers will be specially happy here since the nearby River Bewin is renowned for its salmon and trout, and lovers of unspoilt countryside will revel in the scenery of the Glenveagh National Park a few miles to the south. Also close by is the beautiful Drumatinery Beach; a 9-hole golf course; and The Pottery at Moyra Rectory where you will find a wide variety of handthrown and handformed pottery, both functional and decorative. The Pottery also presents an exclusive range of handmade contemporary jewellery decorated with precious metal lustres and you can complete your visit with a cup of tea or freshly ground coffee and sample The Pottery's tasty home baking.

A few miles to the northeast of Falcarragh is **Horn Head**, a mighty promontory with majestic cliffs rising sheer from the sea to a height of 600ft. The views here are sublime: in one direction the vastness of the Atlantic Ocean broken only by numerous islands and headlands; and inland, mountain ranges with the prominent peaks of Muckish and Errigal.

BLOODY FORELAND
32 miles NW of Letterkenny on the R257

Map 5 ref H2

To enjoy one of the most magnificent views in Ireland go north to Bloody Foreland. The vista over the Atlantic Ocean and the islands is even more spectacular during the blood-red sunsets which have given the area its name.

About 7 miles offshore from Bloody Foreland is **Tory Island**, a barren windswept place reached by a ferry from Magheraroarty. The ferry is supposed to operate year round but the weather can be so bad that the crossing may be impossible for days on end. Indeed, in 1974 the islanders were cut off for 8 weeks by incessant storms so ferocious that even helicopters were prevented from landing. Following that experience two dozen families applied to Donegal County Council for housing on the mainland and it was subsequently revealed that the council had made plans for a total evacuation of the island. Then, as at Glencolmkille, a new priest arrived on the island. Father Diarmuid Ó Péicin encouraged the islanders to lobby every possible source of help, from the US Senator Tip O'Neill to Ian Paisley. Funds began to trickle in and conditions have gradually improved although life is still hard for the 150 or so permanent residents. The main occupation is fishing but the island also boasts a school of primitive painters whose works are displayed at the **James Dixon Gallery** near the harbour.

Less than a 30-minute drive inland towards Letterkenny will take you to **Glenveagh National Park** and Ioad Chois Locha, (the **Dunlewey Lakeside Centre**). Within the National Park is **Poison Glen** which acquired its rather forbidding name from the legend of the cyclops, Balor of the Evil Eye. When Balor was slain by Lugh, his eye rolled to the ground, tainting the whole area. In this Gaelic-speaking area, incidentally, the names on signs also appear in their old Irish form. Bloody Foreland is Cnoc Fola, Gweedore appears as Gaoth Dobhair, and the county name is spelt Dhún na nGall.

IN AND AROUND LETTERKENNY

LETTERKENNY
32 miles NE of Donegal on the N13

Map 5 ref I3

The commercial, administrative and ecclesiastical capital of Co. Donegal, Letterkenny is set beside the River Swilly where it flows into the lough of the same name. A thriving town, Letterkenny has attracted a healthy influx of new businesses on the outskirts but the centre still retains its country town appearance. It boasts one of the longest main streets in Ireland and an attractive feature of the town centre is a group of lifelike statues of naturally posed children. Even by Irish standards, Letterkenny is well-provided with lively pubs, many of them offering Irish music, and the younger generation has a choice of half a dozen nightclubs, a 4-screen cinema and a 10 pin bowling alley.

The town's most impressive building is the late-19th century **St Eunan's Cathedral**, designed in the Gothic style with flying buttresses and a strikingly lofty spire. The cathedral's walls of pearly Donegal sandstone gleam in sunlight and inside there are some interesting Celtic carvings and richly decorated ceilings. The other main place to visit is the **Donegal County Museum** on High Road which is housed in part of the former Workhouse and contains an interesting permanent collection of artefacts from early history and folk life as well as hosting travelling exhibitions.

Incidentally, if you are a devotee of Irish folk dance and music then the ideal time to visit Letterkenny is the middle of August when the **Letterkenny Folk Festival** is in full swing.

TRENTAGH

Map 5 ref I3

6 miles NW of Letterkenny off the R251

Hidden away in the Donegal countryside a few miles from Letterkenny, is the tiny village of Trentagh. It's well worth seeking out if you are looking for bed and breakfast accommodation in the area because it's here you will find **Bridgeburn House**. It takes its name from the old stone bridge that crosses the stream running between the house and the village street. This imposing and attractive house is the home of Donal and Sophia Boyle who had it built a few years ago and have furnished it with style and charm. The 5 spacious guest rooms, 4 of them en suite, are beautifully decorated and well-appointed, complete with television and tea/coffee-making facilities in all rooms. After your day's activities there's a large and comfortable lounge to relax in and evening meals are available on request. Meals are rather special here, with fresh home baking every day. The Boyles are a warm, friendly and helpful family who will do everything they can to make your stay comfortable. Families are welcome and a baby-sitting service sitting is available if required. Bridgeburn House is an ideal touring base for this corner of Donegal, with Glenveagh National Park, the Glebe Gallery, **Colmcille Heritage Centre and Flax Mill** all within a 7-mile radius. Locally, you'll find facilities for golf, horse and pony riding

Bridgeburn House, Trentagh, nr Letterkenny, Co. Donegal
Tel: 074 37167 or 08720 54298

lessons, fishing, swimming and entertainment. The house is situated 15 minutes from Letterkenny on the N56 to the village of Kilmacrenan. Turn left at the signpost for Church Hill and after about 3 miles turn right at the crossroads. Go up the hill and Bridgeburn House is just over half a mile on your right.

STRANORLAR/BALLYBOFEY   MAP 5 REF I4
12 miles S of Letterkenny on the N15/N13

The Finn Valley has been described as "Donegal's best kept secret" - an area of spectacular mountain scenery which is also an angler's paradise. At its heart, standing on opposite banks of the River Finn, stand the Twin Towns of Stranorlar and Ballybofey, and about a mile outside them is Mary McGranaghan's welcoming guest house, **Teevickmoy House** which enjoys a tranquil and scenic location overlooking woodlands. This striking and well-designed house was built in 1995, so the 5 attractive guest bedrooms are all well-equipped with up-to-date amenities. So too is the 2-bedroomed self-catering apartment

Teevickmoy House, Stranorlar/Ballybofey, Co. Donegal
Tel/Fax: 074 31866   e-mail: mmcgranaghan@tinet.ie

which forms part of this spacious house. Mary offers a choice of Irish or continental breakfast and will provide packed lunches on request. Evening meals are not provided but there are many good restaurants in the twin towns.

Teevickmoy House is handily located for exploring the Finn Valley which, in addition to the superb fishing in Ireland's second-largest salmon and trout fishing river, offers a whole range of other activities and attractions. The golfer can enjoy a round on Ballybofey & Stranorlar's 18-hole course, with its tastefully appointed clubhouse and greens. The Finn Valley Athletic Centre is renowned throughout Europe and the centre manager is coach for the Irish team at the Sydney Olympics. The Twin Towns are also home to the

Premier Division League of Ireland team, Finn Harps, and the county gaelic pitch. Rally car events take place annually and walkers can enjoy trails in the Drumboe Woods and around Trusk Lough.

Ballybofey has a theatre and here you'll also find Donegal's largest department store, along with a wide variety of other shops. At Fintown, Donegal's only operational narrow gauge railway runs alongside the crystal waters of Loch Finn where the scenery was described by the actress Meryl Streep as "the most beautiful view she had seen". Near Raphoe stands the fascinating **Beltony Stone Circle**, the "Stonehenge of Donegal" which, in fact, has been dated as being 200 years older than Stonehenge. So it's clearly worth discovering "Donegal's best kept secret" for yourself. Agatha Christie did so in the early 1900s and became a regular visitor to the area.

LIFFORD   Map 5 ref J4
15 miles SE of Letterkenny on the N14

Lifford sits beside the River Finn which separates it from the much larger town of Strabane in Co. Tyrone. The Finn is valued as a good salmon river for spring fish and this tiny town with a population of around 1500 also boasts the only greyhound racing track in Co. Donegal. A more spiritual claim to fame is the fact that Cecil Frances Alexander, the writer of such enduring hymns as *All Things Bright and Beautiful* and *Once in Royal David's City*, was born here in 1818.

The main visitor attraction in Lifford is the **Old Courthouse Visitor Centre**, housed in the superbly restored Courthouse of 1746. With the aid of state-of-the-art audio-visual and talking heads techniques visitors can witness the re-enactment of famous trials in the courtroom and relive the harrowing experiences of prisoners in the cells below.

THE INISHOWEN PENINSULA

One tends to be somewhat sceptical about tourist board literature promoting its own particular area as "undiscovered country" but in the case of the Inishowen peninsula, a great hammerhead of land jutting out into the Atlantic to the northeast of Letterkenny, the claim is entirely credible. Despite being part of the Republic, ("Southern Ireland"), the northern tip of Inishowen, **Malin Head**, is also the most northerly point of all Ireland.

The peninsula has one of the most impressive prehistoric relics in the country, the **Grianan of Aileach**, about 14 miles northeast of Letterkenny. This massive circular stone fort stands on the top of Greenan Mountain (803ft) commanding grand views over Loughs Swilly and Foyle. The Grianan is marked on Ptolemy's 2nd century map of the world and was for several centuries the stronghold of the O'Neill kings. Built around 1700BC the fort has walls 17ft high and 13ft thick at the base, and near the entrance there are passages running inside the walls. The enclosure is 77ft across and three circular embankments form the outer defences. The inside of the walls is terraced which has led to speculation that it was designed for sun-worshipping rituals - *grianan* means a "sun palace". The fort's remarkable state of preservation is due to restoration in the 1870s. The

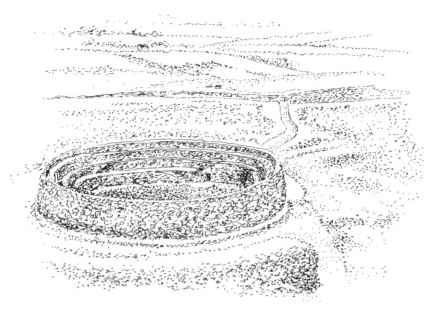

Grianan of Aileach Stone Fort, Co. Donegal

best way to explore this unique part of the country is to follow the 100-mile circular tour that starts at Buncrana in the southwestern corner of the peninsula.

BUNCRANA
Map 5 ref J2

12 miles NW of Londonderry on the R238

The largest town in Inishowen, Buncrana is a favoured resort of holidaymakers from Londonderry and is well-supplied with amusement arcades, shops, bars and a **Vintage Car Museum**. The town is sheltered on three sides by hills and to the south there's a three-mile-long beach. The 15th century **O'Doherty's Keep** stands by Castle Bridge and on the other side of the river are the remains of **Buncrana Castle**, a once handsome building from the early 1600s. Around the town are a number of megalithic monuments, most notably a Bronze Age burial cairn at **Crockcashel**, a mile to the north.

BALLYLIFFIN
Map 5 ref J2

23 miles N of Londonderry on the R238

A busy little resort, Ballyliffin's major out of season attraction is its **Folksong & Ballad Festival** held on the last weekend in March. Just to the north of the town, **Carrickabraghy Castle** is a weather-beaten 16th century fortress of the O'Dohertys overlooking beautiful **Pollan Strand** where huge Atlantic breakers roll in making it dangerous to swim here.

Located on the outskirts of Ballyliffin, **Ard Donn House** is surrounded by lovely scenery and enjoys superb views across Pollan Bay to Malin Head. This is ideal country for walkers and hikers and Ard Donn, offering quality bed and breakfast accommodation, makes an ideal base. The home of Robert and Gráinne Walsh, this large modern villa with

Ard Donn House, Ballyliffin, Inishowen, Co. Donegal
Tel: 077 76156

an attractive conservatory has 6 guest rooms, all en suite and all furnished with style and taste. Breakfast is always rather special at Ard Donn since it includes free range eggs and home made bread. The Walshs will also happily supply a packed lunch. For the evening, there are many fine eating places in the area.

Golfers will be pleased to find that Ballyliffin's two magnificent 18-hole links courses are both less than a mile away and facilities for horse riding, pony trekking, boating and cycle hire are all within easy reach. Walkers will be keen to explore the unspoilt expanses of the Inishowen Peninsula and its wealth of Christian and prehistoric monuments, amongst them the 3000-year-old Bocan Stone Circle near Carndonagh. Another popular attraction in the area is Doagh Farm and Heritage Centre on Doagh Island. Here a mid-19th century Inishowen village has been re-created, providing visitors with a fascinating insight into the hardships experienced by local people during the period of the potato famine. The horrifying story is vividly presented in a series of traditional dwellings although a lighter note is struck in the Fairy House, home to Fergus McArt, one of Inishowen's best-known fairies "who is known to pop up from time to time!" Children will also love the play area, beach, farm zoo and boating pool while parents can indulge themselves in the thatched Tea Room or browse around the Craft Shop. (Doagh Island, incidentally, is not an island any more; the channel which once divided it from the mainland has silted up over the centuries).

CARNDONAGH
MAP 5 REF J2

21 miles N of Londonderry on the R238/R240

This thriving little town stands at Inishowen's main crossroads and is the home of one of the most far-famed Christian relics in Ireland, the **Donagh Cross**. Also known as St Patrick's Cross, it's said to be the oldest standing cross in the country, dating from around 650AD. Richly decorated and well-preserved, the cross stands in the Church of Ireland graveyard where the other interesting monuments include the **Marigold Stone**, so called because of the colouring of the stone.

From Carndonagh, the road runs northwards to the pretty village of **Malin** (another winner of the Tidy Towns competition) and on to **Malin Head**, the most northerly point in Ireland. The views are marvellous, the bird life includes choughs and corncrakes, and there are some good coastal walks here, one of which leads to **Hells Hole**, a 250ft-deep chasm in the cliffs where the inrushing sea pounds and roars. Another leads to the **Wee House of Malin**, a hermit's cliff-side cell once the austere dwelling place of St Muirdealach.

LECKEMY (LECAMY)
MAP 6 REF K2

18 miles NE of Londonderry on the R238

Leckemy village enjoys a peaceful riverside setting a couple of miles from the east coast of Inishowen and provides a good base from which to tour the peninsula.

Staying for bed and breakfast in an old farmhouse is always something rather special and **Trean House** is no exception to the rule. This late-Victorian traditional Irish country house is the home of Joyce Norris and her family who possess a wonderful knack for making their guests feel really welcome. There are 4 comfortable and inviting guest rooms,

Trean House, Tremone, Leckemy, Inishowen, Co. Donegal
Tel: 077 67121   Fax: 077 67227   e-mail: treanhouse@oceanfree.net

2 of them en suite. At breakfast time there's a choice between a hearty full Irish breakfast or a lighter continental version after which you can begin exploring the Inishowen peninsula where, as the local tourist board points out, "less means more". *Less* traffic, so as you drive along the country lanes the only road hogs you are likely to encounter are sheep crossing the road at a leisurely pace. *Fewer* people, so you can enjoy the breathtaking scenery, "pretty much as nature intended, and with plenty of room for you to enjoy it". *Less* noise, but entrancing traditional Irish music and song playing until the small hours in many of the lively pubs. "Fewer inhibitions, more spontaneity. *Less* of the ordinary, *more* of the unexpected".

If you make your way to windswept Malin Head you will have reached the most northerly point in Ireland, but wherever you travel in the Inishowen peninsula you will actually find yourself in the heartland of this enchanting country. To quote once more from Inishowen's colourful brochure: "When you're on holiday, it can be an effort trying to fit in with the locals. Not in Inishowen, where we're happy to take you as we find you and our biggest worry is whether you're having a good enough time". Something you won't have to worry about if you decide to book in at Trean House. To find Trean House, from Moville follow the R238 towards Gleneely. After about 3 miles, turn right at the crossroads, following signs for Carrowmena village for about 2½ miles. Then follow sign for Tremone Bay. Trean House is the first building on the left.

COUNTY SLIGO

Just as the spirit of Robbie Burns seems omnipresent in southwest Scotland, so it is with the poet W.B. Yeats in Co. Sligo. He spent his childhood here, the landscapes and ancient myths of Sligo infuse his best poetry and he is buried at Drumcliffe beneath the huge bulk of Benbulben mountain. One of his best-known poems immortalises the lovely lake isle of Innisfree where *"peace comes dropping slow, / Dropping slow from the veil of the morning to where the cricket sings"*.

Co. Sligo is indeed a peaceful place. It came late to the idea of tourism despite possessing magnificent scenery that rivals Killarney and Donegal, a wealth of medieval remains and the largest concentration of megalithic monuments in Ireland. Because visitors are comparatively few the welcome seems even warmer and more heartfelt than in the more-frequented areas.

SLIGO
40 miles S of Donegal on the N15

MAP 4 REF G6

Attractively set around the Garavogue River as it flows into Sligo Bay, the county town is the most important in northwest Ireland despite having a population of less than 18,000. The town is well-supplied with traditional inns, music pubs and shops, and its racecourse, on the edge of town, is reckoned to be Ireland's most scenic. A popular excursion from the town is a boat trip along **Lough Gill** visiting various places en route that have featured in Yeats' poetry, most notably the Isle of Innisfree. The poems are recited at the appropriate sites and the 2½ excursion includes a 30-minute stop on the island where there's a craft shop and tea room. There's also a 24-mile drive around the lake which provides some superb views.

In the town itself, there are two cathedrals: the Anglican St John's which dates back to the 14th century and was remodelled in 1730 by Richard Castle, and the Catholic cathedral, a Romanesque-style building completed in 1874. **Sligo Abbey** is much older and has endured a more unfortunate history than most such ecclesiastical buildings. Founded in 1252 by Maurice Fitzgerald, Earl of Kildare, the Abbey was destroyed by fire in 1441. It was painstakingly rebuilt but exactly 200 years later was badly damaged during the sack of Sligo in the rebellion of 1641. The nave, choir and central transept have survived as have some striking 15th century carvings. The grassed inner area, surrounded by atmospheric arched cloisters, is a peaceful place for meditation or even a picnic.

Sligo Town has many connections with Ireland's greatest poet, an association most dramatically symbolised by the eye-catching modern **Statue of W.B. Yeats** in the town centre which shows him in a serpentine pose with his jacket splayed out like a cobra's hood. He is also celebrated in the Yeats Memorial Building, across the river from the Abbey, which house both the **Sligo County Museum** and the **Yeats Memorial Museum**. They are both small but crammed with interesting items. The County Museum has some fascinating photographs of old Sligo, a display of appealing 19th century sketches and a remarkable 800-year-old firkin of bog butter. The Yeats Museum has lots of photographs of, and letters by, the poet and the Nobel Prize medal awarded him in 1923 is also on show. A more academic approach to Yeats is pursued at the headquarters of the Yeats Society, just down the road at Douglas Hyde Bridge, which is the venue for the annual Yeats International Summer School.

W. B. Yeats, Sligo

There's more Yeats material on view at the **Model Arts Centre** but here it is the work of Jack Yeats, the poet's brother and the best known Irish painter of the 20th century. His paintings and drawings drew heavily on scenes from Celtic myth and everyday Irish life and the ones on display here have a potent local flavour. Other artists featured include Paul Henry and George Russell, better known as AE. The Centre also hosts three festivals each year: the **Scíobh literary festival** in September, an **Early Music Festival** in October and a **contemporary music festival** in November.

As the major centre for the northwest, Sligo Town offers a wide choice of places to stay. Highly recommended is the **Hotel Silver Swan**, a family-owned hotel which occupies a splendid position on the banks of the soft-flowing Garavogue river in the heart of Sligo town. There are soothing views of the river from the hotel's Cygnet restaurant, a stylish dining room where the menu combines fine European cooking prepared from the best of local produce. On offer are traditional European dishes, including a wide range of sea-foods, with shellfish as the speciality of the house. The hotel takes pride in the quality and presentation of the food served here and your dining pleasure is enhanced by the courteous and efficient service of the restaurant staff. For dining events on a grand scale, the Silver Swan has two function rooms, the Garavogue and the Maple, both of which have private bars and can cater for parties of up to 100 people.

Hotel Silver Swan, Hyde Bridge, Sligo, Co. Sligo
Tel: 071 43231/2/3   Fax: 071 42232

The hotel's traditional Horse-Shoe Bar is noted for its friendly atmosphere and its frequent sessions of live entertainment by local musicians, with the Sunday morning jazz sessions proving especially popular. Every year, the hotel is host to the "Fiddler of Dooney" competition when some of Ireland's most talented musicians compete for this coveted title which is derived from W.B.Yeats' poem of the same name.

The Silver Swan's 35 luxury bedrooms maintain the high standards apparent throughout the hotel. They are all en suite and equipped with direct dial telephone, hospitality tray, garment press, hair dryer, radio, and television complete with video channel. Most bedrooms also pamper their occupants with a therapeutic "aero-spa" bath.

Whether you are looking for a gentle, relaxing holiday or interested in more active pursuits, Sligo has plenty to satisfy your particular preferences. A gentle stroll through this town soaked in history, or a leisurely drive to destinations such as the famous Benbulben mountain, the majestic waterfalls at Glencar; a vigorous game of tennis or a round of golf in breathtaking scenery: Sligo and the surrounding area has it all.

A comfortable 5 minute walk from Sligo town centre will bring you to **Dawnhurst**, a large detached house set in its own grounds. Built in 1934 for a wealthy merchant, Dawnhurst is now the family home of Marie Scanlon who has been welcoming bed and breakfast guests here for some 20 years. Many visitors return again and again, a tribute to Marie's genuine hospitality and to the quality accommodation on offer. Dawnhurst has

Dawnhurst, Pearce Road, Sligo. Co. Sligo
Tel: 071 60595

4 guest rooms, all of them en suite, non-smoking, and well-equipped with such features as television and tea/coffee-making facilities. Children are welcome, with a cot available if required and baby-sitting can also be arranged. Dawnhurst is open all year round except over Christmas and devotees of the Turf will be pleased to know that the house stands right beside the Sligo race course. Amenities for golf, fishing and horse riding are all available within a couple of miles of the house.

Located in a quiet cul de sac less than half a mile from the city centre, **Rosscahill** is the home of Elma O'Halloran, a charming lady who always provides her bed and breakfast visitors with a genuinely warm Irish welcome. Her smart modern house has 3 guest bedrooms, all en suite, comfortable and well-equipped and, like the rest of the house, non-smoking. The inviting residents' lounge is well-stocked with books of every kind, and outside there's a lovely, beautifully-maintained garden, as well as ample parking space. At breakfast time, Elma offers an extensive choice of menu. Open from 1st April to 1st November, Rosscahill offers all the comforts of home in a peaceful location close to Sligo's shops and other attractions. Within a 3-mile radius, you'll also find facilities for

Rosscahill, Marymount, Pearse Road, Sligo, Co. Sligo
Tel: 071 61744

golf, fishing and horse riding, and a short drive will take you to the enchanting Lake Country to the east, or to the wooded hills of the Ox Mountains to the west.

About 4 miles northeast of Sligo, **Glen View** offers select farmhouse accommodation in a modern house which was built with bed and breakfast guests in mind. As the name suggests, Glen View enjoys some splendid vistas which are especially enchanting when viewed from the well-tended gardens. Your host, Mary Coggins, provides excellent home cooking with a choice of dishes such as smoked salmon and scrambled egg at breakfast time, accompanied by home-made bread. Evening meals are also available on request.

Glen View, Drum East, Enniskillen Road, Sligo, Co. Sligo
Tel/Fax: 071 43770

Guests have the use of a large and comfortable residents' lounge which is made very inviting by an open peat fire. The 4 en suite guest rooms at Glen View are also very spacious, fully equipped, and look out onto those marvellous views. Children are welcome and a baby-sitting service is available if required. The house is conveniently placed for mountain walks, and there are beaches, pitch 'n' putt, golf and fishing all within easy reach.

Immediately north of Sligo town is Rosses Point and out in the bay beyond the point is **Coney Island**, so named because of its multitudinous rabbits. It was the inspiration for naming the pleasure park near New York which was also infested with rabbits. Out in the channel is the **Metal Man** which marks the deep water channel into Sligo harbour. It was placed there in 1822 and described by Yeats as "the only Rosses Point man who never told a lie".

ROSSES POINT   Map 4 ref G6
3 miles N of Sligo off the N15

Located near Rosses Point, a truly beautiful seaside village resort boasting magnificent beaches, an 18-hole championship golf course, and great restaurants, Elizabeth and Brendan Kelly's have most aptly named their home, **"Serenity"**. It is in a most spectacular scenic setting overlooking Drumcliffe Bay which mirrors the magic of the magnificent Benbulben Mountain and the varied spectacular sunsets - scenes indeed from Paradise. In the foreground stands Drumcliffe Church where the great poet W.B.Yeats has found his resting place.

"Serenity" itself is most tastefully decorated and well maintained, with 4 guest bedrooms, 3 of which are en suite, and all furnished and decorated to a very high standard. The splendid gardens, surrounded by natural stone walls obviously built by a craftsman, provide a fitting setting for this quite outstanding and very friendly guest house which has recently won an A.I.B./Regional Tourist Board award for the high quality of its

"Serenity", Doonierin, Nr Rosses Point, Kintogher, Co. Sligo
Tel: 071 43351

accommodation, hospitality and good food. Rarely will you find such a wide choice of breakfast menu. If you want to explore this area and discover the abundance of places of exquisite beauty and exceptional interest, the Kellys will provide you with a detailed tour guide of the area which will make your stay in Yeats' Country a most memorable one, with fond memories to cherish for many years to come.

DRUMCLIFF
Map 4 ref G5

4 miles N of Sligo on the N15

Drumcliff, at the northern end of Rosses Point, is dominated by the mighty ramparts of **Benbulben**, 1730ft high. A monastery was founded here by St Columba in the 6th century and two probable relics from it are the stump of a round tower and a 10th century cross. Thirteen feet high, the cross is carved with scenes depicting both Old and New Testament scenes, the only one so decorated in the country.

But the majority of visitors come to visit the small churchyard where a simple stone slab marks the **Grave of W.B. Yeats**. It is inscribed with the epitaph he wrote himself:

> *Cast a cold Eye*
> *On Life, on Death.*
> *Horseman, pass by.*

CARNEY
Map 4 ref G5

6 miles N of Sligo on minor road off the N15

Close to the villages of Drumcliffe and Carney is **Lissadell House**, another location closely associated with Yeats who often visited the Gore-Booth family here. The Gore-Booths still live in this fine but austere mansion in the Greek Revival style. The square 2-storeyed mansion is full of many artefacts gathered by successive generations of the Gore-Booth family displayed in a rather melancholy atmosphere of faded grandeur. Two daughters of the Gore-Booth family were involved in the 1916 rising, one of them, Constance Markiewicz, being condemned to death. Somewhat to her annoyance she was pardoned and went on to become the first British female MP and later Minister of Labour in the Dáil's first cabinet. A famous poem by Yeats recalls the two girls at Lissadell:

> *Light of evening Lissadell*
> *Great windows, open to the south,*
> *Two girls in silk kimonos, both*
> *Beautiful, one a gazelle.*

As its name suggests, **Mountain View** enjoys some grand views of this scenic corner of County Sligo. The mountains in question are those dominated by Benbulben, a dramatic, mist-shrouded mass which was one of W.B. Yeats' favourite locations. Mountain View is the family home of Martina and Brian Murphy who welcomes guests in search of quality bed and breakfast accommodation in this favoured area. Built in 1975 and recently extended, the house is surrounded by superb gardens and enjoys a peaceful position well back from the village road. The house has been fully refurbished and deco-

Mountain View, Carney, Drumcliff, Co. Sligo
Tel: 071 63290

rated to an exceptionally high standard and guests will find a spacious residents' lounge and an attractive dining room. The 5 guest bedrooms are all en suite, comfortable and inviting. Around Carney the countryside is a hikers and bikers' dream with a criss-crossing network of lanes and paths, amongst them a pathway from Mountain View leading to the seashore.

BALLINFULL   MAP 4 REF G5
11 miles NW of Sligo on Drumcliff-Raghly road off the N15

Enjoying a quiet location in beautiful rural surroundings on the north coast of Sligo Bay, **Ardtarmon House** offers visitors a choice of either bed and breakfast or self-catering accommodation. The striking old house, built in the early 1800s, has been the family residence of the Henry family since 1851 and is now the home of Charles and Christa Henry. Set amidst mature gardens, Ardtarmon House offers tranquil, spacious and comfortable accommodation with a 19th century ambience, much original furniture and with four large en suite bedrooms. Evening meals are available on request, an option that is strongly recommended since the dishes are based on home-grown and local produce and prepared by traditional cooking methods.

If you prefer self-catering, there's an interesting choice of 5 varied properties, amongst them a gate lodge, a charming thatched cottage and converted farm buildings. They range in size from one to three bedrooms and are all pleasantly and comfortably furnished, three of them having open fires. Laundry facilities and a pay phone are available.

Amongst other amenities, guests at Ardtarmon House will find a hard tennis court, a games room in a converted stable, an extensive garden and grounds with panoramic

Ardtarmon House, Ballinfull, Co. Sligo
Tel: 071 63156

views of sea and mountains. A 500 yard path through the fields leads to the sea and a beach which is safe for swimming.

The local area, and County Sligo in general, are among the most interesting, varied and scenic locations in the west of Ireland. In the immediate area of the peninsula, there are many opportunities for walking, cycling, boating, (Raghly harbour is just 2 miles away), fishing and bird-watching. Rosses Point (13 miles) has a championship 18-hole golf course and anyone with an interest in Sligo's past will want to visit Lissadell House, the childhood home of Countess Markiewicz, (3 miles), while at Drumcliff there is the grave of W.B.Yeats, a 10th century high cross and an historic round tower.

RAGHLY   MAP 4 REF G5
12 miles NW of Sligo off the N15 at Drumcliffe

From the little harbour at Raghly there are superb views across Sligo Bay to the Ox Mountains. Nearby is a fine sandy beach and if you stroll along it you will find a short path leading to **Seaview Farmhouse** where Mary Herity welcomes guests in search of quality bed and breakfast accommodation. The farmhouse is a smart modern bungalow surrounded by extensive gardens and with a driveway wandering through the 100 acre dairy farm run by her husband, Colm. From the house there are grand views of Drumcliff Bay and the lighthouse on Coney Island. (It was a local man, incidentally, who gave the same name to the famous amusement park on Long Island, New York). Seaview was purpose built as a bed and breakfast establishment so everything is up to date, with 2 of the 4 guest bedrooms en suite and all of them pleasantly furnished, comfortable and relaxing. At breakfast time, there's a choice of a full Irish or continental breakfast and

Seaview Farmhouse, Raghly, Ballinfull, Co. Sligo
Tel: 071 63640

Mary will happily provide an evening meal on request. In addition to the glorious coastline, there are two other well-known attractions close by. Ellen's Pub, about a mile away, is a delightful thatched pub dating back to 1598 where, during summer weekends, musicians gather to make music in traditional Irish style with the time-honoured instruments of fiddles, accordions and banjos. Only a little further away is Lissadell House, famous for its connections with the poet W.B.Yeats who often stayed there during the early 1900s.

SOUTH AND WEST OF SLIGO

Only a couple of miles south of Sligo stands one of the most important prehistoric sites in Europe, the **Carrowmore Megalithic Cemetery**. Scattered across the green fields at the foot of **Knocknarea Mountain** are more than 60 dolmens, standing stones and stone circles. The oldest of them were erected around 4000BC, several hundred years before Stonehenge was built. It's believed that more than half the stones have been removed but Carrowmore is still the second-largest megalithic site in Europe after Carnac in Brittany. Incredibly, a plan was mooted in 1983 to turn the site into a rubbish tip. A restored cottage nearby houses an interesting exhibition relating to the site.

KNOCKNAREA   MAP 4 REF G6
3 miles SW of Sligo off the R292

Built in 1723, **Primrose Grange House** stands about 350 feet up the south slope of Knocknarea, the 1083 feet high mountain from which 5 counties can be seen. For many years, up until 1903, the house operated as Sligo Grammar School but it is now the home of Maisie Carter, a school teacher herself, who welcomes bed and breakfast guests to her spacious house. There are 7 guest bedrooms, including 2 en suite, 3 bathrooms, a large dining room and an equally large sitting room with a log fire. The surrounding farm

Primrose Grange House, Knocknarea, Co. Sligo
Tel: 071 62005

comprises 55 acres on which mixed farming is carried out. The Carters run their farm guest house as a family, with some school girl help during the peak period. The very best of home cooking is the standard fare. Maisie provides her guests with bed and breakfast, and light evening meals with prior notice, packed lunches are also available on request. The house's location is ideal as a base for touring County Sligo and south Donegal and stands just 2 miles from Sligo Riding Centre. Only a mile away is The Glen, a geologist's and botanist's Paradise, and another mile or so brings you to the coastal area, source of inspiration for much of W.B. Yeats' work, where there are many sandy beaches, free from tourist gimmicks.

The walk to the summit of **Knocknarea Mountain** follows a track of strangely moulded limestone with wild flowers growing on either side. At the top rises a huge cairn of weather-beaten stone, 33ft high and 19ft wide, which is reputed to be the burial place of Maeve, Queen of Connaught. She is believed to have lived around the time of Christ but the cairn is considerably older than that, probably dating from the Bronze Age.

STRANDHILL
MAP 4 REF G6
4 miles W of Sligo on the R292

Knocknarea Mountain provides a wonderful backdrop for the popular sea resort of Strandhill where the firm sandy beach stretches for miles and the huge Atlantic breakers attract many bodysurfers here. There are huge sand dunes to the southwest and any pebbles you find on the beach may well contain fossil remains. To the east is Sligo's little airport where you can watch small Aer Lingus planes skimming the top of Knocknarea before landing. At the end of the airstrip is the 10th century **Killaspugbone Church**, reached by way of the beach. It's said that St Patrick tripped on the threshold here and lost a tooth. The tooth was preserved and later enclosed in an exquisite casket, the Fiacal Pádraig, which is now in the National Museum in Dublin although the tooth itself has disappeared.

Knocknarea House B&B is ideally situated in Strandhill with beaches, mountains and megalithic tombs all within easy reach. Being family run, visitors are assured of a warm and friendly welcome from Carmel Connolly and her husband to their substantial detached house, prettily decorated with hanging baskets throughout the season. Knocknarea House has 5 non-smoking guest rooms, 4 of them en suite, with multi-

Knocknarea House B&B, Shore Road, Strandhill, Co. Sligo
Tel: 071 68313   e-mail: connollyma@eircom.ie
website: http://www.dirl.com/sligo/budget-accommodation.htm

channel TV and tea/coffee-making facilities in all rooms. Guests have the use of a private dining room and residents' lounge, and there is ample off-street, secure parking. Local amenities and attractions include golf, fishing, hill and coastal walks, cycling, surfing, watersports, beaches, horse riding and, of course, lively traditional pubs. The house is also convenient for shops and for Sligo Airport. Incidentally, if you are travelling on a tight budget, the Connollys also offer budget accommodation in another house adjacent which has 20+ beds in single, double, family or group rooms. It also provides self-catering.

Nestling at the foot of Knocknarea Mountain and overlooking the Atlantic Ocean, **Ocean View Hotel** is a long-established family hotel offering a unique blend of modern comfort and old-fashioned charm. Here you will find a warm greeting from the proprietors, Shay and Jean Burke, who have been welcoming visitors for some 18 years. Their hotel is exceptionally well-appointed having been recently refurbished to a very high standard, and although Ocean View is comparatively small, (there are just 12 guest bedrooms), it has all the ambience and amenities of a much larger hotel. Amenities like the Rollers Restaurant, renowned for its speciality of locally-caught oak-smoked salmon and

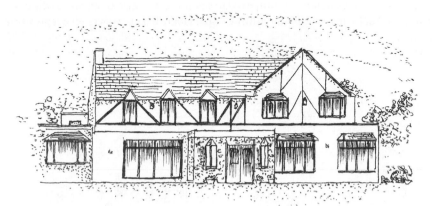

Ocean View Hotel, Strandhill, Co. Sligo
Tel: 071 68115   Fax: 071 68009

for other dishes based on fresh local produce. The hotel also boasts lovely views across the bay where the huge Atlantic rollers from which the restaurant takes its name come crashing in to the shore. This beach is a great favourite with surfers and during the first weekend of August is the setting for the Sligo Open Surfing Championship. For quieter bathing, there's another sandy beach just around the headland at Cullenamore. With Ocean View as your base, most of Sligo's historic sites and popular visitor attractions are within easy reach. At Carrowmore, you can visit the oldest, and one of the largest, megalithic tombs in Europe; then climb 1000 feet to the summit of Knocknarea Mountain to marvel at the colossal 33 feet high cairn containing 40,000 tons of rock which is said to be the tomb of Maeve, Queen of Connacht. If your passion is golf, there are courses at Strandhill itself and at Rosses Point. Or you can rent a pony and go trekking through resplendent scenery, discovering for yourself a region which the poet W.B. Yeats called "the land of heart's desire".

COLLOONEY   Map 4 ref G6
6 miles S of Sligo on the N4

Close to the small town of Collooney, the Owenmore and Unshin rivers combine to force their way through the Collooney Gap between the Ox Mountains and Slieve Daeane. It was near here, during the rebellion of 1798, that a single strategically placed English gun held at bay a combined Franco-Irish force until one of the French officers, the Irish-born Bartholomew Teeling, charged up the hill and shot the gunner dead. The Teeling Monument just north of Collooney commemorates this reckless act of bravery. Teeling was later captured by the English and hanged in Dublin.

Overlooking the River Unshin and approached by a mile-long driveway, **Markree Castle** is a stunning sight with its turrets and battlemented towers, 2-storey oriel windows and arched gatehouse of stone weathered to the colour of pale honey - a complex of glorious buildings surrounded by lush parkland and woods. The oldest parts of the castle date back to 1640 when it was built by the Cooper family who later extended it greatly in

Markree Castle, Collooney, Co. Sligo
Tel: 071 67800 Fax: 071 67840

Victorian times. A magnificent stained-glass window at the top of an impressive oak staircase inside the castle traces the Cooper family tree from the days of King John to the present owner, Charles Cooper - the tenth generation of the family to live here. The oldest inhabited castle in Sligo, Markree is now a superb hotel offering comprehensive amenities and with 30 en suite guest rooms whose furnishings and decoration are in keeping with the grand surroundings. One of the castle's opulent Victorian state rooms, (complete with gilded mirrors and chandelier), is now the Knockmuldowney Restaurant where the cuisine on offer is as sumptuous as the surroundings.

TUBBERCURRY (TOBERCURRY)

MAP 4 REF G7

18 miles SW of Sligo

This orderly market town nestling at the foot of the **Ox Mountains** is well known for its fishing, its music pubs and for hosting the **Western Drama Festival** in March each year. The festival has acquired an excellent reputation for the range and quality of the productions and the local drama group keeps up the good work with its own performances in the spring and autumn.

To savour the authentic atmosphere of the "Real Ireland" a stay at **Cawley's** in Tubbercurry is highly recommended. Visitors will find everything they need here - spacious guest rooms, (most of them en suite), a lively fully-licensed bar, an inviting lounge, and a restaurant famous in the area for its T-bone steaks and its locally-caught fresh fish. The owner, Jean Cawley, is a warm and welcoming lady with a passion for flowers - the

Cawley's, Emmett Street, Tubbercurry, Co. Sligo
Tel: 071 85025 / 85669

handsome 3-storey building is bedecked inside and out with colourful arrangements in tubs, vases and hanging baskets. Cawley's is a popular venue for parties, weddings, dinner dances and other functions, and it provides an excellent base from which to sample the area's diverse range of attractions, activities and places to visit. Tubbercurry's living heritage of traditional music is evident everywhere, with two musical festivals held here every year and a Fair Day during the second week of July when the streets and pubs are filled with music, song and dance.

TEMPLEBOY
Map 4 ref F6
16 miles W of Sligo on the N59

Templeboy enjoys a splendid setting with the Ox Mountains to the south and Sligo Bay to the north and is conveniently placed to explore the grand scenery of west Sligo. Just up the road from Templeboy is **Culkins Emigration Museum** which relives a poignant era when for most people emigration was the only hope of a better life. The museum is housed in what was once the Shipping and Emigration Agency run by the local draper, Daniel Culkin, to assist local people find a passage to the Americas. Founded in the mid-19th century, the Agency continued to operate right up until the 1930s. The purpose-built modern museum has some interesting artefacts and features, including the original shop itself.

Renovated in 1998 as an up-market self-catering accommodation, **Greenfort Cottage** is an attractive bungalow in traditional Irish style, set in extensive gardens and with all the up-to-date amenities. The decor and furnishings are all in pristine condition, with no expense spared to equip the house with every possible extra. The cottage sits close to the sea and even has its own private walkway to the main beach area. It is set amidst spectacular coastal and mountain scenery. Greenfort Cottage can accommodate 8/9

Greenfort Cottage, Rathglass, Templeboy, Co. Sligo
Tel: 096 47108

visitors and is ideal for small groups such as fishermen, surfers or golf enthusiasts, or indeed anyone who would like to explore this charming corner of the country. The garden is there to be enjoyed, equipped with garden furniture as well as a barbecue area for those (hopefully) balmy summer evenings when you can watch the sun set over the Atlantic. The cottage takes its name from the historic Fairy Fort close by which, according to folk lore, is guarded by the fairies.

ENNISCRONE
32 miles W of Sligo on the R297

Map 3 ref F6

This pleasant resort with a sweeping 3-mile-long beach lies close to the Co. Mayo border overlooking Killala Bay and the splendid north Mayo coastline. The town became celebrated for its invigorating hot seaweed baths which can still be experienced at the splendidly Edwardian establishment of **Kilcullen's Bath House**. Patrons immerse themselves in a huge porcelain bath under a blanket of slithery seaweed fronds then rinse off the iodine-rich chocolate-coloured brew with a cold shower. A cup of strong tea in the pleasant tea-room rounds off the experience.

Located about a mile outside the town, **Tara** is a modern bungalow, purpose built in 1976 with bed and breakfast accommodation in mind. It stands in a spacious landscaped garden overlooking a championship golf course and Killala Bay. The peaceful atmosphere of this home is enhanced by a fine reputation for hospitality and excellent cuisine. Tara's owner, Catherine O'Hara has furnished the house with a pleasing mix of antique

Tara, Ballina Road, Enniscrone, Co. Sligo
Tel: 096 36398

and modern. There are 5 guest rooms, 3 of them en suite, and a welcome feature of Tara is an extensive breakfast menu with special emphasis on home cooking. On request, Catherine is happy to provide an evening meal.

Enniscrone is famous for its wonderful beach and hot seaweed baths. A recent addition to the attractions of this popular seaside resort is Waterpoint, an all-weather water leisure complex, ideal for both adults and children. The amenities include a heated swimming pool, a 65 metre water slide, Kiddies' Fun Pool, fitness gym, and an Adult Health Suite with steam room, jacuzzi and sauna.

COUNTY LEITRIM

Even more so than the neighbouring county of Sligo, Leitrim has yet to enter the tourist consciousness. With a total population of less than 26,000 the county is wonderfully uncrowded and unspoilt, sprinkled with lakes offering prime fishing and with rugged mountains sprawling across the northern half. Only the county town, Carrick-on-Shannon has a well-established visitor attraction with its cruises along the River Shannon which, including canal links, is navigable for 240 miles, the longest waterway in Europe. Apart from Parke's Castle near the Sligo border and Lough Rynn House near Mohill the county has few buildings of historical importance - this is, after all, a county where the three main interests are fishing, fishing and fishing.

CARRICK-ON-SHANNON   MAP 4 REF H7
28 miles SE of Sligo on the N4

Incorporated as borough by James I in 1613, Carrick-on-Shannon is a peaceful riverside town set beside a broad stretch of the Shannon and with a population of around 6500. Fishing and river cruising are the major activities as evidenced by the number of fishing tackle shops and the busy marina with its huge fleet of cruisers and pleasure craft.

The town has something of an ecclesiastical oddity in the **Costello Chapel** on Main Street which is reputed to be the second smallest chapel in the world. It was built in 1877 as a mausoleum for Edward Costello and his wife who lie in coffins sunk in the floor either side of the entrance, the lead coffins clearly visible beneath a glass covering.

If you are planning to stay in this pleasant little town, a good place for both food and accommodation is **Aisleigh Guest House**, a smart modern house about a mile from the centre. On arrival, you will receive a warm Irish welcome from Sean and Sharlotte Fearon

Aisleigh Guest House, Dublin Road, Carrick-on-Shannon, Co. Leitrim
Tel: 078 20313

who have owned and run the guest house for some 20 years. Their house is furnished and decorated with a happy blend of modern features and interesting antiques and the 10 guest bedrooms, all en suite, are warm, comfortable and spacious. A popular amenity at Aisleigh is its modern sauna where guests can broil themselves before wandering downstairs to the residents' lounge for a glass of wine from the Fearons' extensive cellar. Evening meals are available on request and the table d'hôte menu will almost certainly include a fresh salmon or freshwater trout dish. And after dinner you might care for a frame or two of pool or snooker in the games room.

MOHILL
9 miles E of Carrick-on-Shannon on the R201/R202 Map 4 ref I7

This busy little fishing centre was the birthplace of the famous blind harpist and composer Turlough O'Carolan (1670-1738). He travelled around the houses of the great chieftains where he entertained his noble hosts with his exquisite playing. He was also an heroic drinker and it's said that on his deathbed he asked for whiskey but finding himself unable to drink it, touched the cup with his lips saying that two old friends should not part without a kiss. A statue on the main street commemorates the last of the court bards.

To the south of Mohill stands one of Leitrim's very few stately homes, **Lough Rynn House**, formerly the hereditary seat of the Clements family, Earls of Leitrim. The older part of the house was built in 1833, an exact copy of a house in Ingestry, Staffordshire, and was greatly extended in the flamboyant Scottish Baronial style in 1878. The interior is richly furnished and decorated in the opulent manner of the period. At that time the house was the centre of a huge 90,000 acre estate and within the grounds there are farm buildings from the 1840s, a picturesque estate office, a charming summerhouse, a dolmen, an arboretum and the ruins of a 17th century castle.

FENAGH
11 miles NE of Carrick-on-Shannon on the R202 Map 4 ref I7

Standing on the northern shore of Fenagh Lough, this little village has the ruins of two Gothic churches, one of them with an unusual east window. They are all that remains of a monastery founded here by St Columba which later became famous as a divinity school under the direction of St Killian. The impressive 17th century Mausoleum nearby was erected by Torna Duignan, a former Rector of Fenagh, for his family.

BALLINAMORE
15 miles NE of Carrick-on-Shannon on the R202/R109 Map 4 ref I7

Like most places of any size in Co. Leitrim, Ballinamore is primarily a centre for anglers. But this former coaching town, with its broad main street, does have a **heritage and folk museum**, housed in the former courthouse. Some of the museum exhibits are distinctly odd - amongst the items on show is the "authentic detachable shirt collar worn by executed 1916 patriot Seán MacDiarmada". The courthouse building also houses the Leitrim Genealogical Centre for those in search of their family roots.

About 3 miles south of Ballinamore, **Wood Island**, an ideally located bungalow, offers excellent self-catering accommodation in peaceful and scenic surroundings. This attractive bungalow is set in its own private grounds surrounded by St John's Lake shore. St John's is one of the many lakes to be found on the newly restored Shannon Erne Waterway and is an excellent lake for fishing. The bungalow can sleep 6 and is fully

For inquiries, contact E. Booth, Tully House, Ballinamore, Co. Leitrim
Tel: 078 44540

equipped with all you will need for your holiday. The owner is on hand if you require assistance of any kind and can guide you to the many attractions of County Leitrim and the surrounding areas. A few miles to the north are the mountains with their scenic views which are ideal for touring. So, whether you want a relaxing holiday, or enjoy a spot of hill walking, golfing, or horse riding, Wood Island provides an ideal base. And if you happen to be an angler, the whole area is a fisherman's paradise.

NORTH LEITRIM

MANORHAMILTON
28 miles N of Carrick-on-Shannon on the N16

MAP 4 REF H6

The only town of any size in north Leitrim, Manorhamilton stands at the meeting of four mountain valleys, surrounded by striking limestone hills. The scenery is magnificent - steep hillsides, narrow ravines and fertile valleys offer a splendid variety of vistas. Five roads branch off from Manorhamilton through the mountain valleys, each one of them providing a wonderfully scenic route. In the town itself, the main feature of interest is a ruined ivy-clad mansion built in 1638 by Sir Frederick Hamilton who founded the settlement here and gave it his name. About a mile to the south of the town, the well-preserved megalithic tomb at **Cashel Bir** is well worth a visit.

DROMAHAIR
Map 4 ref H6
8 miles SW of Manorhamilton on the R288

This attractive little village close to the shore of **Lough Gill** is notable for the ruins of **Creevelea Friary**, the last to be founded in Ireland (in 1508) before Henry VIII's suppression of the monasteries. The monks were Franciscans and some impressive sculptures have survived of St Francis including one of him preaching from a pulpit to a "congregation" of birds.

Beautifully set at the eastern end of Lough Gill, **Parke's Castle** stands just a few yards from the lakeside, an appealing 17th century building that stands on the foundations of a much older moated tower house, the stronghold of the Irish chieftain, Brian O'Rourke.

Parke's Castle, Co. Leitrim

O'Rourke came to an unfortunate end, executed at Tyburn for sheltering a survivor of the wrecked Spanish Armada. His estate was acquired by a certain Robert Parke who cannibalised the walls of O'Rourke's fortress for his own house. The Castle can be reached by boat from Sligo and boat trips around the lake and to the enchanting Isle of Innisfree are available from the castle jetty during the season.

COUNTY CAVAN

Blessed with some of Europe's most beautiful lake scenery, Co. Cavan has also benefitted from the restoration of the old Ballinamore-Ballyconnell canal which now links all four provinces of Ireland. The county has always been a watery place, until comparatively recently an impenetrable tract of lakeland and bog that frustrated potential invaders. But there's plenty of evidence of Neolithic peoples living here as long ago as 4000BC. Their court cairn tombs are still visible but many of their *crannógs*, (artificial islands of branches and brush), have settled into the landscape and are now indistinguishable as man made features. Apart from fishermen, for whom Cavan's lakes and rivers are an angler's dream, few tourists have yet discovered this wonderfully peaceful and unspoilt county.

CAVAN
68 miles NW of ublin on the N3

MAP 4 REF J7

The county town is a pleasant little place with a population of around 3500. It was at one time important as the stronghold of the O'Reillys who ruled the ancient kingdom of East Breffni. Their castle, **Clough Oughter**, stands on an island in Lough Oughter about 3 miles outside Cavan. It's a well-preserved example of a 13th century circular tower castle, rather surprisingly built on a crannóg. It looks very romantic when viewed from the lakeside but in the 1640s the castle served as a prison. Eoghan Roe O'Neill, the great leader of the rebels, was incarcerated and died here, poisoned it is said by his Cromwellian captors. The island can only be reached by hiring a boat.

Of Cavan's **Franciscan Friary**, founded in 1300, only the belfry tower still stands but the modern **Roman Catholic Cathedral**, consecrated in 1942, is well worth visiting for its fine sculptures. Other attractions in the town include **Cavan Crystal**, the second oldest lead crystal factory in Ireland, which offers guided tours during which visitors can observe glass blowing and crystal cutting in progress. A more recent visitor attraction is **Lifeforce Mill**, located in the heart of the town. Erected in 1846, the mill closed down in the 1950s but has now been fully restored and enjoys a new lease of life producing Lifeforce Stoneground Wholemeal Flour. On arrival, visitors are first invited to prepare a loaf of bread using the mill's own flour. This is popped into the oven and by the time the 35-minute tour is over the visitor's very own loaf is ready for collection. The mill also has a coffee shop housed in an old stone building which was transported some 50 miles here from the Boyne valley and re-erected stone by stone.

VIRGINIA
19 miles SE of Cavan on the N3

MAP 4 REF J8

Beautifully situated on the edge of Lough Ramor, Virginia was founded during the reign of James I and named after his aunt, the virgin queen Elizabeth I. It's an orderly little town with rustic cottages lining the main street and a trim avenue of clipped yew trees leading to the Protestant church. The celebrated playwright Richard Brinsley Sheridan lived here for several years and was often visited by his equally famous friend Jonathan Swift. A sandy stretch on the lakeshore provides good bathing and rowing boats can be hired for fishing on Lough Ramor - quantities of pike, perch, rudd and bream are just there for the taking.

Little more than half a mile from Virginia's town centre, **The White House** offers a warm welcome and excellent bed and breakfast accommodation. This spacious modern villa, (painted white, naturally), stands in beautifully maintained gardens in quiet and peaceful surroundings. A recent addition to the amenities is a charming conservatory

The White House, Old Castle Road, Virginia, Co. Cavan
Tel/Fax: 049 854 7515   e-mail: mchugo@csatclear.ie

overlooking the gardens. The White House is the home of Mrs Emily McHugo who, in addition to offering a good breakfast choice of menu, is also happy to provide evening meals if required. The house is non-smoking and the 4 en suite bedrooms are individually designed and furnished to the highest standard. All have TV and tea/coffee-making facilities. The White House is a perfect place to relax but if you prefer to be active there are facilities for forest walks, fishing, golfing and horse riding within easy reach and a choice of interesting places to visit. At **Ballyjamesduff**, the **Cavan County Museum** houses the famous "Pig House Collection" of more than 3,000 items reflecting rural life from the 1700s to the present day, as well as a 1000 year old Dug-Out boat, a collection of "Sheela-na-Gigs" (ancient stone carvings of female figures), and many other items connected with the county. Also about 5 miles away are Fore Abbey, which contains a variety of interesting buildings ranging from the 6th to the 15th centuries, and the village of Kells in Co. Meath, famous for the 9th century illuminated *Book of Kells*. Remains of the monastery where the book was produced can be seen, along with a round tower and several High Crosses. Another popular excursion is a visit to Lough Crew Cairns at Sliabh na Cailligh (The Witches Hill) where the hilltop passage tombs date back to around 3000BC.

Sheela-na-Gigs

DRUMYOUTH

Map 4 ref I7

10 miles SW of Cavan on minor road off the R198

A truly striking modern building, **The Arches** is a large farmhouse surrounded by a 150-acre farm and just 400 metres from Ardra Lake. The house has been purpose built for the comfort of anglers and tourists alike. Guests are greeted on arrival with a welcoming cup of tea and your host, Pearl Kells, makes sure that visitors are guaranteed a friendly atmosphere and delicious home cooking, with evening meals available on request. Centrally heated throughout, The Arches has 4 guest rooms, each with en suite facilities. All the rooms enjoy beautiful country views and all are furnished to an exceptionally high

The Arches, Drumyouth, Arva, Co. Cavan
Tel: 049 43 35460

standard. Guests have the use of a comfortable sitting room, with colour television, and a spacious dining room. Another amenity is a games room where guests can play pool and darts. Outside, there are beautiful gardens and a large parking area.

The Arches is situated in the heart of Ireland's Lakelands - a paradise for the coarse fisherman! The angler's every need is catered for, with a bait shed and fridge, storage facilities for fishing tackle, together with a drying room for clothing. In addition, guests have the use of a small fishing boat.

If you prefer self-catering, there's a charming 3-bedroomed modern cottage on its own private grounds. "The Cottage" is of excellent design and has an ITB 3*** rating. The large fitted kitchen is equipped with electric cooker, fridge/freezer, washing machine and tumble dryer. The living room has an open fire and colour TV and, like the 3 bedrooms, is attractively decorated and furnished. Children and pets are welcome. Like the main house, the cottage is just 400 metres from Ardra Lake, there are country lanes and paths through the tranquil Cavan countryside to explore, while the golfer is spoilt for choice with three 18-hole courses to choose from within a 20-minutes drive.

LOUGH GOWNA

Map 4 ref I8

12 miles SW of Cavan on minor road off the N55

Tucked away in the Cavan countryside, **Sunnyside House** is one of those Hidden Places you feel really pleased with yourself for finding. It's a large, handsome Georgian-style house built in 1899 for the local doctor who, to judge from its proportions, must have had either a very well-paying practice or a substantial private income. Sunnyside House is now the home of Bridget and Dieter Koston - welcoming hosts who make their guests' comfort and happiness their first priority. The countryside air ensures a good night's sleep

Sunnyside House, Lough Gowna, Co. Cavan
Tel: 043 83285

in the comfortable guest rooms, and breakfast is served to suit your schedule and tastes. Evening meals are also available with the tasty dishes based on the freshest and best ingredients - "lovingly prepared to be savoured at leisure!" Pets are welcome at Sunnyside House, but the Kostons do ask you to let them know about your particular friend so they can be sure that their own cat and dog will be happy to see them! This area is, of course, an angler's joy; golf, tennis, and horse-riding facilities are all within easy reach, or you could simply settle down and relax in the lovely gardens of Sunnyside House.

KILLESHANDRA

Map 4 ref I7

11 miles W of Cavan on the R199

Surrounded by a sparkling necklace of small lakes, Killeshandra is as unspoilt a place as you could hope to find in this most traditional of Irish counties. Whether you are looking for a lively traditional Irish pub, a comfortable B&B or independent self-catering accommodation, you'll find them all at or near **The Shamrock Inn**. The inn occupies a prime position in the town centre and is unusually spacious inside. There's a very large lounge, a public bar and a separate games' room. At the time of writing, extensive refurbishing is under way so you can be confident that everything will be spick and span when you arrive. And you can also be sure that on most evenings during the season local musicians will be sending the strains of traditional Irish songs - soft, sentimental and

The Shamrock Inn, Main Street, Killeshandra, Co. Cavan
Tel: 049 433 4139

wistful, or crisp and sharply witty, resounding around the bar. If you are staying for bed and breakfast, the 7 comfortable rooms at The Shamrock, (5 of them en suite), promise and deliver a refreshing night's sleep. If you prefer self-catering accommodation, a few minutes' drive from the pub will bring you to Woodview, a sturdy 2-storey farmhouse located at the heart of an anglers' Paradise. Aughabawn Lake is just 2 minutes' drive from the house, while 5 minutes will take you to all the other networks of lakes which make up the Lake Oughter system. The quality of fishing here is superb: your catch could range through pike, perch, bream, rudd, roach, hybrids, eels and tench. Naturally, Woodview has a tackle shed complete with bait-fridge and the house's other attractions include central heating, beds fitted with continental quilt and sheet sets, a sitting-room with open fireplace, a dining room also with an open fireplace, and a fitted kitchen with electric cooker and refrigerator. The four bedrooms at Woodview can accommodate 8-10 guests: if your immediate family isn't that extended, co-opt some friends!

Set in a lovely rural area about 3 miles from Killeshandra, **Pine Tree Cottage** provides comfortable self-catering accommodation for up to 7 people. The cottage is a smart modern bungalow standing in its own secluded grounds surrounded by the Aughabawn Estate and close to the "hidden" Patterson's Lake. Neat and compact, Pine Tree Cottage has all the charm of a small Irish cottage and has been meticulously maintained. There's

Pine Tree Cottage, Drumany, Killeshandra, Co. Cavan
Tel: 049 433 4531

a large living room, with colour TV, a fully fitted kitchen, 3 bedrooms with vanity units, and 2 bathrooms with showers. Linen is included in the rental. Anglers are well-served, provided with a large storeroom and fridges for bait, and a boat is also available. The cottage is located in the heart of the fishing lakes network and is also close to Killykeen Forest Park, Garadise Park and Lake, and the Woodford Canal. If you are out for the day, the cottage's owner, Bill Murphy, will be happy to arrange packed lunches and, if you grow tired of self-catering, the Slieve Russell Hotel is just a short drive away.

BELTURBET   MAP 4 REF J7
9 miles N of Cavan on the N3

This market town, prettily set on the east bank of the River Erne, is another major centre in Co. Cavan for coarse fishing. There are no conventional visitor attractions here but if you take one of the boat trips along the **Ulster Canal** available during the summer months you glide through an unspoilt countryside where even a single house appears as an intrusion.

A short walk from the town centre brings you to a bridge crossing the River Erne, one of Ireland's most glorious fishing rivers. Just beyond the bridge, overlooking the river,

Erneside Townhouses provide an ideal retreat for fishermen and indeed for anyone in search of a peaceful holiday in idyllic surroundings. A mere 100 yards from these luxury 3-bedroom self-catering houses runs a specially designated Brown Trout Fly Fishing stretch of the river and about 4 miles away is the specially stocked Rainbow Trout facility at the

Erneside Townhouses, Belturbet, Co. Cavan
Tel: 049 95 22781   Fax: 049 95 22555

Holy Lake where licences and boats for hire are available locally. Or you could select any other of the 365 lakes within easy reach of Belturbet. Each of the two Erneside Townhouses, which sleep 5/6 people, has its own fishing tackle store complete with refrigerator and there's a bait shop just 500 yards away. Built in 1997, the houses have a 2** Excellent rating from the Irish Tourist Board and are both comprehensively equipped with extras such as a trouser press, video recorder, cot and baby chair, (and baby sitting service), all available. Guests can also hire a bicycle, rent a boat and engage the services of a Gillie. If angling is not your particular interest, there's a vast range of other activities and attractions all within easy reach: anything from golf and canoeing to canal trips; from ancient castles and abbeys to antique shops and the Carraig Craft Visitor Centre at Mountnugent.

As the name suggests, **Hill Top Farmhouse** occupies an elevated position and so enjoys some enchanting views along the valley of the River Erne. With so many lakes and rivers in the area, this northeast corner of County Cavan is an angler's paradise and the owners of Hill Top Farmhouse, Philomena and Raymond O'Connor, have a boat and engine available for hire and the house has a separate bait and tackle room. Non-anglers will also be happy here since there's a wide range of activities within easy reach: golf, horse-riding, cycle hire and sailing. More leisurely pursuits include walking, bus tours and

Hill Top Farmhouse, Belturbet, Co. Cavan
Tel: 049 9522114   Mobile: 086 839 4322

river trips to Upper Lough Erne from nearby Belturbet. Hill Top Farmhouse has 10 comfortable guest rooms, all of which are en suite. Outside, there's a spacious garden where visitors can settle down to enjoy those superb views. At breakfast time, you'll find a choice of a full Irish or continental meal and the O'Connors will be happy to cook you a tasty evening meal if you wish.

COUNTY MONAGHAN

Drumlins are softly moulded hills created by the melting glaciers of the Ice Age as they retreated northwards. They are found all over northern Europe but nowhere in such profusion as in Co. Monaghan. Viewed from the window of a plane, the landscape has been memorably described as a "basket of eggs". Like the neighbouring county of Cavan, Monaghan is sparsely populated and although well-known to anglers has only recently recognised the need to attract visitors with different interests. Hopefully, the tourism agencies won't try too hard. The real attraction of this neglected area is its authenticity - an unspoiled corner of Ireland completely at ease with itself.

MONAGHAN   MAP 6 REF K6
29 miles NE of Cavan on the N54

A thriving linen industry in the 18th century endowed Monaghan with a fine legacy of classical and Regency buildings around the town's central square, the Diamond. One of them, the handsome **Market House** of 1792 with some fine carved decorations, is now the tourist office. The most striking sight in the Diamond though is the **Rossmore Memorial**, a huge Victorian drinking fountain with 8 grey marble columns and a lofty sandstone canopy. It displaced a 17th century market cross which now stands in another of the town's three squares, Old Cross Square. The third of them, **Church Square**, has a delightful Regency Gothic church and a large obelisk commemorating a colonel killed in the Crimean War, a period when Monaghan was still a British garrison town.

The award-winning **County Museum** on Hill Street has an outstanding collection of prehistoric antiquities, archaeological finds, traditional local crafts, and prints and water-colours from the 18th century to the present day. Housed in the former courthouse of 1829, the museum's most treasured exhibit is the processional **Cross of Clogher**, dating from around 1400 and exquisitely embossed with figures and decoration.

Soaring high above Monaghan is the flamboyant spire of **St Macartan's Catholic Cathedral**, built on a hill just outside the town in the 1860s in the Gothic Revival style popularised by Pugin.

This prosperous little town is well-provided with music pubs and places to eat, one of the best of them being the **Mediterraneo** on Dublin Street. As you might expect from the restaurant's name, the menu here reveals a distinctly Italian flavour. Not just pasta and pizza but also tasty fish, poultry and meat choices, along with tasty vegetarian options. Each day there are also daily specials, imaginative dishes prepared by the owners Paul Deery and his wife, and their team of chefs. The decor at the Mediterraneo has a bright Italian feel to it with pine floors and furniture, fresh flowers on the tables, colourful tablecloths and brilliant white walls hung with attractive paintings. With seating for a maximum of 46 people, the Mediterraneo has a warm and intimate atmosphere. Its

Mediterraneo, Dublin Street, Monaghan, Co. Monaghan
Tel: 047 82335

location in the heart of the town adds to the restaurant's appeal. Combined with the excellent fare on offer, this has made the Mediterraneo a popular venue. It is open every day of the week except Tuesday, all year round, from noon until 2pm for lunch, and from 6pm until 10pm for evening meals, and is strongly recommended.

GLASLOUGH
6 miles NW of Monaghan on the N12/R185

MAP 6 REF K6

Only a small part of the county lies to the north of Monaghan Town, much of it covered by the low-lying flood plain of the River Blackwater with the moorland of Slieve Beagh rising to the west. **Greystones Equestrian Centre** is situated on the Castle Leslie Estate in this hidden, unexploited corner of Ireland that has been described as *"Horse Heaven"*. The countryside is soft green and rolling with ancient forests, lakes and abundant flora and fauna. Here it seems possible to step back in time and escape the pressures of the modern

Greystones Equestrian Centre, Castle Leslie, Glaslough, Co. Monaghan
Tel: 047 88100   Fax: 047 88330   e-mail: gec@eircom.net
website: http://homepage.eircom.net/~horseridingireland/gec

world, enjoying a close harmony with horses, nature and fellow riding companions. The picturesque village of Glaslough lies at the estate gates and has won many awards in the Tidy Town Competition over the years. Its old buildings and character have been preserved along with the village way of life.

The Centre provides a wide variety of programmes to cater for all levels of riders, and non-riders can enjoy excellent fishing, golf, walking or cycling in the surrounding countryside. The horses at Greystones range from the "Baby-sitters" and "Flying Armchairs" for the inexperienced or nervous rider, to typical Irish hunters which provide more of a challenge to the experienced rider. The Centre's aim is for the nervous or novice rider to gain confidence from a team of experienced horses and qualified instructors up to BHSII.

The more experienced rider can ride younger, more challenging horses over extensive trails on the Castle Leslie Estate, with natural and man-made obstacles spread over a wide area. The Centre also has riding on adjacent farmland, there are numerous places of interest to visit within easy riding distance, and a competition course is available with a large number of fences to suit all levels. There's a full set of show jumps, an indoor school and outdoor arenas - both all-weather and grass. All the riding programmes include an initial assessment and rides are graded to ensure that everyone rides at a pace to suit them. The Centre has been approved by both the Association of Irish Riding Establishments and the British Horse Society.

For quality self-catering accommodation and a real sense of stepping back in time, a visit to **Rossarrell House** is strongly recommended. Tucked away in the Monaghan countryside at the end of a long winding lane, the house was built in the 1920s and is a perfect example of a rural Irish dwelling of that time. Rossarrell's owner, Emer Brennan, has taken great care to preserve the original look of the house and the interior fixtures, fittings and furnishings are all in keeping with the 1920s style. The house is splendidly

Rossarrell House, Glaslough, Co. Monaghan
Tel: 047 82073

atmospheric yet nevertheless is fully equipped with all modern amenities and the rental is remarkably reasonable. There are 3 good-sized bedrooms, a spacious lounge and a large kitchen supplied with just about everything you could ever need for a self-catering holiday. The house stands in extensive gardens with ample space for parking. The area around Glaslough is ideal for walking and cycling, and there are facilities for horse-riding and pony trekking within easy reach. Also close by is the 15th century church at Donagh, notable for its fine Celtic Cross.

CASTLEBLAYNEY
15 miles SE of Monaghan on the N2

MAP 6 REF K7

Set in the heart of "Drumlin Country", Castleblayney has adopted the title of "The Killarney of the North". The town stands on a narrow strip of land at the head of Lough Muckno, the county's largest stretch of water covering some 900 acres and the venue for the European Coarse Fishing Championships in 1999.

The handsome little town was built with two broad streets leading to an elegant **Georgian courthouse** at what was the market square. It was established by English colonists to serve the needs of the Hope Castle estate adjoining the lake. The house is now the Hope Castle Hotel (see below) but part of the grounds is now a delightful leisure park set on 900 acres of wooded country, a peaceful place for angling, picnicking and strolling along the waymarked forest walks.

Popular with locals and fishermen, the **Central Hotel**, as its name suggests, stands at the heart of this attractive little town, close to all the shops and restaurants. The hotel was built in the early 1800s and has changed little over the years, retaining the appealing character of a traditional Irish hostelry. Your host is Bridget McCann, a genuinely welcoming lady who presides with charm and warmth over this friendly hotel. Three storeys

Central Hotel, Main Street, Castleblayney, Co. Monaghan
Tel: 042 974 0038

high, the Central has 11 guest bedrooms, with a bathroom on each floor, and provides extremely good value-for-money accommodation. The residents' lounge has its own bar facility and there's also a large function room which has the added attraction of a late night bar licence. An interesting feature of the Central, one that's not found in many hotels, is a genuine coal mine at the rear of the building. Don't be alarmed though! The mine is quite secure and has not been worked for many years.

The Comet restaurant and lounge is also in Main Street and was opened on March 3rd, 1997. The date is significant because it was on that day the Hale-Bopp's comet streaked across the night sky over Ireland. The conjunction of these two events is also reflected in The Comet's Hale-Bopp's Night Club, a popular night spot which is open Wednesday, Friday and Saturday nights. There's more music to be en-

The Comet, Main Street, Castleblayney, Co. Monaghan
Tel: 042 974 9550   Fax: 042 974 0328

joyed in the Comet Bar which is generally reckoned to be the best live venue in Co. Monaghan and has sessions every evening except Tuesday. There are no fewer than 3 separate bars here, each furnished and decorated with a different theme. One is Victorian in character, another has a traditional, olde-worlde atmosphere, while the third is in the style of a gentleman's library. The Comet's restaurant is open 7 days a week with a carvery lunch served daily from noon until 15.00. Breakfast are available from 10.00 until noon, with bar snacks and an à la carte menu on offer until 22.00 every evening. This outstanding bar/restaurant is located in the heart of Castleblayney with all the amenities of the

Lough Muckno Country Park, noted for its excellent angling, virtually on the doorstep.

Occupying a prime position in the centre of the town, **Joan's Pantry** is a popular venue for those in search of good wholesome food, served in pleasant surroundings, and offered at very reasonable prices. This small and friendly restaurant is owned and run by Joan Smyth who also does the cooking. Her menu includes a good choice of varied dishes,

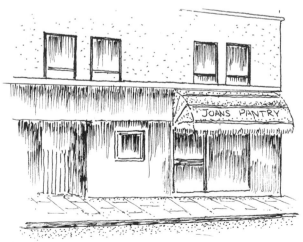

Joan's Pantry, Main Street, Castleblayney,
Co. Monaghan   Tel: 042 974 0294

with quiche and chicken curry amongst the specialities of the house. As well as table service, Joan's also has a take away service. The restaurant building is part of a handsome terrace, which means that parking at the door is not possible, but the town's main car park is just a short walk away.

Appropriately for a major angling centre, Castleblayney boasts the best fish and chip shop in Co. Monaghan - just call in at **Barney's** on Main Street. The owner, Mike Smyth, has been delighting his customers with succulent fish and superlative chips for more than

Barney's, Main Street, Castleblayney, Co. Monaghan
Tel: 042 974 0120

45 years. Well, practice makes perfect, and that's what both locals and visitors consider Mike's fish and chips to be - just perfect! Most customers use the take away service but the continental style premises also have a few sit-in tables. Mike uses only prime quality cod fillets for his cooking and, combined with his skilful preparation, the results are quite delicious.

Beautifully situated overlooking the lake, **Hope Castle Hotel** is a grand Georgian house with a long and interesting history. In the 1600s, the lands around Lough Muckno were owned by the Blayney family and it was they who built the original castle on a site near the present hotel. They also developed the town to which they gave their name. The family continued to prosper and by the early 19th century had added the handsome Courthouse, a market house, a Church of Ireland church and, unusually for those times, a Roman Catholic church. They also built what is now the Hope Castle Hotel, a stately 3-storey building with 5 bays. By the mid-1800s, the Blayneys had fallen on hard times and the house was sold to Henry Thomas Hope, the millionaire owner of the famous Hope

Hope Castle Hotel, Lough Muckno, Castleblayney, Co. Monaghan
Tel: 042 974 9450   Fax: 042 974 9498

Diamond which was reputed to bring bad luck to whoever possessed it. The marriage of Hope's daughter to an English duke doesn't necessarily seem like bad luck but by 1916 the estate was mortgaged and the Hope family departed.

During the 20th century, Hope Castle has played many different rôles. From 1900 to 1904 it was the home of the Duke of Connaught, Queen Victoria's 3rd son, who was Commander in Chief of the British forces in Ireland at that time. Later it was used as an Army barracks, a County Hospital, and a guest house run by Franciscan sisters before being purchased by Monaghan County Council.

Recently, the grand old building has changed hands again and is now owned by Chris Harch. He has completely refurbished the house to the highest standards and created a top-quality hotel offering first class accommodation and a restaurant serving excellent cuisine with an international flavour. Hope Castle Hotel has also established a reputation for live music, with bands playing here 6 nights a week during the summer season.

CARRICKMACROSS
26 miles SE of Monaghan on the N2

MAP 6 REF K7

Carrickmacross is an attractive town with a spacious main street and the sparse remains of a castle built by the Earl of Essex to whom Elizabeth I granted the town. A **Gothic planters church** stands at one end of the street, a gracious Georgian courthouse at the other. Traditional shop fronts and stately Georgian houses all add to the appeal. The town's major industry was once the production of fine lace, appliqué work on tulle. The tradition is still alive and well - the work of today's lacemakers can be seen, and bought, at the **Carrickmacross Lace Gallery** in the **Market Place**.

To the southwest of the town the **Dún a'Rí Forest Park** is an idyllic area, almost 600 acres of woodland looking across to the Mourne Mountains and a ruined Elizabethan fortress. There's a wishing well set into a rocky ledge above the River Cobra, countless places for a peaceful picnic, and a bridge with a story. Apparently, **Sarah's Bridge** is named after a lady who was standing here when a man she had been meeting for 30 years suddenly proposed marriage. She was so startled she fell from the bridge and drowned.

In Gaelic, *shanmullagh* means "ancient hill top" and **Shanmullagh House** is indeed set on the summit of a hill. Margaret and Owen Flannagan's delightful bed and breakfast establishment is located about 1½ miles from Carrickmacross town centre. It stands at the end of a winding country lane in a rural setting with horses grazing in the surrounding fields. Built in 1989, the spacious bungalow has 6 guest bedrooms, 5 of them en suite, and

Shanmullagh House, Killanny Road, Carrickmacross, Co. Monaghan
Tel: 042 966 3038 Fax: 042 966 1915

visitors have their own separate entrance. Margaret is by profession an art teacher and the striking colour schemes throughout the house reflect her flair for attractive combinations of lovely pastel shades and fresh colours. Visitors can enjoy her work at leisure in the comfortable TV lounge and in the dining room with its splendid countryside views. Shanmullagh House has good wheelchair access and children are welcome, with a cot and baby-sitting service available if required. Pets too can be accommodated.

Attractions and activities available locally include coarse and game fishing, an abundance of golf courses, horse riding, forest and country walks, and water sports. This corner of Monaghan was also the inspiration for the poet and novelist Patrick Kavanagh who was born at the nearby village of Inniskeen in 1904. The church where he worshipped for many years is now home to the **Kavanagh Centre** which celebrates the life and work of a gifted writer who was described as "the authentic voice of the Irish poor".

The Centre houses exhibitions on the author and local history, a 60-seat Audio-Visual Theatre, and 12 specially commissioned paintings illustrating Kavanagh's epic poem *The Great Hunger*. A highlight of the year at the Centre is the last weekend in November when the programme is a rich mixture of academia, culture, music, drama and pageantry - and of course "a large helping of pure, undiluted Inniskeen craic!"

A couple of miles south of the town, set in rolling fields and at the end of a long lane, **Nurebeg House** offers comfortable bed and breakfast accommodation in a stylish modern house. It's an interesting building with a horse-shoe shaped entrance to the parking area and an attractive octagonal summer-house standing alongside. Inside the bungalow, the rooms are unusually spacious and inviting. Nurebeg House has 6 non-smoking

Nurebeg House, Ardee Road, Carrickmacross, Co. Monaghan
Tel: 042 966 1044

guest rooms, 5 of them en suite, and all provided with tea and coffee-making facilities. Children are welcome, with a cot and baby sitting service available if required. Pets can also be accommodated. Nurebeg House is open all year except over the Christmas period. Within a 3-mile radius of the house, you will find golf, fishing and horse riding; the attractive landscaped parkland surrounding Lough Fea; and, a little further south, the Dún a Rí Forest Park where there are some delightful woodland walks.

CLONES   Map 5 ref J6
11 miles SW of Monaghan on the N54

Pronounced *clo-nez*, Clones is also a major centre for lace-making. The distinctive variety produced here is crocheted and often features small raised knots known as 'Clones dots'. The town was developed in the early 1600s by English settlers but there are a few survivals from earlier times. In the market place, known as is usual in Monaghan as the Diamond, there's an ancient, deeply carved **High Cross** with scenes from the Old Testament on one side, and New Testament stories depicted on the other.

Just a couple of hundred yards from the town centre, **The Round Tower** pub takes its name from the medieval Round Tower that stands beside the ruins of the Augustinian Abbey founded by St Tiernach in the 6th century. The Round Tower (the pub, that is) has everything you hope to find in a traditional Irish inn. It was built as an ale house well over 150 years ago and while it retains its olde-worlde atmosphere, mine host Peter McClave

The Round Tower, Cara Street, Clones, Co. Monaghan
Tel/Fax: 047 51158

makes sure that the Round Tower provides all the amenities of a modern hostelry. Tasty bar lunches are available every day and they represent excellent value for money. And if you are planning to stay in the area, the Round Tower has 2 comfortable guest rooms, both of them en suite. The pub provides an excellent base for exploring the "County of Little Hills" as well as the Lake Country of neighbouring County Fermanagh.

LATTON   Map 6 ref K7
15 miles S of Monaghan on minor road off the R190

Nestling among the drumlin hills of mid-Monaghan, the three properties of **The Creamery, Granary Loft and Avaghon** provide an excellent choice of self-catering accommodation. The Creamery is a large traditional stone cottage reconstructed in 1999 with a 4**** rating from the Irish Tourist Board and situated on the R190 road from

**Bookings through Joan or Patrick Gibson, Mahon Farmhouse, Latton,
Castleblayney, Co. Monaghan Tel: 042 974 2237 Fax: 042 966 0572
e-mail: k.gibson@iol.ie**

Cootehill to Ballybay. It stands close to the Drumore river system and the local pub is even closer! It was built in 1902 and was used for more than half a century by the farmers of the area to have their milk processed. It contains two separate units: one with 4 bedrooms sleeping up to 8 adults and has all modern conveniences. The 1-bedroom apartment sleeps 2 adults, with the kitchen and living area combined. Granary Loft is a tastefully converted 2-bedroom apartment on the first floor attached to Mahon Farmhouse at Latton. It sleeps four adults. Avaghon is a modern 3-bedroom bungalow, built in 1996. It sleeps up to 7 adults and its excellent design has the needs of the disabled very much in mind. All of these properties contain open fires.

There is a lot to be seen locally. From the top of Mahon hill there's a magnificent view of Lough Avalon which has a shore 5 miles long. This natural, unspoilt environment - a tourist's paradise waiting to be explored, has many outstanding features such as the Billy Fox Memorial Park, the remains of 5 mill wheels along the one river stretch, Mass Rocks, Ring Forts, Famine Graveyards, Black Pig Dikes, and the Cohaw Court Cairn, (a neolithic tomb which dates back to 4000 BC). Numerous attractions within driving distance include the Newgrange tumulus, Marble Arch Caves, the American Folk Park, Carrickmacross and Clones Lace. The surrounding area is an angler's dream with over 50 lakes to choose from. A short tour of the area is included but a tour guide can be pre-arranged. Enjoy a quiet stay in rural Ireland; experience first hand the routine of a working farm.

8 Belfast, Antrim and Londonderry

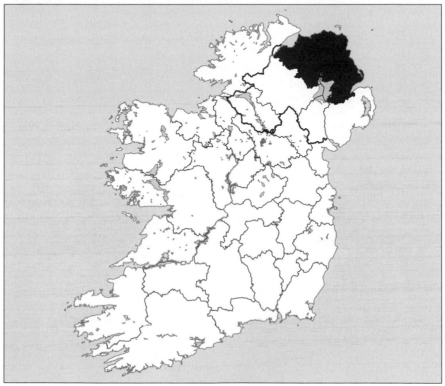

BELFAST

One enthusiastic writer has called Belfast the "Hibernian Rio", a description inspired by the city's fine setting, ringed by high hills, sea lough and river valley. One third of Northern Ireland's population, nearly half a million people, live in this robust, energetic city with its wealth of self-confident Victorian buildings. But the city's growth has been comparatively recent. Four hundred years ago, the small settlement of Beal Feirst ("the mouth of the sandy ford") had grown little since 1177 when the Anglo-Normans built a castle here. The English returned again in 1604 when James I "planted" Sir Arthur Chichester and the town began to expand around the local linen industry. The arrival of French Huguenots later that century, with their powerful work ethic, boosted development greatly.

But it was during the Industrial Revolution that Belfast really boomed. The growth of industries such as linen, rope-making and shipbuilding doubled the size of the town every ten years. The world's largest dry dock is here and the shipyard's giant cranes tower over the port.

Today, the city and river front are being transformed once again. Much of the city centre is pedestrianised, with plenty of benches where visitors can sit and listen to street musicians; smart bars and restaurants have sprung up, and there are inexhaustible opportunities for shopaholics. Music, theatre and the arts have experienced a renaissance in the last few years and the whole city demonstrates an optimism seemingly inspired by the ongoing peace process. What hasn't changed is the people - as friendly, welcoming and eager for craic as they have ever been.

At the heart of the city is Donegall Square, a spacious public area dominated by the imposing **City Hall** (free) and a huge statue of Queen Victoria who visited Belfast in 1849. The Hall was built in 1906 in classical renaissance style with a gleaming Portland

Belfast City Hall

stone exterior and a sumptuous Italian marble interior. There are guided tours available which take in the palatial entrance hall, robing room, council chamber and views of the magnificent 173 feet high dome whose whispering gallery, oddly, cannot be reached.

Located on the north side of Donegall Square, the **Linen Hall Library** is the city's oldest library and has been lending books to Belfast's citizens since 1788. It houses a massive collection of early Belfast printed books and a unique accumulation of more than 80,000 publications covering every aspect of Northern Ireland's political life since 1966. Known as the "Political Collection", it includes election posters, political ephemera, scholarly studies, and even prisoners' letters smuggled out of Long Kesh prison. An unusual amenity at the Linen Hall Library is the café in the Reading Room.

For connoisseurs of architectural fantasies, **St Malachy's Church** in Alfred Street is well worth seeking out. Built in 1844, its exterior is an extravagant medley of turrets and battlements, while the sumptuous, wedding-cake interior is notable for its elaborate fan-vaulted ceiling, modelled on the Henry VII Chapel in Westminster Abbey.

About 300 yards to the west of Donegall Square, the lavish **Grand Opera House** of 1895 is another architectural wonder. It boasts an exotic and opulently decorated interior which draws heavily on images from the Orient, with carved elephants supporting the boxes and a glorious painted ceiling. Also in Great Victoria Street is one of the city's gems, the **Crown Liquor Saloon**, an extraordinary gin palace with a glittering, glazed tile exterior and an interior of dizzying High Victorian excess. Gas lit to this day, it features acres of original wooden panelling, a scrolled ceiling, patterned floor and a long S-shaped bar divided by exuberantly carved screens. A row of wooden snugs, similar to old-style railway compartments, lines one of the walls with carved heraldic beasts at each entry, and the bar staff are dressed appropriately with white aprons and bow ties. This remark-able hostelry is now owned by the National Trust but operates as a normal pub. Just around the corner is another bar that comes a close second to the Crown. **The Britannic** takes its name from the sister ship to the *Titanic* and the bar features plenty of Harland & Wolff shipyard memorabilia along with items from the liner herself.

Great Victoria Street, also known as the **Golden Mile**, leads the visitor out to the University Quarter. The area around the Georgian University Square has rightly been called a "perfect Victorian suburb", with the stately Tudor-style Queen's University build-ing of 1845 as its focal point. The superb sweep of the Upper Terrace dates from the same time, as does the Lower Crescent which, strangely, is not a crescent at all but straight.

Close by are the **Botanic Gardens** where the magnificent Palm House, built in 1829, is one of the earliest curved glass and iron structures in the world, predating the famous one at Kew Gardens by several years. Within the grounds of the gardens, the **Ulster Museum** houses a colossal collection of exhibits relating to the archaeology, ethnogra-phy, art, history and natural sciences of the province. One of the most notable displays is the treasure retrieved from the wreck of the *Girona*, a Spanish Armada galleon which sank off the Giant's Causeway. Some of Belfast's grandest buildings are banks. The Ulster Bank in Waring Street, for example, has an interior resembling a Venetian palace. Rather more restrained in style is **Clifton House**, an elegant Georgian building of 1744 which is better known as the Poor House since it was originally the Charitable Institute for the Aged and Infirm. Designed by an amateur architect, a paper merchant named Robert Joy, it is crowned by a curious octagonal-based stone spire.

Many of Belfast's finest Victorian buildings were designed by the architect Charles Lanyon. His masterpiece is generally reckoned to be the **Custom House** on Donegall Quay. Although not open to the public, you can admire from the outside this imposing Corinthian-style structure of golden stone, designed in the "Italian manner after Palladio". Lanyon was also responsible for the nearby **Sinclair Seamen's Church** which has be-come something of a maritime museum. The pulpit is in the form of a ship's prow while other features include navigation lights and the ship's bell from *HMS Hood*. A couple of hundred yards from the church, the towering **Prince Albert Memorial** stands slightly askew because its foundations have sunk into the clay river bank. It's something of a puzzle why such a huge memorial was erected to the Prince since he never visited the city or ever became involved in its affairs, but the lofty clock tower is useful for getting one's bearings as you stroll around the city.

Also in the port area, **Lagan Lookout Visitor Centre** tells the story of the important rôle played by the River Lagan in the development of the city with the help of models, stories and songs. Interactive displays enable visitors to follow the construction of the Lagan Weir and the regeneration of the River Lagan and the surrounding area. The city spent millions of pounds cleaning up the river with the result that for the first time in many years salmon fishing was possible on the day the weir was inaugurated.

On the outskirts of the city, **Cave Hill** (1182 feet) is a notable landmark, known also as Napoleon's Nose because of its profile. If you climb up to the summit, the entire city and its lough are laid out before you in all their glory. The slopes are dotted with Iron Age forts and in ancient times the hill was mined for flint to make tools and weapons. Set on the side of Cave Hill, **Belfast Castle** is a mansion of 1870 built in the style of Queen Victoria's Scottish residence, Balmoral. Its cellars have been transformed into a re-creation of a typical Belfast street in Victorian times, complete with a bar and restaurant. From the main reception room, a splendid Italianate stairway leads down to attractive gardens enjoying fine views of the harbour area. Nearby, **Belfast Zoo** is home to more than 60 endangered species, housed in enclosures which replicate the wild. Set in pleasantly landscaped parkland, the zoo has won many awards for its emphasis on spacious enclosure, its breeding programme, and its mainly small animal collection. Visitors can view penguins and sea lions from underwater and the zoo provides a rare opportunity to see a spectacled bear and a red panda.

About 5 miles to the east of the city and set in 300 acres of gardens, **Stormont** is a splendid neo-classical building of gleaming white stone. It formerly housed the Northern Ireland Parliament and is now the home of the new Assembly. The building is not open to the public but visitors are free to wander through its extensive grounds which also contain Stormont Castle, the residence of the Secretary of State for Northern Ireland and also not open to visitors.

COUNTY ANTRIM

For most visitors, Antrim is its coast and no tour of Ulster would be complete without a drive along the coastal road. It provides stunning views of the rugged cliffs and passes amazing rock formations, pretty villages, concealed harbours and ancient fortresses. At its north-eastern point, Scotland's Mull of Kintyre is clearly visible just 12 miles away - weather permitting. The road links the 9 beautiful valleys known as the Glens of Antrim, skirts the strange rocks of the Giant's Causeway, and finishes (or starts) at the delightful port and resort of Portrush. Inevitably, this cornucopia of attractions leads to heavy traffic during the summer season, and Sundays are notoriously busy most of the year, but there is so much to enjoy that the journey should definitely not be missed. The interior, by comparison, is quiet and peaceful, a patchwork of fertile fields, rolling hills and gently undulating farming country. We begin this tour of the county by following the coastal road from Portrush in the northwest to Larne in the southeast.

PORTRUSH   MAP 6 REF L2
5 miles N of Coleraine on the A2/A29

This popular family resort enjoys a splendid position on Ramore Head, a mile-long
peninsula jutting out into the Atlantic. Beautiful sandy beaches, (the West and East
Strands), run for miles, ending to the east at **White Rocks** - weirdly shaped limestone
cliffs which have been weathered into caves and arches. The East Strand is backed by the
sand dunes of the famous Royal Portrush Golf Club which provides devotees of the game
with one 9-hole and two 18-hole courses. The town is well-provided with all the usual
seaside amenities including an all-weather holiday centre, **Waterworld**, which offers
flumes, slides, jacuzzis, a sauna, aquarium and restaurant; **Barry's Fairground** with
traditional amusements and rides; **Fantasy Island**, an indoor adventure playground;
and the **Dunluce Centre** which has "virtual reality" family attractions. During the
season, the Portrush Puffer road train carries passengers on a circular tour of the town
and other entertainments include theatre, concerts and firework displays. Towards the
end of May, a hilarious **Raft Race** takes place when contestants race each other across the
harbour on a bizarre assortment of home-made rafts.

Located on the seafront beside Barry's Amusement Park, **Duke's Lodge** is a family-
owned and run B & B offering good food and comfortable accommodation. This large
and imposing Victorian house with an attractive colour-washed frontage has 21 guest
bedrooms, 6 of them en suite. The whole building has recently been refurbished, the
decor bright and everything spick and span. A special attraction at Duke's Lodge is the
food, with meals available all day and breakfast served until 11.00. The building has been

Duke's Lodge, 6 & 7 Kerr Street, Portrush, Co. Antrim BT56 8DG
Tel/Fax: 028 7082 4159

modified to provide disabled access throughout, including a disabled-friendly lift. Another useful amenity at Duke's Lodge is its provision of secure, off-street parking. In Portrush itself, there's a huge choice of things to do and see. One natural feature well worth seeing is the "Cathedral Cave" at the eastern end of the long, sandy beach. The sea and the weather have modelled the soft limestone cliffs into strange shapes and carved out this cave which stretches 180 feet from end to end.

Only one minute from the beach, **Hillrise** is a family home offering quality accommodation with friendly, efficient service. It enjoys a splendid setting in a peaceful and relaxing atmosphere with a view of West Bay and the harbour, and golfers will be pleased to know that the house is located right beside the Portrush and Portstewart golf courses.

Hillrise, 24 Dhu Varren, Portrush, Co. Antrim BT56 8EN
Tel: 028 70822450 Fax: 028 70822493   e-mail: d_moore@lineone.net

The spacious rear garden also enjoys sea views and off-street private parking is provided. The house itself is furnished and decorated to the very highest standard. There are 5 en suite guest bedrooms, some with sea views and all with TV. Children are welcome. Hillrise is the home of Florence Snodden and her daughter, Dianne Moore, and they both take great pains to ensure their guests have a comfortable and relaxing stay. The breakfast they offer deserves a special mention for its huge choice of dishes, ranging from a full Ulster Fry to a dish of mushrooms stuffed with tomato, sausage, sweet pickle and topped with cheese. Freshly baked wheaten bread is served with the meal.

A warm welcome, along with very clean, comfortable accommodation and good home cooked food awaits guests at **Beulah House**, just a short walk from the town's main thoroughfare. This lofty terrace house looks a picture during the summer months when it is bedecked with flowers and hanging baskets. Your hosts at Beulah House are Mr and Mrs Anderson who have been providing excellent bed and breakfast accommodation here since 1993. The house is centrally heated, with en suite and no-smoking rooms available,

Beulah House, 16 Causeway Street, Portrush,
Co. Antrim BT32 8AB Tel: 0280 7082 2412

and all rooms are equipped with satellite TV and tea/coffee-making facilities. There's a spacious residents' lounge and, outside, a lovely walled garden. The extensive choice at breakfast includes a tasty home made porridge and the optional evening meal offers vegetarian options along with other appetising dishes. Children are welcome and there's a reduced rate for senior citizens. The Andersons make every effort to ensure that their guests are comfortable and relaxed. They are happy to arrange golf, fishing, game shooting and water skiing, and there are facilities for pony trekking within easy reach. If you enjoy walking, Beulah House is also convenient for the Ulster Way. In this busy little town, Beulah House provides an additional, useful amenity - a secure locked parking area.

Set in an elegant crescent, **Alexandra Town House** commands grand views of the beach and ocean and is within easy reach of the town's many attractions. The Alexandra's

Alexandra Town House, 11 Lansdowne
Crescent, Portrush, Co. Antrim BT56 8AY
Tel/Fax: 0128 2072 2284

owner, Mary McAllister, has been involved in the guest house business for some 25 years so she knows how to make her guests feel welcome and at home. The ochre-washed Victorian building was built on a generous scale with the spacious dining-room and most of the bedrooms enjoying those lovely sea views. Altogether, there are 10 letting rooms, 5 of them en suite, and they, like the rest of the house, have all been recently refurbished. A full Irish breakfast is included in the tariff. The Alexandra also has a small garden at the front where visitors can settle down and watch the world go by. At the time of writing, Mary is finalising plans for poetry weekends and these should be in place by the time you read this.

Close to all the town's many attractions, **Brookside House** is a large and imposing Victorian terraced house where Peter Fox welcomes guests for bed and breakfast accommodation. Brookside enjoys superb views across the sea to the hills of Donegal, views which are also shared by the 15 guest bedrooms. Like the rest of the house, these rooms are unusually spacious. Most are en suite and some are non-smoking. Children are welcome here, there are reduced rates for senior citizens, and pets can also be accommodated. Brookside has a large residents' lounge and a dining room where a full Irish breakfast is served. Evening meals and packed lunches are also available if required. Guests can stay on either a B & B, half board or full board basis. Brookside has a relaxing home-from-home atmosphere and guests are welcome to make use of the attractive garden to the rear of the house. Brookside is also convenient

Brookside House, 46 Mark Street, Portrush, Co. Antrim Tel/Fax: 028 7082 4498

for joining the Ulster Way, the 450-mile footpath that traverses all six counties of Ulster.

Occupying an excellent position on the sea frontage, overlooking the West Bay and Portrush Harbour and enjoying views of the Donegal Hills, **Casa à la Mar** is a small and friendly family-run guest house. Ideally situated for shops, amusements and the railway station, Casa à la Mar is owned and run by Peter and Rose Larner who hail originally from Liverpool and Birmingham respectively but have lived at Portrush for more than 30 years. Their large Victorian terraced house is bright and attractive with spacious centrally-heated rooms, large dining hall and a visitors' lounge. Casa à la Mar has 6 guest rooms, two of which are en suite, and all equipped with colour television

Casa à la Mar, 21 Kerr Street, Portrush, Co. Antrim BT56 8DG Tel/Fax: 028 7082 2617

and tea/coffee making facilities. Guests can stay on a bed & breakfast, half board or bed only basis, whichever suits.

The Larners describe Portrush as "Northern Ireland's Blackpool", a favourite with Ulster people who "stay at home". There are fine sandy beaches and a wide variety of attractions. The all-weather Waterworld has flumes, slides, sauna, jacuzzis and an aquarium; Fantasy Island is an indoor adventure playground, while Barry's Fairground provides all the traditional seaside amusements. Boating, fishing, water-skiing and wind surfing are all readily available and golfers will no doubt make a beeline for the Royal Portrush Golf Club, Northern Ireland's premier course.

Also located in this convenient street, just yards from all the main attractions, **Harbour Heights** was acquired in early 1999 by Ann and Robin Rossborough. A bubbly and

enthusiastic couple, they have a very "hands on" approach, making sure that everything possible is done to ensure that their guests have a relaxed and comfortable stay. Their large, handsome terrace house looks out across the Atlantic to the Donegal coastline, while from the huge dining room guests have a fine view of the bustling main street of this lively resort. Harbour Heights is attractively furnished, and great attention has been paid to getting the details right. There are 14 guest rooms, 10 of which are en suite. All are pleasantly decorated and well-equipped; most have lovely sea views. Special diets can be catered for and the Rossboroughs also serve high teas and evening meals. The special children's menu is exceptionally good and will surely tempt the pickiest of young eaters.

Harbour Heights, 17 Kerr Street, Portrush,
Co. Antrim BT56 8DG
Tel: 028 70822 765 Fax: 028 7082 2558
e-mail: robin@rossborough.freeserve.co.uk

About 3 miles east of Portrush, **Dunluce Castle** is one of the grandest sights in Ireland. This romantic 13th/16th century ruin clings to a crag, almost entirely surrounded by the sea and with a huge cave right underneath. The castle's defenders could enter the cave which slopes up into the castle precincts and repulse any attack from the drawbridge across the deep chasm which is now

Dunluce Castle, Co. Antrim

spanned by a footbridge. In the late 1500s, Dunluce was the stronghold of the MacDonnells, Lords of the Isles, who ruled all the northeastern corner of Ulster from this seemingly impregnable base. But in 1584, the English under Sir John Perrott battered the castle with artillery, forcing "Sorley Boy" MacDonnell and his clansmen to flee. But with the help of a sympathiser in the castle, Sorley Boy ("Yellow Charles" in Irish) was back a few nights later. His men were hauled up the crag in a basket, the English garrison was annihilated and the constable hanged over the wall. Sorley Boy was able to repair the damage to his castle with the rich pickings gathered from the wreck of the Spanish Armada ship, the *Girona*, which sank near the Giant's Causeway in 1588. Sorley Boy later agreed a peace with the English and his son Randal was created Earl of Antrim by James I.

Dunluce Castle suffered another dramatic disaster in 1639 when a great storm swept the castle's original kitchens off the hilltop, along with the cooks and the dinner they were preparing. A few years later, the MacDonnells moved to a less precarious residence at Glenarm in the Glens of Antrim. The extensive ruins of their abandoned castle include two 13th century towers, a Scottish style gatehouse of around 1600, and the remains of a great hall, part of a 17th century house built within the castle walls. Guided tours are available and in calm weather the sea cave can be visited by boat.

BALLYMACRAE
MAP 6 REF L2
2 miles SE of Portrush on the B62

Just a couple of miles inland from Dunluce Castle, **Shelbourne** is a spacious modern house offering superior bed and breakfast accommodation. Surrounded by a large, beautifully maintained garden, Shelbourne is the home of Thelma Wallace, a lively lady who loves meeting people and really enjoys good "craic", (conversation). Although recently built, Shelbourne has the settled and peaceful look of a much older house. It's a 2-sto-

Shelbourne, 208 Ballybogy Road, Ballymacrea, Portrush, Co. Antrim BT56 8NE Tel: 028 7082 4838

reyed building but both of the two guest rooms are on the ground floor, convenient for anyone who has difficulty with stairs. The rooms are very well-appointed and decorated to the very highest standard. They are also very large, creating a restful sense of space. Each room has a television and tea/coffee making facilities, and they share a bathroom (also very large). A full Irish breakfast is included in the tariff and there's plenty of off-road parking space. Ballymacrae village is just a couple of miles from the bustling holiday resort of Portrush and two of Ulster's prime visitor attractions are only a little further away: the Giants Causeway and the country's oldest distillery, Bushmills, lie just a few miles to the east. Also close by are the striking ruins of Dunluce Castle, the seat of the MacDonnells, "Lords of the Isles", until 1639 when a ferocious storm sent its kitchen, cooks and the dinner they were preparing tumbling down the cliff into the sea. The MacDonnells moved inland and Dunluce has remained empty ever since.

BUSHMILLS
12 miles NE of Coleraine on the A2

MAP 6 REF L2

The quiet little town of Bushmills is known throughout the world for the whiskey that has been legally produced here since 1608, making **Bushmills Distillery** the oldest licit distillery anywhere. Tsar Peter the Great sampled the fiery liquor during his study tour of Europe in 1697 and pronounced himself well-pleased. The distillery offers guided tours which last for about an hour and conclude with a tot of the *usquebeagh*, or you can order a hot toddy if you really need warming up. Bushmills is barely a quarter of a mile out of town and is clearly signposted.

Craig Park Country House Bed and Breakfast, 24 Carnbore Road, Bushmills, Co. Antrim BT57 8YF Tel: 028 2073 2496 Fax: 028 2073 2479 e-mail: jan@craigpark.co.uk website: www.craigpark.co.uk

About 2 miles outside Bushmills, **Craig Park** is a spacious and comfortable country house, close to the Causeway Coast. Set in an elevated position facing west, the house enjoys distant views to the mountains of Donegal, the Antrim hills and, to the northwest, the Scottish islands of Jura and Islay. A modern, Georgian-style house, Craig Park has 3 large guest bedrooms, all with en suite facilities and providing superior accommodation for up to 6 guests. Each bedroom commands wonderful panoramic views and is equipped with colour television and tea/coffee making facilities. There's also a huge residents' lounge which looks very inviting with its deep leather chairs and settees. Craig Park is the home of Jan Cheal and her husband who prefer guests not to smoke in the house.

This peaceful spot is a good base from which to visit the world-famous Giant's Causeway, the Old Bushmills Distillery, Dunluce Castle and the coastal towns of Portrush, Portstewart and Ballycastle. There are magnificent beaches nearby for swimming or surfing, and the dramatic scenery of the coastline provides superb clifftop walks. There are also excellent opportunities for cycling and golf while the nature reserve on the island of Rathlin is a must for ornithologists.

To find Craig Park, leave Bushmills with the Distillery on your left hand side, turn left into Straid Road (the B17), signposted "Ballycastle 11". In half a mile, immediately past the Citroen Garage (Hallidays), turn right into Haw Road, signposted Billy and Liscolman. After one mile, turn left into Carnbore Road. After a quarter of a mile, turn left into a small lane and Craig Park is the second house on the right, up a long lane.

About 3 miles northeast of Bushmills is the spectacular **Giant's Causeway**, the only World Heritage Site in Ireland and one which has been attracting visitors ever since it was

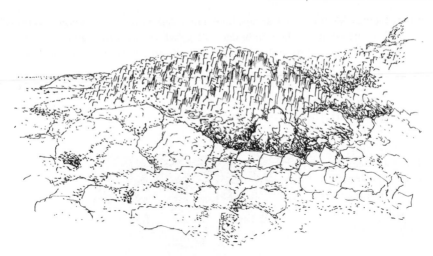

Giant's Causeway, Co. Antrim

pronounced one of the great natural wonders of the world by the Royal Geographical Society in 1693. This extraordinary cluster of black basalt pillars, most of them six-sided although some have as many as ten sides, was formed some 60 million years ago by volcanic activity. As the molten basalt cooled it solidified into some 37,000 columns. Various groups of the stony columns have been given names such as the Organ Pipes, and one, known as Chimney Point has such a strange outline that sailors on the Spanish Armada ship *Girona* mistook it for Dunluce Castle, a mistake which led to the ship's foundering with the loss of more than a thousand lives. The Causeway takes its name from the legend of the Ulster warrior Finn MacCool who built it so that he could reach his beloved, a giantess on the Island of Staffa where the formation resurfaces off the Scottish coast. The Causeway is now in the care of the National Trust which has a Visitor Centre here with a coffee shop, craft shop and audio-visual displays. Next door, the **Causeway School** is an interesting re-creation of a 1920s country school, complete with children's toys such as whipping tops and skipping ropes. It's only open during July and August.

A couple of miles to the east of the Causeway, the sorry looking remains of **Dunseverick Castle** stand on the cliffs of Benbane Head. Only the ruins of a 16th century gatehouse still stand. Between c.500-800AD, this was the capital of the kingdom of Dalriada which, based in north Antrim, colonised much of Scotland. Dunseverick was also the terminus of one of the 5 great roads radiating from Tara, the ancient capital of Ireland.

BALLINTOY
15 miles NE of Coleraine on the B15

MAP 6 REF M2

The dramatic little harbour at Ballintoy with its colourful boats and rock-strewn shore provides a picturesque subject for both amateur and professional painters. The village itself is one of the prettiest along the Antrim coast, its white-painted houses and church creating an almost Mediterranean atmosphere. The village's one-time landlord was Downing Fullerton who endowed the Cambridge college which bears his name and is partly furnished with oak panelling and a staircase taken from Ballintoy Castle, now demolished.

A popular excursion from Ballintoy is the boat trip around **Sheep Island** (National Trust) just offshore, a great stack with a flat grassy top which is home to an enormous colony of cormorants. The original puffin colony was massacred by rats but the rodents in turn were exterminated and a small number of puffins has recently returned. The boat trips usually continue to the nearby **Carrick-a-rede Island**, famous for its nerve-racking rope bridge. Sixty feet long and 80 feet above the sea, the swaying construction of planks and rope links the island to a commercial salmon fishery. Despite a large sign warning of the danger and the absence of any safety netting, there's a regular procession of squealing, giggling or frozen-faced tourists crossing the bridge. Carrick-a-rede means "rock in the road" - the "road" being the sea route taken by Atlantic salmon returning to spawn in the rivers. From Ballintoy harbour, a footpath leads to **Whitepark Bay** (National Trust), a mile-long beach of golden sands backed by grassy dunes. The

The Carrick-a-Rede Rope Bridge, Co. Antrim

path continues to the tiny hamlet of Portbraddan whose slate-roofed church, 12 feet by 6½ feet, lays claim to being the smallest church in Ireland.

For those looking for good quality, value-for-money accommodation, **Sheep Island View** is ideal. This independent holiday hostel is a spanking new purpose built unit with accommodation for up to 56 people as well as space in the grounds for up to 40 tents. All the rooms are en suite, family rooms are available, and there's a large lounge which was formally opened in 1997 by Ballintoy's oldest resident, 101-year-old Annie

Sheep Island View, 42 Main Street, Ballintoy, Co. Antrim BT54 6LX
Tel: 028 2076 9391/2470 Fax: 028 2076 9994

Johnstone. The hostel also provides laundry facilities and the whole building is wheel-chair-friendly. Outside, there's ample parking. This exceptionally well-appointed complex, which is open all year, is owned and run by the McShane family, Josie, Sean and their daughter Aileen. They will provide meals on request, (there are also pubs and restaurants nearby), rent you a bike, or arrange guided walks with local experts. As the name suggests, the hostel looks out to Sheep Island with scenic views extending to the western islands of Scotland. The superb beach at Whitepark Bay is an easy walk, the nerve-racking Rope Bridge at Carrick-a-Rede within easy reach, and one of Ireland's most famous attractions, the Giant's Causeway, lies a few miles to the west. Sheep Island View is ideally located for exploring all of the Causeway Coast as well as the Glens of Antrim.

Just to the north of Ballintoy, the beach at Whitepark Bay is one of the best in Ireland, a mile long stretch of white sands. **Whitepark House** is perfectly placed to make the most of this scenic spot and even has a private path leading down to it. Husband and wife team Bob and Siobhan Isles welcome bed and breakfast guests to their impressive period residence, a "fort"-like dwelling set in a superbly maintained garden. The house is sumptuously furnished, with many Oriental objets d'art accumulated by the Isles during their travels in the Far East.

The huge lounge at Whitepark House is warmed by a massive log fire and the 3 bedrooms, (2 of them en suite), enjoy attractive views of the garden. Breakfast is excellent, served with specially bought in bacon and sausage accompanied by home-made bread. If you are on holiday, there are many attractions in the area. During the summer months, there are boat trips from Ballintoy harbour to Carrick-a-rede Island where, if you are brave, you can tackle the notorious Rope Bridge. Suspended 80 feet above a chasm 60 feet

Whitepark House, 150 Whitepark Road, Ballintoy, Co. Antrim BT54 6NH
Tel: 028 2073 1482 e-mail: bob.isles@virgin.net
website: http://homepage.virgin.net/bob.isles/

wide, this bridge of planks linked by rope bucks and dips alarmingly as you cross. Nerves of steel are recommended. A more conventional attraction is the famous natural wonder of the Giant's Causeway, a few miles to the west of Ballintoy.

Not many guest houses can offer their visitors access to a private fishing lake stocked with rainbow and brown trout from which plump specimens of rainbow trout weighing up to 13 lbs have been landed. The name of this exceptional establishment is **Glenmore House**, located about halfway between Ballintoy and Ballycastle on the B15. You don't have to be an angler to appreciate the many amenities provided at Glenmore House, a

Glenmore House, Whitepark Road, Ballintoy, Ballycastle, Co. Antrim BT54 6LR
Tel/Fax: 028 2076 3584 e-mail:glenmore_house3@lineone.net

modern purpose-built facility designed to provide both quality motel-style accommodation and a range of leisure pursuits. There are 10 guest bedrooms, all en suite, two with a jacuzzi, a residents' lounge, and a licensed bar where visitors can enjoy tasty snacks, lunches, teas and evening meals throughout the day. Packed lunches, picnic baskets and a private barbecue site are also available. The extensive site can also accommodate campers and caravanners who will be pleased to find up-to-date amenities such as a shower block and electrical hook-ups available.

BALLYCASTLE   MAP 6 REF M2
16 miles E of Coleraine on the A2/B67

Ballycastle is a lively little resort town, never more so than in June when it hosts a 3-day festival of Gaelic games, music and dance, the *Fleadh Amhran agus Rince*. In May there's more jollity when the cross-community Northern Lights Festival takes place, but the most time-honoured event occurs on the last Monday and Tuesday of August. **Ould Lammas Fair** has been held here ever since the MacDonnells were granted a charter in 1606, making it Ireland's oldest popular fair. It used to last for a whole week but is now a 2-day event featuring sheep and pony sales along with several hundred street stalls shoehorned into the Diamond (Market Square) and along Fairhill Street. An old, but still popular song, asks:

> *Did you treat your Mary Ann*
> *To dulse and yellow man*
> *At the Ould Lammas Fair in Ballycastle-O?*

"Dulse" is an edible seaweed; "yellow man" a bright yellow toffee so rock-hard it requires a hammer to break it into fragments.

Ballycastle was extensively developed during the mid-1700s by its landowner, Colonel Hugh Boyd, and many attractive houses of that period have survived. The handsome Classical parish church with its octagonal spire was also built at that time. Its square tower is marked by a huge clock face, completely out of proportion to the tower, while inside there's a dazzling star-spangled blue ceiling and some grandiose monuments to the Boyd family.

Another monument, in the form of a picnic site on the sea front, commemorates a crucial moment in the history of telecommunications. It was from here, in 1898, that the 24-year-old Guglielmo Marconi made the world's first successful cross-water wireless transmission to Rathlin Island, about 5 miles distant.

The boomerang-shaped **Rathlin Island** is a popular destination for boat trips from Ballycastle - a 45-minute journey. Girded by high white cliffs for most of its coastline, the island is nowhere more than a mile wide. The cliffs are home to tens of thousands of seabirds whose incessant murmurings sound like the inside of a beehive. The cliffs are perforated by many caves, the most famous of which is Bruce's Cave where Robert the Bruce took refuge after his defeat at Perth by the English in 1306. According to legend, it was here that he observed a spider repeatedly trying to reach the roof of the cave and formulated the apophthegm *"If at first you don't succeed, try, try and try again"*. In calm weather you can visit the cave by boat.

Restrictions on visitor's cars make Rathlin a peaceful place nowadays but the island has witnessed some horrific events. In 795AD its inhabitants were the first victims in Ireland of Viking raiders; in 1575 English forces led by the Earl of Essex slaughtered every one of the women, children and old people whom the MacDonnells had sent here believing it to be a place of safety. In 1642 the MacDonnells on Rathlin Island were again under attack, this time from their Scottish enemies, the Campbells. From a hill in the middle of the island, now called *Cnoc na Screedlin*, "the hill of screaming", the distraught MacDonnell womenfolk looked on helplessly as the Campbells butchered their husbands and sons. For an insight into Rathlin Island's chequered history, its culture and ecology, a visit to the **Boathouse Centre**, just around the bay from the harbour, is recommended.

Back in Ballycastle, **The Strand** restaurant in North Street, with its striking orange and dark-green frontage, is easy to find. It's located in the heart of this attractive coastal resort, overlooking the sea and only yards from the ferry terminals for the boats to Rathlin Island and Campbeltown. The pleasant and attentive staff add to the pleasure of eating here, whether you come in for just a bar snack or for something more substantial from the full menu. Both options represent very good value for money. Comfortable seating and well-spaced tables reflect owner John McQuade's concern for customer satisfaction and his menu specialises in meals based on locally-caught fish such as

The Strand, 9 North Street, Ballycastle, Co. Antrim
Tel: 028 7036 2349

salmon and cod. There's also an excellent choice of dishes for those who prefer vegetarian options. If you enjoy a glass of wine with your meal, The Strand has a comprehensive wine list and the bar is also well-stocked with a wide range of beers and spirits.

The rather olde-worlde Victorian-style frontage of **Harold's Restaurant** in Ann Street looks instantly appealing and the interior is just as inviting. The restaurant takes its name from the owner, Mark Harold who, together with his wife, runs this friendly eatery in the

Harold's Restaurant, 22 Ann Street, Ballycastle, Co. Antrim BT54 6AD Tel: 028 2076 9064

town's main thoroughfare. Mark takes great pride in his food preparation but insists that no-one should be kept waiting for long. The value-for-money menu is available all day with a good choice of home cooked specialities on offer. At Sunday lunchtime, there's a popular Carvery. Children are welcome and a special area of the restaurant has been reserved for families. By the time you read this, Mark's drinks licence should be in place so you can enjoy your favourite beverage with your meal. With its large front door and special toilet, Harold's is very disabled-friendly and has won the town's only Access Award for the disabled. Parking is easy too with the town centre car park close by. Ballycastle is always a lively place but especially during the Northern Lights Festival in May, the 3-day music and dance festival, "Fleadh Amhrán agus Rince", in June, and Ireland's oldest fair, "Ould Lammas", in August when there are sheep and pony sales as well as all the usual amusements.

With its pillared porch and white-painted walls, **Bushbane House** has a rather dignified air but there's nothing starchy about the warm welcome awaiting guests at this friendly bed & breakfast establishment. The house stands on an elevated site enjoying fine views over Ballycastle Bay, surrounded by spacious gardens and well set back from the road leading to the famous Giant's Causeway. Bushbane House is the home of Mary McKiernan who has totally refurbished the building and decorated it to the very highest standards. Each of the 4 letting rooms is en suite, well-equipped with TV and other amenities, and each room shares those superb views. A full range of breakfasts is included in the tariff. Pets are not allowed in the house but adequate kennelling is available where your faithful friend can be accommodated in comfort. Ballycastle itself is a bustling market town and port located at the eastern end of the two most northerly Glens of Antrim, Glenshesk and Glentaisie. The town boasts the oldest fair in Ireland, Ould Lammas Fair, which dates

Bushbane House, 28 Whitepark Road, Ballycastle, Co. Antrim BT54 6IJ
Tel/Fax: 028 2076 3789

back to 1606 and takes place on the last Monday and Tuesday in August. From the harbour, there are regular ferries to Campbeltown on Scotland's Mull of Kintyre, and to Rathlin Island, 5 miles offshore, noted for its rugged scenery and superb birdwatching opportunities.

Continuing eastwards from Ballycastle along the A2 for a couple of miles brings you to **Ballyvoy** and the ruins of **Bonamargy Friary** founded by the MacQuillan family around 1500. It is notable for the tombs of Sorley Boy MacDonnell of Dunluce Castle fame, his son Randal, 1st Earl of Antrim, and his grandson the 2nd Earl who died in 1682. The 2nd Earl's tomb provides evidence that even at this late date Irish was still a living language in this area. As well as English and Latin epitaphs there are two Irish inscriptions. One translates as "Every seventh year a calamity befalls the Irish"; the second, "Now that the Earl has departed, it will occur every year". A slab in the main aisle marks the grave of Julia MacQuillan who insisted on being buried here so that even in death she would be humbled by the feet of passing worshippers.

From Ballyvoy a minor road leads to **Fair Head**, also known as Benmore. From its dizzy summit there are wonderful views over to Rathlin Island and the Scottish islands of Islay and the Paps of Jura, and the Mull of Kintyre, only 13 miles away but seeming much closer. Wild goats live among the rocks below the cliffs. On the top of the headland, Lough na Cranagh is a small lake with a beautiful *crannóg* - a man-made island built in the early Christian period.

CUSHENDUN
MAP 6 REF M3

27 miles N of Larne on the B92

A short detour off the A2 on the B92 leads to the striking little village of Cushendun, once a fashionable watering place and distinguished by its very un-Irish architecture. Most of the buildings were designed by Clough Williams-Ellis, better known for his fantasy village of Portmeirion in Wales. He was commissioned by Ronald McNeill, 1st (and last) Lord Cushendun, and his Cornish wife Maud to create a setting with a Cornish theme. So the houses, built between 1912 and 1925, are of rugged white-washed stone with roofs of slate. Williams-Ellis also designed Lord Cushendun's large neo-Georgian house, fronted by an odd 5-arch arcade, which is now a home for the elderly. The tiny village, (population about 70), is now owned by the National Trust which fussily preserves its pristine appearance.

The Poet Laureate John Masefield knew Cushenden well since he married a daughter of the Crommelin family. The Crommelins lived at Cave House (now a Catholic retreat), a substantial mansion which is set in an amphitheatre of cliffs and can only be reached by passing through a red sandstone cliff 60 feet long. To the west of the village, in Craigagh Wood, is a rock where clandestine Masses were said during the 18th century. The stone is carved with a crucifixion scene and is said to have been brought here from Iona. Nearby, the **Gloonan Stone** is indented with two hollows made, according to legend, by St Patrick when he knelt to pray here. *Glúna* is the Irish word for knees.

Cushendun lies at the head of **Glendun**, the wildest of the Antrim Glens and there's a marvellously scenic walk from the village up to waterfalls.

CUSHENDALL
MAP 6 REF M3

24 miles N of Larne on the A2

This delightful village with trim, colour-washed houses set along a spectacular shore lies at the point where 3 of the nine Glens of Antrim converge, hence its claim to be the "Capital of the Glens". In mid-August the Heart of the Glens Festival takes place here but at any time throughout the year the local pubs offer a good choice of dancing and traditional music. The village's most striking building is **Turnly's Tower** which dominates the main crossroads. It was built in 1809 by a nabob of the East India Company, Francis Turnly, as "a place of confinement for idlers and rioters". After serving as the town's lock-up for more than a century, it became a private dwelling and was inhabited until a few years ago.

Located in the heart of this picturesque coastal village, the **Thornlea Hotel** is an ideal base for touring this beautiful part of Ireland. The hotel is family run so visitors are assured of a warm and friendly welcome, and everything has been done to ensure your stay will be a comfortable and enjoyable experience. All 14 bedrooms are en suite and fully equipped and the whole hotel has been recently refurbished by its new owner, Vincent Jamison. The Thornlea's restaurant is well known for its quality food, especially the steaks and fresh salmon, served with locally grown fresh produce. Bar meals are available, as well as High Tea, A-la-Carte Dinner and Sunday lunch, and the hotel's comfortable lounge

Thornlea Hotel, 6 Coast Road, Cushendall, Co. Antrim BT44 0RU
Tel: 028 2177 1223 Fax: 028 2177 1362

provides a relaxing setting for an after-meal drink. Cushendall's extensive sandy beaches have made the village a popular holiday resort and there are facilities for many other activities: - golf, fishing, pony trekking, cycling, day trips to the bird sanctuary island of Rathlin and many scenic walks. From the village, a delightful cliff-top walk leads to the ruins of **Layde Old Church** which dates back to the 13th century and was the chief burial place of the MacDonnells whose gravestones still fill the churchyard. South of the village, **Ossian's Grave** is even older. This prehistoric court grave is named after the legendary poet Ossian whose supposedly ancient works were in fact the creation of an 18th century fraudster.

A long winding lane leads to **Garron View**, Josie McAuley's modern stone cast bungalow where she provides excellent bed & breakfast accommodation. The house is surrounded by large, well laid out gardens and enjoys splendid views across to Lurig and the Fairy Mountains at Tieverah. Josie named her house because of the fine view of Garron Point on the coast. There are 5 letting rooms (1 family room, 1 twin, and 3 doubles), 3 of which are en suite. All of the rooms share those wonderful vistas. Breakfast at Garron View is a very satisfying experience since Josie is a qualified cook and offers a good choice of breakfast menus. Cushendale itself is an attractive village with brightly colour-washed houses strung along the shoreline. Three of the 9 Glens of Antrim come to a head here which is why Cushendall hosts the popular Heart of the Glens festival in mid-August. The village pubs are lively all year with regular sessions of dancing and traditional music.

Garron View, 14 Cloghs Road, Cushendall, Co. Antrim BT44 0SP
Tel: 028 2177 1018

A mile or so south of Cushendall, the A43 strikes off into Glenariff, a broad and fertile valley flanked by steep mountain sides, a landscape described by William Thackeray as "Switzerland in miniature". About 5 miles along this road is **Glenariff Forest Park** which has several waymarked paths, including a Waterfall Trail leading to a series of spectacular waterfalls bearing evocative names such as *Ess na Larach*, (the Mare's Fall) and *Ess na Crub*, (the Fall of the Hooves). Some of them can be viewed from a timber walkway first erected more than a hundred years ago.

GLENARM   MAP 6 REF M3
12 miles N of Larne on the A2

This appealing little village is one of the oldest of the glen settlements, dating back to the 13th century. Its narrow main street, lined with colour-washed cottages, broadens out as it approaches the impressive gateway of **Glenarm Castle**. The castle, the home of the Earl of Antrim, is not open to the public but if you walk into Glenarm Forest (through the gateway) there's a good view of this curious building which has been likened by many to the Tower of London.

Continuing southwards from Glenarm, the A2 passes through Ballygally where the 17th century plantation castle is now a hotel, its dungeons converted into a welcoming bar, and on to nearby **Carnfunnock Country Park** whose attractions include a walled garden, a "time garden" with an interesting collection of sundials, a maze in the shape of Northern Ireland, a 9-hole golf course, craft shop, miniature railway and many beautiful walks.

LARNE   MAP 6 REF N4
18 miles N of Belfast on the A8

The 60-mile scenic stretch of the Antrim coast comes to an end at the busy industrial port of Larne which is the terminal for ferries to Stranraer and Cairnryan - the shortest sea crossings between Ireland and Scotland. On clear days, the Scottish coast is clearly visible from the promenade and from the Curran, a long gravel spit curving southwards from the town. **The Curran** is an archaeologist's dream. Many thousands of neolithic flint flakes, arrowheads and tools have been discovered here, providing evidence that this was one of the first parts of Ireland to be inhabited. At the southern tip of the Curran stand the ruins of **Olderfleet Castle**, originally a Viking foundation but rebuilt in stone during the 13th century. Its present setting is deeply unromantic, surrounded almost entirely by an industrial park. Perhaps the town's most striking building is the 95 feet high **Round Tower** that overlooks the harbour. Modelled on the lines of an ancient Irish round tower, it was erected in 1888 as a memorial to James Chaine, a County Antrim MP who was the driving force behind the establishment of shipping routes from Larne to Scotland and the Americas. Before his death, James carefully stipulated the manner of his burial. He was to be interred "in an upright position in a private enclosure overlooking the entrance to the lough, so that even in death he could still watch the passing ships". And so he was.

Conveniently located right beside the harbour, **Manor Guest House** is an imposing Victorian villa to which Miss J. A. Graham has been welcoming bed and breakfast guests for almost 40 years. Over the years her visitors have included nationals from every continent and of course the business traveller is always made welcome. The house was built in 1875 and once belonged to the Jacks family, prominent shippers who also owned the harbour. The spacious lounge has a deep bay window extending to some 42 square yards and the entire house is attractively decorated with classic tapestries and Miss Graham's collection of antique dolls. The house has 8 bedrooms, all en suite, one of which is a full Bridal Suite complete with 4-poster bed. An excellent "Ulster Fry" breakfast is included in the tariff and comes accompanied by Miss Graham's own home made bread. Outside, there's a pleasant garden and patio, and private, secure parking.

Manor Guest House, 23 Older Fleet Road,
The Harbour Highway, Larne,
Co. Antrim BT40 1AS
Tel: 028 2827 3305 Fax: 028 2826 0505

In Main Street, **Cellars** is a very distinctive building with a multi-coloured frontage and arched doorway. Built in 1840, the pub was originally a Manse House, a sturdily constructed building many of whose original features have been retained. Cellars central

Cellars, 15 Main Street, Larne, Co. Antrim BT40 1JQ
Tel: 028 2827 2861

location has made it a favourite meeting place in the town. Its popularity is enhanced by the atmospheric interior and by friendly and courteous staff who really do provide service with a smile. The landlord, Roy Craig, is an academic by profession, with degrees in Maths and History, but he finds the licensed trade more to his taste! He is also a local councillor with a wealth of knowledge about the town and its history as well as the attractions of the local area. Foremost amongst these are the famous Glens of Antrim which begin a few miles north of the town, running inland from spruce seaside villages to wild moorland and hills

CARRICKFERGUS
10 miles S of Larne on the A2

Map 6 ref N4

Carrick, a rock; *Fergus*, King of Dalriada: - the name of this seaside town derives from the misfortune of King Fergus when he was shipwrecked nearby during one of his frequent voyages between his Irish and Scottish possessions. The sea front area of the town is dominated by the massive bulk of **Carrickfergus Castle**, its lofty 4-storey tower perched on a rocky promontory above the busy port. Built around 1180 by the Anglo-Norman John de Courcy, the castle was in continual military use until 1928 and is extremely well-preserved. King John slept here in 1210; the French occupied it for a short while in 1760. It now houses the **Cavalry Regimental Museum** which displays an impressive array of weapons and armour. Costumed guides, life-size model figures and a video presentation provide a fascinating insight into the castle's various triumphs and disasters. Visitors can buy a joint ticket which also gives entry to the **Knight Ride** trip, Ireland's only themed

Carrickfergus Castle, Co. Antrim

mono-rail ride, which transports passengers through 1000 years of the town's colourful history, complete with all the appropriate sounds and smells.

American visitors, especially, will find the **Andrew Jackson Centre** of interest. The parents of the 7th President of the United States set sail from Carrickfergus in 1765 and the reconstructed traditional thatched farmhouse here contains exhibits on President Jackson's life and career, his Ulster relations and rural Ulster life. Located within the gardens of the Andrew Jackson Centre, the **US Ranger Centre** tells the story of this elite combat unit whose first unit was formed at Carrickfergus in June 1942. The exhibition material has been donated by Ranger veterans and includes uniforms, vintage radio equipment, documents and photographs.

IN AND AROUND ANTRIM TOWN

Antrim Town is set a little way back from the shores of Lough Neagh, the largest stretch of inland water in the British Isles, 17 miles long and 11 miles wide. The lough is famous for its eels which spawn in the Sargasso Sea, take 3 years to swim across the Atlantic and then wriggle their way up the River Bann during the spring. Some 20 million of them make the transatlantic crossing each year but nowadays as many as possible are caught at Coleraine and transported to Lough Neagh by tankers. Once released into the lough's waters, it takes another 12 years for the eels to fully mature. They are then harvested and treated at the main fishery at Toomebridge, where the River Bann enters the lough. Visitors are welcome at this friendly co-operative managed by local fishermen and farmers.

ANTRIM
MAP 6 REF M4
15 miles NW of Belfast on the A6

Antrim is a prosperous town whose population has rocketed over the last 20 years, with new housing and shopping developments swamping its ancient core of which little now remains. A remarkable survivor is the 9th century **Round Tower**, (just north of the town centre), which is in almost perfect condition. Of Antrim Castle, built in 1662 for Viscount Massereene and Ferrard, only a mutilated tower still stands following a disastrous fire in 1922. But the lovely **Antrim Castle Gardens** surrounding the castle are well worth a visit. They have been carefully restored to the original patterns created by the distinguished French landscape gardener, André Le Nôtre (1613-70), designer of the excruciatingly formal gardens at Versailles. The original design for Antrim Castle Gardens was also pure geometry: a rigid pattern of circular parterres, radial paths and ruler-straight avenues. Fortunately, nature always wins. Overarching trees now soften the harsh lines of Le Nôtre's grid-like view of what a garden should be. Antrim Castle's former carriage house and stable block has also been renovated and is now home to the **Clotworthy Art Centre**, a theatre and art gallery which hosts exhibitions of the work of both local and international artists.

On the Randalstown Road, **Shanes Castle** is the family seat of the O'Neills of Clandeboy. The demesne is regarded as one of the most beautiful and well-maintained in Ireland with a rich variety of fauna, flora, insect and bird life, along with a herd of feral deer. The Castle itself has been in ruins since a fire in 1816 but the peaceful setting, the striking remains and the unique Camellia House make it well worth a visit.

Antrim also boasts an 18-hole golf course on the lake shore, excellent trout fishing, a large indoor sports complex with 2 swimming pools, and there are pleasure boat cruises on Lough Neagh departing from the Six Mile Water marina.

BALLYMENA
MAP 6 REF M4
10 miles N of Antrim on the A26

Set at the heart of a prosperous farming region, Ballymena was mostly settled during the 17th century with incomers from southwest Scotland and the lowland accent and intonation is still very evident. A thriving linen industry formed the basis of the town's steady development, greatly aided by the arrival of Huguenot weavers in the 1680s. There's a lively major market every Saturday but for the rest of the week the blackstone basalt buildings and austere-looking churches make Ballymena seem a rather dour place. Better to travel a few miles east to one of Ireland's most evocative Christian sites, **Slemish Mountain**. It was on the slopes of this extinct volcano that St Patrick herded swine. As a child, he had been captured on the coast of Britain by pirates and brought here where he worked as a slave for 6 years for the local chieftain, Miluic, before making his escape. Slemish is a place of pilgrimage on St Patrick's Day, 17 March, when many thousands of the devout make the steep climb to the summit. If you join them, even if you are not a believer, it's difficult not to succumb to the feeling that there is a truly mystical presence here.

PORTGLENONE
MAP 6 REF L4

10 miles W of Ballymena on the A42

For many years, right up to the mid-18th century, the bridge at Portglenone was the only crossing of the 35-mile-long River Bann apart from Coleraine near the estuary. Originally, it was a drawbridge which would be lifted at night to protect the village from the "tories", or outlaws, infesting the forests on the opposite bank. Canadian visitors may well be interested in the plaque at 48 Main Street, facing the attractive market square. It was in this shop that Timothy Eaton learnt the drapery business during the years 1847-52, working 16 hours a day and sleeping under the counter. He emigrated to Toronto where he made a fortune in retailing.

GLARRYFORD
MAP 6 REF L3

7 miles NW of Ballymena on the A26

The Four Winds is the farmhouse for a mixed working farm which offers home-from-home bed & breakfast accommodation in a convenient location. It's on the A26 with the Giant's Causeway and the Antrim coast within easy reach to the north, Belfast and its airport about the same distance to the south. The modern building has been recently

The Four Winds, 146 Crankill Road, Glarryford, Ballymena, Co. Antrim BT44 9HA
Tel: 028 2568 5360 Mobile: 07803 191436

refurbished and now provides 3 letting rooms, (2 family and 1 double, all with hot and cold). All the rooms are very spacious and have a distinct "farmhouse" appearance. The Four Winds also has a lounge available with television and tea/coffee-making facilities. From the lounge, there are good views of Antrim's famous Slemish Mountain, an extinct volcano which is said to be the place where St Patrick worked as a swineherd after being brought to Ireland as a slave. The Four Winds' proprietor Dorothy Hanna serves her guests a full breakfast menu and packed lunches are also available. Dogs are welcome by prior arrangement and are accommodated in the farm outbuildings.

LISBURN
Map 6 REF M5

10 miles SW of Belfast off the M1

Located in the southern tip of County Antrim, Lisburn was once an important linen town, flourishing under the leadership of the Huguenot Louis Crommelin in the late 17th century. The history of that industry is vividly presented at the **Irish Linen Centre & Museum**, housed in the 18th century Assembly Rooms in the Market Square. Visitors can try their hand at scutching or spinning or watch the only hand loom linen weavers at work in Ireland today in the purpose-built workshop, purchase samples in the craft shop or enjoy refreshments at the café in the modern annex where there are art displays and lunchtime recitals.

Virtually all of Lisburn's older buildings were destroyed by a catastrophic fire in 1707 which, along with most of the town, also laid waste to its 17th century castle. **The Cathedral** was so badly damaged it had to be rebuilt. Only the size of a parish church, the Cathedral contains some interesting tablets and monuments, and the tiny graveyard is the last resting place of Louis Crommelin who brought such prosperity to the town.

Devotees of real ale will want to pay a visit to the **Hilden Brewery**, about a mile outside Lisburn in the village of Hilden. Established in 1981, it's one of only two real ale breweries in Ireland and is housed in the courtyard of a 19th mansion that once belonged to the Barbours, one of Lisburn's greatest linen manufacturing families. Visitors can watch (and smell) the aromatic process, browse through the historical exhibition and refresh themselves in the Tap Room Restaurant.

Just to the south of Lisburn is a much less enticing location - the Long Kesh prison, notorious for its H-block cells, hunger strikes and "dirty protests" by prisoners, and the murder in 1998 of the LVF leader Billy Wright by the INLA that sparked off a wave of retaliatory killings across the north. The prison can be clearly seen from the M1 motorway.

LOWER BALLINDERRY
Map 6 REF M5

9 miles NW of Lisburn on the A26

For top quality bed and breakfast accommodation, **Oakfield Guest House** is hard to beat. This large, modernised farmhouse is surrounded by well-presented gardens, with plenty of parking space, and has 4 guest bedrooms, all en suite. The interior of the house has been completely refurbished and many features introduced which make Oakfield particularly convenient for the disabled. There's easy wheelchair access and a downstairs room is provided with a disabled shower facility. Another recent addition is a downstairs kitchen available for the use of guests who wish to prepare their own food. Rosslyn Faloon, who owns and runs Oakfield with her son John, is happy to provide evening meals and packed lunches on request and, of course, also provides a full Irish breakfast.

**Oakfield Guest House, 9 Crumlin Road, Lower Ballinderry, Lisburn,
Co. Antrim BT28 2JU Tel: 028 9265 1307**

John Faloon is a gifted painter whose striking portraits are for sale and you can even commission him to paint your very own portrait as an unforgettable souvenir of your stay at Oakfield.

COUNTY LONDONDERRY

County Londonderry, or Derry as it is also commonly known, is a beautiful and compact area with a rich and varied scenery. To the south, the Sperrin Mountains sprawl across into County Tyrone with their highest point, Sawel (2240 feet), right on the county border. To the north lies the Atlantic coast, lined with magnificent beaches of surf-washed sand and popular resorts such as Portstewart and Castlerock. Inland lies an inviting landscape of scenic hills, glens and river valleys. These well-wooded acres are the result of the "plantations" of the early 1600s when English Protestant colonists were granted huge tracts of land by James I. The story of that crucial episode in Ulster's history from which so much good and bad has flowed is told in the Plantation of Ulster Visitor Centre at Draperstown. Much of the interest in the area centres on the ancient and historic city of Derry which stands on a commanding site overlooking a broad curve of the River Foyle and is where we begin our tour of the county.

LONDONDERRY   Map 5 ref J3
46 miles NW of Antrim on the A6

In the year 546AD a virulent plague devastated the people of Donegal. Amongst those who fled across the River Foyle into what is now Londonderry was a charismatic monk named Colmcille, better known as St Columba. On a mound surrounded by oak trees, *"doire"*, he established a monastery whose wealth and importance steadily grew over the years, reaching its peak in the 12ᵗʰ and 13ᵗʰ centuries.

Throughout the late Middle Ages the town declined. Elizabeth I tried to establish English rule in Ulster by means of a brutal military campaign which destroyed most of Derry's medieval buildings. It was her successor, James I, who in 1609 granted Derry to the Irish Society of London "for the promotion of religion, order and industry". Along with other English and Scottish Protestant settlers, this energetic body rebuilt the city, laying it out according to the best contemporary principles of town planning, and creating a street plan which has survived almost intact to the present day. They surrounded their new town with walls 25 feet high and 28 feet thick - an impregnable defence which has never been breached. Derry was the last walled city built in Ireland and the only city on the island whose ancient walls survive complete. There are walkways along the 1 mile circuit of the walls which offer some grand views of the city and the River Foyle.

The settlers also built **St Columb's Cathedral** (1633), the first post-Reformation cathedral to be built in Britain. An example of the style known as Planters' Gothic, the cathedral is one of the most important 17ᵗʰ century buildings in the country. This peaceful period of reconstruction and progress was soon shattered. Derry was besieged during the rebellion of 1641, again during the Cromwellian wars and, most significantly for Ulster's subsequent history, in 1689. On this occasion it was the deposed James II who attacked the city. As his troops approached, 13 apprentice boys rushed to the city gates and secured them. During the 135-day siege that followed, the people of Derry were reduced to eating rats, dogs and the starch used for laundering linen. Almost one quarter of the inhabitants perished, a death toll which is commemorated in the skeleton emblazoned on the city's coat-of-arms. Despite their plight, Derry's citizens defiantly proclaimed their policy of "No Surrender", and to this day repeat that slogan during the controversial "Apprentice Boys Marches" through the town that take place each year on 12 August, the day on which troops supporting William of Orange (William III) finally relieved the town. Following William's victory, the 18ᵗʰ and 19ᵗʰ centuries provided an era of comparative prosperity. Now the second largest town in Ulster, Derry offers a wide range of visitor attractions. The **Tower Museum**, which has won awards for both Best Museum in Ireland and Britain, contains a comprehensive display outlining the turbulent development of the city from geological times to the present day; the **Foyle Valley Railway Centre** features a narrow gauge (3 feet) railway with working models and a 1934 diesel railcar on a 2-mile track along the river valley; and the **Harbour Museum** which includes a replica of the 30 feet long curragh in which St Columba sailed to Iona. Also worth a visit is the **Derry Craft Village** in Shipquay Street, a re-created traditional stone village where you'll find a range of traditional craft shops and the stylish Boston Tea Party tea room.

In addition to St Columb's Cathedral, Derry's other buildings of interest include the **Courthouse** of 1813, which is a fine example of Greek Revival architecture; the neo-Gothic Victorian **Guildhall** containing some excellent stained-glass windows depicting the history of Derry and, in a very different vein, **the Free Derry Mural** in the Bogside, a much photographed and repainted emblem of Catholic resistance.

A mile or so outside Derry, the **Ear hart Centre & Wildlife Sanctuary** commemorates Amble Ear hart, the first woman to fly the Atlantic solo in 1932. A sculpture marks the spot in the field where the intrepid American aviator landed after her 13¼ hour flight.

LIMAVADY
15 miles NE of Londonderry on the A2

MAP 6 REF K3

Founded in the early 1600s by an enterprising Welshman, Thomas Phillips, Limavady enjoys a lovely situation in the Roe Valley, surrounded by mountain scenery to the north and southeast. This bustling market town has expanded greatly over recent years but some attractive features of the past have survived. An elegant 6-arch bridge of 1700 spans the River Roe and the Main Street leading to it has some decorous Georgian buildings. One of them, No. 51, was the home of Jane Ross who in 1851 heard a passing itinerant fiddler playing a magically wistful tune. She noted it down and the old folk melody has endured as the *Londonderry Air,* ("Danny Boy"). Jane Ross and her 3 younger sisters, all unmarried, are buried across the road at the 18th century parish church which is notable for its collection of several hundred tapestry kneelers, each one different. A few years before Jane Ross recorded Ireland's most famous tune for posterity, W.M. Thackeray had stopped for ale at an inn in Main Street and was swiftly beguiled by the barmaid's bright eyes. His popular poem *Sweet Peg of Limavady* was the result. The town's most famous son, (in New Zealand at least), was William Massey, Prime Minister of that country from 1912 to 1925. A plaque in Irish Green Street records his birth there in 1856.

A couple of miles south of the town, the **Roe Valley Country Park** is a scenic gem, 3 miles of wooded gorges and floodplain meadows. Ireland's first hydro-electric power station, opened in 1896, is located within the park with much of the original equipment still intact. There's also a small weaving centre and a visitor centre.

Set in farm land overlooking Keady Hill, **Keady View Farm** is a bright, modern house with an elegant, airy conservatory. Sandra and Murray Carmichael have been welcoming

Keady View Farm, 47 Seacoast Road, Limavady, Co. Londonderry BT49 9DW
Tel: 028 7776 4518   Fax: 028 7776 4518
e-mail: sandra.carmichael@tibus.com or keadyview-farm@tibus.com

guests for bed and breakfast here since April 1998 and have two family rooms available plus a single which can sleep two people. The rooms are stylishly furnished and well-equipped. Breakfast is served in the conservatory which looks out onto the large gardens and across to Keady Hill. Guests have the use of the TV lounge and Sandra will provide evening meals if required, packed lunches too. Keady View is on the B69 sea coast road and within easy reach of Limavady, Londonderry and Coleraine. If you enjoy an active holiday, there's a golf course just a couple of miles away, fishing for brown and rainbow trout at Binevenagh Mountain, and sea fishing at Downhill, about 6 miles distant. Also close by, at Bellarena, the Ulster Gliding Club offers full facilities for experienced gliders and trial flights for newcomers. All in all, an ideal base from which to tour west Ireland.

DOWNHILL
10 miles NE of Limavady on the A2

MAP 6 REF K2

One of the most photographed sights in Ireland is **Mussenden Temple** (National Trust) perched on eroding cliffs above the 6-mile-long Magilligan Strand. Modelled on the temples of Vesta at Rome and Tivoli, the elegant domed structure was built in 1783 as a "summer library" by the eccentric Frederick Augustus Hervey, Anglican Bishop of Derry

Mussenden Temple, Downhill, Co. Londonderry

and 4th Earl of Bristol. An unorthodox cleric, he once organised a curates' race along the sands at Downhill, the winners being rewarded with benefices in his diocese. He was also unconventional for his time in his tolerance of Catholics, permitting a weekly Mass in the Temple since there was no local Catholic church. A great traveller and art collector, the Earl-Bishop's progress around the Continent can still be detected by the number of hostelries that re-named themselves the "Hotel Bristol" following a visit by the free-spending English milord. The Temple was originally just a landscape adornment for the Bishop's **Downhill Palace**, a grandiose mansion last occupied by US troops during World War II and now in ruins.

COLERAINE
13 miles NE of Limavady on the A37
MAP 6 REF L2

The county's second largest town after Derry, Coleraine developed around the banks of the River Bann and this area remains the most attractive part of an otherwise unremarkable town. The river splashes noisily over a picturesque weir, whitewashed lock-keepers' cottages maintain watch over the locks upstream at The Cutts, and downstream there's a large and thriving boating marina. Apart from a handsome Town Hall, most of Coleraine's buildings are severely functional but, with the campus of the University of Ulster located here, the town is always lively in term time. About a mile south of the town, **Mountsandel** claims to be the earliest known inhabited place in Ireland. There's not a great deal to see at this 200 feet high oval mound overlooking the river but the post holes and hearths of wooden dwellings are estimated to be 9000 years old.

CASTLEROCK
5 miles NW of Coleraine off the A2
MAP 6 REF K2

This pretty seaside resort is noted for its fine sandy beach that runs for about a mile westwards from the mouth of the River Bann. An open air heated swimming pool by the beach, a championship 18-hole golf course and good sea and river fishing all add to the appeal. About a mile south of the village, **Hezlett House** (National Trust) is a single storey, 17th century thatched rectory with an unusual cruck-truss roof construction. This was a pioneering method of building which involved balancing curved timbers (crucks) in pairs to form a series of arches and building the house around this frame. Smothered in Virginia creeper, the house is now furnished in late Victorian style and has a small display of vintage farm implements.

PORTSTEWART
4 miles N of Coleraine on the A2
MAP 6 REF L2

Two miles of magnificent strand sheltered by rocky headlands, (now protected by the National Trust), attracted Victorian holidaymakers to Portstewart; a century later windsurfers flock here to ride the great breakers which crash down on the long sandy beach firm enough to drive a car along. There's a breezy cliff-side walk which passes trim Victorian villas and an imposing Gothic mansion, now a Dominican nunnery and college.

Portstewart has always had a rather more genteel atmosphere than its twin resort, Portrush, just across the border in County Antrim. Portstewart's Victorian town fathers, for example, insisted that the railway station should be located a good mile from the town centre to discourage the influx of the less desirable class of tourist. It's a much more welcoming place nowadays, offering a choice of two 18-hole golf courses, two 9-hole courses, good bathing, tennis, boating and sea fishing.

The Edgewater Hotel, 88 Strand Road, Portstewart, Co. Londonderry BT55 7LZ
Tel: 028 7083 3314 Fax: 028 7038 3224 e-mail: edgewater.hotel@virgin.net
website: http://freespace.virgin.net/edgewater.hotel/index.htm

Overlooking the Strand Beach, the **Edgewater Hotel** commands grand views of the Donegal Hills, the Atlantic and, on a clear day, southern Scotland. The Edgewater was purpose-built in the 1920s as a guest house and the O'Malley family arrived here in the 1970s. Over the years, they have made many alterations and additions, constantly upgrading the hotel's comfort and amenities. Family-run, the Edgewater is also family-friendly, offering a superb children's menu for example. A wide choice of food is available here, ranging from bar snacks to full meals in the spacious restaurant. The stylishly-furnished Lounge Bar has the additional attraction of looking out across those magnificent views. The Edgewater has 28 letting rooms, all of them en suite, some of them family suites with their own lounges. Anglers will feel at home here since the hotel is the headquarters for the Northern Ireland Sea Anglers' Association, and golfers will find a good choice of courses all within easy reach. But you may well not want to stray far from this pleasing little town and its excellent sandy beach.

Located on the outskirts of the town, **The York** is an attractive building with something of a continental air about it. The York's bars and restaurant overlook the sea, adding to the pleasure of sampling the excellent food on offer. The hotel is owned and run by Richard and Harold Pollock. Richard is the master chef whose first class food and extensive menu has earned The York an enviable reputation for fine dining, with anything from fresh lobster to international dishes amongst the choices. Richard and Harold bought The York in 1997 and have made many improvements, all designed to add to their guests' comfort and enjoyment. They offer an interesting mix of luxury, self-catering apartments, each with 2 bedrooms, a comfortable lounge, and fully equipped kitchen and

The York, 2 Station Road, Portstewart, Co. Londonderry
Tel: 028 7083 3594

bathroom. The York is an ideal base for families, with miles of sandy beaches nearby; the world famous Royal Portrush Golf Club also close at hand; and many other attractions also within easy reach.

A mile or so to the west of Portstewart, **Caralbanagh House** stands in splendid isolation on a hill overlooking Portstewart and Donegal Bay. It's an imposing building with a Roman-style entrance porch and surrounded by a large, lovingly-tended garden

Caralbanagh House, 192 Coleraine Road, Portstewart, Co. Londonderry BT55 7PL
Tel: 028 7083 6294

with its own pond. Caralbanagh is the home of Irene and Shawn Moore, a young couple who have been offering quality bed and breakfast accommodation since 1996. There's a spacious dining room where, in addition to a hearty Irish breakfast, evening meals are available on request. The Moores serve a good selection of home cooking and will also provide a packed lunch if you wish. Caralbanagh has 6 rooms to let, including 1 family room, all of them en suite. The clean, modern interiors are fresh and attractive and the Moores are adept at making guests feel welcome. The house is also equipped with conference facilities for groups of up to 14. If you are touring the area, Caralbanagh is close to two of Northern Ireland's premier attractions: historic Dunluce Castle and the extraordinary Giant's Causeway are both just a few miles away.

AGHADOWEY
MAP 6 REF L3

7 miles S of Coleraine on the B66

This small riverside village lies close to the County Antrim border, conveniently located for exploring both the Causeway Coast and the **Sperrin Mountains**. It's a wonderfully peaceful place for holidaymakers with plenty of activities and attractions within easy reach and some welcoming places with excellent amenities to stay at.

For example, whether you want a drink, a meal, accommodation or a round of golf, the **Brown Trout Golf & Country Club** is well-equipped to provide any or all of them. "Let your hair down, blow away the cobwebs, put your feet up, have some craic" advise the O'Haras whose family has lived here since at least 1817. Accommodation at the Brown Trout is based on the American motel style with modern, easy access rooms. They were the first self-catering rooms to receive a 5-star rating from the Northern Ireland Tourist Board. The Brown Trout's bar offers fresh and exciting food - anything from home made crab chowder to home baked pies. In the restaurant, the focus of the extensive menu is

Brown Trout Golf & Country Club, 209 Agivey Road, Aghadowey,
Co. Londonderry BT51 4AD   Tel: 028 7086 8209

again on excellent home cooking. In addition to the 9-hole golf course which crosses water 7 times, the Brown Trout also has a fully equipped gym, conference facilities for groups of up to 50, and the O'Haras will also happily arrange activities such as horse-riding or game fishing.

Offering bed and breakfast accommodation in rather special surroundings, **Bellevue Country House** is a dignified Georgian-style building of 1840, a listed country house set in 20 acres of farm and woodland and enjoying magnificent views of the north Antrim hills. Bellevue is the home of Elizabeth and Hugo Morrison who have 3 spacious and comfortable letting rooms, all en suite and provided with a radio/clock alarm, hairdryer, tea/coffee-making facilities and television. The relaxing residents' lounge also has television and there's a handy payphone in the hall. Elizabeth is a qualified chef and cooks a

Bellevue Country House, 43 Greenhill Road, Aghadowey, Coleraine,
Co. Londonderry BT51 4EU Tel: 028 7086 8797

good selection of Irish and other dishes. Evening meals are available on request, as are packed lunches. Children are welcome and there are discounts for OAPs. Interestingly, part of the house is powered by a hydro-electric system Hugo has installed in the old mill that stands in the grounds.

KILLYKERGAN   MAP 6 REF L3
7 miles S of Coleraine on the A29

Farmhouse B & Bs seem to have a special appeal all their own and that's certainly true of **Heathfield Farm**, a 17th century stone building set amidst some of Northern Ireland's most charming countryside. Heather Torrens and her husband have been welcoming guests to their relaxed and friendly home since 1988 and their high standards of accommodation and food have brought them a Regional Winner award from the Ulster Tourist

Heathfield Farm, 31 Drumcroone Road, Killykergan, Garvagh, Coleraine, Co. Londonderry BT51 4EB Tel/Fax: 028 2955 8245

Development Association. They are also Ulster winners of an AIB Agri-Tourism Award. Heather is famous for her home cooking - delicious breakfasts served with freshly baked bread, home made marmalade and jams, yoghurts and fresh fruit. Evening meals are available by arrangement - you are welcome to bring your own wine, or you can sample one of the local pubs or restaurants. Heathfield has 3 letting rooms, all en suite and enjoying lovely country views. Guests have the choice of 2 lounges, one non-smoking, and are welcome to relax in the large gardens or stroll around the farm. Heather is a keen golfer, a former club captain, and will be happy to arrange bookings at local courses. If your preference is angling, the nearby River Agivey provides some of the best fishing in the area. Heathfield Farm is an ideal base for exploring the Antrim coast, Derry and Donegal, and of course, the Giant's Causeway.

MAGHERA   Map 6 ref L4
22 miles S of Coleraine on the A29

Pleasantly located at the eastern end of the Sperrin Mountains, the little town of Maghera was once an important ecclesiastical centre, the seat of a bishop. **Maghera Old Church** stands on the site of a 6th century monastery founded by St Lurach. Its fine 12th century west door is decorated with animal and floral designs crowned by a massive lintel carved with a crucifixion scene. The tower, dating back to the 1600s, conveniently provided the priest with a first floor apartment over the shop. Westwards from the town, a scenic route traverses the Glenshane Pass through the Sperrins to Londonderry.

MAGHERAFELT   Map 6 ref L4
27 miles S of Coleraine on the A31

Magherafelt is one of several plantation towns in the area, its spacious and orderly layout created by the Salters' Company of London to whom James I had granted the land. The town provides a convenient angling centre for the Moyola River and there are pleasant drives along the shore of nearby Lough Neagh.

In the bustling little town it-self, **The Dry Dock** pub in Rainey Street, with its bow-windowed upper storey, suggests the bridge of a ship and when you step inside the resemblance is even stronger. This is the Admiral's Room and is modelled on the design of an Officer's Mess as it would have looked in a ship of the line around the time of Admiral Nelson. Lots of rope and port-hole windows add to the nautical character of the room and there's a similar atmosphere in the downstairs bar. Sandra Hawe took over this unusual property in early 1999 and with its town centre location, about 100 yards from the market place, The Dry Dock has become a popular venue with both locals and visitors alike. The pub has its own football team and the local

The Dry Dock, 34-36 Rainey Street, Magherafelt, Co. Londonderry, BT45 5AQ Tel: 028 7963 4129

golf society has made The Dry Dock its meeting place. Food is not normally available but the Admiral's Room can be booked for private functions and conferences (for up to 20 people) and on these occasions catering can be provided.

A popular excursion from Magherafelt is a visit to **Springhill** (National Trust), about 5 miles south. This 17th century whitewashed manor house contains family furniture, paintings, ornaments and curios. An important costume collection is housed in part of the extensive outbuildings which also include a fortified barn also dating from the 17th century and two barns in the Dutch style. There are secluded walled gardens and woodland walks.

DRAPERSTOWN   MAP 6 REF K4
11 miles N of Cookstown on the B41

Draperstown is another of County Derry's plantation villages created, as the name indicates, by the London Company of Drapers. So it's an appropriate location for the **Plantation of Ulster Visitors Centre** where audio-visual technology and computer enhanced images tell the story of James I's attempt to "Anglicize" Ulster by granting huge estates to English and Scottish settlers. The Centre also has displays on Hugh O'Neill and the fateful "Flight of the Earls" in 1607 when Ulster's lords abandoned their homeland.

FEENY
MAP 6 REF K3
15 miles SE of Londonderry on minor road off the A6

The Feeny area, meaning "wooded place", lies in the foothills and valleys of the North Sperrins range, surrounded by some splendid scenery and many sites of archaeological and historical interest. Standing stones, stone circles, a chambered grave, raths (circular earthern defences) and a prehistoric sweathouse are just some of the ancient remains scattered around the area. **Banagher Glen National Nature Reserve**, about 2 miles southwest of Feeny, contains ancient oak woodland of national importance and is one of the last remaining semi-natural woodlands in Northern Ireland. To the northeast are the quietly impressive ruins of **Banagher Old Church**, founded around 1100 by a local saint named Muiredach O'Heney. The saint is buried in a well-preserved mortuary in the churchyard. His tomb stands on a sandhill and if you grasp a handful of the sand from beneath his grave into your possession you will be granted the power to bring luck to yourselves and others.

Half a mile east of Feeny village, the outstanding **Drumcovitt House & Barn** offers a choice of top quality bed & breakfast or self-catering accommodation in idyllic surroundings. The house was built more than 300 years ago on a commanding site between the valleys of the Rivers Roe and Faughan. In 1796, a round-ended Georgian front was added to the house providing two extra reception rooms with two bedrooms over. These rooms enjoy magnificent views down a wooded valley and along the tiny glen to Mullaghmeash. Many of the windowpanes and all the shutters are original, as are the wide Georgian door and its elegant fanlight. This handsome, ivy-clad house has 3 guest bedrooms, two of them benefitting from those grand views. None of the bedrooms is en

Drumcovitt House & Barn, 704 Feeny Road, Feeny, Co. Londonderry BT47 4SU
Tel/Fax: 028 7778 1224 e-mail: drumcovitt.feeny@btinternet.com
website: www.touristnetuk.com/NI/drumcovitt/index.htm

suite, but there are however 2 modern showers, one of which is over a bath. The grounds at Drumcovitt are as inviting as the house. The beech trees in the garden, on the farm, and on the neighbouring farm estate were planted in 1815 to celebrate the victory at Waterloo. These and other mature trees provide an excellent habitat for birds, bats and butterflies.

If your preference is for self-catering, Drumcovitt Barn has been skilfully converted into 3 cottages, each comprehensively equipped and furnished to 4-star standard. In 1998, the complex was a winner of the Ulster Agri Tourism Award. Foyle Cottage sleeps 5, has wheelchair access to the open plan kitchen/diner/sitting room and a ground floor twin-bedded room. Faughan Cottage and Roe Loft both sleep four and are similarly well-equipped, even providing lap-top friendly sockets and direct dial telephones.

If you enjoy hill-walking, time your visit for early August when the Sperrins Hillwalking Festival offers the opportunity of exploring this lovely corner of the country, rich in prehistoric sites, with the help of experienced guides.

DUNGIVEN   MAP 6 REF K3
15 miles SE of Londonderry on the A6

This small market town set beside the River Roe is notable for the ruins of the 12th century **Dungiven Priory**, set on a bluff above the river just south of the town. The shattered remains of the once rich and powerful monastery contain the finest medieval tomb in Ireland. Cooey Na Gall O'Cahan, Chief of the O'Cahan clan, died in 1385. His stone effigy lies under an elaborately traceried canopy; beneath it, in niches sculpted into the sarcophagus, stand six warriors in kilts representing the Scots mercenaries from whom Cooey earned his nickname *Na Gall*, "of the foreigners". It's almost 300 years since the Priory was last in use but it remains something of a shrine for those seeking a cure for illness or disability. An ancient tree within its precincts flutters with votive offerings - handkerchiefs, dresses, even socks.

9 County Down and County Armagh

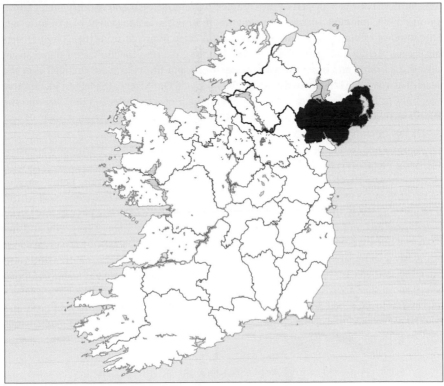

COUNTY DOWN

With farmlands that are among the most fertile in Ireland, more than 200 miles of attractive coastline, the magical Mountains of Mourne and a wealth of interesting historical buildings, Down is indeed a favoured county. The sheltered waters of Strangford Lough are popular with sailing enthusiasts, and for sea anglers there is prime sea-fishing off Ardglass and Portavogie. The county is also rich in prehistoric monuments, with cairns, standing stones and dolmens dating from around 3000BC scattered around Strangford Lough and the Lecale district. As if that weren't enough, the county also claims to have the driest and sunniest climate in Ireland. The area has strong connections with St Patrick who made his final landing on the shore of Strangford Lough in 442AD and is believed to be buried at Downpatrick - at least according to the people of Co. Down but their claim is hotly disputed by Armagh.

HOLYWOOD
4 miles NE of Belfast on the A2

MAP 6 REF N5

This small residential town beside Belfast Lough has some fine sandy beaches and a lovely coastal walk that runs eastwards for 15 miles to Helen's Bay. The major visitor attraction here is the **Ulster Folk & Transport Museum** which ranks among the best museums in the country. The open air part of the complex represents town and country life in Ulster around 1910, complete with a farm using the methods and equipment of a bygone age. The 30-odd buildings are all authentic, painstakingly removed from their original sites throughout Ulster and re-erected here. The indoor galleries show how food preparation, clothing, farming and other everyday occupations and lifestyles have changed over the years. The road and railway transport exhibits include Old Maeve, the largest locomotive ever built in Ireland; a unique collection of vintage motor vehicles and bicycles; and the Titanic Exhibition, a tribute to Belfast's shipbuilding heyday. The museum is open all year round but opening times vary.

Approached by a long driveway lined with rare species of trees, **Carnwood House** is a striking Victorian residence built around 1845 and framed by picturesque gardens with views over woodland. The house enjoys a tranquil environment despite being conveniently located for Belfast and the local City Airport, with the village of Holywood within walking distance. Jenny Foster and her family have lived here for some 11 years and began welcoming bed and breakfast guests in 1996. The house was named by Jenny and her husband since she hails from *Carn*lough, her husband from Holy*wood*. Their spacious home has a warm, cosy family atmosphere, very welcoming and relaxing. In addition to the guest lounge with its lovely garden views, Carnwood House also has a well-equipped games room. The 4 stylishly decorated bedrooms include the Country Suite which boasts a splendid 4-poster bed and all the rooms are en suite with television, trouser press and

**Carnwood House, 85 Victoria Road, Holywood, Co. Down BT18 9BG
Tel/Fax: 028 9042 1745**

tea/coffee-making facilities provided. Jenny is happy to provide packed lunches and also an evening meal if required. This is strongly recommended since Jenny bakes her own bread and cakes and uses only home produce in her cooking.

BANGOR
12 miles E of Belfast on the A2

MAP 6 REF N5

Bangor's attractive Victorian and Edwardian architecture reflects its popularity as a seaside resort during those eras. The town still attracts many day visitors from Belfast and is well provided with all the usual amusements as well as offering some splendid Victorian parks. One of these, **Ward Park**, has two large ponds supporting a range of wildfowl and a resident flock of barnacle geese. Bangor has a weekly open air market, plenty of pubs and eating places, and some good beaches, the best of which is **Ballyholme Bay**.

Of Bangor's once important and influential abbey, founded by St Comgall in 586AD, nothing remains and the oldest building in the town is the fine **Old Custom House** and Tower of 1687 which stands on the seafront and now houses the tourist office.

Within walking distance of the town centre and harbour, **Tara Guest House** offers comfortable bed & breakfast accommodation in a convenient location with all the town's amenities within easy reach. The Tara's owner, Bill Spence, has been in the business since 1991 and knows how to make sure that his guests are well looked after and feel at home. At the Tara, Bill says, "Just kick off your shoes and relax!" The Tara has 10 comfortable guest bedrooms, all of them en suite and all furnished to a high standard. An evening meal is available with a choice that includes a children's menu and vegetarian options,

Tara Guest House, 51 Princetown Road, Bangor, Co. Down BT20 3TA
Tel: 028 9146 8924   Fax: 028 9145 8820   Mobile: 07850 422067

and packed lunches can be supplied if required. Bill knows the town well and can direct you to all the local facilities and attractions. Boating, yachting, sea angling and golf are popular activities here and there are regular boat trips from the harbour to destinations such as Copeland Island and the National Trust property, Lighthouse Island.

Bangor Castle, now the Town Hall, is actually a Victorian mansion built in 1852. Its former outbuildings house the **North Down Heritage Centre** (free), which has some striking displays highlighting the archaeology, early-Christian history and natural history of the area and is enhanced by audio-visual presentations and sound effects tapes. Prize exhibits include the Ballycroghan Swords, dating from 500BC and a 9th century handbell found near Bangor. Uniquely for a local museum, there's also a Jordan Room with a fine collection of Far Eastern wares. The centre also has a rather superior restaurant which is used at times for evening events such as musical recitals and other arts performances.

NEWTOWNARDS
MAP 6 REF N5
9 miles E of Belfast on the A20

A busy manufacturing town, Newtownards stands near the northern tip of Strangford Lough and although the town was founded in 1244 the only ancient remains are those of a ruined Dominican priory which has some striking pillars and semi-circular arches. The most impressive building in Newtownards is the former **market house** of 1765, now the town hall and arts centre, which faces onto the spacious square which is filled with market stalls each Saturday.

About 2 miles outside Newtownards, a turning off a country lane becomes the tree-lined driveway to **Rockhaven**. This beautifully-designed modern house is the home of Jennifer Lindsay and her family, and it's also a very special place to stay for bed and

Rockhaven, 79 Mountain Road, Newtownards, Co. Down BT23 4UL
Tel: 028 9182 3987

breakfast, especially for family groups. If you're spending the evening in, Jennifer is happy to provide an evening meal of home cooked fare, and afterwards there's a spacious guests' lounge to relax in, or you might like to challenge Jennifer to a frame on the pool/snooker table If you plan an evening out, Jennifer will be happy to recommend one of the good bars and restaurants in the neighbourhood. The 2 guest bedrooms at Rockhaven are stylishly furnished, well-equipped with pleasing extras such as toiletries, and both rooms have interesting domed ceilings. The house is surrounded by superb large gardens, (complete with barbecue area), which reindeer visit on a regular basis. And if you're looking for sporting activities such as golf, fishing or horse-riding, Jennifer knows where they all are!

A mile or so southwest of the town rises the prominent landmark of **Scrabo Tower**, built in 1857 as a memorial to the 3rd Marquis of Londonderry for his relief efforts during the Great Famine. If you are prepared to tackle the 122 steps to the top there are some splendid views across Strangford Lough and across to Scotland. The tower stands within the **Scrabo Country Park** (free) which has some splendid woodland walks and also contains the old quarries where the celebrated Scrabo stone was extracted. A couple miles north of Newtownards, the **Somme Heritage Centre** recalls the part played by the Irish and Ulster Divisions in the most horrific and futile battle of World War I. The battle of the Somme lasted for five months and when the Germans finally retreated the British forces had won a few kilometres of shell-pocked mud at the cost of 600,000 lives. At the Centre here, staff in battledress recount the terrible story and the re-created frontline trenches underline the horror. Just across from the Centre, **The Ark** is Ireland's first rare breeds farm and is home to more than 80 rare species of cattle, pigs, sheep, goats, ponies, ducks, poultry and llamas in 40 acres of countryside. There are picnic sites, play areas and a tea room.

THE ARDS PENINSULA

Running east and south from Newtonards, the Ards Peninsula is a long, thin hook of land that almost encloses Strangford Lough with only a narrow channel near Portaferry allowing access from the Irish Sea. The east coast has long stretches of sandy beaches and on the Strangford side there's an endless variety of views from sensitively sited car parks and lay-bys. The area's attractions include one of the only two working windmills in Ireland. It's located near the seaside village of Millisle, at Ballycopeland, and visitors can enjoy a guided tour of the late-18th century windmill and follow the milling process from corn into flour.

BALLYWALTER   MAP 6 REF N5
14 miles SE of Bangor on the A2

A thriving port in the 1600s, Ballywalter still has a busy harbour area which gives the village character and vitality. Just south of the harbour is the Long Strand, a wide stretch of beach offering safe bathing and facilities for all kinds of water sports. Car fanatics will be interested in the **Ballywalter Mini Collection**, a private collection of 30 varieties of this popular car which includes an ex-works Paddy Hopkirk rally car. The display can be visited by arrangement only, (tel: 028 4458098).

Set in an area of outstanding natural beauty and enjoying some grand sea views, **Greenlea Farm** is a working farm which has occupied this location for some 300 years. Parts of the stone built house date back to that time but over the years the original building has been greatly extended and modernised. The present owner, Evelyn McIvor has lived at Greenlea Farm for more than 50 years and has been offering quality bed and

Greenlea Farm, 48 Dunover Road, Ballywalter, Newtonards, Co. Down BT22 2LE   Tel: 028 4275 8218

breakfast accommodation for the last 20 of them. Greenlea's 5 guest rooms are well furnished, comfortable and meticulously clean with a relaxing, peaceful atmosphere. The large residents' lounge has an inviting open fire and there's a piano should you feel in the mood for a sing-a-long! Visitors can stay on either a B & B or full board basis and will find the wholesome home cooking a real treat. Evelyn will provide packed lunches if required and is also happy to cater for small parties.

A few miles south of Ballywalter, near the village of Ballyhalbert, **Burr Point** is the most easterly place in Ireland, and another mile to the south, Portavogie is one of Northern Ireland's most important fishing ports. Few visitors leave without purchasing some of its famous prawns and herrings..

KEARNEY   MAP 6 REF N6
3 miles E of Portaferry off the A2

This small coastal village on the low rocky coastline at the tip of the peninsula owes its spick and span appearance to the fact that it is owned by the National Trust. The Trust has restored some of the houses here to the authentic vernacular style of a traditional fishing village. There are some splendid views across to Scotland, the Isle of Man and the Mountains of Mourne, and a lovely coastal walk leads to **Knockinelder**, a beautiful sandy beach to the south. Seals are regularly seen basking on the rocks between Kearney and Knockinelder.

PORTAFERRY
MAP 6 REF N6
19 miles SE of Belfast on the A2

Portaferry has a magnificent setting looking out across the narrow strait connecting Strangford Lough with the sea. The powerful current which rushes through the Narrows carries 400 million gallons of water with every tide - no wonder the Vikings named the lough "Strong Fjord". A regular car ferry service across the Narrows links the town to the village of Strangford and the county town of Downpatrick.

Portaferry is a busy boating centre, never more so than during the town's annual gala week and regatta in July when the pubs are open 24 hours a day and the traditional Galway boats called hookers sail here to share in the festivities. For an insight into Portaferry's maritime history and the general environment of Strangford Lough, a visit to the **Portaferry Visitor Centre** (free), housed in a former stable, is recommended. The centre also has an informative video introducing the tower houses of Co. Down.

Portaferry is home to **Exploris**, the only aquarium in Northern Ireland, which provides a showcase for thousands of species native to the area, amongst them stingrays which you are invited to touch and sharks which you are not. Thousands of species are on view and in 1999 a new seal sanctuary was added to the attractions.

Located just off the town square, **Fiddlers Green** takes its name from an English folk song. It was christened by landlord Frank McCarthy who, together with his wife Maureen, runs this lively, friendly pub which also offers B & B. A keen folk singer, Frank is always happy to pick up his guitar and entertain his guests. On some evenings, there's also music in the Quarter Deck bar, an interesting room in the shape of a ship's bow. From time to time, the Quarter Deck serves as a function room for parties of up to 60

Fiddlers Green, 10-12 Church Street, Portaferry, Co. Down BT22 1LS Tel: 028 4272 8393/4272 8136

people. The McCarthys also hold a weekly pub quiz, a great opportunity to soak up the local atmosphere. Outside, there's a pleasant Beer Garden overlooking the park and bowling green with a children's play area in view of the garden. The inn's letting rooms are full of character and attractively furnished and decorated. The Ulster Fry breakfast will certainly set you up for the day although packed lunches are available on request.

The comments in the Visitors' Book at **Lough Cowey Lodge** make interesting reading. *"Wonderful location and the craic was good"* writes a lady from Enniskillen; *"Excellent accommodation, excellent hospitality"* is the comment of a visitor from Poland. This modern, purpose-built lodge is owned and run by Mrs Fiona Taggart, (*"Impeccable, great hostess"*), who offers guests a choice of bed and breakfast in the main building or self-

**Lough Cowey Lodge, 9 Lough Cowey Road, Portaferry, Co. Down BT22 1PJ
Tel: 028 4272 8263   Mobile: 077 03221623**

catering accommodation in the adjoining modern villa which is beautifully furnished and decorated, and comprehensively equipped. The Lodge's peaceful garden enjoys magnificent views over Lough Cowey which has excellent seasonal trout and coarse fishing and the house is located close to Strangford Lough, an area of outstanding natural beauty. The Lodge also has a patio area and ample parking. Captivated by its idyllic position and welcoming home-from-home atmosphere, an Italian visitor found just the right word to describe Lough Cowey Lodge: *"bellissimo!"*

GREYABBEY
Map 6 ref N5
7 miles SE of Newtonards on the A20

From Portaferry the A20 runs northwards, hugging the shoreline of Strangford Lough and providing a succession of grand views. Only a handful of small villages stand on this side of the lake, the most interesting of which is Greyabbey which is noted for its clutch of antique shops and art galleries. The village takes its name from **Grey Abbey** whose extensive ruins nestle in beautiful parkland on the edge of the village. Founded in 1193 by

Affreca, daughter of the King of Man, it was the first truly Gothic structure in Ireland, with graceful pointed lancet windows and an impressive west door on which the carved decoration can still be made out. The monks here were Cistercian, an Order with a great knowledge of plants, both wild and cultivated, and made use of this in their practice of medicine. At Grey Abbey they had their own **'physick' garden** and this has been carefully re-created. Based on medieval paintings and texts, the garden contains more than 50 different medicinal plants and herbs. The surroundings are as soothing and tranquil as they would have been when Affreca chose this setting more than 800 years ago.

MOUNT STEWART   Map 6 ref N5
5 miles SE of Newtownards on the A20

The mild micro-climate of Strangford Lough favoured the creation of **Mount Stewart Gardens** (National Trust), the inspired work of Edith, 7th Marchioness of Londonderry, (1879-1959), a leading political hostess of her day. She laid out the gardens in the 1920s with colourful parterres, ornamental lakes, noble trees and many rare and tender plants. There is some striking topiary, including a harp, an appropriately coloured Red Hand of Ulster, and various animals which allude to the marchioness' pet names for her politician friends. Within the grounds there's a lovely Temple of the Winds modelled on the original in Athens and commanding a splendid view of the lough.

Mount Stewart House is also open to the public. It was the birthplace in 1769 of Lord Castlereagh who as chief secretary for Ireland secured the passage of the Act of Union in 1800. The house is richly furnished and contains some interesting political memorabilia, as well as a collection of fine paintings the most notable of which is the huge canvas by George Stubbs depicting the celebrated racehorse, Hambletonian.

IN AND AROUND DOWNPATRICK

DOWNPATRICK   Map 6 ref N6
24 miles SE of Belfast on the A7

Downpatrick and the surrounding area is rich in associations with St Patrick. He sailed up the Slaney River in 432AD, landing near Downpatrick where he is believed to have founded its first church. The present **Downpatrick Cathedral** is comparatively recent, completed in 1826 but incorporating some parts of a 12th century cathedral on the same site. No-one knows for sure where St Patrick was buried - both Downpatrick and Armagh lay claim to being the saint's final resting place. Pilgrims to Downpatrick were so certain that he was buried near the cathedral that they had scrabbled a deep hole in the churchyard. In 1900, the church authorities covered it with a huge granite boulder inscribed with a cross and the single name PATRIC. The saint is also commemorated by a huge 35ft high granite statue on the summit of Slieve Patrick across the valley.

Downpatrick itself is a charming collection of late Georgian and early Victorian buildings set on two low hills. Its 18th century gaol now houses the **Down County**

Museum and the **St Patrick Heritage Centre**. The former has some interesting exhibits of Stone Age artefacts and local history; the latter tells the story of St Patrick using extracts from his autobiography, *Confessions*, and also has a video featuring other locations around the town associated with him.

If you are planning to stay in this restful little town, it's worth seeking out one of the few hostelries in Ireland that can boast a well-documented history going back to 1642. Oak beams, stone floors, meat hooks hanging from the ceiling and a large open fireplace all testify to the antiquity of **Denvir's Hotel**, creating an ambience replete with character and atmosphere. Where else would you find a bar top crafted from the timbers of one of

Denvir's Hotel, 14-16 English Street, Downpatrick, Co. Down BT36 6AB
Tel: 028 4461 2012   Fax: 028 4461 7002   e-mail: Denvirs@btinternet.com
website: www.btinternet.com/~Denvirs

the many ships that, years ago, foundered in the nearby lough? And American visitors will be interested to discover that it was a member of the Denvir family, from which the hotel takes its name, who also gave the family name to the small settlement in Colorado which, (its spelling modified to Denver), later became the capital of that state. Denvir's Hotel is a place to savour, especially in the restaurant where visitors will find an outstanding menu based on prime local produce complemented by interesting extras such as wild mushrooms and a local delicacy called *sloke* - a species of seaweed with a taste rather like spinach. Denvir's Hotel is definitely a place where you will want to linger so it's fortunate that it has 8 cosy and comfortable guest rooms, all of them en suite.

SAUL   MAP 6 REF N6
2 miles NE of Downpatrick off the A25

The small village of Saul overlooks Strangford Lough and holds a special place in Irish history for it was here that St Patrick is said to have made his first landing in Ireland in AD 432. He converted the local lord, a man called Dichu, who presented the saint with a

Saul Church

barn, a "Sabhal", hence the name of the village. A much later **church** now occupies the site with an impressive round tower standing nearby.

An excellent place to stay in this historic spot is **Swan Lodge**, a spacious modern house with a graceful conservatory and large gardens complete with a children's play area and barbecue site. Swan Lodge is the home of Liz and John McMorris who have a truly Irish flair for hospitality. There are splendid views from the charming dining room where, as well as breakfast, guests can enjoy an evening meal. Home-made bread, cakes and jams are part of the wholesome fare and Liz's salmon dishes enjoy a reputation second to none. Packed lunches are also available if required. Swan Lodge has 4 guest

Swan Lodge, 30 St Patrick's Road, Saul, Downpatrick, Co. Down BT30 7JG
Tel: 028 4461 5542

rooms, all en suite, and its location makes it perfect as a base for exploring this part of County Down which in addition to its historic associations with St Patrick offers many other places of interest: Inch Abbey and the Ballynae Stone Circle to mention just two.

STRANGFORD
7 miles NE of Downpatrick on the A25

Map 6 ref N6

Thousands of travellers pass through this tiny village, either boarding or leaving the regular vehicle ferry that links it to the Ards Peninsula. It's worth stopping off though to visit **Castle Ward** (National Trust) - an 18th century mansion which is famed for being divided into two architectural styles. One façade is classical, the other Gothick. This split personality is due to the differences between its original owners, Bernard and Anne Ward, later Lord and Lady Bangor. The interior is equally schizophrenic - half the rooms are classical in style, whilst the others, such as the Saloon and the Boudoir with its fan-vaulted ceiling, are Gothic.

The house is stunningly situated, surrounded by farmland, landscaped gardens and lakes, one of which, Temple Water, is overlooked by a graceful pedimented temple. An underground passage links the house to the stableyard where there's a Victorian pastimes centre where children can dress in clothes from the period and play with popular Victorian toys; a late-19th century laundry; a well-stocked gift shop and a restaurant. Also within the grounds are a defensive tower built in 1610, a sawmill and a recently restored water-powered corn mill which has regular working demonstrations.

BALLYNAHINCH
MAP 6 REF M6
25 miles S of Belfast on the A24/A49

Set among many low, rounded drumlins Ballynahinch is a thriving market town which was laid out in the first half of the 17th century by the Rawdon family who also built a fine mansion for themselves, **Montalto House**. In the following century another family, the Kers, became the landlords of Ballynahinch and it was they who created the town's

Legannany Dolmen, Ballynahinch

pleasant terraces and the large shops with their fine façades. Two miles south of the town is the Spa, two sulphurous springs which enjoyed a few decades of prosperity and, on the south slopes of Cratlieve Mountain, the much-photographed **Legananny Dolmen**. Its tapering capstone is supported by two 6ft portal stones at the front and a smaller stone at the rear.

Occupying an idyllic position just outside Ballynahinch, **Bushymead Country House** is an impressive modern building with a stately pillared entrance. The house stands in spacious grounds with extensive gardens, a children's play area, barbecue site and a large pond with an island in the middle which is a haven for ducks and other wildlife. Bushymead is the home of Sally Murphy and her family who provide quality bed and breakfast accommodation in gracious surroundings and in a wonderfully relaxing atmosphere. Sally does her own baking and if you take your evening meal here you'll find seasonal

Bushymead Country House, 86 Drumaness Road, Ballynahinch,
Co. Down BT24 8LT   Tel/Fax: 028 9756 1171

fruit and vegetables from the garden complementing the menu. A children's menu and vegetarian options are available, but Sally is happy to prepare any meal of your choice - just ask. The house has 8 attractively furnished guest bedrooms, 7 of them en suite, and each named after places in the locality - Ennis, Lecale, Polramer and so on. Situated in the heart of County Down, on the doorstep of Newcastle and the Mountains of Mourne, Bushymead is ideally located close to the area's many tourist attractions.

About 5 miles northeast of Ballynahinch, **Rowallane Garden** near the pretty village of Saintfield has been described as one of the National Trust's finest ornaments. The 50-acre site was created during the first half of the 20th century and is noted for its spectacular displays of rhododendrons, azaleas, rare trees, shrubs and plants.

KILLYLEAGH
5 miles N of Downpatrick on the A22

Map 6 ref N6

Located at the southwest corner of Strangford Lough, Killyleagh is a plantation town and port laid out in a gridiron pattern. Its impressive hilltop castle has **13th century**

Killyleagh Castle

origins but these can hardly be detected now as it was rebuilt in 1666 and again in 1850 when the exuberant Disney-style turrets and cones were added. But its soaring turrets, stalwart battlements, bawn wall and picturesque gatehouse provide an excellent photo-opportunity. Groups can visit the castle by prior arrangement.

Dufferin Arms Coaching Inn stands majestically on the main street of this historic little town. This is a traditional country pub, owned and run by Kitty Stewart and Morris Crawford, lying in the shadow of the 16th century Killyleagh Castle. Renowned throughout Ulster for its excellent food, drink and friendly atmosphere, the Dufferin Arms is a wonderful place where visitors can relax by the open fire and while away the evening. Recommended by Taste of Ulster, the food here in the Cellar Restaurant is absolutely delicious, the very best of country kitchen style cuisine.

The Dufferin Arms, however, is much more than just a pub with a restaurant. The Off Licence stocks a wide range of wines, both New World and the more traditional, and a large selection of

Dufferin Arms Coaching Inn, 35 High Street, Killyleagh, Co. Down BT30 9QF
Tel: 028 4482 8229 Fax: 028 4482 8755
e-mail: dufferin@dial.pipex.com
website: www.nova.co.uk/dufferin

spirits as well as bottled and canned beers. A choice of accommodation is also offered by the Arms. There are 7 luxury en suite bedrooms, some with four-poster beds, and overnight guests have the use of the residents' lounge and a library.

Outside the castle gates, in Frederick Street, a plaque records the achievements of Killyleagh's most famous son, Sir Hans Sloane, who was born here in 1660. He became physician to George II and on his death at the grand old age of 93 bequeathed his fabulous library and collections to the nation. They formed the basis of the British Museum which stands on the site of his London home, Montagu House.

SEAFORDE
6 miles SW of Downpatrick on the A24

MAP 6 REF N6

This tiny village is home to a popular visitor attraction, the **Butterfly House** which has a large flight area with hundreds of free-flying exotic butterflies. There are also reptiles and insects (behind glass!). The surrounding grounds also offer a maze and play area, nursery garden, shop and tea room. An attractive feature is the Moghul Tower from the top of which visitors can survey the attractive gardens.

Set in 60 acres just outside the village, with its own trout-stocked lake, **Drumgooland House** is an impressive country house which has been fully modernised while retaining its splendid 100-year-old character. Whether you come for the beautiful scenery of the Mountains of Mourne, for the area's historic connections with St Patrick, or to ride good Irish horses, Drumgooland House confidently promises visitors the holiday of a lifetime. The McLeigh family, who own and run this hotel and equestrian centre, provide their guests with a unique taste of country living. Their holiday "menu" ranges from 1-hour

**Drumgooland House, 29 Dunnanew Road, Seaforde, Downpatrick,
Co. Down BT30 8PJ Tel: 028 4481 1956 Fax: 028 4481 1265
e-mail: frank.mc_leigh@virgin.net website: http://www.horsetrek-ireland.com**

treks through woodland or along the lake-shore to 6-day itineraries exploring the scenic beauties of this lovely area, with accommodation provided in Drumgooland House, Castlewellan, and Newcastle. The carefully-planned routes wind their way through some of the best scenery in Ireland: a profusion of grand mountains, rugged coastlines, intensely green glens and valleys, mazes of lakes, old fishing villages, castle ruins and historic cities. A special highlight of the tour is the incomparable view where the "Mountains of Mourne sweep down to the sea". After a day travelling through this enchanting countryside, relax in the evening in a traditional Irish pub with local musicians playing their hearts out for you!

The McLeighs take great pride in their trail rides. They take special care of nervous or inexperienced riders and all their mounts are good-natured Irish horses. Their centre is approved by both the British Horse Society and the Department of Agriculture and offers extremely good value for money. All the accommodation on the 6-day trips is Northern Ireland Tourist Board approved and has been chosen because each of them does that little bit extra to ensure the comfort of their guests. The McLeighs will even meet you at either Belfast or Dublin airport so you don't have to bother with car hire.

DUNDRUM

MAP 6 REF N6

9 miles SW of Downpatrick on the A2

Once a thriving fishing port, Dundrum is now mainly of interest because of **Dundrum Castle**, one of the finest Norman castles in Northern Ireland. Built around 1177 as part of John de Courcy's coastal defences, it stands on a steep hill above the town. The circular tower keep is a rare feature in Irish castles and although the fortress was 'slighted' (rendered militarily useless) by Cromwell's troops in 1652, for once they skimped the job and the extensive remains include a fortified gateway, drum towers and a central donjon with a fine spiral stairway winding its way up inside the wall.

About 4 miles to the west of Dundrum, **Castlewellan Forest Park** in the foothills of the Mountains of Mourne is renowned for its arboretum and superb gardens. The arboretum was established in 1740 and its sheltered, south-facing position has encouraged the growth of some magnificent exotic species of trees. There's a 3-mile trail around the lake, marked with sculptures created from the park's natural materials and at the visitor centre the Queen Anne-style courtyard houses a charming tea room.

NEWCASTLE

MAP 6 REF M6

23 miles E of Newry on the A2

One of Northern Ireland's premier seaside resorts, Newcastle is beautifully situated at the western end of the extensive sandy beach that fringes **Dundrum Bay** with the huge bulk of **Slieve Donard** providing a scenic backdrop. The town is also a noted golfing resort boasting two 18-hole courses, one of them the world-famous Royal County Down Club. For family visitors, the **Tropicana Pleasure Beach** provides a whole range of entertainments including a heated outdoor fun pool, giant slides and an adventure playground. For poor weather days, the **Saintfield's Museum of Childhood** has a fine collection of vintage toys and dolls while **Route 66** is Ireland's only museum featuring American automobiles and memorabilia of the 1930s, with jukeboxes and films of cars adding to the nostalgic appeal.

On the outskirts of the town stretches the **Tullymore Forest Park** in the foothills of the Mountains of Mourne. There are some lovely walks here, passing between banks of rhododendrons, over quaint bridges spanning deep ravines and rushing rivers, and past some unusual Gothic follies. In the arboretum there's a magnificent Cork Oak and the visitor centre contains wildlife and forestry exhibits, a lecture theatre and tea room.

This lively resort is also the main tourist centre for the **Mourne mountains**. Only one road leads through the mountains so they can only be fully appreciated on foot. Fortunately, a network of ancient tracks criss-crosses the moorlands and upland pastures - leaflets detailing the most popular walks can be obtained from the tourist information

Mountains of Mourne

centre on the main Promenade. For serious climbers, the Northern Ireland Mountain Centre in Newcastle runs climbing courses but these must be booked at least two weeks in advance.

Overlooking the Promenade and Dundrum Bay, the **Avoca Hotel** is a small licensed hotel which has been owned and run by Isabel Irwin and her family for more than 25 years. It has a relaxed, home-from-home atmosphere with friendly staff always eager to help in any way they can. The Avoca's two bars offer a good choice of bar snacks and a very good restaurant which specialises in locally-caught fish. Vegetarian options and a children's menu are available and for the blind a menu is available in Braille. The enticing menus are complemented by an extensive wine list. The hotel itself is a substantial Edwardian building with 16 guest bedrooms of which 8 are en suite. The Avoca provides

**The Avoca Hotel, 93-97 Central Promenade, Newcastle,
Co. Down BT33 0HH   Tel: 028 4372 2253**

remarkable value for money, and in addition offers reduced rates for children and senior citizens. It is conveniently located for local shops and amenities, and the town is well-known as a handy base for hill and mountain walkers exploring the beautiful Mourne Mountains which are within 5 minutes walking distance.

KILKEEL   MAP 6 REF M7
12 miles S of Newcastle on the N2

Unless you've completely lost your sense of smell, you will quickly realise that Kilkeel's main business is fish. Trawlers crowd the harbour which is surrounded by canneries and the main excitements here are the fish auctions that take place on the quayside. In the summer Kilkeel hosts a **Harbour Festival** and the **Nautilus Centre** has an exhibition on the fishing industry, a fish shop, gift shop, café and conference centre.

In the churchyard here is buried Kilkeel's most infamous son. William Hare was born at Kilkeel sometime around 1800 and as a young man moved to Edinburgh where he owned a lodging house. When one of his lodgers died owing him rent, Hare and his accomplice William Burke sold the body to a medical school for £7.10. Subsequently, they murdered a further 15 people before being caught. Hare turned king's evidence and was released; Burke was hanged. Hare returned under a different name to his home town where he was soon reduced to being an inmate of the workhouse. His identity was only revealed when a former medical student in Edinburgh, a Dr Reid, visited the workhouse and recognised him.

WEST DOWN

NEWRY
MAP 6 REF L6
30 miles SW of Downpatrick on the A1/A25

The most important commercial centre in the area, Newry occupies an anomalous position, straddling the border between Down and Armagh. As if to symbolise this unusual situation, Newry's Town Hall stands on a bridge over the Clanrye river, its offices divided equally between the two counties. Located inside the Hall, the **Newry Museum** (free) has a good local history display and an intriguing collection of other exhibits amongst which is Nelson's table from *HMS Victory*.

When Newry's canal opened in 1741 it was the first in the British Isles and the new waterway established Newry's position as the pre-eminent trading centre for the region, a status it has never lost. The economic boom wasn't translated, as in other prosperous Georgian towns, into stylish squares and terraces, and the most distinctive building in the town is the **Catholic Cathedral**, an uncompromising granite structure with a more attractive Byzantine-style interior and some outstanding stained glass.

BANBRIDGE
MAP 6 REF M6
10 miles N of Newry on the A1/A26

Once an important linen town, Banbridge has little to detain tourists but the town enjoys fame of a kind because of its unusual main street. The street climbs a steep hill which in the days of stage coach travel presented a major travel hazard. When the coach operators threatened to bypass Banbridge the town fathers had a deep underpass cut in the central part of the road and a bridge constructed across it.

GILFORD
MAP 6 REF L6
7 miles NW of Banbridge on the N50

About halfway between Portadown and Banbridge, the sizeable village of Gilford is well worth seeking out if you enjoy outstanding cuisine. You'll find it at **The Yellow Door** restaurant whose unassuming exterior belies the pleasures waiting once you step inside. The two dining-rooms, (the larger one non-smoking), are exquisitely furnished with an ambience that is both luxurious and relaxing. The owner and head chef here is Barry Smyth who has worked extensively in both Germany and Ireland, spending two years with the Rankin family who are famous for their TV cook shows. So it's not surprising to discover that The Yellow Door has a reputation second to none in the area. Barry's menus are always based on fresh local produce and therefore always changing but here's a sample from a typical menu. Amongst the starters, a warm smoked Duck Mille Feuille with Mango Salsa; as a main course, Fillet of Sea Bass served on Orzo Pasta with caramelised vegetables and creamy basil, or a "Vegetarian Trio" which includes Stuffed Peppers, Pasta with Asparagus, and a salad of Tomato, Avocado and Basil. The separate dessert menu might offer a Cherry Clafoutis Tartlet served with Vanilla Ice Cream, or a summer

The Yellow Door, Gilford, Co. Down BT63 6EP
Tel: 028 9783 1543

Peach Cake with whipped cream and Sauce Anglaise. Wine lovers will really feel at home here: The Yellow Door offers an extensive wine list which is one of the best you will find in Ireland. The Yellow Door is closed on Mondays but open every other day from 12.30 until 14.30 for lunch, and from 18.30 until 21.30. *(Please note that The Yellow Door is set to change its name in early 2000: phone ahead to discover the new name!)*

DROMORE   MAP 6 REF M6
14 miles SW of Belfast on the A1

The small town of Dromore stands beside the River Lagan and was for centuries the ecclesiastical capital of the diocese of Dromore. The **cathedral** here was built in the 1660s by Bishop Jeremy Taylor who, unusually, is buried inside the altar. Embodied in the south wall is a stone inscribed with a cross and known as **St Colman's Pillow**. It's believed to be a relic of the monastic foundation created here by St Colman around 600AD. It was one of the saint's successors who erected a High Cross in the Market Square. By the late 1880s it was in a ruinous state so its fragments were incorporated in a restoration of the cross which now stands beside the bridge over the Lagan. Another survival is the **set of stocks** in the market square which are still occasionally used for imprisoning local brides and grooms before a wedding. A good time to visit is on the last Saturday in September when a lively horse fair takes place.

    For almost a quarter of a century, Esther Erwin and her family have been welcoming bed & breakfast guests to their charming home, **Win-Staff House**, located a mile or so south of Dromore. Surrounded by spacious gardens, (complete with a barbecue area), Win-Staff House enjoys a well-deserved reputation for friendliness, hospitality, excellent cuisine and comfortable, relaxing accommodation. Evening meals are available on request and it's definitely a good idea to make that request: Esther is an accomplished cook who changes her menu every day. She is also happy to cater for any celebration with a

**Win-Staff House, 45 Banbridge Road, Dromore, Co. Down BT25 1NE
Tel: 028 9269 2252 Mobile: 0410 203870**

guest list of up to 50 people. On a smaller scale, Esther will provide you with a hearty Irish breakfast, compile a tasty packed lunch, or cook an imaginative evening meal crafted to satisfy your own dietary preferences: vegetarian, carnivorous or a menu designed for children. Win-Staff House is a delightful place to stay with a true home-from-home atmosphere.

HILLSBOROUGH   Map 6 ref M5
4 miles NE of Dromore off the A1

With its fine Georgian architecture, Gothic planter's church, tea rooms and well-stocked antique shops, Hillsborough has been described as one of the most English-looking villages in Ulster. There's a lovely circular walk around the lake which takes about an hour to complete and begins near an impressive ruined fort built in 1650 by Col. Arthur Hill after whom the village is named.

The Hill family seat, **Hillsborough Castle** was built around 1797. Between 1925 and 1973 it was the residence of the Governor of Northern Ireland. Since then it has functioned as a stately home away from home for visiting VIPs and also provided a base for Prime Minister Blair during the April 1997 peace talks.

COUNTY ARMAGH

Although it is the smallest county in Ulster, Armagh has some surprisingly varied scenery. The south is drumlin country, there is wild open moorland in the central area, and to the east, mountains and rocky glens. Around Loughgall in the north the apple orchards are an enchanting sight in May when the trees are in full blossom. A distinctive feature of the Armagh landscape is its network of dry-stone walls dividing the farmland into tiny fields - a legacy of the Gaelic tradition of dividing land equally between all members of the family.

The ancient city of Armagh was in prehistoric times the seat of the kings of Ulster who were crowned at nearby *Emain Macha*, (Navan Fort). Few medieval buildings have survived but there are many good Georgian houses both in Armagh itself and at the National Trust properties of The Argory and Ardress House. While travelling through the county keep an eye open for a game of road bowls in progress. Also known as 'Bullet' this sport is unique to Armagh and Co. Cork and gives a clear indication of the comparative lack of road traffic here.

ARMAGH   MAP 6 REF L6
38 miles SW of Belfast on the A3

The ecclesiastical centre of Ireland for more than 1500 years, Armagh is a delightful place to wander around. The city's prosperity in the 18th century is reflected in its numerous listed Georgian buildings, especially in the Mall - a large expanse of urban parkland, formerly a racecourse, which was one of many gifts to the city from Archbishop Robinson who held the post for 30 years until 1795. On the east side of the Mall, the **Armagh County Museum** (free) occupies one of the most distinctive buildings in Armagh, similar in appearance to a small Greek temple. It was originally built as a school. The exhibits range from prehistoric artefacts, through military costumes, wedding dresses, and natural history specimens to a display recounting the story of Ireland's worst railway accident when two passenger trains collided outside Armagh in 1889. Eighty-nine people lost their lives; many of them are buried in the churchyard of St Mark's nearby.

The city has two cathedrals, both of them dedicated to St Patrick who founded the first church here in 445AD. The **Church of Ireland cathedral** was originally built in 1268 but comprehensively rebuilt in the Gothic style in 1834. It contains some fine monuments, strange and interesting carvings, and in the Library of 1711, just down the hill, there's a copy of *Gulliver's Travels*, annotated by Swift himself. **The Roman Catholic cathedral** with its

Catholic Cathedral, Armagh

soaring twin towers stands impressively atop one of Armagh's seven hills. Built between 1840 and 1873, its inside walls are completely covered with colourful mosaics, including medallions of the saints of Ireland.

At the **St Patrick's Trian Visitor Complex** there are two quite separate exhibitions. One of them, housed in a Presbyterian Meeting House of 1722, explores the Land of Lilliput with the help of a 20ft giant and other models, and also follows Jonathan Swift's associations with Armagh where he lived for a while. The other exhibition, The Armagh Story, offers a multi-media account of the city's development from prehistoric times, through myths and legends, to the coming of St Patrick and Celtic Christianity. The complex also incorporates a former bank, now the tourist information centre, and the bank manager's house of 1800 which has become the Pilgrim's Table Restaurant.

Further insights into Armagh's Georgian past can be gained at the **Palace Stables Heritage Centre & Demesne**. The Palace was another of Archbishop Robinson's 'improving' additions to the city, a somewhat austere Georgian mansion which is now the headquarters of the Armagh District Council. Tours are available by prior arrangement. The Heritage Centre occupies the former stables and courtyard of the palace and includes a 'Day in the Life' exhibition featuring costumed actors portraying life around the stables as it might have appeared on a typical day, July 23rd, 1776. The courtyard also has a craft shop and restaurant. The Demesne, or parkland, surrounding the Palace and stables is beautifully landscaped with laid out walks, orienteering and horse trails, adventure play area, and a Garden of the Senses. The ruins of **Armagh Friary**, the longest friary church in Ireland (163ft) stand near the entrance to the Centre. The extensive grounds also feature a lovely temple-like Chapel with some exquisite wood carvings, an Ice House, a Victorian conservatory, and a Servants' Tunnel which was used to bring food from the detached kitchens - Archbishop Robinson detested the lingering smells from cooking.

Two other visitor attractions in the city are the **Observatory**, built in 1791 and another of the Archbishop's benefactions, and the comparatively recent **Planetarium** of 1968 where digital video technology allows audiences in the Star Theatre to fly through space and a state-of-the-art stereo system provides the appropriate sound effects.

Set in the heart of the countryside, just 5 minutes from the centre of Armagh City, **Ní Eoghain Lodge** offers visitors a choice of either bed and breakfast or self-catering accommodation. Bed and breakfast guests stay in the delightful old farmhouse which has been in the McGeown family for generations and today is in the care of Kathleen McGeown, who looks after her visitors, and her husband who tends the farm. The house abounds in charm and character, its vintage features blending happily with modern facilities. Guests are treated to coffee or tea on arrival, will find an extensive range of choices at breakfast time and, if they wish, enjoy an evening meal based on organic produce and home baking at its best. Vegetarian alternatives are a speciality. The guest bedrooms are all on the ground floor, with Category 3 access provided for the disabled. All the rooms are en suite, with tea and coffee-making facilities, and cots and electric blankets can be provided if required. Children are welcome and a babysitting service is also available. Guests have their own TV room and dining room, both with log fires, and a payphone has been installed for their use. If you prefer self-catering, the McGeowns also have a stylish chalet

Ní Eoghain Lodge, 32 Ennislare Road, Armagh BT60 2AX
Tel: 028 3752 5633 Fax: 028 3751 1246

adjacent to the main house. Ní Eoghain Lodge is set in 2 acres of award-winning gardens of which Alan Titchmarsh would be proud and they offer guests the chance to relax and unwind in tranquil surroundings. Many of those who stay at the Lodge are Americans tracing their family roots, a process in which the McGeowns are happy to assist. Their Visitors' Book contains a host of appreciative comments, all with a common theme: "The best!" says one, "Wonderful food, hospitality and a very special feeling", while another declares that the Lodge is "without doubt the best B & B we have stayed at in Ireland".

A few miles west of Armagh is **Navan Fort**, a colossal earthworks which is all that remains of the great palace built by Queen Macha in 300BC. It was here that Deirdre of the Sorrows met her lover, Noísí, and where the warrior kings of Ulster and the Irish equivalent of the Knights of the Round Table, the Knights of the Red Branch, met and feasted. The feats of these genuine historical figures, and particularly their greatest champion Cuchullain, have passed into legend and are recounted in the songs and stories of the Ulster Cycle. The entire complex of Navan Fort was destroyed in 330AD by the three Cullas brothers so there is little to see apart from the earthen mounds. But the Navan Centre, a grass-covered mound supported inside by columns, re-creates how it is believed the fort would have looked. An audio-visual show brings to life the four main myths connected with Navan, amongst them the Hound of Ulster and the Cattle Raid of Cooley.

PORTADOWN
11 miles NE of Armagh on the N3

Map 6 ref L5

Formerly a prosperous linen manufacturing town, Portadown is set around the River Bann but it was the arrival of the Newry to Lough Neagh canal in the 1730s that provided the basis for its growth. An exhibition detailing the history of the canal and its importance to the town is presented at **Moneypenny's Lock** (free) where there's a restored lock-keeper's house, stables and a bothy. The lock can be reached by a peaceful walk along the canal towpath from the car park in Castle Street.

For quality food served in attractive surroundings the place to make for in Portadown is **Chandlers Café Bistro** located in the heart of the town close to all the main shopping malls. Ivor Beattie is the owner of this stylish eatery which is also a delicatessen selling a wide range of tasty delicacies. Ivor is very much a "hands-on" proprietor, ensuring the smooth running of the Café Bistro and consulting closely with chefs as they plan the menu which varies daily. Today's special might be Ciabatta Bread with Avocado and Crispy Bacon in gourmet salad leaves and redcurrant sauce, for example. All dishes are prepared from fresh local produce with great attention paid to every detail. The smartly uniformed staff are courteous and efficient and the recently refurbished dining rooms, (there are two of them, one upstairs, one down), are bright and attractively decorated with all-new fixtures and fittings. Dinner at Chandlers is also something special, with starters such as spicy chicken tempura, and main dishes ranging from pan-fried chicken and mango with caramelised pineapple and Thai curry. Diners are welcome to bring their own wine

Chandlers Café Bistro, 10 Market Street, Portadown, Co. Armagh BT62 3PB Tel: 028 3839 2998

- there's no extra charge for corkage. If you are anywhere near Portadown around meal-time, you should certainly make a bee-line for this outstanding eatery.

A few miles to the west of Portadown are two fine houses, both of them National Trust properties. **Ardress House** is a 17th century manor house, much altered in the following century so that its appearance is now that of a Georgian mansion. Inside, there's some outstanding plasterwork, a good collection of paintings, a sizeable working farmyard and wooded grounds. Not far away is **The Argory**, a striking neo-classical building overlooking the River Blackwater which has changed little since it was built in the 1820s. Many of the original contents are still in place and there's a charming early-Victorian sundial garden. A curiosity here is the rare acetylene gas plant of 1906 in the laundry yard which still provides light for the interior.

WARINGSTOWN
MAP 6 REF L5

21 miles SW of Belfast on the A26

The attractive village of Waringstown was founded in the 1660s by the Warings family, wealthy linen merchants who built a handsome Jacobean-style mansion for themselves, and sturdy yeoman's houses for their workers. One of the houses they built is now known as **Ivanhoe**, modified over the years but still a place of great charm and character. Since 1960 it has been the home of Mrs Frances Dewart, a lady who absolutely loves welcoming bed and breakfast visitors to this inviting house set in quiet, peaceful surroundings facing a wood. There are 3 spacious guest bedrooms, (2 doubles and 1 twin), all equipped with

**Ivanhoe, 10 Valley Lane, Waringstown, Craigavon, Co. Armagh BT66 7SR
Tel: 028 3888 1287**

hand basins, tea/coffee-making facilities, and electric blankets. Guests have the use of a comfortable residents' lounge and there's a pleasant dining room where at breakfast time you'll find a choice of a full Irish or a continental breakfast. Approved by the Northern Ireland Tourist Board, Ivanhoe is central for touring and convenient for the many leisure facilities in Lurgan, Banbridge and Craigavon.

MOIRA
MAP 6 REF M5

16 miles SW of Belfast off the M1 (Exit 9)

Set right in the heart of this delightful village, the **Maghaberry Arms** is a large imposing building which has been recently renovated to the very highest standard. Andrew Hendron presides over this welcoming traditional hostelry, a free house where the craic is good, the food appetising and very good value for money, and the good choice of ales all maintained in tip-top quality. The menu for the tasty bar meals, all home-cooked and freshly-prepared, changes weekly, and is available Tuesday to Friday between 12.30 and 15.00, and all day on Saturdays. Evening meals are served on Sunday evenings. Food is served in the large public bar where there's also a games room off to one side. The spacious

**Maghaberry Arms, 23 Maghaberry Road, Moira, Craigavon,
Co. Armagh BT67 0JF Tel: 028 9261 1852**

lounge is the setting for live entertainment on Saturday nights when the music on offer ranges from the traditional to the modern.

MARKETHILL
6 miles SE of Armagh on the A28

MAP 6 REF L6

It's difficult to know whether to describe Markethill as a large village or a small town, but whichever term you use it's a pleasant place which takes its name from the twice-weekly livestock market which draws farmers here from all over the county. Business over, many of them find their way to **The Village Inn and Buttery** in the broad main street. With its smart exterior decked with hanging baskets, The Village Inn is a popular venue where locals and visitors alike savour the welcoming atmosphere of a traditional Irish inn. Mine host is William McAllister who arrived here in early 1999 and has built on the pub's well-established reputation for good craic, fine ales and ex-

**The Village Inn and Buttery, 103-105 Main Street,
Markethill, Co. Armagh BT6 1PJ
Tel: 028 3755 1237**

cellent food. Based on local produce, the menu offers a wide choice of high class food, painstakingly prepared, invitingly presented and served in generous portions. Lunches are available Monday to Friday from 12.30 until 14.30: evening meals are served Wednesday to Saturday when there's a steak house menu which represents excellent value for money. This is definitely a pub to seek out and a satisfactory day out can be enjoyed if you combine a visit to The Village Inn with a trip to nearby **Gosford Forest Park**. Several of the nature walks around the estate were first devised by Jonathan Swift when he visited the Earl of Gosford here between 1728 and 1730. The house he stayed in burnt down in 1805 and was replaced by a stunning mock-Norman castle with a large square keep flanked by a sturdy round tower. Within the grounds stand some fine old walnut trees, a walled garden and, in the arboretum, Dean Swift's Chair, a half-moon seat where he would sit in fine weather, writing and composing his poems.

10 County Tyrone and County Fermanagh

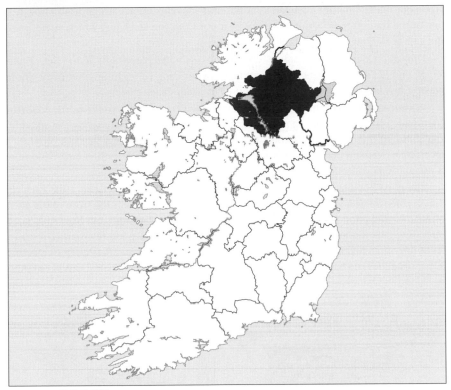

© MAPS IN MINUTES ™ (1998)

COUNTY TYRONE

Lying in the heart of Ulster, Tyrone is one of the most beautiful of the inland counties with the Sperrin Mountains in the north and well-wooded tracts in the southeast which gave rise to the frequently quoted tag, "Tyrone among the bushes, where the Finn and Mourne run". This is primarily a farming county and the whitewashed stone farmhouses with their brightly coloured doors are a distinctive feature of the landscape. The least populated of the Six Counties, Tyrone has a peaceful charm all its own.

The county has a good number of prehistoric remains of which the Beaghmore Stone Circle in the Sperrins is the most remarkable. Very few of the handsome Georgian houses built by the planters are open to the public but Tyrone boasts one of Ireland's major visitor attractions at the Ulster American Folk Park which celebrates the strong links between the peoples of Ulster and North America.

OMAGH
33 miles S of Londonderry on the A5

Map 5 ref J5

Tyrone's county capital is a prosperous, busy place but with a limited number of attractions for the visitor. Two exceptions are the fine classical courthouse and the **Catholic Cathedral of the Sacred Heart** with its irregular twin spires which has been described as "the poor man's Chartres Cathedral". A popular souvenir to take home from Omagh is one of the statuettes or plaques made of peat cut from the Black Bog which stretches to the east of the town.

Omagh incidentally is the home town of the celebrated playwright Brian Friel, *(Translations* and *Philadelphia, Here I Come)*, and also of the song-writer Jimmy Kennedy whose greatest hits were *Red Sails in the Sunset* and *The Teddy Bears' Picnic*.

Within easy reach of the town are some excellent Forest Parks. To the north is **Gortin Glen** which has a 5-mile forest drive with some well-sited lay-bys to enjoy the splendid views and, to the northwest, **Baron's Court Forest Park** where Bessy Bell hill provides a spectacular overview of the Sperrins, Lough Erne and Co. Donegal. To the south, Seskimore is noted for its collection of ornamental birds and domestic fowl.

The most popular visitor attraction however is the **Ulster-American Folk Park** on the A5 three miles north of Omagh. This outstanding museum tells the story of the great waves of emigration from Ulster during the 18th and 19th centuries and how they fared across the Atlantic. In the Old World area of the Park stand some fascinating restored buildings - thatched craftsmen's cottages, a forge, schoolhouse and Presbyterian meeting house. Peat fires still burn in the cottages and there are regular demonstrations of old skills

Ulster-American Folk Park, Omagh

such as candle-making, fish-salting and horse-shoeing. There's also an indoor exhibit recreating an Ulster main street as it would have appeared around 1900.

The New World section displays log houses, a Pennsylvania farmstead, a covered wagon and a full scale replica of an emigrant ship. Disney and others have given theme parks a bad name but the exhibits at the Ulster-American Folk Park have a satisfying stamp of authenticity. The Park was endowed by a generous grant from the Mellon banking family who founded Pittsburgh, Pennsylvania. Their ancestor, Thomas Mellon, was born at the village of Camphill near Omagh and emigrated to America in 1818. His family homestead at Camphill is one of the more substantial of the cottages re-located here.

The Park is open all year round and has a gift shop, café and a major reference and research library containing a wealth of material such as emigrants' letters, ships' passenger lists and newspaper articles of the time.

GORTIN
8 miles N of Omagh on the B48

MAP 5 REF J4

The small village of Gortin lies close to the foot of the Sperrin Mountains, surrounded by woodland and with the Gortin Glen Forest Park a couple of miles to the east. According to legend, St Patrick himself built the local church which is still in use to this day. Gortin

has only the one main street so it's easy to find Peter and Kate McKenna's popular inn, the **Badoney Tavern.** Peter has travelled the world as a textile buyer and has some interesting tales to tell, and both he and Kate are very much "hands on" hosts, keen to make their customers feel welcome. Their tavern is well known for its excellent food with fish, supplied fresh each day, a speciality. A good choice of dishes is available from 12 noon until closing time and at weekends there's an à la carte menu. Parties are catered for and the inn is also a popular

**Badoney Tavern, 16 Main Street, Gortin,
Co. Tyrone BT79 8PH   Tel: 028 8264 8157**

venue for weddings and conferences. At the time of writing, the McKennas are putting the final touches to their self-catering accommodation which should be available by the time you read this.

A couple of miles south of Gortin is one of County Tyrone's major visitor attractions, the **Ulster History Park**. There are full-scale reconstructions of Irish buildings from 7000 BC up to the 17th century, videos and displays, and best of all a guided tour around the site when visitors can enter a foul-smelling deerskin-covered teepee, learn how to make a flint, and explore a ring fort and medieval castle. Gortin village itself lies on the **Ulster**

Ulster History Park, Nr Gortin

Way, not the main 34 mile route which follows an arduous course through the mountains, but a gentler 10 mile stretch which runs through woods and farmland and ends at the Ulster American Folk Park.

NEWTONSTEWART   MAP 5 REF J4
8 miles N of Omagh on the N5

At Newtonstewart the rivers Strule and the Glenelly meet to form the River Mourne, a strategic spot where two medieval castles were built, of which little remains, and attractively laid out in the 1600s as a plantation town.

Co. Tyrone is well-supplied with a diverse range of museums and the one at the **Gateway Centre & Museum** is one of the most fascinating. Much of the collection was a gift from local historian Billy Dunbar and includes a multifarious display of items such as threepenny bit engraved with the Lord's Prayer, a Bordalous (a mini-chamberpot named after a French priest dreaded for his interminable sermons), man traps, vintage packaging, stereoscopes and war memorabilia. Other exhibits include antique toys, and photographic and agricultural equipment dating from the 19th century.

CASTLEDERG
Map 5 ref I4
14 miles NW of Omagh on the B50/B72

Located on the main street of this friendly market town, **The Derg Arms** is a striking building with its black-and-white upper storeys. This family run pub and guest house is well known for its live entertainment with regular performances by bands and artists. It's also home to "The No.1 Disco in Town", Sambo's. The food is good here, too, all home made using top quality fresh ingredients such as locally-caught fish. Lunch is served in the large separate restaurant every day from 12 noon and bar snacks are also available in the snug public bar. Adjoining the pub is the guest house offering 6 bedrooms, all en suite and with complete facilities. The Derg Arms also caters for weddings, private parties and dinner dances.

Castlederg itself is a pleasant place to wander around. It sits on one bank of the River Derg, on the other stand the ruins of **Castlederg Castle** which has one of the shortest

The Derg Arms, 43 Main Street, Castlederg, Co. Tyrone BT81 7AS
Tel: 028 8167 1644 Fax: 028 8167 1202 e-mail: dergarms@ aol.com

histories of any Irish castle. It was built in 1619 and destroyed during the Rebellion of 1641. In the **Castlederg Visitor Centre**, there's an interesting display honouring the American frontiersman and adventurer, Davy Crockett, whose family came from the Castlederg area. The exhibit includes a model of the Alamo fort where Davy made his last stand in 1836.

STRABANE
20 miles N of Omagh on the A5

Map 5 ref J4

This large market town stands beside the River Mourne looking across to its twin town, Lifford in Co. Donegal. To the east stretch the Sperrin Mountains, wonderfully empty of humans but rich in wildlife. The best introduction to this area of solitude and peace, a walker's paradise, is to visit the **Sperrin Heritage Centre** at Cranagh, a few miles east of Strabane. There are hi-tech exhibitions and an audio-visual presentation on the area's natural history and, since there's "gold in them thar hills", visitors can try their luck at panning for it. You can discover the only place where the cloudberry grows and learn about the origins of the St Brigid cross. Made of rushes in the rough shape of a swastika, you will see them hanging above the doors around here to ward off evil. The Centre also has a craft shop and an excellent tea room, the only one for miles around.

About 2½ miles east of Strabane, **Woodend Cottage** is a charming thatched property, built in the 1740s and originally the home of the Duke of Abercorn's bailiff. A listed building, it has recently been refurbished to a very high standard in accordance with the Historical Monuments Department regulations. The bathroom boasts a wonderful antique iron bath and the bay windows at the front still have ancient wooden shutters, all

Woodend Cottage, 42 Woodend Road, Strabane, Co. Tyrone BT82 0BP
Tel: 028 7138 2817

in working order. The owners of Woodend Cottage, Mr and Mrs Hegarty, live nearby and they take great care of their picturesque old property which is now available as self-catering accommodation. The cottage stands on its own grounds of 20 acres, (shared with a family of goats), and there's ample parking space. Inside the centrally-heated cottage there's a sitting room, a well-equipped kitchen and 3 bedrooms, two of them on the ground floor, which between them can sleep up to 5 people. If visitors get tired of self-catering, there's an excellent restaurant in the village and within easy reach there are facilities for fishing in the salmon- rich rivers Finn and Morne, golf, and also a modern Leisure Centre. (Incidentally, the Hegartys have another cottage, Bord Fáilte approved, in a rural setting about 5 miles from Donegal Town).

In Strabane itself, American visitors in particular will be interested in **Gray's Printing Shop** in Main Street, now owned by the National Trust. It was here that John Dunlap, the printer of the American Declaration of Independence and also of America's first daily newspaper, the *Pennsylvania Packet*, learned his trade in the mid-1700s. There's another strong American connection to be found at Dergalt, a couple of miles east of Strabane. **Wilson House** is a small, traditional farmer's house which was the 19th century home of the father of Woodrow Wilson, 28th President of the United States. And 2½ miles from Woodend Cottage, Cowancor is the ancestral home of the 11th President, James Knox Polk, a house which is now owned by a cousin of Mr Hegarty.

SOUTH OF OMAGH

FIVEMILETOWN
MAP 5 REF J5
14 miles S of Omagh on the A4/B122

The village's name came from a popular misconception that it was 5 miles equidistant from the surrounding villages of Clabby, Clogher and Colebrooke, which in fact it isn't. Sir William Stewart built a plantation castle here during the reign of James I, its remains can be seen on the north side of the main street. Fivemiletown stands right on the border with Co. Fermanagh with the mass of Slieve Beagh (1221ft) rising to the south.

A nearby attraction is the **Coach and Carriage Museum** at Blessingbourne. Among the numerous coaches on display is an 1825 London-to-Oxford stage coach, an even older private coach of 1790, and a country doctor's buggy dating from 1910. The museum also has a good collection of horse-drawn farm machinery.

Fivemiletown lies in the lovely valley of the River Black Water and it's here you'll find Claire and Eric Armstrong's exceptionally welcoming **Fourways Hotel**. This is much more than just an inviting place to stay for the night. The restaurant is excellent, offering an all day menu, every day, which specialises in fish. (Don't miss the delicious sea-food chowder or one of the special salmon dishes). All day breakfasts are also available.

Also within the hotel is a grill bar, shop and takeaway as well as a lounge/bar where there's live entertainment each weekend. The Fourways Hotel has 12 comfortable bed-

Fourways Hotel, 41-45 Main Street, Fivemiletown, Co. Tyrone BT75 0PG
Tel: 028 8952 1260 Fax: 028 8952 2061

rooms, all en suite and provided with colour television and direct dial telephone. The hotel's function rooms are designed for various types of reception, from conferences to private parties to public meetings. Coach parties are specially catered for.

The surrounding area has much to offer the visitor. Whether it's fishing, golfing, listening to music or simply enjoying a long walk, everyone is catered for. There are also facilities locally for watersports and equestrian pursuits. Fivemiletown is a good place to join the Clogher Valley Scenic Route, a 25 mile circular drive that wanders on country lanes through woodlands and hills taking in Slieve Beagh and Fardross Forest where there's a spectacular viewpoint across the Clogher Valley. Just beyond Fardross Forest you'll see an extraordinary hilltop tower. This is Brackenridge's Folly, named after George Brackenridge who it built as his mausoleum so that "the squirearchy who had looked down on him during his lifetime were compelled to look up to him after his death".

EAST TYRONE

MOY
5 miles SE of Dungannon on the A29

Map 6 ref L5

Tucked away in the southeast corner of Co. Tyrone, Moy was built in the 18th century by Lord Charlemont, its layout based on the plan of Marengo in Lombardy. The village is attractively set beside the River Blackwater which forms the boundary here with Co. Armagh.

For anyone interested in antiques, there's only one place to stay whilst in Moy. **Charlemont House** is owned and run by Laurence and Margaret McNiece who are also the proprietors of **Moy Antiques** nearby. Their guest house and antique shops enjoy privileged locations in the charming tree-lined square of this award-winning Georgian village. The antique shop carries a vast range of antiques and objets d'art and outside, to the rear of this shop, is Moy Antique Village where you will find the most extensive display of antique furnishings, garden furniture, garden statuary and antique reclaimed pine. Laurence, Margaret and family live at Charlemont House, a handsome Georgian building nearby, where they welcome bed and breakfast guests. They have 5 comfortable rooms, all en suite.

Charlemont House, Moy Antiques & Tomney's Bar, The Square, Moy, Co. Tyrone BT71 7SG
Tel/Fax: 028 8778 4895/4755
Mobile: 07778 373509
e-mail: Sales@Moyantiques.Freeserve.co.uk

To complete your visit, why not pay a visit to **Tomney's Bar**, which is adjacent and where you will be welcome to join in the many traditional music sessions. All combined, these attractions provide one of the most interesting stopover places in Ireland.

DUNGANNON
28 miles SE of Omagh on the A29/A45

MAP 6 REF K5

From their hilltop fortress at Dungannon the O'Neills ruled Ulster for more than 5 centuries but all traces of their medieval castle have disappeared beneath the present **O'Neill's Castle** which is actually a late-Georgian mansion. The town now has the typical appearance of a planter town, with a planned main street, a Royal School founded by James I, and some attractive Georgian terraces. Another building of interest is the police station in the town centre which looks like a castle with projecting apertures for missile throwing. The explanation for this unusual structure is that it was originally intended as a fort for guarding the Khyber Pass but a government clerk mixed up the plans. Presumably, somewhere in southern Afghanistan, there is now a homely police station protecting the wild mountain pass.

Conveniently located in the centre of the town, **The Country Café** offers a huge selection of appetising home-cooked treats served by welcoming staff in relaxing surroundings and at wallet-friendly prices. (The café is also wheelchair-friendly). Dianna Moore is the youthful owner of this inviting eatery which occupies part of a handsome stone-fronted building close to all the shopping malls. Dianna's menu ranges from home-made soups, (the vegetable broth according to one regular is the "best you'll ever taste"), through All Day Breakfasts to substantial meals such as Breast of Chicken with Peppered Sauce or Sirloin Steak. The daily selection of home-made sweets is displayed on the menu board and "Maud's" fa-

The Country Café, Unit 4, Scotch Street Car Park, Dungannon, Co. Tyrone, BT70 1AR Tel: 028 8772 7207

mous ice creams are always available. Children have their own "Kiddies Corner" choices and the extensive regular menu is supplemented by daily specials. An especially attractive feature of The Country Café is the display of hand-painted ceramics on show. These have all been created by Dianna and you may well be tempted to purchase one as a souvenir of your visit.

On the outskirts of the town, **Grange Lodge** has the peaceful, settled look of a house that has occupied its site for many a year. In Grange Lodge's case, since 1698. The original

Grange Lodge, Grange Road, Dungannon, Co. Tyrone BT71 7EJ Tel: 028 8778 4212

tenant was Senator Stevenson of Moygashel fame. A decades-old creeper cloaks the front of the house; to one side an elegant conservatory overlooks spacious lawns. This attractive dwelling is the home of Nora and Ralph Brown who welcome guests to share its tranquil, soothing ambience. A haven where you can arrive depleted in body and soul and leave re-energized. The 5 guest rooms are all en suite and all sumptuously furnished.

Part of the magic emanating from a stay at Grange Lodge is the quality of the cuisine on offer. Nora enjoys a well-deserved reputation as an outstanding cook and, since Grange Lodge is fully licensed, your choice from her imaginative menus can be complemented by an interesting wine list.

Just outside the town, **Tyrone Crystal** at Killybrackey has tours all year round allowing visitors to view the delicate processes of hand-blowing and hand-cutting involved in creating this world-famous product. There's also a factory shop and café.

BALLYGAWLEY   Map 6 ref K5
13 miles SW of Dungannon on the A5/A4

American visitors in particular will be interested in seeking out this village, or rather the smallholding a couple of miles to the east which is now known as the **Grant Ancestral House**. It was once farmed by the maternal ancestors of Ulysses S. Grant (1822-85), hero of the American Civil War and 18th President of the USA. Grant's great-grandfather, John Simpson, was born here in 1738 and the tiny 2-roomed cottage has been restored and furnished in typical 19th century style. There are exhibits and a video recounting Grant's leading rôle in the Civil War while the surrounding working farm has a display of 19th century agricultural implements and is stocked with traditional breeds. The site also includes a wildlife pond and butterfly garden.

COOKSTOWN   Map 6 ref K5
8 miles N of Dungannon on the A29

A planned planter's town built in the early 1600s by one Alan Cook, the town claims to have the longest main street in Ireland, almost 1½ miles long. To the west of the town, the **Drum Manor Forest Park** contains a demonstration shrub garden, a walled butterfly garden and an arboretum. There are nature trails passing lakes and a heronry, a forest trail for the disabled, a perfumed garden for the blind and a café. Nearby is the **Wellbrook Beetling Mill** (National Trust). At this water-powered 18th century linen hammer mill the process of "beetling" took place - the stage in linen manufacture when the cloth is hammered to produce a sheen. Another National Trust property, to the northeast of the town at Moneymore, is **Springhill House**, a charming 17th century manor house complete with family belongings and with a costume museum. There is wheelchair access to the ground floor of the house, delightful gardens and woodland walks.

Back in Cookstown, just off the famous main street in Molesworth Street, **The Black Horse Bar** is a popular venue where you'll find a lively atmosphere, well-tended ales and value-for-money food. Each weekday lunchtime, there's a tasty Carvery with servings to satisfy the heartiest appetite as well as a wide variety of daily specials. There's a large bar and spacious lounge, and in the adjacent building a night club is open on Friday and Saturday evenings from 8pm until 1.30 next morning. The Black Horse also hosts music on Wednesday evenings, offering a wide range of musical styles to suit all tastes. The bar is especially lively on Saturdays which is when Cookstown's broad main street is taken over by the weekly market. Located at the heart of this fertile farming area, Cookstown, incidentally, is a centre of the bacon and sausage industries, something to remember as you sample your bangers and rashers!

The Black Horse Bar, 21-23 Molesworth Street, Cookstown, Co. Tyrone BT80 N8X
Tel: 028 8676 2568

"A sanctuary at the foot of the Sperrins" is how the **Glenavon House Hotel** describes itself, and this luxurious Victorian-style building close to Lough Neagh does indeed provide a wonderful haven for the holiday-maker and the business traveller alike. Set in 9 acres of its own mature grounds on the banks of the Ballinderry River, this 3*** hotel offers 5***** comfort to all its guests with 53 sumptuously appointed en suite bedrooms, providing a range of suites and family rooms along with twins and doubles. Most rooms enjoy an excellent river view.

Great emphasis is placed on the provision of good food, fine wine and courteous, efficient service. Healthy eating is also important and at all times the Glenavon's chefs endeavour to use local seasonal produce. Many guests return again and again to the hotel's two restaurants, The Cellar Grill and Bistro Vino - convincing testimony to the success of the chefs' culinary skills. Families can rest assured that their childrens' requirements are satisfied, with special menus available for all ages and tastes. An additional attraction in the Cellar Bar is the popular sing-along every Saturday and Sunday evening.

All guests at the hotel automatically become members of the "Club Riviera", the only private Leisure Club in the area. This superbly equipped centre has a 20-metre swimming pool, jacuzzi, children's pool, steam room, hair and beauty salon, fitness suite and kiddies' play area.

Conferences and seminars are well catered for at The Glenavon with no fewer than 7 suites capable of accommodating up to 400 delegates available, a wide range of audio-

Glenavon House Hotel, 52 Drum Road, Cookstown, Co. Tyrone BT80 8JQ
Tel: 028 8676 4949   Fax: 028 8676 4396

visual equipment, meals and refreshments, and a full back-up service including fax, photocopying and typing services. This outstanding hotel has also established a fine reputation for its banqueting facilities with 3 suites which can cater for anything from 60 to 400 guests. And Glenavon's central location means that you are never more than one hour's drive from anywhere else in Northern Ireland!

DUNNAMORE   Map 6 ref K4
8 miles W of Cookstown off the A505

For more than 200 years there has been a hostelry at the site of **The Mill Wheel Bar & Restaurant**. The McGurk family were the first licensees, selling groceries, spirits, ales and stout. Today, the host is Michael Loughran who has many years experience as a publican and offers a much wider range of refreshments. Michael has a strong interest in local history in general and The Mill Wheel pub in particular. For example, he can provide you with fascinating details about the massive mill wheel, encased in glass and still turning, which provides such a striking feature of the huge main lounge.

The pub also has a public bar, a games room and a restaurant area serving daily bar lunches and snacks as well as special Sunday lunches with all the food home-cooked and freshly-prepared. The Mill Wheel Bar is a large imposing building with whitewashed walls, a large car park, and farmland all around. This area is famed for its many prehistoric monuments of which the most impressive are the extraordinary **Beaghmore Stone Circles**, a couple of miles to the north. Discovered by peat-cutters in the 1930s, there are

The Mill Wheel Bar & Restaurant, 60 Dunnamore Road, Dungate,
Cookstown, Co. Tyrone BT80 9NX   Tel: 028 8675 1280

7 circles in all, six of them in pairs. The odd one out is scattered with more than 800 upright stones, known as the Dragon's Teeth, and the site also includes ten rows of stones and a dozen burial mounds, some with cremated human remains still inside. The stones are not particularly lofty, (the tallest ones are less than 4 feet high), but the organisation involved in constructing the circles and their uncanny alignment to the movements of the sun, moon and stars testify to the sophistication of the Bronze Age people who occupied this lonely site from 2000 to 1200BC.

COUNTY FERMANAGH

More than a third of Co. Fermanagh lies under water - either lakes or rivers. It's an enchanted landscape, bounded in the northwest by **Lower Lough Erne** and in the southeast by **Upper Lough Erne**, two beautiful lakes linked by the winding River Erne. Tiny wooded islets dot the loughs, many of them with early-Christian ruins and evidence of even older, pagan cultures. Naturally, this is prime fishing country, the quality of the coarse fishing almost legendary.

 This was also plantation country and there are many planters castles scattered around the trim little towns and villages. Fermanagh boasts two outstanding stately homes, Florence Court and Castle Coole, both near Enniskillen. Other places of major interest include the Marble Arch Caves and the famous Belleek Pottery, renowned for its extraordinarily elaborate and delicate wares.

ENNISKILLEN MAP 5 REF I6
27 miles SW of Omagh on the A5

Surrounded by water, the county town of Enniskillen is beautifully located on an island between the Upper and Lower Loughs Erne. Its skyline is dominated by **Enniskillen**

Castle, occupying a picturesque site beside the water. Much modified over the years, the castle's 15th century Keep now houses both a Heritage Centre devoted to Fermanagh life and customs, and the Regimental Museum of the Royal Inniskilling Fusiliers and Dragoons. The town's close connections with these famous regiments have in the past made Enniskillen a target for terrorist attacks, most horrifically on Remembrance Day in 1987 when an IRA bomb killed eleven people and injured another 61. Happily, more peaceful times have returned to the town which has always been noted for the good relations between its Catholic and Protestant communities.

The centre of the town is a tangle of medieval lanes and a winding main street which assumes six different names along its length. Naturally, there are plenty of bait and tackle shops, and the gift shops are well-stocked with the delicate cream-coloured pottery made at Belleek. As an unusual souvenir of the area you might want to buy one of the locally-produced brooches made from fishing flies. More gift possibilities are on offer in the town's former **Buttermarket**, erected in 1835, which is now a crafts and arts centre where you can watch craftspeople at work producing quality pottery, knitwear and leather items. There's also a craft shop displaying quality crafts from all over Ireland, a coffee shop, and the attractive paved courtyard is used in summer for street theatre, buskers and craft fairs.

One of the stateliest buildings in Enniskillen is the Portora Royal School on the edge of the town. Founded by Charles I in 1626, the present building dates from 1777 and its distinguished alumni include Oscar Wilde and Samuel Beckett.

Enniskillen boasts a beautifully maintained open space, **Forthill Park**, set on a steep hill above the town. Crowning the summit is the Cole Monument, built in 1857 to commemorate Sir Galbraith Lowry-Cole who was one of Wellington's Generals. There are superb views from the top of the monument but you will have to negotiate 108 steps before you can enjoy them.

Enniskillen's position at the southern tip of Lower Lough Erne makes it an ideal starting point for boat trips around this fascinating lake. Several of the islands can be visited - Boa Island and Devenish Island both have interesting Celtic or early-Christian relics, and **White Island** is noted for its eerie statues. There are eight of them, ranged against the wall of a 12th century church, and like many of the sculptures discovered in Fermanagh they have a distinctly pagan air about them. **Devenish Island** is famous for its perfect 12th century Round Tower (95ft high), ruined Augustinian priory and an intricately carved 15th century high cross in the graveyard.

Enniskillen is the kind of town one wants to linger in and fortunately it has some pleasant places to stay, most notably **Rossahilly House**. If only one could browse through the Visitors' Book before confirming a reservation at somewhere you've never stayed before. You would then see that the pages of Rossahilly House's guest book display an overwhelming approval. "A little piece of Heaven" in the opinion of one guest; "fantastic, not to be missed" says another entry; a third encapsulates the experience of staying here in just two words, "simply outstanding". In 1998, the high quality and appealing accommodation at Rossahilly House earned it the British Airways Tourism Award for Best Accommodation (other than hotel).

Rossahilly House, Enniskillen, Co. Fermanagh BT94 2FP
Tel: 028 6632 2352   Fax: 028 6632 0277   e-mail: rossahilly.house@virgin.net
website: http://freespace.virgin.net/rossahilly.house/

Built in the 1930s as a gentleman's residence, Rossahilly House occupies a superb position on an elevated site and enjoys one of the best panoramic views of Lower Lough Erne - "the most beautiful spot in a most beautiful country", (Visitors' Book). Your hosts, Eric and Monica Bell, extend a personal welcome to all their visitors and whether your stay is for one night or longer you will leave refreshed, having spent some leisurely time just soaking in the splendour of the surrounding scenery. And perhaps enjoying a few games of tennis on Rossahilly's own court.

All of the bedrooms have been individually decorated and all have private bathrooms. Look out for the breathtaking sunsets which are often a topic of conversation over coffee in the delightful conservatory.

At Rossahilly House, emphasis is placed on good food, simply prepared with natural flavours and taste. Monica is an exceptional cook and meals can be chosen from the Dinner menu or, quick and simple, from the High Tea menu. Ingredients are sourced from local suppliers and from the house's own kitchen gardens and Rossahilly House has its own drinks licence.

Rossahilly's helpful brochure also provides directions for finding the house and they include a rather unusual instruction: "Follow the signs for Airport. 200 yards past Airport entrance, turn left. Follow signs for Rossahilly House and go straight across runway. (If the lights are not working, look left, look right, and look up!)"

A mile or so outside Enniskillen stands a masterpiece of Palladian architecture, **Castle Coole** (National Trust). Built in Portland stone to a design by James Wyatt, the house was completed in 1798 and is generally regarded as the most perfect house of its era in Ireland. It was erected at enormous expense for the Earl of Belmore who spent equally lavishly on its magnificent furnishings. A guided tour of the house includes features such as the ornate State Bedroom, a Servant's Tunnel, and the Earl's luxurious private coach which is garaged in the original 18th century coach house.

Landscaped parkland leads down to the River Erne and nearby is the **Ardhowen Theatre**, occupying a lovely lakeside position. Established in 1986, the theatre offers a lively programme of plays, operas, variety, and dance and jazz performances. Travelling to the theatre by boat from Enniskillen makes a visit even more memorable.

LOWER LOUGH ERNE

An excellent day trip from Enniskillen is to make the drive around the entire expanse of Lower Lough Erne. Driving north from Enniskillen along the A32, the road passes the ferry point for Devenish Island *(see above)*. Fork left on the B32 to pass the town's small airport before reaching the little town of Killadeas.

KILLADEAS   Map 5 ref I5
6 miles N of Enniskillen on the B82

Killadeas is an angling, boating, sailing and cruising centre with a marvellous view of the lake. In the graveyard of the little church here stands the **Bishop's Stone**, one of the most striking examples of an early-Christian carved stone. On one side there's an obviously pagan image of a troubled-looking face; on the other, a bishop with bell and crosier. The graveyard also contains other curiously carved stones which are believed to date from the 7th or 8th centuries, amongst them a rounded pillar which was possibly a pagan phallic image.

A stone plaque outside **The Olde Schoolhouse** records the date that "Killadeas National School" was opened - 1910. For some 60 years it served the children of Killadeas

The Olde Schoolhouse, Tully, Killadeas, Co. Fermanagh BT94 1RE
Tel/Fax: 028 6621688/6628065

before being closed in the 1970s. It has been recently renovated and is now the home of Joan Moore who welcomes bed and breakfast guests to this unusual property. Set in the heart of the Fermanagh lakeland, The Olde Schoolhouse is ideal for touring Fermanagh, Tyrone, Donegal and Cavan. Lough Erne is just 500 yards away where there are facilities for watersports, boat trips and boat hire, or you could just enjoy the scenic drive around this famous lake. The Olde Schoolhouse is right beside Castle Archdale Country Park where there's a striking early 17th century Castle and an embarkation point for boat trips to White Island with its romantic ruined church. The Olde Schoolhouse has 7 guest bedrooms, 5 of them en suite, and all of them exceptionally well laid out and equipped. At breakfast time, there's a choice of either a full Irish or a continental meal. The area around Killadeas provides a wealth of facilities for all kinds of activities, (there's an equestrian centre for example at Irvinestown, just a couple of miles away), and while you are staying at The Olde Schoolhouse you could also stock up on your beauty aids since Joan is also a distributor for the Aloe Vera Forever Living Products.

Continuing northwards from Killadeas, the route passes **Castle Archdale Forest Park** (free) from whose marina there's a ferry to **White Island** *(see above)*. A little further north and beautifully located beside the lough, **Kesh** is a busy little fishing village with facilities for hiring cruise boats.

DRUMSKINNEY   MAP 5 REF I5
18 miles W of Omagh on minor road off the B72

Farmhouse holidays seem to have a special charm of their own and **Montaugh Farm** is no exception. The Loane family have been farming here for some 200 years but within their grounds stands something much, much older. In prehistoric times, an early Irish

Montaugh Farm, Montaughroe, Drumskinney, Kesh, Co. Fermanagh BT93 1EL
Tel: 028 6863 1385

people erected a complex of standing stones and rings here, an open air temple for some long-forgotten and mystical rite. The farmhouse itself, despite its venerable age, has been sensitively modernised to provide every kind of modern amenity. There are just 2 guest bedrooms, both en suite and both attractively decorated and furnished. At breakfast time, guests have the choice of either a full Irish or a continental breakfast and evening meals are available on request. Montaugh Farm provides an excellent base for exploring the scenic delights of the area with Lower Lough Erne heading the list of the county's many attractions. At **Kesh**, about 4 miles south, you can rent motor boats, (and a guide to lead you to the best places to fish for trout), hire a jetski or book yourself on to a banana boat ride.

PETTIGO   Map 5 ref I5
5 miles NW of Kesh off the A35

Just north of Kesh, the road forks. The A47 to the left crosses the long and narrow Boa Island, (the largest of the Lower Lough Erne islands, although it is linked to the mainland by bridges at either end). If you stay on the A35 it will bring you to the little town of Pettigo which is actually in Co. Donegal. Located just ten yards from the Ulster border with Co. Donegal, **Riverview Holiday Cottages** offer excellent self-catering facilities, with bed and breakfast accommodation also available if preferred. The 2 self-catering cottages are part of a smart modern terrace: one with 4 bedrooms, the other with 3. Each

**Riverview Holiday Cottages, Hill Street, Tullyhommon, Pettigo, Co. Donegal
Tel: 028 6863 1224**

cottage has a large lounge, an up-to-date bathroom, and a well-equipped kitchen furnished with just about every feature you can think of. Approved by the Northern Ireland Tourist Board, the cottages are only 20 minutes from Enniskillen and around 25 minutes from Donegal Town. Whatever your particular interests, you will almost certainly find the appropriate facilities nearby - devotees of golf, fishing, boating, horse riding and water sports are all well-provided for. Just yards from the cottages is The Olde Mill which has recently been completely restored and is now a prime tourist attraction. Only a little further away, the brand new Aughnahoo Art Studios are also well worth a visit.

BELLEEK

Map 5 ref H5

25 miles NW of Enniskillen on the A47

From Pettigo, rejoin the A47 as it runs along the lake shore, passing Castle Caldwell Forest (free) which is an RSPB reserve with wildfowl hides, shore walks and an exhibition centre. A short detour from the lakeside road will bring you to Belleek which is also on the border with Co. Donegal. An ancient joke for anglers is that it's possible here to hook a salmon in the Republic and land it in Northern Ireland. But the town is much more famous for its distinctive pottery - beautifully crafted lustreware which is produced primarily for its decorative rather than its utilitarian qualities. At the **Belleek Visitors Centre** (free) a video presentation explains the production process and is followed by a 20-minute guided tour of the pottery which was established in 1857. The Pottery Shop has the complete product range on show and for sale and the Centre also includes an award-winning restaurant where, naturally, your refreshments are served on the finest Belleek tableware.

Skilled craftsmanship of another kind is on view at **Fermanagh Crystal** (free) where you can watch fine pieces being created and even commission a work of your own. Also in Belleek, located on the banks of the River Erne, **Explore Erne** provides the opportunity of exploring the length and breadth of the Lough Erne without getting your feet wet. A huge video wall displays an informative video explaining how the 50 miles of lough were formed; how Lough Erne has influenced the lives of local people; and how the lakes have contributed to travel, recreation and industry in Fermanagh.

LOUGH NAVAR FOREST

Map 5 ref I5

15 miles NW of Enniskillen off the A46

From Belleek, the A46 hugs the southern shore of the lake for most of the 25 mile journey back to Enniskillen. Along the way, it passes the Lough Navar Forest, where there's a 7-mile circular drive through the forest that includes a breathtaking panorama over the lake from the Magho Viewpoint (1000ft).

Two short detours will bring you to the remains of two castles, both of which were destroyed by fire. About 10 miles before Enniskillen, **Tully Castle** was built by Sir John Hume around 1613 and burned by his enemies, the Maguires, in 1641. The Castle has a formal garden and visitor centre. Five miles further on, signposted from the main road, a country lane leads to **Castle Monea** (free), an imposing plantation castle built by Michael Hamilton around 1618. It's remarkable well preserved considering that it has suffered no fewer than three separate fires. It was put to the torch during the Great Rebellion of 1641, again during the Jacobite uprising of 1689, and finally abandoned after another, accidental, fire in 1750.

SOUTH OF ENNISKILLEN

BELLANALECK   MAP 5 REF 16
3 miles S of Enniskillen on the A509

Bellanaleck is a pleasing little town with a marina where you can hire cruisers and rowing boats to explore this little-known wetland area. But if you plan on walking around Bellanaleck, wellington boots are recommended! The town is well-known for Gault's Crafts which specialises in beautiful hand-knit Aran sweaters created by local knitters, but also has a wide range of other items - blackthorn sticks and shillelaghs (made on the premises); hand-woven tweed, rugs, scarves and hats; Belleek and Donegal china; and much more.

Housed in an eye-catching thatched building some 200 years old, **The Sheelin** licensed restaurant is a delightful place where you can enjoy a candlelit dinner and the warmth of open turf fires. Malcolm and Rosemary Cathcart own and run this outstanding eating place as well as **The Sheelin Antique Irish Lace Museum** right next door. All the lace on display here dates from between 1850 to 1900 and includes examples of all the 5 main types of Irish lace. Amongst the 140 items on show are a very rare Irish Crochet

**The Sheelin, Bellanaleck, Enniskillen, Co. Fermanagh BT92 2BA
Tel: 028 6634 8232/6634 8052**

wedding dress, wedding veils, shawls, parasols, baby bonnets, christening gowns, flounces, jackets and much more - all of the highest quality work.

About 5 miles southwest of Bellanaleck, **Florence Court** is regarded as one of the most important houses in Ulster. Beautifully situated beneath the steep mountain of

Florence Court, Nr Bellanaleck

Benaughlin, the house was built for John Cole, father of the 1st Earl of Enniskillen, and completed in 1775. It was named after Florence, his wife. One of the chief glories of Florence Court is the exceptional embellished rococo plasterwork, seen at its best above the stairs and in the dining room. The house contains fine Irish furniture, including an 18th century rococo armchair in the library, an Irish writing cabinet which dates from 1730 and an unusual 18th century bed.

The house is surrounded by a large area of parkland, garden and woodland, including a recently restored walled garden where the pink and white roses are especially attractive in early summer. Florence Court's most notable tree, the Irish yew, grows in a much wilder part of the estate. From its seedlings have grown every other Irish yew anywhere in the world. This 260-year-old original was one of two found in the Fermanagh hills in the 1740s.

Also within the grounds are a recently restored water-powered sawmill, an ice house, a replica of a Victorian summer house, a shop and tea room.

A visit to the house can be combined with an exploration of the **Marble Arch Caves**, three miles to the west. This is one of Europe's finest showcaves, a fascinating underworld of stalactites and stalagmites glistening in winding passages and huge caverns. The 75-minute guided tour begins by boat and then continues on foot past limestone formations, rivers and waterfalls. An especially interesting feature is the "Moses Walk", so-called because the dammed walkway crosses a lake, with more than three feet of water on either side. During the high season the guided tours can be fully booked and after heavy rain the caves may close for safety reasons so it's advisable to telephone before setting out (tel: 028 6634 8855).

HOLYWELL
MAP 5 REF I6
11 miles W of Enniskillen off the A4

Riverside B&B stands close to the famous well from which the village takes its name. The water runs both uphill and downhill and local people swear that the water cures many ills. Riverside enjoys a lovely position, surrounded by a well-established garden with rolling lawns and a beautiful mountain view. The house itself is a spacious modern bungalow with large, comfortable rooms, and just 2 guest bedrooms, one of which is en

Riverside B & B, Holywell, Belcoo, Co. Fermanagh BT94 5DT
Tel/Fax: 028 6638 6303

suite. Riverside is the family home of Patricia Rasdale, a welcoming host who takes great pains to ensure that her guests are as comfortable and relaxed as possible. Tucked away though it is in this scenic corner of Fermanagh, Riverside is within easy reach of such attractions as the famous Marble Arch Caves, just a 10-minute drive away; the castles of Monea and Tully; while a 20-minute drive will bring you to the border town of Belleek and its renowned Pottery.

MAGUIRESBRIDGE
MAP 5 REF J6
8 miles SE of Enniskillen on the A4/A34

The maze of waters around Maguiresbridge present quite a challenge for the explorer so if you plan to explore this wonderfully tranquil area a detailed map is a necessity. Old folk traditions still linger here - you may well come across someone possessing the secret of unorthodox cures for animal and human ailments.

There's a delightful place to stay at near Maguiresbridge, conveniently located within easy reach of all the county's main attractions. **Derryvree Farm Cottage** offers quality self-catering accommodation and there's also the option of excellent B&B in the main house where you can enjoy good home cooking in a relaxed and friendly, non-smoking environment. The cottage is situated on a working sheep farm within walking distance of

Derryvree House, 200 Belfast Road, Maguiresbridge, Co. Fermanagh BT94 4LD
Tel: 028 8953 1251

the village of Maguiresbridge and 8 miles from the county town of Enniskillen. The one-storey building has been cleverly modernised, with much of the original stonework preserved and complemented with a raised pine ceiling and maplewood bedroom floor. It offers all the comforts of a luxurious modern home, equipped with central heating and double glazing. The cottage features an open-plan lounge, kitchen and dining area, all designed to cater for four adults. The double bedroom has en suite facilities suitable for wheelchair users while the lounge has a bed settee for the 3rd and 4th persons. There's also a separate bathroom. The cottage is comprehensively equipped and bed linen, towels, dish towels

Derryvree Farm Cottage

and dish cloths are all provided. Children are welcome with a high chair and cot available if required and outside the lawn provides a safe play area. A picnic table and chairs are also provided and anglers will be pleased to know that the cottage includes a bait house and separate bait fridge. If required, the owners Wendy and Aubrey Bothwell can stock up on groceries for you. Pets can be accommodated but only outside the house. Approved by the NITB, the cottage is available all year round and makes a perfect base for touring Co. Fermanagh and the neighbouring counties of Tyrone, Donegal, Leitrim, Monaghan and Cavan. Amongst the many places of interest within a short drive are the castles at Enniskillen and Crom, Florence Court House and Gardens, the Marble Arch Caves, Castle Archdale Country Park, Colebrooke River and Upper and Lower Loughs Erne.

NEWTOWNBUTLER
Map 5 ref J6
18 miles SE of Enniskillen on the A34

Covering almost two thousand acres of woodland, farmland and loughs which support a wide variety of rare plants and abundant wildlife, the **Crom Estate** (National Trust) is one of Ireland's most important nature conservation areas. Trails around the estate take in the ruins of Crom Old Castle built on the shore of the lough in 1610 by Michael Balfour, Laird of Mountwhinney. The castle withstood two sieges in the troubles of 1689 but was destroyed by an accidental fire in 1764. The yew trees within the ruins are reputed to be the oldest in Ireland. Other buildings of interest within the estate are The Old Farmyard, built as a model farmyard in the 1830s and now the Visitor Centre, a Victorian schoolhouse, summer house, and a splendidly over-the-top Boathouse with decorated bargeboards and battlements. Boats can be hired to explore the islands that form part of the estate or for fishing expeditions. There are good facilities for visitors with disabilities and the Visitor Centre has a tea-room and shop. Crom Estate is open daily from April to September, 10am to 6pm; Sundays, noon until 6pm.

ROSLEA
Map 5 ref J6
9 miles W of Monaghan on the R187

Tucked away in the most easterly corner of the county, Roslea is close to the border of the Republic, with the mountain range of Slieve Beagh stretching for miles to the north and west. This is grand walking country and if you're planning to stay in the area the ideal place is **Annagulgan House.** Both interesting and healthy, farmhouse holidays have a charm of their own and a stay at Annagulgan House is no exception to the rule. Tucked away at the end of a half-mile lane, this is a working dairy farm which means that there's always fresh milk and free range eggs for breakfast. Maureen Callaghan also bakes her own bread, cakes and pies so it's definitely a good idea to take up the option of having an evening meal here. At breakfast time Maureen offers the choice of a wholesome full Irish breakfast or the more abstemious continental variety. The farmhouse itself is a modern building, equipped with all the up-to-date amenities, a comfortable and welcoming place where visitors start to relax as soon as they step inside. The house stands on an elevated site, surrounded by extensive and attractive gardens complete with ponds and a

Annagulgan House, Roslea, Co. Fermanagh BT92 7FN
Tel: 028 6775 1498

barbecue area. If they wish, visitors are welcome to take part in the farm activities but shouldn't miss out on exploring the lovely lakeside scenery around Upper Lough Erne or making the trip to the famous viewpoint of Carnmore. Only 6 miles or so from Annagulgan House, the spectacular panorama from Carnmore on a clear day extends across 32 counties. Another major attraction in the neighbourhood is the Roslea Golf Centre and Driving Range where you can keep your play up to scratch all year round and well into the evening under floodlights.

Also worth visiting while you are in Roslea is the **Roslea Heritage Centre** on the Monaghan road. It's housed in an 1874 schoolhouse, complete with the old school desks, and among the exhibits on display are traditional farming implements, crafts and crochet pieces. The Centre has a genealogical service, tea room and shop.

Calendar of Events

The events listed below are only a selection of the many festivals, fairs shows and other organised activities which take place throughout Ireland each year. We are sure, however, that they will not only provide a very enjoyable insight into the real Irish culture and heritage, but will leave you with fond memories of Ireland and its people.

Most of the events listed occur annually but we suggest that you contact the organisers to confirm dates and times particularly for events in 2001. If you require details of other events taking place in Ireland we recommend that you call in at the nearest **Tourist Information Centre** (listed towards the rear of this edition) or ring **Bord Fáilte - Irish Tourist Board** on 01 602 4000.

JANUARY 2000

27th December - 3rd January
CONNEMARA FOUR SEASONS MILLENNIUM WALKING FESTIVAL

Clifden, Connemara, Co Galway

Hiking in the 12 Bens and Maumturk Mountains. Walking on off-shore islands of Aran, Omey and Inishbofin and bog trotting across ancient buried landscapes with their rich spirit world.

Contact: Michael Gibbons
Tel: 095 21379/21492, Fax: 095 21845,
e-mail: walkwest@indigo.ie
website: www.walkingireland.com

FEBRUARY 2000

4th - 6th February
EIGSE NA BRIDEOIGE – BIDDY FESTIVAL

Waterville, Co Kerry

Cultural weekend celebrating many aspects of local culture.

Contact: Padraig De Buis
Tel: 066 9474123, Fax: 066 9474836
e-mail: debuis@hotmail.com

15th - 28th February
NEWTOWNABBEY ARTS FESTIVAL 2000

Ballyearl Arts Centre, Newtownabbey, Co Antrim

An entertaining programme of artistic events for the new Millennium.

Contact: Tel: (028) 9335 2681

17th February
LACEY CLAN RALLY

Co Tipperary

Contact: Andy Lacey
Tel: 062 33244

MARCH 2000

2nd - 3rd March
JOHN MCCORMACK GOLDEN VOICE OF ATHLONE

Hodson Bay Hotel, Athlone, Co Westmeath

Gala classical singing competition in commemoration of world famous tenor John McCormack.

Contact: Siobhan Bigley
Tel: 0902 73173, Fax: 0902 74386
e-mail: athcci@iol.ie

5th - 12th March
ARKLOW MUSIC FESTIVAL

Various venues in Arklow, Co Wicklow

A competition festival which includes orchestras, choirs, solo singing, drama and verse speaking.

Contact: Eileen Clandillon
Tel: 0402 32732 (W), Tel: 0402 32955 (H)
Fax: 0402 91030

10th - 19th March
BRIDGE HOUSE IRISH FESTIVAL
Tullamore, Co Offaly
Festival celebrating Irish music, food and craic!
Contact: Colm McCabe
Tel: 0506 21704/22000, Fax: 0506 41338

13th - 17th March
ST PATRICK'S FESTIVAL
Downpatrick and various venues in Co Down
A cross-community programme of entertainments, church services and activities climaxed on the Big day with a cavalcade of floats and fancy dress.
Contact: Tel: (028) 4461 3211

14th - 21st March
CELTIC SPRING FESTIVAL
Various venues in Co Derry
St Patrick's Week programme of traditional music, song and dance plus Irish amateur drama.
Contact: Tel: (028) 7126 7234

15th - 19th March
CORK CITY CELTIC FLAME FESTIVAL 2000
This festival will incorporate St. Patrick's Day parade, street entertainment, and traditional Irish music. Celtic Flame concerts in city hotels.
Contact: Frank Donaldson
Tel: 021 273251, Fax: 021 276672

16th - 19th March
ST PATRICK'S FESTIVAL 2000
Dublin
Street theatre carnival and concerts. An intoxicating mix of pageantry, colour, music and madness.
Contact: Grainne Walker
Tel: 01 6763205, Fax: 01 6763208,
e-mail: info@paddyfest.ie
website: www.stpatricksday.ie

16th - 19th March
DAN FOLEY MAGIC WEEKEND
Various venues in Annascaul, Co Kerry
Weekend of music, song and dance.
Contact: Rory O'Shea
Tel: 066 9157419, Fax: 066 9157463,
e-mail: anascaul@indigo.ie
website: www.dingle-peninsula.ie/annascaul

16th - 19th March
ST PATRICK'S WEEKEND FESTIVAL
Banbridge, Co Down
From folklore to farming there's something for everyone.
Contact: Tel: (028) 3884 1234

17th - 20th March
ST PATRICK'S CARNIVAL
Various venues, Belfast
Fun weekend.
Contact: Tel: (028) 9027 0466

17th - 24th March
MARITIME FESTIVAL
Newry Canal, Co Down
Celebrating 150 years of Ireland's oldest canal with a programme of events on land and water.
Contact: Tel: (028) 3025 7864

18th - 19th March
LIMERICK INTERNATIONAL BAND FESTIVAL
University of Limerick and O'Connell Street, Limerick
Celebrating its 30th Anniversary - a memorable weekend when all categories of marching/concert bands and drill teams worldwide converge on the day.
Contact: Caroline Nolan-Diffley
Tel: 061 410777 or Tel: 061 315634 (W)
e-mail: bandfest@shannon-dev.ie
website: http://www.shannon-dev.ie/bandfest

20th March - 2nd April
FEIS CEOIL ASSOCIATION
Royal Dublin Society, Ballsbridge, St. Mary's Church Hall, Christ Church Cathedral, Dublin 8, St. Bartholomews Church, Dublin 4.
The Feis Ceoil Association is a voluntary organisation founded in 1896. Feis Ceoil runs a competitive classical music festival each year.
Contact: Carmel T Byrne
Tel: 01 6767365, Fax: 01 6767429

23rd March - 2nd April
BETWEEN THE LINES 2000
Crescent Arts Centre, Belfast
International literary festival with a millennial theme.
Contact: Tel: (028) 9024 2338

APRIL 2000

20th March - 2nd April
FEIS CEOIL ASSOCIATION
Royal Dublin Society, Ballsbridge, St. Mary's Church Hall, Christ Church Cathedral, Dublin 8, St. Bartholomews Church, Dublin 4

The Feis Ceoil Association is a voluntary organisation founded in 1896. Feis Ceoil runs a competitive classical music festival each year.

Contact: Carmel T Byrne
Tel: 01 6767365, Fax: 01 6767429

23rd March - 2nd April
BETWEEN THE LINES 2000
Crescent Arts Centre, Belfast

International literary festival with a millennial theme.

Contact: Tel: (028) 9024 2338

5th - 16th April
DUBLIN FILM FESTIVAL
Various cinemas throughout Dublin

Exhibits the best in Irish and international cinema.

Contact: Aine O'Halloran
Tel: 01 6792937, Fax: 01 6792939
e-mail: dff@iol.ie
website: http://www.iol.ie/dff/

10th - 16th April
FEIS SHLIGIGH
Hawk's Well Theatre, Sligo.

Festival of drama, Irish language, classical and traditional music, dancing, art and verse speaking.

Contact: Kevin Carroll, Tel: 071 68197

Mid - End April
LAUNCH OF THE JEANIE JOHNSTON SHIP
Blennerville, Tralee, Co Kerry

The Jeanie Johnston Tall Ship and historic replica will sail from Blennerville, Tralee to North America in April 2000 on her millennium voyage. She will visit over 20 cities in the US and Canada celebrating the contribution of Irish People to all spheres of life in the US and Canada.

Contact: Ann Martin
Tel: 066 7181681 or Tel: 066 7181888

14th - 15th April
COLERAINE INTERNATIONAL CHORAL FESTIVAL
University of Ulster, Coleraine, Co Derry

US and European choirs participate in a harmonious event.

Contact: Tel: (028) 7035 3489

12st - 27th April
WORLD IRISH DANCING CHAMPIONSHIPS
Waterfront Hall, Belfast

This event is the highlight of the year for all Irish dancing enthusiasts at which over 4,000 competitors from Ireland, Britian, North America, Australia and New Zealand compete.

Contact: Maire Ni Chorbaid
Tel: 01 4752220, Fax: 01 4751053
e-mail: clrg@tinet.ie

21st - 28th April
CONNEMARA FOUR SEASONS WALKING FESTIVALS
Clifden, Connemara, Co Galway

Hiking in the 12 Bens and Maumturk Mountains. Walking on off-shore islands of Aran, Omey and Inishbofin and bog trotting across ancient buried landscapes with their rich spirit world.

Contact: Michael Gibbons
Tel: 095 21379/21492, Fax: 095 21845,
e-mail: walkwest@Indigo.Ie
website: www.walkingireland.com

22nd - 23rd April
KENMARE EASTER WALKING FESTIVAL
Kenmare, Co Kerry

Guided hill and way walking – Evening entertainment

Contact: Mike Murphy
Tel: 064 41034, Fax: 064 42168
e-mail: murphyma@iol.ie
website: www.walking@kenmare.com

22nd - 24th April [Provisional]
KERRY ARTS FESTIVAL – SAMHLAIOCHT CHIARAI
Various venues in Co Kerry

A festival of music, song, dance, drama, film, literature and photography.

Contact: Maggie Fitzsimons
Tel: 066 7129934, Fax: 066 7125841

23rd April
"OLDE" MACHINERY RALLY
Gleneagle Hotel Grounds, Killarney, Co Kerry

Open Air working Museum – 75 stationary oil engines made during 1905-1940. Vintage tractors, cars, motor cycles, steam engines, collector displays, bottles, tools, phone cards, etc.

Contact: Brendan Griffin
Tel: 064 32530

24th - 28th April
FEIS SHLIGIGH
Summerhill College, Sligo.

Festival of drama, Irish language, classical and traditional music, dancing, art and verse speaking.

Contact: Kevin Carroll
Tel: 071 68197

25th - 30th April
PAN CELTIC INTERNATIONAL FESTIVAL 2000
Tralee, Co Kerry

Celebration of celtic culture, music, song, dance, sport among celtic nations and to promote interceltic tourism and trade.

Contact: Margaret Maunsell
Tel: 066 7180050, Fax: 066 7139449.
e-mail: panceltic.tinet.ie
website: www.panceltic.com

26th - 30th April
FESTIVAL OF CULTURE AND SPORT
Ballymoney Borough, Co Antrim

Representatives from Ireland, Scotland and Wales participate in varied programme venues.

Contact: Tel: (028) 2766 2280.

26th - 30th April
BORD GAIS CORK INTERNATIONAL CHORAL FESTIVAL
Various venues in Cork

Performances by international and national choirs in a competitive and non-competitive capacity throughout city and county.

Contact: John Fitzpatrick
Tel: 021 308308, Fax: 021 308309
e-mail: chorfest@iol.ie
website: www.musweb.com/corkchoral.htm

26th April - 1st May
6TH MAY FESTIVAL – FEILE NA BEALTAINE
Various venues around the Dingle Peninsula, Co Kerry

This festival draws literary figures, artists, politicians, musicians, etc., worldwide.

Contact: Micheal O'Fionnain
Tel: 066 9151465, Fax: 066 9152344

28th - 30th April
THE SHERIDAN CLAN GATHERING
Granard, Co Longford

Contact: Kay Sheridan Cassidy
Tel: 043 86178
e-mail: sheridanclan@oceanfree.net

28th April - 1st May
JOSIE MCDERMOTT MEMORIAL FESTIVAL
Community Hall, Boyle, Co Roscommon
Events include concerts, ceili, feis rince, and talent competitions. The main event is the traditional flute competition.

Contact: Anne Healy/Mary Shivnan
Tel: 078 47024, Fax: 078 47096

28th April - 7th May
JANE ROSS FESTIVAL
Limavady , Co Derry

Celebrating the local woman who gave the world the Londonderry Air. Music, drama, crafts and Mayor's Parade.

Contact: Tel: (028) 7776 0304

29th - 30th April
WICKLOW MOUNTAINS WALKING FESTIVAL
Blessington Lakes, Co Wicklow

Contact: Wicklow County Tourism
Tel: 0404 20100, Fax: 0404 67792,
e-mail: wctr@iol.ie
website: www.wicklow.ie

29th - 30th April
CITY OF BELFAST FLOWER SHOW
Barnett Demense, Belfast

Celebrate the first blooming bulbs of the century among a host of daffodils.

Contact: Tel: (028) 9027 0466

29th April - 1st May
BALLYHOURA INTERNATIONAL WALKING FESTIVAL
Kilfinane, Co Limerick

3-day walking festival with guided walks.

Contact: Thelma Wyngaard
Tel: 063 91300, Fax: 063 91404
e-mail: holidays@ballyhoura.org
website: http://www.foundmark/ballyhoura.html

MAY 2000

26th April - 1st May
6TH MAY FESTIVAL – FEILE NA BEALTAINE
Various venues around the Dingle Peninsula, Co Kerry

This festival draws literary figures, artists, politicians, musicians, etc., worldwide.

Contact: Micheal O'Fionnain
Tel: 066 9151465, Fax: 066 9152344

28th April - 1st May
JOSIE MCDERMOTT MEMORIAL FESTIVAL
Community Hall, Boyle, Co Roscommon
Events include concerts, ceili, feis rince, and talent competitions. The main event is the traditional flute competition.

Contact: Anne Healy/Mary Shivnan
Tel: 078 47024, Fax: 078 47096

28th April - 7th May
JANE ROSS FESTIVAL
Limavady , Co Derry

Celebrating the local woman who gave the world the Londonderry Air. Music, drama, crafts and Mayor's Parade.

Contact: Tel: (028) 7776 0304

29th April - 1st May
BALLYHOURA INTERNATIONAL WALKING FESTIVAL
Kilfinane, Co Limerick

3-day walking festival with guided walks.

Contact: Thelma Wyngaard
Tel: 063 91300, Fax: 063 91404
e-mail: holidays@ballyhoura.org
website: http://www.foundmark/ballyhoura.html

1st - 2nd May
BELFAST MARATHON
Maysfield and city-wide.

Top runners from many countries compete in one of the most popular athletic events in Ireland. Next day, Belfast International Peace Mile will be inaugurated on 2 May in city centre.

Contact: (028) 9027 0466

2nd - 13th May
ALL IRELAND DRAMA FESTIVAL
Dean Crowe Theatre, Athlone, Co Westmeath

Drama competitions which incorporates drama groups from all over Ireland competing for this prestigious competition.

Contact: Colm Kelly
Tel: 0902 72333 – Booking at Royal Hotel Athlone:Tel: 0902 72622

3rd - 9th May
DOYLE & MCDOWELL CLAN GATHERING
Dublin and Wexford

Contact:Clann O DubhGhaill
PO Box 173, Dromana, Victoria 3936, Australia

4th - 7th May
MURPHY'S INTERNATIONAL MUSSEL FAIR,
Bantry, Co Cork

Three day event with free mussels in all bars and restaurants. Quality entertainment free of charge. Family events.

Contact: Eileen O'Shea
Tel/Fax: 027 50360

5th May - 28th July
COUNTY WICKLOW GARDENS FESTIVAL
Gardens throughout the county

Heritage properties and private gardens open to the public. Many events including guided tours, flower arranging classes. etc.

Contact: Wicklow County Tourism
Tel: 0404 20100, Fax: 0404 67792,
e-mail: wctr@iol.ie
website: www.wicklow.ie

6th May
MILLENNIUM LORD MAYOR'S SHOW
Belfast

Parade of floats through downtown streets of Belfast.

Contact: Tel: (028) 9027 0466

6th May
CLOUGH NORMAN DAY

Clough, Downpatrick, Co Down

Costumed enactment in grounds of Castle.

Contact: Tel: (028) 4481 1079

6th - 7th May
KINANE CLAN RALLY

Co Tipperary

Contact: W F Kinane, Tel/Fax: 062 51221

7th May - 24th September
COBH CARILLON RECITALS – 73RD SEASON

St. Colman's Cathedral, Cobh, Co Cork

Free recitals on the 49-bell carillon of St. Colman's Cathedral

Contact: Adrian Patrick Gebruers
Tel: 021 811219, Fax: 021 272121,
e-mail: agebruers@eircom.net
website: http://homepage.eircom.net/~adriange bruers

10th - 12th May
BALMORAL SHOW 2000

Balmoral Showgrounds, Belfast.

One of the great agricultural / entertainment events In the calendar has a special programme for the new century

Contact: Tel: (028) 9066 5225

11th - 14th May
THE GALWAY EARLY MUSIC FESTIVAL "VOLTA 2000"

Various venues in Galway city

Volta 2000 celebrates music, dance and costume from 12th to 17th centuries featuring international, national and local musicians in concert and on the streets in the medieval city of Galway. The festival includes concerts, workshops, street music, dance and historical re-enactment.

Contact: Justina McElligott
Tel: 091 528166
e-mail: justina@iol.ie,
website: http://www.wombat.ie/pages/early-music

13th May
LISBURN MILLENNIUM MAYOR'S PARADE

Lisburn & other venues in Co Antrim

Bigger and better version of regular event that always attracts thousands of visitors. Lisburn Borough Arts Festival in May features Millennium Festival of Dance.

Contact: Tel: (028) 9268 2477

19th - 20th May
A.I.M.S. CHORAL FESTIVAL

New Ross, Co Wexford

Festival for choirs of all kinds. Competitions on 20th May for 11 categories from barbershop to madrigal from male voice to gospel. High standard and friendly atmosphere.

Contact: Connie Tantrum
Tel: 051 421766

20th - 27th May
BALLYCLARE MAY FAIR 2000

Ballyclare, Co Antrim

Traditional annual fair is given the Millennium treatment.

Contact: 028 9335 2681

20th May - 4th June
BELFAST SUMMERFEST 2000

Various venues

Entertainment and activities throughout the capital.

Contact: Tel: (028) 9027 0466

25th - 29th May
BBC MUSIC LIVE

Clotworthy Arts Centre, Antrim and many other venues.

Live performances and workshops.

Contact: Tel: (028) 9342 8000

26th - 28th May
WHITTY CLAN RALLY

Talbot Hotel, Wexford

Contact: Maura Whitty
Tel/Fax: 053 41124
e-mail: mwhitty@tinet.ie

26th - 28th May

SLIGO ARTS FESTIVAL

An explosion of music, street events and exhibitions.

Contact: Danny Kirrane
Tel/Fax: 071 69802

26th May - 4th June

DUNDALK INTERNATIONAL MAYTIME FESTIVAL

Dundalk, Co Louth

International drama, street entertainment and fun.

Contact: Kevin Hall
Tel: 042 9335253
e-mail: dundalkfestival@tinet.ie

27th May - 5th June

KENMARE WHIT WALKING FESTIVAL

Kenmare, Co Kerry

15 Guided hillwalks, - The Kerry Way, Beara Way, Mountain Skills Course. Entertainment and slide shows.

Contact: Mike Murphy
Tel: 064 41034, Fax: 064 42168
e-mail: murphyma@iol.ie
website: www.walking@kenmare.com

29th May

NEWRY MARKET AND THE MILLENNIUM

Newry, Co Down

Take a carriage and go old-time shopping for crafts and gifts in an atmosphere of costumed pageantry.

Contact: Tel: (028) 3026 6232

31st May - 4th June

WRITERS' WEEK LISTOWEL

St John's Arts and Heritage Centre, Listowel, Co Kerry

To promote and celebrate art and literature through readings, music, dance, drama, lectures and comedy.

Contact: Mary Kennelly
Tel: 068 21074, Fax: 068 22893
e-mail: writersweek@tinet.ie

JUNE 2000

5th May - 28th July

COUNTY WICKLOW GARDENS FESTIVAL

Gardens throughout the county

Heritage properties and private gardens open to the public. Many events including guided tours, flower arranging classes. etc.

Contact: Wicklow County Tourism
Tel: 0404 20100, Fax: 0404 67792,
e-mail: wctr@iol.ie
website: www.wicklow.ie

7th May - 24th September

COBH CARILLON RECITALS – 73RD SEASON

St. Colman's Cathedral, Cobh, Co Cork

Free recitals on the 49-bell carillon of St. Colman's Cathedral

Contact: Adrian Patrick Gebruers
Tel: 021 811219, Fax: 021 272121,
e-mail: agebruers@eircom.net
website: http://homepage.eircom.net/~adriangebruers

20th May - 4th June

BELFAST SUMMERFEST 2000

Various venues

Entertainment and activities throughout the capital.

Contact: Tel: (028) 9027 0466

26th May - 4th June

DUNDALK INTERNATIONAL MAYTIME FESTIVAL

Dundalk, Co Louth

International drama, street entertainment and fun.

Contact: Kevin Hall
Tel: 042 9335253
e-mail: dundalkfestival@tinet.ie

27th May - 5th June

KENMARE WHIT WALKING FESTIVAL

Kenmare, Co Kerry

15 Guided hillwalks, - The Kerry Way, Beara Way, Mountain Skills Course. Entertainment and slide shows.

Contact: Mike Murphy
Tel: 064 41034, Fax: 064 42168
e-mail: murphyma@iol.ie
website: www.walking@kenmare.com

31st May - 4th June

WRITERS' WEEK LISTOWEL

St John's Arts and Heritage Centre, Listowel, Co Kerry

To promote and celebrate art and literature through readings, music, dance, drama, lectures and comedy.

Contact: Mary Kennelly
Tel: 068 21074, Fax: 068 22893

1st Jun

CHARITY FUN DAY

Coleraine Marina, Co Derry

Street theatre, music, drama and more. Coleraine town centre. Opening of Millennium Playpark including facilities for disabled children.

Contact: Tel: (028) 7035 3489

1st - 6th Jun

MURPHY'S CAT LAUGHS

Various venues throughout Kilkenny

International comedy festival featuring some of the finest stand up comedians and comic improvisers.

Contact: Richard Cook
Tel: 056 63416, Fax: 056 63679

1st - 30th June

GREATER SHANKILL FESTIVAL

Shankill Area Belfast

Community activities and a special welcome for visitors. Shankill area,

Contact: Tel: (028) 9031 1333

2nd - 4th June

SLIGO COUNTY FLEADH

Ballymote, Co Sligo

A weekend of music, song and dance. Competitions in all traditional musical instruments.

Contact: Kathleen Finn
Tel: 071 83541 or The Secretary, Tel: 071 62763

2nd - 4th June

SLIGO ARTS FESTIVAL

An explosion of music, street events and exhibitions.

Contact: Danny Kirrane
Tel/Fax: 071 69802

2nd - 4th June

Holywood Millennium Jazz Festival:

A swinging weekend celebrates 100 years since the birth of jazz and 10 years of this superb festival. Holywood and Cultra, Co Down

Contact: Tel: (028) 9076 8563

2nd - 5th June

MICK AND MICEAL CARR MEMORIAL TRADITIONAL MUSIC WEEKEND

O'Donnell's Bar, Meenaneary, Carrick, Co Donegal.

A great weekend of music, song and dance. All musicians welcome.

Contact: Rory O'Donnell
Tel: 073 39009

2nd - 5th Jun

JEROME CONNOR ARTS, SCULPTURE AND DRAMA FESTIVAL

Annascaul, Co Kerry

Festival commemorating the life and works of Annascaul born sculptor. Workshops in oils, pastels, sculpture and figure making , youth theatre and drama.

Contact: Marie Kennedy
Tel: 066 9157382
e-mail: dropanchor@tinet.ie

2nd - 5th June

CONNEMARA FOUR SEASONS WALKING FESTIVALS – 12 BENS MOUNTAIN CHALLENGE

Clifden, Connemara, Co Galway

Hiking in the 12 Bens and Maumturk Mountains. Walking on off-shore islands of Aran, Omey and Inishbofin and bog trotting across ancient buried landscapes with their rich spirit world.

Contact: Michael Gibbons
Tel: 095 21379/21492, Fax: 095 21845,
e-mail: walkwest@indigo.ie
website: www.walkingireland.com

2nd - 9th June

MILLENNIUM NEIGHBOURHOOD GAMES

Belfast city-wide.

Serious and not-so-serious sporting activities.

Contact: Tel: (028) 9027 0466

3rd - 4th June [Provisional]
ALL IRELAND SHEEPSHEARING CHAMPIONSHIP
Danesfort, Co Kilkenny

Contact: John Joe Kenny, Tel: 056 29935

3rd - 5th June
KERRY SKELLIG REGIONAL MILLENNIUM FESTIVAL
Kerry/ Skellig Regions

Walking and Gourmet Festival.

Contact: Marc Dourieu
Tel: 066 9473355, Fax: 066 9473366

3rd - 24th June
CASTLEWARD OPERA
Castleward, Strangford, Co Down

Annual season of 18 performances in this magical setting of the famous National Trust property which is a harmonious attraction in its own right.

Contact: Tel: (028) 9066 1090

8th - 17th June
AIB MUSIC FESTIVAL IN GREAT IRISH HOUSES
Classical music played in various great houses throughout Ireland.

Contact: Crawford Tipping
Tel: 01 2781528, Fax: 01 2781529

9th - 11th June
BALLYLICKEY FAILTE WEEKEND
Ballylickey, Bantry, Co Cork

A variety of fun events, competitions and music.

Contact: Elizabeth O'Shea
Tel: 027 50579

9th - 11th June
TEMPO FAIR DAYS
Tempo, Co Fermanagh.

Millennium revival of the town's famous fair of yesteryear. Cattle drive, rare breeds, blacksmithing, butter-churning.

Contact: Tel: (028) 8954 1861

9th - 11th June
WALLED CITY FESTIVAL
Co Derry

Millennium celebration of the sights, sounds and senses of the world, incorporating a homecoming festival for exiles and the Civic Parade.

Contact: Tel: (028) 7126 7284

9th - 11th June
LIMAVADY JAZZ AND BLUES FESTIVAL
Limavady, Co Derry

Local and international musicians swing into summer on a high note.

Contact: Tel: (028) 7776 0304

9th - 11th June
SLIGO ARTS FESTIVAL
An explosion of music, street events and exhibitions.

Contact: Danny Kirrane, Tel/Fax: 071 69802

9th - 17th June
EIGSE CARLOW ARTS FESTIVAL
St. Patrick's College, Carlow

Exhibitions of International/Irish artists. Crafts, drama, classical and pop music.

Contact: Therese Jackman
Tel: 0503 40491, Fax: 0503 30065

10th - 17th June
SAINTFIELD MILLENNIUM FESTIVAL
Saintfield, Co Down

Week of events in this charming floral town.

Contact: Tel: (028) 9756 2509

10th - 25th June
OMAGH CROSS-VILLAGE CHALLENGES
Omagh and other venues in Co Tyrone

Eight communities in and around Omagh celebrate their heritage and environment in a feast of activities which visitors will enjoy.

Contact: Tel: (028) 8224 5321

16th June
BLOOMSDAY
Numerous venues in Dublin

A variety of events take place in Dublin marking the day in 1904 on which all the events of Joyce's "Ulysses" are set.

Contact: James Joyce Cultural Centre
Tel: 01 8788547, Fax: 01 8788488

16th - 18th June
DUNLAVIN FESTIVAL OF ARTS
Market House, Imaal Hall, Dunlavin, Co Wicklow

Dunlavin Festival of Arts has something for everyone, from arts, crafts, music, parades, workshops, horse show, street entertainment and photography.

Contact: Margaret Lynott
Tel: 045 401459

16th - 18th June
O'MAHONY CLAN GATHERING
Castlemahon, Bandon, Co Cork

Contact: John O'Mahony
Tel: 023 41492

16th - 25th June
ANNA LIVIA INTERNATIONAL OPERA FESTIVAL
The Gaiety Theatre, Dublin

Four performances of each of the following two operas: "La Rondine" by Giacomo Puccini and "Herodiade" by Jules Massenet. Also a Celebrity Recital by international soprano – Lynne Dawson and An Operatic Gala Concert with Ireland's finest opera singers.

Contact: Brian Raythorn
Tel: 01 6617544, Fax: 01 6617548
e-mail: operaannalivia@eircom.net

17th June
CITY DANCE 2000
Crescent Arts Centre, Belfast

Festival featuring dances from around the world.

Contact: Tel: (028) 9024 2338

18th June
KILLESHER FESTIVAL
Florencecourt, Co Fermanagh

A summer's day celebrating the rich heritage and culture of a corner of Fermanagh.

Contact: Tel: (028) 6632 1807

20th - 30th June
SIAMSA – AMUSEMENT WITH MUSIC, DANCE ETC.
The Claddagh Hall, Galway

Irish music, singing, dancing and folk drama using harp, flute, fiddles, concertina accordion, banjo, mandolin and bodhran.

Contact: Cepta Byrne
Tel: 091 755479, Fax: 091 755888,
e-mail: siamsa@eircom.net
website: http://homepage.eircom.net/~siamsa

23rd - 25th June
GALWAY HOOKERS REGATTA
Portaferry, Co Down

A fleet of traditional Irish craft, including some venerable 'hookers', have starred in this popular maritime event for 14 years.

Contact: Tel: (028) 9182 4000

23rd - 26th June
O'DONOVAN CLAN GATHERING
Skibbereen, West Cork

e-mail: donovanje@worldnet.att.net

23rd June - 7th August
O'DOCHERTY REUNION
Derry City

People who share the famous North-West. Irish family name come home.

Contact: Tel: (028) 7126 7884

24th June
FESTIVAL OF AIR AND SEA
Bangor Bay, Co Down

Spectacular airshow, the biggest in Ireland, is a highlight of this wide-ranging Millennium celebration organised by award-winning team

Contact: Tel: (028) 9127 8051

24th -30th June
4TH KILLORAN CLAN GATHERING
Tubbercurry, Co Sligo

Contact: Anne Killoran
Tel/Fax: 071 85111, Tel: 071 85679

28th - 30th June

TIERNEY CLAN GATHERING

Co Mayo

Contact: Dr M A Tierney
Tel/Fax: 045 860623
e-mail: drmat@indigo.ie

29th June - 2nd July

THE PORTWEST CASTLEBAR INTERNA-TIONAL FOUR DAYS WALKS

Castlebar, Co Mayo

Four days of walking, talking, rambling, music, song and dance.

Contact: Elaine Devereux
Tel/Fax: 094 24102
e-mail: 4dayswalks@tinet.ie
website: www.castlebar.ie

30th June - 2nd July

DUNNE CLAN GATHERING

Co Laois

Contact: Dr M A Tierney
Tel/Fax: 045 860623
e-mail: drmat@indigo.ie

30th June - 4th July

MURPHY'S IRISH-AMERICAN MUSIC FESTIVAL

Killarney, Co Kerry

A celebration of Irish and American music and their shared origins. The "Fourth of July" – Irish style!

Contact: Rhona Buckley
Tel: 064 36622, Fax: 064 36623
e-mail: welcomes@tinet.ie

JULY 2000

5th May - 28th July

COUNTY WICKLOW GARDENS FESTIVAL

Gardens throughout the county

Heritage properties and private gardens open to the public. Many events including guided tours, flower arranging classes. etc.

Contact: Wicklow County Tourism
Tel: 0404 20100, Fax: 0404 67792,
e-mail: wctr@iol.ie
website: www.wicklow.ie

7th May - 24th September

COBH CARILLON RECITALS – 73RD SEASON

St. Colman's Cathedral, Cobh, Co Cork

Free recitals on the 49-bell carillon of St. Colman's Cathedral

Contact: Adrian Patrick Gebruers
Tel: 021 811219, Fax: 021 272121,
e-mail: agebruers@eircom.net
website:http://homepage.eircom.net/~adria ngebruers

23rd June- 7th August

O'DOCHERTY REUNION

Derry City

People who share the famous North-West. Irish family name come home.

Contact: Tel: (028) 7126 7884

29th June - 2nd July

THE PORTWEST CASTLEBAR INTERNA-TIONAL FOUR DAYS WALKS

Castlebar, Co Mayo

Four days of walking, talking, rambling, music, song and dance.

Contact: Elaine Devereux
Tel/Fax: 094 24102
e-mail: 4dayswalks@tinet.ie
website: www.castlebar.ie

30th June - 2nd July

DUNNE CLAN GATHERING

Co Laois

Contact: Dr M A Tierney
Tel/Fax: 045 860623
e-mail: drmat@indigo.ie

30th June - 4th July

MURPHY'S IRISH-AMERICAN MUSIC FESTI-VAL

Killarney, Co Kerry

A celebration of Irish and American music and their shared origins. The "Fourth of July" – Irish style!

Contact: Rhona Buckley
Tel: 064 36622, Fax: 064 36623
e-mail: welcomes@tinet.ie

1st - 31st July

SIAMSA – AMUSEMENT WITH MUSIC, DANCE ETC.

The Claddagh Hall, Galway

Irish music, singing, dancing and folk drama using harp, flute, fiddles, concertina accordion, banjo, mandolin and bodhran.

Contact: Cepta Byrne
Tel: 091 755479, Fax: 091 755888,
e-mail: siamsa@eircom.net
website: http://homepage.eircom.net/~siamsa

2nd - 7th July

AMERICAN TRIBUTE PARTY

Tullamore, Co Offaly

Selection of the finest live bands play their tributes to the music of the USA.

Contact: Colm McCabe
Tel: 0506 21704/22000, Fax: 0506 41338

3rd - 6th July

CONNEMARA FOUR SEASONS WALKING FESTIVALS

Clifden, Connemara, Co Galway

Hiking in the 12 Bens and Maumturk Mountains. Walking on off-shore islands of Aran, Omey and Inishbofin and bog trotting across ancient buried landscapes with their rich spirit world.

Contact: Michael Gibbons
Tel: 095 21379/21492, Fax: 095 21845,
e-mail: walkwest@indigo.ie
website: www.walkingireland.com

7th - 8th July

LONDONDERRY AND LIMAVADY AGRICULTURAL SHOW

Limavady, Co Derry

Millennium special, grass roots style.

Contact: Tel: (028) 7776 0304

7th - 9th July

COALISLAND MILLENNIUM MUSIC FESTIVAL

Coalisland, Co Tyrone

Annual event bigger than ever with bands from all over Europe.

Contact: Tel: (028) 8774 8052

7th - 10th July

DUNDRUM FAMILY FUN WEEKEND

Dundrum Shorefront, Co Down

Seaside spectacular centring on Millennium regatta.

Contact: Tel: (028) 4375 1295

8th July

SCOTTISH PIPE BANDS MILLENNIUM PAGEANT

Lisburn Leisure Park, Co Antrim

Hoping for a piping hot day to celebrate Scots/Irish music and dance.

Contact: Tel: (028) 9083 3811

8th - 9th July

(MAC) GEOGHEGAN CLAN GATHERING

Castletown Geoghegan, Co Westmeath

Contact: Jack Gargan
PO Box 203, Cedar Key, Fl 32625, USA
e-mail: Throman@aol.com

9th - 15th July [Provisional]

BALLINA ARTS FESTIVAL

Ballina, Co Mayo

Contact: James Geraghty, Tel: 096 21162

9th - 16th July

MULLINGAR BACHELOR FESTIVAL

Various venues in Mullingar, Co Westmeath

Contact: Maria Kearns
Tel: 044 45117

10th July

MULLINGAR SHOW -WESTMEATH SHOW SOCIETY LIMITED

The Show Grounds, Culleen, Mullingar, Co Westmeath

Exhibits in horses, pony showing and jumping. Arts and Crafts.

Contact: Eileen White
Tel/Fax: 0902 32694

11th - 16th July
GALWAY FILM FLEADH
Various venues in Galway

This festival is nationally and internationally recognised for presenting new Irish films alongside cutting edge international cinema.

Contact: Liam Connaire
Tel: 091 751655, Fax: 091 770746
e-mail: gafleadh@iol.ie

12th July
TWELFTH OF JULY PARADES
Belfast and many other venues

Colourful celebration of the anniversary of the 1690 Battle of the Boyne with bands, banners and brethren of the Orange Order.

Contact: Tel: (028) 9032 2801

12th - 15th July
MALLOW INTERNATIONAL GARDEN FESTIVAL
Cork Racecourse Mallow, Co Cork

Contact: Dominic Cullinane
Tel: 021 270657, Mobile: 086 2558931

13th July
CASTLEWELLAN SHOW
Castlewellan Forest Park, Co Down

From sheep to show-jumping

Contact: Tel: (028) 4063 0536

15th July
INISHOWEN AGRICULTURAL SOCIETY CO. LTD
Carndonagh, Co Donegal

The Inishowen Agricultural Show attracts the farming community and public alike. The morning is given to the judging of sheep, cattle, horses and the afternoon is packed with fun and games for all the family.

Contact: Gerard O'Kane
Tel: 077 74066, or Tel: 077 74022

15th - 16th July
FITZPATRICK CLAN GATHERING
Portlaoise, Co Laois

Contact: The Fitzpatrick Clan Society
Tel: 01 4525720
e-mail: fitzpatrick_clan@hotmail.com

16th - 23rd July
LONGFORD SUMMER FESTIVAL
Various locations in Longford

Ireland's biggest free live musical festival.

Contact: Padraig O'Brien
Tel: 043 45241 (W) or 043 45745 (H)

17th - 23rd July
INTERNATIONAL ROSE WEEK
Sir Thomas and Lady Dixon Park, Belfast

Just follow the scent to experience one of the world's greatest floral spectacles, better than ever.

Contact: Tel: (028) 9027 0466

18th - 25th July
13TH SOUTH DOCKS FESTIVAL
St. Andrew's Resource Centre, Pearse Street, Merrion Square (Park), Dublin 2

This is a community festival and visitors are welcome to watch the acts and activities.

Contact: Ann Maher
Tel: 01 6771930, Fax: 01 6715734

19th - 30th July
GALWAY ARTS FESTIVAL
Various venues in Galway City

International festival of the arts, with a strong reputation for innovation, spectacle and fun.

Contact: Fergal McGrath
Tel: 091 509705/6, Fax: 091 562655,
e-mail: info@gaf.iol.ie
website: www.galwayartsfestival.ie

20th July
CARBERY SHOW
Showgrounds, Gortnaclohy, Skibbereen, Co Cork

Showing classes for horses ponies, cattle and sheep. Horticulture, flowers, cookery, crafts and trade displays.

Contact: Eileen O'Sullivan
Tel: 028 38270

20th - 30th July
BOYLE ARTS FESTIVAL
Boyle, Co Roscommon

Contact: Regina Finn
Tel: 079 62066/ 079 63085, Fax: 079 62894

21st - 22nd July

Kinsella Clan Gathering

Ferns, Co Wexford

Contact: D Kinsella
Tel: 054 66442

21st - 26th July

SKIBBEREEN "WELCOME HOME FESTIVAL"

Skibbereen, Co Cork

Family based festival maintaining links with Skibbereen's emigrants and promoting free street entertainment for all plus organised musical events.

Contact: Michael Flynn
Tel: 028 22070

22nd - 28th July

THE GERARD MANLEY HOPKINS SOCIETY INTERNATIONAL SUMMER SCHOOL

Monasterevin, Co Kildare

An international festival which celebrates the poetry and writings of Gerard Manley Hopkins in a rich and diverse contemporary artistic environment.

Contact: Elaine Murphy
Tel/Fax: 045 521715
e-mail: hopkins@iol.ie

23rd - 30th July

BUNCRANA MUSIC FESTIVAL

Buncrana, Co Donegal

Culmination of live street music and lots of fun. Festival ends with barbeque and fireworks display.

Contact: Allison McBride
Tel: 077 74624

23rd July - 5th August

BEARA ARTS FESTIVAL

Castletownbere, Eyeries and Allihies, Beara, Co Cork

Contact: Beara Community Arts Society
Tel: 027 70765

23rd July - 7th August

MARKETHILL FESTIVAL

Markethill, Co Armagh

Lovely county Armagh town puts on fun run, concerts, antiques fair and treasure hunts.

Contact: Tel: (028) 3755 1352

24th - 29th July

PORTSTEWART RED SAILS CARNIVAL

Portstewart, Co Derry

Famous resort of "Red sails in the sunset" enjoys a week of excitement.

Contact: Tel: (028) 7035 2181

26th July

CLOGHER VALLEY SHOW

Augher, Co Tyrone

Agricultural day out in a fertile rural landscape.

Contact: Tel: (028) 8554 8883

28th - 30th July

FESTIVAL OF POPULAR IRISH MUSIC

Co Derry

Large-scale outdoor event over two days featuring top Irish and international artistes.

Contact: Tel: (028) 7126 7284

28th - 30th July

BALLYDAVID FESTIVAL - FEILE BAILE NA NGALL

Various venues in Ballydavid, Co Kerry

Weekend of festivities for both adults and children.

Contact: Sean B O'Conchuir
Tel: 066 9155429
e-mail: tiaracht@iol.ie

28th - 30th July

TIERNEY CLAN GATHERING

Co Mayo

Contact: Dr M A Tierney
Tel/Fax: 045 860623
e-mail: drmat@indigo.ie

28th - 30th July

JAMES MORRISON TRADITIONAL MUSIC FESTIVAL AND FIDDLER OF DOONEY COMPETITION

Riverstown, Co Sligo

Weekend of traditional sessions, ceili, concerts, workshops and lectures.

Contact: Aidan Lyons
Tel: 071 65082
or Martin Enright
Tel: 071 67560

28th - 31st July
LUNASA FESTIVAL – FEILE LUGHNASA

Cloghane and Brandon, Co Kerry

Mount Brandon Walk and Music Song and Dance.

Contact: Clare McMorran/Micheal MacGearailt
Tel: 066 7138277/7138137, Fax: 066 7138356
e-mail: mbmacg@eircom.ie

28th July - 1st August
MITCHELSTOWN MUSIC FESTIVAL

New Square, Mitchelstown, Co Cork

The gig under the Galtees featuring free concerts, street parties, and lots of fun.

Contact: Marie Sheehan
Tel: 025 24811, Fax: 025 84594

28th July - 7th August
BELTURBET FESTIVAL OF THE ERNE

Belturbet, Co Cavan

Festival featuring music, sport, athletics, water based activities, coarse and trout angling competitions, etc.

Contact: Anthony Vesey
Tel: 049 9522781, Fax: 049 9522555
e-mail: apu@eircom.net

29th July
LUGHNASA FAIR

Carrickfergus

Medieval festivities include 'bouncy' castles in the imposing setting of Ireland's best preserved 'real' castle.

Contact: Tel: (028) 4336 6455

29th July - 7th August
MARY FROM DUNGLOE INTERNATIONAL FESTIVAL

Dungloe, Co Donegal

Ten days of magical music, song and craic culminating in the selection of the "Mary" from a dazzling array of truly international girls.

Contact: Anne Marie Doherty, Festival Office, Main Street, Dungloe, Co Donegal.

30th July [Provisional]
LEDWIDGE COTTAGE MUSEUM – "LEDWIDGE DAY"

Museum Garden, The Conyngham Arms Hotel, Slane, Co Meath

Outdoor Irish music, song and dance.

Contact: Mrs Rosemary Yore/Betty Tallon
Tel: 041 9824544

30th July - 13th August
WICKLOW REGATTA FESTIVAL

Wicklow Town

The festival consists of rowing, swimming, sailing and raft races. Singing competitions and Festival Queen Ball.

Contact: Capt. Tom Byrne
Tel: 0404 68391

AUGUST 2000

7th May - 24th September
COBH CARILLON RECITALS – 73RD SEASON

St. Colman's Cathedral, Cobh, Co Cork

Free recitals on the 49-bell carillon of St. Colman's Cathedral

Contact: Adrian Patrick Gebruers
Tel: 021 811219, Fax: 021 272121,
e-mail: agebruers@eircom.net
website: http://homepage.eircom.net/~adriangebruers

23rd June - 7th August
O'DOCHERTY REUNION

Derry City

People who share the famous North-West. Irish family name come home.

Contact: Tel: (028) 7126 7884

23rd July - 5th August
BEARA ARTS FESTIVAL

Castletownbere, Eyeries and Allihies, Beara, Co Cork

Contact: Beara Community Arts Society
Tel: 027 70765

23rd July - 7th August
MARKETHILL FESTIVAL

Markethill, Co Armagh

Lovely county Armagh town puts on fun run, concerts, antiques fair and treasure hunts.

Contact: Tel: (028) 3755 1352

28th July - 1st August
MITCHELSTOWN MUSIC FESTIVAL

New Square, Mitchelstown, Co Cork

The gig under the Galtees featuring free concerts, street parties, and lots of fun.

Contact: Marie Sheehan
Tel: 025 24811, Fax: 025 84594

28th July - 7th August
BELTURBET FESTIVAL OF THE ERNE

Belturbet, Co Cavan

Festival featuring music, sport, athletics, water based activities, coarse and trout angling competitions, etc.

Contact: Anthony Vesey
Tel: 049 9522781, Fax: 049 9522555
e-mail: apu@eircom.net

29th July - 7th August
MARY FROM DUNGLOE INTERNATIONAL FESTIVAL

Dungloe, Co Donegal

Ten days of magical music, song and craic culminating in the selection of the "Mary" from a dazzling array of truly international girls.

Contact: Anne Marie Doherty, Festival Office, Main Street, Dungloe, Co Donegal.

30th July - 13th August
WICKLOW REGATTA FESTIVAL

Wicklow Town

The festival consists of rowing, swimming, sailing and raft races. Singing competitions and Festival Queen Ball.

Contact: Capt. Tom Byrne
Tel: 0404 68391

1st - 31st August
SIAMSA – AMUSEMENT WITH MUSIC, DANCE ETC.

The Claddagh Hall, Galway

Irish music, singing, dancing and folk drama using harp, flute, fiddles, concertina accordion, banjo, mandolin and bodhran.

Contact: Cepta Byrne
Tel: 091 755479, Fax: 091 755888,
e-mail: Siamsa@eircom.net
website: http://homepage.eircom.net/~siamsa

4th - 6th August
CASTLEWELLAN MILLENNIUM FESTIVAL

Castlewellan , Co Down

Millennium Millipede is the centrepiece of family entertainments.

Contact: Tel: (028) 4377 1335

4th - 7th August
O'CAROLAN HARP AND TRADITIONAL MUSIC FESTIVAL

Keadue, Co Roscommon

Festival of Irish music, ceilis, concerts and set dancing.

Contact: Paraic Noone
Tel: 078 47204, Fax: 078 47511

4th - 27th August
GLEN RIVER SUMMER FESTIVAL

O'Donnell's Bar, Meenaneary, Carrick, Co Donegal

A summer festival with lots of traditional, folk and country music. Outdoor dances.

Contact: Rory O'Donnell
Tel: 073 39009

5th August
HILLSBOROUGH HERITAGE FESTIVAL

Hillsborough , Co Down

History vividly comes alive in one of our prettiest villages with spectacular battles and an old-time fair. Millennium groats are the currency of the day!

Contact: Tel: (028) 9268 2477

5th - 6th August
THE FLANNERY CLAN GATHERING

Dublin

e-mail: oflannery@tinet.ie
or The Flannery Clan Society, 81 Woodford Drive, Clondalkin, Dublin 22

5th - 7th August
BALLYSHANNON FOLK AND TRADITIONAL MUSIC FESTIVAL
Ballyshannon, Co Donegal

This is the 23rd annual festival. We provide live music, street entertainment busking competition and workshops and much more.

Contact: Ray Gaughan
Tel: 072 51088, Fax: 072 52832

5th - 8th August
GREYSTONES SUMMER ARTS FESTIVAL
Greystones, Co Wicklow

An extravaganza of workshops from stiltwalking to theatre, mardi-gras, music, international groups – non-stop entertainment.

Contact: Grainne McLoughlin
Tel: 01 2877308, Fax: 01 2878022,
Mobile: 086 8329686
e-mail: gronia@indigo.ie

6th - 14th August
33RD CLONMANY FESTIVAL
Clonmany, Co Donegal

Lots of activities for all ages, various musical acts, sporting activities, etc.

Contact: Hugo Boyce
Tel: 077 76477

7th August
CLOONE AGRICULTURAL SHOW
Cloone, Carrick-on-Shannon, Co Leitrim

One of the leading agricultural shows in the North West. A day out for everyone.

Contact: Martina Mulvey
Tel: 078 36150

7th August
TINAHELY AGRICULTURAL SHOW
Fairwood Park, Tinahely, Co Wicklow

A fun family day out. Full facilities. Craft, food and trade fair. Livestock competitions. Entertainment all day.

Contact: Olivia Grandy
Tel: 0402 34922, Fax: 0402 34923

10th - 12th August
PUCK FAIR
Killorglin, Co Kerry

Puck Fair is one of Ireland's oldest festivals with 15 hours of free family entertainment including a traditional horse fair, busking, open air concerts, parades and fireworks which make it a unique and vibrant festival not to be missed.

Contact: Brid Moriarty
Tel/Fax: 066 9762366
e-mail: info@puckfair.ie
website: www.puckfair.ie

10th - 14th August
FEAKLE INTERNATIONAL TRADITIONAL MUSIC FESTIVAL
Feakle, Co Clare

5 days of traditional music, song, dance, workshops, lectures, concerts, sessions, ceilis.

Contact: Gary Pepper
Tel: 061 924322 or Tel: 061 924288

11th - 20th August
KILKENNY ARTS FESTIVAL
St. Canice's Cathedral, Kilkenny Castle and other venues in Co Kilkenny

Features the very best of music, visual art, theatre, literature, children's arts and outdoor events. Kilkenny's rich medieval heritage with its narrow streets and stunning ancient venues lend a special atmosphere to this fesitve city.

Contact: Maureen Kennelly
Tel: 056 63663, Fax: 056 51704

13th August
TULLAMORE AND POWERS GOLD LABEL NATIONAL LIVESTOCK SHOW
Charleville Estate, Tullamore, Co Offaly

Ireland's premier show. Full programme of events with something for all the family.

Contact: Freda Kinnarney
Tel/Fax: 0506 52141

13th August
MCCABE CLAN RALLY
Slieve Russell Hotel, Ballyconnell, Co Cavan

Contact: Brian McCabe
Tel: 045 894412
e-mail: mccabeb@entemp.irgov.ie

16th - 22nd August
BRIAN BORU FESTIVAL

Killaloe, Co Clare

Annual festival celebrating the crowning of Brian Boru in 1002 as High King of Ireland and Killaloe as the Capital of Ireland!

Contact: John Grimes
Tel: 061 376100

17th - 20th August
POWERS IRISH COFFEE FESTIVAL

Foynes, Co Limerick

World Irish Coffee making championship – 4 days of free street entertainment for all the family.

Contact: Margaret O'Shaughnessy
Tel/Fax: 069 65416
e-mail: famm@tinet.ie

17th - 20th August
MICHAEL SHANLEY TRADITIONAL WEEK-END

Kiltyclogher, Co Leitrim

Festival of traditional music, song and dance.

Contact: Frank Fox
Tel: 072 54222

18th - 22nd August
ROSE OF TRALEE INTERNATIONAL FESTIVAL

Festival Dome, Tralee, Co Kerry

The Rose of Tralee Festival is a celebration of the art of being Irish with family entertainment and a host of activities.

Contact: Noreen Cassidy
Tel: 066 7121322, Fax: 066 7122654
website: www.roseoftralee.ie

19th - 21st August
O'BRIEN FAMILY GATHERING

Glen of Aherlow, Co Tipperary

Contact: Hannah O'Brien
Tel: 062 51298

21st - 27th August
FLEADH CHEOIL NA HEIREANN

Enniscorthy, Co Wexford

This is the biggest annual festival of Irish traditional music worldwide attracting in excess of 160,000 visitors.

Contact: Comhaltas Ceoltoiri Eireann
Tel: 01 2800295, Fax: 01 2803759

24th - 27th August
SHORELINE FESTIVAL 2000

Jordanstown Loughshore Park, Belfast

Family events along scenic Belfast Lough.

Contact: Tel: (028) 9135 2681

26th August
ENNISCRONE AND DISTRICT AGRICULTURAL SHOW

Castlefield, Enniscrone, Co Sligo

An outstanding event where the best of animals, crafts, cookery, flowers, etc., are exhibited. Novelty events draw a large children attendance.

Contact: Martina Grimes, Secretary, Muckduff, Enniscrone, Co Sligo

26th - 27th August
PEOPLE'S PHOTOGRAPHIC EXHIBITION

St. Stephen's Green Railings, Dublin 2

An open air photographic exhibition open to all types of photography by all types of photographers.

Contact: Julian Ashleigh
Tel: 01 8350712
e-mail: jul@iol.ie

26th - 27th August
THE MACCLANCY CLAN

Kinlough, Co Leitrim

Contact: Eamon Clancy
Tel: 01 6282008
e-mail: Eamon.Clancy@ngrid.ie

27th August
GALBALLY GARDEN FETE - OPEN AIR MUSIC FESTIVAL

Co Limerick

Contact: Tel: 062 37920, Fax: 062 37122
e-mail: JimFitz@Hotmail.com

27th - 28th August
GURTEEN AGRICULTURAL AND HORSE SHOW

Gurteen, Co Sligo

Contact: Ann McDonagh
Tel: 071 82158

28th - 29th August

MILLENNIUM OUL' LAMMAS FAIR

Ballycastle, Co Antrim

Ireland's oldest traditional market fair celebrates 400 years as a leading crowd-puller in even more memorable style than usual.

Contact: Tel: (028) 2076 2024

SEPTEMBER 2000

7th May - 24th September

COBH CARILLON RECITALS – 73RD SEASON

St. Colman's Cathedral, Cobh, Co Cork

Free recitals on the 49-bell carillon of St. Colman's Cathedral

Contact: Adrian Patrick Gebruers
Tel: 021 811219, Fax: 021 272121,
e-mail: agebruers@eircom.net
web:http://homepage.eircom.net/~adriangebruers

1st - 3rd September

O'DUBHDA CLAN GATHERING

Enniscrone, Co Sligo

Contact: Conor MacHale
Tel/Fax: 01 2884250
e-mail: heritage@iol.ie

1st - 3rd September

CLANN AINLE (HANLEY-HANLY) MILLENNIUM REUNION CELEBRATION

Athlone, Co Westmeath

e-mail: jphanley@indigo.ie

1st - 3rd September

APPALACHIAN AND BLUEGRASS MUSIC FESTIVAL

Ulster-American Folk Park, Omagh

Celebrating the Ulster-Scots origins of American country music in a superb 'down home' frontier setting.

Tel: (028) 8224 3292

1st - 15th September

THE CAPE CLEAR ISLAND INTERNATIONAL STORYTELLING FESTIVAL

Cape Clear Island, Co Cork

Festival stars international tellers. 40 storytellers in audiences. Concerts, workshops, events for families, story-swapping, music and wholesome fun.

Contact: Chuck Kruger
Tel/Fax: 028 39157
e-mail: ckstory@indigo.ie,

3rd - 10th September

NATIONAL HERITAGE WEEK

Nationwide

There are over 350 events throughout the country. There are all sorts of activities from walks, lectures, mini pageants, re-enactments, music recitals, etc.

Contact: Anne Grady
Tel: 01 6472461, Fax: 01 6616764,
website: www.heritageireland.ie

7th - 10th September

HARVEST TIME BLUES FESTIVAL

Various venues throughout Monaghan

A celebration of blues music and the country from where it originated – America.

Contact: Somhairle MacConghail
Tel: 047 82928, Fax: 047 71189,
e-mail: harvestblues@tlnet.le
website: www.harvestblues.net

7th - 10th September

DINGLE MUSIC FESTIVAL 2000

Various venues in Dingle, Co Kerry

Jazz, blues, folk and traditional music.

Contact: Orna Dunlevy
Tel/Fax: 066 9152427

8th - 10th September

CLARENBRIDGE OYSTER FESTIVAL

Clarenbridge, Co Galway

A celebration of the world's finest oysters, good food, good stout, good company, music and craic.

Contact: Niall Geraghty
Tel: 091 796342, Fax: 091 796016
e-mail: clarenoystfest@esatclear.ie

8th - 10th September
RYAN CLAN RALLY

Various Venues in Co Tipperary

Social events, tour and banquet.

Contact: Christopher Ryan
Tel: 01 2988082
e-mail: ryanc@iol.ie

10th September
AUTUMN HISTORICAL SYMPOSIUM

Boyne Valley Hotel and Country Club, Drogheda, Co Louth

Contact: Donal Healy
Tel: 041 9833097, Fax: 041 9841599

13th - 24th September
KINSALE ARTS FESTIVAL

Various venues in Kinsale, Co Cork

This festival will feature international, national, and local artists including musicians, writers, poets and dramatists.

Contact: Tom O'Hare
Tel: 021 774558/021 774959, Fax: 021 774958,
e-mail: maritime@eirnet.net

15th - 16th September
SOUND AND LIGHT SPECTACULAR

Ulster Folk and Transport Museum, Cultra, Co Down

The grounds and buildings of this outstanding open air museum provide a dramatic location for a Millennium pageant of local history.

Contact: Tel: (028) 9127 8051

15th - 17th September
EIGSE CHORCA DHUIBHNE XIII

Various venues in Ballyferriter, Co Kerry

Contact: Maire Ui Shithigh
Tel: 066 9156100, Fax: 066 9156348,
e-mail: cfcdteo@iol.ie

15th - 17th September
O'LEARY CLAN GATHERING

Rosscarbery, Co Cork

Contact: Peter O'Leary
Tel: 026 49325
e-mail: peteroleary@tinet.ie

16th - 17th September
BYGONE DAYS & AUTUMN FLOWER SHOW

Botanic Gardens, Belfast

Victorian Palm House is the backdrop to a great gardening event with a whiff of nostalgia.

Tel: (028) 9027 0466

19th - 27th September
SEARCHING FOR THAT ELUSIVE IRISH ANCESTOR

Family History Conference

Belfast and Dublin

Tracing your Irish ancestry with expert advice and hands on research in the principal archives and repositories in Ireland.

Contact: Shane McAteer
Tel/Fax: 048 332288,
e-mail: enquiry@uhf.org.uk
website: www.uhf.org.uk

21st - 24th September [Provisional]
GALWAY INTERNATIONAL OYSTER FESTIVAL

Galway City

This festival hosts the Guinness World Oyster Opening Championship.

Contact: Ann Flanagan
Tel: 091 522066, Fax: 091 527282,
website: www.galwayoysterfest.com

21st - 24th Septenber
FOYLE OYSTER FESTIVAL

Moville, Greencastle, Inishowen, Co Donegal

Inaugurated for the purpose of extending the holiday season and the promotion of shell fish in the area.

Contact: Billy Tighe
Tel: 077 82010/82564

21st September - 1st October
WATERFORD INTERNATIONAL FESTIVAL OF LIGHT OPERA

Theatre Royal, Waterford

Competitive professionally adjudicated festival for amateur musical societies.

Contact: Sean Dower
Tel: 051 375437

25th September - 14th October
DUBLIN FRINGE FESTIVAL
Various venues in Dublin

This is a hugely successful showcase for independent theatre and performance.

Contact: Ali Curran
Tel: 01 8729016, Fax: 01 8729138
e-mail: fringe@eircom.ie
website: www.fringefest.com

26th September - 1st October
ASPECTS IRISH LITERATURE FESTIVAL
Bangor Heritage Centre, Bangor, Co Down

Annual wordfest is sure to make a bigger impact than ever for Millennium.

Contact: Tel: (028) 9127 8032

29th September - 1st October
LADY GREGORY OF COOLE – AN AUTUMN GATHERING
Coole Park, Gort, Co Galway

A weekend of literary, cultural and social events to highlight unique contribution of Lady Gregory to life of 20th Century Ireland.

Contact: Sheila O'Donnellan
Tel: 091 521836, Fax: 091 567421

OCTOBER 2000

21st September - 1st October
WATERFORD INTERNATIONAL FESTIVAL OF LIGHT OPERA
Theatre Royal, Waterford

Competitive professionally adjudicated festival for amateur musical societies.

Contact: Sean Dower
Tel: 051 375437

25th September - 14th October
DUBLIN FRINGE FESTIVAL
Various venues in Dublin

This is a hugely successful showcase for independent theatre and performance.

Contact: Ali Curran
Tel: 01 8729016, Fax: 01 8729138
e-mail: fringe@eircom.ie
website: www.fringefest.com

26th September - 1st October
ASPECTS IRISH LITERATURE FESTIVAL
Bangor Heritage Centre, Bangor, Co Down

Annual wordfest is sure to make a bigger impact than ever for Millennium.

Contact: Tel: (028) 9127 8032

29th September - 1st October
LADY GREGORY OF COOLE – AN AUTUMN GATHERING
Coole Park, Gort, Co Galway

A weekend of literary, cultural and social events to highlight unique contribution of Lady Gregory to life of 20th Century Ireland.

Contact: Sheila O'Donnellan
Tel: 091 521836, Fax: 091 567421

1st - 31st October
COMMUNITY AND ARTS FESTIVAL
Venues in Coleraine Borough, Co Derry

A varied programme of arts and cultural activities and performances.

Contact: Tel: (028) 7035 2181

2nd - 14th October
DUBLIN THEATRE FESTIVAL
Various venues in Dublin

Europe's oldest specialist theatre festival offers a unique opportunity to see the best of world theatre alongside new productions from all the major Irish companies including the Abbey and Gate.

Contact: The Director
Tel: 01 6778439. Fax: 01 6797709
e-mail: dubfest@iol.ie
website: www.iftn.ie/dublinfestival

6th - 8th October
ROE VALLEY FOLK FESTIVAL 2000
Dungiven and Limavady, Co Derry

Traditional music in an area steeped in the Irish culture of centuries.

Contact: Tel: (028) 7776 0304

8th - 15th October
CORK FILM FESTIVAL
Cork Opera House, Kino Cinema and Triskel Arts Centre, Cork

Ireland's premier film event includes an electric range of world cinema and a comprehensive programme of new Irish cinema.

Contact: Michael Hannigan
Tel: 021 271711, Fax: 021 275945
e-mail: ciff@indigo.ie
website: www.corkfilmfest.org

10th - 15th October
BABORO GALWAY INTERNATIONAL ARTS FESTIVAL
Town Hall Theatre, Galway City

Ireland's first and biggest international arts festival for children aged 3-12 yrs. Theatre, music, exhibitions, literary events and workshops included.

Contact: Executive Director
Tel: 091 509700, Fax: 091 562655,
e-mail: education@gaf.iol.ie
website: www.iol.ie/baboro

12th - 15th October
KINSALE 24TH INTERNTIONAL GOURMET FESTIVAL
Kinsale, Co Cork

Contact: Peter Barry
Tel: 021 774026, Fax: 021 774438

13th - 15th October
NIRE VALLEY WALKING FESTIVAL
Comeragh Mountains, Co Waterford

An autumn festival of splendid guided walks, traditional music, set dancing, etc.

Contact: Mary Wall
Tel: 052 36134, Fax: 052 36540

16th - 21st October
MILLENNIUM ARTS FESTIVAL
Banbridge, Co Down

Marking the contribution of 25 years dedication by the local arts committee.

Contact: Tel: (028) 4066 2991

19th October - 5th November
WEXFORD FESTIVAL OPERA
Theatre Royal, High Street, Wexford

Wexford Festival Opera is a highly professional undertaking with productions of rare opera performed in one of the most delightful theatres imaginable.

Contact: Jerome Hynes
Tel: 053 22400, Fax: 053 24289
e-mail: info@wexfordopera.com
website: www.wexfordopera.com

21st - 22nd October
LITERATURE OF IRISH EXILE
Ulster-American Folk Park, Omagh, Co Tyrone

New autumn school concentrates on dramatic portrayal of the writings of lesser-known exiles in apt surroundings.

Contact: Tel: (028) 8225 6315

27th - 30th October
CONNEMARA FOUR SEASONS WALKING FESTIVALS
Clifden, Connemara, Co Galway

Hiking in the 12 Bens and Maumturk Mountains. Walking on off-shore islands of Aran, Omey and Inishbofin and bog trotting across ancient buried landscapes with their rich spirit world.

Contact: Michael Gibbons
Tel: 095 21379/21492, Fax: 095 21845,
e-mail: walkwest@indigo.ie
website: www.walkingireland.com

27th - 30th October
GUINNESS CORK JAZZ FESTIVAL
Various venues in Cork City

Jazz from afternoon to late evening in most hotels, pubs, etc. All forms of jazz.

Contact: Ray Fitzgerald
Tel: 021 278979, Tel/Fax: 021 270463

27th - 30th October
TOM CREAN WALKING FESTIVAL
Annascaul, Co Kerry

Annual walking festival with 3 days of walks guided by trained guides. Lectures and discussion workshops with local historians and archaeologists. Community festival with plenty of fun.

Contact: Marie Kennedy
Tel: 066 9157382
e-mail: dropanchor@tinet.ie

27th October - 12th November
BELFAST FESTIVAL AT QUEEN'S
Queen's University, Belfast and other venues in Belfast

Now only second in size to Edinburgh, this 21st Century showcase of the performing arts aims to deliver the best programme in its distinguished history.

Contact: Tel: (028) 9066 7687.

Fringe Festival runs simultaneously. Cathedral Quarter

Contact: Tel: (028) 9027 0466

28th - 29th October
WICKLOW MOUNTAINS WALKING FESTIVAL
Glenmalure and Glendalough, Co Wicklow

Contact: Wicklow County Tourism
Tel: 0404 20100, Fax: 0404 67792
e-mail: wctr@iol.ie
website: www.wicklow.ie

28th - 30th October
KINSALE FRINGE JAZZ FESTIVAL
Various venues in Kinsale, Co Cork

Fun weekend of jazz in Kinsale with free entry to all venues – great entertainment for all the family.

Contact: JackWalsh/Billy Crosbie
Tel: 021 772135, Fax: 021 772231

28th - 30th October
KERRY SKELLIG REGIONAL – DANIEL O'CONNELL WALKING WEEKEND
Kerry/ Skellig Regions

Festival of guided walks for all levels.

Contact: Marc Dourieu
Tel: 066 9473355, Fax: 066 9473366

29th October
BALLINTOGHER 23RD ANNUAL FEIS
Ballintogher, Co Sligo

Competitions in music, singing, dancing, elocution, art and crafts.

Contact: Teresa McCormack
Tel: 071 64250

30th October
98FM DUBLIN CITY MARATHON
Dublin City

A friendly experience of running through the historic streets and scenic suburbs of Ireland's capital city

Contact: Carol McCabe
Tel: 01 6263746
website: www.dublincitymarathon.ie

30th - 31st October
BANKS OF THE FOYLE HALLOWE'EN CARNIVAL
Derry city

Parade through the streets of the walled city plus spectacular riverside displays.

Contact: Tel: (028) 7126 7284

31st October
HALLOWE'EN CAPITAL CELEBRATIONS
Belfast City Centre

Belfast puts on a show to capture the atmosphere of the scariest season of the new century.

Contact: Tel: (028) 9027 0466

NOVEMBER 2000

19th October - 5th November
WEXFORD FESTIVAL OPERA
Theatre Royal, High Street, Wexford

Wexford Festival Opera is a highly professional undertaking with productions of rare opera performed in one of the most delightful theatres imaginable.

Contact: Jerome Hynes
Tel: 053 22400, Fax: 053 24289
e-mail: info@wexfordopera.com
website: www.wexfordopera.com

27th October - 12th November
BELFAST FESTIVAL AT QUEEN'S
Queen's University, Belfast and other venues in Belfast

Now only second in size to Edinburgh, this 21st Century showcase of the performing arts aims to deliver the best programme in its distinguished history.

Tel: (028) 9066 7687.

Fringe Festival runs simultaneously. Cathedral Quarter

Tel: (028) 9027 0466

3rd - 5th November
BALLINTOGHER 3RD TRADITIONAL MUSIC FESTIVAL

Ballintogher, Co Sligo

A weekend of music, song and dance, also commemorating John Egan Flute Player.

Contact: Teresa McCormack
Tel: 071 64250

10th - 12th November
QUEEN OF THE LAND

Tullamore, Co Offaly

Contact: Joan O'Sullivan
Tel: 0405 32718

10th - 19th November
EIGSE SLIABH RUA

Slieverue, Co Kilkenny

This is a festival of local and national history, music and exhibitions.

Contact: Katherine Grant
Tel: 051 832482

17th November
LISBURN SWITCH-ON

Lisburn, Co Antrim

Festivities of the first Christmas of the new century begin.

Contact: Tel: (028) 9268 2477

24th - 26th November
ANNUAL KAVANAGH WEEKEND

Iniskeen, Co Monaghan

Contact: Oliver Keenan
Tel/Fax: 042 9378560

DECEMBER 2000

1st - 24th December
COLERAINE AT CHRISTMAS

Borough-wide venues, Co Derry

Yuletide programme with something for everyone.

Contact: Tel: (01265) 52181

1st - 31st December
SANTA'S UNDERWATER KINGDOM

Lagan Weir, Belfast

The submarine alternative to the shopping mall grotto.

Contact: Tel: (028) 9027 0466

26th - 27th December
WOODFORD MUMMERS FEILE

Woodford, Co Galway

Traditional music, song, dance and mime performed by mummers in traditional colourful costume.

Contact: Marie McMahon
Tel: 0509 49248/49063

Tourist Information Centres

Centres in **Bold** are open all the year around.

Achill
The Sound, Achill Island, Co. Mayo
Tel: 098 45384

Adare
Adare Heritage Centre, Adare, Co. Limerick
Tel: 061 396255 Fax: 061 396610

Antrim
16 High Street, Antrim, Co. Antrim
Tel: 028 9442 8331 Fax: 028 9448 7844 e-mail: abs@antrim.gov.uk

Aran Islands
Kilronan, Inishmore, Co. Galway
Tel: 099 61263

Ardmore
Sea Front Car Park, Ardmore, Co. Waterford
Tel: 024 94444

Arklow
The Parade Ground, Arklow, Co. Wicklow
Tel: 0402 32484

Armagh
40 English Street, Armagh, Co. Armagh BT61 7BA
Tel: 028 3752 1800 Fax: 028 3752 8329

Athlone
Athlone Castle, Market Square, Athlone, Co. Westmeath
Tel: 0902 94630

Ballina
Cathedral Road, Ballina, Co. Mayo
Tel: 096 70848

Ballinasloe
> Keller's Travel Agency, Ballinasloe, Co. Galway
> Tel: 0905 42131

Ballycastle
> 7 Mary Street, Ballycastle, Co. Antrim
> Tel: 028 2076 2024 Fax: 028 2076 2515

Banbridge
> 200 Newry Road, Banbridge, Co. Down
> Tel: 028 4062 3322 Fax: 028 4062 3114

Bangor
> 34 Quay Street, Bangor, Co. Down
> Tel: 028 9127 0069 Fax: 028 9127 4466

Bantry
> Old Courthouse, Bantry, Co. Cork
> Tel: 027 50229

Belfast
> St Anne's Court, 59 North Main Street, Belfast BT1 1NB
> Tel: 028 9023 1221 Fax: 028 9024 0960 e-mail: infor@nitb.com
> website: www.ni-tourism.com

Birr
> Castle Street, Birr, Co. Offaly
> Tel: 0509 20110

Blarney
> Blarney Woollen Mills, Blarney, Co. Cork
> Tel: 021 381624

Boyle
> Market Street, Boyle, Co. Roscommon
> Tel: 079 62145

Buncrana
> Sea Front, Buncrana, Co. Donegal
> Tel: 077 20020

Bundoran
> Main Street, Bundoran, Co. Donegal
> Tel: 072 41350

Caherciveen
RIC Barracks, Caherciveen, Co. Kerry
Tel: 066 72589

Cahir
Castle Street Car Park, Cahir, Co. Tipperary
Tel: 052 41453

Carlow
Kennedy Avenue, Carlow, Co. Carlow
Tel: 0503 31554

Carrickfergus
Heritage Plaza, Carrickfergus, Co. Antrim
Tel: 028 9336 6455 Fax: 028 9335 0350

Carrick-on-Shannon
The Quays, Carrick-on-Shannon, Co. Leitrim
Tel: 078 20170 Fax: 078 20089

Carrick-on-Suir
Heritage Centre, Main Street, Carrick-on-Suir, Co. Leitrim
Tel: 051 640200

Cashel
Town Hall, Cashel, Co. Tipperary
Tel: 062 61333

Castlebar
Linenhall Street, Castlebar, Co. Mayo
Tel: 094 21207

Cavan
1 Farnham Street, Cavan, Co. Cavan
Tel: 049 31942

Clifden
Market Street, Clifden, Co. Galway
Tel: 095 21163

Cliffs of Moher
Liscannor, Co. Clare
Tel: 065 7081171

Clonakilty
Ashe Street, Clonakilty, Co. Cork
Tel: 023 33226

Clonmacnoise
via Shannon Bridge, Clonmacnoise, Co. Offaly
Tel: 0905 74134

Clonmel
8 Sarsfield Street, Clonmel, Co. Tipperary
Tel: 052 22960

Coleraine
Railway Road, Coleraine, Co. Derry
Tel: 028 7034 4723 Fax: 028 7035 1765

Cong
Abbey Street, Cong, Co. Mayo
Tel: 092 46542

Cookstown
48 Molesworth Street, Cookstown, Co. Tyrone
Tel: 028 8676 6727 Fax: 028 8676 1981

Cork
Tourist House, Grand Parade, Cork, Co. Cork
Tel: 021 273251 Fax: 021 273504 e-mail: user@cktourism.ie

Dingle
The Quay, Dingle, Co. Kerry
Tel: 066 51188

Donegal
The Quay, Donegal, Co. Donegal
Tel: 073 21148 Fax: 073 22762

Dongloe
Car Park off Main Street, Dongloe, Co. Donegal
Tel: 075 21297

Drogheda
Bus Eireann Station, West Street, Drogheda, Co. Louth
Tel: 041 9837070

Downpatrick
74 Market Street, Downpatrick, Co. Down
Tel: 028 4461 2233 Fax: 028 4461 2350

Dublin

O'Connell Street. Tel: 01 747733

College Green. Tel: 01 711488

Baggot Street Bridge. 01 765871

Dundalk

Jocelyn Street, Dundalk, Co. Louth

Tel: 042 9335484 Fax: 042 3998070

Dungarvan

The Square, Dungarvan, Co. Waterford

Tel: 058 41741

Ennis

Arthur's Row, Town Centre, Ennis, Co. Clare

Tel: 065 6828366 Fax: 065 6828350

Enniscorthy

Town Centre, Enniscorthy, Co. Wexford

Tel: 054 34699

Enniskillen

Wellington Road, Enniskillen, Co. Fermanagh

Tel: 028 6632 3110 Fax: 028 6632 5511

Galway City

Victoria Place, Eyre Square, Galway, Co. Galway

Tel: 091 563081 Fax: 091 565201 e-mail: user@western-tourism.ie

Giant's Causeway

Bushmills, Co. Antrim

Tel: 028 2073 1855

Glengarriff

Main Street, Glengarriff, Co. Cork

Tel: 027 63084

Gorey

Main Street, Gorey, Co. Wexford

Tel: 055 21248

Hillsborough

Council Offices, Hillsborough, Co. Down

Tel: 028 9268 9717 Fax: 028 9268 9016

Kenmare

Kenmare Heritage Centre, Main Street, Kenmare, Co. Kerry
Tel: 064 41233

Kildare Town

Main Square, Kildare, Co. Kildare
Tel: 045 522696

Kilkee

Main Street, Kilkee, Co. Clare
Tel: 065 376866

Kilkeel

6 Newcastle Street, Kilkeel, Co. Down
Tel/Fax: 028 4176 2525

Kilkenny

Shee Alms House, Kilkenny, Co. Kilkenny
Tel: 056 51500 Fax: 056 63955

Killaloe

The Bridge, Killaloe, Co. Clare
Tel: 061 376866

Killarney

Beech Road, Killarney, Co. Kerry
Tel: 064 31633 Fax: 064 34506

Killymaddy

Ballygawley Road, Killymaddy, Co. Tyrone BT70 1TF
Tel: 028 8776 7259 Fax: 028 8776 7911

Kilrush

Town Hall, Kilrush, Co. Clare
Tel: 065 9051577

Kinsale

Pier Road, Kinsale, Co. Cork
Tel: 021 772234 Fax: 021 774438

Knock

Knock Airport, Knock, Co.Mayo
Tel: 094 67247
Knock Village
Tel: 094 88193

Larne
Narrow Gauge Road, Larne, Co. Antrim
Tel/Fax: 028 2826 0088

Letterkenny
Derry Road, Letterkenny, Co. Donegal
Tel: 074 21160 Fax: 074 25180

Limavady
7 Connell Street, Limavady, Co. Antrim
Tel: 028 7772 2226 Fax: 028 7772 2010

Limerick
Arthurs Quay, Limerick, Co. Limerick
Tel: 061 317522 Fax: 061 317939

Lisburn
Irish Linen Centre, Lisburn, Co. Antrim
Tel: 028 9266 0038 Fax: 028 9260 7889

Lismore
Heritage Centre, Lismore, Co. Waterford
Tel: 058 54975

Listowel
Saint John's Church, Listowel, Co. Kerry
Tel: 068 22590 Fax: 068 23485

Londonderry
44 Foyle Street, Londonderry, Co. Derry
Tel: 028 7126 7284 Fax: 028 7137 7992

Longford
Market Square, Longford, Co. Longford
Tel: 043 46566

Midleton
Jameson Heritage Centre, Midleton, Co. Cork
Tel: 021 613702

Monaghan
Market House, Monaghan, Co. Monaghan
Tel: 047 81122

Mullingar

Market House, Mullingar, Co. Westmeath
Tel: 044 48650

Nenagh

Connolly Street, Nenagh, Co. Tipperary
Tel: 067 31610 Fax: 067 33418

Newcastle

Central Promenade, Newcastle, Co. Down
Tel: 028 4372 2222 Fax: 028 4372 2400

Newgrange

Newgrange Visitor Centre, Newgrange, Co. Meath
Tel: 041 9880305

Newport

Main Street, Newport, Co. Mayo
Tel: 098 41895

New Ross

The Quay, New Ross, Co. Wexford
Tel: 051 421857

Newtownards

31 Regent Street, Newtownards, Co. Down BT23 4AD
Tel: 028 9182 6846 Fax: 028 9182 6681

Omagh

1 Market Street, Omagh, Co. Tyrone BT78 1EE
Tel: 028 8224 7831 (after hours: 028 8224 0774) Fax: 028 8224 0774

Oughterard

Main Street, Oughterard, Co. Galway
Tel: 091 552808 Fax: 091 552811

Portaferry

Castle Street, Portaferry, Co. Down
Tel/Fax: 028 4272 9882

Portlaoise

James Fintan Lawlor Avenue, Portlaoise, Co. Laois
Tel: 0502 21178

Portrush

Sandhill Drive, Portrush, Co. Antrim
Tel: 028 7082 3333 Fax: 028 7082 2256

Roscommon

Harrison Hall, Roscommon, Co. Roscommon
Tel: 0903 26342

Rosslare

Rosslare Harbour, Rosslare, Co. Wexford
Tel: 053 33622/33232 Fax: 053 33421

Salthill

The Promenade, Salthill, Co. Galway
Tel: 091 520500

Shannon Airport

Shannon Airport, Co. Clare
Tel: 061 471664 Fax: 061 471661

Skibbereen

North Street, Skibbereen, Co.Cork
Tel: 028 21766 Fax: 028 21353

Sligo

Temple Street, Sligo, Co. Sligo
Tel: 071 61201 Fax: 071 60360

Strabane

Abercorn Square, Strabane, Co. Tyrone
Tel: 028 7188 3735 Fax: 028 7138 2264

Thoor Ballylee

Yeats Tower, Gort, Thoor Ballylee, Co. Galway
Tel: 091 631436

Tipperary

James Street, Tipperary, Co. Tipperary
Tel: 062 51457

Tralee

Ashe Memorial Hall, Tralee, Co. Kerry
Tel: 066 7121288 Fax: 066 21700

Tramore

Railway Square, Tramore, Co. Waterford
Tel: 051 381572

Trim

Mill Street, Trim, Co. Meath
Tel: 046 37111

Tuam

Mill Museum, Tuam, Co. Galway
Tel: 093 25486

Tullamore

Tullamore Dew, Heritage Centre, Bury Quay, Tullamore, Co. Offaly
Tel: 0506 52617

Waterford

41 The Quay, Waterford, Co. Waterford
Tel: 051 875823 Fax: 051 877388 e-mail: info@southeasttourism.

Westport

The Mall, Westport, Co. Mayo
Tel: 098 25711 Fax: 098 26709

Wexford

Crescent Quay, Wexford, Co. Wexford
Tel: 053 23111 Fax: 053 41743

Wicklow

Rialto Centre, Fitzwilliam Square, Wicklow, Co. Wicklow
Tel: 0404 69117 Fax: 0404 69118

Youghal

Market Square, Youghal, Co. Cork
Tel: 024 92390

Index of Towns, Villages and Places of Interest

Index of Accommodation

Index of
Food and Drink

The Hidden Places
Order Form

To order any of our publications just fill in the payment details below and complete the order form *overleaf*. For orders of less than 4 copies please add £1 per book for postage and packing. Orders over 4 copies are P & P free.

Please Complete Either:

I enclose a cheque for £ .... made payable to Travel Publishing Ltd

Or:

Card No: ⬜⬜⬜⬜ ⬜⬜⬜⬜ ⬜⬜⬜⬜ ⬜⬜⬜⬜

Expiry Date: ⬜⬜ ⬜⬜

Signature: ....

NAME: ....

ADDRESS: ....

....

....

POSTCODE: ....

TEL NO: ....

Please send to: Travel Publishing Ltd
7a Apollo House
Calleva Park
Aldermaston
Berks, RG7 8TN

The Hidden Places
Order Form

	Price	Quantity	Value
Regional Titles			
Cambridgeshire & Lincolnshire	£7.99	....	....
Channel Islands	£6.99	....	....
Cheshire	£7.99	....	....
Chilterns	£7.99	....	....
Cornwall	£7.99	....	....
Derbyshire	£7.99	....	....
Devon	£7.99	....	....
Dorset, Hants & Isle of Wight	£7.99	....	....
Essex	£7.99	....	....
Gloucestershire & Wiltshire	£7.99	....	....
Heart of England	£7.99	....	....
Hereford, Worcs & Shropshire	£7.99	....	....
Highlands & Islands	£7.99	....	....
Kent	£7.99	....	....
Lake District & Cumbria	£7.99	....	....
Lancashire	£7.99	....	....
Norfolk	£7.99	....	....
Northeast Yorkshire	£6.99	....	....
Northumberland & Durham	£6.99	....	....
North Wales	£7.99	....	....
Nottinghamshire	£6.99	....	....
Potteries	£6.99	....	....
Somerset	£6.99	....	....
South Wales	£7.99	....	....
Suffolk	£7.99	....	....
Surrey	£6.99	....	....
Sussex	£6.99	....	....
Thames Valley	£7.99	....	....
Warwickshire & West Midlands	£6.99	....	....
Yorkshire Dales	£6.99	....	....
Set of any 5 Regional titles	**£25.00**	....	....
National Titles			
England	£9.99	....	....
Ireland	£9.99	....	....
Scotland	£9.99	....	....
Wales	£8.99	....	....
Set of all 4 National titles	**£28.00**	....	....
		————	————
		————	————

For orders of less than 4 copies please add £1 per book for postage &
packing. Orders over 4 copies P & P free.

The Hidden Places
Reader Comment Form

The *Hidden Places* research team would like to receive reader's comments on any visitor attractions or places reviewed in the book and also recommendations for suitable entries to be included in the next edition. This will help ensure that the *Hidden Places* series continues to provide its readers with useful information on the more interesting, unusual or unique features of each attraction or place ensuring that their stay in the local area is an enjoyable and stimulating experience.

To provide your comments or recommendations would you please complete the forms below and overleaf as indicated and send to: The Research Department, Travel Publishing Ltd., 7a Apollo House, Calleva Park, Aldermaston, Reading, RG7 8TN.

Your Name:

Your Address:

Your Telephone Number:

Please tick as appropriate: Comments ☐   Recommendation ☐

Name of *"Hidden Place"*:

Address:

Telephone Number:

Name of Contact:

The Hidden Places Reader Comment Form

Comment or Reason for Recommendation:

....

....

....

....

....

....

....

....

....

....

....

....

The Hidden Places
Reader Comment Form

The *Hidden Places* research team would like to receive reader's comments on any visitor attractions or places reviewed in the book and also recommendations for suitable entries to be included in the next edition. This will help ensure that the *Hidden Places* series continues to provide its readers with useful information on the more interesting, unusual or unique features of each attraction or place ensuring that their stay in the local area is an enjoyable and stimulating experience.

To provide your comments or recommendations would you please complete the forms below and overleaf as indicated and send to: The Research Department, Travel Publishing Ltd., 7a Apollo House, Calleva Park, Aldermaston, Reading, RG7 8TN.

Your Name:

Your Address:

Your Telephone Number:

Please tick as appropriate: Comments ☐   Recommendation ☐

Name of *"Hidden Place"*:

Address:

Telephone Number:

Name of Contact:

The Hidden Places
Reader Comment Form

Comment or Reason for Recommendation:

....

....

....

....

....

....

....

....

....

....

....

....

The Hidden Places
Reader Comment Form

The *Hidden Places* research team would like to receive reader's comments on any visitor attractions or places reviewed in the book and also recommendations for suitable entries to be included in the next edition. This will help ensure that the *Hidden Places* series continues to provide its readers with useful information on the more interesting, unusual or unique features of each attraction or place ensuring that their stay in the local area is an enjoyable and stimulating experience.

To provide your comments or recommendations would you please complete the forms below and overleaf as indicated and send to: The Research Department, Travel Publishing Ltd., 7a Apollo House, Calleva Park, Aldermaston, Reading, RG7 8TN.

Your Name:

Your Address:

Your Telephone Number:

Please tick as appropriate: Comments ☐   Recommendation ☐

Name of *"Hidden Place"*:

Address:

Telephone Number:

Name of Contact:

The Hidden Places
Reader Comment Form

Comment or Reason for Recommendation:

....

....

....

....

....

....

....

....

....

....

....

Map Section

The following pages of maps encompass the main cities, towns and geographical features of Ireland, as well as many of the interesting places featured in the guide. Distances are indicated by the use of scale bars located below each of the maps

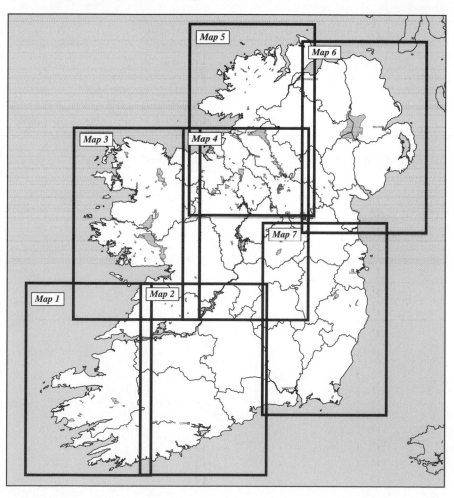

Map 1

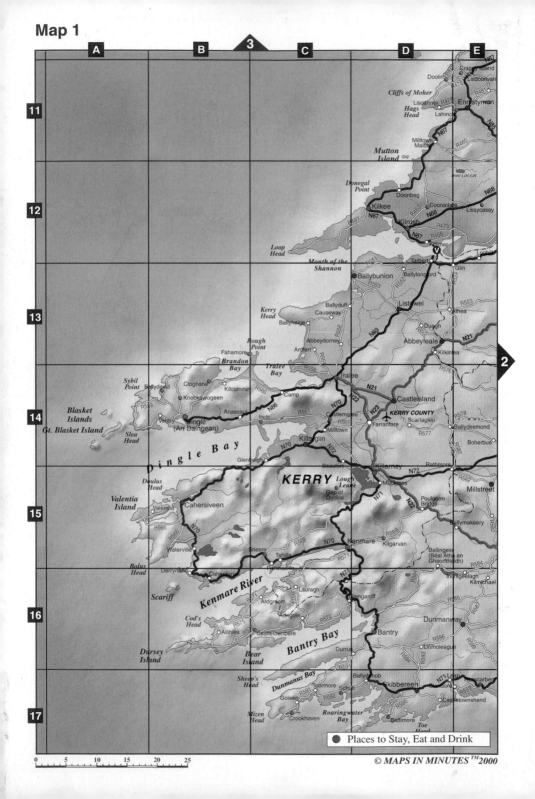

A   B   3   C   D   E

11
Doolin · Cragga Island · Lisdoonvarna
Cliffs of Moher   Liscannor · R478 · Ennistymon · R481
Hags Head   Lahinch · N67 · N85
Milltown · Malbay · R460

12
Mutton Island   DOO LOUGH
Donegal Point   Doonbeg · N68 · N85
Kilkee · R483 · Cooraclare · Lissycasey
Loop Head   Kilrush · N68 · Athea
N67 · R473 · N67 · R466
Mouth of the Shannon   Killimer · V · Tomhil
Tarbert · Glin · N24
Ballylongford · Ballybunion · R553 · R551

13
Kerry Head   Ballyduff · Listowel · R523
Ballyheige · Causeway · Athea
Abbeydorney · R556 · Duagh · N21
Rough Point   Ardfert · Neig · R576
Fahamore · *Brandon Bay* · R551 · R556 · Abbeyfeale · Kilkinlea

14 (grid) **2**
Sybil Point · Ballydavid · Cloghane · Kilcummin · *Tralee Bay* · Tralee
Blasket Islands · Knockavogeen · R560 · Camp · N21 · V22 · N23 · Castleisland
Gt. Blasket Island · Anascaul · R86 · R561 · Castlemaine · R578 · Scartaglen · KERRY COUNTY
Ventry · Dingle (An Daingean) · Inch · Milltown · R561 · Farranfore · Ballydesmond
Slea Head · R549 · Killorglin · R577 · Boherbue
Dingle Bay · N70 · N72 · R565 · Beaufort

15
Doulus Head · Glenbeigh · Killarney · N72
Valentia Island · KERRY · *Lough Leane* · Muckross · N22 · Millstreet
Valentia · Cahersiveen · *Gap of Dunloe* · N71 · Poulgorm Bridge · R582
R565 · R566 · N70 · Ballymakeery · R583
Waterville · Sneem · R568 · N70 · Kenmare · Kilgarvan · Ballingeary (Béal Átha an Ghaorthaidh)

16
Bolus Head · Derrynane · Tahilla · R571 · R584 · Inchigeelagh · Kilmichael
Caherdaniel · Parknasilla · N71 · R585
Scariff · **Kenmare River** · Lauragh · Glengarriff · R587
Ardgroom · R572 · Dunmanway
Cod's Head · Adrigole · Bantry · R586 · Drimoleague · R593
Allihies · Castletownbere · *Bear Island* · **Bantry Bay** · Durrus · R594
Dursey Island · R591 · N71 Leap · Castletownshend

17
Sheep's Head · *Dunmanus Bay* · Toormore · Ballydehob · Skibbereen
Goleen · Schull · R592 · R596
Mizen Head · Crookhaven · *Roaringwater Bay* · Baltimore · *Toe Head*

0   5   10   15   20   25

● Places to Stay, Eat and Drink

© MAPS IN MINUTES ™ 2000

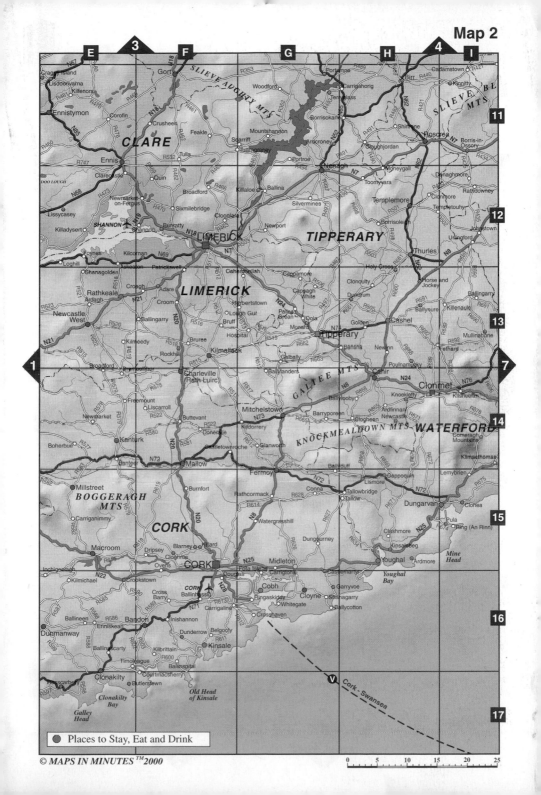

Map 2

3 **4**

E F G H I

N67

Cragvy Island
Lisdoonvarna
R481 Kilfenora
R476
Ennistymon N85
N67 Corofin
R460 R466
Crusheen
R747 Feakle
Ennis R352
Claredale R532 Tulla
R473 Quin
DOO LOUGH Newmarket-
N68 on-Fergus R462
Lissycasey R470 Sixmilebridge
Killadysert Bunratty
SHANNON R463
Poynes Shannon
Loghill N69 Kilcornan N18 LIMERICK
Askeaton Patrickswell N7
Shanagolden
R156 Rathkeale Croagh
R523 Ardagh Adare
Newcastle N21 Croom
West R520 Ballingarry N20
R515 R516
R502 Kilmeedy Bruff
Broadford R519 Rockhill
N21 Dromcollingher R515
Charleville
(Rath Luirc) R515
R579 Freemount R517
Newmarket R580 Liscarroll
Boherbue R577 R522 Buttevant
R580 Donerale
R578 R581
Kanturk N20 Castletownroche
R582 R619 Banteer N72 Mallow
Millstreet Burnfort
BOGGERAGH Rathcormack
MTS N8 R614
Carriganimmy Watergrasshill
CORK N20
Macroom R618 Blarney Killard
Inchigeelagh Dripsey
N22 Cloghroe
Kilmichael Ovens CORK
Crookstown Douglas
Cross Ballinhassig N28
Ballineen R585 Barry CORK
Dunmanway Enniskean R590 Carrigaline
R586 Inishannon
Ballinascarty Bandon
Ballinspittle
Timoleague
Rosscarbery Clonakilty Butlerstown
R597 R598 Courtmacsherry
Clonakilty Old Head
Galley Bay of Kinsale
Head

SLIEVE AUGHTY MTS

Gort R353
R418 Woodford Portumna R489
N18 R461 Mountshannon
Scarriff Borrisokane
Tuamgraney Terryglass
Portroe R494 Carrigahorig
Killaloe Nenagh N7
Ballina R497
Newport Silvermines Toomyvara
Moneygall
Caherconlish Templemore
Cappamore R501 Clonmore
Cappagh Clonoulty Templetouhy
White R497 Dundrum
Herbertstown R503 R661
Lough Gur Pallas Oola Golden Holy Cross
Grean N74 Horse and
Monard Cashel Jockey
Hospital Tipperary R688
Galbally Bansha R692
Ballylanders Newinn Fethard
GALTEE MTS Cahir Mullinahone
Ballylooby N24 Clonmel
Knocklofty Kilsheelan
Mitchelstown Ardfinnan R678
N73 Barryporeen Clogheen Newcastle R671
Kildorrery KNOCKMEALDOWN MTS WATERFORD
Glanworth Ballyduff Comeragh
Fermoy N72 Lismore Mountains
Conna Tallowbridge Cappoquin N72 Kilmacthomas
Dungourney Tallow R627 Lemybrien
Clashmore Dungarvan Clonea
Midleton N25 Pula
Fota Island Kinsalebeg Ring (An Rinn)
Carrigtohill Youghal Mine
Castlemartyr Ardmore Head
Cobh Garryvoe Youghal
Ringaskiddy Cloyne Shanagarry Bay
Whitegate Ballycotton
Crosshaven

Cork - Swansea

SLIEVE BL MTS

Birr R440
Cadamstown R421
Kinnitty
R421 Borris-in-
Roscrea N7 Ossory
Shinrone R434
Cloughjordan
Donaghmore Rathdowney
Clonmore
Johnstown
Borrisoleigh Urlingford
Thurles N8
R690
Ballingarry
Killenaule
Mullinahone

● Places to Stay, Eat and Drink

© *MAPS IN MINUTES* ™ 2000

0   5   10   15   20   25

Map 3

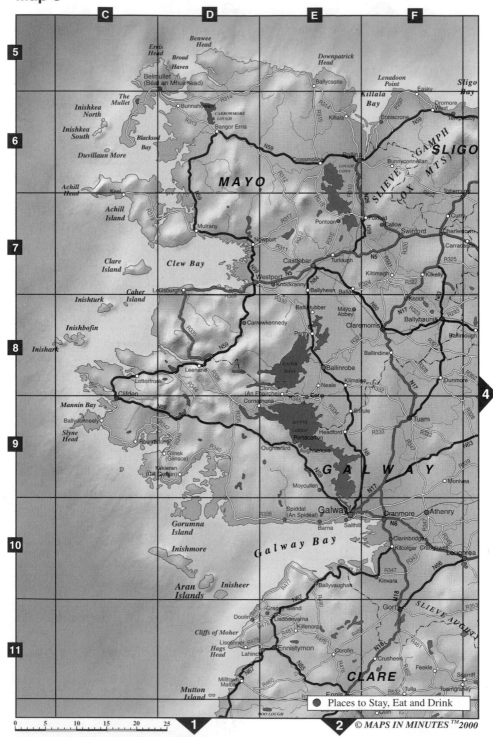

C   **D**   **E**   **F**

5

Erris Head
Benwee Head
Broad Haven
Downpatrick Head
Belmullet (Béal an Mhuirthead)
Ballycastle
Lenadoon Point
Easky
Sligo Bay
The Mullet
Bunnahowen
R314
R314
Killala Bay
Dromore West
Tempebuoy

Inishkea North
CARROWMORE LOUGH
R313
Bangor Erris
Killala
Erriscrone
N59
SLIEVE GAMPH
SLIGO

6

Inishkea South
Blacksod Bay
Crossmolina
Ballina
LOUGH CONN
Bunnyconnellan
SLIEVE OX MTS

Duvillaun More
N59
Tobercurry
R294

Achill Head
Keel
R319
R315
R310
Foxford
N26
Curry

7

Achill Island
Mulrany
R317
Pontoon
Callow
Charlestown
Swinford
Carracastle

Clare Island
Newport
R311
R312
R310
Castlebar
Turlough
N5
Kiltimagh
R320
R322
Kilkelly
R325

Clew Bay
Westport
N59
N5
R324
Knock
R329
N17
Ballyhaunis
R393

Caher Island
Louisburgh
Knockranny
R330
Ballyhean
Balla
Knock
R328

8

Inishturk
Carrowkennedy
Mayo Abbey
Claremorris
Ballinlough
R328

Inishbofin
LOUGH MASK
Partry
R332
R360

Inishark
Leenanes
N59
R335
Ballindine
Dunmore

Inishark
Lettergesh
Lottorfreek
R336
Clonbur (An Fhairche)
Ballinrobe
Neale
Kilmaine
N17

9

Clifden
Cornamona
LOUGH CORRIB
Cong
Shrule
Tuam
R347
N63

Mannin Bay
N59
R342
Portacarron
Headford
R333
R322

Ballyconneely
Roundstone
Glinsk (Glinsce)
Oughterard
Aughnanure
N59
N8
Monivea
R339

Slyne Head
R340
Kilkieran (Cill Chiaráin)
GALWAY
N17

10

Gorumna Island
Moycullen
Galway
Oranmore
Athenry

Inishmore
Spiddal (An Spidéal)
R336
Barna
Salthill
N6
Clarinbridge
R349

Aran Islands
Inisheer
Galway Bay
Kilcolgar
Craughwell
R347
Loughrea
N66

Kinvara
R347
Gort
N18
R353

11

Doolin
Craig Island
Ballyvaughan
R477
SLIEVE AUGHTY
R461

Cliffs of Moher
Lisdoonvarna
R476
Kilfenora
R460
R469

Hags Head
Liscannor
R478
Lahinch
Corofin
Crusheen
N18
Feakle
Scarriff

Milltown Malbay
Ennistymon
R481
Tulla
Tuamgraney
R532

Mutton Island
N67
R460
Ennis
Quin
CLARE

0   5   10   15   20   25   **1**   **2** © MAPS IN MINUTES ™2000

● Places to Stay, Eat and Drink

4

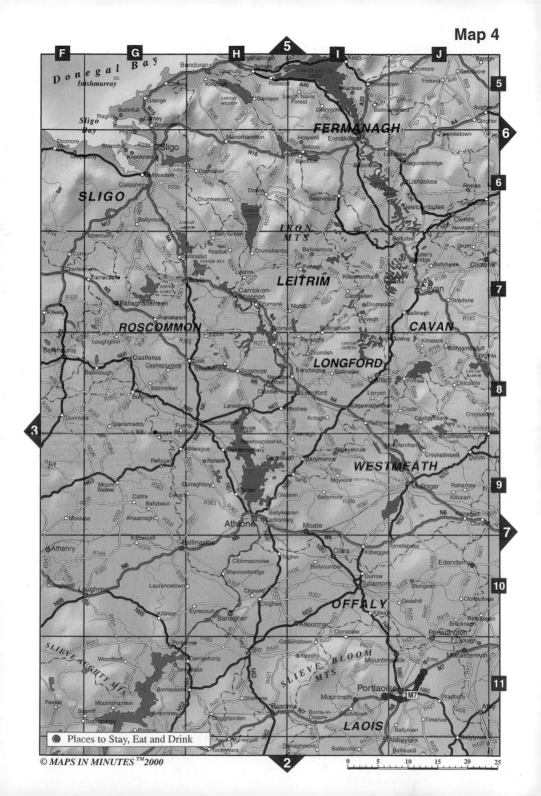

Places to Stay, Eat and Drink

© MAPS IN MINUTES ™ 2000

Map 5

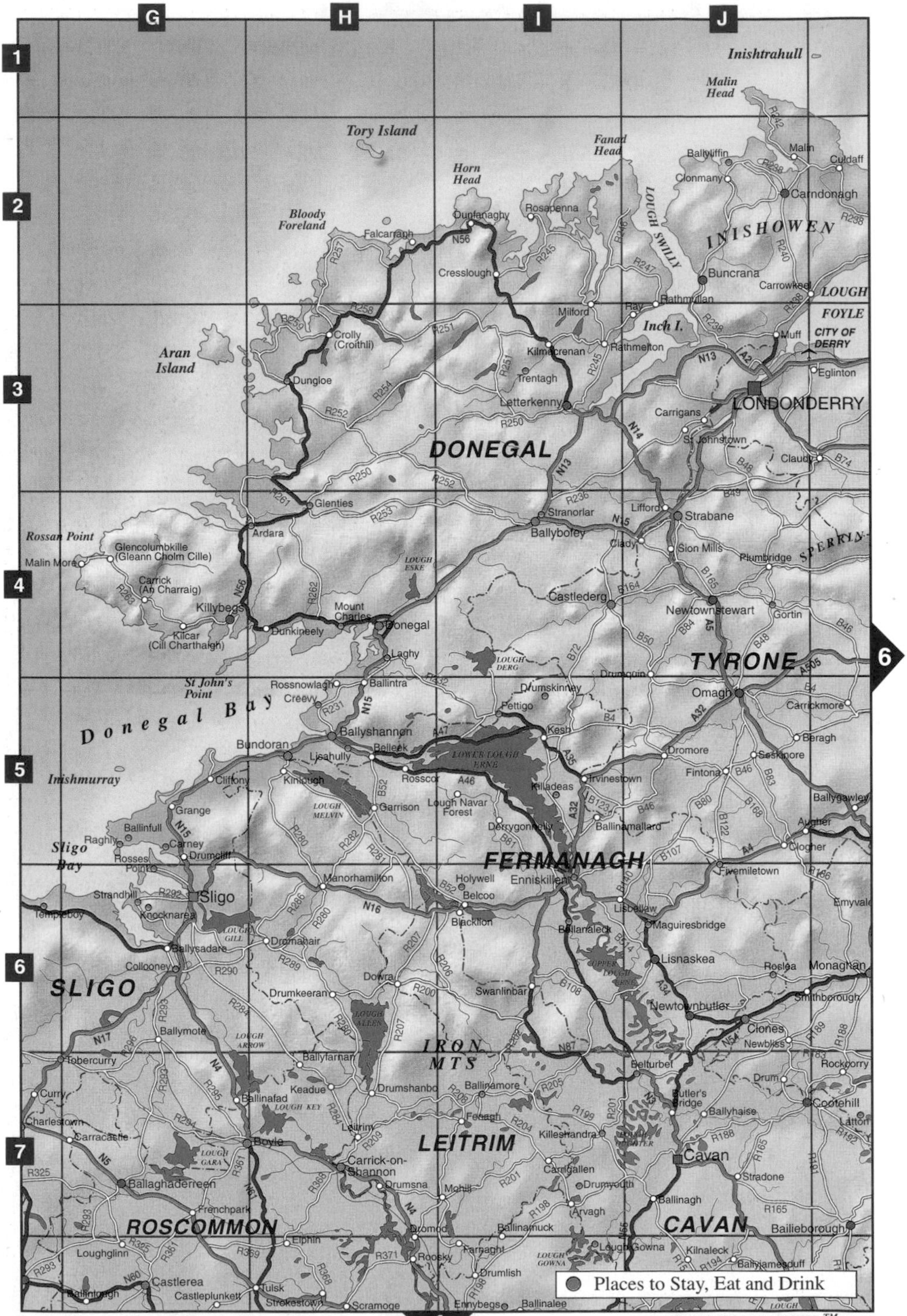

Places to Stay, Eat and Drink

© MAPS IN MINUTES ™ 2000

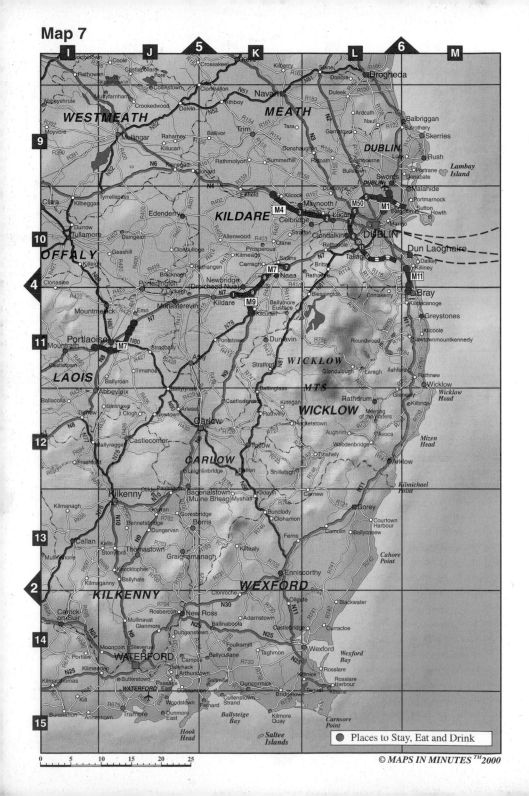

Map 7

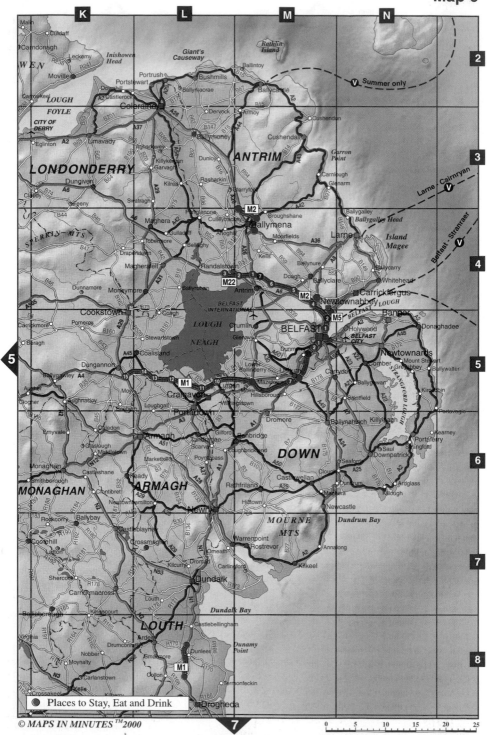

Map 6

Places to Stay, Eat and Drink

© MAPS IN MINUTES ™ 2000